Edited by RICHARD ELLMANN, *Oxford University*

and ROBERT O'CLAIR, *Manhattanville College*

MODERN POEMS

An Introduction to Poetry

W · W · NORTON & COMPANY · INC · *NEW YORK*

PRINTED IN THE UNITED STATES OF AMERICA

Library of Congress Cataloging in Publication Data
Main entry under title:
Modern poems.
Bibliography: p.
Includes indexes.
1. American poetry—20th century. 2. English poetry—20th century. 3. American poetry—19th century. 4. English poetry—19th century. I. Ellmann, Richard, 1918- II. O'Clair, Robert.
PS613.M58 821'.008 75-43773

ISBN 0-393-09187-2

1 2 3 4 5 6 7 8 9 0

Ted Hughes. Originally appeared in *The New Yorker.* "An Otter" from *Lupercal,* copyright © 1960 by Ted Hughes; "Crow's First Lesson" from *Crow,* copyright 1971 by Ted Hughes. "Wodwo" from *Wodwo,* copyright © 1962 by Ted Hughes. Reprinted by permission of Harper & Row, Publishers, Inc., and Faber and Faber Ltd.

Randall Jarrell: "The Death of the Ball Turret Gunner," "Eighth Air Force," "A Girl In A Library," from *The Complete Poems,* copyright © 1945, 1947, 1951, 1955 by Randall Jarrell, copyright renewed 1973, 1975 by Mary von Schrader Jarrell. Reprinted by permission of Farrar, Straus & Giroux, Inc. "Next Day" from *The Lost World,* copyright © Randall Jarrell 1963, 1965. Originally appeared in *The New Yorker.* Reprinted by permission of Macmillan Publishing Co., Inc.

Robinson Jeffers: "Shine Perishing Republic," copyright 1925 and renewed 1953 by Robinson Jeffers; "Fawn's Foster Mother," copyright 1928 and renewed 1956 by Robinson Jeffers, "Hurt Hawks," copyright 1928 and renewed 1956 by Robinson Jeffers, "New Mexican Mountain," copyright 1932 and renewed 1960 by Robinson Jeffers, "Ave Caesar," copyright 1935 and renewed 1963 by Donnan Jeffers and Garth Jeffers. From *The Selected Poetry of Robinson Jeffers.* Reprinted by permission of Random House, Inc.

LeRoi Jones: "Legacy," "Babylon Revisited" from *Black Magic Poetry 1961–1967,* copyright © 1969 by LeRoi Jones. Reprinted by permission of The Bobbs-Merrill Company, Inc. "Political Poem" by Imamu Amiri Baraka (LeRoi Jones), copyright 1964 by LeRoi Jones from *The Dead Lecturer.* Reprinted by permission of The Sterling Lord Agency, Inc.

James Joyce: From *Collected Poems* by James Joyce, copyright 1918 by B. W. Huebsch, Inc., copyright renewed 1946 by Nora Joyce. Copyright 1936 by James Joyce. All rights reserved. Reprinted by permission of The Viking Press, Inc.

Patrick Kavanagh: From *The Collected Poems of Patrick Kavanagh,* copyright 1964 by Patrick Kavanagh. Reprinted by permission of The Devin-Adair Company, Inc.

Weldon Kees: "Robinson" from *The Poetry of Weldon Kees,* copyright © 1967 by John A. Kees. Reprinted by permission of the University of Nebraska Press.

Thomas Kinsella: "Westland Row," "Je t'adore" from *Nightwalker and Other Poems,* copyright © 1966 by Thomas Kinsella. Reprinted by permission of Alfred A. Knopf, Inc.

Lincoln Kirstein: From *Rhymes and More Rhymes of a PFC,* copyright 1964, 1966 by Lincoln Kirstein. Reprinted by the permission of the author.

Etheridge Knight: From *Poems from Prison,* copyright © 1968 by Etheridge Knight. Reprinted by permission of Broadside Press.

Kenneth Koch: From *Thank You and Other Poems,* copyright 1962 by Kenneth Koch. Reprinted by permission of Grove Press, Inc. "Mending Sump," copyright © 1960 by Kenneth Koch, reprinted by permission of International Creative Management and Kenneth Koch.

Stanley Kunitz: From *Selected Poems 1928–1958,* copyright 1958 by Stanley Kunitz; from *The Testing Tree,* copyright © 1966 by Stanley Kunitz. Reprinted by permission of Little, Brown and Co. in association with The Atlantic Monthly Press.

Philip Larkin: "Church Going," "Myxomatosis" from *The Less Deceived.* Reprinted by permission of The Marvell Press, England. "The Whitsun Weddings" from *The Whitsun Weddings,* reprinted by permission of Faber and Faber Limited.

D. H. Lawrence: From *The Complete Poems of D. H. Lawrence* edited by Vivian de Sola Pinto and F. Warren Roberts, copyright © 1964, 1971 by Angelo Ravagli and C. M. Weekley, Executors of the Estate of Frieda Lawrence Ravagli. All rights reserved. Reprinted by permission of The Viking Press, Inc.

Don L. Lee: "But He Was Cool or: He Even Stopped for Green Lights" from *Don't Cry, Scream,* copyright 1969 by Don L. Lee. "Man Thinking About Woman" from *We Walk the Way of the New World,* copyright © 1970, by Don L. Lee. Reprinted by permission of Broadside Press.

Denise Levertov: "The Dog of Art" from *With Eyes at the Back of Our Heads,* copyright © 1959 by Denise Levertov. "Illustrious Ancestors," "Matins," from *The Jacob's Ladder* by Denise Levertov, copyright © 1958, 1961 by Denise Levertov Goodman. "Song for Ishtar," "Losing Track," from *O Taste and See* by Denise Levertov, copyright © 1963, 1962 by Denise Levertov Goodman. "Losing Track" was first published in *Poetry.* Reprinted by permission of New Directions Publishing Corp.

Philip Levine: From *They Feed They Lion,* copyright © 1972 by Philip Levine. Appeared originally in *Kayak.* Reprinted by permission of Atheneum Publishers, Inc. From *Not This Pig,* copyright © 1966 by Philip Levine. Reprinted by permission of Wesleyan University Press.

Cecil Day Lewis: "Sheepdog Trials in Hyde Park" from *Selected Poems,* copyright © 1967 by C. Day Lewis. Reprinted by permission of Harper & Row, Publishers, Inc., the Executors of the Estate of C. Day Lewis and Jonathan Cape Ltd.

Robert Lowell: From *For the Union Dead,* copyright © 1960, 1964 by Robert Lowell; *Life Studies,* copyright © 1956, 1959 by Robert Lowell; *Notebook,* copyright © 1967, 1968, 1969 by Robert Lowell. Reprinted by permission of Farrar, Straus & Giroux, Inc. From *Lord Weary's Castle,* copyright 1946, 1974 by Robert Lowell, Reprinted by permission of Harcourt Brace Jovanovich, Inc.

George Macbeth: From *Collected Poems 1958–1970,* copyright © 1971 by George Macbeth. Reprinted by permission of Atheneum Publishers, Inc. From *The Broken Places,* copyright 1963 by Scorpion Press. Reprinted by permission of the author.

Hugh MacDiarmid: From *Collected Poems* by Hugh MacDiarmid, copyright © Christopher Murray Grieve 1948, 1962. Reprinted by permission of Macmillan Publishing Co., Inc.

Archibald MacLeish: From *Collected Poems 1917–1952,* copyright 1917, 1924, 1925, 1926, 1928, 1929, 1930, 1932, 1933, 1936, 1939, 1943, 1948, 1951, 1952, by Archibald MacLeish. Reprinted by permission of Houghton Mifflin Company.

Louis MacNeice: From *The Collected Poems of Louis MacNeice,* edited by E. R. Dodds.

Copyright © by The Estate of Louis MacNeice 1966. Reprinted by permission of Oxford University Press, Inc. and Faber and Faber Limited.

Edgar Lee Masters: "Elsa Wertman," "Hamilton Greene," "Anne Rutledge," 'Lucinda Matlock," copyright © 1915, 1916, 1942, 1944 by Edgar Lee Masters. Reprinted by permission of Mrs. Edgar Lee Masters.

Roger McGough: "Goodbat Nightman" from *Penguin Modern Poets,* copyright 1967 by Roger McGough. Reprinted by permission of Hope Leresche & Steele. From *After the Merrymaking,* copyright 1971 by Roger McGough. Reprinted by permission of Hope Leresche & Steele and Jonathan Cape Ltd.

Claude McKay: "If We Must Die," "America," from *Selected Poems of Claude McKay,* copyright 1953 by Twayne Publishers and reprinted with permission of Twayne Publishers, A Division of G. K. Hall & Co., Boston.

James Merrill: "The Broken Home" from *Nights and Days,* copyright © 1965 by James Merrill. Appeared originally in *The New Yorker.* Reprinted by permission of Atheneum Publishers, Inc.

W. S. Merwin: "Footprints on the Glacier," from *The Carrier of Ladders,* copyright © 1969 by W. S. Merwin. Appeared originally in *Tri-Quarterly.* Reprinted by permission of Atheneum Publishers, Inc. "Leviathan," "The Drunk in the Furnace," "Footprints on the Glacier," reprinted by permission of David Higham Associates, Ltd. From *The Drunk in the Furnace,* copyright 1958 by W. S. Merwin, published 1960 by The Macmillan Company and reprinted by permission of Harold Ober Associates Incorporated.

Josephine Miles: From *Poems 1930–1960* by Josephine Miles, copyright © 1960 by Indiana University Press. Reprinted by permission of Indiana University Press. "Preliminary to Classroom Lecture" and "Gypsy" reprinted by permission of the author. From *Kinds of Affection,* copyright © 1963 by Josephine Miles. Reprinted by permission of Wesleyan University Press.

Edna St. Vincent Millay: From *Collected Poems,* Harper & Row, copyright 1931, 1958, 1934, 1962 by Edna St. Vincent Millay and Norma Millay Ellis. Reprinted by permission of Norma Millay Ellis, Literary Executor.

Marianne Moore: From *Collected Poems,* copyright 1935 by Marianne Moore, renewed 1963 by Marianne Moore and T. S. Eliot. Copyright 1941 by Marianne Moore, renewed 1969 by Marianne Moore.

Edwin Muir: From *Collected Poems* by Edwin Muir, copyright © 1960 by Willa Muir. Reprinted by permission of Oxford University Press, Inc. and Faber and Faber Ltd.

Howard Nemerov: From *New and Selected Poems,* copyright 1960 by the University of Chicago. Reprinted by permission of Margot Johnson Agency.

Frank O'Hara: "Why I Am Not A Painter" from *Meditations in an Emergency,* copyright 1957 by Frank O'Hara. Reprinted by permission of Grove Press, Inc. Copyright © 1958 by Maureen Granville-Smith, Administratrix of The Estate of Frank O'Hara, from *The Collected Poems of Frank O'Hara,* edited by Donald Allen, reprinted by permission of Alfred A. Knopf, Inc. "The Day Lady Died" from *Lunch Poems,* copyright 1964 by Frank O'Hara. Reprinted by permission of City Lights Books.

Charles Olson: "A Newly Discovered Homeric Hymn" from *The Distances,* copyright 1960 by Charles Olson. Reprinted by permission of Grove Press Inc.

Wilfred Owen: From *Collected Poems of Wilfred Owen,* copyright Chatto & Windus Ltd., 1946, © 1963. Reprinted by permission of the Executors of the Estate of Harold Owen, Chatto & Windus Ltd. and New Directions Publishing Corporation.

Sylvia Plath: From *Ariel,* copyright © 1963 by Ted Hughes, "Ariel," copyright © 1965 by Ted Hughes. Reprinted by permission of Harper & Row, Publishers, Inc. and Olwyn Hughes.

William Plomer: From *Collected Poems* by William Plomer. Reprinted by permission of the Estate of William Plomer and Jonathan Cape Ltd.

Ezra Pound: From *Personae,* copyright 1926 by Ezra Pound, from *The Cantos,* copyright 1934, 1948 by Ezra Pound. All selections reprinted by permission of New Directions Publishing Corporation.

E. J. Pratt: From *The Collected Poems* of E. J. Pratt, Second Edition edited by Northrup Frye, copyright © 1962 by The Macmillan Company of Canada Limited. Reprinted by permission of the publisher.

Alfred Purdy: "Dead Seal" from *North of Summer* by Al Purdy. Reprinted by permission of The Canadian Publishers, McLelland and Stewart Limited, Toronto.

Dudley Randall: "Ballad of Birmingham" and "Booker T. and W.E.B." from *Poem Counterpoem,* copyright 1967 by Dudley Randall. Reprinted by permission of Broadside Press. "Pacific Epitaphs" from *More to Remember* by Dudley Randall. Reprinted by permission of Third World Press.

John Crowe Ransom: "Bells for John Whiteside's Daughter," "Here Lies a Lady," "Captain Carpenter," copyright 1924 by Alfred A. Knopf, Inc., and renewed 1952 by John Crowe Ransom. "Piazza Piece," "The Equilibrists," "Janet Waking," "Here Lies a Lady," versions A and B, and accompanying comments, copyright 1924 by Alfred A. Knopf, Inc., and renewed 1952 by John Crowe Ransom. From *Selected Poems,* Third Edition, Revised and Enlarged, by John Crowe Ransom. Reprinted by permission of Alfred A. Knopf, Inc.

Adrienne Rich: From *Diving into the Wreck, Poems 1971–1972,* © 1973 by W. W. Norton & Company, Inc. From *Leaflets, Poems 1965–1968,* © 1969 by W. W. Norton & Company, Inc. From *The Will to Change, Poems 1968–1970,* © 1971 by W. W. Norton & Company, Inc. Reprinted by permission of W. W. Norton & Company, Inc.

Edwin Arlington Robinson: "Eros Turannos," copyright 1916 by Edwin Arlington Robinson, renewed 1944 by Ruth Nivison. "Mr. Flood's Party," copyright 1921 by Edwin Arlington Robinson, renewed 1949 by Ruth Nevison. "The Sheaves," copyright 1925 by Edwin Arlington Robinson, renewed 1953 by Ruth Nivison and Barbara R. Holt. From *Collected Poems,* reprinted by permission of Macmillan Publishing Co., Inc. "Minever Cheevy," copyright 1907 by Charles Scribner's Sons, "For A Dead Lady," copyright 1910 by Charles Scribner's Sons from *The Town Down the River* by Edwin Arlington Robinson. Reprinted by permission of Charles Scribner's Sons.

Theodore Roethke: "The Waking," copyright 1953 by Theodore Roethke. "Cuttings," "Cuttings (Later)," copyright 1948 by Theodore Roethke. "My Papa's Waltz," copyright 1942 by Hearst Magazines, Inc. "Dolor" copyright 1943 by the Modern Poetry Association, Inc. "The Minimal," copyright 1942 by Theodore Roethke. "Frau Bauman, Frau Schmidt, and Frau Schwartze," copyright 1952 by Theodore Roethke. "I Knew a Woman," copyright 1954 by Theodore Roethke. "Wish for a Young Wife," copyright © 1963 by Beatrice Roethke as Administratrix for the Estate of Theodore Roethke. "In a Dark Time," copyright © 1960 by Beatrice Roethke as Administratrix for the Estate of Theodore Roethke. From *The Complete Poems of Theodore Roethke.* Reprinted by permission of Doubleday & Company, Inc.

Carl Sandburg: "Chicago" from *Chicago Poems* by Carl Sandburg, copyright 1916 by Holt, Rinehart and Winston, Inc.; copyright 1944 by Carl Sandburg, "Grass," "Cool Tombs," "Gargoyle" from *Cornhuskers* by Carl Sandburg, copyright 1918 by Holt, Rinehart and Winston, Inc.; copyright, 1946 by Carl Sandburg. Reprinted by permission of Harcourt Brace Jovanovich, Inc.

Siegfried Sassoon: "Blighters," "The Fathers" from *Collected Poems* by Siegfried Sassoon, copyright 1918 by E. P. Dutton & Co. All rights reserved. Reprinted by permission of The Viking Press, Inc. and G. T. Sassoon.

Delmore Schwartz: "The Heavy Bear Who Goes With Me" from *Selected Poems: Summer Knowledge,* copyright 1938 by New Directions Publishing Corporation, copyright © 1966 by Delmore Schwartz. Reprinted by permission of New Directions Publishing Corporation.

Anne Sexton: "Unknown Girl in the Maternity Ward," copyright © 1960, from *To Bedlam and Part Way Back* by Anne Sexton. "Wanting to Die," copyright © by Anne Sexton, from *Live or Die* by Anne Sexton. Reprinted by permission of Houghton Mifflin Company.

Karl Shapiro: "The Fly," copyright 1942 and renewed 1970 by Karl Shapiro. "Lower the Standard," copyright © 1964 by Karl Shapiro. From *Selected Poems* by Karl Shapiro. Reprinted by permission of Random House, Inc.

Judith Johnson Sherwin: From *Uranium Poems,* copyright © 1969 by Yale University Press. Reprinted by permission of Yale University Press.

John Silkin: From *Poems New and Selected,* copyright © 1954 by Jon Silkin. Reprinted by permission of Jon Silkin and Wesleyan University Press.

Louis Simpson: "The Man Who Married Magdalene," copyright 1955 by Louis Simpson. From *Poets of Today II, Good News of Death and Other Poems.* Reprinted by permission of Charles Scribner's Sons. "American Poetry," from *At the End of the Open Road,* copyright © by Louis Simpson. Reprinted by permission of Wesleyan University Press.

Edith Sitwell: From *Collected Poems,* copyright © 1968 by Vanguard Press, Inc. Copyright © 1949, 1953, 1954, 1959, 1962, 1963 by Dame Edith Sitwell. Reprinted by permission of Vanguard Press, Inc. and David Higham Associates, Ltd.

Stevie Smith: "To Carry the Child" from *The Complete Poems of Stevie Smith* and *The Best Beast,* copyright by Stevie Smith. Originally appeared in *The New Yorker.* Reprinted by permission of James MacGibbons, Literary Executor and Alfred A. Knopf, Inc. "Not Waving But Drowning" and "Was He Married" from *Selected Poems of Stevie Smith,* copyright © 1962, 1964 by Stevie Smith. Reprinted by permission of New Directions Publishing Corporation.

W. D. Snodgrass: "These Trees Stand . . . ," copyright © 1956 by W. D. Snodgrass, from *Heart's Needle,* by W. D. Snodgrass. Reprinted by permission of Alfred A. Knopf, Inc.

Gary Snyder: "Four Poems for Robin" from *The Back Country,* copyright © 1968 by Gary Snyder. Reprinted by permission of New Directions Publishing Corporation.

Stephen Spender: "Icarus," "The Express," copyright 1934 and renewed 1962 by Stephen Spender. Reprinted from *Selected Poems* by permission of Random House, Inc. and Faber and Faber Ltd.

Jon Stallworthy: From *Root and Branch,* copyright © 1969 by Jon Stallworthy. Reprinted by permission of Oxford University Press, Inc. and Chatto and Windus Ltd. Drafts of Yeats's poem "The Second Coming" from Jon Stallworthy, *Between the Lines: Yeats's Poetry in the Making* © Oxford University Press, as reprinted, in a revised version, in Jon Stallworthy's article in *Agenda,* Autumn/Winter issue 1971–72, pp. 24–33. Reprinted by permission of the Oxford University Press, Oxford.

James Stevens: "What Tomas Said in a Pub," copyright 1907 by Macmillan Publishing Co., Inc., "Stephen's Green" ("The Wind"), copyright 1915 by Macmillan Publishing Co., Inc., renewed 1943 by James Stephens. "A Glass of Beer," copyright 1918 by Macmillan Publishing Co., Inc., renewed 1943 by James Stephens. From *Collected Poems,* reprinted by permission of Macmillan Publishing Co., Inc.; Macmillan London & Basingstoke; The Macmillan Company of Canada Limited and Mrs. Iris Wise.

Wallace Stevens: "Thirteen Ways of Looking at a Blackbird," "Anecdote of the Jar," "Sunday Morning," "The Emperor of Ice-Cream," "A High-Toned Old Christian Woman," copyright 1923 and renewed 1951 by Wallace Stevens. "The Idea of Order at Key West," "The Man With the Blue Guitar: 1," copyright 1936 by Wallace Stevens and renewed 1964 by Holly Stevens. "Of Modern Poetry," copyright 1942 and renewed 1970 by Holly Stevens. "To An Old Philosopher In Rome," copyright 1952 by Wallace Stevens. From *The Collected Poems of Wallace Stevens,* reprinted by permission of Alfred A. Knopf, Inc.

Mark Strand: From *Reasons for Moving,* copyright © 1966 by Mark Strand. "Eating Poetry" originally appeared in *The New York Review of Books.* Reprinted by permission of Atheneum Publishers, Inc.

Allen Tate: "Ode to the Confederate Dead" from *Poems* by Allen Tate. Reprinted by permission of The Swallow Press Incorporated.

Dylan Thomas: From *Poems of Dylan Thomas,* copyright 1952 by Dylan Thomas, 1939, 1943, 1946 by New Directions Publishing Corporation. Reprinted by permission of New Directions Publishing Corporation, J. M. Dent Ltd., and the Trustees for the Copyrights of the late Dylan Thomas.

Contents

Preface

Modern Poems: An Introduction to Poetry has come into being because of what we have learned as teachers of American college students and as editors of *The Norton Anthology of Modern Poetry.* Students, when they can choose, often prefer to plunge at once into the poetry of their own century. It responds, after all, to the social and historical conditions in which they find themselves, and its ways of thinking and feeling are those in which they feel most at home. And, of course, much of it is written in contemporary English, the idiom we speak today. In gathering the selections for our longer survey of modern poetry, we came to see that many of these poems would be especially pertinent and moving to students beginning the study of poetry in college, and that their teachers might well share our feeling that such an introduction can be particularly suitable.

Because *Modern Poems* is an *introduction*, we begin the book by presenting, in a section called "Reading Poems," the necessary terms and definitions for the discussion of poetry. Most examples given in these pages are taken from the poems in this book. Teachers may want to use this section as general background, or they may prefer to select one of the topics here and use particular poems from the body of the anthology to illustrate it. The essay has been prepared under the supervision of our editor, John Francis; in trying to make it as useful as possible, we have sought the advice of Albert and Barbara Gelpi (Stanford University), Ronald Sharp (Kenyon College), Robert Phelps, and Scott Elledge (Cornell University), whose sensitive and practical suggestions we acknowledge with thanks.

In selecting the poems themselves, our aim has been to offer a range of work, from the easily accessible to the more difficult, which represents the major modes and aspects of all poetry, regardless of period. We have also sought to represent the principal directions in modern poetry: the most prominent writers and literary groupings appear in sufficient depth so that their interconnections may be studied, and the essay "Modern Poetry in English: A Brief History" offers the setting in which the poems can be regarded.

So that students will be able to read the poems included here without consulting reference books, each poem has been annotated, and each author is briefly introduced in biographical terms. Finally, a bibliography is provided of all the books of poetry and the principal works of prose by each poet.

A note about texts: as a rule, the version here of each poem is the last over which the author may be presumed to have exercised editorial control. Certain exceptions have been made as necessary, and occasionally lines from alternative versions are also given; these textual questions are presented in the footnotes. The poems of each author are arranged chronologically, by the date of first publication in book form. (This date is given immediately following each poem.) Poems without titles are identified by their first lines. Except for a few very long poems, all selections are printed in their entirety; the few exceptions are represented by self-contained excerpts, their omitted portions being indicated by asterisks. Individualities of spelling, punctuation, and typography have been preserved.

This book has profited greatly from the assistance of friends. We wish to thank Professor M. H. Abrams for his timely and valuable counsel. John Francis performed prodigies of editing, and John Benedict, also of W. W. Norton & Company, helped us at crucial junctures; their colleagues Lee Miller and Calvin Towle carried out others of the necessary preparations for this undertaking. We hope that the complete book warrants their manifold exertions.

R. E.
R. O'C.

Reading Poems

Where there are people there are poems. Some of the earliest writings known are in verse, and throughout human history new poets have continued to appear, often without warning or preparation. Even young children can write real poems and like to do it, as the poet Kenneth Koch found when he taught creative writing to sixth-graders in New York's Public School 61. Whatever the reasons for poetry's origins, it has continued to attract people, and our own century has proved to be a great period for it.

Because poetry has consistently figured so large in human culture, many people have tried to define its true nature. It is "painting that speaks"; "the best words in the best order"; "the supreme fiction"; "a criticism of life"; "the breath and finer spirit of all knowledge"; "a little leaf in the drawer of a sublet room"; "a way of taking life by the throat"; and so on, including the down-to-earth "all this fiddle." These observations are well put, but they are incomplete, and the essence of poetry slips through them and escapes. The poet Wallace Stevens, who tried many definitions, once remarked with seeming impatience, "Poetry is the sum of its attributes."

Probably Stevens was right to shrug the question aside. Modern poets and modern readers find it hard to agree which qualities of poems are so typical, and so important, that they belong in a definition of "poetry." Some would argue that poems must be strikingly, artfully shaped; others insist with equal conviction that overtly formal verse is not "true," and that authentic poetry can no longer be written in strict form. This debate has raged for decades, as can be seen in the essay "Modern Poems in English: A Brief History" which follows the selections in this book.

But Stevens' observation implies an important truth: more than philosophical or critical arguments, the qualities of the poems we read shape our idea of poetry. In this respect, the poems in this anthology are offered as a kind of collective "definition" of poetry, which will interact with other poems you may have read or will read in developing your own, personal notion of what poetry is, and why it matters to you.

This essay, "Reading Poems," is no more than it claims to be: a guide to reading. It describes and illustrates some of the most common attributes and techniques to be found in the poems in this book and elsewhere, and it seeks to show how these aspects of poetry can contribute to your understanding of what a poem means. You may also find you enjoy poetry more if you set aside a stretch of time for reading in which you don't expect to be interrupted; most poems begin to yield their full meaning only after several careful, unhurried readings. And try also to keep an open mind as you read: "listen" to what the poem is trying to tell you in its own language.

LANGUAGE

Words

In conversations with friends, our use of language may seem spontaneous to us. But in fact we not only know what we mean but are consciously shaping what we say as we go along. Some people—and they are often the ones we most enjoy listening to—are able to choose striking and appropriate words to express their thoughts and feelings: they are able to shape their language more effectively and colorfully than we can.

Despite all the evidence that poets are especially careful in choosing their words, people often assume that in poetry it is the ideas that matter most. The painter Edgar Degas, who aspired to be a poet as well, found himself perplexed by the difficulties of writing a sonnet, and complained to the poet Stéphane Mallarmé, "I don't see why I can't finish my little poem; after all, I have plenty of ideas." "But, Degas," Mallarmé replied, "poetry is not written with ideas but with words." What Mallarmé meant was that a poem is not an idea decorated with pretty words; the poem is built of words as a musical composition is built of notes. It does, of course, have an intellectual content that may be rewritten as prose, but in the poem that "prose meaning" is inseparable from the emotional content which only certain words in a certain order can express. The manner of saying something affects what is being said, just as the limits of the instruments affect the results of scientific experiments.

Words are therefore the poet's medium, and the ways they can be meaningfully arranged are his tools. This is why W. H. Auden once said of young poets, "As a rule, the sign that a beginner has a genuine original talent is that he is more interested in playing with words than in saying something original." Poets explore and try to use all the expressive resources of words—their "plain" meanings, to be sure, but also their emotional associations, and even their sounds.

Most common English words have, not just one, but a number of plain meanings (or **denotations**). Even in an abridged dictionary, the word *post* has a long list of denotations—"a pole," "one's place of work," "one's job," or "a military bugle call"; "to mail a letter," "to mount notices on a bulletin board," "to put up bail," "to make entries in an accounts ledger," or "to move rhythmically while riding a horse"; or, as a prefix, "after." But *post* doesn't carry all these meanings with it every time it is used, as the context usually eliminates all but one of them. In the sentence "I lost my post at the bank," *post* clearly means "job" (one other denotation is possible, "pole," and that seems pretty unlikely).

When a word in a particular context can still be taken to mean more than one thing, we call it **ambiguous**. Ambiguity can sometimes be confusing. If someone says, "Be sure to take the right road," does he mean the *correct* road or the road *branching to the right*? The right road could be the wrong road, and the left road the right road. Hence, when the aim is to provide clear exposition or instructions, ambiguity is a fault. But writers, and especially poets, sometimes deliberately exploit a word's multiple denotations:

My father, who had flown in World War I,
Might have continued to *invest* his life
In cloud *banks* well above Wall Street and wife.
(Merrill, "The Broken Home")

The poem goes on to say that the poet's father became a stockbroker. In these lines, the poem uses two double meanings: *invest* means "to put money out for financial gain" but also "to surround or envelop," while *banks* are "financial institutions" but also "piled masses." When the possible meanings of a word contrast sharply, as they do here, the result is a **pun**. A pun is often funny but needn't be, as in this example, where the effect is less of a sense of humor than of quick-wittedness and flexibility of mind. In some puns the ambiguity may be between words which have different meanings and are spelled differently but sound the same:

The violence of beast on beast is *read*
As natural law, but *upright* man
Seeks his divinity by inflicting pain.
(Walcott, "A Far Cry from Africa")

Walcott means *read* in the sense of "interpreted," but the sound is the same as *red*, the color of blood, and the first meaning, which is almost bland, is made ominous by the second meaning. *Upright*, too, is ambiguous: man is upright because he stands on two legs rather than four, but the word also means "morally correct," a view of humanity many humans share but which Walcott in the following line seems to question.

Poets are concerned—often obsessively concerned—with much more about a word than its denotations, numerous and suggestive as these may be. They are sensitive to a word's aura of **connotations**, what might be called its atmosphere or "feel," which it acquires from hundreds of years of use in many different contexts. Connotations give a word much of its flavor and its emotional impact.

Take the noun *dust*. Any dictionary will give us its denotation: powdered earth (or other matter), large enough to feel but small enough to be blown about. But poets like the word for its connotations, too. It builds up on furniture; it gets in your eyes; it's useful in phrases like "dry as dust," "dust bowl," "bite the dust." And for hundreds of years it has symbolized distintegration, things wearing away or being ground down to almost nothing. It has also come to stand for human disintegration, or death:

For dust thou art, and unto dust shalt thou return.
(*Genesis* 3:19)

I will show you fear in a handful of dust.
(Eliot, "The Waste Land")

Dust has a near synonym that also sounds much the same: *dirt*. In certain expressions, dust is merely dry dirt: "to shake the dust off one's feet." But substitute one word for the other, and you'll see that dirt has very different connotations:

> For dirt thou art, and unto dirt shalt thou return.
>
> I will show you fear in a handful of dirt.

Dirt's meaning in Old English was "excrement"—some people still use it in this sense—and it carries a connotation of intense disapproval or disgust, as in such expressions as "dirty tricks," "dirty work," "dirty movies." Slanderous or derogatory information about someone is "dirt." One may fear a handful of dirt, but it is defamation rather than death that is threatened. (Dirt also has positive connotations: plants grow in dirt, you can "hit pay dirt." In this sense it means the opposite of dry, sterile dust.)

Though poems as words on the page are visual objects, they are intended to be spoken aloud as well as read, and the full poetic experience involves words' sound-qualities as well as their meanings. The sounds of most words have nothing to do with their meanings: we may say *yes*, but an Italian or Spaniard will say *si*, a Frenchman *oui*, a German *ja*, a Russian *da*, and a Japanese *hai*, and all mean exactly the same thing to their compatriots. Some do sound like their meanings (*buzz, hiss, clickety-clack*); this matching of sound and sense is called **onomatopoeia**. But even onomatopoeic words vary from language to language. English roosters say *Cock-a-doodle-doo,* but French roosters say *Co-co-ri-co*. So, rather than depending on onomatopoeia, poets are likely to interweave the sounds and senses of their words in lines and sentences. This management of sound is illustrated below under RHYME and SOUND EFFECTS WITHIN THE LINE.

Syntax

Syntax is a set of rules for making understandable sentences. Most people find the subject dull and tiresome, and study it only to avoid criticism for using "bad grammar." In this respect, syntax is about as interesting as spelling. But prescribing "correctness" is only one function of syntax, and a fairly minor one at that. Far more important in our daily lives are the various ways syntax enables us to express ourselves, ways we use without necessarily thinking much about it.

She did all the work.	(*A matter-of-fact statement*)
It was she who did all the work.	(*Not he or they or I*)
She it was who did all the work.	(*Pointing the finger*)
All the work was done by her.	(*Emphasizing how much work*)

The basic information is the same. Each sentence, however, focuses on different words through syntactic variation, and therefore each has a subtly different meaning from the others. There are still more ways of varying the basic sentence, for example:

> All the work did she.

This word order, which you would probably never hear in ordinary conversation, is called **inversion,** because it inverts the usual sequence of syntactic units—subject, verb, object—without changing the role each word plays in the sentence. The basic meaning remains unchanged because of a grammatical rule: the word *she* cannot be the object of a verb (though *her* can). Otherwise, the inversion would not be possible: "Susan saw Tom" is not the same as "Tom saw Susan." "All the work did she" has about the same placement of emphasis as "All the work was done by her," but its effect is quite different. The inversion substitutes for the passive voice (which is a way of speaking we routinely use) an unusual word order that calls attention to itself.

These effects, emphasizing particular words and attracting attention to the way it is being done, are constructive uses of inversion. But poets past and present have often used inversion merely to make their rhythms more even or to get rhyming words to the ends of lines; absorbed in solving these technical problems, they may forget about the effect of inversion itself. The technique has consequently acquired a bad reputation in modern poetry. As a young man, W. B. Yeats used inversion in this less rigorous way—"And a small cabin build there," for example, from "The Lake Isle of Innisfree"—and he later regretted the word order as undesirably stilted for the poem, though the rhythm of the line prevented him from revising to eliminate it. But Yeats and other modern poets have also used inversion to powerful expressive effect. Here is the opening of Dylan Thomas' "A Refusal to Mourn the Death, by Fire, of a Child in London":

> Never until the mankind making
> Bird beast and flower
> Fathering and all humbling darkness
> Tells with silence the last light breaking
> And the still hour
> Is come of the sea tumbling in harness
>
> And I must enter again the round
> Zion of the water bead
> And the synagogue of the ear of corn
> Shall I let pray the shadow of a sound
> Or sow my salt seed
> In the least valley of sackcloth to mourn
>
> The majesty and burning of the child's death.

This poem is difficult to understand, partly because the long sentence that stretches across these thirteen lines has been organized so that its parts are out of any usual order. Here it is useful to rearrange them into a more normal prose order:

> I shall never let the shadow of a sound pray
>
> or sow my salt seed in the least valley of sackcloth
>
> to mourn the majesty and burning of the child's death

until

the darkness that makes mankind
that fathers bird beast and flower
and humbles all
tells with silence the breaking of the last light

and the still hour of the sea tumbling in harness is come

and I must enter again the round Zion of the water bead
and the synagogue of the ear of corn.

Note that although this paraphrase makes Thomas' sentence easier to follow, and therefore helps us understand him, it also changes our experience of the poem. If Thomas had begun with the word *I*, as the paraphrase does, he would have immediately focused our attention on the speaker. But he does not. *I*, the subject of the sentence, is placed by inversion in the middle of the sentence, rhetorically the most unobtrusive place for it, and the all-important word which actually begins the sentence is the adverb *Never*. Between these two words Thomas interposes three conditional clauses which taken together imply "until the end of the world"; these clauses not only reinforce the idea of *never*, but imitate it by making us wait ten lines before we are done with it and finally reach the subject of the sentence. This kind of syntactic delaying action is called **suspension**; the reader expects momentarily to come across a grammatically vital word, usually a subject or a verb, but is kept in suspense waiting for it. (It's worth noticing that Thomas never seems to shift sentence elements around merely to make his rhythms or rhymes more symmetrical. In fact, the syntax is so much in the foreground that you might easily overlook, at least in the first reading, that this poem actually is in rhyme.)

A third syntactic technique poets often use is **ellipsis**—leaving out words which prose grammar would require but which need not be there for the poem to make sense:

Sun to his slumber, shadows o'er all the ocean,
Came we then to the bounds of deepest water . . .
(Pound, "Canto I")

We can add what Pound left out: "*When the* sun *had gone* to his slumber, *and* shadows *were* o'er (a contraction for *over*) all the ocean, came we then to the bounds of deepest water." By avoiding routine connectives, Pound creates an effect of decisiveness on the part of the speaker, swiftness of thought, and rhetorical strength.

Some poets use **syntactic ambiguity** as they do verbal ambiguity:

My stare drank deep beauty that still allures.
(Empson, "Villanelle")

Deep can be an adjective: "My stare drank *deep beauty* that still allures." Or it can be an adverb: "My stare *drank deep* beauty that still allures." The line makes sense both ways, and the context does not exclude either meaning, so we may accept both in reading the line. The effect is to put special stress on the ambiguous word *deep*, with its connotations of fullness and profundity.

TONE

Voice

Everyone has a personal way of talking. The choice of words, speech rhythms, breath units, syntax, and all the inflections and signals that go with even the most casual speech, may combine to form a style as distinctive as a fingerprint. Poets, too, have individual verbal styles, some so distinctive that we can identify bits of their work by style alone. Here, for example, are snatches from poems by two modern poets:

> There where it is we do not need the wall:
> He is all pine and I am apple orchard.
> My apple trees will never get across
> And eat the cones under his pines, I tell him.
> He only says, 'Good fences make good neighbors.'
> Spring is the mischief in me, and I wonder
> If I could put a notion in his head:
> '*Why* do they make good neighbors? Isn't it
> Where there are cows? But here there are no cows.
> Before I built a wall I'd ask to know
> What I was walling in or walling out,
> And to whom I was like to give offense.
> Something there is that doesn't love a wall,
> That wants it down.'

> Poetry is the supreme fiction, madame.
> Take the moral law and make a nave of it
> And from the nave build haunted heaven. Thus,
> The conscience is converted into palms,
> Like windy citherns hankering for hymns.
> We agree in principle. That's clear.

If you imagine how each of these passages would sound if someone spoke them to you—or, better yet, if you read them aloud—you'll see that each has a specific, strongly marked verbal style that is quite different from the other's, and that both are probably very different from your own style. And as you read more poems by each poet (Robert Frost and Wallace Stevens, respectively) you'll find that the sound of each of these short selections is typical of other works by its author. This recognizable, typical quality, which we hear in many varied poems by the same poet, is called the poet's **voice**. No matter what the poem is about, no matter whether it's the poet or someone else who seems to be speaking in it, Frost's work has the Frostian voice, as Stevens' work speaks in *his* voice.

The Speaker

But, just because we can recognize Frost's voice in so many of his poems, does that mean that he is always speaking personally and directly in them? Let's look back at the lines by Frost, from "Mending Wall" (above). The situation of the poem suggests that the speaker is a farmer who does his own work. He's not a generalized, abstract farmer, but a distinct personality, articulate (at least as compared with his laconic neighbor), talking in a manner countrified and playful and ironic by turns, with diction that appears rougher than it is, for it contains rather elegant usages such as "to whom" and "spring is the mischief in me." The poem uses a **speaker** who has characteristics of Frost himself, but he does not have all of Frost's characteristics; he is somewhat idealized from the intractable and self-centered man that we now know Frost sometimes was. So, since the portrait of Frost as the poem's speaker is a highly selective or stylized one, it is a mistake to identify the two exactly.

Let's look at another example:

> I am afraid, this morning, of my face.
> It looks at me
> From the rear-view mirror, with the eyes I hate,
> The smile I hate. Its plain, lined look
> Of gray discovery
> Repeats to me: "You're old." That's all, I'm old.
>
> (Jarrell, "Next Day")

This might well be a "confessional" poem, with the author recounting a sudden onset of self-loathing and the sense that the best of life has already passed. Reading other poems by the same poet, we'd recognize the same voice in many of them. And there's nothing improbable about the feelings expressed, while the way they are expressed seems authentic enough. Surely the poet must have gone through this experience; surely the poem is autobiographical. But the rest of the poem identifies the speaker as a woman, while the author, Randall Jarrell, was a man.

We have used the word *speaker,* above; critics, and others who read poetry, have found it a useful term, distinguishing the person who "talks" the poem from its author. Generally, it's safe to assume that the speaker is partly or wholly fictional. Even confessional poetry, a mode of recent years in which poets make apparently direct use of autobiographical situations and intense personal feelings, has a certain distance from the experiences it describes. As Diane Wakoski puts it, "The Diane who's in my poems is not a real person. She's a person I would like to be, that I can imagine myself being; even though I put all my faults in my poems, it doesn't mean [Diane's] not a fantasy or imagined person." This relationship between poet and speaker has led to the speaker sometimes being called a **persona**. *Persona* is the Greek word for *mask*, such as actors wore in performances of classical Greek drama. The term expresses the fact that while the poet may be considered to inhabit a poem, he is there as a voice heard through the mask, creating a character other than himself. It is that character who engages our attention.

There are, of course, times when the poetic mask through which the writer speaks is little more artful or invented than the masks we turn to each other in the ordinary way we go about our lives with other people. In such cases, it may then be a convenient shorthand to call the speaker "the poet" or "Frost" (if that happens to be the case). For clarity's sake, however, we avoid that shorthand in these discussions, for the distinction is a meaningful one.

The Listener

Speech is a means of communication: if there is a speaker, there must be at least one listener. Often the speaker in a poem may seem to be addressing us directly, as in "Mending Wall," which is like a story told to anyone who cares to listen. But as we must bear in mind that poet and persona are never precisely the same, so the listener may not be the same as the reader.

> Let us go, through certain half-deserted streets,
> The muttering retreats
> Of restless nights in one-night cheap hotels
> And sawdust restaurants with oyster-shells:
> Streets that follow like a tedious argument
> Of insidious intent
> To lead you to an overwhelming question . . .
> Oh, do not ask, 'What is it?'
> Let us go and make our visit.
>
> (Eliot, "The Love Song of J. Alfred Prufrock")

Prufrock must be speaking to someone. He uses the words "us" and "you"; he invites someone to accompany him on a journey and even forestalls a question. But is he speaking to us? How could we, outside the poem, enter it to join him on his visit, or ask him a question he could possibly hear? There must be a fictional listener in the poem itself, whose presence influences strongly what Prufrock says and how he says it, and whose reaction (though we can't see or hear it) makes him break off in the middle of a thought.

Eliot's poem is a dramatic monologue, a form which traditionally assumes a listener in the poem with whom the speaker seems to be in conversation. But many other kinds of poems include particular listeners within them:

> I wanted so ably
> to reassure you, I wanted
> the man you took to be me,
>
> to comfort you . . .
>
> (Creeley, "The World")

> Daddy, I have had to kill you.
> You died before I had time . . .
>
> (Plath, "Daddy")

Thy great protruding head-light fix'd in front,
Thy long, pale, floating vapor-pennants, tinged with delicate
  purple,
The dense and murky clouds out-belching from thy smoke-
  stack . . .

(Whitman, "To a Locomotive in Winter")

Thirtyfive years
I lived with my husband.
The plumtree is white today
with masses of flowers.

(Williams, "The Widow's Lament in Springtime")

"The World" is a love poem, which may or may not have been an actual communication from the poet to a woman he loved; to us, strangers to speaker and listener, both are inside the poem, the speaker seeking a particular response from his beloved. "Daddy," however, is addressed to a dead man, who could hardly be expected to hear or respond to what the speaker is saying; and Whitman's poem actually addresses a locomotive as though it were able to understand him. This rhetorical device of speaking to an absent or dead person, or to an object or an abstraction, as though it were present, could hear and understand, is called **apostrophe**; it expresses an attitude more directly and vividly than if the object spoken to were merely spoken about. In Williams' poem, on the other hand, the widow does not seem to be speaking to anyone in the poem or to the readers. She is speaking to herself, a form of inner conversation called a **soliloquy**. The poem, as a poem, is addressed by the poet to the reader, but within the poem a character who is not the poet muses aloud, caught up in a dream of the past, oblivious to the audience of readers who overhear her thoughts.

Varieties of Tone

Suppose you were to receive a love letter that began, "This is to inform you that the state of my feelings toward you as affective object has evolved in a markedly positive direction." It would be hard to believe that your friend loved you more than ever, even though that is what the words say. Suppose that you go to an undertaker about the burial of a beloved relative, and his first remark is, "Where d'yuh wanna dump the stiff?" Once again, it would be hard to believe in the undertaker's concern, even though his question is one that has to be asked and answered before the funeral plans can go forward.

The point must be obvious: in order to communicate successfully, we try to make sure that our words are appropriate, not only to the subject at hand, but also to the situation and to our listeners. Choosing words whose denotations and connotations express the intended meaning is important, but is only the basic, atomic level of organization. Poets in particular take great pains to make their choices consistent (or, if not, to ensure that inconsistencies are intended and meaningful), so that sentences and whole poems may appropriately express attitudes and feelings. This expressive quality is called **tone**.

The broadest and most immediately striking component of tone is the **level of diction**, the degree of formality. Here are some passages at different levels of diction:

And obscure as that heaven of the Jews,
Thy guerdon . . . Accolade thou dost bestow
Of anonymity time cannot raise:
Vibrant reprieve and pardon thou dost show.
(Crane, "Proem: To Brooklyn Bridge")

You were silly like us; your gift survived it all:
The parish of rich women, physical decay,
Yourself. Mad Ireland hurt you into poetry.
(Auden, "In Memory of W. B. Yeats")

I can't help it, she said, pulling a long face,
It's them pills I took, to bring it off, she said.
(She's had five already, and nearly died of young George.)
The chemist* said it would be all right, but I've never been
the same.
(Eliot, "The Waste Land")

cool-cool is so cool he was un-cooled by other niggers' cool
cool-cool ultracool was bop-cool/ice box cool so cool cold cool
his wine didn't have to be cooled, him was air conditioned
cool . . .
cool-cool so cool him nick-named refrigerator.
(Lee, "But He Was Cool")

Crane's diction is what has been called formal or elevated; by it we know that he aspires to present a grand subject in appropriate language. Auden writes in what we might describe as standard or middle diction—the style in which most modern poetry, and indeed much prose, is written. Eliot, in this example, seeks to present the way ordinary people ordinarily talk, which is called informal or colloquial diction (these are two Cockney women in a pub talking about an abortion). Lee writes in what linguists call dialect, specifically Black English. In each case, the poet has sought a level of diction generally suitable to his subject.

Within each of these rather large areas of the language, poets modulate tone so as to convey particular kinds of feeling:

The whiskey on your breath
Could make a small boy dizzy;
But I hung on like death:
Such waltzing was not easy.

We romped until the pans
Slid from the kitchen shelf;

* Pharmacist.

My mother's countenance
Could not unfrown itself.

(Roethke, "My Papa's Waltz")

Sundays too my father got up early
And put his clothes on in the blueblack cold,
then with cracked hands that ached
from labor in the weekday weather made
banked fires blaze. No one ever thanked him.

(Hayden, "Those Winter Sundays")

There's a stake in your fat black heart
And the villagers never liked you.
They are dancing and stamping on you.
They always *knew* it was you.
Daddy, daddy, you bastard, I'm through.

(Plath, "Daddy")

These poems are all written at about the middle level of diction, Hayden's a bit more elevated and Plath's less so, yet the tone of each is quite distinctive. The distinctions result largely from the effect of certain specific words. The son in Roethke's poem speaks to "papa," the daughter in Plath's to "daddy," and the son in Hayden's of "my father," and each of these forms of address affects and agrees with the emotional perspective of its poem. "Papa" and "daddy" suggest an intimacy which "my father" does not; and indeed the tone of Hayden's poem is rather detached and even chilly, an effect reinforced by the word "labor" (instead of "work") and the slightly rhetorical "weekday weather." It's as though the speaker were asserting his adulthood, his independence of his father, by using grown-up words. "Papa," however, is just right for Roethke's poem, which recalls a boisterous occasion in childhood; the warmer tone comes also from words like "hung on" and "romped," which evoke physical closeness and hilarious play. (Mother, on the other hand, is not "mama," and the formality of "countenance" and "unfrown itself" reveals the son's cooler feelings toward her.) The title of Sylvia Plath's poem, "Daddy," accords with the speaker's simple vocabulary, which might suggest a certain childishness, while the slurring epithets "fat" and "black" contribute to the effect of a tantrum, the way in which the speaker of the poem expresses her anger. In these poems and many others, tone rather than description tells us the speaker's (and indeed the poet's) attitude.

Irony

There are many kinds of **irony**. Often irony is a manner of speaking—a special tone—as when a friend says to you sarcastically, "That was just great," when both of you know that whatever it was was dreadful. But irony is more than mere sarcasm: verbally it may be far more subtle, and it may also inform actions, situations, and even a view of the universe.

Irony always involves two levels of meaning. On the surface, there are the actual words. Here, for example, is part of a poem by A. E. Housman:

Smart lad, to slip betimes away
From fields where glory does not stay . . .

Now you will not swell the rout
Of lads that wore their honours out,
Runners whom renown outran
And the name died before the man.

("To an Athlete Dying Young")

The speaker's tone is congratulatory: "smart lad." But the athlete has not retired, he has died, and the occasion for this poem is his funeral: the speaker's words belie the emotions which, as pallbearer and eulogist, he may be presumed to feel, and which are perceptible in the rest of the poem below its ironic surface. At this deeper level, the real meaning of the speaker's words contradicts their apparent meaning. The irony is in the knowing of both meanings, in the double perspective that sees both levels of meaning and the discrepancy between them.

Often an ironic twist may be at the heart of a poem's meaning, as in these lines from Edwin Arlington Robinson's poem, "Mr. Flood's Party":

. . . He raised up to the light
The jug that he had gone so far to fill . . .

Alone, as if enduring to the end
A valiant armor of scarred hopes outworn,
He stood there in the middle of the road
Like Roland's ghost winding a silent horn.

To compare Mr. Flood, a tipsy, elderly, insignificant New Englander, with the heroic knight Roland of the medieval French epic, is unexpected, even startling. Roland, defending the rear of the Emperor Charlemagne's army against an enemy vastly superior in numbers, refused to sound his horn for help until mortally wounded; Mr. Flood, climbing up from town to his hilly retreat, has merely stopped to have a drink. But the ironic comparison offers us a double perspective in which to see Mr. Flood. Next to Roland he seems even smaller and less important than before; yet, for a moment, we are invited to regard his independence of the common herd and his grace in defeat as heroic qualities, worthy of poetic celebration as were those of Roland himself.

Situations and events may be no less ironic than words. The death of an athlete, as in Housman's poem, is ironic because it involves a contradiction between appearances and reality. Athletes in their prime symbolize health, physical vigor, youthfulness—all the qualities that we associate with irrepressible life and the denial of death—yet death will not, finally, be denied, and even youth and beauty may fall victim to accident, murder, suicide. Another poem that presents an ironic view of the universe is Hardy's poem about the sinking of the Titanic, "The Convergence of the Twain":

And as the smart ship grew
In stature, grace, and hue,
In shadowy silent distance grew the Iceberg too.

Alien they seemed to be:
No mortal eye could see
The intimate welding of their later history.

The speaker points up the irony of the situation: while the English were building and fitting out the world's most luxurious and "unsinkable" ocean liner, nature (guided, Hardy believed, by a supernatural force he calls the Immanent Will) was rearing the iceberg to smash the ship on her first voyage.

IMAGERY

In poetry, an **image** is a presentation in words of something the poet has perceived. **Imagery** is the collective word we use for a group of images. The description may be of an object seen, or of a sound, a smell, a taste, a touch or other physical sensation, or the feeling of tensions and movements in one's own body. All of these are nonverbal sensations; to put them into words is to transform them.

it was muggy sunny, the wind from the sea steady and high,
crisp in the running sand,
some breakthroughs of sun

(Ammons, "Corsons Inlet")

. . . the squeal and the blare and the
tweedle of bagpipes, a bugle and fiddles

(Williams, "The Dance")

. . . a sudden sharp hot stink of fox

(Hughes, "The Thought-Fox")

my massive buttocks slipping
like oiled parts with each light step.

(Levine, "Animals Are Passing from Our Lives")

None of these images lists all the sensations you might feel if you were suddenly to change places with the poet. They are details, chosen to evoke the essence of each perception in your imagination. Some poems seem mainly descriptive:

Cavalry Crossing a Ford

A line in long array where they wind betwixt green islands,
They take a serpentine course, their arms flash in the sun—
hark to the musical clank,
Behold the silvery river, in it the splashing horses loitering
stop to drink,
Behold the brown-faced men, each group, each person a
picture, the negligent rest on the saddles,

Some emerge on the opposite bank, others are just entering
the ford—while,
Scarlet and blue and snowy white,
The guidon flags flutter gayly in the wind.

(Whitman)

But poets are not limited to the direct presentation of concrete detail in their effort to transform a perception into words. They may also compare that perception with something else, often quite different. They do this by employing figurative language.

Figurative Language

Figurative language is far from being the exclusive property of poets. Everybody uses it all the time, in order to give freshness and spice to what they say. Slang expressions like "to *background* another *writer*"* are figurative, and so is much of the jargon people use in their work, like the Watergate conspirators' "to *stonewall* it." We also use comparisons to make our point; sometimes it isn't enough to say, "He's happy," you want to say something like "He's happy as a possum up an old gum tree" or "He's happy as a bee in clover."

Often the images that come to mind most quickly when we speak figuratively have had their freshness worn away from overuse. Take the phrase "puppet government." When you think about it, this is a very sharp figure: it suggests that the government is an inert mechanism incapable of action except when someone else "pulls the strings." This expression is so useful that in fact people no longer need to think about it, they know so well the situation it describes. Such worn figures are called clichés. (Still other figures have completely lost the power to evoke comparisons—for example, the "legs" of a chair—though a hundred years ago members of genteel society used to substitute the word "limbs" as somehow less sexually suggestive.)

The simplest form of comparison declares itself by using words such as *like*, *as*, or *as if*, and is called **simile**:

What could have made her peaceful with *a mind*
That nobleness made *simple as a fire*,
With *beauty like a tightened bow* . . . ?

(Yeats, "No Second Troy")

And *life is* too much *like a pathless wood*
Where your face burns and tickles with the cobwebs
Broken across it, and one eye is weeping
From a twig's having lashed across it open.

(Frost, "Birches")

Picking up change, *hands like a walrus*,
and *a face like a barndoor's* . . .

(Creeley, "Wicker Basket")

* "Backgrounding" another "writer" is slang used by graffiti artists ("writers") in New York City. To "background" another writer is to write a new piece of graffiti over his work, reducing it to a background; if you respect his work, you don't do it.

The aquarium is gone. Everywhere,
giant finned cars nose forward like fish . . .
(Lowell, "For the Union Dead")

Another form of figurative comparison, because it does without *like* or *as*, suggests that the thing compared and the thing it's compared with are not merely similar but, for the purposes of the poem, somehow identical. This is called **metaphor**:

. . . a flower stand
Above which *hovers an exploding rose*
Fired from a long-necked crystal vase . . .
(Wilbur, "Playboy")

the Cambridge *ladies who live in furnished souls*
are unbeautiful and *have comfortable minds*
(Cummings, "the Cambridge ladies who live in furnished souls")

The provinces of his body revolted,
The squares of his mind were empty,
Silence invaded the suburbs . . .
(Auden, "In Memory of W. B. Yeats")

That form of figurative language in which an object is given human attributes is called **personification**:

Earth can not count the sons she bore:
The wounded lynx, the wounded man
Come trailing blood unto her door;
She shelters both as best she can.
(Millay, "The Return")

The figure of speech in which a part of a thing or an action stands for the whole is **synechdoche**:

The hand that signed the paper felled a city;
Five sovereign fingers taxed the breath,
Doubled the globe of dead and halved a country . . .
(D. Thomas, "The Hand That Signed the Paper")

There is also a figure in which a thing or action is replaced by one of its attributes, or by something closely associated with it; it is called **metonymy**. It is rarely found in modern poems, but it is fairly common in contemporary usage, as when we speak of a king or queen as "the crown."

When a metaphor is carried beyond the first flash of correspondence, and the comparison is explored in detail, we call the result an **extended metaphor**:

The yellow fog that rubs its back upon the window-panes,

The yellow smoke that rubs its muzzle on the window-
 panes,
Licked its tongue into the corners of the evening,
Lingered upon the pools that stand in drains,
Let fall upon its back the soot that falls from chimneys,
Slipped by the terrace, made a sudden leap,
And seeing that it was a soft October night,
Curled once about the house, and fell asleep.

(Eliot, "The Love Song of J. Alfred Prufrock")

Eliot never says that the fog is *like* a cat; he never uses the word *cat* at all. But he makes the fog behave in so catlike a way that we know with certainty what is being compared to what. This nightmarish image—imagine a cat large enough to curl about a house—helps to characterize the speaker, J. Alfred Prufrock, who has set forth to make a visit he dreads, and who elsewhere in the poem sees the evening as "spread out . . . like a patient etherised upon a table."

A metaphor can be a whole poem:

Oread

Whirl up, sea—
whirl your pointed pines,
splash your great pines
on our rocks,
hurl your green over us,
cover us with your pools of fir.

(H.D.)

Symbol

Symbols, like metaphors, can extend the range of a poem's associations. But a symbol is not simply another kind of figurative language: put most simply, a **symbol** is an object or an action which both represents itself and at the same time has a larger meaning than it ordinarily has—a meaning which can often be multiple or ambiguous. Symbols are more suggestive than figures of speech, usually more complex, and often harder to interpret.

Let's start simply, with an example of symbols outside poetry. The American flag is a symbol. Physically, it is nothing but a rectangle of colored cloth, but it "means" all that Americans have in common and everything they, as a nation, have done or hope to do. Obviously, this symbol draws forth powerful emotions of love, hate, or both, and not only from Americans. How one responds depends on what particular qualities or actions one happens to associate most vividly with the idea of "The United States," as well as one's attitude toward them. A more universal symbol, the cross, is a simple geometric form, but for billions of Christians it stands for Christ's crucifixion—itself a symbolic event which represents the attitude of the Christian God toward humanity and, conversely, Christians' attitudes toward God, the cosmos, and themselves. That two interesecting lines can somehow embody a view of the universe gives some idea of the power symbols have.

A national flag and the cross are conventional symbols, in that while people and nations may fight over the validity of the concepts they symbolize, most or all know, in general, what the symbols mean. (Not all flags or crosses are symbolic: the white flag, which means only one thing—"truce"—and the crosses you use in answering a multiple-choice test are not symbols but signs.) Many other symbols have come to be nearly as well-known through their repeated use in literature. The color green, for example, often stands for the time of fresh leaves and grass, the spring, and therefore indirectly for youth and love.

In older poems it may have been easier for a poet to use a symbol like the cross or green with some confidence that his readers would understand its implications. Nowadays, however, poets are likely to trust their own private symbols (from whatever depths in the poet they may come) as more directly expressing their meaning. This can sometimes make for a problem in reading, as the poet's symbols may be hard to identify. The only clue to a poem's symbolic level of meaning may be that some object in it doesn't act quite naturally, or that the speaker seems interested in it in an odd way. For an example, read Adrienne Rich's "Diving into the Wreck" (p. 435, too long to be reprinted here). Most of the poem seems to be a more or less straightforward account of a scuba dive after sunken treasure. But the very first line is surprising: what has a "book of myths" to do with "diving into the wreck?" And the ladder hanging over the side of the schooner: why is it hanging "innocently," and wherefor the ominous remark, "We know what it is for, we who have used it"? And toward the end, the speaker makes an unexpected identification:

> we are the half-destroyed instruments
> that once held to a course
> the water-eaten log
> the fouled compass
>
> we are, I am, you are
> by cowardice or courage
> the one who find our way
> back to this scene
> carrying a knife, a camera
> a book of myths
> in which
> our names do not appear.

The metaphorical likening between the "we" in this passage and nautical instruments that measure speed, distance, and direction, obliges us to consider that the sunken ship toward which the speaker dives is not merely a sunken ship. Likewise, the observation that it requires "cowardice or courage," not merely curiosity, to "find our way back to this scene," suggests that in "diving into the wreck" the speaker feels an emotional risk. The sunken ship, the schooner on the surface, and the ladder and the water between them seem symbolic of a particular kind of human experience, of going back into one's memories. The surface coherence of the narrative is so strong that one might easily overlook this symbolic meaning altogether—but to do so would be to read a "different" poem than the one the poet wrote.

Some poets have invented private symbologies, or systems of symbols and their associations, that are almost a philosophy or religion. Robert Graves's book *The White Goddess* sets forth a complex interrelationship of supernatural and natural personages, events, and symbols which, he maintains, are inevitably the inspiration of "all true poetry"; "To Juan at the Winter Solstice" (p. 226) is among other things an abstract of Graves's system. William Butler Yeats invented several symbologies, each of which often makes unexpected use of familiar symbols, and adds new ones as well:

> Red Rose, proud Rose, sad Rose of all my days!
> Come near me, while I sing the ancient ways . . .
>
> . . . thine own sadness, whereof stars, grown old
> In dancing silver sandalled on the sea,
> Sing in their high and lonely melody.
> Come near, that no more blinded by man's fate,
> I find under the boughs of love and hate,
> In all poor foolish things that live a day,
> Eternal beauty wandering on her way.
>
> (Yeats, "To the Rose upon the Rood of Time")

Yeats's pervasive use of symbols was one of the needs of his way of thinking; he once wrote, "A symbol is indeed the only possible expression of some invisible essence, a transparent lamp about a spiritual flame." For him the rose was a symbol of transfiguration and fulfillment, as it has been for many religious writers. Here, however, Yeats infuses this traditional symbol with new meaning by imagining it as flowering from the Rood (Christ's cross)—itself a symbol of time and suffering, which the rose transfigures into beauty. The rose is not allowed to behave as roses ordinarily do, nor do any of its attributes except its beauty really apply to the things it stands for.

Myth and Archetype

A **myth** is like a symbol, but involves an extended plot: it is a story which symbolizes something else. Myths once "explained" the origins and qualities of natural forces, the characteristic situations of human life and history, and social customs and observances, through the lives and actions of immortal beings. Such beings are usually imagined in human form, with human passions and ambitions, but exempt from mortal conditions and possessing energies and skills far above our own. Some of these immortals personify natural forces (fertility, the sea); others personify abstract human qualities (love, wisdom). In some mythologies (for example, the American Indian), the idea-beings are associated with animals such as the eagle or the wolf, or actually are those animals.

A **mythology** (that is, a collection of myths), it is now generally agreed, was not merely a series of fictions. It embodied the actual beliefs of a particular culture at a particular time; moreover, most myths were apparently connected with the performance of religious rituals. We, who no longer believe them, may view myths as quaint old stories or as obsolete explanations for phenomena about which we know better. But for many poets over the centuries, and for poets writing today, myths have had an undeniable attraction, because they remain powerful symbols for certain kinds of feeling and experience.

Among the mythologies most commonly used by poets have been the Greek, the Roman, and the Germanic. Poets have also used the stories in the Old and New Testaments in the same way, and even those who disbelieve the literal truth of the Bible may still find it one of the most compelling mythologies. Other, less familiar mythologies have also been drawn on in contemporary poetry, among them the Egyptian, the Irish, the Hindu, and the American Indian.

Within the past hundred years, scholars have compared the mythologies of widely different societies at different times and different places and found that each has many stories, themes, and personages in common with the others. Naturally enough, few mythologies are without a creation myth, giving the physical universe a supernatural origin; but many also have in common a story about the murder and resurrection of a god or king, such as the Nordic god Balder, Osiris in Egyptian religion, and indeed Christ. Another common motif is the quest, a god's or hero's long and dangerous journey to achieve a desired goal. Among the most famous quest stories are Orpheus' descent to the underworld to bring his dead wife Euridice back to life; Odysseus' epic journey home from the Trojan War; and the quest of King Arthur's knights of the Round Table for the Holy Grail. A basic book of comparative mythology, Sir James Frazer's *The Golden Bough*, provided T. S. Eliot with much raw material for *The Waste Land* (p. 179), among whose mythical motifs is the theme of the quest.

Some literary critics call these common mythical elements **archetypes**, from a Greek word meaning "ancient patterns." The term, which the psychologist Carl Jung was the first to apply in this sense, is used to describe such patterns as they occur not only in myths and works of literature but also in ordinary people's dreams and in psychotic fantasies. Literary critics interested in archetypes find them in themes and characters and also in images and even in literary forms and kinds. Perhaps because these "ancient patterns" appear to be so pervasive in religion, literature, and our own minds, they enable us to share deep common human experiences.

Because of this power, then, myths and archetypes have been much used by poets. Rarely, however, will a poet simply retell one of the old stories; more often than not myth will be used fleetingly and by allusion, and the archetypal situation will be buried deep and expressed through seemingly ordinary surface narratives. Yeats's "Leda and the Swan" (p. 45) sets a myth in the foreground, Lawrence's "The Ship of Death" (p. 124) uses archetypal elements as part of its underpinning

Allusion

An **allusion** is a passing, indirect reference to anything outside the poem—a form of words, a work of art, an actual event—which is not precisely identified but which the writer, in most cases, expects or hopes the reader will recognize. Most poetic allusions are meant to bring some aspect of the original context into the poem, and to establish connections between the poem itself and a world outside it.

And then to awake, and the farm, like a wanderer white
With the dew, come back, the cock on his shoulder: it was all
Shining, it was Adam and maiden,
The sky gathered again
And the sun grew round that very day.
So it must have been after the birth of the simple light
In the first, spinning place . . .

(D. Thomas, "Fern Hill")

And can a man his own quietus make
with a bare bodkin?*

With daggers, bodkins, bullets, man can make
a bruise or break of exit for his life;
but is that a quietus, O tell me, is it quietus?

(Lawrence, "The Ship of Death")

If I think of a king at nightfall,
Of three men, and more, on the scaffold

. . .

And of one who died blind and quiet,
Why should we celebrate
These dead men more than the dying?

(Eliot, "Little Gidding")

Who threw potato salad at CCNY lecturers on Dadaism and subsequently presented themselves on the granite steps of the madhouse with shaven heads and harlequin speech of suicide, demanding instanteous lobotomy . . .

(Ginsberg, "Howl")

Each of these allusions is to a different kind of source and for a different purpose. Dylan Thomas, describing the farm where he spent summer holidays as a boy, opens a view of the dew-covered farm at dawn outward into a vision of Eden ("it was Adam and maiden") soon after the Biblical Creation ("after the birth of the simple light / In the first spinning place"). He gives the reader just enough to make the metaphorical identification—not saying Eden, or yet Adam and Eve, but "Adam and maiden"—and moves on swiftly. Lawrence, musing on death, recalls Hamlet's meditation on suicide—quoting, in fact, two lines (III.i.75–6)—and then goes on to use Shakespeare's words to pose to himself Hamlet's own dilemma: is there an existence after death? The allusion suggests the universality of Lawrence's theme, and may even conjure up a vision of a dialogue across the centuries. "Little Gidding" is also a meditative poem, in which Eliot permits the village of Little Gidding, once an Anglican religious community, to evoke its

---

* *quietus:* settlement; *bodkin:* dagger.

historical associations: of King Charles I, who came there after his final defeat in the English Civil War to fortify his spirit; of his execution with his two chief aides in 1649; and of the blind poet John Milton, who had taken Oliver Cromwell's side against the King. The poem was written during the Second World War, and "the dying" are Eliot's contemporaries who were victims of the conflict.

These are relatively familiar allusions, or if not (as in the Eliot passage) the reader can at least tell that something outside the poem is being referred to. The case is different, however, with the potato-salad-thrower in Ginsberg's poem. We now know that he was a real person—the Carl Solomon to whom the poem is dedicated. But this is rather specialized knowledge. Some allusions, in other words, are so subtle that they can easily pass unnoticed or unrecognized, so esoteric that few readers will know their source, or so "private" that the experience in the poet's life to which they refer can only be guessed at. Unless the poet has simply miscalculated, such allusions must make their point by themselves, without support from their sources, as part of the poem. Certainly "Howl" has exerted its power, over the years, on many readers who cannot have known whether or not its many allusions were to real events.

POETIC FORM

Much of what we call poetic form is the management of the sound of a poem—its rhythms, its pace, its pauses, its vowels and consonants. All writers pay attention to these aspects of language, but in most writing the effects are rather subtle and subordinate. In poetry, these effects are often in the foreground, and their study—called **prosody**—is an important part of the experience of poetic meaning.

Lines

The most obvious difference between prose and poetry is that in poetry the lines of type usually don't go all the way across the page. This is a crude distinction, but it still holds; in spite of many changes in verse form, poetry is still written in **lines**. In fact, the line is almost the only device common to all poems, even poems as different as these two:

Stopping by Woods on a Snowy Evening

Whose woods these are I think I know.
His house is in the village, though;
He will not see me stopping here
To watch his woods fill up with snow.

My little horse must think it queer
To stop without a farmhouse near
Between the woods and frozen lake
The darkest evening of the year.

He gives his harness bells a shake
To ask if there is some mistake.
The only other sound's the sweep
Of easy wind and downy flake.

The woods are lovely, dark and deep,
But I have promises to keep,
And miles to go before I sleep,
And miles to go before I sleep.

The Red Wheelbarrow

so much depends
upon

a red wheel
barrow

glazed with rain
water

beside the white
chickens.

The most important fact about the verse line is that it breaks the poem wherever the poet chooses, regardless of grammar, punctuation, or even word division (*wheel / barrow*). When reading poems aloud, most people tend to stress the last word in a line or to hold it longer than usual, then to pause briefly as their eyes travel back to the left to pick up the beginning of the next line. Poets reading their own work usually do the same: listen to recordings by Dylan Thomas or Denise Levertov, and you will seldom be in doubt where the lines end, even if the poems are new to you. (Levertov says that for her the pause between lines has the value of "half a comma.") The line ending, then, is a specialized form of punctuation, and poets use it for rhetorical and musical effects.

Different poets have different uses for the line ending, but most have a few purposes in common. First, all those pauses slow down the reading; the shorter the line, the more often we must pause, and the more deliberate the poetic utterance seems. These rhetorical "pauses for effect" also allow what has just been said to sink in. Williams' "The Red Wheelbarrow" has seven pauses among only fourteen words, and each pause contributes to the weight of his pronouncement. The weight is greatest on the last word of the line, which is underlined not only by the pause that follows it but by that slight emphasis which most readers give it. It's not surprising, then, to find that many poets arrange their poems so that important words come at the ends of lines. (The first word of a line is another strategic spot, since it breaks in on that slight but perceptible silence between the lines and thus receives a bit of extra emphasis.)

The pauses that end poetic lines also have a purpose that might be called "musical." They divide poems into phrasings the way rests divide the melodic line in a piece of music. Sometimes the phrasing agrees with the sentence structure, and the end of a sentence, clause, or other syntactic unit comes at the end of a line. This increases the stress on the last word and the pause after it, and is called **end-stopping**. The lines in the last stanza of Frost's "Stopping by Woods on a Snowy Evening" are all end-stopped. If, on the other hand, the phrasing cuts across a syntactic unit, as in line 11 of Frost's poem, the stress on the last word and the pause after it are still perceptible but less marked, and the result is called **enjambment**. The breaks between lines may be placed in order to ensure that each line will contain a specific number of syllables or stressed syllables, or they may measure the amount of time each line will take to read, or even specify where the reader is to breathe! This rather bewildering range of choices will to some degree be sorted out in the following discussions, but often you will have only the poem itself to show you just what the poet meant by a particular plan of line-divisions and how these should sound when the poem is read aloud.

Rhyme

The largest English dictionaries list over four hundred thousand words, yet linguists set the number of distinct sounds of which these words are composed at about thirty-five. As a result, English is full of words that rhyme. Rhyming is actively avoided in most conversation and prose writing, but for centuries it has been one of the most commonly used formal devices of poetry.

Why should this be? There are many possible answers, none of them definitive. Children find rhyming an entrancing game, and many poets may still feel some of that enjoyment. Light verse almost always rhymes, and sometimes the rhyming is much of the fun, as when the author sets up a seemingly impossible rhyme, then solves the problem with an unexpected but inevitable word. (Ogden Nash did it often: "Farewell, farewell, you old rhinoceros, / I'll stare at something less prepoceros.") Rhymes help you to remember which months have thirty days, or they can keep a commercial jingle rattling around in your head. Most popular songs have rhymed lyrics; poetry and song have long been related, and possibly the recurrences of rhyme are equivalent to the recurrences of melody. And some poets use the requirements of rhyme to make poems harder to write but more engaging to them and their readers; Robert Frost once disparaged composing free verse as like playing tennis without a net.

True rhymes occur when the last stressed syllables of two or more lines share the same vowel sounds, followed by identical-sounding consonants or unstressed syllables. When the last stressed syllable is also the last syllable, as in *sight* / *ignite*, the rhyme is traditionally said to be **masculine**; when the last stressed syllable is followed by one or two unstressed syllables, as is *condition* / *proposition*, the rhyme is **feminine**. (A convention of English poetry called **eye-rhyme** has it that *cough* may sometimes be assumed to rhyme with *enough*, or *sigh* with *sympathy*, though these words do not sound alike when read aloud.)

Poets who like rhyme do not use it randomly, or merely for its own sake. It is part of the web of sound and meaning which all poetic devices help to weave. And the most obvious purpose of rhyme is that it draws still more attention to the end of the poetic line, and to the break between one line and the next. Because of this, poets often put key words into a rhyming position:

> The chestnut casts his flambeaux, and the flowers
> Stream from the hawthorn on the wind away,
> The doors clap to, the pane is blind with showers.
> Pass me the can, lad; there's an end of May.
>
> (Housman, "The Chestnut Casts His Flambeaux")

The inversion which sets "away" at the end of the second line might, in another poem, be merely a convenience of a poet seeking a rhyme for "May." But the theme of these four lines, and of the poem, is that time passes, leaves us, streams *away* like spring flowers; the slight emphasis on "away," then, underlines the poem's meaning. Often words whose sounds rhyme have some relation in meaning as well—they are similar, or opposite, or ask to be compared:

> Miniver Cheevy, born too late,
> Scratched his head and kept on thinking;
> Miniver coughed, and called it fate,
> And kept on drinking.
>
> (Robinson, "Miniver Cheevy")

The rhyme between "born too late" (Miniver Cheevy's situation) and "called it fate" (his response to it) has a kind of unforced conclusiveness about it, while the rhyme between "thinking" and "drinking," emphasized by the short final line, is a witty comment on the quality of Chevy's thinking and seems to "clinch" the poem.

A frequent purpose of rhyme is to unify the poem: to draw you along with rising expectations of an inevitable rhyme, and to fulfill those expectations at a crucial point in the poem. The poems by Housman and Robinson share the same pattern of rhymes, or **rhyme scheme**, and each works the same way: the first two lines begin a thought in such a way that you can predict neither the conclusions nor the rhymes, the third line partly completes the thought and provides one of the rhymes, and the last line is the clincher. Other rhyme schemes work in other ways:

> "It shows a mighty lot of cheek
> To study chemistry and Greek
> When Mister Charlie needs a hand
> To hoe the cotton on his land,
> And when Miss Ann looks for a cook,
> Why stick your nose inside a book?"
>
> (Randall, "Booker T. and W. E. B.")

> Going to second Mass on a summer Sunday—
> You meet me and you say:
> 'Don't forget to see about the cattle—'
> Among your earthiest words the angels stray.
>
> (Kavanagh, "In Memory of My Mother")

One dark night,
my Tudor Ford climbed the hill's skull;
I watched for love-cars. Lights turned down,
they lay together, hull to hull,
where the graveyard shelves on the town. . . .
My mind's not right.

(Lowell, "Skunk Hour")

Dudley Randall's poem is in couplets (pairs of rhymed lines). The rhymes tie together lines closely connected by their meaning and slightly separate them from the other couplets. In couplets the rhymes are very noticeable because they follow upon each other so closely. The couplet is therefore a favorite rhyme scheme when the rhymes themselves are unusual or funny, as in light or comic verse. In Kavanagh's poem only half the lines rhyme, still exploiting the effect of rhyme but more sparingly than do Housman and Robinson.

Robert Lowell, on the other hand, rhymes his poem more complexly, and to keep track of the rhymes it is useful to outline their pattern. Conventionally, the rhyme that begins first is marked *a*, the second is *b*, and so on, while unrhymed lines are all *x*. The rhyme scheme in "Miniver Cheevy" is *abab*; Randall's is *aabbcc*; Kavanagh's, *xaxa*. Lowell's is *abcbca*. The middle four lines set up the same pattern of expectation and fulfillment as in the Housman and Robinson stanzas, but within a much longer arc that takes off from "night" and comes to rest with "right." Such a long wait for the rhyme might be expected to imply a meaningful connection between the rhyming lines, "One dark night," and "My mind's not right," as though the speaker's mind were itself darkened—and in fact Lowell has said that the first line speaks of a "dark night of the soul."

Rhymes may be placed elsewhere than at line endings, in which case they are called **internal rhymes**:

"No, baby, *no*, you may not *go*,
For the dogs are fierce and wild . . ."

(Randall, "Ballad of Birmingham")

The wilderness rose up to it,
And sprawled a*round*, no longer wild.
The jar was *round* upon the *ground*
And tall and of a port in air.

(Stevens, "Anecdote of the Jar")

Since rhyming words command so much attention, their appearance in midline usually signals us that something important is happening, as when the mother in Randall's poem emphatically tells her daughter not to go downtown. Stevens' poem, otherwise unrhymed, clusters three rhyming words in its middle, as though the jar which is said to tame the wilderness were also "taming" the sound of the poem into rhyme.

Some poets like the patterning and underlining effects of rhyme, but find that the sound of true rhyme is a bit too noticeable, the stress too strong for their purposes. They may instead use **near-rhyme** (or **slant rhyme**):

It seemed that out of battle I escaped
Down some profound dull tunnel, long since scooped
Through granites which titanic wars had groined.
Yet also there encumbered sleepers groaned,
Too fast in thought or death to be bestirred.
Then, as I probed them, one sprang up, and stared . . .

(Owen, "Strange Meeting")

Many times man lives and dies
Between his two eternities,
That of race and that of soul,
And ancient Ireland knew it all.

(Yeats, "Under Ben Bulben")

Near-rhyme is rhyme with the vowels slightly "off," but with the final consonants as expected or nearly so. (Note that technically speaking the first two lines of the Yeats selection are in eye-rhyme, not near-rhyme, but the actual effect when the poem is read aloud is the same.)

Many of the examples in the discussion of rhyme are stanzas. **Stanzas** are sections of a poem which are set off from each other by more space than usual. Within a poem, most or all of the stanzas are often the same number of lines long, and often use the same rhythms and rhyme scheme:

Children are dumb to say how hot the day is,
How hot the scent is of the summer rose,
How dreadful the black wastes of evening sky,
How dreadful the tall soldiers drumming by.

But we have speech, to chill the angry day,
And speech, to dull the rose's cruel scent.
We spell away the overhanging night,
We spell away the soldiers and the fright.

(Graves, "The Cool Web")

In many poems, stanzas are like verses of a song, in which the same melody returns accompanying different words. Each encompasses a complete thought, and each ends at the end of a sentence. But poets may play against the stanza divisions, and carry enjambment across the stanza break:

Well, I was ten and very much afraid.
In my kind world the dead were out of range
And I could not forgive the sad or strange
In beast or man. My father took the spade

And buried him. Last night I saw the grass
Slowly divide (it was the same scene
But now it glowed a fierce and mortal green)
And saw the dog emerging. I confess

I felt afraid again, but still he came . . .

(Wilbur, "The Pardon")

It is as if the speaker's strong emotions exerted such a tension on him as to force him to break the formal divisions of the poem.

Many types of stanza have been used so often that their characteristic forms have become fixed; and there are types of poems, such as the sonnet, which are also fixed forms. At the end of these discussions there is a glossary listing and describing the most common forms and kinds of poems, pointing to examples among the selections in this anthology.

Sound Effects Within the Line

The sounds of rhymes stand out in a poem because they echo each other so closely, especially when they come at the ends of lines. But poets take just as much care with the less noticeable sounds of the other words in the poem. "Let's say you have a choice of adjectives," says Denise Levertov, "and one has an onomatopoeic quality which you want, but it also has a couple of s's in it, and the rest of the line, or the line just before it, is already pretty sibilant, but you feel that line is right. You might have to forego the word that you've just found and keep on looking, because you can't have all those s's jammed together." For Levertov, as for many other poets, it's clearly not a matter of watching the sense, and letting the sounds take care of themselves.

The most frequent sound patterns within a line are **alliteration** (in which the consonant sounds, especially at the beginnings of words, are the same) and **assonance** (when several words near to each other have identical or very similar vowel sounds). Here are some examples:

Only the *stutter*ing *r*ifles' *r*apid *r*a*tt*le
Can pa*tt*er ou*t* thei*r* ha*st*y o*r*isons.
(Owen, "Anthem for Doomed Youth")

. . . and bid him whip
In *k*itchen *c*up*s* *c*on*c*upi*s*cent *c*urd*s*.
(Stevens, "The Emperor of Ice Cream")

Now it is *au*tumn and the f*a*lling fruit
and the l*o*ng journey t*o*wards oblivion.
(Lawrence, "The Ship of Death")

Owen's t's and r's imitate the sounds of gunfire; Stevens's hard c's and soft s's sound, if you will, like the spoon or whisk beating the milk. In both cases it is probable that at least one word—"patter" for Owen, "concupiscent" for Stevens—was chosen in large part because it fitted into the sound pattern. The effect of assonance in "The Ship of Death" is less specific, but perhaps the long, open vowels may suggest a drowsiness such as might evoke the coming of winter and of natural death.

Rhythm

There are two species of rhythm in poetry: the pattern of regular rhythmic recurrence called **meter**, and the lack of such pattern, which has come to be called **free verse**. Each differs from the other not only in the way it sounds but in its origins and the kind of poetry that uses it. Meter goes back to poetry's origins as song or chanting to accompany ritual dances; metrical poetry, then, should always be "heard" against an imagined background of ideally regular rhythm, and its divergences from this ideal regularity are like syncopations in music, local effects aimed at producing emphasis and variety. Free verse, however, has nothing to do with music; it is based on the actual rhythms of human speech, in which the stresses and accents of the words fall much less predictably. There is no sustained regular rhythm in ordinary human speech, but sometimes speech may briefly fall into recurring patterns, or **cadences**, for rhetorical effect.

Meter and free verse have each been used to make good poems; neither is inherently better than the other. And like most seeming opposites, they affect each other, and have a rather large expanse of common ground.

Meter

When you listen to the sound of people talking, you can easily notice that their speech varies from syllable to syllable in its degree of **stress.** (Stress is a combination of loudness, duration, and pitch.) This pattern of stress is inherent in all English words of more than one syllable: we always say *syl*lable, not syl*lab*le. (In fact, the placement of an accent in a word may determine its meaning: "*en*trance" is a noun meaning "place of entry," "en*trance*" a verb meaning "to spellbind.") The same is true of groups of words; some one-syllable words receive stress, others do not, according to their importance to the meaning of the sentence.

Meter is a regularized form of verbal rhythm. Except for very special purposes, it does not distort the normal rhythms of speech; rather, it results from words having been arranged so that their natural stresses form a deliberately regular pattern. Meter has an attractiveness of its own, the sensuous appeal of a steady, marked rhythm. It can also enhance poetic meaning.

Since verbal rhythm is invisible in the written language, we make it visible for study by using a system of notation called **scansion.** Scansion recognizes two major degrees of stress, and marks them in this way:

/ strong

◡ weak

(Naturally, there are many degrees of stress between the strongest and the weakest, and if you find it convenient you can mark a syllable that is neither strong or weak with a \ , for intermediate stress.)

These marks, when placed over a line of poetry, reveal its rhythmic pattern:

Wĭth sláppĭng skírts thĕ íslănd wómĕn stánd
Ĭn gárdĕns strípped ănd scáttĕred, péerĭng nórth . . .

(Millay, "Hearing Your Words, and
Not a Word Among Them")

Obviously, these lines are in regular meter: weak and strong stresses alternate one after the other from beginning to end. In scansion, the smallest repeated unit of the rhythmic pattern (in this case, ◡ /) is called a **foot**, and the line is marked off into feet this way:

> Wĭth sláp|pĭng skírts | thĕ ís|lănd wóm|ĕn stánd

The foot is the basic unit of meter. In that imagined, ideally regular meter that we may sense behind the rhythm of the poem itself, each foot always includes one strong stress and one or more weak stresses, and all feet within a line are the same. Not that we pause between feet, as we do between lines. Where a substantial pause occurs naturally within a line, it is called a **caesura** and is marked with another symbol, which does not affect metrical scansion at all:

|| caesura

> A door sunk in a hillside,|| with a bolt
> (Nemerov, "The Icehouse in Summer")

Poets place caesurae so as to vary the meter, in order to avoid monotony and to enhance the poem's meaning. In Nemerov's line, the meter itself is already quite varied, and it would take a reading of the whole poem to know for sure that the ideal meter from which this line departs is the same as that to which Millay's lines conform.

Because they are often discussed, these matters, and the feet of which they are composed, have names:

◡ / the iamb; iambic (examples: prŏpóse, dĕléte)

/ ◡ the trochee; trochaic (examples: sínglĕ; éntĕr)

◡ ◡ / the anapest; anapestic (examples: ăftĕrnoón, ĭn ă hóle)

/ ◡ ◡ the dactyl; dactylic (examples: émphăsĭs, júnĭpĕr)

/ / the spondee; spondaic (examples: hárd tímes, fóul báll)

◡ ◡ the pyrrhic foot (examples: ĭn ă, ŏf thĕ)

The other metrical attribute of a line is its length, which is stated in terms of the number of its feet. A line of two feet is in **dimeter**; three, **trimeter**; four, **tetrameter**; five, **pentameter**; six, **hexameter**; and seven (the longest line normally found in English poetry), **heptameter**. The metrical form of a line or a poem is described by combining the adjective giving the type of foot with the noun giving the number of feet. Thus the line by Millay, and that by Nemerov, are in *iambic pentameter*.

The most common departures from regular meter are substitution—placing a trochee, a spondee, or a pyrrhic foot in an iambic line, for example—and the addition or subtraction of weak stresses at either end of the line. Here are some examples:

> Cléaned, ŏr | rĕstóred? || Sómeŏne | wŏuld knów: || Í dón't.
> (Larkin, "Church Going")

Tŏ plúck | lífe báck. || Thĕ gúns | ŏf thĕ |stéeled fléet
Rĕcoíl . . .
(Lowell, "The Quaker Graveyard at Nantucket")

Thĕ wórld | ĭs chárged | wĭth thĕ | grándĕur | ŏf Gód.
(Hopkins, "God's Grandeur")

Ír|ĭsh pó|ĕts, || léarn | yŏur tráde,
Síng | whătév|ĕr ĭs | wéll máde . . .
(Yeats, "Under Ben Bulben")

By itself the line from Larkin could be either trochaic or iambic; as the poem in which it appears is in iambic pentameter, three of the five feet in this line are substitutions. The spondee at the end makes the words "I don't" seem particularly emphatic. The predominance of strong stresses (which tend to take longer to speak) at the beginning of the line from Lowell slows down the movement of the verse and gives it an air of solemnity. Hopkins' line, on the other hand, has only four strong stresses, and tends to move much more quickly, lightly—surprising when the subject is "God's Grandeur," but that grandeur is not ponderous but volatile, as the next line suggests: "It will flame out, like shining from shook foil." Yeats's line lacks a weak stress either at the beginning or the end of the line (it's impossible to tell, but as most English verse is iambic we conventionally assume that it is dropped from the beginning), and the result—a strong stress on either side of the line break—causes an even longer pause than usual at the end of the line, putting more emphasis on the rhymes and on the meaning of the words placed there.

All this talk of substitution, addition, and subtraction can easily come to sound like algebra rather than poetry, so let's look at a whole poem and the ways in which metrical variation contribute to its meaning:

Range Finding

Thĕ bát|tlĕ rént | ă cób|wĕb día|mŏnd strúng
Ănd cút | ă flów(˘)ĕr | bĕsíde | ă gróund | bírd's nést
Bĕfóre | ĭt stáined | ă síng|lĕ húm | ăn bréast.
Thĕ strí|ckĕn flów(˘)ĕr | bĕnt dóu|blĕ ănd | sŏ húng.
Ănd stíll | thĕ bírd | rĕvís|ĭtéd | hĕr yoúng.
Ă bút|tĕrflý | ĭts fáll | hăd dís|pŏssésed,
Ă móm|ĕnt sóught | ĭn aír | hĭs flów(˘)ĕr | ŏf rést,
Thĕn líght|lý stoóped | tŏ ít | ănd flút|tĕrĭng clúng.
Ón thĕ | báre úp|lănd pás|tŭre thére | hăd spréad
Ŏ'erníght | 'twíxt múl|lĕin stálks | ă whéel | ŏf thréad

Ănd stráin|ĭng cáb|lĕs wét | wĭth síl|vĕr déw.

Ă súd|dĕn pás|sĭng búl|lĕt shóok | ĭt drý.

Thĕ (˘)índwél|lĭng spí|dĕr rán | tŏ gréet | thĕ flý,

Bŭt fínd|ĭng nó|thĭng, súl|lĕnlý | wĭthdréw.

(Frost)

The meter reflects the events in the poem. The first seven lines are all but regular in their iambic movement (if, like Frost among many, you read "flower" as a one-syllable word, like "flour"), as are the last four. The movement is disturbed by the fluttering variation at the end of the eighth line and by the spondees in the next two lines, which slow down the movement slightly and seem to stabilize it. These variations are like the impact of the battle on nature, which otherwise, like the iambic meter, goes on its usual way without disruptions. Frost's use of meter embodies the theme of his poem.

Other Regular Rhythmic Forms

Gerard Manley Hopkins noticed that the ear counts metrical feet not by the number of syllables, whether strong or weak, but by the number of strong stresses in the line. In what he called **sprung rhythm**, the number of strong stresses in the line is kept constant, but the weak stresses vary from foot to foot as the poet desires. Here is an example from Hopkins' friend, Robert Bridges:

For now doors open, and war is waged with the snow;
And trains of sombre men, past tale of number,
Tread long brown paths, as toward their toil they go:
But even for them awhile no cares encumber
Their minds diverted; the daily word is unspoken,
The daily thoughts of labour and sorrow slumber
At the sight of the beauty that greets them, for the charm they have broken.

("London Snow")

The poem seems to fall into iambic movement, but by scanning two or the lines we can see that the meter is not iambic or regular at all:

Ănd tráins | ŏf sóm|brĕ mén, || pást tále | ŏf númbĕr . . .

Ăt thĕ síght | ŏf thĕ béau|tў thăt gréets | thĕm, || fŏr thĕ chárm | thĕy hăve brókĕn.

This kind of metrical variation goes back to older verse, but its reintroduction into modern poetry allowed for greater rhythmic flexibility, and undercut one of the prime tenets of metrical verse: that one kind of regular foot predominate. In fact, the division into feet may itself seem arbitrary in some lines of this kind of verse.

Another departure from metrical verse is called **syllabic meter**. The poet keeps constant the number of syllables in a line, but does not regularize the number or placement of strong stresses. The virtuoso of syllabic meter is Marianne Moore, from whose poem "The Fish" come these stanzas:

The Fish

(syllables:)

wade 1
through black jade. 3
Of the crow-blue mussel shells, one keeps 9
adjusting the ash heaps; 6
opening and shutting itself like 9

an 1
injured fan. 3
The barnacles which encrust the side 9
of the wave, cannot hide 6
there for the submerged shafts of the 8

sun, 1
split like spun 3
glass, move themselves . . . etc.

The rhythm of the poem is casual in effect, like speech. Even the one-syllable line that begins each stanza is sometimes stressed heavily (*wade*), sometimes lightly (*an*); and the longer lines of the first two stanzas scan so irregularly that we can draw no conclusions about the meter:

Ŏf thĕ crów-blúe mússĕl shélls, óne kéeps

Thĕ bárnăclĕs whích ĕncrúst thĕ síde

But Marianne Moore certainly means her lines to be experienced as lines; she even rhymes them: *aabbx*. And lest this kind of versification seem too mathematical, she occasionally adds (or subtracts) a syllable, as in the last line of each of the quoted stanzas. This is playful verse: the poem incorporates the title as part of its first sentence, and each stanza takes an interesting shape on the page (do they look like fish?) Despite the rhyming, and the counting of syllables, we are a long way from metrical rhythm, and toward free verse.

Free Verse

The term "free verse" is a misnomer. Though it is free of certain kinds of metrical regularity, it does not renounce form, and it is as controlled in its way as any other poetry; as T. S. Eliot remarked, no verse is free for the poet who wants to do a good job. Nor is free verse a descriptively specific category, because it includes so great a variety of rhythmic procedures.

Free verse includes poems as varied as these:

After the torchlight red on sweaty faces
After the frosty silence in the gardens
After the agony in stony places
The shouting and the crying
Prison and palace and reverberation
Of thunder of spring over distant mountains
He who was living is now dead

We who were living are now dying
With a little patience

(Eliot, "The Waste Land")

The trees never left
my windows
even when they put on gloves
for age;
they had married the glass
with the thud of falling cones.
They remembered my name
on windy nights.

(Wakoski, "You, Letting the Trees Stand as My Betrayer")

Zeus lies in Ceres' bosom
Taishan is attended of loves
                    under Cythera, before sunrise
and he said: "Hay aquí mucho catolicismo—(sounded
                                        catoli*th*ismo)
                    y muy poco reliHión"
and he said: "Yo creo que los reyes desaparecen"
(Kings will, I think, disappear)
That was Padre José Elizondo
                        in 1906 and 1917
or about 1917

(Pound, "Canto 81")

O sweet spontaneous
earth how often have
the
doting

        fingers of
prurient philosophers pinched
and
poked

thee
, has the naughty thumb
of science prodded
thy

        beauty

(Cummings, "O sweet spontaneous")

What these selections all have in common is that none falls into a regular, predictable meter—not even the Eliot, which begins as though it might. Each poem in free verse finds its own, individual, organic form. The free verse poem can break no "rules" because it exemplifies its own set of rules. But, as we will see, it is sufficiently like metrical poetry in other ways, so that we need not replace all our strategies for reading poems.

Like metrical poetry, free verse is written in lines, and often the breaks between lines have the same purpose in both kinds of writing. And so we may usefully begin looking at the forms of free verse by studying its uses of the line.

TRADITIONAL FORMS OF FREE VERSE

Modern free verse has ancient ancestors. Of these, the most influential has been the Bible, in the seventeenth-century translation called the King James Version. In the poetic books such as the *Song of Solomon* and the *Psalms of David*, there are poems that roll along in irregular lengths and indeterminate meters, but whose rhythm carries great power:

> Behold, thou art fair, my love; behold, thou art fair; thou hast doves' eyes within thy locks: thy hair is as a flock of goats, that appear from Mount Gilead.
> Thy teeth are like a flock of sheep that are even shorn, which came up from the washing; whereof every one bear twins, and none is barren among them.
> Thy lips are like a thread of scarlet, and thy speech is comely: thy temples are like a piece of a pomegranate within thy locks.
> Thy neck is like the tower of David builded for an armory, whereon there hang a thousand bucklers, all shields of mighty men.
> Thy two breasts are like two young roes that are twins, which feed among the lilies.
>
> (*Song of Solomon* 4:1–5)

Walt Whitman, the father of free verse in American poetry, wrote lines which echo these Biblical cadences:

> Just as you feel when you look on the river and sky, so I felt,
> Just as any of you is one of a living crowd, I was one of a crowd,
> Just as you are refreshed by the gladness of the river and the bright flow, I was refreshed,
> Just as you stand and lean on the rail, yet hurry with the swift current, I stood yet was hurried,
> Just as you look on the numberless masts of ships and the thick-stemmed pipes of steamboats, I looked.
>
> ("Crossing Brooklyn Ferry")

Whitman's line is usually a grammatical unit such as a sentence or an independent clause, and is usually end-stopped. His verse is mainly nonmetrical, but in this passage it tends to fall into a dactylic rhythm:

> Júst ăs yóu féel whĕn yŏu lóok ŏn thĕ ríver ănd ský, sŏ Í félt

His rhetoric, which also imitates that of the Old Testament, is one of grammatical parallels reflecting parallel meanings. Whitman's long line has interested poets of our own day, notably Allen Ginsberg.

Another ancient form of free verse is Anglo Saxon (or Old English) alliterative verse. The line is divided by a caesura, before and after which there are usually two strong stresses and a varying number of weak stresses; each line also includes at least one sequence of alliterative words. Ezra Pound imitated Old English strong-stress verse in his "Canto I":

> We *s*ét up má*s*t and *s*áil || on that *s*wárt shíp,
>
> *B*óre shéep a*b*óard her, || and our *b*ódies álso
>
> Héavy *w*ith *w*éeping, || and *w*índs from stérn*w*ard
>
> *B*óre us on oútward || with *b*éllying cánvas,
>
> Círce's this *cráft*, || the trím *coífed* góddess.

MODERN FREE VERSE

> so much depends
> upon
>
> a red wheel
> barrow
>
> glazed with rain
> water
>
> beside the white
> chickens.
>
> (Williams, "The Red Wheelbarrow")

There is probably no poem so famous as "The Red Wheelbarrow" that seems less artful, more prosy, taken word for word. Why, then, this elaborate division of its fourteen words into eight lines? This suggests that the rhythm of the poem may be important, and it may be useful to mark the stresses:

> só múch dĕpénds
>
> ŭpón
>
> ă réd whéel
>
> bárrŏw
>
> glázed wĭth ráin
>
> wátĕr
>
> bĕsíde thĕ whíte
>
> chíckĕns.

There seems to be a pattern here. In each tiny stanza of two dissimilar lines, the first line has two or three strong stresses, one always at the end of the line. On the other hand, the placement of the single strong stress in each second line is less predictable: in the first stanza it is preceded by a weak stress, in the others the weak stress follows. Rhythmically, this means that in the first stanza the first line glides comfortably into the second in a kind of iambic movement. But in the remainder of the poem, the line break within each stanza comes between two strong stresses, making for a slower, more deliberate movement from line to line. The opening declaration contrasts rhythmically with the following description.

How do these intricate relationships express the poem's meaning? Williams does not permit a very definite answer, as he never specifies just what it is that "depends" in the wheelbarrow ("so much" is not very specific) or how. But the rhythm suggests that whatever the importance of wheelbarrow, rainwater, and chickens may be to the farm economy and to society at large, the emphasis of the poem is upon the apprehension of these objects *as objects*. Williams intends us to take in not merely the general effect of the farm landscape but the effect of every detail—rainwater, chickens that are white, a wheelbarrow which is red and which, moreover, is a combination of a wheel and a barrow. Though one may propose a more far-reaching interpretation for the poem, and many have, this aspect of it suggests that "so much depends" at least partly upon accurate observation and freshness of response, even—or especially—to the very familiar.

But free verse is not simply a medium of subtle and elusive effects. Here is a very different kind of poem by Williams:

The Dance

In Breughel's great picture, The Kermess,
the dancers go round, they go round and
around, the squeal and the blare and the
tweedle of bagpipes, a bugle and fiddles
tipping their bellies (round as the thick-
sided glasses whose wash they impound)
their hips and their bellies off balance
to turn them. Kicking and rolling about
the Fair Grounds, swinging their butts, those
shanks must be sound to bear up under such
rollicking measures, prance as they dance
in Breughel's great picture, The Kermess.

The rhythm is a heavy *oom-pah-pah* beat, primarily dactylic, which suggests the sound of the band at the village fair in Pieter Brueghel's painting. Other effects include the imitation of the sounds of the instruments and the pounding of heavy wooden shoes on the dance floor. But though the rhythm is regular enough to suggest meter, there is little connection between the end of a dactylic "foot" and the end of a line. The line-endings cut across the rhythm almost as if they were meant to square off the poem's shape, to make it look a bit like the shape of Brueghel's painting.

The City Limits

When you consider the radiance, that it does not withhold
itself but pours its abundance without selection into every
nook and cranny not overhung or hidden; when you consider

that birds' bones make no awful noise against the light but
lie low in the light as in a high testimony; when you consider
the radiance, that it will look into the guiltiest

swervings of the weaving heart and bear itself upon them,
not flinching into disguise or darkening; when you consider
the abundance of such resource as illuminates the glow-blue

bodies and gold-skeined wings of flies swarming the dumped
guts of a natural slaughter or the coil of shit and in no
way winces from its storms of generosity; when you consider

that air or vacuum, snow or shale, squid or wolf, rose or lichen,
each is accepted into as much light as it will take, then
the heart moves roomier, the man stands and looks about, the

leaf does not increase itself above the grass, and the dark
work of the deepest cells is of a tune with May bushes
and fear lit by the breadth of such calmly turns to praise.

(A. R. Ammons)

Here, on the other hand, for the most part the rhythm flows naturally, as if in a variety of ordinary conversation. The division into lines and stanzas might, on first glance, seem rather casual too. But there's more to it than that. Ammons places each recurrence of the key words "When you consider" at the end of a line, so that his readers won't miss any turn of his elaborate proposal; though each direct object of "when you consider" does not have a stanza of its own, each repetition of those words does. When, having offered his evidence, Ammons turns to his conclusion, he puts the pivotal word "then" at the end of a line (line 14), and another articulation, "and," at the beginning of a line line 18), so that these weighty events in the argument get the benefit of the pause between lines.

but

he" i
staring

into winter twi

light (whisper) "was
my friend" reme
mbering "&

friendship

is a
miracle"

his always
not imaginably

morethanmostgenerous

spirit. Feeling
only
(jesus) every (god)

where

(chr
ist)

what absolute nothing

(e. e. cummings)

Unlike most poems, "but" seems planned more for visual effect than for reading aloud. (Cummings was a painter as well as a poet, and in his poetry he sometimes made the visual effect interact with the verbal.) The meaning of the poem is very difficult to make out from hearing it, but there are visual clues that the discourse is in fact going on simultaneously at more than one level. To disentangle the poem, you must realize that "(whisper)" is the verb of which "i" is the subject, the parentheses being a visual cue, a representation of whispering; that "remembering" connects the words "(whisper)" and "his always," and that lines 14–20 interlock two different phrases, "Feeling only everywhere what absolute nothing" and "(jesus god christ)". By this spatial overlapping, Cummings manages to suggest two levels in the poem: what the speaker is saying, presented first in quotation marks and later, maybe, in those parenthetical whispers, and also what the speaker is thinking, presented with neither quotation marks nor parentheses.

TEXTS AND CONTEXTS

Poems in Contexts

Our discussions, so far, have suggested ways to understand a poem mainly in and for itself—to look at how it is put together, and to develop the fullest sense of what it means. We've said very little about the author's situation, or the reader's. In some ways, this simplification is reasonably true to life. Most people enjoy reading, listening to, or looking at works of art without knowing very much about who made them. And most artists rightly expect that their audience, if any, will consist mainly of strangers. But if you are interested in poetry, or in a particular poem, you may want to go beyond the boundaries of the poem's text and explore its contexts. Here are some suggestions.

If you like a poet's work, it's natural to want to read more of it. At the end of this anthology there is a bibliography which lists all the books of poems by every poet in the anthology, as well as a selection of other books—novels, criticism, stories, plays. (Hardy and Lawrence, for example, were novelists, and if you enjoy their poems you may find their fiction equally affecting.) Or you may want to know more about the poet's life, mind, feelings: all poems are to some extent events in the lives of their creators, and some (such as the "confessional" writing we mentioned earlier) are so personal that they all but demand to be read as autobiography as well as poetry. There are good biographies of many poets, as well as some autobiographies; and a poet's letters, when they have been published, often give you an immediate sense of the person who wrote the poems.

If poems are autobiographical events, they are also events of history, at least of literary history. Most poets read voraciously, and their reading affects their work; you may want to investigate the writers whose work a poet has used (why did T. S. Eliot find the sixteenth- and seventeenth-century English dramatists so stimulating?) or those for whom, in turn, a poet's work has been of use.

Some modern and contemporary poets have made recordings, occasionally with commentary, that might interest you. Poets may also give public readings of their work, often on college campuses, and sometimes accompanied by discussion groups or writing workshops you might be able to join. Not all poets like to present themselves as public figures, but many do want to know how their readers respond to their work.

Then, too, a poem may turn you to thoughts or investigations outside poetry itself. If, for instance, you were excited by Adrienne Rich's "Planetarium," you might want to know more about the life and work of Caroline Herschel, the astronomer who is a central figure in the poem. Or Allen Ginsberg's *Howl* might make you want to know more about the life style of the counterculture it describes. You may have an experience or an idea in common with a poem, and it may lead you to reflections about love, friendship, or hatred, or even politics, economics, or science. There is certainly nothing wrong with being drawn to a poem by your own interests and feelings. In fact, that's why many people start reading a work, because of a need to find their own feeling mirrored or expressed by someone else—to find that the poet, although a stranger, can for a moment be an emotional or intellectual companion. This intimate contact with a poem can be comforting, and sometimes it may prove to be even more important to you than that.

All of these different approaches are ways of reading "creatively": the poem leads you to increase your knowledge or to develop in other ways. When you come back to the poem after such explorations, you are likely to find that it has become a part of your own experience, that it "belongs" to you; this is one of the greatest pleasures that reading has to offer. On the other hand, revisiting a poem may also lead to disappointment and dismay if you then discover that in your earlier readings of it you had misunderstood it. For creative reading also depends on that attentive, patient "listening" to the poem that we have stressed throughout this essay. And in an art as complex and subtle as poetry, misunderstanding is very difficult to avoid.

Some Problems in Reading

Of course, it's not only poems that are easily misunderstood. It sometimes seems so hard to hear correctly even the simplest remarks; we may experience a pang of pleasure (or even relief) when a listener says, "Oh! *Now* I see what you mean." The obstacles to accurate listening and reading have occupied readers, and therefore teachers, for centuries. During the 1920s the critic I. A. Richards asked his students at Cambridge University to read and interpret a number of poems without knowing who wrote them or when. Fifty years later Norman Holland, a specialist in the psychoanalytic aspects of literature, conducted a similar experiment. Both found that their readers tended to overlook important things in the poems, meanwhile imagining others that weren't actually there. Nor is this merely a case of teachers criticizing their students. As Richards sadly observed (in his book *Practical Criticism**), "Not only those whom we would suspect fall victim. Nor is it only the most abstruse poetry which so betrays us. In fact, to set down, for once, the brutal truth, no immunity is possessed on any occasion, not by the most reputable scholar."

How, then, are we to gain the objectivity, the openness to new thoughts and experiences, that allows us to listen sensitively and accurately to the poem itself? True objectivity is as impossible in reading poetry as in any other human activity, but we may be able to correct somewhat for our biases if we know what they are. Richards names a few of the most common ones:

1. Readers often fail to get the plain, prose sense of the poem. It is surprisingly easy to overlook or even to add words that change the whole sense of a poem, or to see one word where the author wrote another (for example, "tinkling" for "tingling"). Ambiguous words cause still more trouble. One student continued to insist that Robert Frost's "The Oven Bird" was about a Thanksgiving turkey, even though this made nonsense of the poem. (Frost was in fact writing about a songbird whose nest looks like a primitive oven.)

2. An irrelevant personal response, or a thoughtless "stock" response, may prevent a reader from understanding a poem. One of Richards' chosen poems was D. H. Lawrence's "Piano" (p. 117); a Cambridge student insisted that "This poem unfortunately associates itself with jazz, and 'coal black mammies' thumping the old piano down in Dixie." To any other reader this association would appear so personal, so foreign to the poem, that it would immediately be dismissed as misleading. Stock responses, on the other hand, are shared by many people, and are triggered by emotionally loaded words for which we have a ready-made response—as when a politician "stands up for America" so as to make a favorable impression while, perhaps, blurring the specifics of his intentions when elected. Lawrence's "Piano" is full of images that aroused Richards' students. The speaker's childhood memories are sentimental, and many concluded that the poem was designed to ap-

* London and New York, 1929.

peal to their own sentimentality—an aim which, as hardheaded college students of the '20s, some said was "nauseating." But Lawrence does not in fact argue that sentimental feelings are a good thing. Quite to the contrary, the speaker says that "in spite of myself," the "insidious mastery" of the music "betrays" him, and that in weeping for his childhood his "manhood is cast down." The poem is *about* sentimentality, but is not itself sentimental, a distinction which stock responses to its language might prevent an unwary reader from making.

3. A reader may be misled by prejudices as to what is or is not suitable for poetry. One student said of the "anonymous" author of "Piano," "He hasn't any idea that hymns in the cozy parlor are somehow wrong in poetry." But *why* are they wrong in poetry? We might better think about how such material is used in *this* poem before concluding that no good use can ever be made of it. Another student protested against the versification, saying that "the continual running over of the lines is irritating." Again, why? Perhaps now, fifty years later, we may have more generous notions of what is or is not "poetic," but the danger of prejudiced or even mistaken readings is always with us.

Mistakes or misunderstandings are not necessarily wholly the fault of the reader. There is no denying that some modern poems, including some of the most important, are difficult to understand—*very* difficult. One major reason may be allusions so private or esoteric that they are beyond most readers' abilities to recognize and interpret, or so numerous that readers have trouble integrating them into the poem. Another hindrance to understanding arises from disjunctiveness, a way of writing in which passages in quite different styles and even about different subjects follow each other abruptly and, it often seems, illogically. These two techniques have probably done more than anything else to discourage readers of such modern poets as T. S. Eliot and Ezra Pound; at the same time, those who persevere often find this kind of poetry especially stimulating to creative reading.

Take these lines from Eliot's *The Waste Land*:

> London Bridge is falling down falling down falling down
> *Poi s'ascose nel foco che gli affina*
> *Quando fiam uti chelidon*—O swallow swallow
> *Le Prince d'Aquitaine à la tour abolie*
> These fragments I have shored against my ruins
> Why then Ile fit you. Hieronymo's mad againe.
> Datta. Dayadhvam. Damyata.
>   Shantih   shantih   shantih

This sequence of quotations in five different languages may look like incoherent nonsense, a mere jumble. It does, however, make sense in terms of the poem as a whole, to readers who have read the poem sensitively and often enough to feel at home with its way of thinking, and who have done a little homework.

The first step, in this poem, might be to obtain an anthology with footnotes which translate the passages in foreign languages and give some information about the sources of the allusions—or, if such help cannot be found, to look in books about the poet or the poem for a commentary which provides this information. (The passage, with notes, is on page 194 of this anthology). You might then come to feel that the line "These fragments I have shored against my ruins" speaks most directly to the readers—it is, after all, the only line that isn't a quotation from elsewhere—and that the other lines, the quotations and bits of quotations, are the "fragments." Then, taking these other lines one at a time and remembering or referring back to the rest of the poem, you would begin to notice that each one alludes to a motif, or theme, or image in an earlier section: London Bridge, the fire ("*foco*") of Purgatory, the swallow ("*chelidon*"), the ruined tower ("*la tour abolie*"), Hieronimo's madness, and even the words in Sanskrit at the end, all have significance in terms of the whole poem if you make yourself open to it.

Even with footnotes and commentary to help, understanding these lines is not easy; critics have argued about them for decades. And Eliot himself was not above a little teasing, challenging readers to make sense of him—even his own footnotes to *The Waste Land* sometimes need footnotes! Such poetry requires the reader's patience and imagination, but perhaps no more patience and imagination than we need to understand our fragmentary modern world, in which space is thought to be discontinuous, time inconstant, and the associations of human thought less rational and more subtle than they used to seem. Disjunctiveness, thought to be bad style in earlier times, has come to seem a particularly appropriate way for modern poets to write. Not itself merely chaotic, it is perhaps a way of showing disorder while controlling it.

Eliot himself had consoling things to say about understanding poetry. One of the most formidably learned critics of our time, he remarked:* "The most seasoned reader . . . does not bother about understanding; not, at least, at first. I know that some of the poetry to which I am most devoted is poetry which I did not understand at first reading; some is poetry which I am not sure I understand yet. . . ."

POETS AT WORK

Like all other craftsmen, poets have their own different ways of working. A few may be able to write out a finished poem in the first draft, with at most a few retouchings, but among serious writers such performances are rare. More often poets have to work their poems into a satisfying shape through successive drafts, sometimes starting with very rough material. Reading these drafts we can see the poet making choices and changes in form, substituting some words for others, refining or even changing the poem's meaning in the process of perfecting it. This kind of revision can reveal to us what matters most to a particular poet writing a particular poem, and deepen our response to that poem, or that poet, or indeed poetry.

* In his essay, "The Use of Poetry and the Use of Criticism."

"The Second Coming" is one of Yeats's most famous and impressive poems, and luckily his drafts for it survive. Jon Stallworthy has transcribed and published them, as well as drafts for other poems by Yeats, in *Between the Lines: W. B. Yeats's Poems in the Making* (1963). The first notes for the poem, which was evidently written in January 1919, are in prose. (The numbers, added for this anthology, refer to corresponding lines in the final version.)

1 Ever more wide sweeps the gyre
1,2 Ever further hawk flies outward
2 from the falconer's hand. scarcely
3? is armed tyranny fallen when
4 when ~~an~~ the mob bred anarchy
4 takes its place. For this
5? Marie Antoinette has
5?/8? mob brutally ( ) & ~~no~~
7? Burke ~~has shook his ( )~~ has answered
7? With his voice, no Pit
7?,10 Arraigns revolution. Surely the second
10 Birth comes near –

(The parentheses represent illegible portions of the manuscript.) Yeats's historical allusions are to Marie Antoinette (1755–1793), wife of Louis XVI of France, who was beheaded for treason during the Reign of Terror that followed the French Revolution; Edmund Burke (1729–1797), the Irish-born British statesman, who opposed the excesses in France in his *Reflections on the French Revolution* (1790); and William Pitt the Younger (1759–1806), Prime Minister of Great Britain from 1783 until his death, who organized two successive coalitions against Napoleon in 1793 and 1798. The first draft, directly below the prose draft, is as follows:

intellectual gyre is ( )
1 The ~~gyres grow wider and more~~ wide
falcon cannot hear
2 The ~~hawk can no more hear~~ the falconer

4? ~~The Germans to Russia to the place~~

Marx
4? The Germany of ( ) has led to Russian ~~( )~~ Com
6 There every day ~~now~~ some innocent has died
Recalls the mob from
8? The common mob to face ( ) & murder
~~( )~~

Stallworthy observes that Yeats must originally have intended to write a rhymed poem (*wide/died*). A *gyre* is a spiral, one of Yeats's principal symbols. The allusion, "The Germans to Russia," refers to the situation in the First World War; in 1918 the new revolutionary government in Russia had made peace with Germany, freeing the German Army to concentrate its force against Britain and France on the western front and increasing the danger of a British defeat. The second line (numbered in boldface) is already in its final form. There follows a further draft of the opening:

1 ~~Broader & broader is the~~

~~Furth~~

1 ~~Ever more wide~~

day by day
1 The gyres sweep wider ~~by year~~
every ~~year day~~

can no more hear the falconer
2 The hawk, ~~flies from the falconer's hand~~

Things have begun to break & f
3 all ~~things are broken up &~~ fall apart

? ~~After they have got the ( )~~

[five illegible lines]

4? The tyrant has the anarch in his pay

5? And murderer to follow murderer

Next comes yet another attempt at this passage:

3 Things fall apart – at every stroke of the clock

6 ~~Of innocence most foully put to death~~

have
6 ~~Old wisdom and young innocence has died~~

6 ~~The gracious and the innocent have~~

5? ~~Or~~ while the mobs fawn upon the murderer

5? And the judge nods before his empty dock

And again:

~~Then~~

3 All things break up – no stroke upon the clock

6 But ceremonious innocence has died,

~~Yet the~~ Yet where
5? While the mob fawns upon the murderer

7? ~~While~~ the judge ~~nods~~ nods before his empty dock,

7? ~~And there's no Burke to cry aloud no Pitt~~

7? And there is none to pluck them by the gown

Yeats still alludes to specific personages and seems to have particular events in mind. In the next draft he presses on to the end of the poem, and though the previously unattempted conclusion takes more working out, the whole is brought very near completion:

widening gyre
1 Turning & turning in the wide gyre

2 The falcon cannot hear the falconer

1 ~~Too wide the the gyres –~~

3 ~~Things fall apart – the centre has lost~~
~~power~~

3 Things fall apart – the centre cannot hold

Mere loose
4 ~~Vile~~ anarchy is ~~loose~~ through out the world

dim tide
5 The blood stained flood is loose & everywhere

6 The ceremony of innocence is drowned

~~uncertainty~~
7 ~~The good are wavering & uncertain~~

lack while
7 The best ~~lose~~ all conviction while the worst

8 Are full of passionate intensity.

~~Surely the great falcon must come~~
10 ~~Surely the hour of the second birth is here~~

12,13? ~~We have the desert – Surely the spiritus mundi leaps~~
~~Surely the spiritus mundi~~ leaps ~~sp shall~~ leap

11 ~~The second Birth! Scarce have those~~
( ) words been spoken

On the following notebook page, Yeats begins again with "Surely." The *spiritus mundi*, or spirit of the world, was for Yeats a kind of divine inspiration, or a storehouse of images which rise into the poet's consciousness.

9 Surely some revelation is at hand

12,13? ~~We have the desert – surely in spiritus~~
~~must leap~~

20 ~~The cradle at Bethlehem has rocked anew~~

the second coming is at
10 Surely ~~the hour of the second birth has~~ struck

are
11 Scarcely ~~have~~ these words

coming have spoken
12 The second ~~Birth. Scarce have the words been spoken~~

? and new intensity ~~( )~~ rent as it were cloth

? ~~Before the dark was cut as with a knife~~

vast
13 And a ~~stark~~ image out of spiritus mundi

14 Troubles my sight. ~~A waste of~~ sand
– A waste of desert sand

14 A shape with lion's body ~~& with woman's~~
and the head of a man ~~breast & head~~

16 ~~Move with a slow slouching step~~

~~And~~ an ~~eye~~ gaze and
15 ~~And eyes,~~ blank & pitiless as the sun

20 ~~Slouches~~

thighs all about it wind ~~swirl~~
16 Moves its slow ~~feet~~ while ~~over it run~~

17 ~~An angry crowd of desert b~~

~~Run~~
17 ~~Fall~~ shadows of the ~~desert birds they~~
indignant desert ~~cry~~
birds

Opposite this page, among drafts for another poem, Yeats drafted a later line:

21 And what rough beast

21 Its turn come ~~up~~ again
round

Finally he concludes his draft:

18 The darkness drops again but now I know
( )
19 ~~weary of its Egyptian sleep at last~~

19 ~~( ) stony~~

19,21? ~~jelous at last, it has thrown off the sleep~~

19,21? ~~jelous at last, it wakens from its sleep~~

That of ~~its~~ stony
19 ~~For~~ twenty centuries a stony sleep

20 ~~Were vexed & all but broken by the second~~
Were vexed

Was
20 ~~Were vexed~~ to night mare by a rocking cradle
( )
21 ~~And now at last, by jelousy stung awake~~

22 ~~It slouches towards Bethlehem to be born~~

22 It has set out for Bethlehem to be born

~~what~~
21 ~~And now at last — knowing its time come round~~

22 It has set out for Bethlehem to be born

~~wild thing~~ – its hour come round at last
21 And what ~~at last~~ – knowing its time ~~come round~~
rough beast

22 ~~Is slouching~~ towards Bethlehem to be born

22 Slouches towards Bethlehem to be born

With a few major revisions—"A waste of desert sand" becomes "somewhere in sands of the desert" (line 13), and "Fall" or "Run" becomes "Reel" (line 17)—and some minor adjustments of punctuation and spelling to the 17 lines that are otherwise in their final form, Yeats has the definitive version:

The Second Coming

Turning and turning in the widening gyre
The falcon cannot hear the falconer;
Things fall apart; the centre cannot hold;
Mere anarchy is loosed upon the world,
The blood-dimmed tide is loosed, and everywhere
The ceremony of innocence is drowned;
The best lack all conviction, while the worst
Are full of passionate intensity.

Surely some revelation is at hand;
Surely the Second Coming is at hand.
The Second Coming! Hardly are those words out
When a vast image out of *Spiritus Mundi*
Troubles my sight: somewhere in sands of the desert
A shape with lion body and the head of a man,
A gaze blank and pitiless as the sun,
Is moving its slow thighs, while all about it
Reel shadows of the indignant desert birds.
The darkness drops again; but now I know
That twenty centuries of stony sleep
Were vexed to nightmare by a rocking cradle,
And what rough beast, its hour come around at last,
Slouches towards Bethlehem to be born?

D. H. Lawrence's poetic drafts have quite a different look from those of Yeats; it's as though he would draft a poem, then completely rewrite it, then rewrite it yet again. Or perhaps he did work on details as well as on the grand outline, and merely saved fair copies of a poem at points where he stopped work, throwing all the other worksheets away. At any rate, his successive drafts of "Bavarian Gentians" show him to have rethought the entire poem two times, and finally to have refined it. Here are the drafts, in the order they appear in his workbooks:

Glory of Darkness

Blue and dark
Oh Bavarian gentians, tall ones
make a dark-blue gloom
in the sunny room.

They have added blueness to blueness, until
it is dark: beauty
blue joy of my soul
Bavarian gentians
your dark blue gloom is so noble!

How deep I have gone
dark gentians
since I embarked on your dark blue fringes
how deep, how deep, how happy!
What a journey for my soul
in the blue dark gloom
of gentians here in the sunny room!

The second version:

. . . .
it is dark
and the door is open
to the depths.

It is so blue, it is so dark
in the dark doorway
and the way is open
to Hades.

Oh, I know—
Persephone has just gone back
down the thickening thickening gloom
of dark-blue gentians to Pluto
to her bridegroom in the dark
and all the dead
and all the dark great ones of the underworld
down there, down there
down the blue depths of mountain gentian flowers
cold, cold
are gathering to a wedding in the [winter] dark
down the dark blue path

what a dark blue gloom
of gentians here in the sunny room!

The allusions are to *Persephone*, daughter of the goddess of natural fertility, Demeter, and to *Pluto*, god of death and the underworld. In the classical myth, Pluto abducted Persephone and carried her off to the underworld. She was allowed to return to earth in April to remain with her mother for six months, during which time Demeter rejoiced and the earth was fruitful, but then in September she had to rejoin her husband, and the earth became barren with Demeter's sorrow. The third version:

Bavarian Gentians

Not every man has gentians in his house
in soft September, at slow, sad Michaelmas.

Bavarian gentians, big and dark, only dark
darkening the day-time, torch-like with the smoking blueness of Pluto's gloom,
ribbed and torch-like, with their blaze of darkness spread blue
down flattening into points, flattened under the sweep of white day
torch-flower of the blue-smoking darkness, Pluto's dark-blue daze,
black lamps from the halls of Dis, burning dark blue,
giving off darkness, blue darkness, as Demeter's pale lamps give off light,
lead me then, lead the way.

Reach me a gentian, give me a torch!
let me guide myself with the blue, forked torch of this flower
down the darker and darker stairs, where blue is darkened on blueness
even where Persephone goes, just now, from the frosted September
to the sightless realm where darkness is awake upon the dark
and Persephone herself is but a voice
or a darkness invisible enfolded in the deeper dark
of the arms Plutonic, and pierced with the passion of dense gloom,
among the spendour of torches of darkness, shedding darkness on the lost bride and her groom.

Michaelmas is the feast celebrating the Archangel Michael, and falls on September 29. *Dis* is the underworld. Here is Lawrence's final version:

Bavarian Gentians

Not every man has gentians in his house
In soft September, at slow, sad Michaelmas.
Bavarian gentians, tall and dark, but dark
darkening the daytime torch-like with the smoking blueness of Pluto's gloom,
ribbed hellish flowers erect, with their blaze of darkness spread blue,
blown flat into points, by the heavy white draught of the day.

Torch-flowers of the blue-smoking darkness, Pluto's dark-blue blaze
black lamps from the halls of Dis, smoking dark blue

giving off darkness, blue darkness, upon Demeter's yellow-
pale day
whom have you come for, here in the white-cast day?

Reach me a gentian, give me a torch!
let me guide myself with the blue, forked torch of a flower
down the darker and darker stairs, where blue is darkened on
blueness
down the way Persephone goes, just now, in first-frosted
September,
to the sightless realm where darkness is married to dark
and Persephone herself is but a voice, as a bride,
a gloom invisible enfolded in the deeper dark
of the arms of Pluto as he ravishes her once again
and pierces her once more with his passion of the utter dark
among the splendour of black-blue torches, shedding fathom-
less darkness on the nuptials.

Give me a flower on a tall stem, and three dark flames,
for I will go to the wedding, and be wedding-guest
at the marriage of the living dark.

Many poets revise their poems even after publication. Often these revisions are only slight retouchings of detail, but several major poets, among them W. B. Yeats, Robert Graves, W. H. Auden, and Robert Lowell, have made more substantial alterations, in some cases changing the effect of the poem altogether. Another such was John Crowe Ransom. In his *Collected Poems,* he went so far as to print some of the early versions on pages facing the revisions, and to give his own explanation for the changes. We reprint his versions and observations on "Here Lies a Lady" without further comment, except to say that as with Lawrence, readers are permitted to disagree with Ransom's preferences:

Here Lies a Lady

A

Here lies a lady of beauty and high degree.
Of chills and fever she died, of fever and chills,
The delight of her husband, her aunt, an infant of three,
And of medicos marveling sweetly on her ills.

For either she burned, and her confident eyes would blaze,
And her fingers fly in a manner to puzzle their heads—
What was she making? Why, nothing; she sat in a maze
Of old scraps of laces, snipped into curious shreds—

Or this would pass, and the light of her fire decline
Till she lay discouraged and cold, like a thin stalk white and
blown,
And would not open her eyes, to kisses, to wine;
The sixth of these states was her last; the cold settled down.

Sweet ladies, long may ye bloom, and toughly I hope ye may
thole,

But was she not lucky? In flowers and lace and mourning,
In love and great honor we bade God rest her soul
After six little spaces of chill, and six of burning.

COMMENT

"The poem was first published in my *Poems and Essays*, Vintage edition, 1945. The *B* poem will follow. . . . I must note that the second line of stanza three here is a hexameter instead of the standard pentameter of the poem, and contains a very dubious phrase, "like a thin stalk white and blown," which hardly describes the image of a beautiful woman even in her ravage. In stanza four the first line is another hexameter; and the archaic 'ye' may be a little too quaint."

B

Here lies a lady of beauty and high degree,
Of chills and fever she died, of fever and chills,
The delight of her husband, an aunt, an infant of three
And medicos marveling sweetly on her ills.

First she was hot, and her brightest eyes would blaze
And the speed of her flying fingers shook their heads.
What was she making? God knows; she sat in those days
With her newest gowns all torn, or snipt into shreds.

But that would pass, and the fire of her cheeks decline
Till she lay dishonored and wan like a rose overblown,
And would not open her eyes, to kisses, to wine;
The sixth of which states was final. The cold came down.

Fair ladies, long may you bloom, and sweetly may thole!
She was part lucky. With flowers and lace and mourning,
With love and bravado, we bade God rest her soul
After six quick turns of quaking, six of burning.

COMMENT

"The opening stanzas of *A* and *B* are alike; in the later stanzas *B* is far superior. The second stanza has the lady sitting among her newest gowns and destroying them; but there may be two interpretations. She may be planning to get a new wardrobe when she has recovered from her illness. That seems at first the sign of a great lady's vanity: why is she not talking with her husband and her child? (The aunt may be hundreds of miles away.) But she must occupy herself somehow while she can; and the husband is a wealthy and busy man, who cannot attend her at all times, while her child is forbidden her bedside. The third stanza, where chill replaces fever, is almost unutterably painful; but I was most intent upon it, and managed to the best of my ability. Lines two and three are the saddest in the poem; perhaps in all my poems. Lne two has her lying 'dishonored and wan like a rose overblown,' where the two phrases almost rhyme. Line three has her at the very point of death; and line four announces the ultimate fact. In stanza four the only thing the friends and relatives can do is to bring their tokens of affection to the coffin; but these are supplemented in line three with 'love and bravado' when they ask God to 'rest her soul.' The 'bravado' may seem strange; until we reflect that any prayer has that constituent, inasmuch as it is addressed to an Unknown God whose designs we cannot thwart. The final line is new and fresh after the twenty-odd years' service of the *A* line. And lines three and four together supply, I suppose, two reasons why she was 'part lucky'; first because of the devotion of her loyal subjects, and then because of the brevity of her illness."

POETIC KINDS, FORMS, AND STANZAS
A GLOSSARY

Though many modern poets often prefer to shape their own "organic" forms out of the flow of their words and ideas, others have chosen to adopt traditional forms which over the centuries have become fixed, as another means of shaping their work. Even if a poet chooses not to use these forms, he may want to write one of the traditional kinds of poetry, which impose no specific scheme of rhyme or meter but which suggest specific ways in which certain subjects may be treated. There follows a glossary defining the most common traditional forms and kinds of poetry.

Ballad A narrative poem, originally an anonymous folk genre. Modern ballads imitate the folk ballad's simple diction, its use of refrain (one or more lines repeated at the close of each stanza), and the ballad stanza form:

Four lines, rhyming *xaxa*

Meter: lines one and three, iambic tetrameter; two and four, iambic trimeter

(Example: Muir, "Ballad of Hector in Hades")

Blank verse Unrhymed iambic pentameter.

(Example: Frost, "Birches")

Canto A large division of a long poem; the term implies no specific formal organization.

(Example: Pound, "Canto I")

Couplet A pair of lines, usually rhymed and in the same meter. **Closed couplets** are end-stopped at the second line; **heroic couplets** are in iambic pentameter.

(Example: Graves, "The Persian Version")

Elegy A poem about a death, often of a friend, a relative, or a famous person; or a meditation on death. The term implies no specific formal organization.

(Example: Auden, "In Memory of W. B. Yeats")

Epigram A short, usually rhymed poem, distinguished by its terseness and usually concluding with a witty surprise.

(Example: Nemerov, 'The Sparrow in the Zoo")

Epistle A letter in verse.
(Example: Stallworthy, "A Letter from Berlin")

Epitaph A poem to be inscribed on a tomb, or an imitation of such.
(Example: Jarrell, "The Death of the Ball Turret Gunner")

Haiku An unrhymed poem of three lines comprising 17 syllables, the first and third lines five syllables each and the second line seven syllables.
(Example: Knight, "Haiku")

Lyric A relatively short poem concerning itself mainly with the speaker's feelings; sometimes specifically a poem to be sung. In modern poetry, the term has been extended to include any poem not primarily narrative, satiric, or instructional in purpose.
(Most short poems in this anthology are lyrics.)

Octave A group of eight lines set off in the poem either by a stanza break or by a distinctive rhyme scheme, as for example in the opening of a Petrarchan Sonnet.
(Example: Robinson, "For a Dead Lady")

Ode A meditative poem of some length, whose subject may be ordinary but gives rise to philosophical reflection. It is usually formally elaborate, but the term implies no specific type of organization. An **Horatian Ode** repeats a stanza form of the poet's choice; the **irregular ode** is composed of stanzas or sections of different patterns.
(Example: Lowell, "To the Union Dead")

Ottava rima A stanza form in eight iambic pentameter lines, rhymed *abababcc.*
(Example: Yeats, "Among School Children")

Parody A poem which humorously mimics and distorts the style or thought of another poem, or of a poet's work in general.
(Example: Koch, "Mending Sump")

Prose poem A poem not divided into lines but "run on" as in prose. It is here that the distinction between prose and poetry blurs, but perhaps the prose poem may be distinguished by its rhythms, its density of imagery, and its brevity.
(Example: Shapiro, "Lower the Standard: That's My Motto")

Quatrain A group of four lines set off in the poem either by a stanza break or by a distinctive rhyme scheme.
(Example: Dickinson, "Because I Could Not Stop for Death")

Sestet A group of six lines set off in the poem either by a stanza break or by a distinctive rhyme scheme, as for example at the conclusion of a Petrarchan sonnet.
(Example: Hardy, "Drummer Hodge")

Sestina An Old French verse form in six sestets and a tercet, usually unrhymed and in iambic pentameter. The end words of the first sestet are repeated as the end words of the other sestets, though for each in a different order; all six end-words are employed in the closing tercet. The permutations by which the order of the end-words was varied are less strictly followed than they once were. Here are the rules for the classic sestina:

Stanza	Order of end-words:
1	1 2 3 4 5 6
2	6 1 5 2 4 3
3	3 6 4 1 2 5
4	5 3 2 6 1 4
5	4 5 1 3 6 2
6	2 4 6 5 3 1
7	2, 5, 4; 3, 6, 1

(Example: Wakoski, "Sestina from the Home Gardener")

Sonnet A lyric in fourteen lines, normally in iambic pentameter, and rhymed according to one of a number of set forms. These are the **Petrarchan sonnet** (*abba abba cdcdcd* or *cdecde* or *cdedce*); the **Shakespearean sonnet** (*abab cdcd efef gg*); and the **Spenserian sonnet** (*ababbcbccdcd cc*). Gerard Manley Hopkins invented a form he called the **curtal** (or shortened) **sonnet** (*abcabc dbcdc*). Characteristically the thought of a sonnet mirrors its form; when the rhyme pattern changes (at the closing sestet in the Petrarchan sonnet, or at the closing couplet in the Shakespearean or Spenserian) the poet also turns from stating propositions to drawing conclusions.

(Examples: Robinson, "The Sheaves"—Petrarchan; Millay, "Hearing Your Words, and Not a Word Among Them"—Shakespearean; Hopkins, "Pied Beauty"—curtal)

Tercet A group of three lines set off in the poem either by a stanza break or by a distinctive rhyme scheme.

(Example: Frost, "Provide, Provide")

Terza rima A sequence of tercets whose rhymes link them together in the pattern *aba bcb cdc ded efe* and so on. Best known as the verse form of Dante's *Divine Comedy*, it is little used in modern English poetry, but a sequence of tercets in blank verse may be made to have a similar effect.

(Examples: Frost, "Acquainted with the Night"; Eliot, "Little Gidding," lines 80–151—blank verse imitation)

Verse paragraph A stretch of verse comparable in function to a prose paragraph, usually set off by a stanza break or indentation.

(Example: Williams, "Tract")

Villanelle An Old French form in six stanzas on two rhymes, usually in iambic pentameter. The first and last lines of the opening tercet serve alternately as the closing line of the following four tercets, and the two together conclude the final quatrain: *AbA′ abA abA′ abA abA′ abAA′*.

(Example: D. Thomas, "Do Not Go Gentle into That Good Night")

WALT WHITMAN
(*1819–1892*)

Walt Whitman was born on May 31, 1819, in then rural Huntington, Long Island. His father was of British, his mother of Dutch ancestry. His indifference to religious orthodoxy, his insistence on the worth of individual experience and on private charity, may owe something to the fact that there were Quakers on both sides of his family. When Whitman was still very young, his father, who was both a farmer and a carpenter, moved the family to Brooklyn, then a city of less than 10,000, where he worked at building houses. Whitman's childhood happily alternated between the growing city and the countryside and seacoast. He attended school for only five years, for in 1830, when he was eleven, he went to work as an office boy, first to an attorney, who encouraged him to read Sir Walter Scott, and then to a physician. He soon turned, however, to printing and journalism, and until the early 1850s—with occasional periods of school teaching—he worked as a newspaperman. From 1846–48 he held the important post of editor of the Brooklyn *Eagle*. He left the paper after a political disagreement with its financial backers, then made his first journey into the interior of America to serve for a few months as editor of the New Orleans *Crescent*.

Whitman had been experimenting with poetry since 1847. In 1851 he moved in with his parents, supported himself with part-time carpentry, and began work on *Leaves of Grass*. The first edition appeared on July 4, 1855; like all but two of the first seven editions, it was privately printed, and the author himself set the type. The book was nearly anonymous; Whitman's name did not appear, but the frontispiece was a photograph of the poet in work clothes, bearded, lounging, unbuttoned. The book did not sell well, but it attracted attention in important quarters. Emerson, to whom Whitman had sent a copy, wrote a famous acknowledgment: "I greet you at the beginning of a great career, which yet must have had a long foreground somewhere, for such a start. I rubbed my eyes a little to see if this sunbeam were no illusion, but the solid sense of the book is a sober certainty. It has the best merits, namely, of fortifying and encouraging."

During the Civil War, Whitman went to the front in Virginia to be with his soldier brother George, who had been reported wounded. George's wounds were slight, but Whitman for a few weeks stayed on near the fighting and then went to Washington. He took a part-time job in the Army paymaster's office in aid of his main activity, the ministering to wounded soldiers, Union and Confederate alike. Whitman's tenderness for the soldiers presages the series of sentimental friendships with young working-class men in which his emotional life found its main expression. He was unaware that his sentiments might be considered unorthodox, and when the English critic John Addington Symons, himself a homosexual, questioned Whitman about his sexual preferences, the poet was horrified and as evidence of his heterosexuality adduced six bastard children, hastily invented for the occasion.

Whitman remained in Washington after the War ended. In 1865 he was appointed to a clerkship in the Office of Indian Affairs, but lost his post within six months when it was discovered that he had written an allegedly indecent book—*Leaves of Grass.* He quickly found employment in the Attorney General's Office, where he remained until he suffered a stroke in 1873. Whitman never completely recovered from his stroke. For a time he lived as an invalid at the home of his brother George in Camden, New Jersey. He was occasionally well enough to do some lecturing—he had a set piece on the death of President Lincoln which he delivered many times—and some traveling. He spent his last eight years in a small house in Camden which he was just prosperous enough to buy for himself. Whitman died on March 26, 1892, in his 73rd year.

Crossing Brooklyn Ferry

1

Flood-tide below me! I see you face to face!
Clouds of the west—sun there half an hour high—I see you also face to face.

Crowds of men and women attired in the usual costumes, how curious you are to me!
On the ferry-boats the hundreds and hundreds that cross, returning home, are more curious to me than you suppose,
And you that shall cross from shore to shore years hence are more to me, and more in my meditations, than you might suppose.

2

The impalpable sustenance of me from all things at all hours of the day,
The simple, compact, well-join'd scheme, myself disintegrated, every one disintegrated yet part of the scheme,
The similitudes of the past and those of the future,
The glories strung like beads on my smallest sights and hearings, on the walk in the street and the passage over the river,
The current rushing so swiftly and swimming with me far away,
The others that are to follow me, the ties between me and them,
The certainty of others, the life, love, sight, hearing of others.

Others will enter the gates of the ferry and cross from shore to shore,
Others will watch the run of the flood-tide,
Others will see the shipping of Manhattan north and west, and the heights of Brooklyn to the south and east,
Others will see the islands large and small;
Fifty years hence, others will see them as they cross, the sun half an hour high,
A hundred years hence, or ever so many hundred years hence, others will see them,
Will enjoy the sunset, the pouring-in of the flood-tide, the falling-back to the sea of the ebb-tide.

3

It avails not, time nor place—distance avails not,
I am with you, you men and women of a generation, or ever so many generations hence,
Just as you feel when you look on the river and sky, so I felt,
Just as any of you is one of a living crowd, I was one of a crowd,
Just as you are refresh'd by the gladness of the river and the bright flow, I was refresh'd,
Just as you stand and lean on the rail, yet hurry with the swift current, I stood yet was hurried,
Just as you look on the numberless masts of ships and the thick-stemm'd pipes of steamboats, I look'd.

I too many and many a time cross'd the river of old,
Watched the Twelfth-month[1] sea-gulls, saw them high in the air floating with motionless wings, oscillating their bodies,
Saw how the glistening yellow lit up parts of their bodies and left the rest in strong shadow,
Saw the slow-wheeling circles and the gradual edging toward the south,
Saw the reflection of the summer sky in the water,
Had my eyes dazzled by the shimmering track of beams,
Look'd at the fine centrifugal spokes of light round the shape of my head in the sunlit water,
Look'd on the haze on the hills southward and south-westward,
Look'd on the vapor as it flew in fleeces tinged with violet,
Look'd toward the lower bay to notice the vessels arriving,
Saw their approach, saw aboard those that were near me,
Saw the white sails of schooners and sloops, saw the ships at anchor,
The sailors at work in the rigging or out astride the spars,
The round masts, the swinging motion of the hulls, the slender serpentine pennants,
The large and small steamers in motion, the pilots in their pilot-houses,
The white wake left by the passage, the quick tremulous whirl of the wheels,
The flags of all nations, the falling of them at sunset,
The scallop-edged waves in the twilight, the ladled cups, the frolicsome crests and glistening,
The stretch afar growing dimmer and dimmer, the gray walls of the granite storehouses by the docks,
On the river the shadowy group, the big steam-tug closely flank'd on each side by the barges, the hay-boat, the belated lighter,
On the neighboring shore the fires from the foundry chimneys burning high and glaringly into the night,
Casting their flicker of black contrasted with wild red and yellow light over the tops of houses, and down into the clefts of streets.

4

These and all else were to me the same as they are to you,
I loved well those cities, loved well the stately and rapid river,

1. The Quaker designation for December.

The men and women I saw were all near to me,
Others the same—others who look back on me because I look'd forward to them,
(The time will come, though I stop here to-day and to-night.)

5

What is it then between us?
What is the count of the scores or hundreds of years between us?

Whatever it is, it avails not—distance avails not, and place avails not,
I too lived, Brooklyn of ample hills was mine,
I too walk'd the streets of Manhattan island, and bathed in the waters around it,
I too felt the curious abrupt questionings stir within me,
In the day among crowds of people sometimes they came upon me,
In my walks home late at night or as I lay in my bed they came upon me,
I too had been struck from the float forever held in solution,
I too had receiv'd identity by my body,
That I was I knew was of my body, and what I should be I knew I should be of my body.

6

It is not upon you alone the dark patches fall,
The dark threw its patches down upon me also,
The best I had done seem'd to me blank and suspicious,
My great thoughts as I supposed them, were they not in reality meagre?
Nor is it you alone who know what it is to be evil,
I am he who knew what it was to be evil,
I too knitted the old knot of contrariety,
Blabb'd, blush'd, resented, lied, stole, grudg'd,
Had guile, anger, lust, hot wishes I dared not speak,
Was wayward, vain, greedy, shallow, sly, cowardly, malignant,
The wolf, the snake, the hog, not wanting in me,
The cheating look, the frivolous word, the adulterous wish, not wanting,
Refusals, hates, postponements, meanness, laziness, none of these wanting,
Was one with the rest, the days and haps of the rest,
Was call'd by my nighest name by clear loud voices of young men as they saw me approaching or passing,
Felt their arms on my neck as I stood, or the negligent leaning of their flesh against me as I sat,
Saw many I loved in the street or ferry-boat or public assembly, yet never told them a word,
Lived the same life with the rest, the same old laughing, gnawing, sleeping,
Play'd the part that still looks back on the actor or actress,
The same old role, the role that is what we make it, as great as we like,
Or as small as we like, or both great and small.

7

Closer yet I approach you,
What thought you have of me now, I had as much of you—I laid in my stores in advance,
I consider'd long and seriously of you before you were born.

Who was to know what should come home to me?
Who knows but I am enjoying this?
Who knows, for all the distance, but I am as good as looking at you now, for all you cannot see me?

8

Ah, what can ever be more stately and admirable to me than mast-hemm'd Manhattan?
River and sunset and scallop-edg'd waves of flood-tide?
The sea-gulls oscillating their bodies, the hay-boat in the twilight, and the belated lighter?
What gods can exceed these that clasp me by the hand, and with voices I love call me promptly and loudly by my nighest name as I approach?
What is more subtle than this which ties me to the woman or man that looks in my face?
Which fuses me into you now, and pours my meaning into you?

We understand then do we not?
What I promis'd without mentioning it, have you not accepted?
What the study could not teach—what the preaching could not accomplish is accomplish'd, is it not?

9

Flow on, river! flow with the flood-tide, and ebb with the ebb-tide!
Frolic on, crested and scallop-edg'd waves!
Gorgeous clouds of the sunset! drench with your splendor me, or the men and women generations after me!
Cross from shore to shore, countless crowds of passengers!
Stand up, tall masts of Mannahatta! stand up, beautiful hills of Brooklyn!
Throb, baffled and curious brain! throw out questions and answers!
Suspend here and everywhere, eternal float of solution!
Gaze, loving and thirsting eyes, in the house or street or public assembly!
Sound out, voices of young men! loudly and musically call me by my nighest name!
Live, old life! play the part that looks back on the actor or actress!
Play the old role, the role that is great or small according as one makes it!
Consider, you who peruse me, whether I may not in unknown ways be looking upon you;
Be firm, rail over the river, to support those who lean idly, yet haste with the hasting current;

Fly on, sea-birds! fly sideways, or wheel in large circles high in the air;
Receive the summer sky, you water, and faithfully hold it till all downcast eyes have time to take it from you!
Diverge, fine spokes of light, from the shape of my head, or any one's head, in the sunlit water!
Come on, ships from the lower bay! pass up or down, white-sail'd schooners, sloops, lighters!
Flaunt away, flags of all nations! be duly lower'd at sunset!
Burn high your fires, foundry chimneys! cast black shadows at nightfall! cast red and yellow light over the tops of the houses!
Appearances, now or henceforth, indicate what you are,
You necessary film, continue to envelop the soul,
About my body for me, and your body for you, be hung our divinest aromas,
Thrive, cities—bring your freight, bring your shows, ample and sufficient rivers,
Expand, being than which none else is perhaps more spiritual,
Keep your places, objects than which none else is more lasting.

You have waited, you always wait, you dumb, beautiful ministers,
We receive you with free sense at last, and are insatiate hence forward,
Not you any more shall be able to foil us, or withhold yourselves from us,
We use you, and do not cast you aside—we plant you permanently within us,
We fathom you not—we love you—there is perfection in you also,
You furnish your parts toward eternity,
Great or small, you furnish your parts toward the soul.

1856

Cavalry Crossing a Ford

A line in long array where they wind betwixt green islands,
They take a serpentine course, their arms flash in the sun—hark to the musical clank,
Behold the silvery river, in it the splashing horses loitering stop to drink,
Behold the brown-faced men, each group, each person a picture, the negligent rest on the saddles,
Some emerge on the opposite bank, others are just entering the ford—while,
Scarlet and blue and snowy white,
The guidon flags flutter gayly in the wind.

1865

A Sight in Camp in the Daybreak Gray and Dim

A sight in camp in the daybreak gray and dim,
As from my tent I emerge so early sleepless,
As slow I walk in the cool fresh air the path near by the hospital tent,

Three forms I see on stretchers lying, brought out there untended lying,
Over each the blanket spread, ample brownish woolen blanket,
Gray and heavy blanket, folding, covering all.

Curious I halt and silent stand,
Then with light fingers I from the face of the nearest the first just lift the blanket;
Who are you elderly man so gaunt and grim, with well-gray'd hair, and flesh all sunken about the eyes?
Who are you my dear comrade?
Then to the second I step—and who are you my child and darling?
Who are you sweet boy with cheeks yet blooming?

Then to the third—a face nor child nor old, very calm, as of beautiful yellow-white ivory;
Young man I think I know you—I think this face is the face of the Christ himself,
Dead and divine and brother of all, and here again he lies.

1865

To a Locomotive in Winter[2]

Thee for my recitative,
Thee in the driving storm even as now, the snow, the winter-day declining,
Thee in thy panoply, thy measur'd dual throbbing and thy beat convulsive,
Thy black cylindric body, golden brass and silvery steel,
Thy ponderous side-bars, parallel and connecting rods, gyrating, shuttling at thy sides,
Thy metrical, now swelling pant and roar, now tapering in the distance,
Thy great protruding head-light fix'd in front,
Thy long, pale, floating vapor-pennants, tinged with delicate purple,
The dense and murky clouds out-belching from thy smoke-stack,
Thy knitted frame, thy springs and valves, the tremulous twinkle of thy wheels,
Thy train of cars behind, obedient, merrily following,
Through gale or calm, now swift, now slack, yet steadily careering;
Type of the modern—emblem of motion and power—pulse of the continent,
For once come serve the Muse and merge in verse, even as here I see thee,
With storm and buffeting gusts of wind and falling snow,
By day thy warning ringing bell to sound its notes,
By night thy silent signal lamps to swing.

Fierce-throated beauty!
Roll through my chant with all thy lawless music, thy swinging lamps at night,

2. Musical declamation between lyrical numbers, as in opera.

Thy madly-whistled laughter, echoing, rumbling like an earthquake, rousing all,
Law of thyself complete, thine own track firmly holding,
(No sweetness debonair of tearful harp or glib piano thine,)
Thy trills of shrieks by rocks and hills return'd,
Launch'd o'er the prairies wide, across the lakes,
To the free skies unpent and glad and strong.

1876

EMILY DICKINSON
(*1830–1886*)

Emily Dickinson was born in Amherst, Massachusetts, on December 19, 1830, the daughter of a respected lawyer, Edward Dickinson, who for many years was the treasurer of Amherst College and for a time was a member of Congress. She had a sister, Lavinia, who like Emily never married, and a brother, Austin, whose wife, Susan Gilbert, a relatively sophisticated New Yorker, was for a time her treasured friend.

From childhood on Emily Dickinson's life was circumscribed: she always lived in her father's house, and rarely left Amherst. Her crucial acquaintance with Thomas Wentworth Higginson she owed to having read one of his magazine articles, which led her to write to him enclosing two poems and asking for critical advice.

When she was seventeen, Emily Dickinson graduated from Amherst Academy, and some months later she entered Mount Holyoke Female Seminary in South Hadley, Massachusetts. It was only six or seven miles away, but she experienced grueling homesickness, and she returned to Amherst joyfully after less than a year. She found her occupations and amusements. In 1856 she won second prize in the Bread Division at the local Cattle Show, and in 1858 she served as one of the judges. She was given to infatuated friendships, though few of the persons she loved can have known the parts they played in her inner life, for she seldom mailed them the letters of admiration she wrote. With Benjamin F. Newton, one of her father's law apprentices, she seems to have had a relationship which went a little beyond an exchange of flirtatious valentines. Newton had an energetic mind, and he encouraged her to question conventional beliefs, but he was poor and otherwise an unsuitable candidate to be her husband. Perhaps the man she most admired was Reverend Charles Wadsworth, whom she met in Philadelphia in 1854 on one of her rare trips beyond Amherst. He visited her at home in 1860 shortly before he was called to a church in San Francisco. She took his departure hard, and her greatest poems, written in the early 1860s, are reenactments of this pain and broodings on it. She became in the 1860s an eccentric recluse; she dressed in white, saw fewer and fewer visitors, and finally none. She died on May 14, 1886. Higginson, her first editor, tidied up some of her roughnesses when he brought out a posthumous volume in 1890. Over the following decades her scope was gradually revealed, as several additional collections appeared, and only in 1955, when all her poems were published for the first time, was her text reproduced without editorial improvements.

258[1]

There's a certain Slant of light,
Winter Afternoons—
That oppresses, like the Heft[2]
Of Cathedral Tunes—

Heavenly Hurt, it gives us—
We can find no scar,
But internal difference,
Where the Meanings, are—

None may teach it—Any—
'Tis the Seal Despair—
An imperial affliction
Sent us of the Air—

When it comes, the Landscape listens—
Shadows—hold their breath—
When it goes, 'tis like the Distance
On the look of Death—[3]

1890

441

This is my letter to the World
That never wrote to Me—
The simple News that Nature told—
With tender Majesty

Her Message is committed
To Hands I cannot see—
For love of Her—Sweet—countrymen—
Judge tenderly—of Me

1890

465

I heard a Fly buzz—when I died—
The Stillness in the Room
Was like the Stillness in the Air—
Between the Heaves of Storm—

The Eyes around—had wrung them dry—
And Breaths were gathering firm
For that last Onset—when the King
Be witnessed—in the Room—

1. The order and numbering of the poems is that established by Thomas H. Johnson in his edition of *The Poems of Emily Dickinson,* Cambridge, Mass., 1955.
2. Weight.
3. "I suppose there are depths in every Consciousness, from which we cannot rescue ourselves—to which none can go with us—which represent to us Mortally—the Adventure of Death—" Letter to Mrs J. G. Holland, June 1878, in *Letters,* Vol. II, p. 555.

I willed my Keepsakes—Signed away
What portion of me be
Assignable—and then it was
There interposed a Fly—

With Blue—uncertain stumbling Buzz—
Between the light—and me—
And then the Windows failed—and then
I could not see to see—

1896

632

The Brain—is wider than the Sky—
For—put them side by side—
The one the other will contain
With ease—and You—beside—

The Brain is deeper than the sea—
For—hold them—Blue to Blue—
The one the other will absorb—
As Sponges—Buckets—do—

The Brain is just the weight of God—
For—Heft them—Pound for Pound—
And they will differ—if they do—
As Syllable from Sound—

1896

712

Because I could not stop for Death—
He kindly stopped for me—
The Carriage held but just Ourselves—
And Immortality.[7]

We slowly drove—He knew no haste
And I had put away
My labor and my leisure too,
For His Civility—

We passed the School, where Children strove
At Recess—in the Ring—
We passed the Fields of Gazing Grain—
We passed the Setting Sun—

7. In a letter to T. W. Higginson, June 9, 1866, she writes: "You mention Immortality. That is the Flood subject. I was told that the Bank was the safest place for a Finless Mind. I explore but little since my mute Confederate, yet the 'infinite Beauty'—of which you speak comes too near to seek. To escape enchantment, one must always flee. Paradise is of the option. Whosoever will Own in Eden notwithstanding Adam and Repeal." *Letters,* II, 454.

Or rather—He passed Us—
The Dews drew quivering and chill—
For only Gossamer, my Gown—
My Tippet[8]—only Tulle—

We paused before a House that seemed
A Swelling of the Ground—
The Roof was scarcely visible—
The Cornice—in the Ground—

Since then—'tis Centuries—and yet
Feels shorter than the Day
I first surmised the Horses' Heads
Were toward Eternity—

1890

1627

The pedigree of Honey
Does not concern the Bee,
Nor lineage of Ecstasy
Delay the Butterfly
On spangled journeys to the peak
Of some perceiveless thing—
The right of way to Tripoli [4]
A more essential thing.

[VERSION II]

The Pedigree of Honey
Does not concern the Bee—
A Clover, any time, to him,
Is Aristocracy—

1890

1670

In Winter in my Room
I came upon a Worm—
Pink, lank and warm—
But as he was a worm
And worms presume
Not quite with him at home—
Secured him by a string
To something neighboring
And went along.

A Trifle afterward
A thing occurred
I'd not believe it if I heard

8. Cape.

4. A Mediterranean port in Libya.

But state with creeping blood—
A snake with mottles rare
Surveyed my chamber floor
In feature as the worm before
But ringed with power—

The very string with which
I tied him—too
When he was mean and new
That string was there—

I shrank—"How fair you are"!
Propitiation's claw—
"Afraid," he hissed
"Of me"?
"No cordiality"—
He fathomed me—
Then to a Rhythm *Slim*
Secreted in his Form
As Patterns swim
Projected him.

That time I flew
Both eyes his way
Lest he pursue
Nor ever ceased to run
Till in a distant Town
Towns on from mine
I set me down
This was a dream.

1914

1732[5]

My life closed twice before its close;
It yet remains to see
If Immortality unveil
A third event to me,

So huge, so hopeless to conceive
As these that twice befell.
Parting is all we know of heaven,
And all we need of hell.

1896

5. The poem perhaps alludes to the death of Emily Dickinson's father and to her love for a Philadelphia clergyman, Charles Wadsworth, whom she met in May 1855, and who went to San Francisco about 1861.

THOMAS HARDY
(*1840–1928*)

Thomas Hardy was born on June 2, 1840, at Upper Bockhampton in Dorset, England, and apart from three long absences it was in this region that he chose to live and die.

Hardy's father was a master mason, and the son's first ambition was to design buildings. At sixteen he was apprenticed to a local ecclesiastical architect. But while he could see the possibilities of a livelihood in this profession, he was extremely interested in his school studies in Latin and his private studies in Greek, a language he had taught himself. William Barnes, a good dialect poet, was a neighbor, and encouraged Hardy's literary interests. But a career in letters did not then present itself as a practical course, and Hardy took no wild risks. Having finished his apprenticeship, Hardy went to London in 1862 and became assistant to an architect there. But after five years he returned to Dorset, and, while continuing his architectural work, he began to write novels; eventually fourteen were published. But when in 1895 *Jude the Obscure* was lampooned as *Jude the Obscene*, Hardy turned altogether to verse. Besides volumes of lyrics and dramatic monologues he published, in the first years of the century, his three-part epic-drama entitled *The Dynasts* about England's wars with Napoleon.

In 1870 he went to Cornwall to restore a church. He there met Emma Lavinia Gifford and in due course (four years) married her. Their marriage did not go well; Mrs. Hardy was more troubled than pleased by her husband's success, especially when this became social as well as literary. She increasingly withheld herself from his friends, preferring to plead illness and stay home alone. Eventually she became mentally deranged. After she died in 1912, however, Hardy wrote his most passionate poems, evocations of her as she was in her "air-blue gown" almost half a century before.

Proud of his longevity, Hardy prepared in 1928 a book called *Winter Words* for the press, and in the preface declared, "So far as I am aware, I happen to be the only English poet who has brought out a new volume of verse on his birthday. . . ." He meant to write in "eighty-eighth," but did not quite make it: the volume appeared after his death on January 11.

Neutral Tones

We stood by a pond that winter day,
And the sun was white, as though chidden of God,
And a few leaves lay on the starving sod;
        —They had fallen from an ash, and were gray.

Your eyes on me were as eyes that rove
Over tedious riddles of years ago;
And some words played between us to and fro
        On which lost the more by our love.

The smile on your mouth was the deadest thing
Alive enough to have strength to die;
And a grin of bitterness swept thereby
Like an ominous bird a-wing. . . .

Since then, keen lessons that love deceives,
And wrings with wrong, have shaped to me
Your face, and the God-curst sun, and a tree,
And a pond edged with grayish leaves.

1898

Drummer Hodge

I

They throw in Drummer Hodge, to rest
Uncoffined—just as found:
His landmark is a kopje-crest[1]
That breaks the veldt[2] around;
And foreign constellations west[3]
Each night above his mound.

II

Young Hodge the Drummer never knew—
Fresh from his Wessex home—[4]
The meaning of the broad Karoo,[5]
The Bush,[6] the dusty loam,
And why uprose to nightly view
Strange stars amid the gloam.

III

Yet portion of that unknown plain
Will Hodge for ever be;
His homely Northern breast and brain
Grow to some Southern tree,
And strange-eyed constellations reign
His stars eternally.

1902

The Subalterns

I

"Poor wanderer," said the leaden sky,
"I fain would lighten thee,

1. A small hill, in Afrikaans, the language used in South Africa. Drummer Hodge is a soldier killed in the Boer War, 1899–1902, when Great Britain fought the Transvaal Republic and the Orange Free State.
2. Plain.
3. The foreign constellations are those with which Hodge, being from a northern country, is unfamiliar. "West" means to set in the west.
4. An ancient Saxon kingdom centered in Salisbury Plain. Hardy revived the name and first used it in his novel, *Far from the Madding Crowd* (1874), to include his native shire of Dorset and all or parts of five adjoining shires.
5. The Karroo is the high plateau in the Cape of Good Hope, South Africa.
6. Tracts of land in South Africa, covered with brushwood and shrubby vegetation.

But there are laws in force on high
Which say it must not be."

II

—"I would not freeze thee, shorn one," cried
The North, "knew I but how
To warm my breath, to slack my stride;
But I am ruled as thou."

III

—"To-morrow I attack thee, wight,"[7]
Said Sickness. "Yet I swear
I bear thy little ark no spite,
But am bid enter there."

IV

—"Come hither, Son," I heard Death say;
"I did not will a grave
Should end thy pilgrimage to-day,
But I, too, am a slave!"

V

We smiled upon each other then,
And life to me had less
Of that fell[8] look it wore ere when
They owned their passiveness.

1902

The Darkling Thrush[9]

I leant upon a coppice[1] gate
When Frost was spectre-gray,
And Winter's dregs made desolate
The weakening eye of day.
The tangled bine-stems[2] scored the sky
Like strings of broken lyres,
And all mankind that haunted nigh
Had sought their household fires.

The land's sharp features seemed to be
The Century's corpse[3] outleant,
His crypt the cloudy canopy,
The wind his death-lament.
The ancient pulse of germ and birth
Was shrunken hard and dry,
And every spirit upon earth
Seemed fervourless as I.

7. Human being (archaic usage).
8. Cruel.
9. The thrush in the dark.
1. Thicket.
2. Stems of a climbing, twisting plant.
3. The poem was written on December 31, 1900.

At once a voice arose among
    The bleak twigs overhead
In a full-hearted evensong
    Of joy illimited;
An aged thrush, frail, gaunt, and small,
    In blast-beruffled plume,
Had chosen thus to fling his soul
    Upon the growing gloom.

So little cause for carolings
    Of such ecstatic sound
Was written on terrestrial things
    Afar or nigh around,
That I could think there trembled through
    His happy good-night air
Some blessed Hope, whereof he knew
    And I was unaware.

1902

A Young Man's Epigram on Existence[9]

A senseless school, where we must give
Our lives that we may learn to live!
A dolt is he who memorizes
Lessons that leave no time for prizes.

1909

Channel Firing

That night your great guns, unawares,
Shook all our coffins as we lay,
And broke the chancel window-squares,
We thought it was the Judgment-day

And sat upright. While drearisome
Arose the howl of wakened hounds:
The mouse let fall the altar-crumb,
The worms drew back into the mounds,

The glebe[1] cow drooled. Till God called, "No;
It's gunnery practice out at sea
Just as before you went below;
The world is as it used to be:

"All nations striving strong to make
Red war yet redder. Mad as hatters
They do no more for Christés sake
Than you who are helpless in such matters.

9. "Printed," according to Hardy, "merely as an amusing instance of early cynicism."

1. A field near the church.

"That this is not the judgment-hour
For some of them's a blessed thing,
For if it were they'd have to scour
Hell's floor for so much threatening. . . .

"Ha, ha. It will be warmer when
I blow the trumpet (if indeed
I ever do; for you are men,
And rest eternal sorely need)."

So down we lay again. "I wonder,
Will the world ever saner be,"
Said one, "than when He sent us under
In our indifferent century!"

And many a skeleton shook his head.
"Instead of preaching forty year,"
My neighbour Parson Thirdly said,
"I wish I had stuck to pipes and beer."

Again the guns disturbed the hour,
Roaring their readiness to avenge,
As far inland as Stourton Tower,
And Camelot, and starlit Stonehenge.[2]

1914

The Convergence of the Twain

Lines on the loss of the "Titanic"[3]

I

In a solitude of the sea
Deep from human vanity,
And the Pride of Life that planned her, stilly couches she.

II

Steel chambers, late the pyres
Of her salamandrine[4] fires,
Cold currents thrid,[5] and turn to rhythmic tidal lyres.

III

Over the mirrors meant
To glass the opulent
The sea-worm crawls—grotesque, slimed, dumb, indifferent.

2. Stourton Tower is a tower erected in the eighteenth century in Stourhead Park, Wiltshire, near where, in 878, King Alfred collected his scattered followers and prepared his decisive victory at Edington in the same year. Camelot, the legendary site of King Arthur's court, is associated usually with Tintagel in Cornwall. Hardy and others associated Stonehenge with pre-Christian rites.

3. On the night of April 14, 1912, the British White Star liner *Titanic*, the largest ship afloat and on her maiden voyage to New York from Southampton, collided with an iceberg in the North Atlantic and sank in less than three hours; 1500 of 2206 passengers were lost.

4. Bright red. The salamander was supposed to be able to live in fire.

5. Thread.

IV

Jewels in joy designed
To ravish the sensuous mind
Lie lightless, all their sparkles bleared and black and blind.

V

Dim moon-eyed fishes near
Gaze at the gilded gear
And query: "What does this vaingloriousness down here?" . . .

VI

Well: while was fashioning
This creature of cleaving wing,
The Immanent Will[6] that stirs and urges everything

VII

Prepared a sinister mate
For her—so gaily great—
A Shape of Ice, for the time far and dissociate.

VIII

And as the smart ship grew
In stature, grace, and hue,
In shadowy silent distance grew the Iceberg too.

IX

Alien they seemed to be:
No mortal eye could see
The intimate welding of their later history,

X

Or sign that they were bent
By paths coincident
On being anon[7] twin halves of one august event,

XI

Till the Spinner of the Years
Said "Now!" And each one hears,
And consummation comes, and jars two hemispheres.

1914

The Voice

Woman much missed, how you call to me, call to me,
Saying that now you are not as you were
When you had changed from the one who was all to me,
But as at first, when our day was fair.

Can it be you that I hear? Let me view you, then,
Standing as when I drew near to the town
Where you would wait for me: yes, as I knew you then,
Even to the original air-blue gown!

6. For Hardy the ultimate cause seemed not the Christian God but a more or less unconscious and harsh natural force rather like Fate or Destiny.

7. Soon (archaic usage).

Or is it only the breeze, in its listlessness
Travelling across the wet mead to me here,
You being ever dissolved to wan wistlessness,[8]
Heard no more again far or near?

Thus I; faltering forward,
Leaves around me falling,
Wind oozing thin through the thorn from norward,
And the woman calling.

1914

The Oxen

Christmas Eve, and twelve of the clock.
"Now they are all on their knees,"[4]
An elder said as we sat in a flock
By the embers in hearthside ease.

We pictured the meek mild creatures where
They dwelt in their strawy pen,
Nor did it occur to one of us there
To doubt they were kneeling then.

So fair a fancy few would weave
In these years! Yet, I feel,
If someone said on Christmas Eve,
"Come; see the oxen kneel,

"In the lonely barton[5] by yonder coomb[6]
Our childhood used to know,"
I should go with him in the gloom,
Hoping it might be so.

1916

In Time of "The Breaking of Nations"[7]

I

Only a man harrowing clods
In a slow silent walk
With an old horse that stumbles and nods
Half asleep as they stalk.

8. Unawareness, ignorance (archaic usage).

4. A folk belief that the oxen kneel every Christmas as the ox kneeled in the manger when Christ was born.

5. Farmyard.

6. Valley.

7. From *Jeremiah* 51:20: "Thou art my battle axe and weapons of war: for with thee will I break in pieces the nations; and with thee will I destroy kingdoms." Hardy commented on this poem, "I believe it would be said by people who knew me well that I have a faculty (possibly not uncommon) for burying an emotion in my heart or brain for forty years, and exhuming it at the end of that time as fresh as when interred. For instance, the poem entitled 'The Breaking of Nations' contains a feeling that moved me in 1870, during the Franco-Prussian war, when I chanced to be looking at such an agricultural incident [the old horse harrowing the arable field in the valley below] in Cornwall. But I did not write the verses till during the war with Germany of 1914, and onwards. Query: where was that sentiment hiding itself during more than forty years?" Florence E. Hardy, *The Life of Thomas Hardy*, New York, 1965, pp. 378–79.

II

Only thin smoke without flame
From the heaps of couch-grass;
Yet this will go onward the same
Though Dynasties pass.

III

Yonder a maid and her wight [8]
Come whispering by:
War's annals will fade into night
Ere their story die.

1916

Proud Songsters

The thrushes sing as the sun is going,
And the finches whistle in ones and pairs,
And as it gets dark loud nightingales
In bushes
Pipe, as they can when April wears,
As if all Time were theirs.

These are brand new birds of twelve-months' growing,
Which a year ago, or less than twain,
No finches were, nor nightingales,
Nor thrushes,
But only particles of grain,
And earth, and air, and rain.

1928

8. Man (archaic usage).

GERARD MANLEY HOPKINS
(*1844–1889*)

Gerard Manley Hopkins was born on July 28, 1844, in Stratford, Essex, a town near London. He was the eldest of eight children of a London marine-insurance adjuster, a man of some cultivation who wrote not only books about marine insurance but also a volume of poems. His mother was conspicuously pious. Hopkins went to Highgate School in London and won a poetry prize. In 1864 he enrolled at Balliol College, Oxford, to read Greats (classics, ancient history, and philosophy). At that time his ambition was to become a painter, like one of his brothers, and he showed proficiency in drawing. But his plans changed because, with three of his friends, he was drawn to Catholicism. His parents were strongly opposed, but he was resolved. He was received into the Church by John Henry (later Cardinal) Newman in October 1866, and the experience of conversion determined the rest of his life. After having taken a first-class degree in 1867, he taught at the Oratory School, Birmingham, under Newman's eye. Two years later he decided to become a Jesuit. It was at this time that he burned all his early verses as too worldly, but in 1875 he resumed the writing of poetry with his Superior's encouragement. In 1877 Hopkins was ordained. He served variously as priest and teacher until 1884, when he was appointed professor of classics at University College, Dublin (founded by Newman as the Catholic University in 1853). Here until his death in 1889 he remained, out of place in the Irish scene but at home in a state of exalted misery. His health was poor and in 1889 he came down with typhoid; he died of that disease and its complications on June 8, at the age of forty-four. His friend from college days, Robert Bridges, the Poet Laureate, collected and edited Hopkins' poetry in 1918, having delayed so long because of his desire to find the propitious moment. The work caught on at once and has been a favorite of the younger poets, from Auden to Lowell.

Heaven-Haven

A nun takes the veil

I have desired to go
Where springs not fail,
To fields where flies no sharp and sided hail
And a few lilies blow.[3]

And I have asked to be
Where no storms come,
Where the green swell is in the havens dumb,
And out of the swing of the sea.

1918

The Habit of Perfection

Elected Silence,[4] sing to me
And beat upon my whorlèd ear,
Pipe me to pastures still and be
The music that I care to hear.

Shape nothing, lips; be lovely-dumb:
It is the shut,[5] the curfew sent
From there where all surrenders come
Which only makes you eloquent.

Be shellèd, eyes, with double dark
And find the uncreated light:[6]

3. Bloom (archaic usage).
4. The priest has elected—or freely chosen—a life of renunciation.
5. Closing in of evening, shut of day.
6. "The creative energy of God's mind." (W. H. Gardner and N. H. MacKenzie, eds., *The Poems of Gerard Manley Hopkins*, 4th ed., London, 1967, p. 252.)

This ruck and reel which you remark[7]
Coils, keeps, and teases simple sight.

Palate, the hutch[8] of tasty lust,
Desire not to be rinsed with wine:
The can[9] must be so sweet, the crust
So fresh that come in fasts divine!

Nostrils, your careless breath that spend
Upon the stir and keep[1] of pride,
What relish shall the censers[2] send
Along the sanctuary side![3]

O feel-of-primrose hands, O feet
That want the yield of plushy sward,
But you shall walk the golden street
And you unhouse and house the Lord.[4]

And, Poverty, be thou the bride
And now the marriage feast begun,
And lily-coloured clothes provide
Your spouse not laboured-at nor spun.[5]

1918

God's Grandeur

The world is charged with the grandeur of God.
  It will flame out, like shining from shook foil;[1]
  It gathers to a greatness, like the ooze of oil
Crushed. Why do men then now not reck his rod?[2]
Generations have trod, have trod, have trod;
  And all is seared with trade; bleared, smeared with toil;
  And wears man's smudge and shares man's smell: the soil
Is bare now, nor can foot feel, being shod.

And for all this, nature is never spent;
  There lives the dearest freshness deep down things;
And though the last lights off the black West went
  Oh, morning, at the brown brink eastward, springs—
Because the Holy Ghost over the bent
  World broods with warm breast and with ah! bright wings.

1918

7. Observe. *Coils:* ensnares.
8. Storage chest.
9. Tankard.
1. Upkeep.
2. Vessels in which incense is burned.
3. In a church, the sanctuary is the space within the altar rails.
4. Remove the Host from the tabernacle and then return it.
5. "And why are you anxious about clothing? Consider the lilies of the field, how they grow; they neither toil nor spin; yet I tell you, even Solomon in all his glory was not arrayed like one of these." *Matthew* 6:28–9.

1. "I mean foil in its sense of leaf or tinsel. . . . Shaken goldfoil gives off broad glares like sheet lightning and also, and this is true of nothing else, owing to its zigzag dints and creasings and network of small many cornered facets, a sort of fork lightning too" (Hopkins' note).
2. Heed his authority.

The Windhover:[3]

To Christ our Lord

I caught this morning morning's minion,[4] king-
  dom of daylight's dauphin,[5] dapple-dawn-drawn Falcon, in his riding
  Of the rolling level underneath him steady air, and striding
High there, how he rung upon the rein[6] of a wimpling wing
In his ecstasy! then off, off forth on swing,
  As a skate's heel sweeps smooth on a bow-bend: the hurl and gliding
  Rebuffed the big wind. My heart in hiding
Stirred for a bird,—the achieve of, the mastery of the thing!

Brute beauty and valour and act, oh, air, pride, plume here
  Buckle![7] AND the fire that breaks from thee then, a billion
  Times told lovelier, more dangerous, O my chevalier!

  No wonder of it: shéer plód makes plough down sillion[8]
Shine, and blue-bleak embers, ah my dear,
  Fall, gall themselves, and gash gold-vermilion.

1918

Pied Beauty

Glory be to God for dappled things—
  For skies of couple-colour as a brinded cow;
    For rose-moles all in stipple upon trout that swim;
Fresh-firecoal chestnut-falls;[9] finches' wings;
  Landscape plotted and pieced—fold, fallow, and plough;
    And áll trádes, their gear and tackle and trim.[1]

All things counter,[2] original, spare, strange;
  Whatever is fickle, freckled (who knows how?)
    With swift, slow; sweet, sour; adazzle, dim;
He fathers-forth whose beauty is past change:
          Praise him.

1918

Felix Randal

Felix Randal the farrier,[3] O he is dead then? my duty all ended,
Who have watched his mould of man, big-boned and hardy-handsome

3. The kestrel, a European falcon resembling the American sparrow hawk; the bird hovers in the air with its head to the wind.

4. Darling, favorite.

5. The heir to the throne of France.

6. To "ring on the rein" is a riding term, "said of a horse that circles at the end of a long rein held by its trainer." Gardner and MacKenzie, p. 267. *Wimpling*: rippling.

7. Of the many senses given for this word by the *Oxford English Dictionary*, at least three are relevant: 1. Equip, get ready for battle; 2. Unite under a single authority; 3. Give way, bend. *Chevalier:* knight.

8. A ridge or narrow strip lying between two furrows. *Selion* is the more common spelling.

9. That is, the chestnuts when they fall from the tree to the ground.

1. Equipment.

2. Contrary, in opposition.

3. One who shoes horses.

Pining, pining, till time when reason rambled in it and some
Fatal four disorders, fleshed there, all contended?

Sickness broke him. Impatient he cursed at first, but mended
Being anointed and all; though a heavenlier heart began some
Months earlier, since I had our sweet reprieve and ransom[4]
Tendered to him. Ah well, God rest him all road ever he offended!

This seeing the sick endears them to us, us too it endears.
My tongue had taught thee comfort, touch had quenched thy tears,
Thy tears that touched my heart, child, Felix, poor Felix Randal;

How far from then forethought of, all thy more boisterous years,
When thou at the random grim forge, powerful amidst peers,
Didst fettle[5] for the great grey drayhorse his bright and battering
sandal!

1918

[No Worst, There Is None. Pitched Past Pitch of Grief]

No worst, there is none. Pitched past pitch of grief,
More pangs will, schooled at forepangs, wilder wring.
Comforter, where, where is your comforting?
Mary, mother of us, where is your relief?
My cries heave, herds-long; huddle in a main, a chief
Woe, world-sorrow; on an age-old anvil wince and sing—
Then lull, then leave off. Fury had shrieked 'No ling-
ering! Let me be fell:[6] force[7] I must be brief'.

O the mind, mind has mountains; cliffs of fall
Frightful, sheer, no-man-fathomed. Hold them cheap
May who ne'er hung there. Nor does long our small
Durance deal with that steep or deep. Here! creep,
Wretch, under a comfort serves in a whirlwind: all
Life death does end and each day dies with sleep.

1918

[I Wake and Feel the Fell of Dark, Not Day]

I wake and feel the fell[8] of dark, not day.
What hours, O what black hoürs we have spent
This night! what sights you, heart, saw; ways you went!
And more must, in yet longer light's delay.
With witness I speak this. But where I say
Hours I mean years, mean life. And my lament
Is cries countless, cries like dead letters[9] sent
To dearest him that lives alas! away.

4. Confession, absolution, and communion.
5. Make ready.
6. Cruel, terrible.
7. Perforce; of necessity.
8. Bitterness or cruelty.
9. Letters which cannot be delivered.

I am gall, I am heartburn. God's most deep decree
Bitter would have me taste: my taste was me;
Bones built in me, flesh filled, blood brimmed the curse.
Selfyeast of spirit a dull dough sours. I see
The lost are like this, and their scourge to be
As I am mine, their sweating selves; but worse.

1918

ROBERT BRIDGES
(*1844–1930*)

Robert Bridges was born on October 3, 1844, at Walmer, Kent. He was educated at Eton and at Corpus Christi College, Oxford. Unvexed by financial worries, Bridges traveled for a time after taking his degree. He then decided that his poetry (which had been his major concern since his days at Eton) would profit from immersion in ordinary life. Accordingly he began a medical course in 1869 and became a surgeon. In 1881 he contracted pneumonia, and spent the winter of 1881–82 in Italy recovering his health. The experience had the effect of making him give up medicine. In 1884 he married and settled with his wife first at Yattenden in Berkshire, then at Boar's Hill, Oxford, and became a well-known figure at his old university.

When a student at Oxford, Bridges had met Gerard Manley Hopkins, and over the years they corresponded and exchanged poems. Bridges found Hopkins' work experimentally rash or "odd," and as Hopkins' literary executor he delayed publication of his friend's work until 1918, on the grounds that the public was not yet ready for it. This delay of almost thirty years has been much criticized, yet it did have the effect of bringing Hopkins from oblivion to instant fame.

In Bridges' later years his public reputation was crowned by appointment as Poet Laureate in 1913. In 1925 he received the Order of Merit. He died on April 21, 1930.

London Snow

When men were all asleep the snow came flying,
In large white flakes falling on the city brown,
Stealthily and perpetually settling and loosely lying,
Hushing the latest traffic of the drowsy town;
Deadening, muffling, stifling its murmurs failing;
Lazily and incessantly floating down and down:
Silently sifting and veiling road, roof and railing;
Hiding difference, making unevenness even,
Into angles and crevices softly drifting and sailing.
All night it fell, and when full inches seven
It lay in the depth of its uncompacted lightness,
The clouds blew off from a high and frosty heaven;
And all woke earlier for the unaccustomed brightness

Of the winter dawning, the strange unheavenly glare:
The eye marvelled—marvelled at the dazzling whiteness;
  The ear hearkened to the stillness of the solemn air;
No sound of wheel rumbling nor of foot falling,
And the busy morning cries came thin and spare.
  Then boys I heard, as they went to school, calling,
They gathered up the crystal manna to freeze
Their tongues with tasting, their hands with snowballing;
  Or rioted in a drift, plunging up to the knees;
Or peering up from under the white-mossed wonder,
'O look at the trees!' they cried, 'O look at the trees!'
  With lessened load a few carts creak and blunder,
Following along the white deserted way,
A country company long dispersed asunder:
  When now already the sun, in pale display
Standing by Paul's[1] high dome, spread forth below
His sparkling beams, and awoke the stir of the day.
  For now doors open, and war is waged with the snow;
And trains of sombre men, past tale of number,
Tread long brown paths, as toward their toil they go:
  But even for them awhile no cares encumber
Their minds diverted; the daily word is unspoken,
The daily thoughts of labour and sorrow slumber
At the sight of the beauty that greets them, for the charm they have broken.

1880

Low Barometer

The south-wind strengthens to a gale,
Across the moon the clouds fly fast,
The house is smitten as with a flail,
The chimney shudders to the blast.

On such a night, when Air has loosed
Its guardian grasp on blood and brain,
Old terrors then of god or ghost
Creep from their caves to life again;

And Reason kens[2] he herits in
A haunted house. Tenants unknown
Assert their squalid lease of sin
With earlier title than his own.

Unbodied presences, the pack'd
Pollution and remorse of Time,
Slipp'd from oblivion reënact
The horrors of unhouseld[3] crime.

1. Refers to St. Paul's Cathedral in central London.
2. Knows. *Herits in:* inherits.
3. Not having received Holy Communion.

Some men would quell the thing with prayer
Whose sightless footsteps pad the floor,
Whose fearful trespass mounts the stair
Or bursts the lock'd forbidden door.

Some have seen corpses long interr'd
Escape from hallowing control,
Pale charnel forms—nay ev'n have heard
The shrilling of a troubled soul,

That wanders till the dawn hath cross'd
The dolorous dark, or Earth hath wound
Closer her storm-spredd cloke, and thrust
The baleful phantoms underground.

1925

A. E. HOUSMAN
(*1859–1936*)

Alfred Edward Housman was born March 26, 1859, in Fockbury, which is in Worcestershire and not, as might be supposed from his verse, in Shropshire. His "sentimental" attachment to Shropshire came, he said, from the fact that "its hills were our western horizon," and he confessed indifferently to having some of his topographical details "quite wrong."

Housman did well at school and won a scholarship to St. John's College, Oxford, where he read Greats, a combination of classics, ancient history, and philosophy. "Oxford had not much effect on me," he said, "except that I there met my greatest friend." The friend was Moses Jackson, a bright and versatile student. He was receptive to friendship, but Housman wanted a more intimate relationship. Enjoined to dismiss his feelings, he had to conceal their intensity in order to enjoy Jackson's company.

At first Housman did well academically, but either because of amorous commotion or because of disaffection from some required studies in his course, he did not even answer many of the examination questions, and was failed. The following fall, 1881, he returned ignominiously to complete a marginal, "pass" degree. Meanwhile Jackson had taken a job in the Patent Office and encouraged Housman to pass a civil service examination and join him there. Housman did so, and for a time the two shared rooms in London. But both had ambitions to transcend their circumstances: Jackson was at work on a doctorate in science, and Housman, scorned for his scholarship by Oxford, was determined to prove himself in classics and spent most of his nights at the British Museum.

Living at such close quarters with Jackson was probably too anguishing. At any rate, Housman in 1886 moved into his own place in Highgate (North London) and lived there a life of total and solitary concentration. Jackson decided upon marriage and upon a career in education, and towards the end of 1887 he resigned from the Patent Office and sailed to India, where he became principal of a small college. Two years later he returned to England to marry the woman who had promised to wait for him. Housman was left to mourn as the Jacksons went to India again. Most of his poems were written in the next few years.

Housman's extraordinary capacity in classical scholarship earned signal recognition in 1892, when he was elected to the chair of Greek and Latin at University College, London. In 1894 his father died, and then occurred a death which afflicted Housman sharply even though he did not know the dead man. It was of a Woolwich cadet, eighteen years old, who committed suicide and left a note reported in a newspaper article that Housman kept for life. It was possible to read the cadet's statement as referring to a hopeless homosexual love, "that one thing I have no hope of obtaining." In the nineties, homosexuals were in danger of victimization by the law. Oscar Wilde was convicted on this charge in 1895 and sentenced to two years in prison; Housman felt for him as well.

Housman's major achievement was a five-volume critical edition of a minor work, the *Astronomicon* of the Roman poet Manilius, which he published sporadically from 1903 to 1930. When in 1910 a chair of classics fell vacant at Cambridge, Housman was elected to it, and he lived there from 1911 until his death. His later life is almost bare of incident. His friend Jackson died in 1923. Housman lived a retired life at Cambridge, though in 1933 he delivered his famous Leslie Stephen lecture, "The Name and Nature of Poetry," which created a profound impression. He died April 30, 1936.

Loveliest of Trees, the Cherry Now

Loveliest of trees, the cherry now
Is hung with bloom along the bough,
And stands about the woodland ride
Wearing white for Eastertide.

Now, of my threescore years and ten,
Twenty will not come again,
And take from seventy springs a score,
It only leaves me fifty more.

And since to look at things in bloom
Fifty springs are little room,
About the woodlands I will go
To see the cherry hung with snow.

1896

To an Athlete Dying Young

The time you won your town the race
We chaired you through the market-place;
Man and boy stood cheering by,
And home we brought you shoulder-high.

To-day, the road all runners come,
Shoulder-high we bring you home,
And set you at your threshold down,
Townsman of a stiller town.

Smart lad, to slip betimes[1] away
From fields where glory does not stay
And early though the laurel[2] grows
It withers quicker than the rose.

Eyes the shady night has shut
Cannot see the record cut,
And silence sounds no worse than cheers
After earth has stopped the ears:

Now you will not swell the rout
Of lads that wore their honours out,
Runners whom renown outran
And the name died before the man.

So set, before its echoes fade,
The fleet foot on the sill of shade,
And hold to the low lintel up
The still-defended challenge-cup.

And round that early-laurelled head
Will flock to gaze the strengthless dead
And find unwithered on its curls
The garland briefer than a girl's.

1896

Terence, This Is Stupid Stuff

'Terence,[1] this is stupid stuff:
You eat your victuals fast enough;
There can't be much amiss, 'tis clear,
To see the rate you drink your beer.
But oh, good Lord, the verse you make,
It gives a chap the belly-ache.
The cow, the old cow, she is dead;
It sleeps well, the horned head:
We poor lads, 'tis our turn now
To hear such tunes as killed the cow.
Pretty friendship 'tis to rhyme
Your friends to death before their time
Moping melancholy mad:
Come, pipe a tune to dance to, lad.'

1. Early.

2. In ancient Greece, the emblem of victory in athletics or preeminence in poetry.

1. The original title of *A Shropshire Lad* was *The Poems of Terence Hearsay.*

Why, if 'tis dancing you would be,
There's brisker pipes than poetry.
Say, for what were hop-yards meant,
Or why was Burton built on Trent?
Oh many a peer of England brews
Livelier liquor than the Muse,[2]
And malt does more than Milton can
To justify God's ways to man.[3]
Ale, man, ale's the stuff to drink
For fellows whom it hurts to think:
Look into the pewter pot
To see the world as the world's not.
And faith, 'tis pleasant till 'tis past:
The mischief is that 'twill not last.
Oh I have been to Ludlow[4] fair
And left my necktie God knows where,
And carried half-way home, or near,
Pints and quarts of Ludlow beer:
Then the world seemed none so bad,
And I myself a sterling lad;
And down in lovely muck I've lain,
Happy till I woke again.
Then I saw the morning sky:
Heigho, the tale was all a lie;
The world, it was the old world yet,
I was I, my things were wet,
And nothing now remained to do
But begin the game anew.

Therefore, since the world has still
Much good, but much less good than ill,
And while the sun and moon endure
Luck's a chance, but trouble's sure,
I'd face it as a wise man would,
And train for ill and not for good.
'Tis true, the stuff I bring for sale
Is not so brisk a brew as ale:
Out of a stem that scored the hand
I wrung it in a weary land.
But take it: if the smack is sour,
The better for the embittered hour;
It should do good to heart and head
When your soul is in my soul's stead;
And I will friend you, if I may,
In the dark and cloudy day.

2. A comparison of the fountains of Mount Ida, tended by the Muses, with the breweries of Burton-on-Trent, some of whose owners were raised to the peerage, as sources of poetic inspiration.

3. An allusion to Milton's promise in *Paradise Lost* (I:17–26) to "justify the ways of God to men."

4. A Shropshire town.

There was a king reigned in the East:
There, when kings will sit to feast,
They get their fill before they think
With poisoned meat and poisoned drink.
He gathered all that springs to birth
From the many-venomed earth;
First a little, thence to more,
He sampled all her killing store;
And easy, smiling, seasoned sound,
Sate the king when healths went round.
They put arsenic in his meat
And stared aghast to watch him eat;
They poured strychnine in his cup
And shook to see him drink it up:
They shook, they stared as white's their shirt:
Them it was their poison hurt.
—I tell the tale that I heard told.
Mithridates, he died old.[5]

1896

The Chestnut Casts His Flambeaux

The chestnut casts his flambeaux,[6] and the flowers
Stream from the hawthorn on the wind away,
The doors clap to, the pane is blind with showers.
Pass me the can,[7] lad; there's an end of May.

There's one spoilt spring to scant our mortal lot,
One season ruined of our little store.
May will be fine next year as like as not:
Oh ay, but then we shall be twenty-four.

We for a certainty are not the first
Have sat in taverns while the tempest hurled
Their hopeful plans to emptiness, and cursed
Whatever brute and blackguard made the world.

It is in truth iniquity on high
To cheat our sentenced souls of aught they crave,
And mar the merriment as you and I
Fare on our long fool's-errand to the grave.

Iniquity it is; but pass the can.
My lad, no pair of kings our mothers bore;
Our only portion is the estate of man:
We want the moon, but we shall get no more.

5. Mithridates VI, a pre-Christian king of Pontus, was said to have made himself immune to attempts to poison him by taking poison in small quantities.

6. Torches; chestnut blossoms are a vivid red in color.

7. Tankard.

If here to-day the cloud of thunder lours[8]
  To-morrow it will hie[9] on far behests;
The flesh will grieve on other bones than ours
  Soon, and the soul will mourn in other breasts.

The troubles of our proud and angry dust
  Are from eternity, and shall not fail.
Bear them we can, and if we can we must.
  Shoulder the sky, my lad, and drink your ale.

1922

Eight O'Clock

He stood, and heard the steeple
  Sprinkle the quarters on the morning town.
One, two, three, four, to market-place and people
  It tossed them down.

Strapped, noosed, nighing his hour,
  He stood and counted them and cursed his luck;
And then the clock collected in the tower
  Its strength, and struck.

1922

Epitaph on an Army of Mercenaries

These, in the day when heaven was falling,
  The hour when earth's foundations fled,
Followed their mercenary calling
  And took their wages and are dead.

Their shoulders held the sky suspended;
  They stood, and earth's foundations stay;
What God abandoned, these defended,
  And saved the sum of things for pay.

1922

8. Or "lowers": looks dark and threatening.

9. Hasten.

W. B. YEATS
(*1865–1939*)

William Butler Yeats was born in Dublin on June 13, 1865, the son of John Butler Yeats, later well known as a portrait-painter. His mother came from the Pollexfen family which lived near Sligo, and Yeats spent much of his childhood with them. In Dublin Yeats attended high school and then art school, the latter from 1884 to 1886. He gave up painting abruptly and threw himself into literary work. From now on his life expanded in many different directions. He founded Irish literary societies in both Dublin and London. In 1889 he met Maud Gonne and "the troubles of my life began." A nationalist, and a beauty, she became his ideal love and his coadjutor in various nationalistic activities. But eventually, in 1903, she married Major John MacBride. Her political extremism completed her separation from Yeats. She remained a figure in his poetry till the end.

To some extent Yeats fell under the spell of two famous occultists of the time, Madame Helena Petrovna Blavatsky, founder of the Theosophical movement, and MacGregor Mathers, founder of a magical order called the Golden Dawn. Yeats found their doctrines helpful in his own esoteric symbolism. That he was not totally credulous, however, is clear from his having been expelled from the Theosophists by Madame Blavatsky herself; he would have been expelled by Mathers as well if he had not succeeded in expelling Mathers first.

The Irish dramatic movement, which Yeats began to organize in 1899, took up more and more of his time, especially after the founding of the Abbey Theatre in 1904. The Easter Rebellion in 1916, though put down at once by the British, awoke his sympathy and his best political poems. The following year, 1917, Yeats married an Englishwoman, Georgie (changed by Yeats to George) Hyde-Lees. The early days of their marriage were troubled by his concern that his marriage was ill-advised. Mrs. Yeats, in an endeavor to distract her husband, attempted automatic writing, and his doubts evaporated.

The Yeatses had a son and a daughter, both memorialized in verse, and they lived off and on in a Norman tower called Thoor (Castle) Ballylee near Lady Augusta Gregory's house at Coole. After the Irish Free State was formed Yeats served six years in the Senate, and after his term he continued to devote himself to various schemes for invigorating the country. Some of these were harebrained, but they always came back to his own ideal of a nation of men free to cultivate their imaginative capacities. All governments began to appall him, and the grim prophecy in his poem "The Second Coming" seemed to him more and more apt. He died on January 28, 1939, in southern France, just before the Second World War began. After it was over, his body was exhumed and brought back to Ireland by an Irish destroyer. He was buried, as his poem had directed, near Sligo, "under Ben Bulben."

To the Rose upon the Rood of Time[9]

Red Rose, proud Rose, sad Rose of all my days!
Come near me, while I sing the ancient ways:
Cuhoollin[1] battling with the bitter tide;
The Druid, gray, wood-nurtured, quiet-eyed,
Who cast round Fergus dreams, and ruin untold;[2]
And thine own sadness, whereof stars, grown old

9. The rose, as an image of transfiguration and fulfillment, is a frequent symbol in Yeats's poetry of this period. The title indicates, and line 12 confirms, that the rose is here a symbol of eternal beauty, which flowers from the cross *(rood)* of time and sacrifice.

1. Cuchulain, the Irish mythological hero. His name means "Hound of Culain."

2. Priest of the ancient Druidic religion. According to Yeats's poem "Fergus and the Druid" he gave King Fergus, in response to the latter's entreaties, a bag of dreams. These made the king know everything but feel that he had grown to be nothing.

In dancing silver sandalled on the sea,
Sing in their high and lonely melody.
Come near, that no more blinded by man's fate,
I find under the boughs of love and hate,
In all poor foolish things that live a day,
Eternal beauty wandering on her way.

Come near, come near, come near—Ah, leave me still
A little space for the rose-breath to fill!
Lest I no more hear common things that crave;
The weak worm hiding down in its small cave,
The field mouse running by me in the grass,
And heavy mortal hopes that toil and pass;
But seek alone to hear the strange things said
By God to the bright hearts of those long dead,
And learn to chaunt a tongue men do not know.
Come near; I would, before my time to go,
Sing of old Eire[4] and the ancient ways:
Red Rose, proud Rose, sad Rose of all my days.

1892

The Lake Isle of Innisfree[5]

I will arise and go now, and go to Innisfree,
And a small cabin build there, of clay and wattles made;
Nine bean rows will I have there, a hive for the honey bee,
And live alone in the bee-loud glade.

And I shall have some peace there, for peace comes dropping slow,
Dropping from the veils of the morning to where the cricket sings;
There midnight's all a glimmer, and noon a purple glow,
And evening full of the linnet's[7] wings.[8]

4. Ireland.

5. Innisfree, which means "Heather Island" in Irish, is a small island in Lough Gill near Sligo in the west of Ireland. In his *Autobiography* Yeats writes: "I had still the ambition, formed in Sligo in my teens, of living in imitation of Thoreau on Innisfree . . . and when walking through Fleet Street [in London] very homesick I heard a little tinkle of water and saw a fountain in a shop-window which balanced a little ball upon its jet, and began to remember lake water. From the sudden remembrance came my poem *Innisfree*, my first lyric with anything in its rhythm of my own music. I had begun to loosen rhythm as an escape from rhetoric and from that emotion of the crowd rhetoric brings, but I only understood vaguely and occasionally that I must for my special purpose use nothing but the common syntax. A couple of years later I would not have written that first line with its conventional archaism—'Arise and go'—nor the inversion in the last stanza."

7. A songbird of the finch family.

8. An early draft of the poem read as follows:

I will arise and go now and go to the island of Innisfree
And live in a dwelling of wattles, of woven wattles and wood-work made.
Nine bean-rows will I have there, a yellow hive for the honey-bee,
And this old care shall fade.

There from the dawn above me peace will come down dropping slow,
Dropping from the veils of the morning to where the household cricket sings;
And noontide there be all a glimmer, and midnight be a purple glow,
And evening full of the linnet's wings.

I will arise and go now, for always night and day
I hear lake water lapping with low sounds by the shore;
While I stand on the roadway, or on the pavements gray,
I hear it in the deep heart's core.

1892

When You Are Old[9]

When you are old and gray and full of sleep,
And nodding by the fire, take down this book,
And slowly read, and dream of the soft look
Your eyes had once, and of their shadows deep;

How many loved your moments of glad grace,
And loved your beauty with love false or true;
But one man loved the pilgrim soul in you,
And loved the sorrows of your changing face.

And bending down beside the glowing bars
Murmur, a little sadly, how love fled
And paced upon the mountains overhead
And hid his face amid a crowd of stars.

1892

Who Goes with Fergus?[1]

Who will go drive with Fergus now,
And pierce the deep wood's woven shade,
And dance upon the level shore?
Young man, lift up your russet brow,
And lift your tender eyelids, maid,
And brood on hopes and fears no more.

And no more turn aside and brood
Upon Love's bitter mystery;
For Fergus rules the brazen cars,[2]
And rules the shadows of the wood,
And the white breast of the dim sea
And all dishevelled wandering stars.

1892

9. An adaptation from a poem by Pierre Ronsard (1524–1585), which begins: "Quand vous serez bien vieille, au soir à la chandelle" (When you are quite old, in the evening by candle-light).

1. According to one story, King Fergus of Ulster decided to abdicate his throne and live with a few companions in the woods.

2. Brass chariots.

Michael Robartes Bids His Beloved Be at Peace[6]

I hear the Shadowy Horses, their long manes a-shake,
Their hoofs heavy with tumult, their eyes glimmering white;
The North unfolds above them clinging, creeping night,
The East her hidden joy before the morning break,
The West weeps in pale dew and sighs passing away,
The South is pouring down roses of crimson fire:
O vanity of Sleep, Hope, Dream, endless Desire,
The Horses of Disaster plunge in the heavy clay:
Beloved, let your eyes half close, and your heart beat
Over my heart, and your hair fall over my breast,
Drowning love's lonely hour in deep twilight of rest,
And hiding their tossing manes and their tumultuous feet.

1899

No Second Troy[7]

Why should I blame her that she filled my days
With misery, or that she would of late
Have taught to ignorant men most violent ways,
Or hurled the little streets upon the great,
Had they but courage equal to desire?[8]
What could have made her peaceful with a mind
That nobleness made simple as a fire,
With beauty like a tightened bow, a kind
That is not natural in an age like this,
Being high and solitary and most stern?
Why, what could she have done, being what she is?
Was there another Troy for her to burn?

1910

6. Yeats's elaborate note on this poem in *The Wind among the Reeds* gave this explanation: "November, the old beginning of winter, or of the victory of the Fomor, or powers of death, and dismay, and cold, and darkness, is associated by the Irish people with the horse-shaped Púcas, who are now mischievous spirits, but were once Fomorian divinities. I think that they may have some connection with the horses of Mannannan, who reigned over the country of the dead, where the Fomorian Tethra reigned also; and the horses of Mannannan, though they could cross the land as easily as the sea, are constantly associated with the waves. Some neo-platonist, I forget who, describes the sea as a symbol of the drifting indefinite bitterness of life, and I believe there is like symbolism intended in the many Irish voyages to the islands of enchantment, or that there was, at any rate, in the mythology out of which these stories have been shaped. I follow much Irish and other mythology, and the magic tradition, in associating the North with night and sleep, and the East, the place of sunrise, with hope, and the South, the place of the sun when at its height, with passion and desire, and the West, the place of sunset, with fading and dreaming things." A reference to the Four Horsemen of the Apocalypse may also be intended. Michael Robartes, whose name appears in several poems by Yeats, was a character in some of his early stories. In later versions of this poem its title became, "He Bids His Beloved Be at Peace."

7. This poem, based upon the unnamed Maud Gonne, who is compared with Helen of Troy, is one of the several poems reshaping Greek legend for contemporary purposes which Yeats wrote in middle life.

8. The reference is to Maud Gonne's revolutionary activities.

On Hearing that the Students of Our New University Have Joined the Agitation Against Immoral Literature[9]

Where, where but here have Pride and Truth,
That long to give themselves for wage,
To shake their wicked sides at youth
Restraining reckless middle-age?

1912

Friends

Now must I these three praise—
Three women[1] that have wrought
What joy is in my days:
One because no thought,
Nor those unpassing cares,
No, not in these fifteen
Many-times-troubled years,
Could ever come between
Mind and delighted mind;
And one because her hand
Had strength that could unbind
What none can understand,
What none can have and thrive,
Youth's dreamy load, till she
So changed me that I live
Labouring in ecstasy.
And what of her that took
All till my youth was gone
With scarce a pitying look?
How could I praise that one?
When day begins to break
I count my good and bad,
Being wakeful for her sake,
Remembering what she had,
What eagle look still shows,
While up from my heart's root
So great a sweetness flows
I shake from head to foot.

1912

9. The "new university" was founded as the Catholic University, but soon became known as the Royal University. In 1908 it was renamed the National University and made the parent body of colleges in Cork, Dublin, Galway, and Maynooth. Yeats has the Dublin students in mind.

1. The first is Lady Gregory (1852–1932), Irish playwright and Yeats's collaborator in the Abbey Theatre; after their meeting in 1896, they shared an interest in folklore and the drama. The second is Olivia Shakespear, a novelist; with her Yeats had his first love affair about 1895. The third is Maud Gonne.

September 1913[6]

What need you,[7] being come to sense,
But fumble in a greasy till
And add the halfpence to the pence
And prayer to shivering prayer, until
You have dried the marrow from the bone?
For men were born to pray and save:
Romantic Ireland's dead and gone,
It's with O'Leary[8] in the grave.

Yet they were of a different kind,
The names that stilled your childish play,
They have gone about the world like wind,
But little time had they to pray
For whom the hangman's rope was spun,
And what, God help us, could they save?
Romantic Ireland's dead and gone,
It's with O'Leary in the grave.

Was it for this the wild geese[9] spread
The grey wing upon every tide;
For this that all that blood was shed,
For this Edward Fitzgerald died,
And Robert Emmet and Wolfe Tone,[1]
All that delirium of the brave?
Romantic Ireland's dead and gone,
It's with O'Leary in the grave.

Yet could we turn the years again,
And call those exiles as they were
In all their loneliness and pain,
You'd cry, 'Some woman's yellow hair
Has maddened every mother's son':
They weighed so lightly what they gave.
But let them be, they're dead and gone,
They're with O'Leary in the grave.

1913

6. Originally entitled "Romance in Ireland (On Reading Much of the Correspondence against the Art Gallery)" and published in the *Irish Times*, 8 September 1913. Sir Hugh Lane had offered to give his valuable collection of paintings to Dublin if the city would build a proper gallery. There was unexpected opposition, and he withdrew the gift, though an unwitnessed codicil to his will renewed his benefaction.

7. The new Catholic middle class.

8. John O'Leary (1830–1907) was a heroic nationalist who, after five years' imprisonment and fifteen years' exile, returned to Dublin in 1885. Yeats, then twenty, was one of the young men and women whom O'Leary rallied to the cause of literary nationalism.

9. A widely-used name for the Irishmen who, because of the penal laws against Catholics, were forced to go to the continent from 1691 until Catholic Emancipation.

1. Lord Edward Fitzgerald (1763–1798), the Irish rebel and patriot. He joined the United Irishmen to foment a rising but was taken prisoner and died of wounds received in the struggle over his arrest. Robert Emmet (1778–1803), another Irish patriot, and also a member of the United Irishmen, started an unsuccessful rising in 1802, but was captured, tried, and executed. Wolfe Tone (1763–1798) brought a French force to Ireland but was captured and died in prison, perhaps at his own hand, before execution.

The Wild Swans at Coole[2]

The trees are in their autumn beauty,
The woodland paths are dry,
Under the October twilight the water
Mirrors a still sky;
Upon the brimming water among the stones
Are nine-and-fifty swans.

The nineteenth autumn has come upon me
Since I first made my count;
I saw, before I had well finished,
All suddenly mount
And scatter wheeling in great broken rings
Upon their clamorous wings.

I have looked upon those brilliant creatures,
And now my heart is sore.
All's changed since I, hearing at twilight,
The first time on this shore,
The bell-beat of their wings above my head,
Trod with a lighter tread.

Unwearied still, lover by lover,
They paddle in the cold
Companionable streams or climb the air;
Their hearts have not grown old;
Passion or conquest, wander where they will,
Attend upon them still.

But now they drift on the still water,
Mysterious, beautiful;
Among what rushes will they build,
By what lake's edge or pool
Delight men's eyes when I awake some day
To find they have flown away?[8]

1917

An Irish Airman Foresees His Death[1]

I know that I shall meet my fate
Somewhere among the clouds above;
Those that I fight I do not hate,
Those that I guard I do not love;
My country is Kiltartan Cross,[2]

2. Coole Park was the estate of Lady Gregory, Yeats's friend and associate at Dublin's Abbey Theatre. It is in the western county of Galway.

8. When the poem was first published, this stanza came immediately after the second.

1. Lady Gregory's son, Major Robert Gregory, was killed in action on the Italian front on January 23, 1918. This is one of the poems Yeats wrote in his memory.

2. Near Coole.

My countrymen Kiltartan's poor,
No likely end could bring them loss
Or leave them happier than before.
Nor law, nor duty bade me fight,
Nor public men, nor cheering crowds,
A lonely impulse of delight
Drove to this tumult in the clouds;
I balanced all, brought all to mind,

The years to come seemed waste of breath,
A waste of breath the years behind
In balance with this life, this death.

1919

Easter 1916[5]

I have met them at close of day
Coming with vivid faces
From counter or desk among grey
Eighteenth-century houses.
I have passed with a nod of the head
Or polite meaningless words,
Or have lingered awhile and said
Polite meaningless words,
And thought before I had done
Of a mocking tale or a gibe[6]
To please a companion
Around the fire at the club,
Being certain that they and I
But lived where motley[7] is worn:
All changed, changed utterly:
A terrible beauty is born.

That woman's days were spent
In ignorant good-will,
Her nights in argument
Until her voice grew shrill.
What voice more sweet than hers
When, young and beautiful,
She rode to harriers?[8]
This man had kept a school

5. Yeats was moved by the Easter Rebellion on April 24, 1916, when republicans seized buildings and a park in the center of Dublin. They were killed or captured by April 29 and the leaders were executed in May. Yeats plays on Easter as the day of Christ's resurrection as well as the day of the Irish insurrection.

6. A sarcastic or scornful remark.

7. A many-colored garment worn by the professional jester or fool.

8. Dogs trained to hunt rabbits; to "ride to harriers" is to ride among huntsmen following a pack of harriers at the chase. 'That woman" is Countess Markiewicz, née Constance Gore-Booth (1868–1927), who took a prominent part in the rebellion. She was sentenced to execution but her sentence was commuted to imprisonment.

And rode our wingèd horse;[9]
This other his helper and friend
Was coming into his force;
He might have won fame in the end,
So sensitive his nature seemed,
So daring and sweet his thought.
This other man I had dreamed
A drunken, vainglorious lout.[1]
He had done most bitter wrong
To some who are near my heart,
Yet I number him in the song;
He, too, has resigned his part
In the casual comedy;
He, too, has been changed in his turn,
Transformed utterly:
A terrible beauty is born.

Hearts with one purpose alone
Through summer and winter seem
Enchanted to a stone
To trouble the living stream.
The horse that comes from the road,
The rider, the birds that range
From cloud to tumbling cloud,
Minute by minute they change;
A shadow of cloud on the stream
Changes minute by minute;
A horse-hoof slides on the brim,
And a horse plashes within it;
The long-legged moor-hens dive,
And hens to moor-cocks call;
Minute by minute they live:
The stone's in the midst of all.

Too long a sacrifice
Can make a stone of the heart.
O when may it suffice?
That is Heaven's part, our part
To murmur name upon name,
As a mother names her child
When sleep at last has come
On limbs that had run wild.
What is it but nightfall?
No, no, not night but death;

9. Patrick Pearse (1879–1916) had founded St. Enda's School for Boys at Rathfarnham, near Dublin. He was the leader of the insurrection. The winged horse is Pegasus, the poet's mythical charger; Pearse wrote verse in Irish and English. The "helper and friend" was Thomas MacDonagh (1878–1916), a poet and dramatist.

1. Major John MacBride, Maud Gonne's husband. He and his wife had separated long since because of his drinking and other alleged offenses.

Was it needless death after all?
For England may keep faith
For all that is done and said.[2]
We know their dream; enough
To know they dreamed and are dead;
And what if excess of love
Bewildered[3] them till they died?
I write it out in a verse—
MacDonagh and MacBride
And Connolly and Pearse
Now and in time to be,
Wherever green is worn,
Are changed, changed utterly:
A terrible beauty is born.

1916

The Second Coming[4]

Turning and turning in the widening gyre[5]
The falcon cannot hear the falconer;
Things fall apart; the centre cannot hold;
Mere anarchy is loosed upon the world,
The blood-dimmed tide is loosed, and everywhere
The ceremony of innocence is drowned;
The best lack all conviction, while the worst
Are full of passionate intensity.

Surely some revelation is at hand;
Surely the Second Coming is at hand.
The Second Coming! Hardly are those words out
When a vast image out of *Spiritus Mundi*[6]
Troubles my sight: somewhere in sands of the desert
A shape with lion body and the head of a man,
A gaze blank and pitiless as the sun,
Is moving its slow thighs, while all about it
Reel shadows of the indignant desert birds.
The darkness drops again; but now I know
That twenty centuries[8] of stony sleep
Were vexed to nightmare by a rocking cradle,[9]

2. England had promised Home Rule for Ireland.

3. Both "confused" and "made wild."

4. Written in January 1919, this poem reflects Yeats's attitude toward the First World War and the Black and Tan war in Ireland. The title fuses Christ's prediction of his second coming in *Matthew* 24 and John's vision of the coming of the Beast of the Apocalypse, or Antichrist (*1 John* 2:18).

5. The upward, spiraling motion of the falcon, but Yeats also used two interlocking gyres or cones as symbolic of the conflicting forces in life. In this poem he uses a single gyre which is widening towards its maximum, at which point the age will turn upon itself, there will be violence and a new era.

6. Spirit of the World (Lat.), a Yeats term for a kind of divine inspiration, or the collective unconscious.

8. That is, the twenty centuries of Christianity.

9. Of Christ, as if Christianity prepared its own opposite.

And what rough beast, its hour come round at last,
Slouches towards Bethlehem[1] to be born?

1921

A Prayer for My Daughter[2]

Once more the storm is howling, and half hid
Under this cradle-hood and coverlid
My child sleeps on. There is no obstacle
But Gregory's wood[3] and one bare hill
Whereby the haystack- and roof-levelling wind,
Bred on the Atlantic, can be stayed;
And for an hour I have walked and prayed
Because of the great gloom that is in my mind.

I have walked and prayed for this young child an hour
And heard the sea-wind scream upon the tower,
And under the arches of the bridge, and scream
In the elms above the flooded stream;
Imagining in excited reverie
That the future years had come,
Dancing to a frenzied drum.
Out of the murderous innocence of the sea.

May she be granted beauty and yet not
Beauty to make a stranger's eye distraught,
Or hers before a looking-glass, for such,
Being made beautiful overmuch,
Consider beauty a sufficient end,
Lose natural kindness and maybe
The heart-revealing intimacy
That chooses right, and never find a friend.

Helen being chosen found life flat and dull
And later had much trouble from a fool,[4]
While that great Queen,[5] that rose out of the spray,
Being fatherless could have her way
Yet chose a bandy-leggèd smith for man.
It's certain that fine women eat
A crazy salad with their meat
Whereby the Horn of Plenty[6] is undone.

In courtesy I'd have her chiefly learned;
Hearts are not had as a gift but hearts are earned
By those that are not entirely beautiful;
Yet many, that have played the fool

1. Christ's birthplace, here ironically made the birthplace of the Antichrist.

2. Yeats's daughter was Anne Butler Yeats, born February 26, 1919.

3. Lady Gregory's wood at Coole, not far from the tower, Thoor Ballylee, where Yeats was then living.

4. Paris, Helen's lover, for whom she deserted her husband, Menelaus, causing the Trojan War.

5. Venus, goddess of love, born from the sea, married Vulcan, the gods' blacksmith.

6. Or cornucopia. According to myth, it was always filled with fruit and grain.

For beauty's very self, has charm made wise,
And many a poor man that has roved,
Loved and thought himself beloved,
From a glad kindness cannot take his eyes.

May she become a flourishing hidden tree
That all her thoughts may like the linnet[7] be,
And have no business but dispensing round
Their magnanimities of sound,
Nor but in merriment begin a chase,
Nor but in merriment a quarrel.
O may she live like some green laurel
Rooted in one dear perpetual place.

My mind, because the minds that I have loved,
The sort of beauty that I have approved,
Prosper but little, has dried up of late,
Yet knows that to be choked with hate
May well be of all evil chances chief.
If there's no hatred in a mind
Assault and battery of the wind
Can never tear the linnet from the leaf.

An intellectual hatred is the worst,
So let her think opinions are accursed.
Have I not seen the loveliest woman[8] born
Out of the mouth of Plenty's horn,
Because of her opinionated mind
Barter that horn and every good
By quiet natures understood
For an old bellows full of angry wind?

Considering that, all hatred driven hence,
The soul recovers radical innocence
And learns at last that it is self-delighting,
Self-appeasing, self-affrighting,
And that its own sweet will is Heaven's will;
She can, though every face should scowl
And every windy quarter howl
Or every bellows burst, be happy still.

And may her bridegroom bring her to a house
Where all's accustomed, ceremonious;
For arrogance and hatred are the wares
Peddled in the thoroughfares.
How but in custom and in ceremony
Are innocence and beauty born?
Ceremony's a name for the rich horn,
And custom for the spreading laurel tree.

1921

7. A songbird.
8. Maud Gonne, whose political attitudes became increasingly militant (and less and less to Yeats's taste).

Leda and the Swan[1]

A sudden blow: the great wings beating still
Above the staggering girl, her thighs caressed
By the dark webs, her nape caught in his bill,
He holds her helpless breast upon his breast.[2]

How can those terrified vague fingers push
The feathered glory from her loosening thighs?
And how can body, laid in that white rush,
But feel the strange heart beating where it lies?

A shudder in the loins engenders there
The broken wall, the burning roof and tower
And Agamemnon dead.
Being so caught up,
So mastered by the brute blood of the air,
Did she put on his knowledge with his power
Before the indifferent beak could let her drop?

1924

Sailing to Byzantium[5]

I

That[6] is no country for old men. The young
In one another's arms, birds in the trees
—Those dying generations—at their song,
The salmon-falls, the mackerel-crowded seas,

1. According to legend, Leda bore, as a result of her rape by Zeus disguised as a swan, two eggs, containing the twins Castor and Pollux, Helen, and Clytemnestra. Helen deserted her husband, King Menelaus, to go with Paris to Troy, and so caused the Trojan War; Clytemnestra became the wife of the Greek king Agamemnon, and after the latter's return from Troy murdered him. 'I wrote Leda and the Swan because the editor of a political review [George Russell] asked me for a poem. I thought, "After the individualist, demagogic movement [of the Eighteenth Century] we have a soil so exhausted that it cannot grow that crop again for centuries.' Then I thought, 'Nothing is now possible but some movement from above preceded by some violent annunciation.' My fancy began to play with Leda and the Swan for metaphor, and I began this poem; but as I wrote, bird and lady took such possession of the scene that all politics went out of it, and my friend tells me that his 'conservative readers would misunderstand the poem.' " (Yeats's note.) For Yeats Leda's rape by the Swan is the beginning of a new age, as was the annunciation to Mary by the Dove of Christ's conception.

2. A first draft of the first four lines reads: "Now can the swooping godhead have his will / Yet hovers, though her helpless thighs are pressed / By the webbed toes; and that all-powerful bill / Has suddenly bowed her face upon his breast."

5. Byzantium (Constantinople) was for Yeats a kind of city of the soul, especially of the artist's soul; he admired its stylization and assurance. (See also "Byzantium," p. 49.) As he said in *A Vision* (1937, pp. 279–80), he would, if given a month to spend in antiquity, have chosen to spend it in Byzantium, "a little before Justinian opened St. Sophia and closed the Academy of Plato. I think I could find in some little wine-shop some philosophic worker in mosaic who could answer all my questions, the supernatural descending nearer to him than to Plotinus even. . . . I think that in early Byzantium, maybe never before or since in recorded history, religious, aesthetic and practical life were one, that architect and artificers . . . spoke to the multitude and the few alike. The painter, the mosaic worker, the worker in gold and silver, the illuminator of sacred books, were almost impersonal, almost perhaps without the consciousness of individual design, absorbed in their subject-matter and that the vision of a whole people. They would copy out of old gospel books those pictures that seemed as sacred as the text, and yet weave all into a vast design, the work of many that semed the work of one, that made building, picture, pattern, metalwork of rail and lamp, seem but a single image. . . ."

6. Ireland, as suggested by the salmon-falls (line 4).

Fish, flesh, or fowl, commend all summer long
Whatever is begotten, born, and dies.
Caught in that sensual music all neglect
Monuments of unageing intellect.

II

An aged man is but a paltry thing,
A tattered coat upon a stick, unless
Soul clap its hands and sing, and louder sing
For every tatter in its mortal dress,
Nor is there singing school but [8] studying
Monuments of its own magnificence;
And therefore I have sailed the seas and come
To the holy city of Byzantium.

III

O sages standing in God's holy fire
As in the gold mosaic of a wall,[1]
Come from the holy fire, perne in a gyre,[2]
And be the singing-masters of my soul.
Consume my heart away; sick with desire
And fastened to a dying animal
It knows not what it is; and gather me
Into the artifice of eternity.

IV

Once out of nature I shall never take
My bodily form from any natural thing,
But such a form as Grecian goldsmiths make
Of hammered gold and gold enamelling
To keep a drowsy Emperor awake;[4]
Or set upon a golden bough to sing
To lords and ladies of Byzantium
Of what is past, or passing, or to come.

1927

Among School Children[8]

I

I walk through the long schoolroom questioning;
A kind old nun in a white hood replies;

8. That is, except for studying.

1. The church of St. Sophia is famous for its enormous mosaics of Biblical subjects.

2. "Perne" refers to the winding or unwinding of thread on a bobbin. The poet asks the sages to spiral down *(in a gyre)* from their timeless setting to his point in time.

4. In a note to this poem, Yeats writes, "I have read somewhere that in the Emperor's palace at Byzantium was a tree made of gold and silver, and artificial birds that sang."

8. Yeats wrote in a notebook, about March 14, 1926: "Topic for poem—School children and the thought that life will waste them perhaps that no possible life can fulfill our dreams or even their teacher's hope. Bring in the old thought that life prepares for what never happens."

Yeats visited some schools as part of his work in the Irish Senate.

The children learn to cipher[9] and to sing,
To study reading-books and history,
To cut and sew, be neat in everything
In the best modern way—the children's eyes
In momentary wonder stare upon
A sixty-year-old smiling public man.

II

I dream of a Ledaean body,[1] bent
Above a sinking fire, a tale that she
Told of a harsh reproof, or trivial event
That changed some childish day to tragedy—
Told, and it seemed that our two natures blent
Into a sphere from youthful sympathy,
Or else, to alter Plato's parable,[2]
Into the yolk and white of the one shell.

III

And thinking of that fit of grief or rage
I look upon one child or t'other there
And wonder if she stood so at that age—
For even daughters of the swan can share
Something of every paddler's heritage—
And had that colour upon cheek or hair,
And thereupon my heart is driven wild:
She stands before me as a living child.

IV

Her present image[3] floats into the mind—
Did Quattrocento finger[4] fashion it
Hollow of cheek as though it drank the wind
And took a mess of shadows for its meat?
And I though never of Ledaean kind
Had pretty plumage once—enough of that,
Better to smile on all that smile, and show
There is a comfortable kind of old scarecrow.

V

What youthful mother, a shape upon her lap
Honey of generation[7] had betrayed,

9. Do arithmetic.

1. A body like Leda's, the lover of Zeus. (See "Leda and the Swan," p. 45.) Yeats has Maud Gonne in mind, though he does not name her.

2. In Plato's *Symposium*, it is suggested that man was originally both male and female, but fell into division, and that the resulting two beings come together and embrace each other to become one again.

3. In old age, Maud Gonne was thin and almost skeletal.

4. That is, the skill of a fifteenth-century Italian painter.

7. The pleasure of sexual intercourse. Yeats's note says, "I have taken the 'honey of generation' from Porphyry's essay on 'The Cave of the Nymphs,' but find no warrant in Porphyry for considering it the 'drug' that destroys the 'recollection' of prenatal freedom. He blamed a cup of oblivion given in the zodiacal sign of Cancer." Porphyry (233–c.304), a Neo-platonist philosopher, tried to explain the soul's passage from the blissful state of eternity into the prison of time.

And that must sleep, shriek, struggle to escape
As recollection or the drug decide,
Would think her son, did she but see that shape
With sixty or more winters on its head,
A compensation for the pang of his birth,
Or the uncertainty of his setting forth?

VI[8]

Plato thought nature but a spume that plays
Upon a ghostly paradigm[9] of things;
Solider Aristotle played the taws
Upon the bottom of a king of kings;
World-famous golden-thighed Pythagoras[1]
Fingered upon a fiddle-stick or strings
What a star sang and careless Muses heard:
Old clothes upon old sticks to scare a bird.

VII

Both nuns and mothers worship images,
But those the candles light are not as those
That animate a mother's reveries,
But keep a marble or a bronze repose.
And yet they too break hearts—O Presences
That passion, piety or affection knows,
And that all heavenly glory symbolise—
O self-born mockers of man's enterprise;

VIII

Labour is blossoming or dancing where
The body is not bruised to pleasure soul,
Nor beauty born out of its own despair,[2]
Nor blear-eyed wisdom out of midnight oil.
O chestnut-tree, great-rooted blossomer,
Are you the leaf, the blossom or the bole?
O body swayed to music, O brightening glance,
How can we know the dancer from the dance?

1927

8. On September 24, 1926, Yeats wrote Mrs. Olivia Shakespear, "Here is a fragment of my last curse upon old age. It means that even the greatest men are owls, scarecrows, by the time their fame has come. Aristotle, remember, was Alexander's tutor, hence the taws (form of birch) . . . Pythagoras made some measurement of the intervals between notes on a stretched string. It is a poem of seven or eight similar verses." *Letters*, p. 719. Plato thought nature merely an image, an imitation of a world that exists elsewhere; Aristotle was "solider" because he regarded the world we perceive as the authentic one.

9. Pattern.

1. Iamblichus, in his life of his teacher Pythagoras, said that the philosopher had once shown a friend that he had a golden thigh.

2. That is, out of despair at its own lack.

Byzantium[4]

The unpurged images of day[5] recede;
The Emperor's drunken soldiery are abed;
Night resonance recedes, night-walkers' song
After great cathedral gong;
A starlit or a moonlit dome[6] disdains
All that man is,
All mere complexities,
The fury and the mire of human veins.[7]

Before me floats an image, man or shade,
Shade more than man, more image than a shade;
For Hades' bobbin bound in mummy-cloth[8]
May unwind the winding path;[9]
A mouth that has no moisture and no breath
Breathless mouths[1] may summon;
I hail the superhuman;
I call it death-in-life and life-in-death.[2]

Miracle, bird or golden handiwork,
More miracle than bird or handiwork,
Planted on the star-lit golden bough,
Can like the cocks of Hades crow,[3]
Or, by the moon embittered, scorn aloud
In glory of changeless metal
Common bird or petal
And all complexities of mire or blood.[4]

At midnight on the Emperor's pavement flit
Flames that no faggot feeds, nor steel has lit,
Nor storm disturbs, flames begotten of flame,
Where blood-begotten spirits come
And all complexities of fury leave,

4. In Yeats's 1930 Diary he noted, as "subject for a poem," "Describe Byzantium as it is in the system towards the end of the first Christian millennium. A walking mummy. Flames at the street corners where the soul is purified, birds of hammered gold singing in the golden trees, in the harbour [dolphins] offering their backs to the wailing dead that they may carry them to Paradise." In this poem Byzantium is both the city of art and the valley of the blest. (Also see "Sailing to Byzantium," p. 45.)

5. As distinguished from the imaginative images of midnight which are purged.

6. Of the great church of St. Sophia.

7. The first stanza of the poem read in its first draft:

When the emperor's brawling soldiers are abed
The last benighted victims dead or fled—
When silence falls on the cathedral gong
And the drunken harlot's song
A cloudy silence, or a silence lit
Whether by star or moon
I tread the emperor's tower
All my intricacies grown clear and sweet.

8. "Hades' bobbin" is the soul, which winds up the mummy-cloth of experience during life.

9. That is, even in life the soul can communicate with the timeless world.

1. The mouths of the living, enraptured by vision.

2. Such images are dead from the point of view of our life, but under the aspect of eternity it is they that are alive and we who are dead.

3. On Roman tombstones the cock is a herald of rebirth.

4. The golden birds are another form of art, which scorns earthly life ("mire or blood").

Dying into a dance,
An agony of trance,
An agony of flame that cannot singe a sleeve.[5]

Astraddle on the dolphin's mire and blood,
Spirit after spirit. The smithies break the flood,
The golden smithies of the Emperor!
Marbles of the dancing floor
Break bitter furies of complexity,
Those images that yet
Fresh images beget,
That dolphin-torn, that gong-tormented sea.

1932

Crazy Jane Talks with the Bishop[6]

I met the Bishop on the road
And much said he and I.
'Those breasts are flat and fallen now,
Those veins must soon be dry;
Live in a heavenly mansion,
Not in some foul sty.'

'Fair and foul are near of kin,
And fair needs foul,' I cried.
'My friends are gone, but that's a truth
Nor grave nor bed denied,
Learned in bodily lowliness
And in the heart's pride.

'A woman can be proud and stiff
When on love intent;
But Love has pitched his mansion in
The place of excrement;
For nothing can be sole or whole
That has not been rent.'

1933

Lapis Lazuli

(FOR HARRY CLIFTON)[7]

I have heard that hysterical[8] women say
They are sick of the palette and fiddle-bow,

5. In notes for *A Vision*, Yeats spoke of how the dead are at first subject to destiny, but at a later stage, "the point . . . where . . . we may escape from the constraint of our nature and that of external things, entering upon a state where all fuel becomes flame, where there is nothing but the state itself, nothing to constrain it or end it." Quoted in Ellmann, *The Identity of Yeats*, p. 221.

6. Crazy Jane was modeled to some extent upon an old woman who lived near Lady Gregory. Yeats used her as a speaker in a group of poems.

7. Yeats had received from Harry Clifton a piece of lapis lazuli, a bluish gemstone, carved by some Chinese sculptor into the semblance of a mountain with temple, trees, paths, and an ascetic and pupil about to climb the mountain."

8. Because Europe was (in 1936) close to war.

Of poets that are always gay,
For everybody knows or else should know
That if nothing drastic is done
Aeroplane and Zeppelin[7] will come out,
Pitch like King Billy bomb-balls in[8]
Until the town lie beaten flat.

All perform their tragic play,
There struts Hamlet, there is Lear,
That's Ophelia, that Cordelia;
Yet they, should the last scene be there,
The great stage curtain about to drop,
If worthy their prominent part in the play,
Do not break up their lines to weep.
They know that Hamlet and Lear are gay;
Gaiety transfiguring all that dread.
All men have aimed at, found and lost;
Black out; Heaven blazing into the head:
Tragedy wrought to its uttermost.
Though Hamlet rambles and Lear rages,
And all the drop-scenes[1] drop at once
Upon a hundred thousand stages,
It cannot grow by an inch or an ounce.

On their own feet they came, or on shipboard,
Camel-back, horse-back, ass-back, mule-back,[2]
Old civilisations put to the sword.
Then they and their wisdom went to rack:[3]
No handiwork of Callimachus,[4]
Who handled marble as if it were bronze,
Made draperies that seemed to rise
When sea-wind swept the corner, stands;
His long lamp-chimney shaped like the stem
Of a slender palm, stood but a day;
All things fall and are built again,
And those that build them again are gay.

Two Chinamen, behind them a third,
Are carved in lapis lazuli,
Over them flies a long-legged bird,
A symbol of longevity;
The third, doubtless a serving-man,
Carries a musical instrument.

Every discoloration of the stone,
Every accidental crack or dent,

7. The German Zeppelins (dirigibles) seemed at this time to be formidable weapons.

8. King William III, who routed the forces of James II at the Battle of the Boyne in Ireland in 1690. A popular ballad says, "King William he threw his bomb-balls in, / And set them all on fire."

1. Scenery lowered into place from above the stage.

2. Egyptians, Arabians, Christians, Mohammedans.

3. Destruction.

4. An Athenian sculptor (5th century B.C.).

Seems a water-course or an avalanche,
Or lofty slope where it still snows
Though doubtless plum or cherry-branch
Sweetens the little half-way house
Those Chinamen climb towards, and I
Delight to imagine them seated there;
There, on the mountain and the sky,
On all the tragic scene they stare.
One asks for mournful melodies;
Accomplished fingers begin to play.
Their eyes mid many wrinkles, their eyes,
Their ancient, glittering eyes, are gay.

1938

Long-Legged Fly

That civilisation may not sink,
Its great battle lost,
Quiet the dog, tether the pony
To a distant post;
Our master Caesar is in the tent
Where the maps are spread,
His eyes fixed upon nothing,
A hand under his head.
Like a long-legged fly upon the stream
His mind moves upon silence.

That the topless towers be burnt
And men recall that face,[1]
Move most gently if move you must
In this lonely place.
She thinks, part woman, three parts a child,
That nobody looks; her feet
Practise a tinker[2] shuffle
Picked up on a street.
Like a long-legged fly upon the stream
Her mind moves upon silence.

That girls at puberty may find
The first Adam in their thought,
Shut the door of the Pope's chapel,
Keep those children out.
There on that scaffolding reclines
Michael Angelo.[3]
With no more sound than the mice make
His hand moves to and fro.

1. Of Helen of Troy. Yeats alludes to Marlowe's *Dr. Faustus:* "Was this the face that launched a thousand ships / And burnt the topless towers of Ilium?"

2. An itinerant mender of pots and pans.

3. Yeats refers to the painting of "The Creation of Man" on the Sistine Chapel ceiling in the Vatican.

Like a long-legged fly upon the stream
His mind moves upon silence.

1939

The Circus Animals' Desertion

I

I sought a theme and sought for it in vain,
I sought it daily for six weeks or so.
Maybe at last, being but a broken man,
I must be satisfied with my heart, although
Winter and summer till old age began
My circus animals were all on show,
Those stilted boys, that burnished chariot,
Lion and woman and the Lord knows what.[4]

II

What can I but enumerate old themes?
First that sea-rider Oisin led by the nose
Through three enchanted islands,[5] allegorical dreams,
Vain gaiety, vain battle, vain repose,
Themes of the embittered heart, or so it seems,
That might adorn old songs or courtly shows;
But what cared I that set him on to ride,
I, starved for the bosom of his faery bride?[6]

And then a counter-truth filled out its play,
The Countess Cathleen[7] was the name I gave it;
She, pity-crazed, had given her soul away,
But masterful Heaven had intervened to save it.
I thought my dear must her own soul destroy,
So did fanaticism and hate enslave it,
And this brought forth a dream and soon enough
This dream itself had all my thought and love.

And when the Fool and Blind Man stole the bread
Cuchulain fought the ungovernable sea;[8]
Heart-mysteries there, and yet when all is said
It was the dream itself enchanted me:

4. Yeats alludes to the ancient Irish heroes of his early work ("Those stilted boys") and to the making of an elaborate carriage in his play, *The Unicorn from the Stars.* The lion appears in several poems of Yeats.

5. In "The Wanderings of Oisin," the fairy Niamh leads Oisin to the Islands of Delight, of Many Fears, and of Forgetfulness.

6. Niamh. Yeats suggests that it was his own unsatisfied longing for a beloved that led him to write about Oisin.

7. A play, first published in 1892, in which the Countess (modelled on an idealized version of Maud Gonne) sells her soul to save the people of Ireland.

8. An allusion to his play, *On Baile's Strand,* in which Cuchulain, crazed by his discovery that he has killed his son, goes out to do battle with the sea. Yeats implies that the play reflected his own anguish, presumably at losing Maud Gonne. The Fool and Blind Man are also characters in the play.

Character isolated by a deed
To engross the present and dominate memory.
Players and painted stage took all my love,
And not those things that they were emblems of.

III

Those masterful images because complete
Grew in pure mind, but out of what began?
A mound of refuse or the sweepings of a street,
Old kettles, old bottles, and a broken can,
Old iron, old bones, old rags, that raving slut
Who keeps the till. Now that my ladder's gone,
I must lie down where all the ladders start,
In the foul rag-and-bone shop of the heart.

1939

Under Ben Bulben[1]

I

Swear by what the sages spoke
Round the Mareotic Lake
That the Witch of Atlas knew,[2]
Spoke and set the cocks a-crow.
Swear by those horsemen,[3] by those women
Complexion and form prove superhuman,
That pale, long-visaged company
That air in immortality
Completeness of their passions won;
Now they ride the wintry dawn
Where Ben Bulben sets the scene.

Here's the gist of what they mean.

II

Many times man lives and dies
Between his two eternities,
That of race and that of soul,[4]
And ancient Ireland knew it all.
Whether man die in his bed
Or the rifle knocks him dead,
A brief parting from those dear
Is the worst man has to fear.

1. Ben Bulben is a mountain near Sligo. Yeats is in fact buried within sight of it, in Drumcliff Churchyard.

2. "The Witch of Atlas" is a poem by Shelley. Yeats, in an essay on Shelley, writes: "When the Witch has passed in her boat from the caverned river, that is doubtless her own destiny, she passes along the Nile 'by Moeris and the Mareotic lakes,' and sees all human life shadowed upon its waters . . . and because she can see the reality of things she is described as journeying 'in the calm depths' of 'the wide lake' we journey over unpiloted." Lake Mareotis was near Alexandria, Egypt.

3. Superhuman beings.

4. Yeats wrote Dorothy Wellesley on June 22, 1938, "This is the proposition on which I write: There is now overwhelming evidence that man stands between two eternities, that of his family and that of his soul." *Letters*, p. 911.

Though grave-diggers' toil is long,
Sharp their spades, their muscles strong,
They but thrust their buried men
Back in the human mind again.

III

You that Mitchel's prayer have heard,
'Send war in our time, O Lord!'[5]
Know that when all words are said
And a man is fighting mad,
Something drops from eyes long blind,
He completes his partial mind,
For an instant stands at ease,
Laughs aloud, his heart at peace.
Even the wisest man grows tense
With some sort of violence
Before he can accomplish fate,
Know his work or choose his mate.

IV

Poet and sculptor, do the work,
Nor let the modish painter shirk
What his great forefathers did,
Bring the soul of man to God,
Make him fill the cradles right.

Measurement began our might:
Forms a stark Egyptian thought,
Forms that gentler Phidias wrought.
Michael Angelo left a proof
On the Sistine Chapel roof,
Where but half-awakened Adam
Can disturb globe-trotting Madam[6]
Till her bowels are in heat,
Proof that there's a purpose set
Before the secret working mind:
Profane perfection of mankind.

Quattrocento[7] put in paint
On backgrounds for a God or Saint
Gardens where a soul's at ease;
Where everything that meets the eye,
Flowers and grass and cloudless sky,
Resemble forms that are or seem
When sleepers wake and yet still dream,
And when it's vanished still declare,
With only bed and bedstead there,

5. John Mitchel (1815–1875), an Irish nationalist. After having been transported to Australia, he escaped to the United States, but returned to Ireland in 1874. Yeats is quoting from Mitchel's *Jail Journal*; the words parody a sentence in the *Book of Common Prayer*.

6. Compare "Long-Legged Fly," lines 21–6.

7. Fifteenth-century Italian art.

That heavens had opened.
                                        Gyres[8] run on;
When that greater dream had gone
Calvert and Wilson, Blake and Claude,[9]
Prepared a rest for the people of God,
Palmer's phrase,[1] but after that
Confusion fell upon our thought.

V

Irish poets, learn your trade,
Sing whatever is well made,
Scorn the sort now growing up
All out of shape from toe to top,
Their unremembering hearts and heads
Base-born products of base beds.
Sing the peasantry, and then
Hard-riding country gentlemen,
The holiness of monks, and after
Porter-drinkers'[2] randy laughter;
Sing the lords and ladies gay
That were beaten into the clay
Through seven heroic centuries;[3]
Cast your mind on other days
That we in coming days may be
Still the indomitable Irishry.

VI

Under bare Ben Bulben's head
In Drumcliff churchyard Yeats is laid.
An ancestor was rector there
Long years ago,[4] a church stands near,
By the road an ancient cross.
No marble, no conventional phrase;
On limestone quarried near the spot
By his command these words are cut:
Cast a cold eye
On life, on death.
Horseman, pass by!

1939

8. Spirals. Yeats uses the image of interlocking gyres, with now one and now the other dominant, as his symbol for cyclical human life.

9. Edward Calvert (1799–1883) was an English painter and a follower of the poet and engraver William Blake. Richard Wilson (1714–1782), an English painter, was a disciple of Claude of Lorraine (1600–1682), the French landscape painter.

1. Samuel Palmer (1805–1881), an English landscape painter, said of Blake's illustrations to Virgil, "They are like all this wonderful artist's work, the drawing aside of the fleshly curtain, and the glimpse which all the most holy, studious saints and sages have enjoyed, of the rest which remains to the people of God."

2. Porter is a strong dark ale.

3. Since the conquest of Ireland by the Normans in the twelfth-century reign of Henry II.

4. Rev. John Yeats (1774–1846), Rector of Drumcliff, Sligo, from 1805.

EDGAR LEE MASTERS
(*1868–1950*)

Edgar Lee Masters was born on August 23, 1868, in Garnett, Kansas. His family soon moved to Illinois, and he grew up in Lewistown, near Springfield. His childhood was rendered difficult by his father's unsuccess as a lawyer. Masters managed to attend Knox College in Galesburg for a year, but was then obliged by his father to withdraw and study law privately. In 1892 he went to Chicago, and as he struggled for a foothold took a job collecting bills for the Edison Company there, but gradually he built up a successful law practice. For eight years he was a partner of the greatest criminal lawyer and defender of lost causes of the day, Clarence Darrow.

For some time Masters had been submitting conventional poems to William Marion Reedy, the editor of *Reedy's Mirror* in St. Louis. Reedy sent them back, but kept up the acquaintance, and in 1913 gave him a copy of J. W. Mackail's *Selected Epigrams from the Greek Anthology*, which had been revised and reissued in 1907. Masters felt the challenge to see what he could do with adapting the mode to modern circumstances. His first efforts were perhaps intended as parodic updatings of classical epitaphs, but Reedy received them so enthusiastically that Masters went forward in a burst of creative force.

As the poems came to be written and sometimes published, they were discovered by Harriet Monroe, the editor of *Poetry*. She published some of them and helped Masters to issue them in book form in 1915 as *Spoon River Anthology*. Spoon River in the title is the name of an actual river in Illinois, but the town is a combination of Lewistown and Petersburg, where Masters' grandparents lived, and the river itself includes the Saugamon River as well. The book had an instant and undreamed-of success; perhaps no book of verse has gone so quickly through so many editions.

Masters' later life proved to be anticlimactic. He published thirty-nine books (none destined to last) during the thirty-five years he lived after the *Spoon River Anthology*. In 1923 Masters left Chicago and settled, for most of his remaining years, in New York. He died on March 5, 1950, in a convalescent home in Philadelphia.

From *SPOON RIVER ANTHOLOGY*[1]

Elsa Wertman

I was a peasant girl from Germany,
Blue-eyed, rosy, happy and strong.

1. The title derives from the *Greek Anthology*, a collection of poems—many of them epitaphs—written from the 7th century B.C. to the 10th century A.D. An epigram on love from a 1906 translation of the anthology reads: "Within my heart Love himself has moulded Heliodora with her lovely voice, the soul of my soul." A sailor's epitaph: "Not dust nor the light weight of a stone, but all this sea that you behold is the tomb of Erasippus; for he perished with his ship, and in some unknown place his bones moulder, and the seagulls alone know them to tell." Another epitaph: "I Dionysius of Tarsus lie here at sixty, having never married; and I would that my father had not."

And the first place I worked was at Thomas Greene's.
On a summer's day when she was away
He stole into the kitchen and took me
Right in his arms and kissed me on my throat,
I turning my head. Then neither of us
Seemed to know what happened.
And I cried for what would become of me.
And cried and cried as my secret began to show.
One day Mrs. Greene said she understood,
And would make no trouble for me,
And, being childless, would adopt it.
(He had given her a farm to be still.)
So she hid in the house and sent out rumors,
As if it were going to happen to her.
And all went well and the child was born—They were so kind to me.
Later I married Gus Wertman, and years passed.
But—at political rallies when sitters-by thought I was crying
At the eloquence of Hamilton Greene—
That was not it.
No! I wanted to say:
That's my son! That's my son!

1915

Hamilton Greene

I was the only child of Frances Harris of Virginia
And Thomas Greene of Kentucky,
Of valiant and honorable blood both.
To them I owe all that I became,
Judge, member of Congress, leader in the State.
From my mother I inherited
Vivacity, fancy, language;
From my father will, judgment, logic.
All honor to them
For what service I was to the people!

1915

Anne Rutledge[3]

Out of me unworthy and unknown
The vibrations of deathless music;
"With malice toward none, with charity for all."[4]
Out of me the forgiveness of millions toward millions,
And the beneficent face of a nation
Shining with justice and truth.
I am Anne Rutledge who sleep beneath these weeds,

3. Ann Rutledge was a girl Abraham Lincoln knew in New Salem, Illinois. She died at the age of 19, and one of Lincoln's biographers insisted that she was the only true love of his life.

4. From Lincoln's second Inaugural Address, March 4, 1865.

Beloved in life of Abraham Lincoln,
Wedded to him, not through union,
But through separation.
Bloom forever, O Republic,
From the dust of my bosom!

1915

Lucinda Matlock[5]

I went to the dances at Chandlerville,
And played snap-out[6] at Winchester.
One time we changed partners,
Driving home in the moonlight of middle June,
And then I found Davis.
We were married and lived together for seventy years,
Enjoying, working, raising the twelve children,
Eight of whom we lost
Ere I had reached the age of sixty.
I spun, I wove, I kept the house, I nursed the sick,
I made the garden, and for holiday
Rambled over the fields where sang the larks,
And by Spoon River gathering many a shell,
And many a flower and medicinal weed—
Shouting to the wooded hills, singing to the green valleys.
At ninety-six I had lived enough, that is all,
And passed to a sweet repose.
What is this I hear of sorrow and weariness,
Anger, discontent and drooping hopes?
Degenerate sons and daughters,
Life is too strong for you—
It takes life to love Life.

1915

5. Lucinda Matlock was the maiden name of Masters' grandmother.

6. Perhaps the same as "crack the whip."

EDWIN ARLINGTON ROBINSON
(*1869–1935*)

Edwin Arlington Robinson was born in Head Tide, Maine, on December 22, 1869. At the age of one he was taken by his parents to another small, bleak Maine town, Gardiner. It was here that he spent his childhood, and it was in Gardiner, which he renamed Tilbury Town, that he situated much of his poetry. Robinson had a difficult childhood. He wrote Amy Lowell that at the age of six, as he remembered, he sat in a rocking chair and wondered why he had been born. His life seems to have been singularly lacking in happiness, a matter instead of family ties and low-pitched affections for men and women friends.

In 1890 he formed the ambition to be a writer. As a boy he had an older friend, Dr. Alanson Tucker Schumann, who gave him assignments in common and uncommon verse forms, and this experience seems to have suited Robinson's need for the settling effect of known patterns.

Robinson attended Harvard as a special student (rather than a degree candidate) from 1891 to 1893. He committed himself increasingly to literature: "I never could do anything but write verse," he was to tell his biographer, Chard Powers Smith, on his deathbed. He published in 1896, at his own expense ($52), *The Torrent and the Night Before*, and dedicated it with modesty to "any man, woman or critic who will cut the pages." The people to whom he sent copies replied encouragingly. A later book, *Captain Craig* (1902), came to the notice of President Theodore Roosevelt, who resolved to be of help. He wrote a magazine article in praise of Robinson and found him a sinecure in the New York Custom House. Robinson wrote a friend, "The strenuous man has given me some of the most powerful loafing that has ever come my way." He stayed in the Custom House five years, from 1905 to 1909. The "job" seems to have encouraged him in his drinking, which was a regular habit, though he never started until six o'clock in the evening.

When Roosevelt left office in 1909, Robinson was forced to resign his post, and for the rest of his life he never sought further employment. For years he was sustained by the generosity of friends and, during the summers, by regular invitations to live and work at the MacDowell Artists' Colony in New Hampshire. Unexpectedly, the publication of his *Collected Poems* in 1921 made him famous; it was awarded the Pulitzer Prize, and he was given an honorary degree by Yale University. He won the Pulitzer prize twice again, the last time for his long Arthurian poem *Tristram* (1927). *Tristram* was also a bestseller, and for the first time in his life Robinson became financially independent, as he was to remain. Though none of his later books repeated the success of *Tristram*, they consolidated his position; in 1933 Allen Tate described him as "the most famous of living American poets." He died in New York on April 6, 1935.

Miniver Cheevy

Miniver Cheevy, child of scorn,
  Grew lean while he assailed the seasons;
He wept that he was ever born,
  And he had reasons.

Miniver loved the days of old
  When swords were bright and steeds were prancing;
The vision of a warrior bold
  Would set him dancing.

Miniver sighed for what was not,
  And dreamed, and rested from his labors;
He dreamed of Thebes and Camelot,
  And Priam's neighbors.[3]

3. Thebes was the setting of many Greek legends, including that of King Oedipus; Camelot was the location of King Arthur's court; Priam was the last king of Troy, and his neighbors included Helen, Aeneas, and Hector.

Miniver mourned the ripe renown
  That made so many a name so fragrant;
He mourned Romance, now on the town,
  And Art, a vagrant.

Miniver loved the Medici,[4]
  Albeit he had never seen one;
He would have sinned incessantly
  Could he have been one.

Miniver cursed the commonplace
  And eyed a khaki[5] suit with loathing;
He missed the mediæval grace
  Of iron clothing.

Miniver scorned the gold he sought,
  But sore[6] annoyed was he without it;
Miniver thought, and thought, and thought,
  And thought about it.

Miniver Cheevy, born too late,
  Scratched his head and kept on thinking;
Miniver coughed, and called it fate,
  And kept on drinking.

1910

For a Dead Lady

No more with overflowing light
Shall fill the eyes that now are faded,
Nor shall another's fringe with night
Their woman-hidden world as they did.
No more shall quiver down the days
The flowing wonder of her ways,
Whereof no language may requite
The shifting and the many-shaded.

The grace, divine, definitive,
Clings only as a faint forestalling;
The laugh that love could not forgive
Is hushed, and answers to no calling;
The forehead and the little ears
Have gone where Saturn keeps the years;[7]
The breast where roses could not live
Has done with rising and with falling.

4. Florentine merchant-princes of the Renaissance who were famous both as powerful rulers and as patrons of the arts.

5. Formerly the material of which army uniforms were made.

6. Greatly (archaic usage).

7. Saturn, or Cronos, the deposed ruler of the gods, was often erroneously associated with time ("Chronos").

The beauty, shattered by the laws
That have creation in their keeping,
No longer trembles at applause,
Or over children that are sleeping;
And we who delve in beauty's lore
Know all that we have known before
Of what inexorable cause
Makes Time so vicious. in his reaping.

1910

Eros Turannos[8]

She fears him, and will always ask
  What fated her to choose him;
She meets in his engaging mask
  All reasons to refuse him;
But what she meets and what she fears
Are less than are the downward years,
Drawn slowly to the foamless weirs[9]
  Of age, were she to lose him.

Between a blurred sagacity
  That once had power to sound him,
And Love, that will not let him be
  The Judas that she found him,
Her pride assuages her almost,
As if it were alone the cost.—
He sees that he will not be lost,
  And waits and looks around him.

A sense of ocean and old trees
  Envelops and allures him;
Tradition, touching all he sees,
  Beguiles and reassures him;
And all her doubts of what he says
Are dimmed with what she knows of days—
Till even prejudice delays
  And fades, and she secures him.

The falling leaf inaugurates
  The reign of her confusion;
The pounding wave reverberates
  The dirge of her illusion;
And home, where passion lived and died,
Becomes a place where she can hide,
While all the town and harbor side
  Vibrate with her seclusion.

8. Love, the tyrant (Greek). Eros is the god of love.

9. Dams or fences in rivers.

We tell you, tapping on our brows,
The story as it should be,—
As if the story of a house
Were told, or ever could be;
We'll have no kindly veil between
Her visions and those we have seen,—
As if we guessed what hers have been,
Or what they are or would be.

Meanwhile we do no harm; for they
That with a god have striven,
Not hearing much of what we say,
Take what the god has given;
Though like waves breaking it may be
Or like a changed familiar tree,
Or like a stairway to the sea
Where down the blind are driven.

1916

Mr. Flood's Party

Old Eben Flood, climbing alone one night
Over the hill between the town below
And the forsaken upland hermitage
That held as much as he should ever know
On earth again of home, paused warily.
The road was his with not a native near;
And Eben, having leisure, said aloud,
For no man else in Tilbury Town[1] to hear:

"Well, Mr. Flood, we have the harvest moon
Again, and we may not have many more;
The bird is on the wing, the poet says,[2]
And you and I have said it here before.
Drink to the bird." He raised up to the light
The jug that he had gone so far to fill,
And answered huskily: "Well, Mr. Flood,
Since you propose it, I believe I will."

Alone, as if enduring to the end
A valiant armor of scarred hopes outworn,
He stood there in the middle of the road
Like Roland's ghost winding a silent horn.[3]

1. The imaginary Maine town in which many of Robinson's poems are set.

2. Alludes to Edward Fitzgerald's translation of *The Rubáiyát of Omar Khayyám:* "Come, fill the Cup, and in the fire of Spring / Your Winter-garment of Repentance fling: / The Bird of Time has but a little way / To flutter—and the Bird is on the Wing."

3. In the *Chanson de Roland*, a medieval French poem, Roland and the soldiers under his command were trapped and killed in a battle at the mountain pass of Roncevaux. He refused to blow his horn, the signal for help from Charlemagne's army, until the moment of his death.

Below him, in the town among the trees,
Where friends of other days had honored him,
A phantom salutation of the dead
Rang thinly till old Eben's eyes were dim.

Then, as a mother lays her sleeping child
Down tenderly, fearing it may awake,
He set the jug down slowly at his feet
With trembling care, knowing that most things break;
And only when assured that on firm earth
It stood, as the uncertain lives of men
Assuredly did not, he paced away,
And with his hand extended paused again:

"Well, Mr. Flood, we have not met like this
In a long time; and many a change has come
To both of us, I fear, since last it was
We had a drop together. Welcome home!"
Convivially returning with himself,
Again he raised the jug up to the light;
And with an acquiescent quaver said:
"Well, Mr. Flood, if you insist, I might.

"Only a very little, Mr. Flood—
For auld lang syne. No more, sir; that will do."
So, for the time, apparently it did,
And Eben evidently thought so too;
For soon amid the silver loneliness
Of night he lifted up his voice and sang,
Secure, with only two moons listening,
Until the whole harmonious landscape rang—

"For auld lang syne." The weary throat gave out,
The last word wavered, and the song was done.
He raised again the jug regretfully
And shook his head, and was again alone.
There was not much that was ahead of him,
And there was nothing in the town below—
Where strangers would have shut the many doors
That many friends had opened long ago.

1920

The Sheaves

Where long the shadows of the wind had rolled,
Green wheat was yielding to the change assigned;
And as by some vast magic undivined
The world was turning slowly into gold.
Like nothing that was ever bought or sold
It waited there, the body and the mind;

And with a mighty meaning of a kind
That tells the more the more it is not told.

So in a land where all days are not fair,
Fair days went on till on another day
A thousand golden sheaves were lying there,
Shining and still, but not for long to stay—
As if a thousand girls with golden hair
Might rise from where they slept and go away.

1925

WALTER DE LA MARE
(*1873–1956*)

Walter de la Mare was born at Charlton, Kent, on April 25, 1873. He attended St. Paul's Cathedral Choir School in London and founded the school magazine, *The Choristers' Journal.* Unable to afford further education, he became a bookkeeper at the London branch of the Anglo-American Oil Company, a branch of Standard Oil. He continued at this work for twenty years, and learned to contrast this immersion in affairs with the true life of the imagination. He began to publish poems in 1895, and his first book of verse appeared, under a pseudonym, in 1902. Two years later he published the first of five novels. In 1908 the Asquith government granted him a Civil List pension of a hundred pounds a year, which enabled him to give up keeping books for writing them. In 1912 his book, *The Listeners and Other Poems*, brought him fame. For more than fifty years he lived the life, unremarkable in its externals, of the successful and established man of letters. At 75 he was made a Companion of Honour, and at 80 he was awarded the Order of Merit. De la Mare died on June 22, 1956, in his home at Twickenham, and was buried in Westminster Abbey.

The Listeners

'Is there anybody there?' said the Traveller,
  Knocking on the moonlit door;
And his horse in the silence champed the grasses
  Of the forest's ferny floor:
And a bird flew up out of the turret,
  Above the Traveller's head:
And he smote upon the door again a second time;
  'Is there anybody there?' he said.
But no one descended to the Traveller;
  No head from the leaf-fringed sill
Leaned over and looked into his grey eyes,
  Where he stood perplexed and still.
But only a host of phantom listeners
  That dwelt in the lone house then

Stood listening in the quiet of the moonlight
  To that voice from the world of men:
Stood thronging the faint moonbeams on the dark stair,
  That goes down to the empty hall,
Hearkening in an air stirred and shaken
  By the lonely Traveller's call.
And he felt in his heart their strangeness,
  Their stillness answering his cry,
While his horse moved, cropping the dark turf,
  'Neath the starred and leafy sky;
For he suddenly smote on the door, even
  Louder, and lifted his head:—
'Tell them I came, and no one answered,
  That I kept my word,' he said.
Never the least stir made the listeners,
  Though every word he spake
Fell echoing through the shadowiness of the still house
  From the one man left awake:
Ay, they heard his foot upon the stirrup,
  And the sound of iron on stone,
And how the silence surged softly backward,
  When the plunging hoofs were gone.

1912

The Song of the Mad Prince

Who said, 'Peacock Pie'?
  The old King to the sparrow:
Who said, 'Crops are ripe'?
  Rust to the harrow:
Who said, 'Where sleeps she now?
  Where rests she now her head,
Bathed in eve's loveliness'?—
  That's what I said.

Who said, 'Ay, mum's the word'?
  Sexton to willow:
Who said, 'Green dusk for dreams,
  Moss for a pillow'?
Who said, 'All Time's delight
  Hath she for narrow bed;
Life's troubled bubble broken'?—
  That's what I said.

1913

ROBERT FROST
(1874–1963)

Robert Frost was born on March 26, 1874, in San Francisco. His father, William Prescott Frost Jr., had been born in New Hampshire, the state to which Robert Frost made his devious way back. As a boy he tried to enlist in the Confederate army, a passionate displaced regionalism which his son (appropriately named Robert Lee after the general) emulated, though he found it necessary to change the region. William Frost determined to go west, but to earn money for a year first as headmaster at a small private school in Pennsylvania. The school had only one other teacher, Isabelle Moodie, a woman six years older than himself, whom he courted and married. In May 1885 he died of tuberculosis; his instructions were that he be buried in Lawrence, Massachusetts, and his widow discharged this wish and then remained in the East. Her son attended high school there from 1888 to 1892. He was an excellent student of classics, and he also began to be known as a poet. In the school another student of equal excellence was Elinor White. Frost resolved to marry her, and it was characteristic of his tenacity that he succeeded in doing so in spite of her delays and doubts. He won a scholarship to Dartmouth, and she went to St. Lawrence College. Before a semester was over, Frost had dropped out. He had hoped to persuade Elinor White to marry him at once, but she insisted upon waiting until she had finished college. The ceremony did not occur until 1895.

In 1897 Frost decided he must have his Harvard education after all, and persuaded the authorities to admit him as a special student (rather than a degree candidate). He was to say in later life that this was a turning-point for him. At Harvard he could try himself against the cultural powers of his time, and he could listen to philosophers like Santayana and James. But again, in March 1899, he withdrew of his own accord. On medical advice he thought he would live in the country, and his grandfather bought him a farm in Derry, New Hampshire. These years, when money was short and family life was especially difficult—the Frosts had five children by 1905—were gloomy ones for Frost. He more than once meditated suicide. A lift came when in 1906 he took a teaching job at Pinkerton Academy. During the next five years he reformed its English syllabus, directed plays, and wrote most of the poems later included in his first book.

In 1911 he sold his farm, and in October he took ship with his family to Glasgow and then went on to London. There was little reason to hope that publication of his verse would be any easier in England than in the United States, but a month after his arrival he submitted his poems to an English publisher and had them accepted. *A Boy's Will* was published in 1913 and a second book, *North of Boston*, in 1914.

In England Frost came to know the poets of the time. Ezra Pound introduced him to Yeats, whom he had long admired, and Frost also met imagists like F. S. Flint and Amy Lowell and became friendly with the Georgian poets. Among these last his closest friend was Edward Thomas, in whom he recognized something like an *alter ego*. This pleasant idyll in England was broken into by the war, which forced him to return in 1915 to the United

States. There his luck held: the publisher Henry Holt was easily persuaded to publish both his earlier books as well as subsequent ones. Although Frost could not live on his poems, his poetry made him much sought after by colleges and universities. In 1917 he began to teach at Amherst, and he kept up for many years a loose association with this college, intermixed with periods as professor or poet-in-residence elsewhere. He was a frequent lecturer around the country and eventually became a goodwill emissary to South America and then, at his friend President John F. Kennedy's request, to the Soviet Union.

Frost's personal life was never easy. He demanded great loyalty and was quick to suspect friends of treachery. In 1938 his wife died, and in 1940 a son committed suicide. Nonetheless he was showered with honors. Perhaps the most conspicuous was, at John F. Kennedy's invitation, to read a poem at the presidential inauguration ceremony in 1961. He had become by far the most recognized poet in America by the time of his death, at the age of eighty-eight, on January 29, 1963.

Mending Wall

Something there is that doesn't love a wall,
That sends the frozen-ground-swell under it
And spills the upper boulders in the sun,
And makes gaps even two can pass abreast.
The work of hunters is another thing:
I have come after them and made repair
Where they have left not one stone on a stone,
But they would have the rabbit out of hiding,
To please the yelping dogs. The gaps I mean,
No one has seen them made or heard them made,
But at spring mending-time we find them there.
I let my neighbor know beyond the hill;
And on a day we meet to walk the line
And set the wall between us once again.
We keep the wall between us as we go.
To each the boulders that have fallen to each.
And some are loaves and some so nearly balls
We have to use a spell to make them balance:
'Stay where you are until our backs are turned!'
We wear our fingers rough with handling them.
Oh, just another kind of outdoor game,
One on a side. It comes to little more:
There where it is we do not need the wall:
He is all pine and I am apple orchard.
My apple trees will never get across
And eat the cones under his pines, I tell him.
He only says, 'Good fences make good neighbors.'
Spring is the mischief in me, and I wonder
If I could put a notion in his head:
'*Why* do they make good neighbors? Isn't it

Where there are cows? But here there are no cows.
Before I built a wall I'd ask to know
What I was walling in or walling out,
And to whom I was like to give offense.
Something there is that doesn't love a wall,
That wants it down.' I could say 'Elves' to him,
But it's not elves exactly, and I'd rather
He said it for himself. I see him there
Bringing a stone grasped firmly by the top
In each hand, like an old-stone savage armed.
He moves in darkness as it seems to me,
Not of woods only and the shade of trees.
He will not go behind his father's saying,
And he likes having thought of it so well
He says again, 'Good fences make good neighbors.'

1914

After Apple-Picking

My long two-pointed ladder's sticking through a tree
Toward heaven still,
And there's a barrel that I didn't fill
Beside it, and there may be two or three
Apples I didn't pick upon some bough.
But I am done with apple-picking now.
Essence of winter sleep is on the night,
The scent of apples: I am drowsing off.
I cannot rub the strangeness from my sight
I got from looking through a pane of glass
I skimmed this morning from the drinking trough
And held against the world of hoary grass.
It melted, and I let it fall and break.
But I was well
Upon my way to sleep before it fell,
And I could tell
What form my dreaming was about to take.
Magnified apples appear and disappear,
Stem end and blossom end,
And every fleck of russet showing clear.
My instep arch not only keeps the ache,
It keeps the pressure of a ladder-round.
I feel the ladder sway as the boughs bend.
And I keep hearing from the cellar bin
The rumbling sound
Of load on load of apples coming in.
For I have had too much
Of apple-picking: I am overtired
Of the great harvest I myself desired.
There were ten thousand thousand fruit to touch,
Cherish in hand, lift down, and not let fall.
For all

That struck the earth,
No matter if not bruised or spiked with stubble,
Went surely to the cider-apple heap
As of no worth.
One can see what will trouble
This sleep of mine, whatever sleep it is.
Were he not gone,
The woodchuck could say whether it's like his
Long sleep, as I describe its coming on,
Or just some human sleep.

1914

The Road Not Taken[2]

Two roads diverged in a yellow wood,
And sorry I could not travel both
And be one traveler, long I stood
And looked down one as far as I could
To where it bent in the undergrowth;

Then took the other, as just as fair,
And having perhaps the better claim,
Because it was grassy and wanted wear;
Though as for that the passing there
Had worn them really about the same,

And both that morning equally lay
In leaves no step had trodden black.
Oh, I kept the first for another day!
Yet knowing how way leads on to way,
I doubted if I should ever come back.

I shall be telling this with a sigh
Somewhere ages and ages hence:
Two roads diverged in a wood, and I—
I took the one less traveled by,
And that has made all the difference.

1916

The Oven Bird

There is a singer everyone has heard,
Loud, a mid-summer and a mid-wood bird,

2. According to Lawrance Thompson, this poem was a slightly mocking parody of the behavior of Frost's friend, Edward Thomas (p. 88), who used to choose a direction for their country walks, then, before they had finished, berate himself for not having chosen a different, more interesting way. Frost, says Thompson, did not approve of romantic "sighing over what might have been."

On the other hand, E. S. Sergeant, in *Robert Frost: The Trial by Existence* (New York, 1960, pp. 87–88), quotes a letter from Frost, written February 10, 1912, in which he describes how, going down a lonely cross-road on a recent evening, he saw someone who "looked for all the world like myself coming down the other, his approach to the point where our paths must intersect being so timed that unless one of us pulled up we must inevitably collide. I felt as if I was going to meet my own image in a slanting mirror. . . . I stood still in wonderment and let him pass by."

Who makes the solid tree trunks sound again.
He says that leaves are old and that for flowers
Mid-summer is to spring as one to ten.
He says the early petal-fall is past,
When pear and cherry bloom went down in showers
On sunny days a moment overcast;
And comes that other fall we name the fall.
He says the highway dust is over all.
The bird would cease and be as other birds
But that he knows in singing not to sing.
The question that he frames in all but words
Is what to make of a diminished thing.

1916

Birches

When I see birches bend to left and right
Across the lines of straighter darker trees,
I like to think some boy's been swinging them.
But swinging doesn't bend them down to stay
As ice-storms do. Often you must have seen them
Loaded with ice a sunny winter morning
After a rain. They click upon themselves
As the breeze rises, and turn many-colored
As the stir cracks and crazes[3] their enamel.
Soon the sun's warmth makes them shed crystal shells
Shattering and avalanching on the snow-crust—
Such heaps of broken glass to sweep away
You'd think the inner dome of heaven had fallen.
They are dragged to the withered bracken by the load,
And they seem not to break; though once they are bowed
So low for long, they never right themselves:
You may see their trunks arching in the woods
Years afterwards, trailing their leaves on the ground
Like girls on hands and knees that throw their hair
Before them over their heads to dry in the sun.
But I was going to say when Truth broke in
With all her matter-of-fact about the ice-storm,
I should prefer to have some boy bend them
As he went out and in to fetch the cows—
Some boy too far from town to learn baseball,
Whose only play was what he found himself,
Summer or winter, and could play alone.
One by one he subdued his father's trees
By riding them down over and over again
Until he took the stiffness out of them,
And not one but hung limp, not one was left
For him to conquer. He learned all there was
To learn about not launching out too soon

3. Forms many tiny cracks in, as with old glazed pottery.

And so not carrying the tree away
Clear to the ground. He always kept his poise
To the top branches, climbing carefully
With the same pains you use to fill a cup
Up to the brim, and even above the brim.
Then he flung outward, feet first, with a swish,
Kicking his way down through the air to the ground.
So was I once myself a swinger of birches.
And so I dream of going back to be.
It's when I'm weary of considerations,
And life is too much like a pathless wood
Where your face burns and tickles with the cobwebs
Broken across it, and one eye is weeping
From a twig's having lashed across it open.
I'd like to get away from earth awhile
And then come back to it and begin over.
May no fate willfully misunderstand me
And half grant what I wish and snatch me away
Not to return. Earth's the right place for love:
I don't know where it's likely to go better.
I'd like to go by climbing a birch tree,
And climb black branches up a snow-white trunk
Toward heaven, till the tree could bear no more,
But dipped its top and set me down again.
That would be good both going and coming back.
One could do worse than be a swinger of birches.

1916

Range-Finding[4]

The battle rent a cobweb diamond-strung
And cut a flower beside a ground bird's nest
Before it stained a single human breast.
The stricken flower bent double and so hung.
And still the bird revisited her young.
A butterfly its fall had dispossessed,
A moment sought in air his flower of rest,
Then lightly stooped to it and fluttering clung.
On the bare upland pasture there had spread
O'ernight 'twixt mullein[5] stalks a wheel of thread
And straining cables wet with silver dew.
A sudden passing bullet shook it dry.
The indwelling spider ran to greet the fly,
But finding nothing, sullenly withdrew.

1916

4. Frost wrote to Amy Lowell, "Would it amuse you to learn that Range Finding belongs to a set of war poems I wrote in time of profound peace (circa 1902)? Most of them have gone the way of waste paper. Range Finding was only saved from going the same way by Edward Thomas who liked it . . . he thought it so good a description of No Man's Land." *Letters*, p. 220.

5. An herb with coarse stalks and small flowers.

The Witch of Coös[6]

I stayed the night for shelter at a farm
Behind the mountain, with a mother and son,
Two old-believers. They did all the talking.

MOTHER. Folks think a witch who has familiar spirits[7]
She could call up to pass a winter evening,
But won't, should be burned at the stake or something.
Summoning spirits isn't "Button, button,
Who's got the button," I would have them know.

SON. Mother can make a common table rear
And kick with two legs like an army mule.

MOTHER. And when I've done it, what good have I done?
Rather than tip a table for you, let me
Tell you what Ralle the Sioux Control[8] once told me.
He said the dead had souls, but when I asked him
How could that be—I thought the dead were souls—
He broke my trance. Don't that make you suspicious
That there's something the dead are keeping back?
Yes, there's something the dead are keeping back.

SON. You wouldn't want to tell him what we have
Up attic, mother?

MOTHER. Bones—a skeleton.

SON. But the headboard of mother's bed is pushed
Against the attic door: the door is nailed.
It's harmless. Mother hears it in the night,
Halting perplexed behind the barrier
Of door and headboard. Where it wants to get
Is back into the cellar where it came from.

MOTHER. We'll never let them, will we, son! We'll never!

SON. It left the cellar forty years ago
And carried itself like a pile of dishes
Up one flight from the cellar to the kitchen,
Another from the kitchen to the bedroom,
Another from the bedroom to the attic,
Right past both father and mother, and neither stopped it.
Father had gone upstairs; mother was downstairs.
I was a baby: I don't know where I was.

MOTHER. The only fault my husband found with me—
I went to sleep before I went to bed,

6. A county in New Hampshire.
7. A "control" is a ghostly intermediary who, in spiritualist séances, facilitates the communication between the medium and the spirits of the dead.
8. Supernatural beings who attend and protect human witches.

Especially in winter when the bed
Might just as well be ice and the clothes snow.
The night the bones came up the cellar stairs
Toffile had gone to bed alone and left me,
But left an open door to cool the room off
So as to sort of turn me out of it.
I was just coming to myself enough
To wonder where the cold was coming from,
When I heard Toffile upstairs in the bedroom
And thought I heard him downstairs in the cellar.
The board we had laid down to walk dry-shod on
When there was water in the cellar in spring
Struck the hard cellar bottom. And then someone
Began the stairs, two footsteps for each step,
The way a man with one leg and a crutch,
Or a little child, comes up. It wasn't Toffile:
It wasn't anyone who could be there.
The bulkhead double-doors were double-locked
And swollen tight and buried under snow.
The cellar windows were banked up with sawdust
And swollen tight and buried under snow.
It was the bones. I knew them—and good reason.
My first impulse was to get to the knob
And hold the door. But the bones didn't try
The door; they halted helpless on the landing,
Waiting for things to happen in their favor.
The faintest restless rustling ran all through them.
I never could have done the thing I did
If the wish hadn't been too strong in me
To see how they were mounted for this walk.
I had a vision of them put together
Not like a man, but like a chandelier.
So suddenly I flung the door wide on him.
A moment he stood balancing with emotion,
And all but lost himself. (A tongue of fire
Flashed out and licked along his upper teeth.
Smoke rolled inside the sockets of his eyes.)
Then he came at me with one hand outstretched,
The way he did in life once; but this time
I struck the hand off brittle on the floor,
And fell back from him on the floor myself.
The finger-pieces slid in all directions.
(Where did I see one of those pieces lately?
Hand me my button box—it must be there.)
I sat up on the floor and shouted, "Toffile,
It's coming up to you." It had its choice
Of the door to the cellar or the hall.
It took the hall door for the novelty,
And set off briskly for so slow a thing
Still going every which way in the joints, though,
So that it looked like lightning or a scribble,

From the slap I had just now given its hand.
I listened till it almost climbed the stairs
From the hall to the only finished bedroom,
Before I got up to do anything;
Then ran and shouted, "Shut the bedroom door,
Toffile, for my sake!" "Company?" he said,
"Don't make me get up; I'm too warm in bed."
So lying forward weakly on the handrail
I pushed myself upstairs, and in the light
(The kitchen had been dark) I had to own
I could see nothing. "Toffile, I don't see it.
It's with us in the room though. It's the bones."
"What bones?" "The cellar bones—out of the grave."
That made him throw his bare legs out of bed
And sit up by me and take hold of me.
I wanted to put out the light and see
If I could see it, or else mow the room,
With our arms at the level of our knees,
And bring the chalk-pile down. "I'll tell you what—
It's looking for another door to try.
The uncommonly deep snow has made him think
Of his old song, 'The Wild Colonial Boy.'
He always used to sing along the tote road.[9]
He's after an open door to get outdoors.
Let's trap him with an open door up attic."
Toffile agreed to that, and sure enough,
Almost the moment he was given an opening,
The steps began to climb the attic stairs.
I heard them. Toffile didn't seem to hear them.
"Quick!" I slammed to the door and held the knob.
"Toffile, get nails." I made him nail the door shut
And push the headboard of the bed against it.
Then we asked was there anything
Up attic that we'd ever want again.
The attic was less to us than the cellar.
If the bones liked the attic, let them have it.
Let them stay in the attic. When they sometimes
Come down the stairs at night and stand perplexed
Behind the door and headboard of the bed,
Brushing ther chalky skull with chalky fingers,
With sounds like the dry rattling of a shutter,
That's what I sit up in the dark to say—
To no one any more since Toffile died.
Let them stay in the attic since they went there.
I promised Toffile to be cruel to them
For helping them be cruel once to him.

SON. We think they had a grave down in the cellar.

9. A rough road for hauling supplies, especially to a lumber camp.

MOTHER. We know they had a grave down in the cellar.

SON. We never could find out whose bones they were.

MOTHER. Yes, we could too, son. Tell the truth for once.
They were a man's his father killed for me.
I mean a man he killed instead of me.
The least I could do was to help dig their grave.
We were about it one night in the cellar.
Son knows the story: but 'twas not for him
To tell the truth, suppose the time had come.
Son looks surprised to see me end a lie
We'd kept all these years between ourselves
So as to have it ready for outsiders.
But tonight I don't care enough to lie—
I don't remember why I ever cared.
Toffile, if he were here, I don't believe
Could tell you why he ever cared himself. . . .

She hadn't found the finger-bone she wanted
Among the buttons poured out in her lap.
I verified the name next morning: Toffile.
The rural letter box said Toffile Lajway.

1923

Fire and Ice

Some say the world will end in fire,
Some say in ice.
From what I've tasted of desire
I hold with those who favor fire.
But if it had to perish twice,
I think I know enough of hate
To say that for destruction ice
Is also great
And would suffice.

1923

Stopping by Woods on a Snowy Evening

Whose woods these are I think I know.
His house is in the village, though;
He will not see me stopping here
To watch his woods fill up with snow.

My little horse must think it queer
To stop without a farmhouse near
Between the woods and frozen lake
The darkest evening of the year.

He gives his harness bells a shake
To ask if there is some mistake.
The only other sound's the sweep
Of easy wind and downy flake.

The woods are lovely, dark and deep,
But I have promises to keep,
And miles to go before I sleep,
And miles to go before I sleep.[1]

1923

To Earthward

Love at the lips was touch
As sweet as I could bear;
And once that seemed too much;
I lived on air

That crossed me from sweet things,
The flow of—was it musk
From hidden grapevine springs
Downhill at dusk?

I had the swirl and ache
From sprays of honeysuckle
That when they're gathered shake
Dew on the knuckle.

I craved strong sweets, but those
Seemed strong when I was young;
The petal of the rose
It was that stung.

Now no joy but lacks salt,
That is not dashed with pain
And weariness and fault;
I crave the stain

Of tears, the aftermark
Of almost too much love,
The sweet of bitter bark
And burning clove.

When stiff and sore and scarred
I take away my hand
From leaning on it hard
In grass and sand,

1. Frost always insisted that the repetition of the line in the last stanza was not supposed to invoke death but only to imply a somnolent dreaminess in the speaker.

The hurt is not enough:
I long for weight and strength
To feel the earth as rough
To all my length.

1923

Acquainted with the Night

I have been one acquainted with the night.
I have walked out in rain—and back in rain.
I have outwalked the furthest city light.

I have looked down the saddest city lane.
I have passed by the watchman on his beat
And dropped my eyes, unwilling to explain.

I have stood still and stopped the sound of feet
When far away an interrupted cry
Came over houses from another street,

But not to call me back or say good-by;
And further still at an unearthly height
One luminary clock against the sky

Proclaimed the time was neither wrong nor right.
I have been one acquainted with the night.

1928

Two Tramps in Mud Time

Out of the mud two strangers came
And caught me splitting wood in the yard.
And one of them put me off my aim
By hailing cheerily "Hit them hard!"
I knew pretty well why he dropped behind
And let the other go on a way.
I knew pretty well what he had in mind:
He wanted to take my job for pay.

Good blocks of oak it was I split,
As large around as the chopping block;
And every piece I squarely hit
Fell splinterless as a cloven rock.
The blows that a life of self-control
Spares to strike for the common good,
That day, giving a loose to my soul,
I spent on the unimportant wood.

The sun was warm but the wind was chill.
You know how it is with an April day

When the sun is out and the wind is still,
You're one month on in the middle of May.
But if you so much as dare to speak,
A cloud comes over the sunlit arch,
A wind comes off a frozen peak,
And you're two months back in the middle of March.

A bluebird comes tenderly up to alight
And turns to the wind to unruffle a plume
His song so pitched as not to excite
A single flower as yet to bloom.
It is snowing a flake: and he half knew
Winter was only playing possum.
Except in color he isn't blue,
But he wouldn't advise a thing to blossom.

The water for which we may have to look
In summertime with a witching wand,
In every wheelrut's now a brook,
In every print of a hoof a pond.
Be glad of water, but don't forget
The lurking frost in the earth beneath
That will steal forth after the sun is set
And show on the water its crystal teeth.

The time when most I loved my task
These two must make me love it more
By coming with what they came to ask.
You'd think I never had felt before
The weight of an ax-head poised aloft,
The grip on earth of outspread feet,
The life of muscles rocking soft
And smooth and moist in vernal heat.

Out of the woods two hulking tramps
(From sleeping God knows where last night,
But not long since in the lumber camps).
They thought all chopping was theirs of right.
Men of the woods and lumberjacks,
They judged me by their appropriate tool.
Except as a fellow handled an ax,
They had no way of knowing a fool.

Nothing on either side was said.
They knew they had but to stay their stay
And all their logic would fill my head:
As that I had no right to play
With what was another man's work for gain.
My right might be love but theirs was need.
And where the two exist in twain
Theirs was the better right—agreed.

But yield who will to their separation,
My object in living is to unite
My avocation and my vocation
As my two eyes make one in sight.
Only where love and need are one,
And the work is play for mortal stakes,
Is the deed ever really done
For Heaven and the future's sakes.

1936

Desert Places

Snow falling and night falling fast, oh, fast
In a field I looked into going past,
And the ground almost covered smooth in snow,
But a few weeds and stubble showing last.

The woods around it have it—it is theirs.
All animals are smothered in their lairs.
I am too absent-spirited to count;
The loneliness includes me unawares.

And lonely as it is, that loneliness
Will be more lonely ere it will be less—
A blanker whiteness of benighted snow
With no expression, nothing to express.

They cannot scare me with their empty spaces
Between stars—on stars where no human race is.
I have it in me so much nearer home
To scare myself with my own desert places.

1936

Neither Out Far nor In Deep

The people along the sand
All turn and look one way.
They turn their back on the land.
They look at the sea all day.

As long as it takes to pass
A ship keeps raising its hull;
The wetter ground like glass
Reflects a standing gull.

The land may vary more;
But wherever the truth may be—
The water comes ashore,
And the people look at the sea.

They cannot look out far.
They cannot look in deep.
But when was that ever a bar
To any watch they keep?

1936

Design[2]

I found a dimpled spider, fat and white,
On a white heal-all, holding up a moth
Like a white piece of rigid satin cloth—
Assorted characters of death and blight
Mixed ready to begin the morning right,
Like the ingredients of a witches' broth—
A snow-drop spider, a flower like a froth,
And dead wings carried like a paper kite.

What had that flower to do with being white,
The wayside blue and innocent heal-all?[3]
What brought the kindred spider to that height,
Then steered the white moth thither in the night?
What but design of darkness to appall?—
If design govern in a thing so small.

1936

Provide, Provide

The witch that came (the withered hag)
To wash the steps with pail and rag,
Was once the beauty Abishag[4],

The picture pride of Hollywood.
Too many fall from great and good
For you to doubt the likelihood.

Die early and avoid the fate.
Or if predestined to die late,
Make up your mind to die in state.

2. The original version, entitled "In White," was written early in 1912 and sent in a letter, as Lawrance Thompson points out. It read as follows:

A dented spider like a snowdrop white
On a white Heal-all, holding up a moth
Like a white peace of lifeless satin cloth—
Saw ever curious eye so strange a sight?
Portent in little, assorted death and blight
Like the ingredients of a witches' broth?
The beady spider, the flower like a froth,
And the moth carried like a paper kite.

What had that flower to do with being white,
The blue Brunella every child's delight?
What brought the kindred spider to that height?
(Make we no thesis of the miller's [miller-moth's] plight.)
What but design of darkness and of night?
Design, design! Do I use the word aright?

3. The name of a flower usually blue in color, thought to have medicinal properties.

4. A beautiful young woman who nursed King David in his old age.

Make the whole stock exchange your own!
If need be occupy a throne,
Where nobody can call *you* crone.

Some have relied on what they knew;
Others on being simply true.
What worked for them might work for you.

No memory of having starred
Atones for later disregard
Or keeps the end from being hard.

Better to go down dignified
With boughten friendship at your side
Than none at all. Provide, provide!

1936

The Bearer of Evil Tidings

The bearer of evil tidings,
When he was halfway there,
Remembered that evil tidings
Were a dangerous thing to bear.

So when he came to the parting
Where one road led to the throne
And one went off to the mountains
And into the wild unknown,

He took the one to the mountains.
He ran through the Vale of Cashmere,
He ran through the rhododendrons
Till he came to the land of Pamir.

And there in a precipice valley
A girl of his age he met
Took him home to her bower,
Or he might be running yet.

She taught him her tribe's religion:
How ages and ages since
A princess en route from China
To marry a Persian prince

Had been found with child; and her army
Had come to a troubled halt.
And though a god was the father
And nobody else at fault,

It had seemed discreet to remain there
And neither go on nor back.

So they stayed and declared a village
There in the land of Yak.

And the child that came of the princess
Established a royal line,
And his mandates were given heed to
Because he was born divine.

And that was why there were people
On one Himalayan shelf;
And the bearer of evil tidings
Decided to stay there himself.

At least he had this in common
With the race he chose to adopt:
They had both of them had their reasons
For stopping where they had stopped.

As for his evil tidings,
Belshazzar's overthrow,
Why hurry to tell Belshazzar
What soon enough he would know?[1]

1936

The Subverted Flower

She drew back; he was calm;
'It is this that had the power.'
And he lashed his open palm
With the tender-headed flower.
He smiled for her to smile,
But she was either blind
Or willfully unkind.
He eyed her for a while
For a woman and a puzzle.
He flicked and flung the flower,
And another sort of smile
Caught up like finger tips
The corners of his lips
And cracked his ragged muzzle.
She was standing to the waist
In goldenrod and brake,[2]
Her shining hair displaced.
He stretched her either arm
As if she made it ache
To clasp her—not to harm;

1. Though Frost uses the names of a real place (Pamir, bounded by Kashmir, Afghanistan, China, and Russia) and a real person (Belshazzar, the last great king of Babylonia), he invented the rest.
2. A species of fern.

As if he could not spare
To touch her neck and hair.
'If this has come to us
And not to me alone—'
So she thought she heard him say;
Though with every word he spoke
His lips were sucked and blown
And the effort made him choke
Like a tiger at a bone.
She had to lean away.
She dared not stir a foot,
Lest movement should provoke
The demon of pursuit
That slumbers in a brute.
It was then her mother's call
From inside the garden wall
Made her steal a look of fear
To see if he could hear
And would pounce to end it all
Before her mother came.
She looked and saw the shame:
A hand hung like a paw,
An arm worked like a saw
As if to be persuasive,
An ingratiating laugh
That cut the snout in half,
An eye become evasive.
A girl could only see
That a flower had marred a man,
But what she could not see
Was that the flower might be
Other than base and fetid:
That the flower had done but part,
And what the flower began
Her own too meager heart
Had terribly completed.
She looked and saw the worst.
And the dog or what it was,
Obeying bestial laws,
A coward save at night,
Turned from the place and ran.
She heard him stumble first
And use his hands in flight.
She heard him bark outright.
And oh, for one so young
The bitter words she spit
Like some tenacious bit
That will not leave the tongue.
She plucked her lips for it,
And still the horror clung.

Her mother wiped the foam
From her chin, picked up her comb,
And drew her backward home.

1942

The Gift Outright

The land was ours before we were the land's.
She was our land more than a hundred years
Before we were her people. She was ours
In Massachusetts, in Virginia,
But we were England's, still colonials,
Possessing what we still were unpossessed by,
Possessed by what we now no more possessed.
Something we were withholding made us weak
Until we found out that it was ourselves
We were withholding from our land of living,
And forthwith found salvation in surrender.
Such as we were we gave ourselves outright
(The deed of gift was many deeds of war)
To the land vaguely realizing westward,
But still unstoried, artless, unenhanced,
Such as she was, such as she would become.

1942

CARL SANDBURG
(*1878–1967*)

Carl Sandburg was born in Galesburg, Illinois, on January 8, 1878. His father and mother had come from Sweden. At first he exhibited little of the tenacity that marked his father's work as a machinist's blacksmith: he left school after the eighth grade and took on all kinds of jobs. When he was twenty the Spanish-American War gave him an opportunity to enlist as a volunteer. He served as a private in Puerto Rico and sent back letters about his army experiences for a Galesburg newspaper. The war ended, he applied to West Point, and would have been appointed if he had not abjectly failed the examinations in grammar and mathematics.

Sandburg now entered Lombard College in Illinois and supported himself by working in the town fire department. At college he distinguished himself by his writing, but he left in 1902 without a degree. The next ten years took him to many places and many jobs. At first he traveled about the country selling stereoscopic photographs. But he also rode the rails, enjoying the company of hobos; on one occasion he was arrested and made to serve ten days in a Pittsburgh jail. His sympathy for underdogs was fixed by such experiences. In 1904 he returned to work for a Galesburg newspaper, and in this year published his first poems. He took other jobs: in 1907 he became assistant editor of *Tomorrow Magazine* in Chicago, and began to do itinerant lecturing on such subjects as Whitman and Bernard Shaw. In 1907–08 he worked as an organizer for the Social Democratic Party and campaigned with Eugene Victor Debs, the presidential candidate. He returned to Chicago and worked for various newspapers for the next dozen years until he was able to support himself entirely as a writer.

By 1920 Sandburg had become a popular figure. He toured the country giving ballad concerts, he wrote articles, books for children, an autobiography, his biographies of the Lincolns, and a series of books of verse. Like Robert Frost, he enjoyed in old age extraordinary acclaim. The governor of Illinois proclaimed his seventy-fifth birthday as "Carl Sandburg Day," the King of Sweden decorated him, the United States Congress invited him to address a joint session in 1959 on Lincoln Day, schools bearing his name were opened in Illinois, and in 1964 he received from President Lyndon B. Johnson the Presidential Medal of Freedom. Sandburg died on July 22, 1967.

Chicago[1]

Hog Butcher for the World,
Tool Maker, Stacker of Wheat,
Player with Railroads and the Nation's Freight Handler;
Stormy, husky, brawling,
City of the Big Shoulders:

They tell me you are wicked and I believe them, for I have seen your painted women under the gas lamps luring the farm boys.
And they tell me you are crooked and I answer: Yes, it is true I have seen the gunman kill and go free to kill again.
And they tell me you are brutal and my reply is: On the faces of women and children I have seen the marks of wanton hunger.
And having answered so I turn once more to those who sneer at this my city, and I give them back the sneer and say to them:
Come and show me another city with lifted head singing so proud to be alive and coarse and strong and cunning.
Flinging magnetic curses amid the toil of piling job on job, here is a tall bold slugger set vivid against the little soft cities;
Fierce as a dog with tongue lapping for action, cunning as a savage pitted against the wilderness,
Bareheaded,
Shoveling,
Wrecking,
Planning,
Building, breaking, rebuilding,
Under the smoke, dust all over his mouth, laughing with white teeth,

1. Sandburg wrote of Chicago to a friend on July 30, 1913, "You might say at first shot that this is the hell of a place for a poet but the truth is it is a good place for a poet to get his head knocked when he needs it. In fact, it is so good a place for a healthy man who wants to watch the biggest, most intense, brutal and complicated game in the world—the game by which the world gets fed and clothed—the method of control—the economics and waste—so good a place is it from this viewpoint that I think you will like it." *The Letters of Carl Sandburg*, ed. Herbert Mitgang, New York, 1968, pp. 99–100.

Under the terrible burden of destiny laughing as a young man laughs,
Laughing even as an ignorant fighter laughs who has never lost a battle,
Bragging and laughing that under his wrist is the pulse, and under his ribs the heart of the people,
Laughing!
Laughing the stormy, husky, brawling laughter of Youth, half-naked, sweating, proud to be Hog Butcher, Tool Maker, Stacker of Wheat, Player with Railroads and Freight Handler to the Nation.

1916

Grass

Pile the bodies high at Austerlitz and Waterloo.[2]
Shovel them under and let me work—
I am the grass; I cover all.

And pile them high at Gettysburg[3]
And pile them high at Ypres and Verdun.[4]
Shovel them under and let me work.
Two years, ten years, and passengers ask the conductor:
What place is this?
Where are we now?

I am the grass.
Let me work.

1918

Cool Tombs

When Abraham Lincoln was shoveled into the tombs, he forgot the copperheads[5] and the assassin . . . in the dust, in the cool tombs.

And Ulysses Grant lost all thought of con men and Wall Street, cash and collateral turned ashes . . . in the dust, in the cool tombs.

Pocahontas' body, lovely as a poplar, sweet as a red haw[5] in November or a pawpaw in May, did she wonder? does she remember? . . . in the dust, in the cool tombs?

Take any streetful of people buying clothes and groceries, cheering a hero or throwing confetti and blowing tin horns . . . tell me if the lovers are losers . . . tell me if any get more than the lovers . . . in the dust . . . in the cool tombs.

1918

Gargoyle

I saw a mouth jeering. A smile of melted red iron ran over it. Its laugh was full of nails rattling. It was a child's dream of a mouth.

2. Austerlitz (Slavkov, Czechoslovakia) was in 1805 the scene of one of Napoleon's great victories, while Waterloo, in Belgium, was where he met his final defeat in 1815.
3. The city in Pennsylvania near which the Confederate army suffered a major defeat in 1863.
4. Ypres, Belgium, and Verdun, in France, were the centers of some of the fiercest fighting in the First World War.
5. Hawthorn berry.

A fist hit the mouth: knuckles of gun-metal driven by an electric wrist
and shoulder. It was a child's dream of an arm.
The fist hit the mouth over and over, again and again. The mouth bled
melted iron, and laughed its laughter of nails rattling.
And I saw the more the fist pounded the more the mouth laughed. The
fist is pounding and pounding, and the mouth answering.

1918

EDWARD THOMAS
(*1878–1917*)

Edward Thomas was born in Lambeth, a section of London, on March 3, 1878, and he spent most of his early life in the city. Both of his parents were Welsh; his father, a dour man, discouraged Thomas's early interest in poetry and urged the wisdom of a career in the Civil Service. Thomas was educated at St. Paul's School and Lincoln College, Oxford. At 16 he fell in love with a girl two years his senior, and he married her while still in his third year at Oxford. Thomas was poor, he soon had a family to support, and he was given to periods of terrible self-doubt and melancholy. He supported himself as a reviewer and hack writer, and when he died at 39 he had written thirty books of prose and edited many others. He came to poetry late, and he lived to see only six of his poems in print.

A transforming moment in Thomas's life was his reading of the poetry of Robert Frost and his meeting soon thereafter with the poet himself, who had come to England. Frost's poems seem to have suggested to Thomas a way that he might himself write poetry. Frost convinced Thomas that he had long neglected his true vocation, which was poetry. And Thomas was proud to say of a poem that it "sounded" like Frost.

In 1915 Thomas enlisted as a private soldier to fight for England in the First World War. He went to France, where the experience of war both alleviated his chronic depression and encouraged his writing. Easter Sunday, 1917 found him in Arras; he wrote his wife, "You would have laughed to see us dodging shells to-day." The next day, April 9, 1917, he was killed.

The Owl

Downhill I came, hungry, and yet not starved;
Cold, yet had heat within me that was proof
Against the North wind; tired, yet so that rest
Had seemed the sweetest thing under a roof.

Then at the inn I had food, fire, and rest,
Knowing how hungry, cold, and tired was I.
All of the night was quite barred out except
An owl's cry, a most melancholy cry

Shaken out long and clear upon the hill,
No merry note, nor cause of merriment,
But one telling me plain what I escaped
And others could not, that night, as in I went.

And salted was my food, and my repose,
Salted and sobered, too, by the bird's voice
Speaking for all who lay under the stars,
Soldiers and poor, unable to rejoice.

1917

The Gallows

There was a weasel lived in the sun
With all his family,
Till a keeper shot him with his gun
And hung him up on a tree,
Where he swings in the wind and rain,
In the sun and in the snow,
Without pleasure, without pain,
On the dead oak tree bough.

There was a crow who was no sleeper,
But a thief and a murderer
Till a very late hour; and this keeper
Made him one of the things that were,
To hang and flap in rain and wind,
In the sun and in the snow.
There are no more sins to be sinned
On the dead oak tree bough.

There was a magpie, too,
Had a long tongue and a long tail;
He could both talk and do—
But what did that avail?
He, too, flaps in the wind and rain
Alongside weasel and crow,
Without pleasure, without pain,
On the dead oak tree bough.

And many other beasts
And birds, skin, bone, and feather,
Have been taken from their feasts
And hung up there together,
To swing and have endless leisure
In the sun and in the snow,
Without pain, without pleasure,
On the dead oak tree bough.

1917

WALLACE STEVENS
(1879–1955)

Wallace Stevens was born on October 2, 1879, in Reading, Pennsylvania. He attended high school in Reading and then entered Harvard as a special student, like Robert Frost. He remained for three years, 1897 to 1900, during which he studied French and German and, following his philosophical bent, became friendly with the philosopher-poet George Santayana. Stevens became president of the *Harvard Advocate*, and like Eliot published his early poems in it.

Apart from his interest in writing, he was not sure how to make a livelihood. His first job was on the *New York Herald Tribune*, and he did not like it. At his father's suggestion he resigned and entered the New York Law School in the fall of 1901. In 1904 he was admitted to the New York Bar and began, unsuccessfully, to practice law. A partnership failed, and then he worked in several other law firms. In January 1908 he entered the legal staff of an insurance firm and at last felt secure enough to marry, in 1909, Elsie Moll, a young woman whom he had met in Reading five years before. In 1916 he joined the New York office of the Hartford Accident and Indemnity Company and a few months later moved to Hartford. In 1934 he became vice president. He was extraordinarily self-effacing; he never presented himself as a literary figure to his business associates. The events of his subsequent life are scanty. He traveled a good deal, chiefly for his company but sometimes on his own. He bought a few paintings by French artists like Tal Coat; he built up an impressive collection of phonograph records of classical music; he grew fond of gardening. He continued to work at the insurance company until his death on August 2, 1955.

A High-Toned Old Christian Woman

Poetry is the supreme fiction, madame.
Take the moral law and make a nave[2] of it
And from the nave build haunted heaven. Thus,
The conscience is converted into palms,
Like windy citherns[3] hankering for hymns.
We agree in principle. That's clear. But take
The opposing law and make a peristyle,
And from the peristyle project a masque[4]
Beyond the planets. Thus, our bawdiness,[5]
Unpurged by epitaph, indulged at last,
Is equally converted into palms,[6]

2. The principal part of a Christian church, where the congregation sits. A peristyle, with which Stevens contrasts the nave, is a colonnade surrounding a building or a court, associated with classical Greek architecture and often part of a pagan temple.

3. Aeolian harps—stringed instruments played upon by the wind.

4. An elaborate courtly entertainment involving drama, music and dance.

5. Including its older meaning, boldness.

6. Palm leaves are part of pagan as well as Christian ritual.

Squiggling like saxophones. And palm for palm,
Madame, we are where we began. Allow,
Therefore, that in the planetary scene
Your disaffected flagellants, well-stuffed,
Smacking their muzzy bellies in parade,
Proud of such novelties of the sublime,
Such tink and tank and tunk-a-tunk-tunk,
May, merely may, madame, whip from themselves
A jovial hullabaloo among the spheres.[7]
This will make widows wince. But fictive things
Wink as they will. Wink most when widows wince.

1923

The Emperor of Ice-Cream[8]

Call the roller of big cigars,
The muscular one, and bid him whip
In kitchen cups concupiscent curds.[9]
Let the wenches dawdle in such dress
As they are used to wear, and let the boys
Bring flowers in last month's newspapers.
Let be be finale of seem.[1]
The only emperor is the emperor of ice-cream.
Take from the dresser of deal,[2]
Lacking the three glass knobs, that sheet
On which she embroidered fantails[3] once
And spread it so as to cover her face.
If her horny feet protrude, they come
To show how cold she is, and dumb.
Let the lamp affix its beam.
The only emperor is the emperor of ice-cream.

1923

Sunday Morning

I

Complacencies of the peignoir,[4] and late
Coffee and oranges in a sunny chair,
And the green freedom of a cockatoo

7. "Music of the spheres" was believed, until the 17th century, to result from the vibrations of stellar and planetary motion.

8. In 1933 Stevens wrote to William Rose Benét: "I think I should select from my poems as my favorite the Emperor of Ice Cream. This wears a deliberately commonplace costume, and yet seems to me to contain something of the essential gaudiness of poetry; that is the reason why I like it."

9. "The words 'concupiscent curds' have no genealogy; they are merely expressive: at least, I hope they are expressive. They express the concupiscence of life, but, by contrast with the things in relation in the poem, they express or accentuate life's destitution, and it is this that gives them something more than a cheap lustre." *Letters*, p. 500.

1. ". . . the true sense of Let be be the finale of seem is let being become the conclusion or denouement of appearing to be: in short, ice cream is an absolute good. The poem is obviously not about ice cream, but about being as distinguished from seeming to be." *Letters*, p. 341.

2. Fir or pine boards.

3. ". . . the word fantails does not mean fans, but fantail pigeons . . ." *Letters*, p. 500.

4. Dressing gown.

Upon a rug mingle to dissipate
The holy hush of ancient sacrifice.
She dreams a little, and she feels the dark
Encroachment of that old catastrophe,
As a calm darkens among water-lights.
The pungent oranges and bright, green wings
Seem things in some procession of the dead,
Winding across wide water, without sound.
The day is like wide water, without sound,
Stilled for the passing of her dreaming feet
Over the seas, to silent Palestine,
Dominion of the blood and sepulchre.[5]

II

Why should she give her bounty to the dead?
What is divinity if it can come
Only in silent shadows and in dreams?
Shall she not find in comforts of the sun,
In pungent fruit and bright, green wings, or else
In any balm or beauty of the earth,
Things to be cherished like the thought of heaven?
Divinity must live within herself:
Passions of rain, or moods in falling snow;
Grievings in loneliness, or unsubdued
Elations when the forest blooms; gusty
Emotions on wet roads on autumn nights;
All pleasures and all pains, remembering
The bough of summer and the winter branch.
These are the measures destined for her soul.

III

Jove[6] in the clouds had his inhuman birth.
No mother suckled him, no sweet land gave
Large-mannered motions to his mythy mind
He moved among us, as a muttering king,
Magnificent, would move among his hinds,[7]
Until our blood, commingling, virginal,
With heaven, brought such requital to desire
The very hinds discerned it, in a star.
Shall our blood fail? Or shall it come to be
The blood of paradise? And shall the earth
Seem all of paradise that we shall know?
The sky will be much friendlier then than now,
A part of labor and a part of pain,
And next in glory to enduring love,
Not this dividing and indifferent blue.

5. Alluding to the crucifixion, burial, and resurrection of Christ.

6. Or Jupiter, in Roman myth ruler of the gods.

7. Shepherds.

IV

She says, "I am content when wakened birds,
Before they fly, test the reality
Of misty fields, by their sweet questionings;
But when the birds are gone, and their warm fields
Return no more, where, then, is paradise?"
There is not any haunt of prophecy,
Nor any old chimera[8] of the grave,
Neither the golden underground, nor isle
Melodious, where spirits gat them home,
Nor visionary south, nor cloudy palm
Remote on heaven's hill, that has endured
As April's green endures; or will endure
Like her remembrance of awakened birds,
Or her desire for June and evening, tipped
By the consummation of the swallow's wings.

V

She says, "But in contentment I still feel
The need of some imperishable bliss."
Death is the mother of beauty; hence from her,
Alone, shall come fulfillment to our dreams
And our desires. Although she strews the leaves
Of sure obliteration on our paths,
The path sick sorrow took, the many paths
Where triumph rang its brassy phrase, or love
Whispered a little out of tenderness,
She makes the willow shiver in the sun
For maidens who were wont to sit and gaze
Upon the grass, relinquished to their feet.
She causes boys to pile new plums and pears
On disregarded plate.[9] The maidens taste
And stray impassioned in the littering leaves.

VI

Is there no change of death in paradise?
Does ripe fruit never fall? Or do the boughs
Hang always heavy in that perfect sky,
Unchanging, yet so like our perishing earth,
With rivers like our own that seek for seas
They never find, the same receding shores
That never touch with inarticulate pang?
Why set the pear upon those river-banks
Or spice the shores with odors of the plum?
Alas, that they should wear our colors there,
The silken weavings of our afternoons,
And pick the strings of our insipid lutes!
Death is the mother of beauty, mystical,

8. Fantasy.

9. "Plate is used in the sense of so-called family plate. Disregarded refers to the disuse into which things fall that have been possessed for a long time. I mean, therefore, that death releases and renews" [*Letters of Wallace Stevens,* New York, 1966, pp. 183–184].

Within whose burning bosom we devise
Our earthly mothers waiting, sleeplessly.

VII

Supple and turbulent, a ring of men
Shall chant in orgy on a summer morn
Their boisterous devotion to the sun,
Not as a god, but as a god might be,
Naked among them, like a savage source.
Their chant shall be a chant of paradise,
Out of their blood, returning to the sky;
And in their chant shall enter, voice by voice,
The windy lake wherein their lord delights,
The trees, like serafin,[1] and echoing hills,
That choir among themselves long afterward.
They shall know well the heavenly fellowship
Of men that perish and of summer morn.
And whence they came and whither they shall go
The dew upon their feet shall manifest.

VIII

She hears, upon that water without sound,
A voice that cries, "The tomb in Palestine
Is not the porch of spirits lingering.
It is the grave of Jesus, where he lay."
We live in an old chaos of the sun,
Or old dependency of day and night,
Or island solitude, unsponsored, free,
Of that wide water, inescapable.
Deer walk upon our mountains, and the quail
Whistle about us their spontaneous cries;
Sweet berries ripen in the wilderness;
And, in the isolation of the sky,
At evening, casual flocks of pigeons make
Ambiguous undulations as they sink,
Downward to darkness, on extended wings.

1923

Anecdote of the Jar

I placed a jar in Tennessee,
And round it was, upon a hill.
It made the slovenly wilderness
Surround that hill.

The wilderness rose up to it,
And sprawled around, no longer wild.
The jar was round upon the ground
And tall and of a port in air.

1. Or seraphim, six-winged angels.

It took dominion everywhere.
The jar was gray and bare.
It did not give of bird or bush,
Like nothing else in Tennessee.

1923

Thirteen Ways of Looking at a Blackbird[3]

I

Among twenty snowy mountains,
The only moving thing
Was the eye of the blackbird.

II

I was of three minds,
Like a tree
In which there are three blackbirds.

III

The blackbird whirled in the autumn winds.
It was a small part of the pantomime.

IV

A man and a woman
Are one.
A man and a woman and a blackbird
Are one.

V

I do not know which to prefer,
The beauty of inflections,
Or the beauty of innuendoes,
The blackbird whistling
Or just after.

VI

Icicles filled the long window
With barbaric glass.
The shadow of the blackbird
Crossed it, to and fro.
The mood
Traced in the shadow
An indecipherable cause.

VII

O thin men of Haddam,[4]
Why do you imagine golden birds?

3. "This group of poems is not meant to be a collection of epigrams or of ideas, but of sensations." *Letters*, p. 251.

4. A town in Connecticut. "The thin men of Haddam are entirely fictitious although some years ago one of the citizens of that place wrote to me to ask what I had in mind. I just like the name." *Letters*, p. 786.

Do you not see how the blackbird
Walks around the feet
Of the women about you?

VIII

I know noble accents
And lucid, inescapable rhythms;
But I know, too,
That the blackbird is involved
In what I know.

IX

When the blackbird flew out of sight,
It marked the edge
Of one of many circles.

X

At the sight of blackbirds
Flying in a green light,
Even the bawds of euphony
Would cry out sharply.[5]

XI

He rode over Connecticut
In a glass coach.
Once, a fear pierced him,
In that he mistook
The shadow of his equipage[6]
For blackbirds.

XII

The river is moving.
The blackbird must be flying.

XIII

It was evening all afternoon.
It was snowing
And it was going to snow.
The blackbird sat
In the cedar-limbs.

1923

The Idea of Order at Key West

She sang beyond the genius of the sea.
The water never formed to mind or voice,
Like a body wholly body, fluttering
Its empty sleeves; and yet its mimic motion

5. "Naturally, with pleasure, etc." *Letters*, p. 340.

6. Carriage.

Made constant cry, caused constantly a cry,
That was not ours although we understood,
Inhuman, of the veritable ocean.

The sea was not a mask. No more was she.
The song and water were not medleyed sound
Even if what she sang was what she heard,
Since what she sang was uttered word by word.
It may be that in all her phrases stirred
The grinding water and the gasping wind;
But it was she and not the sea we heard.

For she was the maker of the song she sang.
The ever-hooded, tragic-gestured sea
Was merely a place by which she walked to sing.
Whose spirit is this? we said, because we knew
It was the spirit that we sought and knew
That we should ask this often as she sang.

If it was only the dark voice of the sea
That rose, or even colored by many waves;
If it was only the outer voice of sky
And cloud, of the sunken coral water-walled,
However clear, it would have been deep air,
The heaving speech of air, a summer sound
Repeated in a summer without end
And sound alone. But it was more than that,
More even than her voice, and ours, among
The meaningless plungings of water and the wind,
Theatrical distances, bronze shadows heaped
On high horizons, mountainous atmospheres
Of sky and sea.

It was her voice that made
The sky acutest at its vanishing.
She measured to the hour its solitude.
She was the single artificer of the world
In which she sang. And when she sang, the sea,
Whatever self it had, became the self
That was her song, for she was the maker. Then we,
As we beheld her striding there alone,
Knew that there never was a world for her
Except the one she sang and, singing, made.

Ramon Fernandez,[7] tell me, if you know,
Why, when the singing ended and we turned
Toward the town, tell why the glassy lights,
The lights in the fishing boats at anchor there,

7. Stevens pointed out to a correspondent that in choosing this name he had simply combined two common Spanish names at random, without conscious reference to Ramon Fernandez the French critic: "Ramon Fernandez was not intended to be anyone at all."

As the night descended, tilting in the air,
Mastered the night and portioned out the sea,
Fixing emblazoned zones and fiery poles,
Arranging, deepening, enchanting night.

Oh! Blessed rage for order, pale Ramon,
The maker's rage to order words of the sea,
Words of the fragrant portals, dimly-starred,
And of ourselves and of our origins,
In ghostlier demarcations, keener sounds.

1935

From The Man with the Blue Guitar[8]

I

The man bent over his guitar,
A shearsman of sorts.[9] The day was green.

They said, "You have a blue guitar,
You do not play things as they are."

The man replied, "Things as they are
Are changed upon the blue guitar."

And they said then, "But play, you must,
A tune beyond us, yet ourselves,

A tune upon the blue guitar
Of things exactly as they are."

1937

Of Modern Poetry

The poem of the mind in the act of finding
What will suffice. It has not always had
To find: the scene was set; it repeated what
Was in the script.
Then the theatre was changed
To something else. Its past was a souvenir.
It has to be living, to learn the speech of the place.
It has to face the men of the time and to meet
The women of the time. It has to think about war

8. "[The sections of 'The Man with the Blue Guitar'] deal with the relation or balance between imagined things and real things which, as you know, is a constant source of trouble to me. . . . Actually, they are not abstractions, even though what I have just said about them suggests that. Perhaps it would be better to say that what they really deal with is the painter's problem of realization: I have been trying to see the world about me both as I see it and as it is." *Letters*, p. 316. Though the title describes a painting from Picasso's "blue period," *Blind Guitar-Player* (1903), Stevens asserted in 1953, "I had no particular painting of Picasso's in mind." *Letters*, p. 786.

9. "This refers to the posture of the speaker, squatting like a tailor (a shearsman) as he works on his cloth." *Letters*, p. 783.

And it has to find what will suffice. It has
To construct a new stage. It has to be on that stage
And, like an insatiable actor, slowly and
With meditation, speak words that in the ear,
In the delicatest ear of the mind, repeat,
Exactly, that which it wants to hear, at the sound
Of which, an invisible audience listens,
Not to the play, but to itself, expressed
In an emotion as of two people, as of two
Emotions becoming one. The actor is
A metaphysician[9a] in the dark, twanging
An instrument, twanging a wiry string that gives
Sounds passing through sudden rightnesses, wholly
Containing the mind, below which it cannot descend,
Beyond which it has no will to rise.

It must
Be the finding of a satisfaction, and may
Be of a man skating, a woman dancing, a woman
Combing. The poem of the act of the mind.

1942

To an Old Philosopher in Rome[1]

On the threshold of heaven, the figures in the street
Become the figures of heaven, the majestic movement
Of men growing small in the distances of space,
Singing, with smaller and still smaller sound,
Unintelligible absolution and an end—

The threshold, Rome, and that more merciful Rome
Beyond, the two alike in the make of the mind.
It is as if in a human dignity
Two parallels become one, a perspective, of which
Men are part both in the inch and in the mile.

How easily the blown banners change to wings . . .
Things dark on the horizons of perception,
Become accompaniments of fortune, but
Of the fortune of the spirit, beyond the eye,
Not of its sphere, and yet not far beyond,

9a. Philosopher who studies the nature of reality and of fundamental causes and processes.

1. The poem is addressed to the Spanish-born American philosopher, George Santayana (1863–1952), also a poet, who retired from teaching at Harvard in 1912 and went to Italy to live. Stevens met Santayana while an undergraduate at Harvard. "While I did not take any of his courses and never heard him lecture, he invited me to come to see him a number of times and, in that way, I came to know him a little. I read several poems to him and he expressed his own view of the subject of them in a sonnet ['Cathedrals by the Sea: Reply to a sonnet beginning "Cathedrals are not built along the sea" '] which he sent me, and which is in one of his books." *Letters*, pp. 481–2. This poem was written less than a year before Santayana's death in the nursing home of a Roman Catholic order in Rome: "He seems to have gone to live at the convent, in which he died, in his sixties, probably gave them all he had and asked them to keep him, body and soul." *Letters*, pp. 761–2.

The human end in the spirit's greatest reach,
The extreme of the known in the presence of the extreme
Of the unknown. The newsboys' muttering
Becomes another murmuring; the smell
Of medicine, a fragrantness not to be spoiled . . .

The bed, the books, the chair, the moving nuns,
The candle as it evades the sight, these are
The sources of happiness in the shape of Rome,
A shape within the ancient circles of shapes,
And these beneath the shadow of a shape

In a confusion on bed and books, a portent
On the chair, a moving transparence on the nuns,
A light on the candle tearing against the wick
To join a hovering excellence, to escape
From fire and be part only of that of which

Fire is the symbol: the celestial possible.
Speak to your pillow as if it was yourself.
Be orator but with an accurate tongue
And without eloquence, O, half-asleep,
Of the pity that is the memorial of this room,

So that we feel, in this illumined large,
The veritable small, so that each of us
Beholds himself in you, and hears his voice
In yours, master and commiserable man,
Intent on your particles of nether-do,[2]

Your dozing in the depths of wakefulness,
In the warmth of your bed, at the edge of your chair, alive
Yet living in two worlds, impenitent
As to one, and, as to one, most penitent,
Impatient for the grandeur that you need

In so much misery; and yet finding it
Only in misery, the afflatus[3] of ruin,
Profound poetry of the poor and of the dead,
As in the last drop of the deepest blood,
As it falls from the heart and lies there to be seen,

Even as the blood of an empire, it might be,
For a citizen of heaven though still of Rome.
It is poverty's speech that seeks us out the most.
It is older than the oldest speech of Rome.
This is the tragic accent of the scene.

2. A coinage based on the expression "derring-do," itself according to the O.E.D. a misreading of Chaucer's usage for "daring to do." A paraphrase might be, "doings or happenings on the lowest level or smallest scale of existence," not forgetting the original expression's connotation of "courageous feats at arms."

3. Inspiration.

And you—it is you that speak it, without speech,
The loftiest syllables among loftiest things,
The one invulnerable man among
Crude captains, the naked majesty, if you like,
Of bird-nest arches and of rain-stained-vaults.

The sounds drift in. The buildings are remembered.
The life of the city never lets go, nor do you
Ever want it to. It is part of the life in your room.
Its domes are the architecture of your bed.
The bells keep on repeating solemn names

In choruses and choirs of choruses,
Unwilling that mercy should be a mystery
Of silence, that any solitude of sense
Should give you more than their peculiar chords
And reverberations clinging to whisper still.

It is a kind of total grandeur at the end,
With every visible thing enlarged and yet
No more than a bed, a chair and moving nuns,
The immensest theatre, the pillared porch,
The book and candle in your ambered room,

Total grandeur of a total edifice,
Chosen by an inquisitor of structures
For himself. He stops upon this threshold,
As if the design of all his words takes form
And frame from thinking and is realized.

1954

JAMES STEPHENS
(*1880–1950*)

James Stephens was probably born on February 9, 1880, in Dublin. Having been abandoned by his mother when he was three, Stephens may have taken a curious revenge by claiming his parentage was unknown. Because of some childish theft, Stephens was sent at a very young age to the Meath Protestant Industrial School for Boys, but this punishment proved beneficial, for he received a very good education there. Although he never grew to more than four feet ten inches, Stephens became an expert gymnast and a member of a prizewinning team. After finishing school he must have worked at various nondescript jobs, such as the one he settled in during 1906, as clerk-typist in a law office. He remained there, but in 1907 at the invitation of Arthur Griffith, the Irish nationalist, Stephens began also to contribute to Griffith's newspaper, *Sinn Féin.* He learned Irish and translated beautifully from that language, but his more conspicuous talent was for humorous fantasy. This was often taken more lightly than Stephens intended, as in *The Crock of Gold* (1912), which he based upon a mystical scheme involving opposites and their reconciliation. The success of this novel enabled him to quit his job and devote himself to writing. After the Irish Free State was founded in 1922 Stephens seems to have felt disaffected for social or political reasons. Two years later he and his wife (once his landlady) bought a house in London and lived there for the rest of their lives. But Stephens was lonely, and would haunt Euston Station, where the trains from Ireland came in, hoping to see old friends. In his later years he gave excellent talks for the BBC and was also much sought after for his marvelous conversational powers. He died in London on December 26, 1950.

What Tomas Said in a Pub

I saw God! Do you doubt it?
Do you dare to doubt it?
I saw the Almighty Man! His hand
Was resting on a mountain! And
He looked upon the World, and all about it:
I saw Him plainer than you see me now
—You mustn't doubt it!

He was not satisfied!
His look was all dissatisfied!
His beard swung on a wind, far out of sight
Behind the world's curve! And there was light
Most fearful from His forehead! And He sighed—
—That star went always wrong, and from the start
I was dissatisfied!—

He lifted up His hand!
I say He heaved a dreadful hand
Over the spinning earth! Then I said, —Stay,
You must not strike it, God! I'm in the way!
And I will never move from where I stand!—
He said,—Dear child, I feared that you were dead,—
. . . And stayed His hand!

1909

The Wind

The wind stood up, and gave a shout;
He whistled on his fingers, and

Kicked the withered leaves about,
And thumped the branches with his hand,

And said he'll kill, and kill, and kill;
And so he will! And so he will!

1915

A Glass of Beer[4]

The lanky hank of a she in the inn over there
Nearly killed me for asking the loan of a glass of beer;
May the devil grip the whey-faced slut by the hair,
And beat bad manners out of her skin for a year.

That parboiled ape, with the toughest jaw you will see
On virtue's path, and a voice that would rasp the dead,
Came roaring and raging the minute she looked at me,
And threw me out of the house on the back of my head!

If I asked her master he'd give me a cask a day;
But she, with the beer at hand, not a gill would arrange!
May she marry a ghost and bear him a kitten, and may
The High King of Glory permit her to get the mange.

1918

4. Adapted from a poem in Irish by David O'Bruadair (c. 1650–1694), a poet born in Limerick, Ireland.

JAMES JOYCE
(*1882–1941*)

James Joyce was born in Rathgar, a Dublin suburb, on February 2, 1882. He was educated at Jesuit private schools and then at University College, Dublin, also under Jesuit supervision. He soon declared himself an artist and an unbeliever, and determined to go into self-imposed exile. After one abortive early attempt in 1902–03, he finally eloped in 1904 with Nora Barnacle. Because of his contempt for convention, the couple were not married until twenty-seven years later. In the meantime they had lived in various places in Europe: Pola (now Yugoslavia), 1904–05; Trieste, 1905–15 (except for nine months in Rome and three trips to Dublin); Zurich, 1915–19; Trieste again, 1919–20; and in Paris, 1920–39. During these peregrinations Joyce wrote and published the works of fiction which are his chief claim to greatness as a writer: *A Portrait of the Artist as a Young Man* (published serially 1914–15), *Ulysses* (1922), and *Finnegans Wake* (1939). The Second World War drove Joyce first to unoccupied France and then to Zurich, where he died on January 13, 1941.

[Though I Thy Mithridates[4] Were]

Though I thy Mithridates were,
  Framed to defy the poison-dart,
Yet must thou fold[5] me unaware

4. The ancient king of Persia who is supposed to have taken small therapeutic doses of poison and thus to have thwarted attempts on his life.

5. Enfold.

To know the rapture of thy heart,
And I but render and confess
The malice of thy tenderness.

For elegant and antique phrase,
Dearest, my lips wax[6] all too wise;
Nor have I known a love whose praise
Our piping poets solemnize,
Neither a love where may not be
Ever so little falsity.

1907

[I Hear an Army Charging upon the Land]

I hear an army charging upon the land,
And the thunder of horses plunging, foam about their knees:
Arrogant, in black armour, behind them stand,
Disdaining the reins, with fluttering whips, the charioteers.

They cry unto the night their battle-name:
I moan in sleep when I hear afar their whirling laughter.
They cleave the gloom of dreams, a blinding flame,
Clanging, clanging upon the heart as upon an anvil.

They come shaking in triumph their long, green hair:
They come out of the sea and run shouting by the shore.
My heart, have you no wisdom thus to despair?
My love, my love, my love, why have you left me alone?

1907

Ecce Puer[7]

Of the dark past
A child is born
With joy and grief
My heart is torn

Calm in his cradle
The living lies.
May love and mercy
Unclose his eyes!

Young life is breathed
On the glass;
The world that was not
Comes to pass.

6. Grow.

7. "Behold the boy" (Lat). Joyce wrote the poem in 1932 on the birth of his grandson Stephen; the old man (line 14) is Joyce's father, who had recently died.

A child is sleeping:
An old man gone.
O, father forsaken,
Forgive your son!

1936

E. J. PRATT
(*1883–1964*)

Edwin John Pratt was born on February 4, 1883, in the small fishing village of Western Bay, Newfoundland, the son of a Methodist clergyman. He was educated at St. John's Methodist College. Afterwards he taught and preached in remote parts of the island, then in 1907 entered Victoria College, University of Toronto. Until he was almost forty Pratt wavered between a career in teaching and the ministry. He was ordained in 1913 and took a Ph.D. in Philosophy four years later. He finally decided on teaching and in 1920 joined the Department of English at Victoria College, where he remained until his retirement in 1953. He received many honors for his contributions to the development of a Canadian culture. He died in Toronto on April 26, 1964 at the age of 81.

The Ritual

I

She took her name beneath according skies,
With ringing harbour cheers, and in the lee[1]
Of hills derived her birthright to the sea—
The adoration of a thousand eyes.
Each bulwark[2] ran its way from stern to prow,
With the slim tracery of a sea-gull's wing,
And—happy augury for the christening—
The bottle broke in rainbows on her bow.

Beyond the port in roll and leap and curl,
In the rich hues of sunlight on the spray,
And in the march of tides—swept down the bay
The pageant of the morning, to the skirl
Of merry pipers as the rising gale
Sounded a challenge to her maiden sail.

II

She left her name under revolted skies,
Before the break of day, upon a rock
Whose long and sunken ledge met the full shock

1. That is, protected from the wind.

2. That part of a ship's side above the water line.

Of an Atlantic storm, and with the cries
Of the curlews[3] issuing from dark caves,
Accompanied by the thud of wings from shags[4]
That veered down from their nests upon the crags
To pounce on bulwarks shattered by the waves.
And the birthright that was granted for a brief,
Exultant hour with cheers and in the lee
Of hills was now restored unto the sea,
Amidst the grounded gutturals of the reef,
And with the grind of timbers on the sides
Of cliffs resounding with the march of tides.

1932

The Prize Cat

Pure blood domestic, guaranteed,
Soft-mannered, musical in purr,
The ribbon had declared the breed,
Gentility was in the fur.

Such feline culture in the gads[1]
No anger ever arched her back—
What distance since those velvet pads
Departed from the leopard's track!

And when I mused how Time had thinned
The jungle strains within the cells,
How human hands had disciplined
Those prowling optic parallels;

I saw the generations pass
Along the reflex of a spring,
A bird had rustled in the grass,
The tab had caught it on the wing;

Behind the leap so furtive-wild
Was such ignition in the gleam,
I thought an Abyssinian[2] child
Had cried out in the whitethroat's scream.

1937

3. A seaside bird known for the forlorn cry after which it is named.
4. Cormorants.

1. Claws.
2. Ethiopian.

WILLIAM CARLOS WILLIAMS
(*1883–1963*)

William Carlos Williams was born on September 17, 1883, in Rutherford, New Jersey. His father had emigrated from Birmingham, England, and his mother (whose mother was Basque and whose father was of Dutch-Spanish-Jewish descent) from Puerto Rico. Williams attended schools in Rutherford until 1897, when he was sent for two years to a school near Geneva and to the Lycée Condorcet in Paris. On his return he attended the Horace Mann High School in New York City. After having passed a special examination, he was admitted in 1902 to the medical school of the University of Pennsylvania. There he met two poets, Hilda Doolittle and Ezra Pound. The latter friendship had a permanent effect; Williams said he could divide his life into *Before Pound* and *After Pound.*

Williams did his internship in New York City from 1906 to 1909, writing verse in between patients. He published a first book, *Poems,* in 1909. Then he went to Leipzig in 1909 to study pediatrics, and after that returned to Rutherford to practice medicine there for the rest of his life. In 1912 he married Florence Herman (or "Flossie"). In 1913 Pound secured a London publisher for Williams' second book, *The Tempers.* But his first distinctly original book was *Al Que Quiere!* (To Him Who Wants It!), published in Boston in 1917. In the following years he wrote not only poems but short stories, novels, essays, and an autobiography. In 1946 he began the fulfillment of a long-standing plan, to write an epic poem, with the publication of *Paterson,* Book I. The three following books appeared in 1948, 1949, and 1951; in 1952 he suffered a crippling stroke, which forced him to give up his medical practice and drastically limited his ability to write. Nonetheless he continued to do so, producing an unanticipated fifth book of *Paterson* in 1958 as well as shorter poems. He died in Rutherford on March 4, 1963. Two months later his last book of lyrics won the Pulitzer prize for poetry.

Tract

I will teach you my townspeople
how to perform a funeral
for you have it over a troop
of artists—
unless one should scour the world—
you have the ground sense necessary.

See! the hearse leads.
I begin with a design for a hearse.
For Christ's sake not black—
nor white either—and not polished!
Let it be weathered—like a farm wagon—
with gilt wheels (this could be
applied fresh at small expense)

or no wheels at all:
a rough dray to drag over the ground.

Knock the glass out!
My God—glass, my townspeople!
For what purpose? Is it for the dead
to look out or for us to see
how well he is housed or to see
the flowers or the lack of them—
or what?
To keep the rain and snow from him?
He will have a heavier rain soon:
pebbles and dirt and what not.
Let there be no glass—
and no upholstery, phew!
and no little brass rollers
and small easy wheels on the bottom—
my townspeople what are you thinking of?

A rough plain hearse then
with gilt wheels and no top at all.
On this the coffin lies
by its own weight.

No wreaths please—
especially no hot house flowers.
Some common memento is better,
something he prized and is known by:
his old clothes—a few books perhaps—
God knows what! You realize
how we are about these things
my townspeople—
something will be found—anything
even flowers if he had come to that.
So much for the hearse.

For heaven's sake though see to the driver!
Take off the silk hat! In fact
that's no place at all for him—
up there unceremoniously
dragging our friend out to his own dignity!
Bring him down—bring him down!
Low and inconspicuous! I'd not have him ride
on the wagon at all—damn him—
the undertaker's understrapper!
Let him hold the reins
and walk at the side
and inconspicuously too!

Then briefly as to yourselves:
Walk behind—as they do in France,
seventh class, or if you ride

Hell take curtains! Go with some show
of inconvenience; sit openly—
to the weather as to grief.
Or do you think you can shut grief in?
What—from us? We who have perhaps
nothing to lose? Share with us
share with us—it will be money
in your pockets.
Go now
I think you are ready.

1917

The Widow's Lament in Springtime[1]

Sorrow is my own yard
where the new grass
flames as it has flamed
often before but not
with the cold fire
that closes round me this year.
Thirtyfive years
I lived with my husband.
The plumtree is white today
with masses of flowers.
Masses of flowers
loaded the cherry branches
and color some bushes
yellow and some red
but the grief in my heart
is stronger than they
for though they were my joy
formerly, today I notice them
and turned away forgetting.
Today my son told me
that in the meadows,
at the edge of the heavy woods
in the distance, he saw
trees of white flowers.
I feel that I would like
to go there
and fall into those flowers
and sink into the marsh near them.

1921

The Great Figure

Among the rain
and lights

1. The poem is a tribute to Williams's mother.

I saw the figure 5
in gold
on a red
firetruck
moving
tense
unheeded
to gong clangs
siren howls
and wheels rumbling
through the dark city.

1921

Spring and All

By the road to the contagious hospital
under the surge of the blue
mottled clouds driven from the
northeast—a cold wind. Beyond, the
waste of broad, muddy fields
brown with dried weeds, standing and fallen

patches of standing water
the scattering of tall trees

All along the road the reddish
purplish, forked, upstanding, twiggy
stuff of bushes and small trees
with dead, brown leaves under them
leafless vines—

Lifeless in appearance, sluggish
dazed spring approaches—

They enter the new world naked,
cold, uncertain of all
save that they enter. All about them
the cold, familiar wind—

Now the grass, tomorrow
the stiff curl of wildcarrot leaf
One by one objects are defined—
It quickens: clarity, outline of leaf

But now the stark dignity of
entrance—Still, the profound change
has come upon them: rooted, they
grip down and begin to awaken

1923

The Red Wheelbarrow

so much depends
upon

a red wheel
barrow

glazed with rain
water

beside the white
chickens.

1923

At the Ball Game

The crowd at the ball game
is moved uniformly

by a spirit of uselessness
which delights them—

all the exciting detail
of the chase

and the escape, the error
the flash of genius—

all to no end save beauty
the eternal—

So in detail they, the crowd,
are beautiful

for this
to be warned against

saluted and defied—
It is alive, venomous

it smiles grimly
its words cut—

The flashy female with her
mother, gets it—

The Jew gets it straight—it
is deadly, terrifying—

It is the Inquisition, the
Revolution

It is beauty itself
that lives

day by day in them
idly—

This is
the power of their faces

It is summer, it is the solstice
the crowd is

cheering, the crowd is laughing
in detail

permanently, seriously
without thought

1923

Portrait of a Lady

Your thighs are appletrees
whose blossoms touch the sky.
Which sky? The sky
where Watteau hung a lady's
slipper.[4] Your knees
are a southern breeze—or
a gust of snow. Agh! what
sort of man was Fragonard?
—as if that answered
anything. Ah, yes—below
the knees, since the tune
drops that way, it is
one of those white summer days,
the tall grass of your ankles
flickers upon the shore—
Which shore?—
the sand clings to my lips—
Which shore?
Agh, petals maybe. How
should I know?

4. Jean Antoine Watteau (1684–1721), a French painter, was famous for his pictures of outdoor gatherings of people. However, Williams evidently has in mind "The Swing," a famous painting by another French artist, Jean Honoré Fragonard (1732–1806, line 8), in which the girl on the swing has kicked off her slipper, which hangs perpetually in mid-air.

Which shore? Which shore?
I said petals from an appletree.

1934

The Yachts

contend in a sea which the land partly encloses
shielding them from the too-heavy blows
of an ungoverned ocean which when it chooses

tortures the biggest hulls, the best man knows
to pit against its beatings, and sinks them pitilessly.
Mothlike in mists, scintillant in the minute

brilliance of cloudless days, with broad bellying sails
they glide to the wind tossing green water
from their sharp prows while over them the crew crawls

ant-like, solicitously grooming them, releasing,
making fast as they turn, lean far over and having
caught the wind again, side by side, head for the mark.

In a well guarded arena of open water surrounded by
lesser and greater craft which, sycophant, lumbering
and flittering follow them, they appear youthful, rare

as the light of a happy eye, live with the grace
of all that in the mind is fleckless, free and
naturally to be desired. Now the sea which holds them

is moody, lapping their glossy sides, as if feeling
for some slightest flaw but fails completely.
Today no race. Then the wind comes again. The yachts

move, jockeying for a start, the signal is set and they
are off. Now the waves strike at them but they are too
well made, they slip through, though they take in canvas.[5]

Arms with hands grasping seek to clutch at the prows.
Bodies thrown recklessly in the way are cut aside.
It is a sea of faces about them in agony, in despair

until the horror of the race dawns staggering the mind,
the whole sea become an entanglement of watery bodies
lost to the world bearing what they cannot hold. Broken,

beaten, desolate, reaching from the dead to be taken up
they cry out, failing, failing! their cries rising
in waves still as the skillful yachts pass over.

1935

5. That is, reduce the area of their sails, thus go slower.

These

are the desolate, dark weeks
when nature in its barrenness
equals the stupidity of man.

The year plunges into night
and the heart plunges
lower than night

to an empty, windswept place
without sun, stars or moon
but a peculiar light as of thought

that spins a dark fire—
whirling upon itself until,
in the cold, it kindles

to make a man aware of nothing
that he knows, not loneliness
itself—Not a ghost but

would be embraced—emptiness,
despair—(They
whine and whistle) among

the flashes and booms of war;
houses of whose rooms
the cold is greater than can be thought,

the people gone that we loved,
the beds lying empty, the couches
damp, the chairs unused—

Hide it away somewhere
out of the mind, let it get roots
and grow, unrelated to jealous

ears and eyes—for itself.
In this mine they come to dig—all.
Is this the counterfoil[6] to sweetest

music? The source of poetry that
seeing the clock stopped, says,
The clock has stopped

that ticked yesterday so well?
and hears the sound of lakewater
splashing—that is now stone.

1938

6. For example, a check stub.

The Dance

In Breughel's great picture, The Kermess,[8]
the dancers go round, they go round and
around, the squeal and the blare and the
tweedle of bagpipes, a bugle and fiddles
tipping their bellies (round as the thick-
sided glasses whose wash they impound)
their hips and their bellies off balance
to turn them. Kicking and rolling about
the Fair Grounds, swinging their butts, those
shanks must be sound to bear up under such
rollicking measures, prance as they dance
in Breughel's great picture, The Kermess.

1944

Burning the Christmas Greens

Their time past, pulled down
cracked and flung to the fire
—go up in a roar

All recognition lost, burnt clean
clean in the flame, the green
dispersed, a living red,
flame red, red as blood wakes
on the ash—

and ebbs to a steady burning
the rekindled bed become
a landscape of flame

At the winter's midnight
we went to the trees, the coarse
holly, the balsam and
the hemlock for their green

At the thick of the dark
the moment of the cold's
deepest plunge we brought branches
cut from the green trees

to fill our need, and over
doorways, about paper Christmas
bells covered with tinfoil
and fastened by red ribbons

8. Pieter Brueghel the Elder (c. 1525–1569), the Flemish painter, was most famous for his pictures of peasant life, set in ordinary Dutch farms and villages. A kermess is an outdoor festival or fair held to benefit a church on the town's patron saint's day.

we stuck the green prongs
in the windows hung
woven wreaths and above pictures
the living green. On the

mantle we built a green forest
and among those hemlock
sprays put a herd of small
white deer as if they

were walking there. All this!
and it seemed gentle and good
to us. Their time past,
relief! The room bare. We

stuffed the dead grate
with them upon the half burnt out
log's smoldering eye, opening
red and closing under them

and we stood there looking down.
Green is a solace
a promise of peace, a fort
against the cold (though we

did not say so) a challenge
above the snow's
hard shell. Green (we might
have said) that, where

small birds hide and dodge
and lift their plaintive
rallying cries, blocks for them
and knocks down

the unseeing bullets of
the storm. Green spruce boughs
pulled down by a weight of
snow—Transformed!

Violence leaped and appeared.
Recreant![9] roared to life
as the flame rose through and
our eyes recoiled from it.

In the jagged flames green
to red, instant and alive. Green!
those sure abutments . . . Gone!
lost to mind

9. One who has renounced formerly held principles or faith.

and quick in the contracting
tunnel of the grate
appeared a world! Black
mountains, black and red—as

yet uncolored—and ash white,
an infant landscape of shimmering
ash and flame and we, in
that instant, lost,

breathless to be witnesses,
as if we stood
ourselves refreshed among
the shining fauna of that fire.

1944

D. H. LAWRENCE
(*1885–1930*)

David Herbert Lawrence was born on September 11, 1885, in Eastwood, Nottinghamshire. His mother was a schoolteacher, his father a miner; their personalities clashed and marked their son's, whose Oedipal feelings play a prominent part in his novel *Sons and Lovers*. Lawrence tended to think of his life as in two parts, the first of them dominated by his mother. Like her he became a schoolteacher, after he had attended the University of Nottingham. He published his first poems in a magazine in 1909. His first novel, *The White Peacock*, appeared in 1911. A month before, in December, his mother had died, and Lawrence felt very conscious of this "wound," as he called it. The second part of his life, a process of recovery, began in April 1912, when he met Frieda von Richthofen Weekley, the wife of a professor of philology at the University of Nottingham and daughter of a German baron. Almost at once they determined to elope to the continent, although Frieda would have to leave her three children behind. Eventually Frieda secured a divorce and Lawrence married her in 1914. Back in England, Lawrence opposed the First World War and was suspected of being a spy. He also encountered legal opposition to his novel *The Rainbow* (1915), which was declared obscene; all copies of the book were seized by the police. The obscenity question bedeviled him for the rest of his life. As soon as the war was over, he and his wife left for Italy. They were to travel about a great deal during the remaining years of Lawrence's life. One extended sojourn was at Taos, New Mexico, where he was surrounded by women admirers. He died at Vence, France, on March 4, 1930, of tuberculosis.

Piano

Softly, in the dusk, a woman is singing to me;
Taking me back down the vista of years, till I see
A child sitting under the piano, in the boom of the tingling strings
And pressing the small, poised feet of a mother who smiles as she sings.

In spite of myself, the insidious mastery of song
Betrays me back, till the heart of me weeps to belong
To the old Sunday evenings at home, with winter outside
And hymns in the cosy parlour, the tinkling piano our guide.

So now it is vain for the singer to burst into clamour
With the great black piano appassionato.[1] The glamour
Of childish days is upon me, my manhood is cast
Down in the flood of remembrance, I weep like a child for the past.

1918

Tortoise Gallantry

Making his advances
He does not look at her, nor sniff at her,
No, not even sniff at her, his nose is blank.

Only he senses the vulnerable folds of skin
That work beneath her while she sprawls along
In her ungainly pace,
Her folds of skin that work and row
Beneath the earth-soiled hovel in which she moves.

And so he strains beneath her housey walls
And catches her trouser-legs in his beak
Suddenly, or her skinny limb,
And strange and grimly drags at her
Like a dog,
Only agelessly silent, with a reptile's awful persistency.

Grim, gruesome gallantry, to which he is doomed.
Dragged out of an eternity of silent isolation
And doomed to partiality, partial being,
Ache, and want of being,
Want,
Self-exposure, hard humiliation, need to add himself on to her.

Born to walk alone,
Fore-runner,
Now suddenly distracted into this mazy side-track,
This awkward, harrowing pursuit,
This grim necessity from within.

Does she know
As she moves eternally slowly away?
Or is he driven against her with a bang, like a bird flying in the dark
against a window,
All knowledgeless?

1. A musical direction, meaning "impassioned."

The awful concussion,
And the still more awful need to persist, to follow, follow, continue,

Driven, after æons of pristine, fore-god-like singleness and oneness,
At the end of some mysterious, red-hot iron,
Driven away from himself into her tracks,
Forced to crash against her.

Stiff, gallant, irascible, crook-legged reptile,
Little gentleman,
Sorry plight,
We ought to look the other way.

Save that, having come with you so far,
We will go on to the end.

1923

Snake

A snake came to my water-trough
On a hot, hot day, and I in pyjamas for the heat,
To drink there.

In the deep, strange-scented shade of the great dark carob-tree [2]
I came down the steps with my pitcher
And must wait, must stand and wait, for there he was at the trough before me.

He reached down from a fissure in the earth-wall in the gloom
And trailed his yellow-brown slackness soft-bellied down, over the edge of the stone trough
And rested his throat upon the stone bottom,
And where the water had dripped from the tap, in a small clearness,
He sipped with his straight mouth,
Softly drank through his straight gums, into his slack long body,
Silently.

Someone was before me at my water-trough,
And I, like a second comer, waiting.

He lifted his head from his drinking, as cattle do,
And looked at me vaguely, as drinking cattle do,
And flickered his two-forked tongue from his lips, and mused a moment,
And stooped and drank a little more,
Being earth-brown, earth-golden from the burning bowels of the earth
On the day of Sicilian July, with Etna[3] smoking.

2. A Mediterranean evergreen. 3. The great Sicilian volcano.

The voice of my education said to me
He must be killed,
For in Sicily the black, black snakes are innocent, the gold are venomous.

And voices in me said, If you were a man
You would take a stick and break him now, and finish him off.

But must I confess how I liked him,
How glad I was he had come like a guest in quiet, to drink at my water-trough
And depart peaceful, pacified, and thankless,
Into the burning bowels of this earth?

Was it cowardice, that I dared not kill him?
Was it perversity, that I longed to talk to him?
Was it humility, to feel so honoured?
I felt so honoured.

And yet those voices:
If you were not afraid, you would kill him!

And truly I was afraid, I was most afraid,
But even so, honoured still more
That he should seek my hospitality
From out the dark door of the secret earth.

He drank enough
And lifted his head, dreamily, as one who has drunken,
And flickered his tongue like a forked night on the air, so black;
Seeming to lick his lips,

And looked around like a god, unseeing, into the air,
And slowly turned his head,
And slowly, very slowly, as if thrice adream,
Proceeded to draw his slow length curving round
And climb again the broken bank of my wall-face.

And as he put his head into that dreadful hole,
And as he slowly drew up, snake-easing his shoulders, and entered farther,
A sort of horror, a sort of protest against his withdrawing into that horrid black hole,
Deliberately going into the blackness, and slowly drawing himself after,
Overcame me now his back was turned.

I looked round, I put down my pitcher,
I picked up a clumsy log
And threw it at the water-trough with a clatter.

I think it did not hit him,
But suddenly that part of him that was left behind convulsed in undignified haste,
Writhed like lightning, and was gone
Into the black hole, the earth-lipped fissure in the wall-front,
At which, in the intense still noon, I stared with fascination.

And immediately I regretted it.
I thought how paltry, how vulgar, what a mean act!
I despised myself and the voices of my accursed human education.

And I thought of the albatross,[4]
And I wished he would come back, my snake.

For he seemed to me again like a king,
Like a king in exile, uncrowned in the underworld,
Now due to be crowned again.

And so, I missed my chance with one of the lords
Of life.
And I have something to expiate;
A pettiness.

1923

When I Went to the Circus——

When I went to the circus that had pitched on the waste lot
it was full of uneasy people
frightened of the bare earth and the temporary canvas
and the smell of horses and other beasts
instead of merely the smell of man.

Monkeys rode rather grey and wizened
on curly plump piebald ponies
and the children uttered a little cry—
and dogs jumped through hoops and turned somersaults
and then the geese scuttled in in a little flock
and round the ring they went to the sound of the whip
then doubled, and back, with a funny up-flutter of wings—
and the children suddenly shouted out.
Then came the hush again, like a hush of fear.

The tight-rope lady, pink and blonde and nude-looking, with a few gold spangles
footed cautiously out on the rope, turned prettily, spun round
bowed, and lifted her foot in her hand, smiled, swung her parasol

4. In Coleridge's *Rime of the Ancient Mariner,* a ship and its crew fall under a curse when the Mariner wantonly shoots an albatross.

to another balance, tripped round, poised, and slowly sank
her handsome thighs down, down, till she slept her splendid body on the rope.
When she rose, tilting her parasol, and smiled at the cautious people
they cheered, but nervously.

The trapeze man, slim and beautiful and like a fish in the air
swung great curves through the upper space, and came down like a star
—And the people applauded, with hollow, frightened applause.

The elephants, huge and grey, loomed their curved bulk through the dusk
and sat up, taking strange postures, showing the pink soles of their feet
and curling their precious live trunks like ammonites [5]
and moving always with a soft slow precision
as when a great ship moves to anchor.
The people watched and wondered, and seemed to resent the mystery that lies in beasts.

Horses, gay horses, swirling round and plaiting
in a long line, their heads laid over each other's necks;
they were happy, they enjoyed it;
all the creatures seemed to enjoy the game
in the circus, with their circus people.

But the audience, compelled to wonder
compelled to admire the bright rhythms of moving bodies
compelled to see the delicate skill of flickering human bodies
flesh flamey and a little heroic, even in a tumbling clown,
they were not really happy.
There was no gushing response, as there is at the film.

When modern people see the carnal body dauntless and flickering gay
playing among the elements neatly, beyond competition
and displaying no personality,
modern people are depressed.
Modern people feel themselves at a disadvantage.
They know they have no bodies that could play among the elements.
They have only their personalities, that are best seen flat, on the film,
flat personalities in two dimensions, imponderable and touchless.

And they grudge the circus people the swooping gay weight of limbs
that flower in mere movement,
and they grudge them the immediate, physical understanding they have with their circus beasts,
and they grudge them their circus-life altogether.
Yet the strange, almost frightened shout of delight that comes now and then from the children

5. Flat spiral shellfish of the Mesozoic age.

shows that the children vaguely know how cheated they are of their
birthright
in the bright wild circus flesh.

1929

When I Read Shakespeare——

When I read Shakespeare I am struck with wonder
that such trivial people should muse and thunder
in such lovely language.

Lear, the old buffer, you wonder his daughters
didn't treat him rougher,
the old chough, the old chuffer!

And Hamlet, how boring, how boring to live with,
so mean and self-conscious, blowing and snoring
his wonderful speeches, full of other folks' whoring!

And Macbeth and his Lady, who should have been choring,
such suburban ambition, so messily goring
old Duncan with daggers!

How boring, how small Shakespeare's people are!
Yet the language so lovely! like the dyes from gas-tar.

1929

Bavarian Gentians[8]

Not every man has gentians in his house
in Soft September, at slow, sad Michaelmas.[9]

Bavarian gentians, big and dark, only dark
darkening the day-time, torch-like with the smoking blueness of Pluto's
gloom,[1]
ribbed and torch-like, with their blaze of darkness spread blue
down flattening into points, flattened under the sweep of white day
torch-flower of the blue-smoking darkness, Pluto's dark-blue daze,
black lamps from the halls of Dis, burning dark blue,
giving off darkness, blue darkness, as Demeter's pale lamps give off
light,
lead me then, lead the way.

Reach me a gentian, give me a torch!
let me guide myself with the blue, forked torch of this flower

8. A blue, trumpet-shaped, Alpine flower.

9. September 29, the feast celebrating the Archangel Michael.

1. Pluto, in Roman mythology, ruled the underworld (or Dis). He abducted Persephone, daughter of the grain goddess Demeter, and made her his queen; she was allowed to return from the underworld in April and remain with her mother for six months, but in September had to rejoin her husband.

down the darker and darker stairs, where blue is darkened on blueness
even where Persephone goes, just now, from the frosted September
to the sightless realm where darkness is awake upon the dark
and Persephone herself is but a voice
or a darkness invisible enfolded in the deeper dark
of the arms Plutonic, and pierced with the passion of dense gloom,
among the splendour of torches of darkness, shedding darkness on the
lost bride and her groom.

1932

The Ship of Death[2]

I

Now it is autumn and the falling fruit
and the long journey towards oblivion.

The apples falling like great drops of dew
to bruise themselves an exit from themselves.

And it is time to go, to bid farewell
to one's own self, and find an exit
from the fallen self.

II

Have you built your ship of death, O have you?
O build your ship of death, for you will need it.

The grim frost is at hand, when the apples will fall
thick, almost thundrous, on the hardened earth.

And death is on the air like a smell of ashes!
Ah! can't you smell it?

And in the bruised body, the frightened soul
finds itself shrinking, wincing from the cold
that blows upon it through the orifices.

III

And can a man his own quietus make
with a bare bodkin?[3]

With daggers, bodkins, bullets, man can make
a bruise or break of exit for his life;
but is that a quietus, O tell me, is it quietus?

2. This poem was written near the end of 1929; Lawrence died on March 2, 1930. In his travel book, *Etruscan Places* (1927), Lawrence described ancient Italian tombs in which had been buried, near the body of the dead man, "the little bronze ship that should bear him over to the other world, the vases of jewels for his arraying, the vases of small dishes, the little bronze statuettes and tools, the weapons, the armor: all the amazing impedimenta [heavy baggage] of the important dead."

3. Paraphrased from *Hamlet*, III.i.75–6, in which Prince Hamlet contemplates suicide. *Quietus:* extinguishment of life; *bodkin:* a dagger or stiletto.

Surely not so! for how could murder, even self-murder
ever a quietus make?

IV

O let us talk of quiet that we know,
that we can know, the deep and lovely quiet
of a strong heart at peace!
How can we this, our own quietus, make?

V

Build then the ship of death, for you must take
the longest journey, to oblivion.

And die the death, the long and painful death
that lies between the old self and the new.

Already our bodies are fallen, bruised, badly bruised,
already our souls are oozing through the exit
of the cruel bruise.

Already the dark and endless ocean of the end
is washing in through the breaches of our wounds,
already the flood is upon us.

Oh build your ship of death, your little ark
and furnish it with food, with little cakes, and wine
for the dark flight down oblivion.

VI

Piecemeal the body dies, and the timid soul
has her footing washed away, as the dark flood rises.

We are dying, we are dying, we are all of us dying
and nothing will stay the death-flood rising within us
and soon it will rise on the world, on the outside world.

We are dying, we are dying, piecemeal our bodies are dying
and our strength leaves us,
and our soul cowers naked in the dark rain over the flood,
cowering in the last branches of the tree of our life.

VII

We are dying, we are dying, so all we can do
is now to be willing to die, and to build the ship
of death to carry the soul on the longest journey.

A little ship, with oars and food
and little dishes, and all accoutrements
fitting and ready for the departing soul.

Now launch the small ship, now as the body dies
and life departs, launch out, the fragile soul

in the fragile ship of courage, the ark of faith
with its store of food and little cooking pans
and change of clothes,
upon the flood's black waste
upon the waters of the end
upon the sea of death, where still we sail
darkly, for we cannot steer, and have no port.

There is no port, there is nowhere to go
only the deepening blackness darkening still
blacker upon the soundless, ungurgling flood

darkness at one with darkness, up and down
and sideways utterly dark, so there is no direction any more
and the little ship is there; yet she is gone.
She is not seen, for there is nothing to see her by.
She is gone! gone! and yet
somewhere she is there.
Nowhere!

VIII

And everything is gone, the body is gone
completely under, gone, entirely gone.
The upper darkness is heavy as the lower,
between them the little ship
is gone
she is gone.

It is the end, it is oblivion.

IX

And yet out of eternity, a thread
separates itself on the blackness,
a horizontal thread
that fumes a little with pallor upon the dark.

Is it illusion? or does the pallor fume
A little higher?
Ah wait, wait, for there's the dawn,
the cruel dawn of coming back to life
out of oblivion.

Wait, wait, the little ship
drifting, beneath the deathly ashy grey
of a flood-dawn.

Wait, wait! even so, a flush of yellow
and strangely, O chilled wan soul, a flush of rose.

A flush of rose, and the whole thing starts again.

X

The flood subsides, and the body, like a worn sea-shell
emerges strange and lovely.
And the little ship wings home, faltering and lapsing
on the pink flood,
and the frail soul steps out, into her house again
filling the heart with peace.

Swings the heart renewed with peace
even of oblivion.

Oh build your ship of death, oh build it!
for you will need it.
For the voyage of oblivion awaits you.

1932

EZRA POUND
(*1885–1972*)

Ezra Pound was born on October 30, 1885, in Hailey, Idaho; at the age of two he was taken to Pennsylvania and brought up in the East. He retained a frontiersman's pleasure in thinking about the opening up of the West, and prided himself on the exploits of a grandfather who built a railway; he kept up a rough-and-ready manner, an American bluntness in effete Europe. At the age of sixteen Pound enrolled as a special student (rather than as a degree candidate) at the University of Pennsylvania, to study (as he said) what he thought important. Then in 1903 he matriculated more conventionally at Hamilton College, and took a Ph.B. in 1905. His interests were in romance languages and literatures; he returned as a fellow in these to the University of Pennsylvania in 1905. He took a master of arts degree that year, but much more consequential was his meeting with two poets also just getting started, William Carlos Williams and Hilda Doolittle. Miss Doolittle later became a member of Pound's Imagist group, and Williams and Pound remained friends and critics of each other all their lives.

The next year Pound won a fellowship to go to Provence, Italy, and especially Spain, in preparation for a dissertation on Lope de Vega. This was never to be written. On his return he became an instructor in romance languages at Wabash College in Crawfordsville, Indiana. His generosity in offering his bed to a girl stranded from a burlesque show was construed by his landladies, and then by the college authorities, as immoral behavior; he was discharged but was given the rest of his year's salary, and with this he went to Gibraltar and Venice. From Venice Pound went to London, where for twelve years he remained a continuing sensation, a poetic one-man band. He was extraordinarily generous and disinterestedly critical on behalf of other artists. W. B. Yeats asked Pound's help when in 1912 he felt his style had become abstract. Even Robert Frost was obliged to admit that two or three changes which Pound proposed in "The Death of the Hired Man" were acceptable. Pound may also be said to have discovered James Joyce, first as a poet and then as a prose writer, and to have made possible all his later work.

In 1912, with Hilda Doolittle, Richard Aldington, and F. S. Flint, he founded the Imagist group. Their purpose was to sanction experimentation in verse form and to aim at new modes of perception. But Pound's most congruent literary relationship in England was with T. S. Eliot, whom he met in September 1914. He was astonished to discover that Eliot had "modernized himself on his own," and he quickly obliged Harriet Monroe to publish "Prufrock" and persuaded the editor of the *Egoist*, Harriet Weaver, to publish Eliot's first book, *Prufrock and Other Observations.* Eliot asked Pound's help when in 1921 he had to sift *The Waste Land* out of a mass of ill-assorted material.

Pound did not confine himself to literature: he was friendly with the sculptors Jacob Epstein and Henri Gaudier-Brzeska (about whom he wrote a book), the painter and writer Wyndham Lewis, and others, including, later, Constantin Brancusi; he wrote an opera, *Villon*, and did a book on the American composer George Antheil.

In 1920 Pound left England for Paris, where he lived until 1924. Then he moved to Italy, and by 1928 he had settled in Rapallo. In 1939 he visited the United States for the first time since 1910. The next year he began to give talks on the Rome radio, denouncing President Roosevelt and supporting various activities of Mussolini as conducive to a new society no longer based on money grubbing. After the United States entered the war he continued to give these talks, and so was indicted in 1943 for treason. The following year the U.S. Army arrested him, and he suffered confinement in a stockade in Pisa. This experience was reflected in some of his best poems, the *Pisan Cantos*. In 1945 he was flown to Washington to stand trial but was remanded to St. Elizabeth's Hospital for the criminally insane. When in 1949 he was awarded the Bollingen Prize for poetry, a great furore was raised, and Pound's adherents and detractors argued the merits of his case, and of the poems, for a long time afterwards. In 1958, because of the intercession of various poets, including Frost and MacLeish, and of other sympathizers, the indictment for treason was dismissed. Pound went to Italy and resided for a time with his daughter at Schloss Brunnenburg, near Merano, and then with his longtime companion, Olga Rudge, in Venice. He died there on November 1, 1972.

Portrait d'une Femme[5]

Your mind and you are our Sargasso Sea,[6]
London has swept about you this score years
And bright ships left you this or that in fee:
Ideas, old gossip, oddments of all things,
Strange spars[7] of knowledge and dimmed wares of price.
Great minds have sought you—lacking someone else.
You have been second always. Tragical?

5. Portrait of a woman (Fr).

6. A sea in the north Atlantic which is choked with seaweed; it was widely believed, though eventually disproved, that many ships had been inextricably tangled in the weeds.

7. Bits of a wrecked wooden ship.

No. You preferred it to the usual thing:
One dull man, dulling and uxorious,[8]
One average mind—with one thought less, each year.
Oh, you are patient, I have seen you sit
Hours, where something might have floated up.
And now you pay one. Yes, you richly pay.
You are a person of some interest, one comes to you
And takes strange gain away.
Trophies fished up; some curious suggestion;
Fact that leads nowhere; and a tale or two,
Pregnant with mandrakes,[9] or with something else
That might prove useful and yet never proves,
That never fits a corner or shows use,
Or finds its hour upon the lóom of days:
The tarnished, gaudy, wonderful old work;
Idols and ambergris[1] and rare inlays,
These are your riches, your great store; and yet
For all this sea-hoard of deciduous things,
Strange woods half sodden, and new brighter stuff:
In the slow float of differing light and deep,
No! there is nothing! In the whole and all,
Nothing that's quite your own.
Yet this is you.

1912

The Return

See, they return; ah, see the tentative
Movements, and the slow feet,
The trouble in the pace and the uncertain
Wavering!

See, they[2] return, one, and by one,
With fear, as half-awakened;
As if the snow should hesitate
And murmur in the wind,
and half turn back;
These were the "Wing'd-with-Awe,"
Inviolable.

Gods of the wingèd shoe![3]
With them the silver hounds,
sniffing the trace of air!

8. Excessively fond of or submissive to a wife.

9. An herb whose fleshy, forked root somewhat resembles a human form; traditionally, when pulled from the earth it was believed to scream. Eating it was thought to promote pregnancy.

1. A waxy substance secreted by the sperm whale, and used in making perfumes. It is sometimes found floating in the ocean.

2. A deliberately indistinct reference to the pagan gods.

3. A Homeric epithet, coined by Pound, to identify the gods; Hermes, their messenger, wore winged shoes.

Haie! Haie!
These were the swift to harry;
These the keen-scented;
These were the souls of blood.

Slow on the leash,
pallid the leash-men!

1912

The River-Merchant's Wife: A Letter[4]

While my hair was still cut straight across my forehead
I played about the front gate, pulling flowers.
You came by on bamboo stilts, playing horse,
You walked about my seat, playing with blue plums.
And we went on living in the village of Chokan:
Two small people, without dislike or suspicion.

At fourteen I married My Lord you.
I never laughed, being bashful.
Lowering my head, I looked at the wall.
Called to, a thousand times, I never looked back.

At fifteen I stopped scowling,
I desired my dust to be mingled with yours
Forever and forever and forever.
Why should I climb the look out?

At sixteen you departed,
You went into far Ku-tō-en,[5] by the river of swirling eddies,
And you have been gone five months.
The monkeys make sorrowful noise overhead.

You dragged your feet when you went out.
By the gate now, the moss is grown, the different mosses,
Too deep to clear them away!
The leaves fall early this autumn, in wind.
The paired butterflies are already yellow with August

Over the grass in the West garden;
They hurt me. I grow older.
If you are coming down through the narrows of the river Kiang,

4. This is one of Pound's versions of Chinese poems, based on notes made by the American sinologist Ernest Fenollosa, for whom the Chinese originals were interpreted by various Japanese scholars; Pound uses Japanese spellings of Chinese place-names, and even of the name of the poet, Li Po (701–762), who in Japanese is called Rihaku. This poem is a translation of the first of Li Po's "Two Letters from Chang-Kan" (a suburb of Nanking, called "Chokan" in line 5).

5. An island in the river Ch'ü-t'ang (or Kiang, in Japanese, as in line 26).

Please let me know beforehand,
And I will come out to meet you
As far as Chō-fū-Sa.[6]

1915

A Pact

I make a pact with you, Walt Whitman—
I have detested you long enough.
I come to you as a grown child
Who has had a pig-headed father;
I am old enough now to make friends.
It was you that broke the new wood,
Now is a time for carving.
We have one sap and one root—
Let there be commerce between us.

1916

In a Station of the Metro[7]

The apparition of these faces in the crowd;
Petals on a wet, black bough.

1916

Hugh Selwyn Mauberley

LIFE AND CONTACTS

"Vocat æstus in umbram"
***Nemesianus* Ec. IV.**

E. P. Ode pour L'Election de Son Sepulchre[8]

I

For three years, out of key with his time,
He strove to resuscitate the dead art

6. A beach several hundred miles upstream of Nanking.

7. Of this poem Pound writes in *Gaudier-Brzeska: A Memoir* (1916): "Three years ago in Paris I got out of a 'metro' train at La Concorde, and saw suddenly a beautiful face, and then another and another, and then a beautiful child's face, and then another beautiful woman, and I tried all that day to find words for what this had meant to me, and I could not find any words that seemed to me worthy, or as lovely as that sudden emotion. And that evening . . . I was still trying and I found, suddenly, the expression. I do not mean that I found words, but there came an equation . . . not in speech, but in little splotches of colour. . . . The 'one-image poem' is a form of super-position, that is to say, it is one idea set on top of another. I found it useful in getting out of the impasse in which I had been left by my metro emotion. I wrote a thirty-line poem, and destroyed it. . . . Six months later I made a poem half that length; a year later I made the following *hokku*-like sentence."

8. "Ode on the Choice of His Tomb." Adapted from the title of a poem by Pierre de Ronsard (1524–1585), "De l'election de son sepulchre." The Latin epigraph is from the Fourth Eclogue of Nemesianus, a third-century poet, and means "Summer heat calls us into the shade"; it suggests Mauberley's alienation from the contemporary scene. Pound's note to this poem describes it as "a farewell to London."

Of poetry; to maintain "the sublime"
In the old sense. [8] Wrong from the start—

No, hardly, but seeing he had been born
In a half savage country,[9] out of date;
Bent resolutely on wringing lilies from the acorn;
Capaneus;[1] trout for factitious bait;

Ἴδμεν γάρ τοι πάνθ', ὅσ' ἐνὶ Τροίῃ[2]
Caught in the unstopped ear;
Giving the rocks small lee-way [2a]
The chopped seas held him, therefore, that year.

His true Penelope was Flaubert,[3]
He fished by obstinate isles;
Observed the elegance of Circe's[4] hair
Rather than the mottoes on sun-dials.[5]

Unaffected by "the march of events,"
He passed from men's memory in *l'an trentuniesme*
De son eage; [6] the case presents
No adjunct to the Muses' [7] diadem.

II

The age demanded an image
Of its accelerated grimace,
Something for the modern stage,
Not, at any rate, an Attic [8] grace;

Not, not certainly, the obscure reveries
Of the inward gaze;
Better mendacities
Than the classics in paraphrase!

8. That is, according to Longinus (fl. 1st cent. A.D.) the purported author of the Greek critical work *On the Sublime.* To be sublime, Longinus wrote, a literary work must display excellence in the use of language, express a noble spirit, and delight and move any reader even after frequent readings.

9. The United States.

1. One of the seven warriors who attacked Thebes. Having defied Zeus, he was struck down by a thunderbolt.

2. **Idmen gár toi pánth hós** enì Troíe (Greek): "For we know all the things that in Troy . . ." Part of the Sirens' song in *Odyssey* XII. Odysseus filled the ears of his shipmates with wax so that they would be untempted by the song, but he left his own ears open and had himself lashed to the mast so that he might experience the temptation. "Troíe," pronounced Troh-*ee*-ay, rhymes with "leeway;" bilingual rhymes are a recurring device of the poem.

2a. Clearance, so that the wind would not blow the ship onto the rocks.

3. Gustave Flaubert (1821–1880), the French novelist, is here a symbol of artistic perfectionism. Penelope, Odysseus' wife, was famous for her long faithfulness to her husband.

4. Circe was the sorceress with whom Odysseus spent a year, delaying his return home from the Trojan War.

5. A sundial often carried an inscription warning that time is passing.

6. "In the thirty-first year of his life" (Old French); Pound adapts the first line of the *Grand Testament* by François Villon (1431–c. 1485). Pound was 31 when his book of early poems, *Lustra,* was published.

7. The nine Greek goddesses of song, poetry, and knowledge, to whom the poet conventionally appeals for inspiration.

8. Athenian; usually refers to purity and elegance of style.

The "age demanded" chiefly a mould in plaster,
Made with no loss of time,
A prose kinema,[9] not, not assuredly, alabaster
Or the "sculpture" of rhyme.

III

The tea-rose tea-gown, etc.
Supplants the mousseline of Cos,[7]
The pianola "replaces"
Sappho's barbitos.[8]

Christ follows Dionysus,
Phallic and ambrosial
Made way for macerations;[9]
Caliban casts out Ariel.[1]

All things are a flowing,
Sage Heracleitus says;[2]
But a tawdry cheapness
Shall outlast our days.

Even the Christian beauty
Defects—after Samothrace;[3]
We see *τὸ καλὸν*[4]
Decreed in the market place.

Faun's[5] flesh is not to us,
Nor the saint's vision.
We have the press for wafer;
Franchise for circumcision.[6]

All men, in law, are equals.
Free of Pisistratus,[7]
We choose a knave or an eunuch
To rule over us.

9. Movement (Greek).

7. Cos, a Greek island, was famous in Roman times for its muslin.

8. Lyre (Greek). Sappho (6th century B.C.), the Greek poet, is Pound's type of the classical poet; most of her works survive only in fragments.

9. That is, the ecstatic, sensual celebrations of Dionysus, the Greek god of wine, have been succeeded by the "macerations"—excessive fasting—of Christianity.

1. Caliban, a monstrous creature, and Ariel, a spirit of the air, are characters in Shakespeare's *The Tempest*.

2. Heraclitus (c. 535–475 B.C.), the Greek philosopher, held that everything is in eternal flux and therefore cannot ultimately escape dissolution.

3. A Greek island which was visited by St. Paul on his way to convert the Macedonian Jews to Christianity; perhaps Pound objects to the stern ethic formulated by Paul from Christ's teachings.

4. Tò kalón (Greek): "The Beautiful."

5. In Roman myth, fauns were country deities combining the physical attributes of goats and men.

6. In Christian ritual, the wafer is a thin piece of unleavened bread used in Communion; the circumcision of Christ is a feast day.

7. Pisistratus (d. 527 B.C.), an Athenian tyrant.

O bright Apollo,
τίν' ἄνδρα, τίν' ἥρωα, τίνα θεόν,[8]
What god, man, or hero
Shall I place a tin wreath upon!

IV

These fought in any case,
and some believing,
                    pro domo,[9] in any case . . .

Some quick to arm,
some for adventure,
some from fear of weakness,
some from fear of censure,
some for love of slaughter, in imagination,
learning later . . .
some in fear, learning love of slaughter;

Died some, pro patria,
                    non "dulce" non "et decor" . . .
walked eye-deep in hell
believing in old men's lies, then unbelieving
came home, home to a lie,
home to many deceits,
home to old lies and new infamy;
usury age-old and age-thick
and liars in public places.

Daring as never before, wastage as never before.
Young blood and high blood,
fair cheeks, and fine bodies;

fortitude as never before

frankness as never before,
disillusions as never told in the old days,
hysterias, trench confessions,
laughter out of dead bellies.

V

There died a myriad,
And of the best, among them,
For an old bitch gone in the teeth,
For a botched civilization,

8. Tín ándra, tín hèroa, tína theón (Greek): "What man, what hero, what god," a phrase from the Second Olympian Ode by Pindar (c. 522–c. 402 B.C.), the Greek lyric poet; the original reads, "What god, what hero, what man." Pindar's tone is one of genuine eulogy; Pound puns on "tin," which is the sound of the Greek word for "what."

9. For [one's] home (Latin), a substitution in the phrase from Horace (65–8 B.C.), *Odes*, III, ii, line 13: "Dulce et decorum est pro patria mori"—"It is sweet and fitting to die for one's country." Pound attacks this sentiment in lines 71–2, inserting the negative "non."

Charm, smiling at the good mouth,
Quick eyes gone under earth's lid,

For two gross of broken statues,
For a few thousand battered books.

* * *

Envoi (1919)[6]

Go, dumb-born book,
Tell her that sang me once that song of Lawes:[7]
Hadst thou but song
As thou hast subjects known,
Then were there cause in thee that should condone
Even my faults that heavy upon me lie,
And build her glories their longevity.

Tell her that sheds
Such treasure in the air,
Recking[8] *naught else but that her graces give*
Life to the moment,
I would bid them live
As roses might, in magic amber laid,
Red overwrought with orange and all made
One substance and one colour
Braving time.

Tell her that goes
With song upon her lips
But sings not out the song, nor knows
The maker of it, some other mouth,
May be as fair as hers,
Might, in new ages, gain her worshippers,
When our two dusts with Waller's shall be laid,
Siftings on siftings in oblivion,
Till change hath broken down
All things save Beauty alone.

1920

6. In literary convention, an envoi is a postscript to a poem commending it to its readers. The poem, presumably written by Mauberley, is an adaptation of "Go, Lovely Rose," a poem by Edmund Waller (1606–1687), part of which reads: "Go, lovely rose! / Tell her that wastes her time and me / That now she knows, / When I resemble her to thee, / How sweet and fair she seems to be. . . . / Then die! that she / The common fate of all things rare / May read in thee; / How small a part of time they share / That are so wondrous sweet and fair!"

7. Henry Lawes (1598–1662), an English composer, set Waller's poem to music; poet and musician are mentioned, with other Elizabethan composers, in the "libretto" (lines 95–111) of Canto 81, p. 369.

8. Caring for.

The Cantos

Ezra Pound began to publish the *Cantos* in 1917, when early versions of the first three appeared. In the end, there were 109 complete Cantos and "drafts and fragments" of eight more. From the beginning he was vague about the final dimensions of the work; his decision in 1969 to publish incomplete versions of the latest additions may have meant that he thought he could do no more.

Pound's intention was to develop a modern epic, a "poem including history," that encompasses not only the world's literature but its art and architecture, myths, economics, the lives of historical figures—in effect "the tale of the tribe"—in a profuse assemblage of particular details that may, or may not, make connections with each other. Underlying this concept are didactic purposes: to present materials which he thinks a civilized reader ought to absorb, and to point, by means of documents and achievements of the past and present, towards a good civilization ruled by right-thinking men of action. The famous obscurity of the *Cantos* results partly from Pound's disjunctive arrangement of his materials, but partly also from the obscurity of the materials themselves; Pound, formidably traveled and read, usually assumes that his readers are as familiar with 16th-century Italian architecture, Provençal lyrics, Confucian philosophy, and medieval economic history as he is, as well as with the nearly dozen languages from which he draws, or into which he translates, many of his allusions.

Cantos 1–7 indicate the poem's procedures and some of its themes. Cantos 8–11 present Sigismundo Malatesta (d. 1468), the Venetian soldier and art patron, as a type of the man of action. Cantos 12–13 contrast modern economic exploitation with the tranquil order of Confucian moral philosophy. Cantos 14–16 describe a passage through hell (in the guise of modern London), ending with a vision of medieval Venice as paradise in Canto 17. American presidents whose policies and personal styles Pound admires are presented in Cantos 31–3 (Jefferson), 34 (John Quincy Adams), 37 (Van Buren), and 62–71 (John Adams); Canto 41 introduces Mussolini, whom Pound, sympathizing with the Fascist economic program and seeming patronage of art, thought the best contemporary leader. As Pound identifies humane civilization and government with Confucian ethics, he sketches a history of ancient China (Cantos 52–61) to show that Chinese prosperity and peace only attended rule by Confucian moral principles—a conclusion that modern historians find dubious. In counterpoint to these "historical" Cantos Pound sets those of the *Fifth Decad of Cantos,* which inveigh against usurious monetary systems (those, according to Pound, based on paper values rather than real ones) and exalt those principles, from the Eleusinian mysteries of ancient Greece to the "social credit" theories of Pound's contemporary C. H. Douglas, which encourage the growth of natural fertility and wealth. During the Second World War Pound wrote two Cantos in Italian which have not been published; at the war's end he was imprisoned near Pisa by the U.S. Army on charges of treason arising from his wartime broadcasts on the Italian radio.

The *Pisan Cantos,* written in the prison camp under great physical and psychological duress while Pound was waiting to be returned to the United States for trial and quite possibly execution, record a "dark night of the soul" through which the poet passes toward a vision of Aphrodite, the goddess of love, and the acceptance of his own death. Available to him were the scenes and events of the detention camp, the Bible, an edition of Confucius, a poetry anthology, and the resources of his extraordinary memory. Under extreme pressure these elements combine, in a "magic moment" recorded in Canto 81. The *Pisan Cantos* are both impressive and difficult, and when they won the Bollingen Prize in 1949 (given by the Library of Congress; the distinguished jury included T. S. Eliot), a controversy was set off involving not only the charge of treason which was still pending against Pound, and the undeniably Fascist and antisemitic passages in parts of the poems, but also a reaction against the aesthetic of post-symbolist "modernism" as exemplified in all the works of Pound and Eliot.

The later Cantos—*Section: Rock Drill* (1955) and *Thrones* (1959)—consolidate the insights of the earlier Cantos and are yet more cryptic. The *Drafts and Fragments of Cantos CX–CXVII* (1969) hint at an apologia: "But the beauty is not the madness / Tho' my errors and wrecks lie about me./ And I am not a demigod, / I cannot make it cohere." (From Canto 116.) In a 1968 conversation with Daniel Cory, Pound said that he had "botched" the work. But despite its unevenness and obscurity, the *Cantos* remains for readers and for other poets one of the great literary challenges and inspirations of the century.

I[5]

And then went down to the ship,
Set keel to breakers, forth on the godly sea, and
We[6] set up mast and sail on that swart ship,
Bore sheep aboard her, and our bodies also
Heavy with weeping, and winds from sternward
Bore us out onward with bellying canvas,
Circe's this craft, the trim-coifed goddess.[7]
Then sat we amidships, wind jamming the tiller,
Thus with stretched sail, we went over sea till day's end.
Sun to his slumber, shadows o'er all the ocean,
Came we then to the bounds of deepest water,
To the Kimmerian lands,[8] and peopled cities
Covered with close-webbed mist, unpierced ever
With glitter of sun rays
Nor with stars stretched, nor looking back from heaven
Swartest night stretched over wretched men there.
The ocean flowing backward, came we then to the place
Aforesaid by Circe.
Here did they rites, Perimedes and Eurylochus,[9]
And drawing sword from my hip

5. This Canto is, until line 68, a free translation of the opening of *Odyssey*, XI, which describes Odysseus' voyage to the end of the earth, where he summons up spirits from the underworld. The verse is alliterative, resembling that of Old English poetry, perhaps to suggest the archaic and archetypal character of this Odyssean experience.

6. Odysseus and his shipmates. *Swart:* dark.

7. Odysseus has just left the island where he lived for a year with the goddess Circe. Following her instructions, he is to go to the mouth of the underworld and there consult the prophet Tiresias about his return to his native Ithaca.

8. The Cimmerii were a mythical people living on the edge of the world.

9. Two of Odysseus' men.

I dug the ell-square pitkin;[1]
Poured we libations unto each the dead,
First mead[1a] and then sweet wine, water mixed with white flour.
Then prayed I many a prayer to the sickly death's-heads;
As set in Ithaca, sterile bulls of the best
For sacrifice, heaping the pyre with goods,
A sheep to Tiresias only, black and a bell-sheep.[2]
Dark blood flowed in the fosse,[3]
Souls out of Erebus,[4] cadaverous dead, of brides
Of youths and of the old who had borne much;
Souls stained with recent tears, girls tender,
Men many, mauled with bronze lance heads,
Battle spoil, bearing yet dreory[5] arms,
These many crowded about me; with shouting,
Pallor upon me, cried to my men for more beasts;
Slaughtered the herds, sheep slain of bronze;
Poured ointment, cried to the gods,
To Pluto the strong, and praised Proserpine;[6]
Unsheathed the narrow sword,
I sat to keep off the impetuous impotent dead,
Till I should hear Tiresias.
But first Elpenor[7] came, our friend Elpenor,
Unburied, cast on the wide earth,
Limbs that we left in the house of Circe,
Unwept, unwrapped in sepulchre, since toils urged other.
Pitiful spirit. And I cried in hurried speech:
"Elpenor, how art thou come to this dark coast?
Cam'st thou afoot, outstripping seamen?"

And he in heavy speech:
"Ill fate and abundant wine. I slept in Circe's ingle.[7a]
Going down the long ladder unguarded,
I fell against the buttress,
Shattered the nape-nerve, the soul sought Avernus.[8]
But thou, O King, I bid remember me, unwept, unburied,
Heap up mine arms, be tomb by sea-bord, and inscribed:
A man of no fortune, and with a name to come.
And set my oar up, that I swung mid fellows."
And Anticlea[9] came, whom I beat off, and then Tiresias Theban,

1. A pitkin is Pound's coinage for a small pit; an ell is a measure of length, varying from two to four feet.

1a. A fermented beverage of water, malt, and honey.

2. A bell-sheep is the one which leads the herd. Tiresias, a Theban, was granted the gift of prophecy by the gods. Compare *The Waste Land*, III (p. 465).

3. Ditch (Latin).

4. Primeval darkness, Hades.

5. Bloody. (The Old English word is *dreorig*.)

6. Pluto was the Roman god of the underworld; Proserpine was his wife.

7. One of Odysseus' companions. He broke his neck in an accidental fall from the roof of Circe's house; because his companions did not discover his death they failed to perform the burial rites.

7a. Hearth.

8. A lake near Cumae and Naples, beside which was the cave through which the Trojan hero Aeneas descended to Hades to learn the future. It is also a name given to the underworld itself.

9. The mother of Odysseus. In the *Odyssey*, Odysseus weeps at the sight of his mother (a detail omitted by Pound), but at Circe's instruction will not allow her to drink the blood, and so to speak with him, until Tiresias has done so.

Holding his golden wand, knew me, and spoke first:
"A second time?[1] why? man of ill star,
Facing the sunless dead and this joyless region?
Stand from the fosse, leave me my bloody bever[2]
For soothsay."
And I stepped back,
And he strong with the blood, said then: "Odysseus
Shalt return through spiteful Neptune,[3] over dark seas,
Lose all companions." And then Anticlea came.
Lie quiet Divus. I mean, that is Andreas Divus,
In officina Wecheli, 1538, out of Homer.[4]
And he sailed, by Sirens and thence outward and away
And unto Circe.[5]
Venerandam,[6]
In the Cretan's phrase, with the golden crown, Aphrodite,
Cypri munimenta sortita est,[7] mirthful, orichalchi,[8] with golden
Girdles and breast bands, thou with dark eyelids
Bearing the golden bough of Argicida.[9] So that:

1917, 1925

LXXXI

Zeus lies in Ceres' bosom[3]
Taishan[4] is attended of loves
under Cythera,[5] before sunrise
and he said: "Hay aquí mucho catolicismo—(sounded catoli*th*ismo)
y muy poco reliHión"[6]
and he said: "Yo creo que los reyes desaparecen"[7]
(Kings will, I think, disappear)

1. They have met before, in the upper world.
2. Potation (Middle English).
3. An allusion to the shipwreck Odysseus was to undergo. Neptune was the Roman sea-god.
4. Pound here acknowledges that he has been following not the original Greek but a medieval Latin translation of Homer by Andreas Divus, published by the workshop of Wechel in Paris in 1538. Hence also Pound's use of the Roman names for the gods. With these words he abruptly turns from the *Odyssey*.
5. Actually, Odysseus first returned to Circe and then went on past the Sirens, creatures whose singing had often lured sailors to wreck their boats on the rocks.
6. Commanding reverence (Latin). This is the epithet given to Aphrodite in what is known as the second Homeric Hymn. (These Greek hymns were not in fact written by Homer.) Pound is again working from a Latin translation, this one by Georgius Dartona Cretensis ("the Cretan"); it was included in Pound's copy of Divus' Latin *Odyssey*.
7. The citadels of Cyprus were her appointed realm (Latin).
8. Of copper (Latin). The Hymn recounts how a votive gift of copper and gold was made, by the attendant hours, to Aphrodite.
9. Argicida, an epithet usually given to Hermes, the gods' messenger, means "Slayer of Argus" (a mythical herdsman with eyes all over his body, whose watchfulness the goddess Hera had counted on to prevent her husband Zeus from an affair with the mortal woman Io). But Pound is perhaps conferring the epithet upon Aphrodite as slayer of the Argi (Greeks) during the Trojan War. The golden bough was Aeneas' offering to Proserpina before his descent to Hades, and is usually associated with Diana and the sacred wood of Nemi rather than Aphrodite. The Canto's abrupt ending may be taken to suggest that it is not complete in itself, but part of a larger work—the *Cantos*.

3. Zeus, the ruler of the Greek gods, is sometimes said to have married his sister Ceres, the goddess of agriculture and natural fertility.
4. A sacred mountain in China, which Pound identified with a cone-shaped mountain visible from his cage in the Disciplinary Training Center near Pisa.
5. Aphrodite, goddess of love; Cythera was an island sacred to her.
6. "There is much Catholicism here and very little religion" (Spanish). The parenthetical instruction is a direction for reading the Canto aloud, and is not itself to be spoken.
7. Translated in the next line.

That was Padre José Elizondo[8]
in 1906 and in 1917
or about 1917
and Dolores said "Come pan, niño," (eat bread, me lad)
Sargent[9] had painted her
before he descended
(i.e. if he descended)
but in those days he did thumb sketches,
impressions of the Velásquez in the Museo del Prado
and books cost a peseta,
brass candlesticks in proportion,
hot wind came from the marshes
and death-chill from the mountains.
And later Bowers[1] wrote: "but such hatred,
I had never conceived such"
and the London reds wouldn't show up his friends
(i.e. friends of Franco
working in London) and in Alcázar[2]
forty years gone, they said: "Go back to the station to eat,
you can sleep here for a peseta"
goat bells tinkled all night
and the hostess grinned: "Eso es luto, *haw*!
mi marido es muerto"[3]
(it is mourning, my husband is dead)
when she gave me paper of the locanda[3a] to write on
with a black border half an inch or more deep, say 5/8ths,
"We call *all* foreigners frenchies"
and the egg broke in Cabranez' pocket,
thus making history.[4] Basil says
they beat drums for three days
till all the drumheads were busted
(simple village fiesta)
and as for his life in the Canaries . . .[5]
Possum[6] observed that the local portagoose folk dance
was danced by the same dancers in divers localities
in political welcome . . .
the technique of demonstration
Cole studied that (not G.D.H., Horace)[7]

8. A Spanish priest who had helped Pound to obtain a photostat of manuscripts by Guido Cavalcanti from the Escorial, the palace of the Spanish kings.

9. John Singer Sargent (1856–1925) was much influenced by Velasquez' paintings even before 1880, when he travelled to Spain and copied "The Maids of Honor" and other paintings in the Prado. Dolores is presumably the subject of one of Sargent's Spanish paintings; later he specialized in portraits of important people.

1. Claude Gernade Bowers (1878–1958) was the American ambassador to Spain during the Spanish Civil War, 1936–9, won by the right-wing faction led by Francisco Franco.

2. Probably Alcazar de San Juan, a town in central Spain.

3. Translated in the following line.

3a. Inn or boarding house (Ital).

4. Perhaps a joke involving one of Pound's Spanish friends; the meaning of this allusion has not been traced.

5. Basil Bunting, the English poet and friend of Pound, lived in the Canary Islands (a Spanish possession off the northwest coast of Africa) from 1933 to 1936 because it was inexpensive, but found the food bad and the Spanish inhabitants cruel.

6. T. S. Eliot (author of *Old Possum's Book of Practical Cats*).

7. Horace Cole was a writer for magazines and a contributor to *20th Century Business Practice;* G. D. H. Cole (1880–1959) was an English economist and novelist.

"You will find" said old André Spire,[8]
"that every man on that board (Crédit Agricole)[9]
has a brother-in-law."
                    "You the one, I the few"
                    said John Adams
speaking of fears in the abstract
        to his volatile friend Mr. Jefferson.
(To break the pentameter, that was the first heave)
or as Jo Bard[1] says: "They never speak to each other,
if it is baker and concierge visibly
            it is La Rochefoucauld and de Maintenon audibly."[2]
"Te caverò le budella"
                    "La corata a te"[3]
In less than a geological epoch
                        said Henry Mencken[4]
"Some cook, some do not cook,
        some things cannot be altered"
Ἴυγξ . . . ἐμὸν ποτί δῶμα τὸν ἄνδρα[5]
What counts is the cultural level,
        thank Benin for this table ex packing box[6]
        "doan yu tell no one I made it"
                    from a mask fine as any in Frankfurt
"It'll get you offn th' groun"
                    Light as the branch of Kuanon[7]
And at first disappointed with shoddy
the bare ramshackle quais,[7a] but then saw the
high buggy wheels
                    and was reconciled,
George Santayana[8] arriving in the port of Boston
and kept to the end of his life that faint *thethear*[9]
of the Spaniard
                    as a grace quasi imperceptible,
as did Muss the *v* for *u* of Romagna,[1]

8. André Spire (1868–1966), a French writer and advocate of Zionism.

9. The French agricultural bank.

1. Joseph Bard, an English essayist.

2. The Duc de la Rochefoucauld (1747–1827) and Madame de Maintenon (1635–1719) here not presented as historical figures but as exemplars of elegant prose style, which, Pound indicates, is inherent in the French language.

3. "I'll cut your guts out!" "And I'll tear the liver out of you!" (Ital) In Canto X this passage is part of an exchange between Sigismondo Malatesta (1417–1468) and his sworn enemy Federigo d'Urbino (1422–1482).

4. ". . . I believe that all schemes of monetary reform collide inevitably with the nature of man in the mass. He can't be convinced in anything less than a geological epoch." (Quoted as part of a letter from Mencken to Pound in *Guide to Kulchur,* p. 182.) Pound observed, "Above statement does not invalidate geological process."

5. Iünx, emòn potí doma ton ándra (Greek): Little wheel, [bring back] that man to my house. From the second Idyll of Theocritus, a dramatic monologue in which a girl uses a magic wheel to cast a spell on her unfaithful lover.

6. A district in Nigeria, famous for its bronze masks; a collection of them was made by the German anthropologist Leo Frobenius (1873–1938) at the Institute for Cultural Morphology in Frankfurt. The incident Pound tells of occurred in the DTC, where a black prisoner named Edwards made him a table.

7. The Chinese goddess of mercy.

7a. Or quays, paved landings in a harbor where ships may tie up for loading and unloading.

8. (1863–1952), the American philosopher; lines 70–80 are based on his *Autobiography.*

9. *Cecear* (Spanish) means the Castilian pronunciation of the soft *c,* with a lisp.

1. Mussolini's dialect, in which the sound *w* was pronounced as *v.*

and said the grief was a full act
        repeated for each new condoleress
working up to a climax.
And George Horace[2] said he wd/ "get Beveridge" (Senator)
Beveridge wouldn't talk and he wouldn't write for the papers
but George got him by campin' in his hotel
and assailin' him at lunch breakfast an' dinner
            three articles
and my ole man went on hoein' corn
    while George was a-tellin' him,
come across a vacant lot
        where you'd occasionally see a wild rabbit
or mebbe only a loose one
    AOI!
    a leaf in the current
                at my grates no Althea[3]

libretto[4]

Yet
Ere the season died a-cold
Borne upon a zephyr's shoulder
I rose through the aureate sky
            Lawes and Jenkins guard thy rest
            Dolmetsch ever be thy guest,[5]
Has he tempered the viol's wood
To enforce both the grave and the acute?
Has he curved us the bowl of the lute?
            Lawes and Jenkins guard thy rest
            Dolmetsch ever be thy guest,
Hast 'ou fashioned so airy a mood
    To draw up leaf from the root?
Hast 'ou found a cloud so light
    As seemed neither mist nor shade?

            Then resolve me, tell me aright
            If Waller sang or Dowland played.[6]

        Your eyen two wol sleye me sodenly
        I may the beauté of hem nat susteyne[7]

2. George Horace Lorimer (1868–1937) was editor of the Saturday Evening Post for over 35 years. He was trying to interview Albert Jeremiah Beveridge (1862–1927), the American Senator and historian.
3. From the poem by Richard Lovelace (1618–1657), "To Althea, from Prison": "When Love with unconfined wings / Hovers within my Gates; / And my divine Althea brings / To whisper at the grates . . ."
4. A text to be sung to music.
5. Henry Lawes (1596–1662) and John Jenkins (1592–1678) were English composers; Lawes made a setting of Waller's poem, "Go, Lovely Rose," which is the source of "Envoi" in Pound's *Hugh Selwyn Mauberley*. Arnold Dolmetsch (1858–1940), the musicologist and builder of modern reconstructions of old instruments, advocated a revival of interest in pre-baroque music.
6. Edmund Waller (1606–1687), the English poet, and John Dowland (1563–1626), the composer and lutenist.
7. From Chaucer's "Merciles Beauté": "Your two eyes will slay me quickly; I may not withstand their beauty."

And for 180 years almost nothing.

Ed ascoltando il leggier mormorio[8]
        there came new subtlety of eyes into my tent,
whether of spirit or hypostasis,[9]
        but what the blindfold hides
or at carnival
                nor any pair showed anger
        Saw but the eyes and stance between the eyes,
colour, diastasis,[1]
        careless or unaware it had not the
    whole tent's room
nor was place for the full Ειδὼς[2]
interpass, penetrate
        casting but shade beyond the other lights
            sky's clear
            night's sea
            green of the mountain pool
            shone from the unmasked eyes in half-mask's space.
What thou lovest well remains,
                        the rest is dross
What thou lov'st well shall not be reft from thee
What thou lov'st well is thy true heritage
Whose world, or mine or theirs
                    or is it of none?
First came the seen, then thus the palpable
        Elysium, though it were in the halls of hell,
What thou lovest well is thy true heritage
What thou lov'st well shall not be reft from thee

The ant's a centaur in his dragon world.
Pull down thy vanity,[3] it is not man
Made courage, or made order, or made grace,
        Pull down thy vanity, I say pull down.
Learn of the green world what can be thy place
In scaled invention or true artistry,
Pull down thy vanity,
                    Paquin pull down!
The green casque has outdone your elegance.[4]

"Master thyself, then others shall thee beare"[5]
        Pull down thy vanity

8. And listening to the light murmur (Ital). Pound has remarked that this is "Not a quotation, merely the author using handy language."
9. The substance of the Godhead; here, possibly Aphrodite.
1. Separation.
2. Eidòs (Greek): knowing.
3. The tone and language of the following passage are reminiscent of *Ecclesiastes* 1: "Saith the preacher, vanity of vanities, all is vanity."
4. The shell of a green insect. Pound had ended the previous Canto with the words, "sunset grand couturier"; Paquin is a Parisian dress designer.
5. A variation on Chaucer's "Ballade of Good Counsel": "Subdue thyself, and others thee shall hear."

Thou art a beaten dog beneath the hail,
A swollen magpie in a fitful sun,
Half black half white
Nor knowst'ou wing from tail
Pull down thy vanity
                How mean thy hates
Fostered in falsity,
                Pull down thy vanity,
Rathe[6] to destroy, niggard in charity,
Pull down thy vanity,
                I say pull down.

But to have done instead of not doing
                this is not vanity
To have, with decency, knocked
That a Blunt[7] should open
            To have gathered from the air a live tradition
or from a fine old eye the unconquered flame
This is not vanity.
        Here error is all in the not done,
all in the diffidence that faltered . . .

1948

6. Quick (Middle English).

7. Wilfred Scawen Blunt (1840–1922), English poet and political writer; in 1914 Pound and Yeats organized a testimonial dinner for him at his house, and Pound's address on the occasion reads in part: "We who are little given to respect, / Respect you."

H. D. (Hilda Doolittle)
(*1886–1961*)

Hilda Doolittle was born in Bethlehem, Pennsylvania, on September 10, 1886. Her father was a professor of mathematics and of astronomy at Lehigh University and later at the University of Pennsylvania. She was educated at private schools in Philadelphia and she studied at Bryn Mawr for a time, but because of ill health she left the college in her sophomore year.

In 1911 H. D. went to Europe for what she thought would be a brief summer's stay. In England she renewed her friendship with Ezra Pound, who several years before had been momentarily in love with her, and he encouraged her to write. At about the same time H. D. met the English poet Richard Aldington, whom she soon married. They collaborated on some translations from the Greek, and after he had gone off to war, she was an assistant editor of the magazine called the *Egoist*. Several years after the war H. D. and Aldington were divorced, and she moved to Switzerland, where she spent most of the remainder of her life. However, she returned to London in 1939 and remained there for six years; inspired by her experience of the Blitz, she composed a trilogy of long meditative poems, *The Walls Do Not Fall* (1944), *Tribute to the Angels* (1945), and *The Flowering of the Rod*

(1946). Her later books include *A Tribute to Freud* (1956)—H. D. had been one of Freud's patients—and *By Avon River* (1949), a celebration of Shakespeare in prose and verse. After the war she returned to Switzerland and died in Zurich on September 29, 1961.

Heat

O wind, rend open the heat,
cut apart the heat,
rend it to tatters.

Fruit cannot drop
through this thick air—
fruit cannot fall into heat
that presses up and blunts
the points of pears
and rounds the grapes.

Cut the heat—
plough through it,
turning it on either side
of your path.

1916

Oread[1]

Whirl up, sea—
whirl your pointed pines,
splash your great pines
on our rocks,
hurl your green over us,
cover us with your pools of fir.

1924

1. A nymph of the mountains.

SIEGFRIED SASSOON (1886–1967)

Siegfried Sassoon was born in London on September 8, 1886, into a prosperous family of English Sephardic Jews. His parents separated when Sassoon was a child; his father died soon thereafter, and he was raised by his mother. He was educated at Marlborough Grammar School and at Clare College, Cambridge, and then spent a few years in London. Sassoon was an attractive young man, well connected and comfortably situated, and his main interests were hunting and poetry. He was taken up by Sir Edward Marsh, a patron of the arts, and for a time figured in the collections of Georgian poetry he began to publish in 1912.

When war broke out in 1914, Sassoon immediately enlisted and went to France as a second lieutenant. His fellow officer Robert Graves showed him his own poems about the war, and Sassoon objected that they were too "realistic," though he would soon change his mind about the war and the proper way to write about it. In 1917 Sassoon was wounded and he was sent home; outraged by the war and the civilians who were profiting from it financially and emotionally, he threw his Military Cross into the sea and did his best to get court-martialed so that he could make his views public. Instead he was judged to be "temporarily insane" and thus denied a hearing; he eventually returned to France, where he was wounded for a second time.

When the war was over, Sassoon, a declared pacifist, toured the United States, reading his poems and speaking against war. He became a Roman Catholic in 1957; he died on September 1, 1967.

"Blighters"

The House is crammed: tier beyond tier they grin
And cackle at the Show, while prancing ranks
Of harlots shrill the chorus, drunk with din;
"We're sure the Kaiser[1] loves the dear old Tanks!"

I'd like to see a Tank come down the stalls,[2]
Lurching to ragtime tunes, or "Home, sweet Home,"—
And there'd be no more jokes in Music-halls
To mock the riddled corpses round Bapaume.[3]

1917

The Fathers

Snug at the club two fathers sat,
Gross, goggle-eyed, and full of chat.
One of them said: "My eldest lad
Writes cheery letters from Bagdad.[5]
But Arthur's getting all the fun
At Arras[6] with his nine-inch gun."

"Yes," wheezed the other, "that's the luck!
My boy's quite broken-hearted, stuck
In England training all this year.
Still, if there's truth in what we hear,
The Huns[7] intend to ask for more

1. Kaiser Wilhelm II, ruler of Germany during the First World War.

2. Orchestra seats

3. A town in northern France, one of the main objectives in the costly but successful Allied offensive against the Hindenburg Line in 1918.

5. Captured by the British in their 1917 campaign against the Turks (then allied with Germany).

6. City in northern France and a key point in the western front in World War I; it was the site of a futile British offensive in April 1917 which cost 132,000 British casualties.

7. The German army.

Before they bolt across the Rhine."
I watched them toddle through the door—
These impotent old friends of mine.

1918

ROBINSON JEFFERS
(*1887–1962*)

Robinson Jeffers was born January 10, 1887, in Pittsburgh; his father was a professor at the Western Theological Seminary there. As a boy Jeffers was sent to boarding schools on the continent in Geneva, Lausanne, Zurich, and Leipzig. He mastered French, Italian, and German, though his work scarcely suggests this cosmopolitanism. He was brought back from school in 1903, and the next year his family moved from Pittsburgh to California. Jeffers entered Occidental College and was graduated at the age of eighteen. He began graduate work at the University of Southern California, and there, in his nineteenth year, his future was determined; he met, in a German class, Mrs. Una Call Kuster. From now on she was his lodestar, but her husband stood in Jeffers' way. The next years passed in a series of false starts: he went off to the University of Zurich in 1906 but came quickly back in 1907 to resume studies at Southern California, though in a different course, medicine. His medical interest flagged, and in 1910 he decided to try forestry at the University of Washington. But in 1911 he was back in California. In 1912 he received a modest legacy and published a book entitled *Flagons and Apples.* Una Kuster's husband began to fade from the scene, and on August 2, 1913, Jeffers married her.

They had planned to go to England, but war broke out. In September 1914 they went to the village of Carmel on the California coast and decided it was there they must live. Jeffers immediately began to have a house built; he was later to build Hawk Tower beside it with his own hands. The rocky coast, the seabirds, the comparative isolation, all suited him.

Jeffers lived intensely but with few outward incidents. Perhaps his greatest fame came when he translated Euripedes' *Medea* into his own manner, and Judith Anderson played the leading role on Broadway. He risked opprobrium by opposing American participation in the Second World War. Since his death on January 20, 1962, he has become a coterie hero, identified with the spectacular Pacific coastline and with basic, violent emotions.

Shine, Perishing Republic

While this America settles in the mould of its vulgarity, heavily thickening to empire,
And protest, only a bubble in the molten mass, pops and sighs out, and the mass hardens,

I sadly smiling remember that the flower fades to make fruit, the fruit rots to make earth.

Out of the mother; and through the spring exultances, ripeness and decadence; and home to the mother.

You making haste haste on decay: not blameworthy; life is good, be it stubbornly long or suddenly
A mortal splendor: meteors are not needed less than mountains: shine, perishing republic.

But for my children, I would have them keep their distance from the thickening center; corruption
Never has been compulsory, when the cities lie at the monster's feet there are left the mountains.

And boys, be in nothing so moderate as in love of man, a clever servant, insufferable master.
There is the trap that catches noblest spirits, that caught—they say—God, when he walked on earth.

1925

Fawn's Foster-Mother

The old woman sits on a bench before the door and quarrels
With her meager pale demoralized daughter.
Once when I passed I found her alone, laughing in the sun
And saying that when she was first married
She lived in the old farmhouse up Garapatas Canyon.
(It is empty now, the roof has fallen
But the log walls hang on the stone foundation; the redwoods
Have all been cut down, the oaks are standing;
The place is now more solitary than ever before.)
"When I was nursing my second baby
My husband found a day-old fawn hid in a fern-brake [1]
And brought it; I put its mouth to the breast
Rather than let it starve, I had milk enough for three babies.
Hey, how it sucked, the little nuzzler,
Digging its little hoofs like quills into my stomach.
I had more joy from that than from the others."
Her face is deformed with age, furrowed like a bad road
With market-wagons, mean cares and decay.
She is thrown up to the surface of things, a cell of dry skin
Soon to be shed from the earth's old eyebrows,
I see that once in her spring she lived in the streaming arteries,
The stir of the world, the music of the mountain.

1928

1. Thicket of ferns.

Hurt Hawks

I

The broken pillar of the wing jags from the clotted shoulder,
The wing trails like a banner in defeat,
No more to use the sky forever but live with famine
And pain a few days: cat nor coyote
Will shorten the week of waiting for death, there is game without talons.
He stands under the oak-bush and waits
The lame feet of salvation; at night he remembers freedom
And flies in a dream, the dawns ruin it.
He is strong and pain is worse to the strong, incapacity is worse.
The curs of the day come and torment him
At distance, no one but death the redeemer will humble that head,
The intrepid readiness, the terrible eyes.
The wild God of the world is sometimes merciful to those
That ask mercy, not often to the arrogant.
You do not know him, you communal people, or you have forgotten him;
Intemperate and savage, the hawk remembers him;
Beautiful and wild, the hawks, and men that are dying, remember him.

II

I'd sooner, except the penalties, kill a man than a hawk; but the great redtail
Had nothing left but unable misery
From the bone too shattered for mending, the wing that trailed under his talons when he moved.
We had fed him six weeks, I gave him freedom,
He wandered over the foreland hill and returned in the evening, asking for death,
Not like a beggar, still eyed with the old
Implacable arrogance. I gave him the lead gift in the twilight.
What fell was relaxed,
Owl-downy, soft feminine feathers; but what
Soared: the fierce rush: the night-herons by the flooded river cried fear at its rising
Before it was quite unsheathed from reality.

1928

New Mexican Mountain

I watch the Indians dancing to help the young corn at Taos[4] pueblo. The old men squat in a ring
And make the song, the young women with fat bare arms, and a few shame-faced young men, shuffle the dance.

4. A town in New Mexico.

The lean-muscled young men are naked to the narrow loins, their breasts and backs daubed with white clay,
Two eagle-feathers plume the black heads. They dance with reluctance, they are growing civilized; the old men persuade them.

Only the drum is confident, it thinks the world has not changed; the beating heart, the simplest of rhythms,
It thinks the world has not changed at all; it is only a dreamer, a brainless heart, the drum has no eyes.

These tourists have eyes, the hundred watching the dance, white Americans, hungrily too, with reverence, not laughter;
Pilgrims from civilization, anxiously seeking beauty, religion, poetry; pilgrims from the vacuum.

People from cities, anxious to be human again. Poor show how they suck you empty! The Indians are emptied,
And certainly there was never religion enough, nor beauty nor poetry here . . . to fill Americans.

Only the drum is confident, it thinks the world has not changed. Apparently only myself and the strong
Tribal drum, and the rockhead of Taos mountain, remember that civilization is a transient sickness.

1932

Ave Caesar[7]

No bitterness: our ancestors did it.
They were only ignorant and hopeful, they wanted freedom but wealth too.
Their children will learn to hope for a Caesar.
Or rather—for we are not aquiline Romans but soft mixed colonists—
Some kindly Sicilian tyrant who'll keep
Poverty and Carthage off until the Romans arrive.[8]
We are easy to manage, a gregarious people,
Full of sentiment, clever at mechanics, and we love our luxuries.

1935

7. Hail, Caesar!
8. For over 200 years the towns of Sicily were ruled by tyrants; this was ended by the First Punic War (264–241 B.C.), in which Rome defeated Carthage and annexed Sicily.

EDWIN MUIR
(*1887–1959*)

Edwin Muir was born on May 15, 1887, in Deerness in the Orkney Islands off the coast of Scotland. He was the son of a small tenant farmer and spent his boyhood, as he later came to recognize, in a society which had changed little since the Middle Ages. Muir's recollections of this primitive agricultural life, its daily and seasonal rituals, its folk beliefs and superstitions, are the material for much of his poetry.

When he was thirteen Muir's family had to give up their farm and move to the industrial city of Glasgow, then famous for its prosperity and for its terrible slums, which were thought to be the worst in the British Isles. His parents found life in the city unbearable and by the time Muir was 18 both were dead. Muir moved from one shabby job to another. He had left school at 14 and was forced to continue his education on his own. In June 1919 Muir married Willa Anderson, and he was frequently to say that his marriage was the most important single event of his life. She gave him the courage to devote himself to writing, heartening him to leave Glasgow and move to London, and some years later collaborated with him on their translations of twentieth-century German writers, notably Franz Kafka, whose work had previously been little known in the English-speaking world.

Muir made his living as a journalist—for years he reviewed novels—and as an occasional teacher. He and his wife spent some time in Prague both before and after the Second World War when he lectured on English literature, and for five years he was the Warden of Newbattle, a residential adult education college in Scotland. In 1955–56 he was Charles Eliot Norton Professor at Harvard. He died on January 3, 1959.

Ballad of Hector in Hades[1]

Yes, this is where I stood that day,
  Beside this sunny mound.
The walls of Troy are far away,
  And outward comes no sound.

I wait. On all the empty plain
  A burnished stillness lies,
Save for the chariot's tinkling hum,
  And a few distant cries.

His helmet glitters near. The world
  Slowly turns around,
With some new sleight compels my feet
  From the fighting ground.

I run. If I turned back again
  The earth must turn with me,
The mountains planted on the plain,
  The sky clamped to the sea.

1. Hector, leader of the Trojan army, was killed in battle by the Greek hero Achilles, who dragged the dead body behind his chariot around the walls of Troy. Muir, in his *Autobiography* (1954, pp. 42–3), tells of an incident in his own childhood which inspired this poem. Another boy had chased him home from school: "What I was afraid of I did not know; it was not Freddie, but something else. . . . I was seven at the time, and in the middle of my guilty fears. On that summer afternoon they took the shape of Freddie Sinclair, and turned him into a terrifying figure of vengeance. . . . I got rid of that terror almost thirty years later in a poem describing Achilles chasing Hector round Troy, in which I pictured Hector returning after his death to run the deadly race over again."

The grasses puff a little dust
  Where my footsteps fall.
I cast a shadow as I pass
  The little wayside wall.

The strip of grass on either hand
  Sparkles in the light;
I only see that little space
  To the left and to the right,

And in that space our shadows run,
  His shadow there and mine,
The little flowers, the tiny mounds,
  The grasses frail and fine.

But narrower still and narrower!
  My course is shrunk and small,
Yet vast as in a deadly dream,
  And faint the Trojan wall.
The sun up in the towering sky
  Turns like a spinning ball.

The sky with all its clustered eyes
  Grows still with watching me,
The flowers, the mounds, the flaunting weeds
  Wheel slowly round to see.

Two shadows racing on the grass,
  Silent and so near,
Until his shadow falls on mine.
  And I am rid of fear.

The race is ended. Far away
  I hang and do not care,
While round bright Troy Achilles whirls
  A corpse with streaming hair.

1925

The Horses

Barely a twelvemonth after
The seven days war that put the world to sleep,
Late in the evening the strange horses came.
By then we had made our covenant with silence,
But in the first few days it was so still
We listened to our breathing and were afraid.
On the second day
The radios failed; we turned the knobs; no answer.
On the third day a warship passed us, heading north,
Dead bodies piled on the deck. On the sixth day
A plane plunged over us into the sea. Thereafter

Nothing. The radios dumb;
And still they stand in corners of our kitchens,
And stand, perhaps, turned on, in a million rooms
All over the world. But now if they should speak,
If on a sudden they should speak again,
If on the stroke of noon a voice should speak,
We would not listen, we would not let it bring
That old bad world that swallowed its children quick [7]
At one great gulp. We would not have it again.
Sometimes we think of the nations lying asleep,
Curled blindly in impenetrable sorrow,
And then the thought confounds us with its strangeness.
The tractors lie about our fields; at evening
They look like dank sea-monsters couched and waiting.
We leave them where they are and let them rust:
'They'll moulder away and be like other loam'.
We make our oxen drag our rusty ploughs,
Long laid aside. We have gone back
Far past our fathers' land.
And then, that evening
Late in the summer the strange horses came.
We heard a distant tapping on the road,
A deepening drumming; it stopped, went on again
And at the corner changed to hollow thunder.[8]
We saw the heads
Like a wild wave charging and were afraid.
We had sold our horses in our fathers' time
To buy new tractors. Now they were strange to us
As fabulous steeds set on an ancient shield
Or illustrations in a book of knights.
We did not dare go near them. Yet they waited,
Stubborn and shy, as if they had been sent
By an old command to find our whereabouts
And that long-lost archaic companionship.
In the first moment we had never a thought
That they were creatures to be owned and used.
Among them were some half-a-dozen colts
Dropped in some wilderness of the broken world,
Yet new as if they had come from their own Eden.
Since then they have pulled our ploughs and borne our loads,
But that free servitude still can pierce our hearts.
Our life is changed; their coming our beginning.

1956

7. Alive.

8. In 1958 Muir wrote to a student who had sent him an essay on this poem: "I think you have gone wrong in thinking of the horses as wild horses, or as stampeding. It is less than a year since the seven days' war happened. So the horses are good plough-horses and still have a memory of the world before the war. . . . As for the 'tapping': have you ever listened, on a still evening, to horses trotting in the distance? The sound is really a pretty tapping. The drumming sound indicated that they were drawing nearer: the hollow thunder when they turned the corner meant that they saw the village or farmstead and found their home." (Quoted in P. H. Butter, *Edwin Muir*, p. 260.)

EDITH SITWELL
(1887–1964)

Edith Sitwell was born on September 7, 1887. She was the first child of Sir George Sitwell, baronet, and of Lady Ida, herself the daughter of an earl. She and her two brothers, Osbert and Sacheverell, were inseparable as children and remained so later. It must not be thought that aristocratic surroundings bred happiness. Her father was an extreme eccentric and an impossible parent; as for her mother, she was upset by Edith's unusual features and then by her great height. These might have made for ungainliness, but Edith Sitwell exploited them, by headdresses, jewelry, and Elizabethan or medieval costume, so they became assets. She was often photographed and painted.

Her first poems were published in 1915. In 1916 she became editor of a literary review, *Wheels*, the purpose of which was to stir up the poetic scene. In 1923 Edith Sitwell's *Façade*, with music by William Walton, was performed at the Aeolian Hall in London. She stood behind a painted curtain and intoned the lines. The critics were generally baffled or exasperated; she was to boast afterwards, "Never . . . was a larger and more imposing shower of brickbats hurled at any new work."

In later life, however, she was much honored. She was created a Dame Grand Cross of the British Empire by Elizabeth II and received honorary degrees from Oxford, Cambridge, and other universities. She and her brother Osbert toured the United States to great applause. She died on December 9, 1964.

Aubade[1]

Jane, Jane,
Tall as a crane,
The morning light creaks down again;

Comb your cockscomb[2]-ragged hair,
Jane, Jane, come down the stair.

Each dull blunt wooden stalactite
Of rain creaks, hardened by the light,

Sounding like an overtone
From some lonely world unknown.

1. A morning love song; it laments the coming of day, when lovers part. "The poem is about a country servant, a girl on a farm, plain and neglected and unhappy, and with a sad bucolic stupidity, coming down in the dawn to light the fire; and this phrase means that to her mind the light is an empty thing which conveys nothing. It cannot bring sight to her—she is not capable of seeing anything; it can never bring overtones to her mind, because she is not capable of hearing them. She scarcely knows even that she is suffering." (Sitwell's note).

2. A cockscomb, besides the comb on a rooster's head, is also a spiky red or yellow flower common in England, and further the emblem of a jester or fool.

But the creaking empty light
Will never harden into sight,

Will never penetrate your brain
With overtones like the blunt rain.

The light would show (if it could harden)
Eternities of kitchen garden,

Cockscomb flowers that none will pluck,
And wooden flowers that 'gin to cluck.

In the kitchen you must light
Flames as staring, red and white,

As carrots or as turnips, shining
Where the cold dawn light lies whining.

Cockscomb hair on the cold wind
Hangs limp, turns the milk's weak mind. . . .
Jane, Jane,
Tall as a crane,
The morning light creaks down again!

1923

Country Dance

That hobnailed goblin, the bobtailed Hob,
Said, 'It is time I began to rob.'
For strawberries bob, hob-nob with the pearls
Of cream (like the curls of the dairy girls),
And flushed with the heat and fruitish-ripe
Are the gowns of the maids who dance to the pipe.
Chase a maid?
She's afraid!
'Go gather a bob-cherry kiss from a tree,
But don't, I prithee, come bothering me!'
She said,
As she fled.
The snouted satyrs drink clouted cream[8]
'Neath the chestnut-trees as thick as a dream;
So I went,
And leant,
Where none but the doltish coltish wind
Nuzzled my hand for what it could find.
As it neighed,
I said,
'Don't touch me, sir, don't touch me, I say,

8. Satyrs are ancient Greek deities of the wood, half goat and half man. *Clouted*: clotted.

You'll tumble my strawberries into the hay.'
Those snow-mounds of silver that bee, the spring,
Has sucked his sweetness from, I will bring
With fair-haired plants and with apples chill
For the great god Pan's[9] high altar . . . I'll spill
Not one!
So, in fun,
We rolled on the grass and began to run,
Chasing that gaudy satyr the Sun;
Over the haycocks, away we ran,
Crying, 'Here be berries as sunburnt as Pan!'
But Silenus[1]
Has seen us. . . .
He runs like the rough satyr Sun.
Come away!

1923

Still Falls the Rain

The Raids, 1940.[8] Night and Dawn

Still falls the Rain—
Dark as the world of man, black as our loss—
Blind as the nineteen hundred and forty nails
Upon the Cross.

Still falls the Rain
With a sound like the pulse of the heart that is changed to the hammer-beat
In the Potter's Field,[9] and the sound of the impious feet

On the Tomb:
Still falls the Rain
In the Field of Blood where the small hopes breed and the human brain
Nurtures its greed, that worm with the brow of Cain.

Still falls the Rain
At the feet of the Starved Man hung upon the Cross.
Christ that each day, each night, nails there, have mercy on us—
On Dives and on Lazarus.[1]
Under the Rain the sore and the gold are as one.

9. Pan, a rural god of the Greeks and kin to the satyrs, ruled Arcadia, a mythical pastoral country inhabited by shepherds and shepherdesses.

1. Silenus was Pan's father, and foster-father of Dionysus, Greek god of wine.

8. During the Battle of Britain, the German Air Force carried out many heavy bombing raids on England.

9. A cemetery for foreigners, on land near Jerusalem bought with the blood money thrown away by Judas; it was also called the Field of Blood.

1. In a parable told by Jesus (*Luke* 16:19–31), the rich man Dives was sent to hell, while the leprous beggar Lazarus went to heaven. (This is *not* the same Lazarus who was raised from the dead.)

Still falls the Rain—
Still falls the Blood from the Starved Man's wounded Side:
He bears in His Heart all wounds—those of the light that died,
The last faint spark
In the self-murdered heart, the wounds of the sad uncomprehending
    dark,
The wounds of the baited bear—[2]
The blind and weeping bear whom the keepers beat
On his helpless flesh . . . the tears of the hunted hare.

Still falls the Rain—
Then—O Ile leape up to my God: who pulles me doune—[3]
See, see where Christ's blood streames in the firmament:
It flows from the Brow we nailed upon the tree
Deep to the dying, to the thirsting heart
That holds the fires of the world—dark-smirched with pain
As Caesar's laurel crown.[4]

Then sounds the voice of One who like the heart of man
Was once a child who among beasts has lain—
'Still do I love, still shed my innocent light, my Blood, for thee.'

1942

2. A medieval entertainment in which a pack of dogs fought a bear chained to a post.

3. Faust's cry of despair at the end of Marlowe's play *Dr. Faustus*, when he realizes that he has been damned for his compact with the devil Mephistopheles.

4. A token of victory or preeminence.

MARIANNE MOORE
(*1887–1972*)

Marianne Moore was born on November 15, 1887, in St. Louis, ten months before T. S. Eliot was born in the same city. She was educated in the Metzger Institute, then at Bryn Mawr College. After taking a degree in 1909, she thought of becoming a painter, a profession for which her extraordinary visual sense might seem to have equipped her. But, perhaps as a stopgap, she went to the Carlisle Commercial College and then taught stenography at the government Indian school in Carlisle, Pennsylvania, from 1911 to 1915. In 1918 she moved to New York and worked as a private tutor, as a secretary, and then, from 1921 to 1925, as an assistant in a branch of the New York Public Library. She spent a lot of time in the Bronx Zoo and also at Ebbets Field, where for many years she applauded the Brooklyn Dodgers until their unhappy translation to Los Angeles. From 1926 to 1929, when it ceased publication, she was editor of the *Dial*, a leading review of the time. In later life she did a good deal of public reading of her poems, which she continued to write, impervious to changing modes. She died in New York on February 5, 1972.

The Fish

wade
through black jade.
Of the crow-blue mussel shells, one keeps
adjusting the ash heaps;
opening and shutting itself like

an
injured fan.
The barnacles which encrust the side
of the wave, cannot hide
there for the submerged shafts of the

sun,
split like spun
glass, move themselves with spotlight swiftness
into the crevices—
in and out, illuminating

the
turquoise sea
of bodies. The water drives a wedge
of iron through the iron edge
of the cliff; whereupon the stars,[1]

pink
rice-grains, ink-
bespattered jellyfish, crabs like green
lilies, and submarine
toadstools, slide each on the other.

All
external
marks of abuse are present on this
defiant edifice—
all the physical features of

ac-
cident—lack
of cornice, dynamite grooves, burns, and
hatchet strokes, these things stand
out on it; the chasm side is

dead.
Repeated
evidence has proved that it can live
on what can not revive
its youth. The sea grows old in it.

1921

1. Starfish.

Poetry

I, too, dislike it: there are things that are important beyond all this fiddle.
Reading it, however, with a perfect contempt for it, one discovers in
it after all, a place for the genuine.[2]
Hands that can grasp, eyes
that can dilate, hair that can rise
if it must, these things are important not because a

high-sounding interpretation can be put upon them but because they are
useful. When they become so derivative as to become unintelligible,
the same thing may be said for all of us, that we
do not admire what
we cannot understand: the bat
holding on upside down or in quest of something to
eat, elephants pushing, a wild horse taking a roll, a tireless wolf under
a tree, the immovable critic twitching his skin like a horse that feels a flea, the base-
ball fan, the statistician—
nor is it valid
to discriminate against 'business documents and

school-books';[3] all these phenomena are important. One must make a distinction
however: when dragged into prominence by half poets, the result is not poetry,
nor till the poets among us can be
'literalists of
the imagination'[4]—above
insolence and triviality and can present

for inspection, 'imaginary gardens with real toads in them', shall we have
it. In the meantime, if you demand on the one hand,
the raw material of poetry in
all its rawness and
that which is on the other hand
genuine, you are interested in poetry.

1921

2. In the last edition of her *Collected Poems,* Miss Moore omitted all the poem following this line.

3. Miss Moore's note quotes the *Diaries of Tolstoy*, New York, 1917, p. 94: "Where the boundary between prose and poetry lies, I shall never be able to understand. The question is raised in manuals of style, yet the answer to it lies beyond me. Poetry is verse: prose is not verse. Or else poetry is everything with the exception of business documents and school books."

4. "The limitation of his [Blake's] view was from the very intensity of his vision; he was a too literal realist of imagination as others are of nature; and because he believed that the figures seen by the mind's eye, when exalted by inspiration, were 'eternal existences,' symbols of divine essences, he hated every grace of style that might obscure their lineaments." W. B. Yeats, "William Blake and His Illustrations," in *Ideas of Good and Evil,* London, 1903, p. 182. (Miss Moore gives this reference.)

A Grave

Man looking into the sea,
taking the view from those who have as much right to it as you have to yourself,
it is human nature to stand in the middle of a thing,
but you cannot stand in the middle of this;
the sea has nothing to give but a well excavated grave.
The firs stand in a procession, each with an emerald turkey-foot at the top,
reserved as their contours, saying nothing;
repression, however, is not the most obvious characteristic of the sea;
the sea is a collector, quick to return a rapacious look.
There are others besides you who have worn that look—
whose expression is no longer a protest; the fish no longer investigate them
for their bones have not lasted:
men lower nets, unconscious of the fact that they are desecrating a grave,
and row quickly away—the blades of the oars
moving together like the feet of water-spiders as if there were no such thing as death.
The wrinkles progress among themselves in a phalanx—beautiful under networks of foam,
and fade breathlessly while the sea rustles in and out of the seaweed;
the birds swim through the air at top speed, emitting catcalls as heretofore—
the tortoise-shell scourges about the feet of the cliffs, in motion beneath them;
and the ocean, under the pulsation of lighthouses and noise of bell-buoys,
advances as usual, looking as if it were not that ocean in which dropped things are bound to sink—
in which if they turn and twist, it is neither with volition nor consciousness.

1924

The Pangolin[8]

Another armored animal—scale
lapping scale with spruce-cone regularity until they
form the uninterrupted central
tail-row! This near artichoke with head and legs and grit-equipped gizzard,
the night miniature artist engineer is,
yes, Leonardo da Vinci's replica[9]—
impressive animal and toiler of whom we seldom hear.
Armor seems extra. But for him,

8. The pangolin is an anteater.
9. Leonardo da Vinci (1452–1519) created not only works of art but also designs for armored war vehicles.

the closing ear-ridge—
or bare ear lacking even this small
eminence and similarly safe

contracting nose and eye apertures
impenetrably closable, are not; a true ant-eater,
not cockroach-eater, who endures
exhausting solitary trips through unfamiliar ground at night,
returning before sunrise; stepping in the moonlight,
on the moonlight peculiarly, that the outside
edges of his hands may bear the weight and save the claws
for digging. Serpentined about
the tree, he draws
away from danger unpugnaciously,
with no sound but a harmless hiss; keeping

the fragile grace of the Thomas-
of-Leighton Buzzard Westminster Abbey wrought-iron vine,[1] or
rolls himself into a ball that has
power to defy all effort to unroll it; strongly intailed, neat
head for core, on neck not breaking off, with curled-in feet.
Nevertheless he has sting-proof scales; and nest
of rocks closed with earth from inside, which he can thus
darken.
Sun and moon and day and night and man and beast
each with a splendor
which man in all his vileness cannot
set aside; each with an excellence!

"Fearful yet to be feared," the armored
ant-eater met by the driver-ant[2] does not turn back, but
engulfs what he can, the flattened sword-
edged leafpoints on the tail and artichoke set leg- and body-plates
quivering violently when it retaliates
and swarms on him. Compact like the furled fringed frill
on the hat-brim of Gargallo's[3] hollow iron head of a
matador, he will drop and will
then walk away
unhurt, although if unintruded on,
he cautiously works down the tree, helped

by his tail. The giant-pangolin-
tail, graceful tool, as prop or hand or broom or ax, tipped like
an elephant's trunk with special skin,
is not lost on this ant- and stone-swallowing uninjurable
artichoke which simpletons thought a living fable

1. Describes a grate above the tomb of Eleanor of Castile (d. 1290) near the main altar; its design is the intertwining of 28 vines. The maker was a master smith named Thomas from the ancient market town of Leighton Buzzard, 40 miles from London.

2. A species of ant that moves in vast armies and eats plants and small animals.

3. Pablo Gargallo (1881–1934), Spanish sculptor who worked in iron.

whom the stones had nourished, whereas ants had done
so. Pangolins are not aggressive animals; between
dusk and day they have the not unchain-like machine-like
form and frictionless creep of a thing
made graceful by adversities, con-

versities.[4] To explain grace requires
a curious hand. If that which is at all were not forever,
why would those who graced the spires
with animals and gathered there to rest, on cold luxurious
low stone seats—a monk and monk and monk—between the thus
ingenious roof supports, have slaved to confuse
grace with a kindly manner, time in which to pay a debt,
the cure for sins, a graceful use
of what are yet
approved stone mullions[5] branching out across
the perpendiculars? A sailboat

was the first machine. Pangolins, made
for moving quietly also, are models of exactness,
on four legs; on hind feet plantigrade,[6]
with certain postures of a man. Beneath sun and moon, man slaving
to make his life more sweet, leaves half the flowers worth having,
needing to choose wisely how to use his strength;
a paper-maker like the wasp; a tractor of foodstuffs,
like the ant; spidering a length
of web from bluffs
above a stream; in fighting, mechanicked
like the pangolin; capsizing in

disheartenment. Bedizened or stark
naked, man, the self, the being we call human, writing-
master to this world, griffons[7] a dark
"Like does not like like that is obnoxious"; and writes error with four
r's. Among animals, *one* has a sense of humor.
Humor saves a few steps, it saves years. Unignorant,
modest and unemotional, and all emotion,
he has everlasting vigor,
power to grow,
though there are few creatures who can make one
breathe faster and make one erecter.

Not afraid of anything is he,
and then goes cowering forth, tread paced to meet an obstacle
at every step. Consistent with the
formula—warm blood, no gills, two pairs of hands and a few hairs—
that

4. A coinage; perhaps, "turnings back."
5. Nonstructural, decorative bars in the design of a window.
6. Walking on the soles of the feet, with the heel touching the ground.
7. A griffon is a mythical monster, half eagle and half lion.

is a mammal; there he sits in his own habitat,
serge-clad, strong-shod. The prey of fear, he, always
curtailed, extinguished, thwarted by the dusk, work partly done,
says to the alternating blaze,
"Again the sun!
anew each day; and new and new and new,
that comes into and steadies my soul."

1936

What Are Years?

What is our innocence,
what is our guilt? All are
naked, none is safe. And whence
is courage: the unanswered question,
the resolute doubt—
dumbly calling, deafly listening—that
is misfortune, even death,
encourages others
and in its defeat, stirs

the soul to be strong? He
sees deep and is glad, who
accedes to mortality
and in his imprisonment rises
upon himself as
the sea in a chasm, struggling to be
free and unable to be,
in its surrendering
finds its continuing.

So he who strongly feels,
behaves. The very bird,
grown taller as he sings, steels
his form straight up. Though he is captive,
his mighty singing
says, satisfaction is a lowly
thing, how pure a thing is joy.
This is mortality,
this is eternity.

1941

JOHN CROWE RANSOM
(*1888–1974*)

John Crowe Ransom was born on April 30, 1888, in Pulaski, Tennessee. He received an A.B. degree from Vanderbilt in 1909, and as a Rhodes scholar took a B.A. at Christ Church, Oxford in 1913. Ransom was a lieutenant in the First World War. Afterwards he returned to Vanderbilt, where he had already done some teaching, and remained there until 1937. While there, he was joined by fellow teachers and by such students as Allen Tate and Robert Penn Warren in a group calling itself "the Fugitives"; they read and criticized each others' poems, and published them (and others) in a periodical they called *The Fugitive.*

In 1937, to the surprise of many, Ransom moved north to Kenyon College and became founder and editor of the *Kenyon Review*, which was to be the best known, and very likely the best, literary review in the United States from 1937 until Ransom's retirement in 1959. He also published two important books of criticism, *The World's Body* (1938) and *The New Criticism* (1941), the second of which gave its name to the critical theory which after the Second World War came to dominate literary scholarship and teaching. In his later years Ransom reviewed and revised his earlier poems, and their issuance in 1963 as a new volume of *Selected Poems* was the occasion for him to receive the Bollingen Prize. He died on July 3, 1974.

Bells for John Whiteside's Daughter

There was such speed in her little body,
And such lightness in her footfall,
It is no wonder her brown study[1]
Astonishes us all.

Her wars were bruited[2] in our high window.
We looked among orchard trees and beyond
Where she took arms against her shadow,
Or harried unto the pond

The lazy geese, like a snow cloud
Dripping their snow on the green grass,
Tricking and stopping, sleepy and proud,
Who cried in goose, Alas,

For the tireless heart within the little
Lady with rod that made them rise
From their noon apple-dreams and scuttle
Goose-fashion under the skies!

But now go the bells, and we are ready,
In one house we are sternly stopped
To say we are vexed at her brown study,
Lying so primly propped.

1924

1. A state of serious, absorbed mental activity.

2. Reported, made known.

Here Lies a Lady

Here lies a lady of beauty and high degree,
Of chills and fever she died, of fever and chills,
The delight of her husband, an aunt, an infant of three
And medicos marveling sweetly on her ills.

First she was hot, and her brightest eyes would blaze
And the speed of her flying fingers shook their heads.
What was she making? God knows; she sat in those days
With her newest gowns all torn, or snipt into shreds.

But that would pass, and the fire of her cheeks decline
Till she lay dishonored and wan like a rose overblown,
And would not open her eyes, to kisses, to wine;
The sixth of which states was final. The cold came down.

Fair ladies, long may you bloom, and sweetly may thole!
She was part lucky. With flowers and lace and mourning,
With love and bravado, we bade God rest her soul
After six quick turns of quaking, six of burning.

1924, 1945

Captain Carpenter

Captain Carpenter rose up in his prime
Put on his pistols and went riding out
But had got wellnigh nowhere at that time
Till he fell in with ladies in a rout.[3]

It was a pretty lady and all her train
That played with him so sweetly but before
An hour she'd taken a sword with all her main
And twined[4] him of his nose for evermore.

Captain Carpenter mounted up one day
And rode straightway into a stranger rogue
That looked unchristian but be that as may
The Captain did not wait upon prologue.

But drew upon him out of his great heart
The other swung against him with a club
And cracked his two legs at the shinny part
And let him roll and stick like any tub.

Captain Carpenter rode many a time
From male and female took he sundry harms
He met the wife of Satan crying "I'm
The she-wolf bids you shall bear no more arms."

3. Crowd.

4. Separated.

Their strokes and counters whistled in the wind
I wish he had delivered half his blows
But where she should have made off like a hind
The bitch bit off his arms at the elbows.

And Captain Carpenter parted with his ears
To a black devil that used him in this wise
O Jesus ere his threescore and ten years
Another had plucked out his sweet blue eyes.

Captain Carpenter got up on his roan
And sallied from the gate in hell's despite
I heard him asking in the grimmest tone
If any enemy yet there was to fight?

"To any adversary it is fame
If he risk to be wounded by my tongue
Or burnt in two beneath my red heart's flame
Such are the perils he is cast among.

"But if he can he has a pretty choice
From an anatomy with little to lose
Whether he cut my tongue and take my voice
Or whether it be my round red heart he choose."

It was the neatest knave that ever was seen
Stepping in perfume from his lady's bower
Who at this word put in his merry mien[5]
And fell on Captain Carpenter like a tower.

I would not knock old fellows in the dust
But there lay Captain Carpenter on his back
His weapons were the old heart in his bust
And a blade shook between rotten teeth alack.

The rogue in scarlet and grey soon knew his mind
He wished to get his trophy and depart
With gentle apology and touch refined
He pierced him and produced the Captain's heart.

God's mercy rest on Captain Carpenter now
I thought him Sirs an honest gentleman
Citizen husband soldier and scholar enow
Let jangling kites eat of him if they can.

But God's deep curses follow after those
That shore him of his goodly nose and ears
His legs and strong arms at the two elbows
And eyes that had not watered seventy years.

5. Expression.

The curse of hell upon the sleek upstart
That got the Captain finally on his back
And took the red red vitals of his heart
And made the kites to whet their beaks clack clack.

1924

Piazza Piece[8]

—I am a gentleman in a dustcoat trying
To make you hear. Your ears are soft and small
And listen to an old man not at all,
They want the young men's whispering and sighing.

But see the roses on your trellis dying
And hear the spectral singing of the moon;
For I must have my lovely lady soon,
I am a gentleman in a dustcoat trying.

—I am a lady young in beauty waiting
Until my truelove comes, and then we kiss.
But what grey man among the vines is this
Whose words are dry and faint as in a dream?
Back from my trellis, Sir, before I scream!
I am a lady young in beauty waiting.

1927

Janet Waking

Beautifully Janet slept
Till it was deeply morning. She woke then
And thought about her dainty-feathered hen,
To see how it had kept.

One kiss she gave her mother.
Only a small one gave she to her daddy
Who would have kissed each curl of his shining baby;
No kiss at all for her brother.

"Old Chucky, old Chucky!" she cried,
Running across the world upon the grass
To Chucky's house, and listening. But alas,
Her Chucky had died.

It was a transmogrifying bee
Came droning down on Chucky's old bald head
And sat and put the poison. It scarcely bled,
But how exceedingly

8. A reenactment of the old folk tale of Death and the Maiden.

And purply did the knot
Swell with the venom and communicate
Its rigor! Now the poor comb stood up straight
But Chucky did not.

So there was Janet
Kneeling on the wet grass, crying her brown hen
(Translated[6] far beyond the daughters of men)
To rise and walk upon it.

And weeping fast as she had breath
Janet implored us, "Wake her from her sleep!"
And would not be instructed in how deep
Was the forgetful kingdom of death.

1927

The Equilibrists

Full of her long white arms and milky skin
He had a thousand times remembered sin.
Alone in the press of people traveled he,
Minding her jacinth,[7] and myrrh, and ivory.

Mouth he remembered: the quaint orifice
From which came heat that flamed upon the kiss,
Till cold words came down spiral from the head,
Grey doves from the officious tower illsped.

Body: it was a white field ready for love,
On her body's field, with the gaunt tower above,
The lilies grew, beseeching him to take,
If he would pluck and wear them, bruise and break.

Eyes talking: Never mind the cruel words,
Embrace my flowers, but not embrace the swords.
But what they said, the doves came straightway flying
And unsaid: Honor, Honor, they came crying.

Importunate her doves. Too pure, too wise,
Clambering on his shoulder, saying, Arise,
Leave me now, and never let us meet,
Eternal distance now command thy feet.

Predicament indeed, which thus discovers
Honor among thieves, Honor between lovers.

6. Carried across.

7. An orange-colored precious stone.

O such a little word is Honor, they feel!
But the grey word is between them cold as steel.[8]

At length I saw these lovers fully were come
Into their torture of equilibrium;
Dreadfully had forsworn each other, and yet
They were bound each to each, and they did not forget.

And rigid as two painful stars, and twirled
About the clustered night their prison world,
They burned with fierce love always to come near,
But Honor beat them back and kept them clear.

Ah, the strict lovers, they are ruined now!
I cried in anger. But with puddled brow
Devising for those gibbeted and brave
Came I descanting: Man, what would you have?

For spin your period out, and draw your breath,
A kinder sæculum[1] begins with Death.
Would you ascend to Heaven and bodiless dwell?
Or take your bodies honorless to Hell?

In Heaven you have heard no marriage is,
No white flesh tinder to your lecheries,
Your male and female tissue sweetly shaped
Sublimed[2] away, and furious blood escaped.

Great lovers lie in Hell, the stubborn ones
Infatuate of the flesh upon the bones;
Stuprate,[3] they rend each other when they kiss,
The pieces kiss again, no end to this.

But still I watched them spinning, orbited nice.[4]
Their flames were not more radiant than their ice.
I dug in the quiet earth and wrought the tomb
And made these lines to memorize[5] their doom:—

EPITAPH

Equilibrists lie here; stranger, tread light;
Close, but untouching in each other's sight;
Mouldered the lips and ashy the tall skull.
Let them lie perilous and beautiful.

1927

8. In the Romance of Tristram and Iseult, the two lovers flee together from Iseult's betrothed, King Mark, who is Tristram's liege lord. Their sense of honor prevents them from consummating their love, and Mark eventually finds them sleeping in a forest with a sword between them. This motif is found in several other stories and myths as well.

1. Age (Lat).

2. Converted from the solid to the vapor state; purified.

3. A coinage meaning "infamous."

4. Precisely.

5. Memorialize (archaic usage).

T. S. ELIOT
(*1888–1965*)

Thomas Stearns Eliot was born in St. Louis on September 26, 1888. He was one of seven children, and the youngest son. His family had come from Massachusetts and "jealously guarded," as Eliot wrote, its New England connections. His grandfather, William Greenleaf Eliot, after graduation from the Harvard Divinity School, went to St. Louis in 1834; he founded the first Unitarian church there. His ability rapidly made him a shaper of the city's intellectual life, and he founded Washington University in 1859. His son, the poet's father (1843–1919), was a successful industrialist. He married in 1860 a woman of literary interests, Charlotte Champe Stearns (1843–1929).

Eliot's geographical movements may reflect his private turbulence. After living for his first seventeen years in St. Louis, except for annual summer holidays in New England, he went to Milton Academy in Massachusetts and then entered Harvard in 1906. He completed his course at Harvard in three years instead of four. After taking his first degree in 1909, Eliot entered the graduate school in the department of philosophy.

In 1910 he took a master's degree and then went to the Sorbonne for a year, after which he returned to Harvard to write a doctoral dissertation on the philosophy of F. H. Bradley, the author of *Appearance and Reality*. Meanwhile he ranged about in what may have seemed a haphazard way: he read French poetry, he studied the Sanskrit and Pali languages, he took a great interest in Indic religion. It was in 1910 also that he wrote his earliest mature poem, "The Love Song of J. Alfred Prufrock." During the academic year 1913–1914 Eliot was an assistant at Harvard. He was then awarded a traveling fellowship, and went to study for the summer at Marburg in Germany. The outbreak of war forced him to Oxford. The year 1914–1915 proved to be pivotal, as he then came to three interrelated decisions: to give up the appearance of the philosopher for the reality of the poet, to marry, and to settle in England.

He obtained much encouragement in all three from Ezra Pound, whom he met in September 1914. Pound read the poems which no one had been willing to publish, and pronounced his verdict, that Eliot "has actually trained himself *and* modernized himself *on his own*." He told Harriet Monroe, the editor of *Poetry*, that she must publish them, beginning with "Prufrock." It took some time to persuade her, and it was not until June 1915 that Eliot's first publication took place. This was also the month of his first marriage, on June 26th. His wife was Vivien Haigh-Wood, and Eliot remained, like Merlin with another Vivian, under her spell, beset and possessed by her intricacies for fifteen years and more. (They separated in 1932; Mrs. Eliot died in 1947.)

He resisted his parents' urging that he return to the United States for a career in teaching philosophy. He would be a poet, and England offered a better atmosphere in which to write. His family did not cut him off, but they offered insufficient help to support the couple. Eliot took a teaching job at the High Wycombe Grammar School, then at Highgate Junior School. He deferred to his parents' wishes so far as to complete his dissertation, and was booked to sail on April 1, 1916, to take his oral examination at Harvard. The crossing was canceled because of wartime complications, and his academic gestures came to an end. In March 1917 he took a job as clerk with Lloyd's Bank in London, and stayed at it for eight years, while he struggled with literary and marital problems too.

The personal life out of which in 1921 came Eliot's poem, *The Waste Land,* began now to be lived in earnest. Vivien Eliot suffered obscurely from nerves, her health was subject to frequent collapses, she complained of neuralgia, of insomnia. Ezra Pound regarded the passage in *The Waste Land* which begins, "My nerves are bad tonight," as a transcript of her talk. Eliot was put under great strain. The death of his father in January 1919 was another blow, especially since his father died thinking that Eliot had wasted his ability.

Much of *The Waste Land* was written by early 1921. Then Eliot had a breakdown, and was advised by a neurologist to take three months away from Lloyd's Bank. When the Bank had agreed, he went first to Margate and to Lausanne, where he had psychiatric treatment. He consulted Pound in Paris, and with Pound's brilliant aid was able to piece *The Waste Land* out of various drafts. When the poem itself was published in 1922, it gave Eliot his central position in modern poetry. In the year that *The Waste Land* appeared, Eliot founded a new review, *The Criterion,* which became a leading cultural magazine. He also joined the firm of Faber and Gwyer in 1925. As editor of the leading literary journal, as a director of a publishing firm, and as poet and critic, he was a magisterial figure in English letters.

Eliot became a British citizen in 1927, and in the same year joined the Anglican church. Some of his plays, notably *The Cocktail Party,* achieved a success ordinarily reserved in modern times for plays in prose rather than in verse. In 1948 he was awarded the Nobel Prize for Literature. He died in London on January 4, 1965.

The Love Song of J. Alfred Prufrock[1]

S'io credessi che mia risposta fosse
a persona che mai tornasse al mondo,
questa fiamma staria senza più scosse.
Ma per ciò che giammai di questo fondo
non tornò vivo alcun, s'i'odo il vero,
senza tema d'infamia ti rispondo.[2]

Let us go then, you and I,
When the evening is spread out against the sky
Like a patient etherised upon a table;
Let us go, through certain half-deserted streets,
The muttering retreats

1. Eliot probably finished this poem in 1911, when he was twenty-three, but was not able to have it published until Ezra Pound placed it with *Poetry* in 1915.

2. The epigraph is from Dante's *Inferno,* Canto XXVII, where the poet asks Guido da Montefeltro, who like the other Counsellors of Fraud is wrapped in a tall flame, to identify himself. Guido, having sinned with his tongue, has to speak through the tongue of the flame. He replies, "If I thought that I was speaking / to someone who would go back to the world, / this flame would shake no more. / But since nobody has ever / gone back alive from this place, if what I hear is true, / I answer you without fear of infamy."

Of restless nights in one-night cheap hotels
And sawdust restaurants with oyster-shells:
Streets that follow like a tedious argument
Of insidious intent
To lead you to an overwhelming question . . .
Oh, do not ask, 'What is it?'
Let us go and make our visit.

In the room the women come and go
Talking of Michelangelo.

The yellow fog that rubs its back upon the window-panes,
The yellow smoke that rubs its muzzle on the window-panes,
Licked its tongue into the corners of the evening,
Lingered upon the pools that stand in drains,
Let fall upon its back the soot that falls from chimneys,
Slipped by the terrace, made a sudden leap,
And seeing that it was a soft October night,
Curled once about the house, and fell asleep.

And indeed there will be time
For the yellow smoke that slides along the street
Rubbing its back upon the window-panes;
There will be time, there will be time
To prepare a face to meet the faces that you meet;
There will be time to murder and create,
And time for all the works and days[4] of hands
That lift and drop a question on your plate;
Time for you and time for me,
And time yet for a hundred indecisions,
And for a hundred visions and revisions,
Before the taking of a toast and tea.

In the room the women come and go
Talking of Michelangelo.

And indeed there will be time
To wonder, 'Do I dare?' and, 'Do I dare?'
Time to turn back and descend the stair,
With a bald spot in the middle of my hair—
(They will say: 'How his hair is growing thin!')
My morning coat, my collar mounting firmly to the chin,
My necktie rich and modest, but asserted by a simple pin—
(They will say: "But how his arms and legs are thin!')
Do I dare
Disturb the universe?
In a minute there is time
For decisions and revisions which a minute will reverse.

4. The title of a poem by Hesiod (8th century B.C.), the Greek poet, which celebrates farm work.

For I have known them all already, known them all—
Have known the evenings, mornings, afternoons,
I have measured out my life with coffee spoons;
I know the voices dying with a dying fall
Beneath the music from a farther room.
  So how should I presume?

And I have known the eyes already, known them all—
The eyes that fix you in a formulated phrase,
And when I am formulated, sprawling on a pin,
When I am pinned and wriggling on the wall,
Then how should I begin
To spit out all the butt-ends of my days and ways?
  And how should I presume?

And I have known the arms already, known them all—
Arms that are braceleted and white and bare
(But in the lamplight, downed with light brown hair!)
Is it perfume from a dress
That makes me so digress?
Arms that lie along a table, or wrap about a shawl.
  And should I then presume?
  And how should I begin?

. . . . .

Shall I say, I have gone at dusk through narrow streets
And watched the smoke that rises from the pipes
Of lonely men in shirt-sleeves, leaning out of windows? . . .

I should have been a pair of ragged claws
Scuttling across the floors of silent seas.

. . . . .

And the afternoon, the evening, sleeps so peacefully!
Smoothed by long fingers,
Asleep . . . tired . . . or it malingers,
Stretched on the floor, here beside you and me.
Should I, after tea and cakes and ices,
Have the strength to force the moment to its crisis?
But though I have wept and fasted, wept and prayed,
Though I have seen my head (grown slightly bald) brought in upon a
  platter,[5]
I am no prophet—and here's no great matter;
I have seen the moment of my greatness flicker,
And I have seen the eternal Footman hold my coat, and snicker,
And in short, I was afraid.

5. John the Baptist was beheaded by order of King Herod, and his head was brought in upon a silver dish to please Herod's stepdaughter Salome. (*Matthew* 14: 3–11.)

And would it have been worth it, after all,
After the cups, the marmalade, the tea,
Among the porcelain, among some talk of you and me,
Would it have been worth while,
To have bitten off the matter with a smile,
To have squeezed the universe into a ball[8]
To roll it towards some overwhelming question,
To say: 'I am Lazarus,[9] come from the dead,
Come back to tell you all, I shall tell you all'—
If one, settling a pillow by her head,
  Should say: 'That is not what I meant at all.
  That is not it, at all.'

And would it have been worth it, after all,
Would it have been worth while,
After the sunsets and the dooryards and the sprinkled streets,
After the novels, after the teacups, after the skirts that trail along the floor—
And this, and so much more?—
It is impossible to say just what I mean!
But as if a magic lantern threw the nerves in patterns on a screen:
Would it have been worth while
If one, settling a pillow or throwing off a shawl,
And turning toward the window, should say:
  'That is not it at all,
  That is not what I meant, at all.'

. . . . .

No! I am not Prince Hamlet, nor was meant to be;
Am an attendant lord, one that will do
To swell a progress,[1] start a scene or two,
Advise the prince; no doubt, an easy tool,
Deferential, glad to be of use,
Politic, cautious, and meticulous;
Full of high sentence,[2] but a bit obtuse;
At times, indeed, almost ridiculous—[3]
Almost, at times, the Fool.

I grow old . . . I grow old . . .
I shall wear the bottoms of my trousers rolled.[4]

Shall I part my hair behind? Do I dare to eat a peach?
I shall wear white flannel trousers, and walk upon the beach.
I have heard the mermaids singing, each to each.

8. In a poem, "To His Coy Mistress," Andrew Marvell (1621–1678) wrote: "Let us roll all our strength and all / Our sweetness up into a ball, / And tear our pleasures with rough strife / Thorough the iron gates of life."

9. Raised by Christ from the dead. (*John* 11:1–44.)

1. A progress was a royal journey, usually made by most of the court as well as by the sovereign.

2. Lofty judgment.

3. Prufrock appears to have in mind Polonius, the king's adviser in *Hamlet*.

4. Prufrock is eager to keep up with the latest fashion, which was to wear cuffs on trousers.

I do not think that they will sing to me.

I have seen them riding seaward on the waves
Combing the white hair of the waves blown back
When the wind blows the water white and black.

We have lingered in the chambers of the sea
By sea-girls wreathed with seaweed red and brown
Till human voices wake us, and we drown.

1917

Sweeney Among the Nightingales

ὤμοι, πέπληγμαι καιρίαν πληγὴν ἔσω.[8]

Apeneck Sweeney spreads his knees
Letting his arms hang down to laugh,
The zebra stripes along his jaw
Swelling to maculate[9] giraffe.

The circles of the stormy moon
Slide westward toward the River Plate,[1]
Death and the Raven[2] drift above
And Sweeney guards the hornèd gate.[3]

Gloomy Orion and the Dog[4]
Are veiled; and hushed the shrunken seas;
The person in the Spanish cape
Tries to sit on Sweeney's knees

Slips and pulls the table cloth
Overturns a coffee-cup,
Reorganised upon the floor
She yawns and draws a stocking up;

The silent man in mocha brown
Sprawls at the window-sill and gapes;
The waiter brings in oranges
Bananas figs and hothouse grapes;

The silent vertebrate in brown
Contracts and concentrates, withdraws;
Rachel *née* Rabinovitch
Tears at the grapes with murderous paws;

8. The epigraph is from Aeschylus' *Agamemnon;* when Agamemnon is struck by his wife Clytemnestra, he cries, "Alas, I have been struck a mortal blow." Eliot once remarked that all he consciously set out to create in this poem was a sense of foreboding.

9. Spotted.

1. A South American river.

2. The constellation Corvus, with overtones of the raven as a bird of ill omen.

3. The gate of Hades through which true dreams come.

4. Orion, constellation of the hunter, is close in the sky to Canis Major, the constellation of the dog.

She and the lady in the cape
Are suspect, thought to be in league;
Therefore the man with heavy eyes
Declines the gambit, shows fatigue,

Leaves the room and reappears
Outside the window, leaning in,
Branches of wistaria
Circumscribe a golden grin;

The host with someone indistinct
Converses at the door apart,
The nightingales are singing near
The Convent of the Sacred Heart,[6]

And sang within the bloody wood[7]
When Agamemnon cried aloud
And let their liquid siftings fall
To stain the stiff dishonoured shroud.

1919

Gerontion[8]

Thou hast nor youth nor age
But as it were an after dinner sleep
Dreaming of both.[9]

Here I am, an old man in a dry month,
Being read to by a boy, waiting for rain.[1]
I was neither at the hot gates
Nor fought in the warm rain
Nor knee deep in the salt marsh, heaving a cutlass,
Bitten by flies, fought.[2]
My house is a decayed house,
And the Jew squats on the window sill, the owner,
Spawned in some estaminet[4] of Antwerp,
Blistered in Brussels, patched and peeled in London.
The goat coughs at night in the field overhead;
Rocks, moss, stonecrop, iron, merds.[6]

6. A Roman Catholic conventual order devoted to the worship of the heart of Jesus Christ as a symbol of his love for humanity.

7. Eliot has said he was thinking here of Orpheus, torn apart by the Thracian women for rejecting them. He telescopes this death with that of Agamemnon.

8. Written in 1919, and once proposed by Eliot as a prologue to *The Waste Land.* The title means "little old man" (in Greek).

9. The epigraph comes from Shakespeare's *Measure for Measure,* III.i, in which the Duke consoles Claudio, who is about to be executed.

1. Based on a description of Edward Fitzgerald: "Here he sits, in a dry month, old and blind, being read to by a country boy, longing for rain." A. C. Benson *Edward FitzGerald,* New York and London, 1905, p. 142. Eliot borrows the words, but has more than Fitzgerald in mind.

2. Probably references to specific battles: Thermopylae (Greek for "hot gates"), 480 B.C.; Waterloo, 1815; and Cannae, 216 B.C. Compare Prufrock, "No, I am not Prince Hamlet, nor was meant to be."

4. Tavern.

6. Excrement (Fr).

The woman keeps the kitchen, makes tea,
Sneezes at evening, poking the peevish gutter.[7]
                                          I an old man,
A dull head among windy spaces.

Signs are taken for wonders. 'We would see a sign!'
The word within a word, unable to speak a word,
Swaddled with darkness.[8] In the juvescence of the year
Came Christ the tiger[9]

In depraved May,[1] dogwood and chestnut, flowering judas,
To be eaten, to be divided, to be drunk
Among whispers; by Mr. Silvero
With caressing hands, at Limoges
Who walked all night in the next room;

By Hakagawa, bowing among the Titians;
By Madame de Tornquist, in the dark room
Shifting the candles; Fräulein von Kulp
Who turned in the hall, one hand on the door.
      Vacant shuttles
Weave the wind. I have no ghosts,
An old man in a draughty house
Under a windy knob.

After such knowledge,[2] what forgiveness? Think now
History has many cunning passages, contrived corridors
And issues, deceives with whispering ambitions,
Guides us by vanities. Think now
She gives when our attention is distracted
And what she gives, gives with such supple confusions
That the giving famishes the craving. Gives too late

7. British usage for "drain."

8. Eliot is alluding to several passages in the Gospels, and to Lancelot Andrewes' (1555–1626) commentary on them in *Works*, I, 204. *Matthew* 12:38: "Then some of the scribes and Pharisees said to [Christ], 'Master, we would see a sign from you,' " as a proof of his divinity. *John* 1:1, 14: "In the beginning was the Word, and the Word was with God, and the Word was God. . . . And the Word became flesh and dwelt among us, full of grace and truth." *Luke* 2:12, "And this will be a sign for you: you will find a babe [Jesus] wrapped in swaddling cloths and lying in a manger." The passage from Andrewes: "Signs are taken for wonders. 'Master, we would fain see a sign,' that is a miracle. And in this sense it [the Gospel] is a sign to wonder at. Indeed, every word here is a wonder. . . . *Verbum infans* [the infant Word, or the Christ child] the Word without a word; the eternal Word not able to speak a word; 1. a wonder sure. 2. And . . . swaddled; and that a wonder too." Grover Smith, *T. S. Eliot's Poetry and Plays*, Chicago, 1956, p. 306.

9. Christ's resurrection at Easter reminds Gerontion of power and awesomeness rather than of benevolence and love. "Juvescence" is Eliot's elision of "juvenescence," or youth.

1. That is, depraved in these days. Henry Adams, in *The Education of Henry Adams*, Boston and New York, 1918, p. 400, speaks of settling in Washington: "The Potomac and its tributaries squandered beauty. . . . Here and there a Negro log cabin alone disturbed the dogwood and the judas-tree. . . . The tulip and the chestnut tree gave no sense of struggle against a stingy nature. . . . No European spring had shown him [Adams] the same intermixture of delicate grace and passionate depravity that marked the Maryland May. He loved it too much as if it were Greek and half human."

2. The knowledge, however imperfect, of Christ.

What's not believed in, or is still believed,
In memory only, reconsidered passion. Gives too soon
Into weak hands, what's thought can be dispensed with
Till the refusal propagates a fear. Think
Neither fear nor courage saves us. Unnatural vices
Are fathered by our heroism. Virtues
Are forced upon us by our impudent crimes.
These tears are shaken from the wrath-bearing tree.[3]

The tiger springs in the new year. Us he devours.[4] Think at last
We have not reached conclusion, when I
Stiffen in a rented house. Think at last
I have not made this show purposelessly
And it is not by any concitation[5]
Of the backward devils.
I would meet you upon this honestly.
I that was near your heart was removed therefrom
To lose beauty in terror, terror in inquisition.
I have lost my passion: why should I need to keep it
Since what is kept must be adulterated?
I have lost my sight, smell, hearing, taste and touch:
How should I use them for your closer contact?

These with a thousand small deliberations
Protract the profit of their chilled delirium,
Excite the membrane, when the sense has cooled,
With pungent sauces, multiply variety
In a wilderness of mirrors. What will the spider do,
Suspend its operations, will the weevil
Delay? De Bailhache, Fresca, Mrs. Cammel, whirled
Beyond the circuit of the shuddering Bear[6]
In fractured atoms. Gull against the wind, in the windy straits
Of Belle Isle, or running on the Horn.
White feathers in the snow, the Gulf claims,
And an old man driven by the Trades
To a sleepy corner.[7]

Tenants of the house,
Thoughts of a dry brain in a dry season.

1920

3. A symbol encompassing the Tree of the Knowledge of Good and Evil in the garden of Eden; the flowering judas (line 21), traditionally held to be the tree on which Judas hanged himself in remorse for having betrayed Christ; and the Cross itself, on which Christ was crucified.

4. Instead of the Communion, in which the worshipers "devour" him.

5. Stirring up.

6. The Great Bear, a northern constellation.

7. The gull is compared with Gerontion who is probably a sailor. While it attempts the dangerous passage to the extreme north (the Belle Isle straits off eastern Canada) or south (Cape Horn, at the tip of South America), he sails with the steady trade-winds towards the equator.

The Waste Land

Eliot says of *The Waste Land* itself that "Not only the title, but the plan and a good deal of the incidental symbolism of the poem were suggested by Miss Jessie L. Weston's book on the Grail legend: *From Ritual to Romance* [1920]. Indeed, so deeply am I indebted, Miss Weston's book will elucidate the difficulties of the poem much better than my notes can do; and I recommend it (apart from the great interest of the book itself) to any who think such elucidation of the poem worth the trouble. To another work of anthropology I am indebted in general, one which has influenced our generation profoundly; I mean [Sir James Frazer's] *The Golden Bough* [1890–1915]; I have used especially the two volumes *Adonis, Attis, Osiris*. Anyone who is acquainted with these works will immediately recognize in the poem certain references to vegetation ceremonies." Miss Weston contends that the Arthurian romances of the quest for the Holy Grail are underlain by pre-Christian fertility myths and rituals such as those described by Frazer. In the Arthurian legend a Fisher King (the fish being an ancient symbol of life) has been maimed or killed, and his country has therefore become a dry Waste Land; he can only be regenerated and his land restored to fertility by a knight (Perceval or Parsifal) who perseveres through various ordeals to the Perilous Chapel and learns the answers to certain ritual questions about the Grail. The Fisher King is seen as analogous to vegetation gods such as Adonis of Greece, Attis of Phrygia, Osiris of Egypt, and perhaps also the Greek deity Hyacinthus, all of whose deaths and rebirths are represented in ancient ritual ceremonies intended to bring about the regeneration of plants after the sterile winter. Miss Weston also connects the symbols of the Arthurian stories with the suits of the Tarot deck, today used to tell fortunes but perhaps originally designed by the Egyptians to predict the flooding of the Nile, and the restoration of its valley to fertility.

Eliot wrote most of *The Waste Land* while at Lausanne in 1921, but it had been on his mind since 1919. Indeed, parts of the poem antedate the final version by several years: lines 26–9 were taken from "The Death of Saint Narcissus" (1915), lines 312–321 are adapted from Eliot's French poem "Dans le Restaurant" (1916–17), and Conrad Aiken remarks that lines 377–384 and other passages had "long been familiar" to him "as poems, or part-poems, in themselves" (*A Reviewer's ABC*, 1958).

From the first Eliot gave Ezra Pound much credit for his help in shaping *The Waste Land*, and the manuscript reveals how extensive and crucial this help was. Pound persuaded Eliot to delete 72 lines in rhymed couplets at the beginning of "The Fire Sermon" imitating the style of Pope's "The Rape of the Lock" and the defecation scene in Joyce's *Ulysses* (a book which Eliot had recently read in manuscript and thought "magnificent") and another 82 lines, preceding line 312, based on Dante's description of Ulysses' last voyage and describing the wreck of a New England fishing boat. Pound also disapproved of three short lyrics which Eliot planned as interludes, and dissuaded him from adding "Gerontion" as a preface. Smaller emendations were proposed in order to eliminate patches of conventionally poetic diction and to cut out nonessential verbiage; the effect was often to distort previously regular meter and rhyme. In gratitude for Pound's help Eliot dedicated the poem to him, quoting Dante's tribute to the Provençal poet Arnaut Daniel, "The better craftsman [*il miglior fabbro*] of the mother tongue." (*Purgatorio*, XXVI.)

Eliot's 52 footnotes to *The Waste Land,* reproduced here, were prepared for its publication as a book in 1922; they do not accompany the poem in *The Criterion* (London), Eliot's own magazine, or in *The Dial* (New York). He later remarked, "I have sometimes thought of getting rid of these notes; but now they can never be unstuck. They have had almost greater popularity than the poem itself." But Eliot was not unaware of the difficulties his work presented to its readers. In *The Use of Poetry and the Use of Criticism* he emphasized that such difficulties may come from various causes and be of different kinds. "The more seasoned reader . . . does not bother about understanding; not, at least, at first. I know that some of the poetry to which I am most devoted is poetry which I did not understand at first reading; some is poetry which I am not sure I understand yet: for instance, Shakespeare's." He mentions "the difficulty caused by the author's having left out something which the reader is used to finding; so that the reader, bewildered, gropes about for what is absent, and puzzles his head for a kind of 'meaning' which is not there, and is not meant to be there." These remarks, which are somewhat introductory to *The Waste Land,* may be supplemented by Eliot's remark in an interview, "In *The Waste Land* I wasn't even bothering whether I understood what I was saying." (*Writers at Work,* Second Series, 1963, p. 105). And, though critics immediately began to interpret the poem as Eliot's expression of a generation's spiritual alienation, Eliot himself soon felt the need to disavow any such intention, and is reported to have remarked, "To me it was only the relief of a personal and wholly insignificant grouse against life; it is just a piece of rhythmical grumbling." [T. S. Eliot, *The Waste Land* (Facsimile and Transcript of the Original Drafts . . .), ed. by Valerie Eliot, New York, 1971.]

The Waste Land

'Nam Sibyllam quidem Cumis ego ipse oculis meis vidi in ampulla pendere, et cum illi pueri dicerent: Σίβυλλα τί θέλεις; respondebat illa: ἀποθανεῖν θέλω.'[8]

For Ezra Pound
il miglior fabbro.

I. The Burial of the Dead[9]

April is the cruellest month, breeding
Lilacs out of the dead land, mixing
Memory and desire, stirring

8. "For I saw with my own eyes the Sibyl hanging in a jar at Cumae, and when the acolytes said, 'Sibyl, what do you wish?' she replied, 'I wish to die.' " (Petronius, *Satyricon,* ch. 48.) Apollo had granted the Sibyl eternal life but not eternal youth, and consequently her body shrivelled up until she could be put in a bottle.

9. A phrase from the Anglican burial service.

Dull roots with spring rain.
Winter kept us warm, covering
Earth in forgetful snow, feeding
A little life with dried tubers.
Summer surprised us, coming over the Starnbergersee[1]
With a shower of rain; we stopped in the colonnade,
And went on in sunlight, into the Hofgarten,
And drank coffee, and talked for an hour.
Bin gar keine Russin, stamm' aus Litauen, echt deutsch.[2]
And when we were children, staying at the arch-duke's,
My cousin's, he took me out on a sled,
And I was frightened. He said, Marie,
Marie, hold on tight. And down we went.
In the mountains, there you feel free.
I read, much of the night, and go south in the winter.

What are the roots that clutch, what branches grow
Out of this stony rubbish? Son of man,[3]
You cannot say, or guess, for you know only
A heap of broken images, where the sun beats,
And the dead tree gives no shelter, the cricket no relief,[4]
And the dry stone no sound of water. Only
There is shadow under this red rock,[5]
(Come in under the shadow of this red rock),
And I will show you something different from either
Your shadow at morning striding behind you
Or your shadow at evening rising to meet you;
I will show you fear in a handful of dust.
Frisch weht der Wind
Der Heimat zu
Mein Irisch Kind,
Wo weilest du?[6]
'You gave me hyacinths first a year ago;
'They called me the hyacinth girl.'
—Yet when we came back, late, from the hyacinth garden,
Your arms full, and your hair wet, I could not
Speak, and my eyes failed, I was neither

1. A lake near Munich; the Hofgarten is a park in the city. Lines 8–18 resemble some autobiographical reminiscences of Countess Marie Larisch, confidante of Empress Elizabeth of Austria, of the years before Austria's defeat in the First World War lessened the nobility's wealth and influence. According to Valerie Eliot, Eliot based this passage on a conversation he had had with the countess.

2. "I'm not a Russian woman at all; I come from Lithuania, a true German."

3. "Cf. *Ezekiel* II:1" (Eliot's note): "Son of man, stand upon thy feet, and I will speak of thee," says God to Ezekiel. In *Ezekiel* 37, in the valley of the dry bones, God asks Ezekiel, "Son of man, can these bones live?" and is answered, "O Lord God, thou knowest."

4. "Cf. *Ecclesiastes* 12:5" (Eliot's note), in which the preacher evokes the evil days "when they shall be afraid of that which is high, and fears shall be in the way, and the almond tree shall flourish, and the grasshopper shall be a burden, and desire shall fail . . ."

5. Compare *Isaiah* 32:2, which tells of a savior who "shall be . . . as rivers of water in a dry place, as the shadow of a great rock in a weary land."

6. "V. *Tristan und Isolde,* I, verses 5–8" (Eliot's note). A sailor on the ship which brings Isolde from Ireland to her unloved husband-to-be, King Mark of Cornwall, sings wistfully of a girl he left behind: "Fresh blows the wind / To the homeland; / My Irish darling, / Where do you linger?"

Living nor dead, and I knew nothing,
Looking into the heart of light, the silence.
Oed' und leer das Meer.[8]

Madame Sosostris,[9] famous clairvoyante,
Had a bad cold, nevertheless
Is known to be the wisest woman in Europe,
With a wicked pack of cards.[1] Here, said she,
Is your card, the drowned Phoenician Sailor,[2]
(Those are pearls that were his eyes. Look!)[3]
Here is Belladonna,[4] the Lady of the Rocks,
The lady of situations.
Here is the man with three staves, and here the Wheel,[5]
And here is the one-eyed merchant,[6] and this card,
Which is blank, is something he carries on his back,
Which I am forbidden to see. I do not find
The Hanged Man. Fear death by water.
I see crowds of people, walking round in a ring.
Thank you. If you see dear Mrs. Equitone,
Tell her I bring the horoscope myself:
One must be so careful these days.

Unreal City,[7]
Under the brown fog of a winter dawn,
A crowd flowed over London Bridge, so many,
I had not thought death had undone so many.[8]

8. "Id. III, verse 24" (Eliot's note). Tristan, having been caught in adultery with Isolde and badly wounded, awaits her coming to heal him; but a shepherd, posted as lookout for her ship, says sadly, "Desolate and empty the sea."

9. A fortune-teller who uses the name of the Egyptian pharaoh Sesostris. (Eliot came across it in a comic scene in Aldous Huxley's *Crome Yellow* [1921].)

1. The Tarot deck of cards, with their vestiges of an ancient vegetation myth. Eliot notes: "I am not familiar with the exact constitution of the Tarot pack of cards, from which I have obviously departed to suit my own convenience. The Hanged Man, a member of the traditional pack, fits my purpose in two ways: because he is associated in my mind with the Hanged God of Frazer, and because I associate him with the hooded figure [Christ] in the passage of the disciples to Emmaus in Part V. The Phoenician Sailor and the Merchant appear later; also the 'crowds of people,' and Death by Water is executed in Part IV. The Man with Three Staves (an authentic member of the Tarot pack) I associate quite arbitrarily, with the Fisher King himself."

2. The Phoenicians were ancient seamen and merchants of the Mediterranean. The sailor reappears as Phlebas in Part IV.

3. From Shakespeare's *The Tempest,* I.ii; while the young prince Ferdinand is "Sitting on a bank, / Weeping again the king my father's wrack, / This music crept by me on the waters . . ." The music is a song by the spirit Ariel, who tells Ferdinand (falsely): "Full fathom five thy father lies, / Of his bones are coral made, / Those are pearls that were his eyes. / Nothing of him that doth fade, / But doth suffer a sea-change, / Into something rich and strange."

4. Lovely lady (Ital), but also a poison. Calling her "the Lady of the Rocks" is an ironic allusion to Leonardo da Vinci's "Madonna of the Rocks," a picture of the Virgin Mary.

5. That is, the Wheel of Fortune, and perhaps also the Buddhist "Wheel of Existence" from which the soul endeavors to escape.

6. Mr. Eugenides of Part III. This card, like that of the drowned Phoenician Sailor, is not part of the Tarot deck.

7. "Cf. Baudelaire: '*Fourmillante cité, cité pleine de rêves / Où le spectre en plein jour raccroche le passant*' (Eliot's note). From Baudelaire's poem, "*Les Sept Vieillards*" (The Seven Old Men). "Swarming city, city full of dreams, / Where the spectre in full daylight accosts the passer-by."

8. "Cf. *Inferno* III, 55–57 . . ." (Eliot's note); Dante describes souls in limbo as "So long a train of people / That I should never have believed / That death had undone so many." They are in limbo because they "lived without praise or blame" or did not know the faith.

Sighs, short and infrequent, were exhaled,[9]
And each man fixed his eyes before his feet.
Flowed up the hill and down King William Street,
To where Saint Mary Woolnoth kept the hours
With a dead sound on the final stroke of nine.[1]
There I saw one I knew, and stopped him, crying: 'Stetson!
'You who were with me in the ships at Mylae![2]
'That corpse you planted last year in your garden,
'Has it begun to sprout? Will it bloom this year?
'Or has the sudden frost disturbed its bed?
'O keep the Dog far hence, that's friend to men,
'Or with his nails he'll dig it up again![3]
'You! hypocrite lecteur!—mon semblable,—mon frère!'[4]

II. A Game of Chess[5]

The Chair she sat in, like a burnished throne,
Glowed on the marble,[6] where the glass
Held up by standards wrought with fruited vines
From which a golden Cupidon peeped out
(Another hid his eyes behind his wing)
Doubled the flames of sevenbranched candelabra
Reflecting light upon the table as
The glitter of her jewels rose to meet it,
From satin cases poured in rich profusion.
In vials of ivory and coloured glass
Unstoppered, lurked her strange synthetic perfumes,
Unguent, powdered, or liquid—troubled, confused
And drowned the sense in odours; stirred by the air
That freshened from the window, these ascended
In fattening the prolonged candle-flames,

9. "Cf. *Inferno* IV, 25–27 . . ." (Eliot's note): "Here, so far as I could tell by listening, / There was no lamentation except sighs, / Which caused the eternal air to tremble." The sighs are uttered by the souls of the virtuous heathen who lived before Christ.

1. "A phenomenon I have often noticed" (Eliot's note). The people cross London Bridge and pass St. Mary Woolnoth (at the corner of King William and Lombard streets) on their way to the financial district of London, known as "the City."

2. A battle in the first Punic War between Rome and Carthage. It merges with the First World War, in which the speaker and Stetson fought.

3. "Cf. the Dirge in Webster's *White Devil*" (Eliot's note): "But keep the wolf far thence, that's foe to man / Or with his nails he'll dig them up again." The dirge is sung by a woman to one of her sons, who has killed the other and is burying him. In fertility rituals, the death of the god heralds his rebirth, but in the Waste Land such rituals are twisted to the point of parody. The god's burial becomes a grim murder, and the dog, perhaps Anubis (the dog-headed Egyptian god of the underworld who helped Isis to reassemble her dismembered brother Osiris), is to be kept away. Webster: John Webster (1580–1625), Jacobean playwright.

4. "V. Baudelaire, Preface to *Fleurs du Mal* [Flowers of Evil]" (Eliot's note). This is the last line of "*Au Lecteur*" ("To the Reader"), which describes boredom as man's worst sin, and well-known to the reader: "Hypocrite reader!—my double—my brother!"

5. The title comes from Thomas Middleton's (c. 1570–1627) play, *A Game at Chess,* but refers particularly to another play by Middleton, *Women Beware Women,* in which a girl is seduced in one room while her mother-in-law is kept busy at a chess game in the next. The chess moves are an eerie reflection of the erotic maneuvers next door.

6. "Cf. *Antony and Cleopatra,* II.ii.190" (Eliot's note). An ironic adaptation of the famous description of Cleopatra in Shakespeare's play.

Flung their smoke into the laquearia,[7]
Stirring the pattern on the coffered ceiling.
Huge sea-wood fed with copper
Burned green and orange, framed by the coloured stone,
In which sad light a carvèd dolphin swam.
Above the antique mantel was displayed
As though a window gave upon the sylvan scene[8]
The change of Philomel,[9] by the barbarous king
So rudely forced;[1] yet there the nightingale
Filled all the desert with inviolable voice
And still she cried, and still the world pursues,
'Jug Jug' to dirty ears.[2]
And other withered stumps of time
Were told upon the walls; staring forms
Leaned out, leaning, hushing the room enclosed.
Footsteps shuffled on the stair.
Under the firelight, under the brush, her hair
Spread out in fiery points
Glowed into words, then would be savagely still.

'My nerves are bad to-night. Yes, bad. Stay with me.
'Speak to me. Why do you never speak. Speak.
　'What are you thinking of? What thinking? What?
'I never know what you are thinking. Think.'

I think we are in rats' alley[3]
Where the dead men lost their bones.

'What is that noise?'
　　　　　　　　The wind under the door.[4]
'What is that noise now? What is the wind doing?'
　　　　　　　　Nothing again nothing.
　　　　　　　　　　　　　　　　　　'Do
'You know nothing? Do you see nothing? Do you remember
'Nothing?'

　　I remember
Those are pearls that were his eyes.

7. "Laquearia. V. *Aeneid,* I, 726 . . ." (Eliot's note). The word means "panelled ceiling," and Eliot refers to Virgil's description of the banquet given by the Carthaginian queen Dido for her lover Aeneas: "Burning lamps hang from the gold-panelled ceiling, / And torches dispel the night with their flames."

8. "Sylvan scene. V. Milton *Paradise Lost,* IV, 140" (Eliot's note). The source is Satan's description of Eden.

9. "V. Ovid, *Metamorphoses,* VI, Philomela" (Eliot's note). In the Greek legend of the nightingale, Philomela was raped by her sister Procne's husband, King Tereus. He cut out her tongue to insure her silence, but she depicted his crime on a piece of needlework and sent it to Procne. Procne, to revenge her sister, killed her own son Itys and served up his flesh to Tereus. When he attempted to kill the sisters, Philomela was changed into a nightingale and Procne into a swallow.

1. "Cf. Part III, line 204" (Eliot's note).

2. Though a familiar representation in Elizabethan literature of the nightingale's song (see note 2, p. 187), it appears here as a further degradation of Philomela's grief.

3. "Cf. Part III, line 195" (Eliot's note).

4. "Cf. Webster: 'Is the wind in that door still?' " (Eliot's note). In Webster's *The Devil's Law Case,* a physician asks this question on finding that the victim of a murderous attack is still breathing.

'Are you alive, or not? Is there nothing in your head?'
But
O O O O that Shakespeherian Rag—
It's so elegant
So intelligent[5]
'What shall I do now? What shall I do?'
'I shall rush out as I am, and walk the street
'With my hair down, so. What shall we do tomorrow?
'What shall we ever do?'
The hot water at ten.
And if it rains, a closed car at four.
And we shall play a game of chess,[6]
Pressing lidless eyes and waiting for a knock upon the door.

When Lil's husband got demobbed,[7] I said—
I didn't mince my words, I said to her myself,
HURRY UP PLEASE ITS TIME[8]
Now Albert's coming back, make yourself a bit smart.
He'll want to know what you done with that money he gave you
To get yourself some teeth. He did, I was there.
You have them all out, Lil, and get a nice set,
He said, I swear, I can't bear to look at you.
And no more can't I, I said, and think of poor Albert,
He's been in the army four years, he wants a good time,
And if you don't give it him, there's others will, I said.
Oh is there, she said. Something o' that, I said.
Then I'll know who to thank, she said, and give me a straight look.
HURRY UP PLEASE ITS TIME
If you don't like it you can get on with it, I said.
Others can pick and choose if you can't.
But if Albert makes off, it won't be for lack of telling.
You ought to be ashamed, I said, to look so antique.
(And her only thirty-one.)
I can't help it, she said, pulling a long face,
It's them pills I took, to bring it off, she said.
(She's had five already, and nearly died of young George.)
The chemist[9] said it would be all right, but I've never been the same.
You *are* a proper fool, I said.
Well, if Albert won't leave you alone, there it is, I said,
What you get married for if you don't want children?
HURRY UP PLEASE ITS TIME
Well, that Sunday Albert was home, they had a hot gammon,[1]
And they asked me in to dinner, to get the beauty of it hot—

5. Bruce R. McElderry has identified the "Shakespearian Rag" as an actual American ragtime song which was a hit of Ziegfeld's Follies of 1912.

6. "Cf. the game of chess in Middleton's *Women Beware Women*" (Eliot's note), described in note 5, p. 183. Between this and the next line Eliot's manuscript includes another: "The ivory men make company between us." It was cut from the poem at Vivien Eliot's request before publication, but Eliot restored it from memory in a fair copy he wrote out in 1960.

7. Demobilized; discharged from the army after the First World War. (The following passage, according to Eliot, was based on a story told the Eliots by their maid; the manuscript shows that lines 153 and 164 were suggested by Vivien Eliot.)

8. The barkeeper's call at closing time in an English pub.

9. Druggist.

1. Ham.

HURRY UP PLEASE ITS TIME
HURRY UP PLEASE ITS TIME
Goonight Bill. Goonight Lou. Goonight May. Goonight.
Ta ta. Goonight. Goonight.
Good night, ladies, good night, sweet ladies, good night, good night.[2]

III. The Fire Sermon[3]

The river's tent is broken; the last fingers of leaf
Clutch and sink into the wet bank. The wind
Crosses the brown land, unheard. The nymphs are departed.
Sweet Thames, run softly, till I end my song.[4]
The river bears no empty bottles, sandwich papers,
Silk handkerchiefs, cardboard boxes, cigarette ends
Or other testimony of summer nights. The nymphs are departed.
And their friends, the loitering heirs of City directors;
Departed, have left no addresses.
By the waters of Leman I sat down and wept . . .[5]
Sweet Thames, run softly till I end my song,
Sweet Thames, run softly, for I speak not loud or long.
But at my back in a cold blast I hear[6]
The rattle of the bones, and chuckle spread from ear to ear.

A rat crept softly through the vegetation
Dragging its slimy belly on the bank
While I was fishing in the dull canal
On a winter evening round behind the gashouse
Musing upon the king my brother's wreck[7]
And on the king my father's death before him.
White bodies naked on the low damp ground
And bones cast in a little low dry garret,
Rattled by the rat's foot only, year to year.
But at my back from time to time I hear
The sound of horns and motors, which shall bring

2. From *Hamlet* IV.v, these words conclude Ophelia's mad speech before her suicide by drowning.

3. In the *Fire Sermon*, Buddha counsels his followers to conceive an aversion for the burning flames of passion and physical sensation, and thus live a holy life, attain freedom from earthly things, and finally leave the cycle of rebirth for Nirvana. "The complete text of the Buddha's Fire Sermon (which corresponds in importance to the Sermon on the Mount) . . . will be found translated in the late Henry Clarke Warren's *Buddhism in Translation* (Harvard Oriental Series) . . ." (Eliot's note).

4. "V. Spenser, *Prothalamion*" (Eliot's note). This line is the refrain of the Elizabethan poet Edmund Spenser's marriage-song. The nymphs (in the preceding line) are described by Spenser as "lovely Daughters of the Flood", or "Thames-Daughters" as Eliot calls them in his note to line 266.

5. The Psalmist describes the exiled Hebrews mourning for their homeland: "By the rivers of Babylon, there we sat down, yea, we wept, when we remembered Zion." (*Psalm* 137) Leman is the Swiss name for Lake Geneva, near which, in Lausanne, Eliot was convalescing when he was completing *The Waste Land;* in Elizabethan and earlier English, the common noun meant a lover.

6. "Cf. Marvell, *To His Coy Mistress*" (Eliot's note). Eliot's note, intended for line 196, applies here as well; both are ironic paraphrases of Marvell's lines, "But at my back I always hear / Time's winged chariot hurrying near . . ."

7. "Cf. *The Tempest,* I, ii" (Eliot's note). See line 48.

Sweeney to Mrs. Porter in the spring.[8]
O the moon shone bright on Mrs. Porter
And on her daughter
They wash their feet in soda water[9]
Et O ces voix d'enfants, chantant dans la coupole![1]

Twit twit twit
Jug jug jug jug jug jug
So rudely forc'd.
Tereu[2]

Unreal City
Under the brown fog of a winter noon
Mr. Eugenides, the Smyrna merchant
Unshaven, with a pocket full of currants
C.i.f. London: documents at sight,[3]
Asked me in demotic[3a] French
To luncheon at the Cannon Street Hotel[4]
Followed by a weekend at the Metropole.

At the violet hour, when the eyes and back
Turn upward from the desk, when the human engine waits
Like a taxi throbbing waiting,
I Tiresias,[5] though blind, throbbing between two lives,

8. "Cf. Day, *Parliament of Bees:* 'When of the sudden, listening, you shall hear, / A noise of horns and hunting, which shall bring, / Actaeon to Diana in the spring, / Where all shall see her naked skin . . .' " (Eliot's note). Diana, the virgin goddess of the woods and hunting, was seen naked by Actaeon the hunter; she then changed him into a stag, to be hunted to death by his own dogs. She was equivalent to the Greek goddess Artemis, whom Frazer discusses as a type of the Hanged God (see note to line 46).

9. "I do not know the origin of the ballad from which these lines are taken: it was reported to me from Sydney, Australia" (Eliot's note). It was sung by Australian troops during the Dardanelles Campaign of World War I; a fuller version reads: "O the moon shone bright on Mrs. Porter / And on the daughter / Of Mrs. Porter. / They wash their feet in soda water / And so they oughter / To keep them clean." As the note for the next line suggests, this may parody the ceremonial washing of feet which is part of the liturgy of Holy Thursday; the act's symbolic meaning is of humility and love, and recapitulates Christ's washing of his disciples' feet as recounted in *John* 13:1–17.

1. "V. Verlaine, *Parsifal*" (Eliot's note): "And O those children's voices singing in the dome!" Verlaine's poem evokes Wagner's opera about the Grail quest. Parsifal has withstood the enchantress's efforts to seduce him; humbled and purified, she washes his feet to prepare him to enter the Grail Castle, where he heals the Fisher King Amfortas and becomes king himself. The opera ends with the sound of children's voices singing Christ's praise from the heights of the castle.

2. Another conventional representation of the nightingale's song, alluding to King Tereus and his brutality to Philomel. Compare a song in John Lyle's play, *Campaspe* (1584): "O 'tis the ravished nightingale. / Jug, jug, jug, jug, tereu! she cries. . . ."

3. "The currants were quoted at a price 'carriage and insurance free to London'; and the Bill of Lading etc. were to be handed to the buyer on payment of the sight draft" (Eliot's note).

3a. Common, colloquial.

4. Next to the Cannon Street Station in the City, this hotel was used by businessmen going to or from the continent by boat-train; it was also a locale for homosexual liaisons. The Metropole is a luxurious hotel in the seaside resort of Brighton.

5. "Tiresias, although a mere spectator and not indeed a 'character,' is yet the most important personage in the poem uniting all the rest. Just as the one-eyed merchant, seller of currants, melts into the Phoenician Sailor, and the latter is not wholly distinct from Ferdinand Prince of Naples [in *The Tempest*], so all the women are one woman, and the two sexes meet in Tiresias. What Tiresias *sees*, in fact, is the substance of the poem . . ." (Eliot's note). Eliot then quotes a passage in Ovid's *Metamorphoses* (III. 316–38) which tells how Tiresias struck and so separated two snakes that were coupling, and was thereupon turned into a woman; eight years later he saw them again, struck them once more, and was changed back into a man. Jupiter and Juno asked him, since he had been both man and woman, to decide a dispute between them as to whether men or women more enjoyed sexual intercourse. Tiresias infuriated Juno by saying that women did, and was blinded. Jupiter palliated this affliction by granting him the gift of prophecy.

Old man with wrinkled female breasts, can see
At the violet hour, the evening hour that strives
Homeward, and brings the sailor home from sea,[6]
The typist home at teatime, clears her breakfast, lights
Her stove, and lays out food in tins.
Out of the window perilously spread
Her drying combinations touched by the sun's last rays,
On the divan are piled (at night her bed)
Stockings, slippers, camisoles,[6a] and stays.
I Tiresias, old man with wrinkled dugs
Perceived the scene, and foretold the rest—
I too awaited the expected guest.
He, the young man carbuncular, arrives,
A small house agent's clerk, with one bold stare,
One of the low on whom assurance sits
As a silk hat on a Bradford millionaire.[7]
The time is now propitious, as he guesses,
The meal is ended, she is bored and tired,
Endeavours to engage her in caresses
Which still are unreproved, if undesired.
Flushed and decided, he assaults at once;
Exploring hands encounter no defence;
His vanity requires no response,
And makes a welcome of indifference.
(And I Tiresias have foresuffered all
Enacted on this same divan or bed;
I who have sat by Thebes below the wall[8]
And walked among the lowest of the dead.)
Bestows one final patronising kiss,
And gropes his way, finding the stairs unlit . . .

She turns and looks a moment in the glass,
Hardly aware of her departed lover;
Her brain allows one half-formed thought to pass:
'Well now that's done: and I'm glad it's over.'
When lovely woman stoops to folly and
Paces about her room again, alone,
She smoothes her hair with automatic hand,
And puts a record on the gramophone.[9]

6. "This may not appear as exact as Sappho's lines, but I had in mind the 'long-shore' or 'dory' fisherman, who returns at nightfall" (Eliot's note). Sappho wrote, "Hesperus [the evening star], thou bringest home all things bright morning scattered: thou bringest the sheep, the goat, the child to the mother." Also involved is "Home is the sailor, home from the sea," a line in Robert Louis Stevenson's "Requiem."

6a. Slips.

7. War profiteer. Bradford is an industrial town in the north of England.

8. Tiresias, who prophesied in the marketplace by the wall of Thebes, foretold the fall of two Theban kings, Oedipus and Creon. After his death he remained a prophet; Odysseus summoned him from Hades and was given advice to aid his voyage home.

9. "V. Goldsmith, the song in *The Vicar of Wakefield*" (Eliot's note). The seduced Olivia sings, "When lovely woman stoops to folly / And finds too late that men betray, / What charm can soothe her melancholy, / What art can wash her guilt away? / The only art her guilt to cover, / To hide her shame from every eye, / To give repentance to her lover / And wring his bosom—is to die."

'This music crept by me upon the waters'[1]
And along the Strand, up Queen Victoria Street.
O City city, I can sometimes hear
Beside a public bar in Lower Thames Street,
The pleasant whining of a mandoline
And a clatter and a chatter from within
Where fishmen lounge at noon: where the walls
Of Magnus Martyr[2] hold
Inexplicable splendour of Ionian white and gold.

The river sweats[3]
Oil and tar
The barges drift
With the turning tide
Red sails
Wide
To leeward, swing on the heavy spar.
The barges wash
Drifting logs
Down Greenwich reach
Past the Isle of Dogs.[4]
Weialala leia
Wallala leialala

Elizabeth and Leicester[5]
Beating oars
The stern was formed
A gilded shell
Red and gold
The brisk swell
Rippled both shores
Southwest wind
Carried down stream
The peal of bells

1. "V. *The Tempest* as above" (Eliot's note). See note for l. 48.

2. "The interior of St. Magnus Martyr is to my mind one of the finest among [Sir Christopher] Wren's interiors. See *The Proposed Demolition of Nineteen City Churches:* (P. S. King & Son, Ltd.)" (Eliot's note). The church, built in 1676, still stands at the corner of Lower Thames and Fish Streets, between London Bridge and London's fish market. It is here another intimation of a world separated from the Waste Land.

3. "The Song of the (three) Thames-daughters begins here. From line 292 to 306 inclusive they speak in turn. V. *Götterdämmerung,* III, i: the Rhine-daughters" (Eliot's note). In Wagner's opera *The Twilight of the Gods,* the three Rhine-maidens try in vain to seduce and then frighten the hero Siegfried into returning their gold, which brings both power and death to its possessor; since its theft the beauty of their river has gone. Lines 277–8 quote the refrain of their song.

4. A peninsula in East London formed by a sharp bend in the Thames called Greenwich Reach; Greenwich is a borough on the south bank. It was in Greenwich House that Queen Elizabeth I was born and that she entertained the Earl of Leicester (lines 279–289).

5. "V. [J. A.] Froude, [*The Reign of*] *Elizabeth,* Vol. I, ch. iv, letter of De Quadra [Spanish bishop and ambassador to England] to [King] Philip of Spain: 'In the afternoon we were in a barge, watching the games on the river. (The queen) was alone with Lord Robert [Earl of Leicester] and myself on the poop, when they began to talk nonsense, and went so far that Lord Robert at last said, as I was on the spot there was no reason why they should not be married if the Queen pleased' " (Eliot's note).

White towers
                Weialala leia
                Wallala leialala

'Trams and dusty trees.
Highbury bore me. Richmond and Kew
Undid me.[6] By Richmond I raised my knees
Supine on the floor of a narrow canoe.'

'My feet are at Moorgate, and my heart
Under my feet. After the event
He wept. He promised "a new start."
I made no comment. What should I resent?'

'On Margate Sands.[7]
I can connect
Nothing with nothing.
The broken fingernails of dirty hands.
My people humble people who expect
Nothing.'
            la la

To Carthage then I came[8]

Burning burning burning burning[9]
O Lord Thou pluckest me out[1]
O Lord Thou pluckest

burning

IV. Death by Water[2]

Phlebas the Phoenician, a fortnight dead,
Forgot the cry of gulls, and the deep sea swell
And the profit and loss.
                A current under sea
Picked his bones in whispers. As he rose and fell

6. "Cf. *Purgatorio,* V, 133 . . ." (Eliot's note). Dante meets the spirit of Pia de' Tolomei of Siena, who tells him that "Siena made me, Maremma unmade me," a reference to her violent death in Maremma at her husband's hands.

7. Margate, and the other places mentioned above, are in or near London and the Thames.

8. "V. St. Augustine's *Confessions:* 'To Carthage then I came, where a cauldron of unholy loves sang all about mine ears' " (Eliot's note).

9. Eliot's note (see note 3, p. 186) to this line alludes to the Buddha's Fire Sermon, but the line is not quoted from it.

1. "From St. Augustine's *Confessions* again. The collocation of these two representatives of eastern and western asceticism, as the culmination of this part of the poem, is not an accident" (Eliot's note). Augustine wrote, "I entangle my steps with these outward beauties, but Thou pluckest me out, O Lord, Thou pluckest me out."

2. The death of Phlebas by drowning was predicted by Madame Sosostris in Part I. Some readers feel that he dies in order to be reborn, as a fertility god; others, that his death is sterile and without hope of resurrection. The likeliest view is that Phlebas represents the principal speaker's urge to find oblivion, and that his death is not to be taken as a real drowning.

He passed the stages of his age and youth
Entering the whirlpool.
                                        Gentile or Jew
O you who turn the wheel and look to windward,
Consider Phlebas, who was once handsome and tall as you.

V. What the Thunder Said[3]

After the torchlight red on sweaty faces
After the frosty silence in the gardens
After the agony in stony places
The shouting and the crying
Prison and palace and reverberation
Of thunder of spring over distant mountains
He who was living is now dead[4]
We who were living are now dying
With a little patience

Here is no water but only rock
Rock and no water and the sandy road
The road winding above among the mountains
Which are mountains of rock without water
If there were water we should stop and drink
Amongst the rock one cannot stop or think
Sweat is dry and feet are in the sand
If there were only water amongst the rock
Dead mountain mouth of carious teeth that cannot spit
Here one can neither stand nor lie nor sit
There is not even silence in the mountains
But dry sterile thunder without rain
There is not even solitude in the mountains
But red sullen faces sneer and snarl
From doors of mudcracked houses
                                        If there were water
   And no rock
   If there were rock
   And also water
   And water
   A spring
   A pool among the rock
   If there were the sound of water only
   Not the cicada
   And dry grass singing
   But sound of water over a rock
   Where the hermit-thrush sings in the pine trees

3. "In the first part of Part V three themes are employed: the journey to Emmaus, the approach to the Chapel Perilous (see Miss Weston's book) and the present decay of eastern Europe" (Eliot's note).

4. Christ's agony in the Garden of Gethsemane, his imprisonment, trial, and death on the cross are alluded to here.

Drip drop drip drop drop drop drop[5]
But there is no water

Who is the third who walks always beside you?[6]
When I count, there are only you and I together
But when I look ahead up the white road
There is always another one walking beside you
Gliding wrapt in a brown mantle, hooded
I do not know whether a man or a woman
—But who is that on the other side of you?

What is that sound high in the air
Murmur of maternal lamentation
Who are those hooded hordes swarming
Over endless plains, stumbling in cracked earth
Ringed by the flat horizon only
What is the city over the mountains
Cracks and reforms and bursts in the violet air
Falling towers
Jerusalem Athens Alexandria
Vienna London
Unreal[7]

A woman drew her long black hair out tight
And fiddled whisper music on those strings
And bats with baby faces in the violet light
Whistled, and beat their wings
And crawled head downward down a blackened wall
And upside down in air were towers
Tolling reminiscent bells, that kept the hours
And voices singing out of empty cisterns and exhausted wells

In this decayed hole among the mountains
In the faint moonlight, the grass is singing
Over the tumbled graves, about the chapel[8]
There is the empty chapel, only the wind's home.

5. "This is *Turdus aonalaschkae pallasii,* the hermit-thrush which I have heard in Quebec Province. Chapman says (*Handbook of Birds of Eastern North America*) 'it is most at home in secluded woodland and thickety retreats. . . . Its notes are not remarkable for variety or volume, but in purity and sweetness of tone and exquisite modulation they are unequalled.' Its 'water-dripping song' is justly celebrated" (Eliot's note).

6. "The following lines were stimulated by the account of one of the Antarctic expeditions (I forget which, but I think one of Shackleton's): it was related that the party of explorers, at the extremity of their strength, had the constant delusion that there was *one more member* than could actually be counted" (Eliot's note). In *Luke* 24:13–16 two disciples, on their way to Emmaus, discuss Christ's resurrection, and "Jesus himself drew near, and went with them. But their eyes were holden [constrained], that they should not know him."

7. Eliot's note for lines 367–77: "Cf. Hermann Hesse, *Blick ins Chaos* [A Glimpse into Chaos]": "Already half of Europe, and at least half of Eastern Europe, is on the way to Chaos, travels drunk in sacred madness along the brink of the abyss and moreover sings drunken hymns as Dmitri Karamazov sang. The bourgeois, shocked, laughs at these songs; the saint and seer hears them with tears." The "maternal lamentation" is of the women weeping over Christ and perhaps over the deaths of other vegetation gods.

8. The Perilous Chapel, which the knight must enter on his way to the Grail.

It has no windows, and the door swings,
Dry bones can harm no one.
Only a cock stood on the rooftree
Co co rico co co rico[9]
In a flash of lightning. Then a damp gust
Bringing rain

Ganga[1] was sunken, and the limp leaves
Waited for rain, while the black clouds
Gathered far distant, over Himavant.[2]
The jungle crouched, humped in silence.
Then spoke the thunder
DA[3]
Datta: what have we given?
My friend, blood shaking my heart
The awful daring of a moment's surrender
Which an age of prudence can never retract
By this, and this only, we have existed
Which is not to be found in our obituaries
Or in memories draped by the beneficent spider[4]
Or under seals broken by the lean solicitor[4a]
In our empty rooms
DA
Dayadhvam: I have heard the key
Turn in the door once and turn once only[5]
We think of the key, each in his prison
Thinking of the key, each confirms a prison
Only at nightfall, aethereal rumours
Revive for a moment a broken Coriolanus[6]
DA
Damyata: The boat responded
Gaily, to the hand expert with sail and oar
The sea was calm, your heart would have responded

9. The cock crows to announce the coming dawn and the departure of evil spirits which shun daylight.

1. The sacred Indian river Ganges.

2. The Himalayan mountain range.

3. The sound of thunder. " 'Datta, dayadhvam damyata' (Give, sympathize, control). The fable of the meaning of the Thunder is found in the Brihadaranyaka-Upanishad, 5, 1 . . ." (Eliot's note). In the Hindu fable of "The Three Great Disciplines," the Creator God instructs the lesser gods to "control" their unruly natures, men to "give" alms despite their natural miserliness, and the cruel demons to "sympathize"; "That very thing is repeated even today by the heavenly voice, in the form of thunder as 'Da,' 'Da,' 'Da.'. . . Therefore one should practice these three things: self-control, giving, and mercy."

4. "Cf. Webster, *The White Devil,* V, vi: ' . . . they'll remarry / Ere the worm pierce your winding-sheet, ere the spider / Make a thin curtain for your epitaphs' " (Eliot's note).

4a. Here, family lawyer.

5. "Cf. *Inferno,* XXXIII 46 . . ." (Eliot's note), which is translated: "And I heard below me the door of the horrible tower being locked." The traitor Ugolino tells Dante that his enemies imprisoned him and his children in a tower to die of starvation. Eliot continues: "Also F. H. Bradley, *Appearance and Reality,* p. 346. 'My external sensations are no less private to myself than are my thoughts or my feelings. In either case my experience falls within my own circle, a circle closed on the outside; and, with all its elements alike, every sphere is opaque to the others which surround it. . . . In brief, regarded as an existence which appears in a soul, the whole world for each is peculiar and private to that soul.' "

6. Roman general, the hero of a play by Shakespeare, who was exiled by the Roman people and then from injured pride led the enemy against Rome.

Gaily, when invited, beating[6a] obedient
To controlling hands

I sat upon the shore
Fishing,[7] with the arid plain behind me
Shall I at least set my lands in order?[8]
London Bridge is falling down falling down falling down
Poi s'ascose nel foco che gli affina[9]
Quando fiam uti chelidon—O swallow swallow[1]
Le Prince d'Aquitaine à la tour abolie[2]
These fragments I have shored against my ruins
Why then Ile fit you. Hieronymo's mad againe.[3]
Datta. Dayadhvam. Damyata.
Shantih shantih shantih[4]

1922

Little Gidding[8]

I

Midwinter spring is its own season
Sempiternal[9] though sodden towards sundown,
Suspended in time, between pole and tropic.
When the short day is brightest, with frost and fire,
The brief sun flames the ice, on pond and ditches,
In windless cold that is the heart's heat,
Reflecting in a watery mirror
A glare that is blindness in the early afternoon.
And glow more intense than blaze of branch, or brazier,

6a. In sailing, heading into the wind.

7. "V. Weston: *From Ritual to Romance;* chapter on the Fisher King" (Eliot's note).

8. *Isaiah* 38:1 : "Thus saith the Lord, Set thine house in order: for thou shalt die, and not live."

9. "V. *Purgatorio,* XXVI, 28 . . ." (Eliot's note). In this passage the soul of the poet Arnaut Daniel speaks to Dante, "Now I pray you, by the goodness that guides you to the top of this staircase [out of Purgatory], be mindful in time of my suffering." Dante continues, "Then he hid himself in the fire which refines them."

1. "V. *Pervigilium Veneris.* Cf. Philomela in Parts II and III" (Eliot's note). In the late Latin poem. "The Vigil of Venus," Philomel asks, "When shall I be like the swallow," continuing, "that I may cease to be silent?" A. C. Swinburne's "Itylus" begins, "Swallow, my sister, O sister swallow, / How can thy heart be full of spring?"

2. "V. Gerard de Nerval, Sonnet *El Desdichado*" (Eliot's note). From Nerval's poem, "The Disinherited," in which the poet compares himself to "The prince of Aquitaine at the ruined tower".

3. "V. Kyd's *Spanish Tragedy*" (Eliot's note). The play's subtitle is "Hieronymo Is Mad Againe"; to avenge his son's murder he feigns madness, and writes a play in which, acting one of the parts, he kills the murderer. "Why then Ile fit you!" (that is, accommodate you) is his answer when requested to write the play.

4. "Repeated as here, a formal ending to an Upanishad. 'The Peace which passeth understanding' is our equivalent to this word" (Eliot's note). In the 1922 edition of this poem, Eliot phrased his note as "our feeble equivalent to this word."

8. This poem, published in 1942, is the last of Eliot's *Four Quartets,* and Eliot considered it the best part of that work, as that work was the best of his poetry. Like the late quartets of Beethoven, they are thematically interwoven with each other. Each of Eliot's *Quartets* is divided into five parts or movements which develop the central theme in quite different ways. Each quartet is based upon one of the four elements, that of *Little Gidding* being fire. Here, as in *The Waste Land* (The Fire Sermon), fire is the torturing element in which we live, but it is also the refining fire which can bring man to salvation. Little Gidding was an Anglican religious community founded in 1625 by Nicholas Ferrar; it is now a village in Huntingdonshire. Although the community lasted only twenty-two years, the memory of its devotion persisted, and the chapel was rebuilt in the nineteenth century.

9. Everlasting.

Stirs the dumb spirit: no wind, but pentecostal fire[1]
In the dark time of the year. Between melting and freezing
The soul's sap quivers. There is no earth smell
Or smell of living thing. This is the spring time
But not in time's covenant. Now the hedgerow
Is blanched for an hour with transitory blossom
Of snow, a bloom more sudden
Than that of summer, neither budding nor fading,
Not in the scheme of generation.
Where is the summer, the unimaginable
Zero summer?

If you came this way,[3]
Taking the route you would be likely to take
From the place you would be likely to come from,
If you came this way in may[4] time, you would find the hedges
White again, in May, with voluptuary sweetness.
It would be the same at the end of the journey,
If you came at night like a broken king,[5]
If you came by day not knowing what you came for,
It would be the same, when you leave the rough road
And turn behind the pig-sty to the dull façade
And the tombstone. And what you thought you came for
Is only a shell, a husk of meaning
From which the purpose breaks only when it is fulfilled
If at all. Either you had no purpose
Or the purpose is beyond the end you figured
And is altered in fulfilment. There are other places
Which also are the world's end, some at the sea jaws,
Or over a dark lake, in a desert or a city—
But this is the nearest, in place and time,
Now and in England.

If you came this way,
Taking any route, starting from anywhere,
At any time or at any season,
It would always be the same: you would have to put off
Sense and notion. You are not here to verify,
Instruct yourself, or inform curiosity
Or carry report. You are here to kneel
Where prayer has been valid. And prayer is more
Than an order of words, the conscious occupation
Of the praying mind, or the sound of the voice praying.

1. On the feast of Pentecost, the disciples of Christ were assembled, "And suddenly there came a sound from heaven, as of a rushing mighty wind, and it filled all the house where they were sitting. And there appeared unto them cloven tongues, like as of fire. . . . And they were all filled with the Holy Ghost . . ." (*Acts* 2:2–4).

3. To Little Gidding.

4. A shrub bearing white flowers in spring.

5. King Charles I, who after his final defeat at the battle of Naseby in the English Civil War came to Little Gidding to fortify his spirit.

And what the dead had no speech for, when living,
They can tell you, being dead: the communication
Of the dead is tongued with fire beyond the language of the living.
Here, the intersection of the timeless moment
Is England and nowhere. Never and always.

II

Ash on an old man's sleeve[6]
Is all the ash the burnt roses leave.
Dust in the air suspended
Marks the place where a story ended.
Dust inbreathed was a house—
The wall, the wainscot and the mouse.
The death of hope and despair,
    This is the death of air.

There are flood and drouth
Over the eyes and in the mouth,
Dead water and dead sand
Contending for the upper hand.
The parched eviscerate soil
Gapes at the vanity of toil,
Laughs without mirth.
    This is the death of earth.

Water and fire succeed
The town, the pasture and the weed.
Water and fire deride
The sacrifice that we denied.
Water and fire shall rot
The marred foundations we forgot,
Of sanctuary and choir.
    This is the death of water and fire.

In the uncertain hour before the morning[7]
  Near the ending of interminable night
  At the recurrent end of the unending
After the dark dove with the flickering tongue[8]
  Had passed below the horizon of his homing
  While the dead leaves still rattle on like tin
Over the asphalt where no other sound was
  Between three districts whence the smoke arose
  I met one walking, loitering and hurried
As if blown towards me like the metal leaves

6. The second movement meditates on the death of the four elements—air, earth, water, and fire—which were once thought to make up the physical universe.

7. Lines 80–151 are meant to suggest, if not exactly to imitate, the stanzaic pattern of Dante's *Divine Comedy*. Eliot was an air raid warden during the German raids on London in the Second World War, and represents himself here as patrolling the streets after such a raid.

8. The German dive-bomber.

Before the urban dawn wind unresisting.
And as I fixed upon the down-turned face
That pointed scrutiny with which we challenge
The first-met stranger in the waning dusk
I caught the sudden look of some dead master
Whom I had known, forgotten, half recalled
Both one and many; in the brown baked features
The eyes of a familiar compound ghost[9]
Both intimate and unidentifiable.
So I assumed a double part, and cried
And heard another's voice cry: 'What! are *you* here?'
Although we were not. I was still the same,
Knowing myself yet being someone other—
And he a face still forming; yet the words sufficed
To compel the recognition they preceded.
And so, compliant to the common wind,
Too strange to each other for misunderstanding,
In concord at this intersection time
Of meeting nowhere, no before and after,
We trod the pavement in a dead patrol.
I said: 'The wonder that I feel is easy,
Yet ease is cause of wonder. Therefore speak:
I may not comprehend, may not remember.'
And he: 'I am not eager to rehearse [1]
My thoughts and theory which you have forgotten.
These things have served their purpose: let them be.
So with your own, and pray they be forgiven
By others, as I pray you to forgive
Both bad and good. Last season's fruit is eaten
And the fullfed beast shall kick the empty pail.
For last year's words belong to last year's language
And next year's words await another voice.
But, as the passage now presents no hindrance
To the spirit unappeased and peregrine [1a]
Between two worlds become much like each other,
So I find words I never thought to speak
In streets I never thought I should revisit
When I left my body on a distant shore.
Since our concern was speech, and speech impelled us
To purify the dialect of the tribe[2]
And urge the mind to aftersight and foresight,
Let me disclose the gifts reserved for age
To set a crown upon your lifetime's effort.
First, the cold friction of expiring sense
Without enchantment, offering no promise
But bitter tastelessness of shadow fruit

9. Eliot said that he had principally in mind here W. B. Yeats and Jonathan Swift.

1. Repeat.

1a. Wandering.

2. A reference to the line in Stéphane Mallarmé, "Le Tombeau d'Edgar Poe," "Donner un sens plus pur aux mots de la tribu" (To give the words of the tribe a more exact meaning).

As body and soul begin to fall asunder.
Second, the conscious impotence of rage[3]
At human folly, and the laceration
Of laughter at what ceases to amuse.[4]
And last, the rending pain of re-enactment
Of all that you have done, and been; the shame
Of motives late revealed, and the awareness
Of things ill done and done to others' harm
Which once you took for exercise of virtue.
Then fools' approval stings, and honour stains.
From wrong to wrong the exasperated spirit
Proceeds, unless restored by that refining fire[5]
Where you must move in measure, like a dancer.'
The day was breaking. In the disfigured street
He left me, with a kind of valediction,
And faded on the blowing of the horn.[6]

III

There are three conditions which often look alike
Yet differ completely, flourish in the same hedgerow:
Attachment to self and to things and to persons, detachment
From self and from things and from persons; and, growing between them, indifference
Which resembles the others as death resembles life,
Being between two lives—unflowering, between
The live and the dead nettle. This is the use of memory:
For liberation—not less of love but expanding
Of love beyond desire, and so liberation
From the future as well as the past. Thus, love of a country
Begins as attachment to our own field of action
And comes to find that action of little importance
Though never indifferent. History may be servitude,
History may be freedom. See, now they vanish,
The faces and places, with the self which, as it could, loved them,
To become renewed, transfigured, in another pattern.

Sin is Behovely,[7] but
All shall be well, and
All manner of thing shall be well.
If I think, again, of this place,
And of people, not wholly commendable,

3. In Yeats's poem, "The Spur," he spoke of lust and rage as the two aspects of old age.

4. Swift's epitaph, written by himself in Latin (and translated by Yeats) says that "Savage indignation now / Cannot lacerate his breast."

5. See note 8, p. 194. But Eliot has also in mind the purgative fires in Yeats's poem, "Byzantium," p. 49.

6. Spirits usually vanish at the crowing of the cock. The horn is the "All Clear" siren after the air raid. Eliot echoes Shakespeare's description of the disappearance of Hamlet's father's ghost: "It faded on the crowing of the cock." (*Hamlet* I.ii. 157.)

7. Necessary to the divine plan. In one of her visions the 14th-century English mystic, Dame Juliana of Norwich, was told that "sin is behovable but all shall be well . . . and all manner of things shall be well."

Of no immediate kin or kindness,
But some of peculiar genius,
All touched by a common genius,
United in the strife which divided them;
If I think of a king at nightfall,
Of three men, and more, on the scaffold[8]
And a few who died forgotten
In other places, here and abroad,
And of one who died blind and quiet,[9]
Why should we celebrate
These dead men more than the dying?
It is not to ring the bell backward
Nor is it an incantation
To summon the spectre of a Rose.[1]
We cannot revive old factions
We cannot restore old policies
Or follow an antique drum.
These men, and those who opposed them
And those whom they opposed
Accept the constitution of silence
And are folded in a single party.
Whatever we inherit from the fortunate
We have taken from the defeated
What they had to leave us—a symbol:
A symbol perfected in death.
And all shall be well and
All manner of thing shall be well
By the purification of the motive
In the ground of our beseeching.[2]

IV

The dove descending breaks the air
With flame of incandescent terror
Of which the tongues declare
The one discharge from sin and error.[3]
The only hope, or else despair
  Lies in the choice of pyre or pyre—
  To be redeemed from fire by fire.

Who then devised the torment? Love.
Love is the unfamiliar Name

8. King Charles I and his two chief aides, Thomas Wentworth, Earl of Strafford, and Archbishop Laud, who were executed by the Puritans in 1649.

9. John Milton, who took Cromwell's side against the King.

1. The phrase is the title of a sentimental ballet, in which a girl dreams of the ghost of a rose she once wore to the ball, and a reference to the Wars of the Roses, Lancaster being the white and York the red, to determine which family would rule England.

2. Dame Juliana of Norwich was instructed in a vision that "the ground of our beseeching" is love.

3. The dove is both dive bomber and the symbol of the Holy Ghost with its pentecostal tongues of fire. The two kinds of fire, destructive and refining, form the basis of this lyrical movement.

Behind the hands that wove
The intolerable shirt of flame
Which human power cannot remove.[4]
  We only live, only suspire [5]
  Consumed by either fire or fire.

V

What we call the beginning is often the end
And to make an end is to make a beginning.
The end is where we start from. And every phrase
And sentence that is right (where every word is at home,
Taking its place to support the others,
The word neither diffident nor ostentatious,
An easy commerce of the old and the new,
The common word exact without vulgarity,
The formal word precise but not pedantic,
The complete consort[5a] dancing together)
Every phrase and every sentence is an end and a beginning,
Every poem an epitaph. And any action
Is a step to the block, to the fire, down the sea's throat
Or to an illegible stone: and that is where we start.
We die with the dying:
See, they depart, and we go with them.
We are born with the dead:
See, they return, and bring us with them.
The moment of the rose and the moment of the yew-tree[6]
Are of equal duration. A people without history
Is not redeemed from time, for history is a pattern
Of timeless moments. So, while the light fails
On a winter's afternoon, in a secluded chapel[7]
History is now and England.

With the drawing of this Love and the voice of this Calling[8]

We shall not cease from exploration
And the end of all our exploring
Will be to arrive where we started
And know the place for the first time.
Through the unknown, remembered gate
When the last of earth left to discover
Is that which was the beginning;
At the source of the longest river
The voice of the hidden waterfall

4. The shirt of Nessus, which Hercules' wife had him put on because she had been falsely informed that it would win back his love for her, clung to his flesh and caused such suffering that he had himself placed on a pyre and burned himself to death.

5. Sigh or breathe.

5a. Fellowship.

6. The rose is a symbol of love and life, as the yew-tree of grief and death.

7. At Little Gidding.

8. Quoted from *The Cloud of Unknowing*, an anonymous 14th-century religious work.

And the children in the apple-tree
Not known, because not looked for
But heard, half-heard, in the stillness
Between two waves of the sea.[9]
Quick now, here, now, always—
A condition of complete simplicity
(Costing not less than everything)
And all shall be well and
All manner of thing shall be well
When the tongues of flame are in-folded
Into the crowned knot[1] of fire
And the fire and the rose are one.[2]

1942

9. The voices of the children and the thrush (the "hidden waterfall"), which occur in the first of the *Four Quartets*, "Burnt Norton," are intimations of the crossing of the time world by the timeless one, of now by always.

1. A nautical term, as George Williamson points out, for a knot finished by interweaving the strands so as to prevent untwisting.

2. The fire suggests the power and intensity of the divine spirit, the rose suggests mercy and love. Whatever meaning is given to the symbols, their union implies the visionary experience within human life.

CLAUDE McKAY
(1890–1948)

Claude McKay was born at Sunny Ville, Jamaica on September 15, 1890. His parents were poor farm workers. At six he went to live with an older brother, from whom he received all the education he was to have until he emigrated to the United States. McKay began while still a boy to write poems in the Jamaican dialect. Many of them were collected in two books published in 1912. For his work he won a prize which enabled him to come to the United States, where he studied briefly at the Tuskeegee Institute and for two years at Kansas State College. In 1914 he moved to Harlem, supporting himself with odd jobs, most often as a restaurant waiter, and during the First World War began to publish some of his most famous poems under the pseudonym "Eli Edwards." By 1920 his poems were being published regularly in England, and he was living there; the next year McKay returned to the United States as an editor of the radical newspapers *The Liberator* and *The Masses*.

Like many other writers of the time, both black and white, McKay was attracted to Communism; he traveled to Moscow in 1922 to meet Lenin and Trotsky, and represented the American Workers' Party at the Third Internationale. He remained in Europe, mainly in France and Morocco, and turned to writing fiction. Finally, McKay returned to the United States for the rest of his life. In his later years he was a well-known figure in American letters, though he wrote little; his poem "If We Must Die," a response to the Harlem race riots of 1919, was read to the British people by Winston Churchill and into the Congressional Record by American Senator Henry Cabot Lodge, Sr., as a World War II rallying cry. In 1942 he was converted to Catholicism and (like Richard Wright at about the same time) repudiated his earlier commitment to Communism. He died in Chicago on May 2, 1948.

If We Must Die

If we must die, let it not be like hogs
Hunted and penned in an inglorious spot,
While round us bark the mad and hungry dogs,
Making their mock at our accursed lot.
If we must die, O let us nobly die,
So that our precious blood may not be shed
In vain; then even the monsters we defy
Shall be constrained to honor us though dead!
O kinsmen! we must meet the common foe!
Though far outnumbered let us show us brave,
And for their thousand blows deal one deathblow!
What though before us lies the open grave?
Like men we'll face the murderous, cowardly pack,
Pressed to the wall, dying, but fighting back!

1922

America

Although she feeds me bread of bitterness,
And sinks into my throat her tiger's tooth,
Stealing my breath of life, I will confess
I love this cultured hell that tests my youth!
Her vigor flows like tides into my blood,
Giving me strength erect against her hate.
Her bigness sweeps my being like a flood.
Yet as a rebel fronts a king in state,
I stand within her walls with not a shred
Of terror, malice, not a word of jeer.
Darkly I gaze into the days ahead,
And see her might and granite wonders there,
Beneath the touch of Time's unerring hand,
Like priceless treasures sinking in the sand.

1922

EDNA ST. VINCENT MILLAY
(*1892–1950*)

Edna St. Vincent Millay was born on February 22, 1892, in Rockland, Maine. Her parents were divorced when she was a child, and her mother encouraged her literary interests. Edna Millay wrote her first poem when she was five, and as a child she regularly submitted poems to *St. Nicholas Magazine*. She studied for a short time at Barnard, then attended Vassar, where she spent a good part of her time enjoying the role of the young poet and baiting the college authorities. In 1917, the year of her Vassar degree, her first book of poems was published. She moved to Greenwich Village, then (as to a lesser degree now) a refuge for young people newly liberated from home and school, and her poems helped to create the legend of an American Bohemia. She joined the Provincetown Players and published three plays in verse. In 1923 she was awarded the Pulitzer Prize for *The Harp-Weaver;* in the same year she married Eugen Boissevain, a Dutch importer, and moved with her husband to a farm in the southern Berkshires. She died in 1950 at the age of fifty-eight.

[Hearing Your Words, and Not a Word Among Them]

Hearing your words, and not a word among them
Tuned to my liking, on a salty day
When inland woods were pushed by winds that flung them
Hissing to leeward[1] like a ton of spray,
I thought how off Matinicus[2] the tide
Came pounding in, came running through the Gut,
While from the Rock the warning whistle cried,
And children whimpered, and the doors blew shut;
There in the autumn when the men go forth,
With slapping skirts the island women stand
In gardens stripped and scattered, peering north,
With dahlia tubers dripping from the hand:
The wind of their endurance, driving south,
Flattened your words against your speaking mouth.

1931

The Return

Earth does not understand her child,
　Who from the loud gregarious town
Returns, depleted and defiled,
　To the still woods, to fling him down.

Earth can not count the sons she bore:
　The wounded lynx, the wounded man
Come trailing blood unto her door;
　She shelters both as best she can.

But she is early up and out,
　To trim the year or strip its bones;
She has no time to stand about
　Talking of him in undertones

Who has no aim but to forget,
　Be left in peace, be lying thus
For days, for years, for centuries yet,
　Unshaven and anonymous;

1. With the wind.
2. An island off the coast of Maine. The other allusions are to local geographical features.

Who, marked for failure, dulled by grief,
Has traded in his wife and friend
For this warm ledge, this alder leaf:
Comfort that does not comprehend.

1934

ARCHIBALD MACLEISH
(*1892–*)

Archibald MacLeish was born in Glencoe, Illinois on May 7, 1892. He describes his father as a "devout, cold, rigorous man of very beautiful speech." His mother was his father's third wife; before her marriage she had taught at Vassar College. MacLeish was educated at Hotchkiss School, at Yale (B.A., 1915), and at Harvard Law School, where he led his class. During the First World War, despite the fact that he had a wife and one child, he served as a volunteer ambulance driver and then at the front as a Captain of Field Artillery.

In the years just after the war MacLeish worked as a lawyer in Boston. His work distracted him from his poetry, and in 1923 he moved with his family to France, where he participated in the modernist revolution. Between 1924 and 1928 he published four books of poetry. In 1928 MacLeish returned to America, and in the winter of the following year, as preparation for the writing of his long poem *Conquistador*, he retraced by foot and mule-back the route of Cortez's conquering army through Mexico. The poem won the Pulitzer Prize for 1932.

During the early Depression years MacLeish worked for *Fortune* magazine. In the later Thirties he produced a series of works designed to warn his fellow citizens of the imminent war with Fascism and to restore their love of country. In 1940 MacLeish, in his highly controversial pamphlet *The Irresponsibles*, charged the great writers of his generation with weakening the moral fiber of their readers and leaving them prey to Fascism. MacLeish had come to believe that the poetry of Eliot and Pound was inadequate to the needs of a country which would shortly be at war.

As the Second World War approached, MacLeish became a very public man; the career of no other American man of letters displays so many connections with government offices and agencies. In 1939 President Roosevelt appointed him Librarian of Congress. The appointment was criticized by professional librarians, who viewed MacLeish as an amateur, and by politicians, who charged him with writing obscure poetry, but he held the post for five years. In 1941 he was made Director of the Office of Facts and Figures, a wartime agency with special responsibilities in the area of propaganda, and in 1944-45 he was Assistant Secretary of State. After the war he worked for the formation of UNESCO, and in 1946 served as chairman of the first UNESCO conference in Paris.

In 1949 MacLeish retired to the academy to become Boylston Professor of English Rhetoric at Harvard, and he held that post until 1962.

L'An Trentiesme de Mon Eage[1]

And I have come upon this place
By lost ways, by a nod, by words,
By faces, by an old man's face
At Morlaix[2] lifted to the birds,

By hands upon the tablecloth
At Aldebori's, by the thin
Child's hands that opened to the moth
And let the flutter of the moonlight in,

By hands, by voices, by the voice
Of Mrs. Whitman on the stair,
By Margaret's "If we had the choice
To choose or not—" through her thick hair,

By voices, by the creak and fall
Of footsteps on the upper floor,
By silence waiting in the hall
Between the doorbell and the door,

By words, by voices, a lost way—
And here above the chimney stack
The unknown constellations sway—
And by what way shall I go back?

1926

You, Andrew Marvell[5]

And here face down beneath the sun
And here upon earth's noonward height
To feel the always coming on
The always rising of the night:

To feel creep up the curving east
The earthy chill of dusk and slow
Upon those under lands the vast
And ever climbing shadow grow

And strange at Ecbatan[6] the trees
Take leaf by leaf the evening strange
The flooding dark about their knees
The mountains over Persia change

1. "In the thirtieth year of my age" (Old Fr), the opening of the *Great Testament* of François Villon (1431–c.1485), hence a traditional phrase for the end of youth.

2. A French city near the tip of Brittany.

5. An English poet (1621–1678). MacLeish extends and develops the idea expressed in two lines of Marvell's "To His Coy Mistress": "But at my back I always hear / Time's winged chariot hurrying near."

6. The ancient capital of Media (now part of Iran).

And now at Kermanshah[7] the gate
Dark empty and the withered grass
And through the twilight now the late
Few travelers in the westward pass

And Baghdad darken and the bridge
Across the silent river gone
And through Arabia the edge
Of evening widen and steal on

And deepen on Palmyra's street[8]
The wheel rut in the ruined stone
And Lebanon fade out and Crete
High through the clouds and overblown

And over Sicily the air
Still flashing with the landward gulls
And loom and slowly disappear
The sails above the shadowy hulls

And Spain go under and the shore
Of Africa the gilded sand
And evening vanish and no more
The low pale light across that land

Nor now the long light on the sea:

And here face downward in the sun
To feel how swift how secretly
The shadow of the night comes on . . .

1930

7. A district and city in Iran.

8. In ancient times this city in Syria was a great center of power and culture, but it is now a poor Arab village.

HUGH MacDIARMID (C. M. Grieve) (*1892–*)

Hugh MacDiarmid was born Christopher Murray Grieve on August 11, 1892, at Langholm, Dumfriesshire in the Scottish border country. He was educated at a local school and at Edinburgh University, then served in the First World War, after which he worked for many years as a journalist. His first poems, which were written in English, appeared in an anthology of Scottish verse in 1920, and two years later some poems in Scots, signed "Hugh MacDiarmid," were published in a periodical called *The Scottish Chapbook;* since that time he has been best known by his pseudonym. His *First Hymn to Lenin* (1931) announced his commitment to Marxist Communism, and he was one of the founders of the Scottish Nationalist Party in 1934; he has maintained a tempestuous relationship with each, in part because he belongs to both. Since his retirement as a journalist, MacDiarmid has lectured extensively in Europe, the Orient, and North America.

Parley of Beasts

Auld[2] Noah was at hame wi' them a',
The lion and the lamb,
Pair by pair they entered the Ark
And he took them as they cam'.

If twa o' ilka[3] beist there is
Into this room sud[4] come,
Wad[5] I cud welcome them like him,
And no' staun' gowpin'[6] dumb!

Be chief[7] wi' them and they wi' me
And a' wi' ane anither
As Noah and his couples were
There in the Ark thegither.

It's fain I'd mell wi' tiger and tit,[8]
Wi' elephant and eel,
But noo-a-days e'en wi' ain's se[9]
At hame it's hard to feel.

1926

O Wha's[10] the Bride?

O wha's the bride that cairries the bunch
O' thistles blinterin'[11] white?
Her cuckold bridegroom little dreids
What he sall ken[12] this nicht.

For closer than gudeman[13] can come
And closer to'r than hersel',
Wha didna need her maidenheid
Has wrocht his purpose fell.

O wha's been here afore me, lass,
And hoo did he get in?
—*A man that deed or*[14] *was I born*
This evil thing has din.

2. Old.
3. Every.
4. Should.
5. Would.
6. Gaping.
7. Friendly.
8. I'd eagerly mix with tiger and titmouse.
9. Even with one's self.
10. Who's.
11. Shining. The thistle is the emblem of Scotland.
12. Shall know.
13. Husband.
14. Died before.

And left, as it were on a corpse,
Your maidenheid to me?
—Nae lass,[15] *gudeman, sin' Time began*
'S hed ony mair to gi'e.[16]

But I can gi'e ye kindness, lad,
And a pair o' willin' hands,
And you sall ha'e my breists like stars,
My limbs like willow wands.

And on my lips ye'll heed nae mair,
And in my hair forget,
The seed o' a' the men that in
My virgin womb ha'e met. . . .

1926

Another Epitaph on an Army of Mercenaries[4]

It is a God-damned lie to say that these
Saved, or knew, anything worth any man's pride.
They were professional murderers and they took
Their blood money and impious risks and died.
In spite of all their kind some elements of worth
With difficulty persist here and there on earth.

1935

15. No girl.
16. Has had any more to give.

4. "In reply to A. E. Housman's" (MacDiarmid's note; see p. 32).

WILFRED OWEN
(*1893–1918*)

Wilfred Owen was born at Oswestry, England, on March 18, 1893. His father had a modest job with the railway, and the family's limited means had their effect on Owen's life. His mother was strict and Calvinistic. Owen attended Birkenhead Institute from 1900 to 1907, then Shrewsbury Technical School. He did some work at University College, Reading, in botany, then matriculated at the University of London. Unfortunately there was no money for fees, so he had to withdraw. He then went to Dunsden, Oxfordshire, as a pupil and lay assistant to the vicar; at first the notion was that he should become a priest, but Owen developed sympathy for the sufferings of the parishioners without a compatible confidence in Christianity's power to relieve them.

As a result of his disaffection, he left this post in August 1913 and went to teach at the Berlitz school in Bordeaux. He stayed in the city for two years, the second as tutor for two boys. The coming of war made him restive at "this deflowering of Europe," as he called. it. So he returned to England in August or September 1915 in order to enlist. He was trained and then commissioned in the Manchester Regiment, which went to the western front in January 1917. The weather was extremely cold, the fighting was fierce. In June Owen became ill and had to be moved to a hospital and then sent back to England to recuperate. Moved again, to a hospital in Edinburgh, he met Siegfried Sassoon, an army captain already known as a war poet. Sassoon encouraged him to write more poems and introduced him to other writers. He also optimistically assured him, when the time came for Owen to return to the front, that his new experiences would help his poetry. Owen went back to France on August 31, 1918, and was killed a week before the Armistice, on November 4. His poems, collected by Sassoon, were published in 1920.

Strange Meeting

It seemed that out of battle I escaped
Down some profound dull tunnel, long since scooped
Through granites which titanic wars had groined.[1]
Yet also there encumbered sleepers groaned,
Too fast in thought or death to be bestirred.
Then, as I probed them, one sprang up, and stared
With piteous recognition in fixed eyes,
Lifting distressful hands as if to bless.
And by his smile, I knew that sullen hall,
By his dead smile I knew we stood in Hell.
With a thousand pains that vision's face was grained;
Yet no blood reached there from the upper ground,
And no guns thumped, or down the flues made moan.
"Strange friend," I said, "here is no cause to mourn."
"None," said that other, "save the undone years,
The hopelessness. Whatever hope is yours,
Was my life also; I went hunting wild
After the wildest beauty in the world,
Which lies not calm in eyes, or braided hair,
But mocks the steady running of the hour,
And if it grieves, grieves richlier than here.
For of my glee might many men have laughed,
And of my weeping something had been left,
Which must die now. I mean the truth untold,
The pity of war, the pity war distilled.
Now men will go content with what we spoiled,
Or, discontent, boil bloody, and be spilled.
They will be swift with swiftness of the tigress.
None will break ranks, though nations trek from progress.
Courage was mine, and I had mystery,
Wisdom was mine, and I had mastery:
To miss the march of this retreating world

1. Cut into vaulted caverns.

Into vain citadels that are not walled.
Then, when much blood had clogged their chariot-wheels,
I would go up and wash them from sweet wells,
Even with truths that lie too deep for taint.
I would have poured my spirit without stint
But not through wounds; not on the cess[2] of war.
Foreheads of men have bled where no wounds were.
I am the enemy you killed, my friend.
I knew you in this dark: for so you frowned
Yesterday through me as you jabbed and killed.
I parried; but my hands were loath and cold.
Let us sleep now. . . ."

1920

Greater Love[3]

Red lips are not so red
As the stained stones kissed by the English dead.
Kindness of wooed and wooer
Seems shame to their love pure.
O Love, your eyes lose lure
When I behold eyes blinded in my stead!

Your slender attitude
Trembles not exquisite like limbs knife-skewed,
Rolling and rolling there
Where God seems not to care;
Till the fierce love they bear
Cramps them in death's extreme decrepitude.

Your voice sings not so soft,—
Though even as wind murmuring through raftered loft,—
Your dear voice is not dear,
Gentle, and evening clear,
As theirs whom none now hear,
Now earth has stopped their piteous mouths that coughed.

Heart, you were never hot
Nor large, nor full like hearts made great with shot;
And though your hand be pale,
Paler are all which trail
Your cross through flame and hail:
Weep, you may weep, for you may touch them not.

1920

Anthem for Doomed Youth

What passing-bells for these who die as cattle?
Only the monstrous anger of the guns.

2. As in cesspool.
3. From *John* 15:13, "Greater love hath no man than this, that a man lay down his life for his friends."

Only the stuttering rifles' rapid rattle
Can patter out their hasty orisons.
No mockeries now for them; no prayers nor bells,
Nor any voice of mourning save the choirs,—
The shrill, demented choirs of wailing shells;
And bugles calling for them from sad shires.

What candles may be held to speed them all?
Not in the hands of boys, but in their eyes
Shall shine the holy glimmers of good-byes.
The pallor of girls' brows shall be their pall;
Their flowers the tenderness of patient minds,
And each slow dusk a drawing-down of blinds.

1920

Disabled

He sat in a wheeled chair, waiting for dark,
And shivered in his ghastly suit of grey,
Legless, sewn short at elbow. Through the park
Voices of boys rang saddening like a hymn,
Voices of play and pleasure after day,
Till gathering sleep had mothered them from him.

. . .

About this time Town used to swing so gay
When glow-lamps budded in the light blue trees,
And girls glanced lovelier as the air grew dim,—
In the old times, before he threw away his knees.
Now he will never feel again how slim
Girls' waists are, or how warm their subtle hands;
All of them touch him like some queer disease.

. . .

There was an artist silly for his face,
For it was younger than his youth, last year.
Now, he is old; his back will never brace;
He's lost his colour very far from here,
Poured it down shell-holes till the veins ran dry,
And half his lifetime lapsed in the hot race,
And leap of purple spurted from his thigh.

. . .

One time he liked a blood-smear down his leg,
After the matches, carried shoulder-high.
It was after football, when he'd drunk a peg,[4]
He thought he'd better join.—He wonders why.
Someone had said he'd look a god in kilts,[5]

4. A drink, a shot.
5. Like "jewelled hilts for daggers in plaid socks" (lines 32–3), part of the dress uniform of a Scottish regiment.

That's why; and may be, too, to please his Meg;
Aye, that was it, to please the giddy jilts
He asked to join. He didn't have to beg;
Smiling they wrote his lie; aged nineteen years.
Germans he scarcely thought of; all their guilt,
And Austria's, did not move him. And no fears
Of Fear came yet. He thought of jewelled hilts
For daggers in plaid socks; of smart salutes;
And care of arms; and leave; and pay arrears;
Esprit de corps; and hints for young recruits.
And soon, he was drafted out with drums and cheers.

. . .

Some cheered him home, but not as crowds cheer Goal.
Only a solemn man who brought him fruits
Thanked him; and then inquired about his soul.

. . .

Now, he will spend a few sick years in Institutes,
And do what things the rules consider wise,
And take whatever pity they may dole.
To-night he noticed how the women's eyes
Passed from him to the strong men that were whole.
How cold and late it is! Why don't they come
And put him into bed? Why don't they come?

1920

E. E. CUMMINGS
(*1894–1962*)

Edward Estlin Cummings was born in Cambridge, Massachusetts, on October 14, 1894. He was the son of a Congregational minister who preached in Boston at the Old South Church and also taught at the Harvard Divinity School. Cummings took a B.A. degree at Harvard in 1915 and an M.A. in 1916. He then volunteered to go to France as a member of the Norton Harjes Ambulance Corps. A foolish mail censor, his suspicions roused by a letter written in Cummings' special style, caused him to be arrested and then interned for three months in a concentration camp. Cummings commemorated this experience in the semifictional work, *The Enormous Room* (1922), where he celebrates the courageous idiosyncrasies that persisted among the prisoners even in this spirit-destroying situation.

After the war Cummings lived in Paris and took up painting as well as writing. He exhibited his paintings several times with the Society of Independent Artists there, and in 1931 published a book of his paintings and drawings as *CIOPW*. A trip made to Russia in the early Thirties confirmed Cummings in his dislike of that country, which he found to be another enormous room and excoriated in a book called *Eimi* (Greek for "I am") (1933). He had returned to the United States and settled in Greenwich Village, New York City, then still the haunt of artists and bohemians.

In his last years Cummings was asked to be Norton Professor at Harvard, and agreed on condition that his lectures should be "nonlectures"; they appeared under this title in 1954. He died in New York City in 1963.

[All in green went my love riding]

All in green went my love riding
on a great horse of gold
into the silver dawn.

four lean hounds crouched low and smiling
the merry deer ran before.

Fleeter be they than dappled dreams
the swift sweet deer
the red rare deer.

Four red roebuck at a white water
the cruel bugle sang before.

Horn at hip went my love riding
riding the echo down
into the silver dawn.

four lean hounds crouched low and smiling
the level meadows ran before.

Softer be they than slippered sleep
the lean lithe deer
the fleet flown deer.

Four fleet does at a gold valley
the famished arrow sang before.

Bow at belt went my love riding
riding the mountain down
into the silver dawn.

four lean hounds crouched low and smiling
the sheer peaks ran before.

Paler be they than daunting death
the sleek slim deer
the tall tense deer.

Four tall stags at a green mountain
the lucky hunter sang before.

All in green went my love riding
on a great horse of gold
into the silver dawn.

four lean hounds crouched low and smiling
my heart fell dead before.

1923

[O sweet spontaneous]

O sweet spontaneous
earth how often have
the
doting

          fingers of
prurient philosophers pinched
and
poked

thee
, has the naughty thumb
of science prodded
thy

        beauty   how
often have religions taken
thee upon their scraggy knees
squeezing and

buffeting thee that thou mightest conceive
gods
        (but
true

to the incomparable
couch of death thy
rhythmic
lover

        thou answerest

them only with

                    spring)

1923

[the Cambridge ladies who live in furnished souls]

the Cambridge ladies who live in furnished souls
are unbeautiful and have comfortable minds
(also, with the church's protestant blessings
daughters, unscented shapeless spirited)

they believe in Christ and Longfellow, both dead,
are invariably interested in so many things—
at the present writing one still finds
delighted fingers knitting for the is it Poles?
perhaps. While permanent faces coyly bandy
scandal of Mrs. N and Professor D
. . . . the Cambridge ladies do not care, above
Cambridge if sometimes in its box of
sky lavender and cornerless, the
moon rattles like a fragment of angry candy

1923

[she being Brand]

she being Brand

-new;and you
know consequently a
little stiff i was
careful of her and(having

thoroughly oiled the universal
joint tested my gas felt of
her radiator made sure her springs were O.

K.)i went right to it flooded-the-carburetor cranked her

up,slipped the
clutch(and then somehow got into reverse she
kicked what
the hell)next
minute i was back in neutral tried and

again slo-wly; bare,ly nudg.   ing(my

lev-er Right-
oh and her gears being in
A 1 shape passed
from low through
second-in-to-high like
greasedlightning)just as we turned the corner of Divinity

avenue i touched the accelerator and give

her the juice,good

                    (it
was the first ride and believe i we was
happy to see how nice she acted right up to
the last minute coming back down by the Public
Gardens i slammed on
the

internalexpanding
&
externalcontracting
brakes Bothatonce and

brought allofher tremB
-ling
to a:dead.

stand-
;Still)

1926

[a man who had fallen among thieves[2]]

a man who had fallen among thieves
lay by the roadside on his back
dressed in fifteenthrate ideas
wearing a round jeer for a hat

fate per a somewhat more than less
emancipated evening
had in return for consciousness
endowed him with a changeless grin

whereon a dozen staunch and leal[3]
citizens did graze at pause
then fired by hypercivic zeal
sought newer pastures or because

swaddled with a frozen brook
of pinkest vomit out of eyes
which noticed nobody he looked
as if he did not care to rise

one hand did nothing on the vest
its wideflung friend clenched weakly dirt
while the mute trouserfly confessed
a button solemnly inert.

Brushing from whom the stiffened puke
i put him all into my arms
and staggered banged with terror through
a million billion trillion stars

1926

2. A modern version of Christ's parable of the Good Samaritan (*Luke* 10:30–37).

3. Loyal.

[i sing of Olaf glad and big]

i sing of Olaf glad and big
whose warmest heart recoiled at war:
a conscientious object-or

his wellbelovéd colonel(trig[4]
westpointer most succinctly bred)
took erring Olaf soon in hand;
but—though an host of overjoyed
noncoms(first knocking on the head
him)do through icy waters roll
that helplessness which others stroke
with brushes recently employed
anent this muddy toiletbowl,
while kindred intellects evoke
allegiance per blunt instruments—
Olaf(being to all intents
a corpse and wanting any rag
upon what God unto him gave)
responds,without getting annoyed
"I will not kiss your f.ing flag"
straightway the silver bird[5] looked grave
(departing hurriedly to shave)

but—though all kinds of officers
(a yearning nation's blueeyed pride)
their passive prey did kick and curse
until for wear their clarion
voices and boots were much the worse,
and egged the firstclassprivates on
his rectum wickedly to tease
by means of skilfully applied
bayonets roasted hot with heat—
Olaf(upon what were once knees)
does almost ceaselessly repeat
"there is some s. I will not eat"

our president,being of which
assertions duly notified
threw the yellowsonofabitch
into a dungeon,where he died

Christ(of His mercy infinite)
i pray to see;and Olaf,too

preponderatingly because
unless statistics lie he was
more brave than me:more blond than you.

1931[1]

4. Primly neat.

5. The insignia of an Army colonel.

[my father moved through dooms of love]

my father[8] moved through dooms of love
through sames of am through haves of give,
singing each morning out of each night
my father moved through depths of height

this motionless forgetful where
turned at his glance to shining here;
that if(so timid air is firm)
under his eyes would stir and squirm

newly as from unburied which
floats the first who,his april touch
drove sleeping selves to swarm their fates
woke dreamers to their ghostly roots

and should some why completely weep
my father's fingers brought her sleep:
vainly no smallest voice might cry
for he could feel the mountains grow.

Lifting the valleys of the sea
my father moved through griefs of joy;
praising a forehead called the moon
singing desire into begin

joy was his song and joy so pure
a heart of star by him could steer
and pure so now and now so yes
the wrists of twilight would rejoice

keen as midsummer's keen beyond
conceiving mind of sun will stand,
so strictly(over utmost him
so hugely)stood my father's dream

8. Rev. Edward Cummings, a Unitarian minister in Boston. His son described him in this way: "He was a New Hampshire man, 6 foot 2, a crack shot & a famous fly-fisherman & a firstrate sailor (his sloop was named The Actress) & a woodsman who could find his way through forests primeval without a compass & a canoist who'd still paddle you up to a deer without ruffling the surface of a pond & an ornithologist & taxidermist & (when he gave up hunting) an expert photographer (the best I've ever seen) & an actor who portrayed Julius Caesar in Sanders Theatre & a painter (both in oils & watercolors) & a better carpenter than any professional & an architect who designed his own houses before building them & (when he liked) a plumber who just for the fun of it installed all his own waterworks & (while at Harvard) a teacher with small use for professors—by whom (Royce, Lanman, Taussig, etc.) we were literally surrounded (but not defeated)—& later (at Doctor Hale's socalled South Congregational really Unitarian church) a preacher who announced, during the last war, that the Gott Mit Uns [God with us] boys were in error since the only thing which mattered was for man to be on God's side (& one beautiful Sunday in Spring remarked from the pulpit that he couldn't understand why anyone had come to hear him on such a day) & horribly shocked his pewholders by crying 'the Kingdom of Heaven is no spiritual roofgarden: it's inside you.'" Quoted by Charles Norman, *E. E. Cummings*, New York, 1967, pp. 12–13.

his flesh was flesh his blood was blood:
no hungry man but wished him food;
no cripple wouldn't creep one mile
uphill to only see him smile.

Scorning the pomp of must and shall
my father moved through dooms of feel;
his anger was as right as rain
his pity was as green as grain

septembering arms of year extend
less humbly wealth to foe and friend
than he to foolish and to wise
offered immeasurable is

proudly and(by octobering flame
beckoned)as earth will downward climb,
so naked for immortal work
his shoulders marched against the dark

his sorrow was as true as bread:
no liar looked him in the head;
if every friend became his foe
he'd laugh and build a world with snow.

My father moved through theys of we,
singing each new leaf out of each tree
(and every child was sure that spring
danced when she heard my father sing)

then let men kill which cannot share,
let blood and flesh be mud and mire,
scheming imagine,passion willed, 
freedom a drug that's bought and sold

giving to steal and cruel kind,
a heart to fear,to doubt a mind,
to differ a disease of same,
conform the pinnacle of am 

though dull were all we taste as bright,
bitter all utterly things sweet,
maggoty minus and dumb death
all we inherit,all bequeath

and nothing quite so least as truth
—i say though hate were why men breathe—
because my father lived his soul
love is the whole and more than all

1940

[plato told]

plato told

him:he couldn't
believe it(jesus

told him;he
wouldn't believe
it)lao

tsze[1]
certainly told
him,and general
(yes

mam)
sherman;[2]
and even
(believe it
or

not)you
told him:i told
him;we told him
(he didn't believe it,no

sir)it took
a nipponized bit of
the old sixth

avenue
el;in the top of his head:to tell

him[3]

1944

1. Lao Tse, the ancient Chinese philosopher and originator of the doctrine of Taoism.

2. William Tecumseh Sherman (1820–1891), Union general in the Civil War, who is reported to have told a military academy's graduating class that "War is hell."

3. A scandal of the late Thirties arose over the sale to Japan of scrap metal obtained when the elevated railway over New York's Sixth Avenue was pulled down; it was made into weapons and ammunition which were subsequently used against American forces in the Second World War.

JEAN TOOMER
(*1894–1967*)

Jean Toomer was born on December 26, 1894, in Washington, D.C., the grandson of P. B. S. Pinchback, a black man who during Reconstruction served as acting Governor of Louisiana. As a boy he was much interested in physical culture and worked to build up his body; later, after sampling courses in physical education, agriculture, medicine, sociology and history at five different colleges, he decided on a literary career, and found the roots of his inspiration in the black community of Sparta, Georgia, where he was a teacher in the local schools from 1918 to 1921. The poems and prose sketches which comprise Toomer's only book, *Cane* (1923), were written in Sparta and Washington, D.C., and were first published separately as magazine pieces. *Cane* attracted much attention in the white literary community, and proved to be a spearhead of the Harlem Renaissance of the Twenties.

However, Toomer was not to consolidate his early success, and in fact he dropped from sight for most of the remaining 45 years of his life. He began to direct his efforts towards his psychological development and integration, and in 1924 he spent a summer at Fontainebleau studying the ideas of George Gurdjieff, a Russian mystic whose ethical and psychological philosophy had great impact on Toomer's later styles of life and art. In the United States he taught Gurdjieffian mysticism and conducted experiments in community living. In 1932 he married a member of one of his communes, Marjorie Latimer, a white woman of impeccable New England credentials who was herself a promising writer, but a year later she died in giving birth to their only child; in 1934 Toomer married again, this time Marjorie Content, the daughter of a New York stockbroker. Toomer's experiments and marriages led to some scandalmongering in the press, and he was occasionally evasive about whether he actually was a black. He died in 1967.

Reapers

Black reapers with the sound of steel on stones
Are sharpening scythes. I see them place the hones
In their hip-pockets as a thing that's done,
And start their silent swinging, one by one.
Black horses drive a mower through the weeds,
And there, a field rat, startled, squealing bleeds,
His belly close to ground. I see the blade,
Blood-stained, continue cutting weeds and shade.

1923

November Cotton Flower

Boll-weevil's coming, and the winter's cold,
Made cotton-stalks look rusty, seasons old,
And cotton, scarce as any southern snow,
Was vanishing; the branch, so pinched and slow,
Failed in its function as the autumn rake;
Drouth fighting soil had caused the soil to take
All water from the streams; dead birds were found
In wells a hundred feet below the ground—
Such was the season when the flower bloomed.
Old folks were startled, and it soon assumed
Significance. Superstition saw

Something it had never seen before:
Brown eyes that loved without a trace of fear,
Beauty so sudden for that time of year.

1923

ROBERT GRAVES
(*1895–*)

Robert Graves was born on July 26, 1895 at Wimbledon near London. His father, Alfred Perceval Graves, was Irish and himself a poet; his mother was German and related to the historian von Ranke. Through two world wars Graves's German connections got him into trouble, and as a schoolboy and soldier he self-protectively insisted on his Irish paternity. He went to a succession of preparatory schools where he learned to "keep a straight bat at cricket, and to have a high moral sense." His public school was Charterhouse; Graves found it conventional, hypocritical, and anti-intellectual. He left school a week before the outbreak of the War in 1914 and joined the Royal Welch Fusiliers as an officer, went to France soon after, and saw a good deal of action. Of Graves's school generation one in three died in the war, and on his 21st birthday he was himself reported killed in action. Though Graves was disgusted with both the officer caste and those civilians, his father among them, who enjoyed the war from a safe distance, he maintained respect for bravery and soldierly values. He became friends with the poet Siegfried Sassoon, and when the latter made a public declaration of his disgust with the pointless fighting, Graves, unknown to Sassoon, connived at his being sent to a mental hospital as an alternative to a probable court-martial and prison sentence.

Towards the end of the war Graves married Nancy Nicholson, an artist and member of a family of artists. She was a feminist; after the marriage she insisted on keeping her own name, and she soon began to include Graves "in her universal condemnation of men." After the armistice, Graves studied at Oxford. His thesis, written for an Oxford B. Litt. and published as *Poetic Unreason* (1925), argues that there is in poetry a "supralogical element" and that the "latent associations" of the words used in a poem often contradict its prose sense.

By the late Twenties Graves felt he had reached a dead end. He was rescued from his poetic irresolution by his association with the American poet Laura Riding. They collaborated as critics in such books as *A Survey of Modernist Poetry* (1927) and *A Pamphlet Against Anthologies* (1928); then, having in 1929 left England for Majorca, they founded the Seizin Press, an imprint under which they published a select list of impeccably produced books. Graves also began a series of vigorous and successful historical novels with *I, Claudius* (1934). Graves and Riding eventually separated in 1938, and except during the Second World War he has continued to live on Majorca. In 1948 Graves completed his "historical grammar of poetic myth," *The White Goddess*, a matriarchal study of history, personality, and poetic inspiration. He was Professor of Poetry at Oxford University from 1961 to 1966.

The Cool Web

Children are dumb to say how hot the day is,
How hot the scent is of the summer rose,
How dreadful the black wastes of evening sky,
How dreadful the tall soldiers drumming by.

But we have speech, to chill the angry day,
And speech, to dull the rose's cruel scent.
We spell away the overhanging night,
We spell away the soldiers and the fright.

There's a cool web of language winds us in,
Retreat from too much joy or too much fear:
We grow sea-green at last and coldly die
In brininess and volubility.

But if we let our tongues lose self-possession,
Throwing off language and its watery clasp
Before our death, instead of when death comes,
Facing the wide glare of the children's day,
Facing the rose, the dark sky and the drums,
We shall go mad no doubt and die that way.

1927

Ogres and Pygmies

Those famous men of old, the Ogres—
They had long beards and stinking arm-pits,
They were wide-mouthed, long-yarded and great-bellied
Yet not of taller stature, Sirs, than you.
They lived on Ogre-Strand, which was no place
But the churl's terror of their vast extent,
Where every foot was three-and-thirty inches
And every penny bought a whole hog.
Now of their company none survive, not one,
The times being, thank God, unfavourable
To all but nightmare shadows of their fame;
Their images stand howling on the hill
(The winds enforced against those wide mouths),
Whose granite haunches country-folk salute
With May Day kisses, and whose knobbed knees.
So many feats they did to admiration:
With their enormous throats they sang louder
Than ten cathedral choirs, with their grand yards
Stormed the most rare and obstinate maidenheads,
With their strong-gutted and capacious bellies
Digested stones and glass like ostriches.
They dug great pits and heaped huge mounds,
Deflected rivers, wrestled with the bear

And hammered judgements for posterity—
For the sweet-cupid-lipped and tassel-yarded
Delicate-stomached dwellers
In Pygmy Alley, where with brooding on them
A foot is shrunk to seven inches
And twelve-pence will not buy a spare rib.
And who would judge between Ogres and Pygmies—
The thundering text, the snivelling commentary—
Reading between such covers he will marvel
How his own members bloat and shrink again.

1931

Ulysses[2]

To the much-tossed Ulysses, never done
With woman whether gowned as wife or whore,
Penelope and Circe seemed as one:
She like a whore made his lewd fancies run,
And wifely she a hero to him bore.

Their counter-changings terrified his way:
They were the clashing rocks, Symplegades,
Scylla and Charybdis too were they;
Now they were storms frosting the sea with spray
And now the lotus island's drunken ease.

They multiplied into the Sirens' throng,
Forewarned by fear of whom he stood bound fast
Hand and foot helpless to the vessel's mast,
Yet would not stop his ears: daring their song
He groaned and sweated till that shore was past.[3]

One, two and many: flesh had made him blind,
Flesh had one pleasure only in the act,
Flesh set one purpose only in the mind—
Triumph of flesh and afterwards to find
Still those same terrors wherewith flesh was racked.

His wiles were witty and his fame far known,
Every king's daughter[4] sought him for her own,
Yet he was nothing to be won or lost.
All lands to him were Ithaca: love-tossed
He loathed the fraud, yet would not bed alone.

1933

2. The Greek hero of the Trojan War, whose long journey homeward to Ithaca and his faithful wife Penelope is the subject of Homer's *Odyssey*.

3. Circe, the temptress with whom he stayed a year and who changed his companions into swine; Symplegades, the clashing rocks; Scylla and Charybdis, a man-eating monster and a dangerous whirlpool between which Ulysses' ship had to pass; the land of the drugged lotus-eaters; and the Sirens, fabulous creatures whose singing lured men to sail their ships onto the rocks, were hazards which Ulysses successfully negotiated on his voyage.

4. For example Nausicaa, daughter of King Alcinoos of the Phaeacians, in whose court Ulysses recounted his adventures.

Down, Wanton, Down!

Down, wanton, down! Have you no shame
That at the whisper of Love's name,
Or Beauty's, presto! up you raise
Your angry head and stand at gaze?

Poor bombard-captain, sworn to reach
The ravelin and effect a breach—
Indifferent what you storm or why,
So be that in the breach you die!

Love may be blind, but Love at least
Knows what is man and what mere beast;
Or Beauty wayward, but requires
More delicacy from her squires.

Tell me, my witless, whose one boast
Could be your staunchness at the post,
When were you made a man of parts
To think fine and profess the arts?

Will many-gifted Beauty come
Bowing to your bald rule of thumb,
Or Love swear loyalty to your crown?
Be gone, have done! Down, wanton, down!

1933

The Devil's Advice to Story-Tellers

Lest men suspect your tale to be untrue,
Keep probability—some say—in view.
But my advice to story-tellers is:
Weigh out no gross of probabilities,
Nor yet make diligent transcriptions of
Known instances of virtue, crime or love.
To forge a picture that will pass for true,
Do conscientiously what liars do—
Born liars, not the lesser sort that raid
The mouths of others for their stock-in-trade:
Assemble, first, all casual bits and scraps
That may shake down into a world perhaps;
People this world, by chance created so,
With random persons whom you do not know—
The teashop sort, or travellers in a train
Seen once, guessed idly at, not seen again;
Let the erratic course they steer surprise
Their own and your own and your readers' eyes;
Sigh then, or frown, but leave (as in despair)
Motive and end and moral in the air;
Nice contradiction between fact and fact
Will make the whole read human and exact.

1938

To Juan at the Winter Solstice[5]

There is one story and one story only
That will prove worth your telling,
Whether as learned bard or gifted child;[6]
To it all lines or lesser gauds belong
That startle with their shining
Such common stories as they stray into.

Is it of trees you tell, their months and virtues,[7]
Or strange beasts[8] that beset you,
Of birds that croak at you the Triple will?[9]
Or of the Zodiac and how slow it turns
Below the Boreal Crown,
Prison of all true kings that ever reigned?[1]

Water to water, ark again to ark,
From woman back to woman:
So each new victim treads unfalteringly
The never altered circuit of his fate,
Bringing twelve peers as witness
Both to his starry rise and starry fall.[2]

Or is it of the Virgin's silver beauty,
All fish below the thighs?
She in her left hand bears a leafy quince;

5. This poem epitomizes Graves's "historic grammar of poetic myth," *The White Goddess* (1948), an intuitive study of ancient mythologies (especially Greek and Celtic) which finds the only theme for true poetry in the story of the life-cycle of the Sun-God or -Hero, his marriage with the Goddess and inevitable death at her hands or by her command. Juan is Graves's youngest son; he was born on December 21, 1945, one day before the Winter Solstice, which (as it is the time when the sun gives least heat and light to the North) is in many religions the birthday of the Solar Hero. Some of these heroes are Apollo, Dionysus, Zeus, Hermes, and Hercules of Greek mythology; Horus, the Egyptian sun-god; Merlin and King Arthur; and perhaps Jesus Christ, whose life often parallels that of the Solar Hero, and whose mother Mary shares some characteristics of the Goddess.

6. Graves "decoded" the Celtic riddle-poem, "The Battle of the Trees," by the bard Taliesin, who as a "gifted child" outmatched twenty-four experienced court poets; this insight began the series of researches and intuitions which resulted in *The White Goddess.*

7. Besides "The Battle of the Trees" (see note 6 above) Graves also cites an ancient Druidic "tree-calendar" which describes the natural and magic properties of various trees and associates each tree with a month or season of the year.

8. For example, the unicorn, the chimera, and the phoenix, some of the fabulous animals associated with the Goddess.

9. The Goddess sometimes speaks through "prophetic" birds, such as the owl, the crane, and the eagle. She was sometimes called the Triple Goddess or Triple Muse because of her threefold aspect as Goddess of the Underworld, the Earth, and the Sky; further, each of these aspects includes three stages of an infinite cycle—as Goddess of the Underworld she symbolizes birth, procreation, and death; as Earth-Goddess she is, in turn, Spring, Summer, and Winter; and, perhaps most important, as Goddess of the Sky she is the Moon-Goddess, proceeding through the cycle of New Moon, Full Moon, and Old Moon.

1. "*Boreal Crown* is Corona Borealis, . . . which in Thracean-Libyan mythology, carried to Bronze Age Britain, was the purgatory where Solar Heroes went after death" (Graves's note). The progression or "turning" of the twelve signs of the Zodiac corresponds to the cycle of months.

2. The King (or Solar Hero), reincarnated, reappears at the Winter Solstice floating in an ark on the water. The "twelve peers" may be, for example, the twelve knights of King Arthur's round table, Christ's apostles, or even the twelve Zodiacal constellations (as suggested by line 18).

When with her right she crooks a finger, smiling,[3]
How may the King hold back?
Royally then he barters life for love.

Or of the undying snake from chaos hatched,
Whose coils contain the ocean,
Into whose chops with naked sword he springs,
Then in black water, tangled by the reeds,
Battles three days and nights,
To be spewed up beside her scalloped shore?[4]

Much snow is falling, winds roar hollowly,
The owl hoots from the elder,
Fear in your heart cries to the loving-cup:
Sorrow to sorrow as the sparks fly upward.
The log groans and confesses:[5]
There is one story and one story only.

Dwell on her graciousness, dwell on her smiling,
Do not forget what flowers
The great boar trampled down in ivy time.[6]
Her brow was creamy as the crested wave,
Her sea-blue eyes were wild[7]
But nothing promised that is not performed.

1945

The Persian Version

Truth-loving Persians do not dwell upon
The trivial skirmish fought near Marathon.[8]

3. Two forms of the Goddess are Aphrodite, Greek goddess of love, whose emblem is the quince (the mythical or Biblical "apple," since the modern apple was not then known), and Rahab, the Hebraic sea-goddess who resembled the modern idea of a mermaid.

4. The snake is Ophion, who was created by the Goddess and mated with her; from their egg the world was hatched by the sun's rays. The Sun-King must kill the serpent to win the Goddess; in turn, in October, the serpent (perhaps reincarnated as the boar of line 39) inevitably kills the King.

5. The owl and the elder tree are occult emblems of death. "The *log* is the Yule log, burned at the year's end" (Graves's note).

6. The boar is another symbol of death; Aphrodite's lover Adonis was killed by a boar. Ivy was eaten as an intoxicant by the priestesses of Dionysus in ancient Greece; if their October revels were interrupted by any man, they tore him to pieces.

7. In another version of this poem, "the crested wave" was replaced by "the long ninth wave"; the ninth wave is said to be the whitest. In the poem to *The White Goddess,* Graves gives a fuller description:

Whose broad high brow was white as any leper's,
Whose eyes were blue, with rowan-berry lips,
With hair curled honey-coloured to white hips.

This recalls not only Botticelli's famous painting, "The Birth of Venus," but some lines from "The Rime of the Ancient Mariner" by Coleridge:

Her lips were red, her looks were free,
Her locks were yellow as gold,
Her skin was white as leprosy.
The Nightmare Life-in-Death was she,
Who thicks man's blood with cold.

8. The decisive battle of the first war between Persia and Greece, in which an Athenian force routed part of the Persian army. Modern historians consider this war far less significant than the second one, in which the allied Greek city-states defeated an enormous Persian army and navy of 400,000 men. "The Greek theatrical tradition" consists mainly of a play about the wars by Aeschylus; no information has survived about the Persian view of the affair.

As for the Greek theatrical tradition
Which represents that summer's expedition
Not as a mere reconnaissance in force
By three brigades of foot and one of horse
(Their left flank covered by some obsolete
Light craft detached from the main Persian fleet)
But as a grandiose, ill-starred attempt
To conquer Greece—they treat it with contempt;
And only incidentally refute
Major Greek claims, by stressing what repute
The Persian monarch and the Persian nation
Won by this salutary demonstration:
Despite a strong defence and adverse weather
All arms combined magnificently together.

1945

AUSTIN CLARKE
(*1896–1974*)

Austin Clarke was born in Dublin on May 9, 1896. He was educated at Belvedere College, a Catholic school where James Joyce had also been a student, and then at University College, Dublin. His parents were nationalists, and he must have been strengthened in his own patriotic feelings by the Easter Rebellion of 1916, which occurred when he was at the University. He had been taught by Donagh MacDonagh, a lecturer and poet who was executed for his part in the rising. In 1917 Clarke took MacDonagh's place at University College.

Difficulties ensuing from an unhappy marriage obliged Clarke to move to England in the Twenties, and to remain there "in exile," as he said, until 1937. He supported himself by writing leaders for *T.P.'s Weekly* and anonymous reviews, often severe and crotchety, for the *Times Literary Supplement*. He also wrote four novels, which were banned for a time by the Irish Censorship Board. After returning to Dublin, he continued to write as a freelance, and often broadcast on the Irish radio. He died in the summer of 1974.

The Young Woman of Beare[1]

Through lane or black archway,
The praying people hurry,
When shadows have been walled,
At market hall and gate,
By low fires after nightfall;

1. Beare is an Irish port on Bantry Bay. The poem is set in southern Ireland in the mid-sixteenth century. "The episodes of this allegory are fanciful, but the Old Woman of Beare is a well-known figure in country stories. She had seven periods of youth before the climacteric of her grief. She speaks in a famous and classic poem: 'the lament of an old hetaira [courtesan] who contrasts the privation and suffering of her old age with the pleasure of her youth when she had been the delight of kings' (Kuno Meyer). . . . In Glendalough, that holy place, a man told me of a poor crone who had lived in the ruined settlement below the abandoned mines. She refused even the consolations of religion, for she remembered with great anger her own times of merriment and the strong mortals she had held, when silver and lead were brought down the mountainside, more than half a century ago" (Clarke's note).

The bright sodalities [1]
Are bannered in the churches;
But I am only roused
By horsemen of de Burgo[2]
That gallop to my house.

Gold slots of the sunlight
Close up my lids at evening.
Half clad in silken piles
I lie upon a hot cheek.
Half in dream I lie there
Until bad thoughts have bloomed
In flushes of desire.
Drowsy with indulgence,
I please a secret eye
That opens at the Judgment.

I am the bright temptation
In talk, in wine, in sleep.
Although the clergy pray,
I triumph in a dream.
Strange armies tax the south,
Yet little do I care
What fiery bridge or town
Has heard the shout begin—
That Ormond's men are out
And the Geraldine is in.[3]

The women at green stall
And doorstep on a weekday,
Who have been chinned with scorn
Of me, would never sleep
So well, could they but know
Their husbands turn at midnight,
And covet in a dream
The touching of my flesh.
Small wonder that men kneel
The longer at confession.

Bullies, that fight in dramshop
For fluttered rags and bare side,
At beggars' bush, may gamble
To-night on what they find.
I laze in yellow lamplight—
Young wives have envied me—

1. Lay associations of the Catholic Church, usually for charitable or devotional purposes.

2. An Irish noble family that ruled the province of Connacht in northwest Ireland; later they assumed the name MacWilliam (line 114).

3. Thomas, Earl of Ormonde, and Gerald, Earl of Desmond, fought over control of Munster (the southwest province of Ireland, whose capital is Limerick) from 1564 until Desmond's death in 1579. The province was then made a Presidency. The "strange armies" of line 25 may be the Spanish and Italian troops that fought for the Geraldines.

And laugh among lace pillows,
For a big-booted captain
Has poured the purse of silver
That glitters in my lap.

Heavily on his elbow,
He turns from a caress
To see—as my arms open—
The red spurs of my breast.
I draw fair pleats around me
And stay his eye at pleasure,
Show but a white knee-cap
Or an immodest smile—
Until his sudden hand
Has dared the silks that bind me.

See! See, as from a lathe
My polished body turning!
He bares me at the waist
And now blue clothes uncurl
Upon white haunch. I let
The last bright stitch fall down
For him as I lean back,
Straining with longer arms
Above my head to snap
The silver knots of sleep.

Together in the dark—
Sin-fast—we can enjoy
What is allowed in marriage.
The jingle of that coin
Is still the same, though stolen:
But are they not unthrifty,
Who spend it in a shame
That brings ill and repentance,
When they might pinch and save
Themselves in lawful pleasure?

. . .

Young girls, keep from dance-hall
And dark side of the road;
My common ways began
In idle thought and courting.
I strayed the mountain fields
And got a bad name down
In Beare. Yes, I became
So careless of my placket,[4]
That after I was blamed,
I went out to the islands.

4. An opening in a skirt; thus, her virtue.

Pull the boats on the roller
And rope them in the tide!
For the fire has got a story
That while the nets were drying,
I stretched to plank and sun
With strong men in their leather;
In scandal on the wave,
I fled with a single man
And caught behind a sail
The air that goes to Ireland.

He drew me from the seas
One night, without an oar,
To strip between the beach
And dark ribs of that boat.
Hard bed had turned to softness—
We drowsed into small hours.
How could I tell the glancing
Of men that awakened me,
When daylight in my lashes
Thickened with yellow sleep?

My fear was less than joy
To gallop from the tide;
Hooded among his horsemen,
MacWilliam bore me tighter.
The green land by Lough Corrib[5]
Spoke softly and all day
We followed through a forest
The wet heel of the axe,
Where sunlight had been trestled
In clearing and in gap.

At dark a sudden threshold
Was squared in light. Men cast
Their shadows as we rode up
That fiery short-cut. Bench
And board were full at night.
Unknown there to the clergy,
I stayed with him to sin.
Companies of carousing—
Was I not for a winter
The darling of your house?

. . .

Women, obey the mission—
Be modest in your clothes.
Each manly look and wish
Is punished but the more.

5. A large lake in Connacht.

In king's house, I have called
Hurlers[5a] and men that fight.
It is my grief that time
Cannot appease my hunger;
I flourish where desire is
And still, still I am young.

I prosper, for the towns
Have made my skin but finer.
Hidden as words in mouth,
My fingers can entice
Until the sight is dim
And conscience lost in flame.
Then, to a sound of bracelets,
I look down and my locks
Are curtailed on a nape
That leads men into wrong.

Ships glide in Limerick
Between tall houses, isled
By street and castle: there
Are flighted steps to climb.
Soon with a Flemish merchant
I lodged at Thomond Gate.[6]
I had a painted bedpost
Of blue and yellow ply,
A bright pot and rich curtains
That I could pull at night.

But in that corner house
Of guilt, my foreign face
Shook voices in the crowd,
As I leaned out to take
The twilight at my sill.
When tide had filled the boat-rings,
Few dealers could be tempted
Who drank upon the fair-day:
The black friars[6a] preached to them
And frightened me with prayers.

As I came to the Curragh[7]
I heard how, at their ease,
Bands of the Geraldine
Gather with joy to see
The going of young horses
At morning on the plain.
A mile from Scholars Town[8]

5a. Players of hurling, a violent game like field hockey popular in Ireland.

6. A suburb of Limerick.

6a. Of the ascetic Dominican order.

7. A large open plain, southwest of Dublin, used as a battleground and for horse races.

8. That is, Dublin.

I turned to ask the way,
And laughing with the chapmen,[9]
I rode into the Pale.[1]

The summer had seen plenty;
I saw but a black crop
And knew the President
Of Munster had come back.
All day, in high and low street,
His orderlies ran by.
At night I entertained him
Between the wine and map;
I whispered with the statesmen,
The lawyers that break land.

. . .

I am the dark temptation
Men know—and shining orders
Of clergy have condemned me.
I fear, alone, that lords
Of diocese[2] are coped
With gold, their staven hands
Upraised again to save
All those I have corrupted:
I fear, lost and too late,
The prelates of the Church.

In darker lane or archway,
I heard an hour ago
The men and women murmur;
They came back from Devotions.
Half-wakened by the tide,
Ships rise along the quay
As though they were unloading.
I turn a drowsy side—
That dreams, the eye has known,
May trouble souls to-night.

1929

9. Merchants.

1. The English Pale in Ireland was the area around Dublin which was directly under English governance.

2. Bishops, who wear copes (ecclesiastical cloaks) and carry croziers, or staffs.

HART CRANE
(1899–1933)

Hart Crane was born on July 21, 1899, in Garretsville, Ohio, a small town near the Pennsylvania border. He was the son of a candy manufacturer, a stormy, affectionate man who felt insufficiently loved by his wife and stirred up quarrel after quarrel. The two parents separated in 1908, and Mrs. Crane promptly broke down. Then some months later they were reconciled and lived disharmoniously together until their divorce in 1917. Hart Crane took his mother's part, but his own relations with her were troubled and ended eventually in rupture. After his death, however, she played widow to his memory, seeking to solicit fame for him even while she herself scrubbed floors for a living.

In 1917, following the divorce of his parents, Crane went to live and work in New York instead of finishing high school. He had little success with jobs, and his personal life was unhappy. For some years he moved back to Ohio whenever his money ran out, but eventually, in 1923, he settled in New York for good. His love affairs with men were short lived, including that with a sailor which became the groundwork of a group of poems called "Voyages."

In his last year he made some attempt to change his sexual direction; he had a love affair in Mexico with a woman, but on the ship back he suddenly went to her stateroom to bid her goodbye—she thought he was joking, but he went on deck and jumped into the sea. Accounts differ as to whether or not he tried to catch the life preserver that was thrown to him. He died on April 27, 1933.

Chaplinesque[1]

We make our meek adjustments,
Contented with such random consolations

As the wind deposits
In slithered and too ample pockets.

For we can still love the world, who find
A famished kitten on the step, and know
Recesses for it from the fury of the street,
Or warm torn elbow coverts.

We will sidestep, and to the final smirk
Dally the doom of that inevitable thumb[2]

1. Crane was delighted to see Charlie Chaplin in *The Kid* in 1921. He considered Chaplin "a dramatic genius that truly approaches the fabulous sort." In a letter to William Wright of October 17, 1921, he wrote: "As you did not 'get' my idiom in 'Chaplinesque,' I feel rather like doing my best to explain myself. I am moved to put Chaplin with the poets (of today); hence the 'we.' In other words, he, especially in *The Kid*, made me feel myself, as a poet, as being 'in the same boat' with him. Poetry, the human feelings, 'the kitten,' is so crowded out of the humdrum, rushing, mechanical scramble of today that the man who would preserve them must duck and camouflage for dear life to keep them or keep himself from annihilation. I have since learned that I am by no means alone in seeing these things in the buffooneries of the tragedian, Chaplin . . . and in the poem I have tried to express these 'social sympathies' in words corresponding somewhat to the antics of the actor." (*Letters*, p. 68.) To Gorham Munson, who objected that the film was sentimental, he replied, "Chaplin may be a sentimentalist, after all, but he carries the theme with such power and universal portent that sentimentality is made to transcend itself into a new kind of tragedy, eccentric, homely and yet brilliant. It is because I feel that I have captured the arrested climaxes and evasive victories of his gestures in words, somehow, that I like the poem as much as anything I have done." (*Letters*, p. 69.)

2. Of the policeman.

That slowly chafes its puckered index toward us,
Facing the dull squint with what innocence
And what surprise!

And yet these fine collapses are not lies
More than the pirouettes of any pliant cane;
Our obsequies[3] are, in a way, no enterprise.
We can evade you, and all else but the heart:
What blame to us if the heart[4] live on.

The game enforces smirks; but we have seen
The moon in lonely alleys make
A grail[5] of laughter of an empty ash can,
And through all sound of gaiety and quest
Have heard a kitten in the wilderness.

1926

At Melville's Tomb[6]

Often beneath the wave, wide from this ledge
The dice of drowned men's bones he saw bequeath
An embassy.[7] Their numbers as he watched,
Beat on the dusty shore and were obscured.

And wrecks passed without sound of bells,
The calyx of death's bounty giving back
A scattered chapter, livid hieroglyph,
The portent wound in corridors of shells.[8]

Then in the circuit calm of one vast coil,
Its lashings charmed and malice reconciled,
Frosted eyes there were that lifted altars;[9]
And silent answers crept across the stars.

3. Funeral rites, but also acts of compliance.

4. According to Crane, a deliberate pun on his first name.

5. The cup used by Christ at the Last Supper, traditionally the object of knightly quests. It was thought to glow of its own radiance.

6. Herman Melville (1819–1891), the American writer, is buried at Woodlawn Cemetery in New York City.

7. In a letter to Harriet Monroe, editor of *Poetry*, Crane explained: "Dice bequeath an embassy, in the first place, by being ground (in this connection only, of course) in little cubes from the bones of drowned men by the action of the sea, and are finally thrown around the sand, giving 'numbers' but no identification. These being the bones of dead men who never completed their voyage, it seems legitimate to refer to them as the only surviving evidence of certain things, experiences that the dead mariners might have had to deliver. Dice as a symbol of chance and circumstance is also implied." (In Philip Horton, *Hart Crane*, New York, 1937, pp. 333–4.)

8. "This calyx refers in a double ironic sense both to a cornucopia and the vortex made by a sinking vessel. As soon as the water has closed over a ship this whirlpool sends up broken spars, wreckage, etc., which can be alluded to as *livid hieroglyphs,* making a *scattered chapter* so far as any complete record of the recent ship and her crew is concerned. In fact, about as much definite knowledge might come from all this as anyone might gain from the roar of his own veins, which is easily heard (haven't you ever done it?) by holding a shell close to one's ear." *Calyx:* the cup-like set of leaves that surround the base of a flower. *Cornucopia:* the horn of plenty, in Greek myth a goat's horn filled with fruit and grain.

9. "Refers simply to a conviction that a man, not knowing perhaps a definite god yet being endowed with a reverence for deity—such a man naturally postulates a deity somehow, and the altar of that deity by the very *action* of the eyes *lifted* in searching."

Compass, quadrant and sextant contrive
No farther tides[1] . . . High in the azure steeps
Monody[1a] shall not wake the mariner.
This fabulous shadow only the sea keeps.

1926

Voyages[2]

I

Above the fresh ruffles of the surf
Bright striped urchins flay each other with sand.
They have contrived a conquest for shell shucks,
And their fingers crumble fragments of baked weed
Gaily digging and scattering.

And in answer to their treble interjections
The sun beats lightning on the waves,
The waves fold thunder on the sand;
And could they hear me I would tell them:

O brilliant kids, frisk with your dog,
Fondle your shells and sticks, bleached
By time and the elements; but there is a line
You must not cross nor ever trust beyond it
Spry cordage[2a] of your bodies to caresses
Too lichen-faithful from too wide a breast.[3]
The bottom of the sea is cruel.

II

—And yet this great wink of eternity,[4]
Of rimless floods, unfettered leewardings, [4a]
Samite[5] sheeted and processioned where
Her undinal vast belly moonward bends,
Laughing the wrapt inflections of our love;

Take this Sea, whose diapason[5a] knells
On scrolls of silver snowy sentences,[6]
The sceptred terror of whose sessions rends
As her demeanors motion well or ill,
All but the pieties of lovers' hands.[7]

1. "Hasn't it often occurred that instruments originally invented for record and computation have inadvertently so extended the concepts of the entity they were invented to measure (concepts of space etc.) in the mind and imagination that employed them, that they may metaphorically be said to have extended the original boundaries of the entity measured?

1a. An elegy chanted by a single mourner.

2. The poem consists of six love poems, the outcome of a passionate affair with Emil Opffer, a merchant seaman.

2a. Ropes that make up the rigging of a ship.

3. The sea's.

4. The sea, as if eternity were unshuttered for an instant. The imperative verb, "Take," is understood here, though it does not appear until the next stanza.

4a. In sailing, running before the wind.

5. A silken fabric, sometimes interwoven with gold and silver threads. In sailing, "sheeted" means hauled in tight by sheets, or ropes: with sails set. *Undinal:* rippling her waves, as if winding a clock.

5a. The entire range of musical notes.

6. "Snowy sentences" is the object of "knells."

7. Object of "rends."

And onward, as bells off San Salvador[8]
Salute the crocus lustres[9] of the stars,
In these poinsettia meadows of her tides,—
Adagios of islands,[1] O my Prodigal,
Complete the dark confessions her veins spell.

Mark how her turning shoulders wind the hours,
And hasten while her penniless rich palms
Pass superscription of bent foam and wave,—
Hasten, while they are true,—sleep, death, desire,
Close round one instant in one floating flower.[2]

Bind us in time, O Seasons clear, and awe.
O minstrel galleons[3] of Carib fire,
Bequeath us to no earthly shore until
Is answered in the vortex of our grave
The seal's wide spindrift[3a] gaze toward paradise.

III

Infinite consanguinity[4] it bears—
This tendered theme of you that light
Retrieves from sea plains where the sky
Resigns a breast that every wave enthrones;
While ribboned water lanes I wind[5]
Are laved and scattered with no stroke
Wide from your side, whereto this hour
The sea lifts, also, reliquary[6] hands.

And so, admitted through black swollen gates
That must arrest all distance otherwise,—[7]
Past whirling pillars and lithe pediments,
Light wrestling there incessantly with light,
Star kissing star through wave on wave unto
Your body rocking!
                                        and where death, if shed,
Presumes no carnage, but this single change,—

8. Crane alludes to a legend, of which he had heard from Opffer, of a buried city beneath the Pacific Ocean off San Salvador.

9. Reflections of the stars in the sea. *Crocus:* A yellow or purple flowering plant. The plants commonly grow in clusters.

1. In an essay, "General Aims and Theories," Crane explained, "When . . . I speak of 'adagios of islands,' the reference is to the motion of a boat through islands clustered thickly, the rhythm of the motion, etc. And it seems a much more direct and creative statement than any more logical employment of words such as 'coasting slowly through the islands,' besides ushering in a whole world of music." *Adagio:* a musical instruction, meaning "slow." *Prodigal:* extravagant or lavish, with particular allusion to the biblical parable of the prodigal son, who in his travels in the world spent or lost all that he had, and yet was welcomed home by his father even more joyfully than his more prudent brothers. (Luke 15: 11–32.)

2. The sea seems to control the hours by her waves, as if winding a clock. She offers a kind of authentication of love.

3. Harmonious structures of the sea. The fire paradoxically means the water.

3a. Sea spray.

4. Love and the sea are interknit.

5. As if he were swimming. *Laved:* washed.

6. Pious. A reliquary is a container holding a relic, such as a piece of Christ's cross or the bone of a saint.

7. A voyage of love which, if unsuccessful, would have rendered futile all amorous quests.

Upon the steep floor flung from dawn to dawn
The silken skilled transmemberment of song;[8]

Permit me voyage, love, into your hands . . .

IV

Whose counted smile[9] of hours and days, suppose
I know as spectrum of the sea and pledge[1]
Vastly now parting gulf on gulf of wings
Whose circles bridge, I know, (from palms to the severe
Chilled albatross's white immutability)[2]
No stream of greater love advancing now
Than, singing, this mortality alone
Through clay aflow immortally to you.

All fragrance irrefragibly,[2a] and claim
Madly meeting logically in this hour
And region that is ours to wreathe again,
Portending eyes and lips and making told
The chancel port[3] and portion of our June—

Shall they[4] not stem and close in our own steps
Bright staves of flowers and quills to-day as I
Must first be lost in fatal tides to tell?[5]

In signature of the incarnate word[6]
The harbor shoulders to resign[7] in mingling
Mutual blood, transpiring as foreknown
And widening noon within your breast for gathering
All bright insinuations that my years have caught
For islands where must lead inviolably
Blue latitudes and levels of your eyes,—

In this expectant,[8] still exclaim receive
The secret oar and petals[9] of all love.

V

Meticulous, past midnight in clear rime,
Infrangible[9a] and lonely, smooth as though cast
Together in one merciless white blade—
The bay estuaries fleck the hard sky limits.

8. Death, if it should come to such lovers, would be only harmonized transmutation.

9. The sea's tides.

1. Subject is "I."

2. From the tropics to the polar regions.

2a. Incontestably.

3. The chancel is the part of the church that includes the sanctuary, hence the most sacred or cherished part.

4. The waves.

5. He can only tell of the amorous fusion after separation has occurred.

6. Of love.

7. The harbor seeks to leave the shore for the sea and islands of love.

8. Though separation must occur.

9. Sexual imagery.

9a. Inviolable, unbreakable. *Estuaries:* Places at a river's mouth where the river current meets the ocean tide.

—As if too brittle or too clear to touch!
The cables of our sleep so swiftly filed,
Already hang, shred ends from remembered stars.
One frozen trackless smile . . . What words
Can strangle this deaf moonlight? For we

Are overtaken. Now no cry, no sword
Can fasten or deflect this tidal wedge,
Slow tyranny of moonlight, moonlight loved
And changed . . . "There's

Nothing like this in the world," you say,
Knowing I cannot touch your hand and look
Too, into that godless cleft of sky
Where nothing turns but dead sands[1] flashing.

"—And never to quite understand!" No,
In all the argosy of your bright hair I dreamed
Nothing so flagless as this piracy.[2]

But now
Draw in your head, alone and too tall here.
Your eyes already in the slant of drifting foam;
Your breath sealed by the ghosts I do not know:
Draw in your head and sleep the long way home.

VI

Where icy and bright dungeons lift
Of swimmers their lost morning eyes,
And ocean rivers, churning, shift
Green borders under stranger skies,

Steadily as a shell secretes
Its beating leagues of monotone,
Or as many waters trough the sun's
Red kelson[3] past the cape's wet stone;

O rivers mingling toward the sky
And harbor of the phœnix' breast—[4]
My eyes pressed black against the prow,
—Thy derelict and blinded guest[5]

Waiting, afire, what name, unspoke,
I cannot claim:[6] let thy waves rear

1. Of the turning moon.
2. The stealing away of love.
3. A horizontal wooden structure bolted to the keel of a ship to give it greater strength.
4. The sea is itself the harbor of the phoenix' breast. The phoenix, a mythical bird, is an emblem of rebirth.
5. Himself.
6. He waits, afire like the phoenix (who can be reborn from its own ashes), for the unspoken name of the love he cannot claim to possess.

More savage than the death of kings,
Some splintered garland for the seer.[7]

Beyond siroccos[8] harvesting
The solstice thunders, crept away,
Like a cliff swinging or a sail
Flung into April's inmost day—

Creation's blithe and petalled word
To the lounged goddess when she rose
Conceding dialogue with eyes
That smile unsearchable repose—

Still fervid covenant, Belle Isle,[9]
—Unfolded floating dais before
Which rainbows twine continual hair—
Belle Isle, white echo of the oar![1]

The imaged Word, it is, that holds
Hushed willows anchored in its glow.
It is the unbetrayable reply[2]
Whose accent no farewell can know.

1926

From *THE BRIDGE*

Proem: To Brooklyn Bridge

How many dawns, chill from his rippling rest
The seagull's wings shall dip and pivot him,
Shedding white rings of tumult, building high
Over the chained bay waters Liberty—

Then, with inviolate curve, forsake our eyes
As apparitional as sails that cross[3]
Some page of figures to be filed away;
—Till elevators drop us from our day . . .

I think of cinemas, panoramic sleights
With multitudes bent toward some flashing scene

7. He asks for some poetic message. *Garland:* Here, a mark of distinction.

8. Hot, oppressive winds of the Mediterranean and Caribbean. *Solstice:* The longest or shortest day of the year; here, the longest.

9. Straits off the northeast coast of Canada.

1. The meaning appears to be that creation's blithe and petalled word is sounded apart from the siroccos, is like a cliff swinging or a sail flung into the heart of a spring day, as when Venus rose from the sea (that word of creation holds dialogue with her reposeful eyes) or as Belle Isle stands as covenant for love.

2. The imaged Word is the poet's reply to the creation's word, and it cannot be betrayed or dismissed, as can transitory love.

3. In the imagination of some office worker.

Never disclosed, but hastened to again,
Foretold to other eyes on the same screen;

And Thee, across the harbor, silver-paced
As though the sun took step[4] of thee, yet left
Some motion ever unspent in thy stride,—
Implicitly thy freedom staying thee!

Out of some subway scuttle, cell or loft
A bedlamite[5] speeds to thy parapets,
Tilting there momently, shrill shirt ballooning,
A jest falls from the speechless caravan.

Down Wall,[6] from girder into street noon leaks,
A rip-tooth of the sky's acetylene;
All afternoon the cloud-flown derricks turn . . .
Thy cables breathe the North Atlantic still.

And obscure as that heaven of the Jews,[7]
Thy guerdon[8] . . . Accolade thou dost bestow
Of anonymity time cannot raise:
Vibrant reprieve and pardon thou dost show.

O harp and altar, of the fury[9] fused,
(How could mere toil align thy choiring strings!)
Terrific threshold of the prophet's pledge,[1]
Prayer of pariah, and the lover's cry,—

Again the traffic lights that skim thy swift
Unfractioned idiom, immaculate sigh of stars,
Beading thy path—condense eternity:
And we have seen night lifted in thine arms.

Under thy shadow by the piers I waited;
Only in darkness is thy shadow clear.
The City's fiery parcels[2] all undone,
Already snow submerges an iron year . . .

O Sleepless as the river under thee,
Vaulting the sea, the prairies' dreaming sod,
Unto us lowliest sometime sweep, descend
And of the curveship[3] lend a myth to God.[4]

4. Followed the lead.
5. Madman.
6. Wall Street in Manhattan.
7. Heaven in the Jewish tradition is much vaguer than in the Christian.
8. Reward.
9. The imagination.

1. Of heaven on earth. *Pariah:* One rejected by society, an outcast.
2. Skyscrapers.
3. Like "kingship."
4. A new mythological embodiment of God.

Royal Palm

FOR GRACE HART CRANE[8]

Green rustlings, more-than-regal charities
Drift coolly from that tower of whispered light.
Amid the noontide's blazed asperities
I watched the sun's most gracious anchorite[9]

Climb up as by communings, year on year
Uneaten of the earth or aught earth holds,
And the grey trunk, that's elephantine, rear
Its frondings sighing in æthereal folds.

Forever fruitless, and beyond that yield
Of sweat the jungle presses with hot love
And tendril till our deathward breath is sealed—
It grazes the horizons, launched above

Mortality—ascending emerald-bright,
A fountain at salute, a crown in view—
Unshackled, casual of its azured height
As though it soared suchwise through heaven too.

1933

8. Hart Crane's mother. A royal palm is a tall palm with a white trunk, native to the Caribbean area.

9. Hermit.

ALLEN TATE
(*1899–*)

Allen Tate was born in Winchester, Clarke County, Kentucky, on November 19, 1899. His schooling was desultory, with a year at a school in Nashville, three years at one in Louisville, a half year each at two public high schools, a final year at a preparatory school in Washington, D.C. He entered Vanderbilt University in 1919. His readings in philosophy and literature were sufficiently varied to impress John Crowe Ransom, from whom he took two courses and the sense of a way of life. Tate, and later his roommate Robert Penn Warren, were the two undergraduates favored by an invitation to join an adult group who met to discuss poetry and other subjects in Nashville. They called themselves the Fugitives and published a magazine, *The Fugitive,* to which Tate contributed a number of poems. One of these brought him a letter from Hart Crane, who thought he detected in it the influence of Eliot. A long and momentous friendship then began.

Because of a skirmish with tuberculosis, Tate had to take his degree a year later, in 1923. He then did some school teaching in West Virginia, but moved on to New York in the hope of a writing career. To make ends meet he worked on a semi-pornographic magazine called *Telling Tales.* He had meanwhile married Caroline Gordon, also a writer, and they moved to a large house in Patterson, New York, in late 1925 to pursue their writing careers. Hart Crane was invited to stay with them and remained for several months, but the quarrel over his housekeeping chores—which he could not abide—led to his departure.

The Tates moved back to live in Greenwich Village after a year in Patterson. Allen Tate became a well-known and highly respected figure in the literary world. He edited the *Sewanee Review* from 1944 to 1946. In 1950 he became a Roman Catholic. From 1951 until his retirement in 1968 he was a professor of English at the University of Minnesota.

Ode to the Confederate Dead[5]

Row after row with strict impunity
The headstones yield their names to the element,
The wind whirrs without recollection;
In the riven troughs the splayed leaves
Pile up, of nature the casual sacrament
To the seasonal eternity of death;
Then driven by the fierce scrutiny
Of heaven to their election in the vast breath,
They sough[5a] the rumour of mortality.

Autumn is desolation in the plot
Of a thousand acres where these memories grow
From the inexhaustible bodies that are not
Dead, but feed the grass row after rich row.
Think of the autumns that have come and gone!—
Ambitious November with the humors of the year,
With a particular zeal for every slab,
Staining the uncomfortable angels that rot
On the slabs, a wing chipped here, an arm there:
The brute curiosity of an angel's stare
Turns you, like them, to stone,
Transforms the heaving air
Till plunged to a heavier world below
You shift your sea-space blindly
Heaving, turning like the blind crab.[6]

5. In an essay "Narcissus as Narcissus," Tate explains that this poem "is 'about' solipsism, a philosophical doctrine which says that we create the world in the act of perceiving it; or about Narcissism, or any other *ism* that denotes the failure of the human personality to function objectively in nature and society."

5a. Sigh. *Rumour:* in addition to the usual sense, Tate uses the older meaning of "a soft noise."

6. "The structure of the Ode is simple. Figure to yourself a man stopping at the gate of a Confederate graveyard on a late autumn afternoon. The leaves are falling; his first impressions bring him the 'rumor of mortality'; and the desolation barely allows him, at the beginning of the second stanza, the conventionally heroic surmise that the dead will enrich the earth, 'where these memories grow.' From those quoted words to the end of that passage he pauses for a baroque meditation on the ravages of time, concluding with the figure of the 'blind crab.' This figure has mobility but no direction, energy but, from the human point of view, no purposeful world to use it in: in the entire poem there are only two explicit symbols for the looked-in ego; the crab is the first and less explicit symbol, a mere hint, a planting of the idea that will become overt in its second instance—the jaguar towards the end. The crab is the first intimation of the nature of the moral conflict upon which the drama of the poem develops: the cut-off-ness of the modern 'intellectual man' from the world" (Tate's note).

Dazed by the wind, only the wind
The leaves flying, plunge

You know who have waited by the wall
The twilight certainty of an animal,
Those midnight restitutions of the blood
You know—the immitigable pines, the smoky frieze
Of the sky, the sudden call: you know the rage,
The cold pool left by the mounting flood,
Of muted Zeno and Parmenides.[7]
You who have waited for the angry resolution
Of those desires that should be yours tomorrow,
You know the unimportant shrift of death
And praise the vision
And praise the arrogant circumstance
Of those who fall
Rank upon rank, hurried beyond decision—
Here by the sagging gate, stopped by the wall.[8]

Seeing, seeing only the leaves
Flying, plunge and expire

Turn your eyes to the immoderate past,
Turn to the inscrutable infantry rising
Demons out of the earth—they will not last.
Stonewall,[9] Stonewall, and the sunken fields of hemp,[1]
Shiloh, Antietam, Malvern Hill, Bull Run.[2]

7. Parmenides and his follower Zeno, both of Elea, were Greek philosophers of the fifth century B.C. They held that the real universe is a single and unchanging whole, while the apparent universe of mutable things is illusory and unknowable.

8. "The next long passage or 'strophe' . . . states the other term of the conflict. It is the theme of heroism, not merely moral heroism, but heroism in the grand style, elevating even death from mere physical dissolution into a formal ritual: this heroism is a formal ebullience of the human spirit in an entire society, not private, romantic illusion—something better than moral heroism, great as that may be, for moral heroism, being personal and individual, may be achieved by certain men in all ages, even ages of decadence. But the late Hart Crane . . . described the theme as the 'theme of chivalry, a tradition of excess (not literally excess, rather active faith) which cannot be perpetuated in the fragmentary cosmos of today—"those desires which should be yours tomorrow," but which, you know, will not persist nor find any way into action.' The structure then is the objective frame for the tension between the two themes, 'active faith' which has decayed, and the 'fragmentary cosmos' which surrounds us. . . . In contemplating the heroic theme the man at the gate never quite commits himself to the illusion of its availability to him. The most that he can allow himself is the fancy that the blowing leaves are charging soldiers, but he rigorously returns to the refrain: 'Only the wind'—or the 'leaves flying.'. . . More than this, he cautions himself, reminds himself repeatedly, of his subjective prison, his solipsisms, by breaking off the half-illusion and coming back to the refrain of wind and leaves, a refrain that, as Hart Crane said, is necessary to the 'subjective continuity' " (Tate's note).

9. Thomas Jonathan Jackson (1824–1863), Confederate general in the Civil War, earned the nickname Stonewall at the first battle of Bull Run (Virginia), July 21, 1861. He was killed in 1863 at the Battle of Chancellorsville.

1. Sunken because not cultivated during the war.

2. Famous battles of the Civil War, slightly out of chronological order. Shiloh (Tennessee), April 6–7, 1862, ended with the Confederate troops in retreat; Antietam or Sharpsburg (Maryland), September 17, 1862, and Malvern Hill (Virginia), July 2, 1862, also were disadvantageous to the South; the two battles of Bull Run, in 1861 and on August 29–30, 1862, were both victories for the Confederate armies.

Lost in that orient of the thick-and-fast
You will curse the setting sun.

Cursing only the leaves crying
Like an old man in a storm

You hear the shout, the crazy hemlocks point
With troubled fingers to the silence which
Smothers you, a mummy, in time.

The hound bitch
Toothless and dying, in a musty cellar
Hears the wind only.

Now that the salt of their blood
Stiffens the saltier oblivion of the sea,
Seals the malignant purity of the flood,
What shall we who count our days and bow
Our heads with a commemorial woe
In the ribboned coats of grim felicity,
What shall we say of the bones, unclean,
Whose verdurous anonymity will grow?
The ragged arms, the ragged heads and eyes
Lost in these acres of the insane green?
The gray lean spiders come, they come and go;
In a tangle of willows without light
The singular screech-owl's tight
Invisible lyric seeds the mind
With the furious murmur of their chivalry.

We shall say only the leaves
Flying, plunge and expire

We shall say only the leaves whispering
In the improbable mist of nightfall
That flies on multiple wing;
Night is the beginning and the end
And in between the ends of distraction
Waits mute speculation, the patient curse
That stones the eyes, or like the jaguar leaps
For his own image in a jungle pool, his victim.[4]

What shall we say who have knowledge
Carried to the heart?[5] Shall we take the act

4. "This figure of the jaguar is the only explicit rendering of the Narcissus motif in the poem, but instead of a youth gazing into a pool, a predatory beast stares at a jungle stream, and leaps to devour himself" (Tate's note).

5. "This is Pascal's war between heart and head, between *finesse* and *géometrie*" (Tate's note). The allusion is to Blaise Pascal (1623–1662), the philosopher who wrote in his *Pensées* (Thoughts), #277, "The heart has reasons that the reason does not know."

To the grave? Shall we, more hopeful, set up the grave
In the house? The ravenous grave?[6]

Leave now
The shut gate and the decomposing wall:
The gentle serpent, green in the mulberry bush,
Riots with his tongue through the hush—
Sentinel of the grave who counts us all![7]

1928, 1937

6. "These two themes struggle for mastery up to [lines 77–78]. . . . It will be observed that the passage begins with a phrase taken from the wind-leaves refrain —the signal that it has won. The refrain has been fused with the main stream of the man's reflections dominating them; and he cannot return even to an ironic vision of the heroes. There is nothing but death, the mere naturalism of death at that—spiritual extinction in the decay of the body. Autumn and the leaves are death; the men who exemplified in a grand style an 'active faith' are dead; there are only the leaves. Shall we then worship death . . . that will take us before our time? The question is not answered, although as a kind of morbid romanticism it might, if answered affirmatively, provide the man with an illusory escape from his solipsism; but he cannot accept it. Nor has he been able to live in his immediate world, the fragmentary cosmos. There is no practical solution, no solution offered for the edification of moralists. . . . The main intention of the poem has been to make dramatically visible the conflict, to concentrate it . . ." (Tate's note).

7. "The closing image, that of the serpent, is the ancient symbol of time, and I tried to give it the credibility of the commonplace by placing it in a mulberry bush —with the faint hope that the silkworm would somehow be implicit. But time is also death. If that is so, then space, or the Becoming, is life; and I believe there is not a single spatial symbol in the poem. 'Seaspace' is allowed the 'blind crab'; but the sea, as appears plainly in the passage beginning, 'Now that the salt of their blood . . .' is life only insofar as it is the source of the lowest forms of life, the source perhaps of all life, but life undifferentiated, halfway between life and death. This passage is a contrasting inversion of the conventional

. . . inexhaustible bodies that are not
Dead, but feed the grass . . .

the reduction of the earlier, literary conceit to a more naturalistic figure derived from modern biological speculation. Those 'buried Caesars' will not bloom in the hyacinth but will only make saltier the sea" (Tate's note).

YVOR WINTERS
(*1900–1968*)

Yvor Winters was born in Chicago on October 17, 1900. He spent his childhood in California and Oregon, then returned to Chicago, where he went to high school and began studies at the University of Chicago. In his freshman year he was discovered to have tuberculosis, and he was sent to Santa Fe, New Mexico, where he convalesced, taught primary school, and worked as a manual laborer. In 1925 he took an M.A. in romance languages at the University of Colorado, and in 1928 he became an instructor at Stanford University, where he taught until his retirement in 1966. He became known as an abrasive but honest and penetrating critic, as well as a poet. He died in Palo Alto on January 26, 1968.

John Sutter[1]

I was the patriarch of the shining land,
Of the blond summer and metallic grain;
Men vanished at the motion of my hand,
And when I beckoned they would come again.

The earth grew dense with grain at my desire;
The shade was deepened at the springs and streams;
Moving in dust that clung like pillared fire,[2]
The gathering herds grew heavy in my dreams.

Across the mountains, naked from the heights,
Down to the valley broken settlers came,
And in my houses feasted through the nights,
Rebuilt their sinews and assumed a name.

In my clear rivers my own men discerned
The motive for the ruin and the crime—
Gold heavier than earth, a wealth unearned,
Loot, for two decades, from the heart of Time.

Metal, intrinsic value, deep and dense,
Preanimate, inimitable, still,
Real, but an evil with no human sense,
Dispersed the mind to concentrate the will.

Grained by alchemic change,[3] the human kind
Turned from themselves to rivers and to rocks;
With dynamite broke metal unrefined;
Measured their moods by geologic shocks.

With knives they dug the metal out of stone;
Turned rivers back, for gold through ages piled,
Drove knives to hearts, and faced the gold alone;
Valley and river ruined and reviled;

Reviled and ruined me, my servant slew,
Strangled him from the figtree by my door.
When they had done what fury bade them do,
I was a cursing beggar, stripped and sore.

1. John Sutter (1803–1880), American pioneer, born in Switzerland, was in 1838 granted a huge tract of land on the Sacramento river by the Mexican governor on condition that he develop and fortify it. His settlement, "New Helvetia," became powerful. After California was acquired by the United States, Sutter prepared a new mill; but in the course of digging, gold was found. The news leaked out against his will, the gold rush began, and his property was overrun. When the U.S. Supreme Court found the title to most of his land invalid, he went bankrupt. From 1871 to 1880, when he died, he petitioned Congress annually for redress.

2. Alludes to the Israelites' journey through the desert to the Promised Land; they were guided by a pillar of cloud by day, and a pillar of fire by night.

3. Alchemy, a medieval precursor of chemistry, sought to transmute "base" metal to gold.

What end impersonal, what breathless age,
Incontinent of quiet and of years,
What calm catastrophe will yet assuage
This final drouth of penitential tears?

1941

Sir Gawaine and the Green Knight[4]

Reptilian green the wrinkled throat,
Green as a bough of yew the beard;
He bent his head, and so I smote;
Then for a thought my vision cleared.

The head dropped clean; he rose and walked;
He fixed his fingers in the hair;
The head was unabashed and talked;
I understood what I must dare.

His flesh, cut down, arose and grew.
He bade me wait the season's round,
And then, when he had strength anew,
To meet him on his native ground.

The year declined; and in his keep
I passed in joy a thriving yule;
And whether waking or in sleep,
I lived in riot like a fool.

He beat the woods to bring me meat.
His lady, like a forest vine,
Grew in my arms; the growth was sweet;
And yet what thoughtless force was mine!

By practice and conviction formed,
With ancient stubbornness ingrained,
Although her body clung and swarmed,
My own identity remained.

Her beauty, lithe, unholy, pure,
Took shapes that I had never known;
And had I once been insecure,
Had grafted laurel in my bone.

And then, since I had kept the trust,
Had loved the lady, yet was true,

4. Winters' poem is based upon a Middle English poem of the same name. Sir Gawaine cuts off the head of the Green Knight, who tells him to come in a year's time to a castle so as to receive a similar blow. Gawaine arrives, and while his host is out hunting, the lady of the castle woos him. He keeps his virtue, and the Green Knight allows him to depart unscathed.

The knight withheld his giant thrust
And let me go with what I knew.

I left the green bark and the shade,
Where growth was rapid, thick, and still;
I found a road that men had made
And rested on a drying hill.

1941

LANGSTON HUGHES
(*1902–1967*)

Langston Hughes was born on February 1, 1902, in Joplin, Missouri. His early years were spent in Missouri and Kansas. His parents separated and remarried, but always kept an eye out for him. He lived mostly with his mother in Lawrence, Kansas, until his twelfth year, and then went to Lincoln, Illinois, to live with his father and stepmother. While there he completed grammar school and was elected class poet, a distinction which compelled him to try writing verse for the first time. He then went to join his mother, also remarried, in Cleveland, and attended high school.

In 1919 a sudden telegram from his father enjoined him to be ready next day to travel to Mexico for the summer. His father had found he could do better at business in Mexico than in the United States. His expectation was that Langston Hughes would become an engineer, and when the boy protested that this was not his interest, his father insisted that he could do well at anything. But eventually Langston was sent, as he had wished, to Columbia University. After one year (1921–22), he dropped out and shipped out to Africa, and then, on another vessel, to France. The year 1924 was spent in various odd jobs in Paris, the best being that of assistant cook in a fashionable restaurant.

On his return to the United States, Hughes joined his mother, now living in Washington, and took a job as busboy in a hotel. It happened that Vachel Lindsay was dining there, and Hughes, too shy to present himself directly, left some poems beside Lindsay's plate. The famous poet read some of them to an audience that night, and the busboy poet became locally renowned.

With considerable sense of himself and his future, Hughes accepted a scholarship to Lincoln University in Pennsylvania. He received a B.A. there in 1929, and in the same year published his first novel, *Not Without Laughter*. He became a succesful writer and was also well known for his excellent reading of his poetry. He died May 22, 1967.

The Weary Blues

Droning a drowsy syncopated tune,
Rocking back and forth to a mellow croon,
    I heard a Negro play.
Down on Lenox Avenue[1] the other night

1. A major street in Harlem.

By the pale dull pallor of an old gas light
He did a lazy sway. . . .
He did a lazy sway. . . .
To the tune o' those Weary Blues.
With his ebony hands on each ivory key
He made that poor piano moan with melody.
O Blues!
Swaying to and fro on his rickety stool
He played that sad raggy tune like a musical fool.
Sweet Blues!
Coming from a black man's soul.
O Blues!
In a deep song voice with a melancholy tone
I heard that Negro sing, that old piano moan—
"Ain't got nobody in all this world,
Ain't got nobody but ma self.
I's gwine to quit ma frownin'
And put ma troubles on the shelf."
Thump, thump, thump, went his foot on the floor.
He played a few chords then he sang some more—
"I got the Weary Blues
And I can't be satisfied.
Got the Weary Blues
And can't be satisfied—
I ain't happy no mo'
And I wish that I had died."
And far into the night he crooned that tune.
The stars went out and so did the moon.
The singer stopped playing and went to bed
While the Weary Blues echoed through his head.
He slept like a rock or a man that's dead.

1926

Morning After[2]

I was so sick last night I
Didn't hardly know my mind.
So sick last night I
Didn't know my mind.
I drunk some bad licker that
Almost made me blind.

Had a dream last night I
Thought I was in hell.
I drempt last night I
Thought I was in hell.

2. This poem is in the form of a Blues.

Woke up and looked around me—
Babe, your mouth was open like a well.

I said, Baby! Baby!
Please don't snore so loud.
Baby! Please!
Please don't snore so loud.
You jest a little bit o' woman but you
Sound like a great big crowd.

1942

Madam's Past History

My name is Johnson—
Madam Alberta K.
The Madam stands for business.
I'm smart that way.

I had a
HAIR-DRESSING PARLOR
Before
The depression put
The prices lower.

Then I had a
BARBECUE STAND
Till I got mixed up
With a no-good man.

Cause I had a insurance
The WPA[3]
Said, We can't use you
Wealthy that way.

I said,
DON'T WORRY 'BOUT ME!
Just like the song,
You WPA folks take care of yourself—
And I'll get along.

I do cooking,
Day's work, too!
Alberta K. Johnson—
Madam to you.

1949

3. The Works Progress Administration, a Federal agency that during the Thirties created jobs for the unemployed.

Theme for English B

The instructor said,

Go home and write
a page tonight.
And let that page come out of you—
Then, it will be true.

I wonder if it's that simple?
I am twenty-two, colored, born in Winston-Salem.
I went to school there, then Durham,[4] then here
to this college[5] on the hill above Harlem.
I am the only colored student in my class.
The steps from the hill lead down into Harlem,
through a park, then I cross St. Nicholas,[6]
Eighth Avenue, Seventh, and I come to the Y,
the Harlem Branch Y, where I take the elevator
up to my room, sit down, and write this page:

It's not easy to know what is true for you or me
at twenty-two, my age. But I guess I'm what
I feel and see and hear, Harlem, I hear you:
hear you, hear me—we two—you, me, talk on this page.
(I hear New York, too.) Me—who?

Well, I like to eat, sleep, drink, and be in love.
I like to work, read, learn, and understand life.
I like a pipe for a Christmas present,
or records—Bessie,[7] bop, or Bach.
I guess being colored doesn't make me *not* like
the same things other folks like who are other races.
So will my page be colored that I write?

Being me, it will not be white.
But it will be
a part of you, instructor.
You are white—
yet a part of me, as I am a part of you.
That's American.
Sometimes perhaps you don't want to be a part of me.
Nor do I often want to be a part of you.
But we are, that's true!
As I learn from you,
I guess you learn from me—

4. Cities in North Carolina.
5. Columbia University.
6. An avenue east of Columbia University.
7. Bessie Smith (1894–1937), Blues singer. *Bop:* a style of modern jazz, especially popular during the Forties and Fifties.

although you're older—and white—
and somewhat more free.

This is my page for English B.

1959

STEVIE SMITH
(*1902–1971*)

Stevie Smith was born Florence Margaret Smith in Hull, Yorkshire, England in 1902. (Her nickname "Stevie" refers to her smallness; it was borrowed from a famous jockey of the time.) At the age of three she moved to London with her family, and she lived in the same house there until her death. Until 1953 she worked in a publisher's office in London; after that she devoted her time to writing and to broadcasting for the BBC. In 1966 she was given the Cholmondely Award, in 1969 the Queen's Gold Medal for Poetry. She died in March 1971.

Not Waving But Drowning

Nobody heard him, the dead man,
But still he lay moaning:
I was much further out than you thought
And not waving but drowning.

Poor chap, he always loved larking
And now he's dead
It must have been too cold for him his heart gave way,
They said.

Oh, no no no, it was too cold always
(Still the dead one lay moaning)
I was much too far out all my life
And not waving but drowning.

1957

Was He Married?

Was he married, did he try
To support as he grew less fond of them
Wife and family?

No,
He never suffered such a blow.

Did he feel pointless, feeble and distrait,
Unwanted by everyone and in the way?

From his cradle he was purposeful,
His bent strong and his mind full.

Did he love people very much
Yet find them die one day?

He did not love in the human way.

Did he ask how long it would go on,
Wonder if Death could be counted on for an end?

He did not feel like this,
He had a future of bliss.

Did he never feel strong
Pain for being wrong?

He was not wrong, he was right,
He suffered from others', not his own, spite.

But there *is* no suffering like having made a mistake
Because of being of an inferior make.

He was not inferior,
He was superior.

He knew then that power corrupts but some must govern?

His thoughts were different.

Did he lack friends? Worse,
Think it was for his fault, not theirs?

He did not lack friends,
He had disciples he moulded to his ends.

Did he feel over-handicapped sometimes, yet must draw even?

How could he feel like this? He was the King of Heaven.

. . . find a sudden brightness one day in everything
Because a mood had been conquered, or a sin?

I tell you, he did not sin.

Do only human beings suffer from the irritation
I have mentioned? learn too that being comical
Does not ameliorate the desperation?

Only human beings feel this,
It is because they are so mixed.

All human beings should have a medal,
A god cannot carry it, he is not able.

A god is Man's doll, you ass,
He makes him up like this on purpose.

He might have made him up worse.

He often has, in the past.

To choose a god of love, as he did and does,
Is a little move then?

Yes, it is.

A larger one will be when men
Love love and hate hate but do not deify them?

It will be a larger one.

1962

To Carry the Child

To carry the child into adult life
Is good? I say it is not,
To carry the child into adult life
Is to be handicapped.

The child in adult life is defenceless
And if he is grown-up, knows it,
And the grown-up looks at the childish part
And despises it.

The child, too, despises the clever grown-up,
The man-of-the-world, the frozen,
For the child has the tears alive on his cheek
And the man has none of them.

As the child has colours, and the man sees no
Colours or anything,
Being easy only in things of the mind,
The child is easy in feeling.

Easy in feeling, easily excessive
And in excess powerful,
For instance, if you do not speak to the child
He will make trouble.

You would say a man had the upper hand
Of the child, if a child survive,

But I say the child has fingers of strength
To strangle the man alive.

Oh it is not happy, it is never happy,
To carry the child into adulthood,
Let children lie down before full growth
And die in their infanthood
And be guilty of no man's blood.

But oh the poor child, the poor child, what can he do,
Trapped in a grown-up carapace,[1]
But peer outside of his prison room
With the eye of an anarchist?

1966

1. Shell.

WILLIAM PLOMER
(*1903–1973*)

William Plomer was born on December 10, 1903, in Pietersburg, Transvaal, South Africa. His parents were English, and he was sent to Rugby School. He returned to Africa for reasons of health, and he was variously a farmer in the Stormberg Mountains and a trader in Zululand. In 1925 he published his first novel, *Turbott Wolfe*, an outraged account of racial discrimination in South Africa. During his twenties he spent two years traveling and teaching in Japan, returned to England for a time, then settled in Greece. He served in the British Admiralty during the Second World War, and from then on he lived in England until his death on September 21, 1973.

The Widow's Plot: or, She Got What Was Coming to Her

Troubled was a house in Ealing [1]
Where a widow's only son
Found her fond maternal feeling
    Overdone.

She was fussy and possessive;
Lennie, in his teens,
Found the atmosphere oppressive;
    There were scenes.

Tiring one day of her strictures
Len went down the street,

1. A western part of London, here associated with dull respectability.

Took a ticket at the pictures,
Took his seat.

The picture was designed to thrill
But oh, the girl he sat beside!
If proximity could kill
He'd have died.

Simple, sweet, sixteen and blonde,
Unattached, her name was Bess.
Well, boys, how would *you* respond?
I can guess.

Len and Bessie found each other
All that either could desire,
But the fat, when he told Mother,
Was in the fire.

The widow, who had always dreaded
This might happen, hatched a scheme
To smash, when they were duly wedded,
Love's young dream.

One fine day she murmured, 'Sonny,
It's not for me to interfere,
You may think it rather funny
But I hear

'Bess goes out with other men'
'I don't believe it! It's a lie!
Tell me who with, where, and when?
Tell me why?'

'Keep cool, Lennie. I suspected
That the girl was far from nice.
What a pity you rejected
My advice.'

Suspicion from this fatal seed
Sprang up overnight
And strangled, like a poisonous weed,
The lilies of delight.

Still unbelieving, Len believed
That Bess was being unchaste,
And a man that feels himself deceived
May act in haste.

Now Bess was innocence incarnate
And never thought of other men;

She visited an aunt at Barnet[2]
Now and then,

But mostly stayed at home and dusted,
Crooning early, crooning late,
Unaware of being distrusted
By her mate.

Then one day a wire was sent:
MEET ME PALACEUM AT EIGHT
URGENT AUNTIE. Bessie went
To keep the date.

Slightly anxious, Bessie came
To the unusual rendezvous.
Desperate, Lennie did the same,
He waited too,

Seeing but unseen by Bessie,
And in a minute seeing red—
For a stranger, fat and dressy,
A trilby on his head,

In his tie a tasteful pearl,
On his face a nasty leer,
Sidled up towards the girl
And called her 'Dear.'

At this juncture Len stepped in,
Made a bee-line for the lout,
With a straight left to the chin
Knocked him out.

He might have done the same for Bess
Thinking still that she had tricked him,
But she was gazing in distress
At the victim.

'It's a *her*!' she cried (but grammar
Never was her strongest suit):
'She's passed out!' he heard her stammer,
'Lennie, scoot!'

'It's *what*? A *her*? Good God, it's *Mum*!
Ah, now I see! A wicked plan
To make me think my Bess had come
To meet a *man*—'

2. A suburb in the north of London.

'Now what's all this?' a copper said,
Shoving the crowd aside. 'I heard a
Rumour somebody was dead.
Is it murder?'

Len quite candidly replied,
'No, officer, it's something less.
It's justifiable matricide,
Isn't it, Bess?'

1940

RICHARD EBERHART
(*1904–*)

Richard Eberhart was born in Austin, Minnesota, on April 5, 1904. His father was a well-off businessman, and he grew up contentedly on the family's forty-acre estate, Burr Oaks. Eberhart was graduated from high school in 1921 and duly entered the University of Minnesota. But the following year marked an abrupt change. His mother died of cancer, and he said afterwards that her death made him into a poet. Soon after, and with even greater suddenness, his father's fortune was largely wiped out; an employee had embezzled over a million dollars. Perhaps in refuge from this turmoil, Eberhart left the University of Minnesota and enrolled at Dartmouth. He received his B.A. degree there in 1926. Then, not sure what to do next besides write verse, he worked in Chicago as a floorwalker in a department store, as an advertising copywriter, then shipped out as a deck hand on a tramp steamer going around the world. At Port Said, to escape a tyrannical captain, he jumped ship and made his way to England. In 1927 he went up to St. John's College, Cambridge, and took a second B.A. there in 1929.

The following year (1930–31), he returned to the United States and served as tutor to the son of King Prajadhipok of Siam, the king being then in New York for a cataract operation. Eberhart spent 1932–33 as a graduate student at Harvard, and in 1933 received an M.A. from Cambridge University. Then he decided not to become a university teacher, and instead taught English at St. Mark's School in Southboro from 1933 to 1941. During the Second World War he was an aerial gunnery officer in the Navy.

Eberhart's wife's family controlled the Butcher Polish Company. On leaving the Navy, Eberhart became assistant manager. He worked actively for the company for six years, and remained on its board of directors. But the academic life, of which he had so long disapproved, had become a more favorable environment for poets, and he was invited back into it. After various university posts he accepted the position of professor of English and poet-in-residence at Dartmouth, where he has been since 1956.

The Groundhog

In June, amid the golden fields,
I saw a groundhog lying dead.
Dead lay he; my senses shook,

And mind outshot our naked frailty.
There lowly in the vigorous summer
His form began its senseless change,
And made my senses waver dim
Seeing nature ferocious in him.
Inspecting close his maggots' might
And seething cauldron of his being,
Half with loathing, half with a strange love,
I poked him with an angry stick.
The fever arose, became a flame
And Vigour circumscribed the skies,
Immense energy in the sun,
And through my frame a sunless trembling.
My stick had done nor good nor harm.
Then stood I silent in the day
Watching the object, as before;
And kept my reverence for knowledge
Trying for control, to be still,
To quell the passion of the blood;
Until I had bent down on my knees
Praying for joy in the sight of decay.
And so I left; and I returned
In Autumn strict of eye, to see
The sap gone out of the groundhog,
But the bony sodden hulk remained.
But the year had lost its meaning,
And in intellectual chains
I lost both love and loathing,
Mured up [1] in the wall of wisdom.
Another summer took the fields again
Massive and burning, full of life,
But when I chanced upon the spot
There was only a little hair left,
And bones bleaching in the sunlight
Beautiful as architecture;
I watched them like a geometer,
And cut a walking stick from a birch.
It has been three years, now.
There is no sign of the groundhog.
I stood there in the whirling summer,
My hand capped a withered heart,
And thought of China and of Greece,
Of Alexander in his tent;
Of Montaigne in his tower,
Of Saint Theresa [2] in her wild lament.

1936

1. Walled.

2. Three types of human enterprise: Alexander the Great, conqueror of the world; Montaigne, the ironic commentator on all human affairs; and St. Theresa of Avila, mystic and founder of a religious order.

The Fury of Aerial Bombardment

You would think the fury of aerial bombardment
Would rouse God to relent; the infinite spaces
Are still silent. He looks on shock-pried faces.
History, even, does not know what is meant.

You would feel that after so many centuries
God would give man to repent; yet he can kill
As Cain could, but with multitudinous will,
No farther advanced than in his ancient furies.

Was man made stupid to see his own stupidity?
Is God by definition indifferent, beyond us all?
Is the eternal truth man's fighting soul
Wherein the Beast ravens in its own avidity?

Of Van Wettering I speak, and Averill,
Names on a list, whose faces I do not recall
But they are gone to early death, who late in school
Distinguished the belt feed lever from the belt holding pawl.

1947

C. DAY LEWIS
(*1904–1972*)

Cecil Day Lewis was born in Ballintubber, Queen's County, in Northern Ireland, on April 17, 1904. On his mother's side he could claim, like Yeats, to be descended from a noble family, the Butlers. His father was a priest of the Church of Ireland, for a time an army chaplain.

When he was four, his mother died, and Day Lewis attributed to her loss some of his later tension with his father. Sent to "public" school, he had the usual nightmares associated with British schools of this type. But at Wadham College, Oxford, he was much happier. His tutor Maurice Bowra was kind to him; he came to know Robert Graves. In his last year as a student at Oxford, Day Lewis became acquainted with W. H. Auden, his junior by two years. The friendship which then began led to these two, along with Stephen Spender and Louis MacNeice, being lumped by critics into a school. With Auden he compiled and edited an anthology, *Oxford Poetry 1927*; they wrote alternate paragraphs of the pretentious introduction while sitting in a Wharfedale pub, as Auden recalled. Day Lewis studied classics—he was later to translate Virgil—and ancient history and philosophy.

After Oxford, Day Lewis became a schoolteacher at Larchfield Academy in Scotland, a post in which Auden succeeded him. He married, and in part to make up the added expenses, he wrote a detective story under the pseudonym of Nicholas Blake. It proved so successful that he continued to write detective stories at the rate of one a year. He also wrote several serious novels. But poetry was his constant interest.

During the Second World War, Day Lewis served in the Ministry of Information. He was named Professor of Poetry at Oxford University in 1951. He was appointed Poet Laureate in 1970. He died, after a year's illness, on May 22, 1972.

Sheepdog Trials in Hyde Park [1]

A shepherd stands at one end of the arena.
Five sheep are unpenned at the other. His dog runs out
In a curve to behind them, fetches them straight to the shepherd,
Then drives the flock round a triangular course
Through a couple of gates and back to his master: two
Must be sorted there from the flock, then all five penned.
Gathering, driving away, shedding[2] and penning
Are the plain words for the miraculous game.
An abstract game. What can the sheepdog make of such
Simplified terrain?—no hills, dales, bogs, walls, tracks,
Only a quarter-mile plain of grass, dumb crowds
Like crowds on hoardings[3] around it, and behind them
Traffic or mounds of lovers and children playing.
Well, the dog is no landscape-fancier: his whole concern
Is with his master's whistle, and of course
With the flock—sheep are sheep anywhere for him.

The sheep are the chanciest element. Why, for instance,
Go through this gate when there's on either side of it
No wall or hedge but huge and viable space?
Why not eat the grass instead of being pushed around it?
Like a blob of quicksilver on a tilting board
The flock erratically runs, dithers, breaks up,
Is reassembled: their ruling idea is the dog;
And behind the dog, though they know it not yet, is a shepherd.

The shepherd knows that time is of the essence
But haste calamitous. Between dog and sheep
There is always an ideal distance, a perfect angle;
But these are constantly varying, so the man
Should anticipate each move through the dog, his medium.
The shepherd is the brain behind the dog's brain,
But his control of dog, like dog's of sheep,
Is never absolute—that's the beauty of it.

For beautiful it is. The guided missiles,
The black-and-white angels follow each quirk and jink of
The evasive sheep, play grandmother's-steps[4] behind them,
Freeze to the ground, or leap to head off a straggler
Almost before it knows that it wants to stray,
As if radar-controlled. But they are not machines—

1. A large park in the West End of London.
2. Setting some apart from others.
3. Billboards.
4. In this game, the players try to creep up behind "granny," who may look back at any time; anyone caught moving is out of the game.

You can feel them feeling mastery, doubt, chagrin:
Machines don't frolic when their job is done.

What's needfully done in the solitude of sheep-runs—
Those rough, real tasks become this stylised game,
A demonstration of intuitive wit
Kept natural by the saving grace of error.
To lift, to fetch, to drive, to shed, to pen
Are acts I recognise, with all they mean
Of shepherding the unruly, for a kind of
Controlled woolgathering [5] is my work too.

1957

5. Daydreaming.

PATRICK KAVANAGH
(*1905–1967*)

Patrick Kavanagh was born in the village of Inniskeen, County Monaghan, Ireland in 1905. Though he remained a Roman Catholic, Kavanagh blamed the Church for causing much unhappiness, his own included, through its repression of natural feelings. In 1939 he went to Dublin. Ferociously independent, forever in a rage with readers who accepted the delusions promoted by successful authors and critics, Kavanagh eked out a meager living as a columnist, movie critic, and, in 1952, as publisher of his own magazine *Kavanagh's Weekly*. His first book of poems to attract much attention, *The Great Hunger* (1942), got him into trouble with the censor because of its alleged obscenity and anti-Catholicism.

In 1954 he was gravely ill: he suffered from lung cancer, and one of his lungs had to be surgically removed. During his convalescence, in the summer of 1955, he resigned himself to obscurity and failure, finding consolation in the thought that great men "are not concerned with whether or not their work is involved with the ephemeral." Kavanagh married for the first time early in 1967. He died the same year, on November 30, in a Dublin nursing home.

Tinker's Wife [9]

I saw her amid the dunghill debris
Looking for things
Such as an old pair of shoes or gaiters.
She was a young woman,
A tinker's wife.
Her face had streaks of care
Like wires across it,
But she was supple

9. A tinker repairs pots and other household utensils.

As a young goat
On a windy hill.

She searched on the dunghill debris,
Tripping gingerly
Over tin canisters
And sharp-broken
Dinner plates.

1936

Inniskeen Road: July Evening[1]

The bicycles go by in twos and threes—
There's a dance in Billy Brennan's barn to-night,
And there's the half-talk code of mysteries
And the wink-and-elbow language of delight.
Half-past eight and there is not a spot
Upon a mile of road, no shadow thrown
That might turn out a man or woman, not
A footfall tapping secrecies of stone.

I have what every poet hates in spite
Of all the solemn talk of contemplation.
Oh, Alexander Selkirk[2] knew the plight
Of being king and government and nation.
A road, a mile of kingdom, I am king
Of banks and stones and every blooming thing.

1936

Canal Bank Walk

Leafy-with-love banks and the green waters of the canal
Pouring redemption for me, that I do
The will of God, wallow in the habitual, the banal,
Grow with nature again as before I grew.
The bright stick trapped, the breeze adding a third
Party to the couple kissing on an old seat,
And a bird gathering materials for the nest for the Word
Eloquently new and abandoned to its delirious beat.
O unworn world enrapture me, encapture me in a web
Of fabulous grass and eternal voices by a beech,
Feed the gaping need of my senses, give me ad lib
To pray unselfconsciously with overflowing speech
For this soul needs to be honoured with a new dress woven
From green and blue things and arguments that cannot be proven.

1960

1. Inniskeen, in the south of County Monaghan, was Kavanagh's native village.
2. Eighteenth century seaman whose experiences on an uninhabited island off the coast of Chile were used by Daniel Defoe for *Robinson Crusoe*.

Come Dance with Kitty Stobling

No, no, no, I know I was not important as I moved
Through the colourful country, I was but a single
Item in the picture, the namer not the beloved.
O tedious man with whom no gods commingle.
Beauty, who has described beauty? Once upon a time
I had a myth that was a lie but it served:
Trees walking across the crests of hills and my rhyme
Cavorting on mile-high stilts and the unnerved
Crowds looking up with terror in their rational faces.
O dance with Kitty Stobling I outrageously
Cried out-of-sense to them, while their timorous paces
Stumbled behind Jove's page boy[3] paging me.
I had a very pleasant journey, thank you sincerely
For giving me my madness back, or nearly.

1960

In Memory of My Mother

I do not think of you lying in the wet clay
Of a Monaghan[4] graveyard; I see
You walking down a lane among the poplars
On your way to the station, or happily

Going to second Mass on a summer Sunday—
You meet me and you say:
'Don't forget to see about the cattle—'
Among your earthiest words the angels stray.

And I think of you walking along a headland
Of green oats in June,
So full of repose, so rich with life—
And I see us meeting at the end of a town

On a fair day by accident, after
The bargains are all made and we can walk
Together through the shops and stalls and markets
Free in the oriental streets of thought.

O you are not lying in the wet clay,
For it is a harvest evening now and we
Are piling up the ricks against the moonlight
And you smile up at us—eternally.

1960

3. Jove was the king of the Roman gods.

4. The rural Irish county where Kavanagh grew up.

ROBERT PENN WARREN
(*1905–*)

Robert Penn Warren was born in Guthrie, Kentucky, on April 24, 1905. At sixteen he entered Vanderbilt University, planning to major in the sciences; however, he found freshman English to be more absorbing, and better taught, than freshman chemistry, and decided instead to study literature. Among his teachers were John Crowe Ransom and Donald Davidson, who in 1922 founded a literary magazine called *The Fugitive*, and who brought together a number of Vanderbilt teachers and students to read and discuss each other's poetry. As a sophomore, Warren was brought into this circle by his friend Allen Tate, also a student, and he maintained his identification with the Fugitives for years after he graduated in 1925 and went to California, Yale, and Oxford to continue his studies.

While at Oxford on a Rhodes Scholarship, Warren wrote his first book, a biography of John Brown. He also contributed as essay defending racial segregation in the South to the symposium *I'll Take My Stand* (1930), compiled by Ransom to defend Southern and agrarian principles in the face of growing Northern derision and antagonism. (Later, Warren reversed his position on segregation, and it is characteristic of his sense of honor that he was quick to publish his new attitude.) Returning to the United States, he taught at Vanderbilt, Louisiana State, and Minnesota before joining the Yale faculty in 1950. His style of teaching, as rigorous and detailed as that of his own teacher, John Crowe Ransom, is embodied in *Understanding Poetry* (1938), the textbook he wrote with Cleanth Brooks and which has exerted a commanding inffuence on the study of literature in American colleges. He has worked with equal commitment and success in fiction and verse, and is unique in having won the Pulitzer Prize in both genres, for *All the King's Men* in 1947 and for *Promises* in 1958.

Bearded Oaks

The oaks, how subtle and marine,
Bearded, and all the layered light
Above them swims; and thus the scene,
Recessed, awaits the positive night.

So, waiting, we in the grass now lie
Beneath the languorous tread of light:
The grasses, kelp-like, satisfy
The nameless motions of the air.

Upon the floor of light, and time,
Unmurmuring, of polyp made,
We rest; we are, as light withdraws,
Twin atolls on a shelf of shade.

Ages to our construction went,
Dim architecture, hour by hour:
And violence, forgot now, lent
The present stillness all its power.

The storm of noon above us rolled,
Of light the fury, furious gold,
The long drag troubling us, the depth:
Dark is unrocking, unrippling, still.

Passion and slaughter, ruth,[5] decay
Descend, minutely whispering down,
Silted down swaying streams, to lay
Foundation for our voicelessness.

All our debate is voiceless here,
As all our rage, the rage of stone;
If hope is hopeless, then fearless is fear,
And history is thus undone.

Our feet once wrought the hollow street
With echo when the lamps were dead
At windows, once our headlight glare
Disturbed the doe that, leaping, fled.

I do not love you less that now
The caged heart makes iron stroke,
Or less that all that light once gave
The graduate dark should now revoke.

We live in time so little time
And we learn all so painfully,
That we may spare this hour's term
To practice for eternity.

1942

Mexico Is a Foreign Country: Four Studies in Naturalism

IV. The Mango on the Mango Tree

The mango on the mango tree—
I look at it, it looks at me,
And thus we share our guilt in decent secrecy

(As once in the crowd I met a face
Whose lineaments were my disgrace
And whose own shame my forehead bore from place to place).

5. Pity.

The mango is a great gold eye,
Like God's, set in the leafy sky
To harry heart, block blood, freeze feet, if I would fly.

For God has set it there to spy
And make report, and here am I,
A cosmic Hawkshaw[6] to track down its villainy.

Gumshoe, *agent provocateur,*[7]
Stool, informer, whisperer
—Each pours his tale into the Great Schismatic's[8] ear.

For God well works the Roman plan,
Divide and rule,[8] mango and man,
And on hate's axis the great globe grinds in its span.

I do not know the mango's crime
In its far place and different time,
Nor does it know mine committed in a frostier clime.

But what to God's were ours, who pay,
Drop by slow drop, day after day,
Until His monstrous, primal guilt be washed away,

Who till that time must thus atone
In pulp and pit, in flesh and bone,
By our vicarious sacrifice[1] fault not our own?

For, ah, I do not know what word
The mango might hear, or if I've heard
A breath like *pardon, pardon,* when its stiff lips stirred.

If there were a word that it could give,
Or if I could only say *forgive,*
Then we might lift the Babel curse[2] by which we live,

And I could leap and laugh and sing
And it could leap, and everything
Take hands with us and pace the music in a ring,

6. A detective in a comic strip.

7. A secret agent who incites those he spies on to illegal activity, so that they may be arrested and punished.

8. One who divides.

9. The strategy by which Julius Caesar won and controlled the Roman empire, which at its greatest extent took in nearly all of the known world.

1. For example, the sacrifice of Christ, by which alone humanity is held to have been redeemed from the original sin of Adam and Eve.

2. The inability to communicate, by extension from the Biblical legend which attributes the different languages of the earth to God, who thereby confounded the builders of the Tower of Babel.

And sway like the multitudinous wheat
In a blessedness so long in forfeit—
Blest in that blasphemy of love we cannot now repeat.

1944

STANLEY KUNITZ
(*1905–*)

Stanley Kunitz was born in Worcester, Massachusetts, on July 29, 1905. He studied at Harvard, receiving his B.A. in 1926 and his M.A. the next year. He then joined the staff of the H. W. Wilson company in New York to edit the Wilson Library Bulletin, and also collaborated with Howard Haycraft to edit four invaluable biographical dictionaries of major English and American authors. In 1942 Kunitz joined the Army to serve during the Second World War. On being released from the Army, he joined the faculty of Bennington College, and has taught at various colleges, since 1963 at Columbia. His *Selected Poems* (1958) won the Pulitzer Prize. He has continued to edit dictionaries of literary biography, most recently *European Authors, 1000–1900* (1967). In 1969 he succeeded Dudley Fitts as editor of the Yale Series of Younger Poets.

Father and Son

Now in the suburbs and the falling light
I followed him, and now down sandy road
Whiter than bone-dust, through the sweet
Curdle of fields, where the plums
Dropped with their load of ripeness, one by one.
Mile after mile I followed, with skimming feet,
After the secret master of my blood,
Him, steeped in the odor of ponds, whose indomitable love
Kept me in chains. Strode years; stretched into bird;
Raced through the sleeping country where I was young,
The silence unrolling before me as I came,
The night nailed like an orange to my brow.

How should I tell him my fable and the fears,
How bridge the chasm in a casual tone,
Saying, "The house, the stucco one you built,
We lost. Sister married and went from home,
And nothing comes back, it's strange, from where she goes.
I lived on a hill that had too many rooms:
Light we could make, but not enough of warmth,
And when the light failed, I climbed under the hill.
The papers are delivered every day;
I am alone and never shed a tear."

At the water's edge, where the smothering ferns lifted
Their arms, "Father!" I cried, "Return! You know
The way. I'll wipe the mudstains from your clothes;
No trace, I promise, will remain. Instruct
Your son, whirling between two wars,
In the Gemara[1] of your gentleness,
For I would be a child to those who mourn
And brother to the foundlings of the field
And friend of innocence and all bright eyes.
O teach me how to work and keep me kind."
Among the turtles[2] and the lilies he turned to me
The white ignorant hollow of his face.

1944

River Road

That year of the cloud, when my marriage failed,
I slept in a chair, by the flagstone hearth,
fighting my sleep,
and one night saw a Hessian soldier
stand at attention there in full
regalia, till his head broke into flames.
My only other callers were the FBI
sent to investigate me as a Russian spy
by patriotic neighbors on the river road;
and flying squirrels parachuting from the elms
who squeaked in rodent heat between the walls
and upstairs rumbled at their nutty games.
I never dared open the attic door.
Even my nervous Leghorns joined the act,
indulging their taste for chicken from behind.
A glazed look swam into the survivors' eyes;
they caught a sort of dancing-sickness,
a variation of the blind staggers,
that hunched their narrow backs, and struck
a stiffened wing akimbo,
as round and round the poultry yard
they flapped and dropped and flapped again.
The county agent shook his head:
not one of them was spared the cyanide.

That year of the cloud, when my marriage failed,
I paced up and down the bottom-fields,
tamping the mud-puddled nurslings in
with a sharp blow of the heel
timed to the chop-chop of the hoe:
red pine and white, larch, balsam fir,

1. That part of the Talmud which amplifies and discusses the Mishnah, which in turn collects judicial decisions developing the laws of the Old Testament. Much of both parts is obscure.

2. Turtle doves.

one stride apart, two hundred to the row,
until I heard from Rossiter's woods
the downward spiral of a veery's song
unwinding on the eve of war.

Lord! Lord! who has lived so long?
Count it ten thousand trees ago,
five houses and ten thousand trees,
since the swallows exploded from Bowman Tower
over the place where the hermit[3] sang,
while I held a fantail of squirming roots
that kissed the palm of my dirty hand,
as if in reply to a bird.
The stranger who hammers No Trespass signs
to the staghorn sumac along the road
must think he owns this property.
I park my car below the curve
and climbing over the tumbled stones
where the wild foxgrape perseveres,
I walk into the woods I made,
my dark and resinous, blistered land,
through the deep litter of the years.

1971

3. Hermit thrush.

JOHN BETJEMAN
(*1906–*)

John Betjeman was born in London on August 28, 1906. At the Highgate School in North London, he showed his poems to one of the teachers, T. S. Eliot by name, who failed to comment on them. Betjeman then attended Marlborough School and finally Oxford. Desperate to avoid a business career, he became a schoolteacher, though later he was also an insurance broker. He has written travel guides to three English counties, as well as books on Oxford and on English landscape, and he has worked to preserve monuments of Victorian architecture, among them country houses, railway stations, and prisons. During the Second World War he held various government posts, one of them as press attaché at the British Embassy in Ireland. His *Collected Poems*, published in 1958, had an astonishing success. In 1969 he was knighted, and in 1972 was named Poet Laureate.

The Arrest of Oscar Wilde at the Cadogan Hotel[1]

He sipped at a weak hock and seltzer[1a]
  As he gazed at the London skies

1. The poet and playwright Oscar Wilde (1856–1900) was convicted of homosexuality in 1895 and jailed for two years. The circumstances of his arrest were as Betjeman describes them.

1a. Rhine wine and soda water.

Through the Nottingham lace of the curtains
  Or was it his bees-winged[2] eyes?

To the right and before him Pont Street
  Did tower in her new built red,
As hard as the morning gaslight
  That shone on his unmade bed,

"I want some more hock in my seltzer,
  And Robbie,[3] please give me your hand—
Is this the end or beginning?
  How can I understand?

"So you've brought me the latest *Yellow Book:*
  And Buchan has got in it now:[4]
Approval of what is approved of
  Is as false as a well-kept vow.

"More hock, Robbie—where is the seltzer?
  Dear boy, pull again at the bell!
They are all little better than *cretins,*
  Though this *is* the Cadogan Hotel.

"One astrakhan coat is at Willis's—
  Another one's at the Savoy:[5]
Do fetch my morocco portmanteau,
  And bring them on later, dear boy."

A thump, and a murmur of voices—
  ("Oh why must they make such a din?")
As the door of the bedroom swung open
  And TWO PLAIN CLOTHES POLICEMEN came in:

"Mr. Woilde, we 'ave come for tew take yew
  Where felons and criminals dwell:
We must ask yew tew leave with us quoietly
  For this *is* the Cadogan Hotel."

He rose, and he put down *The Yellow Book.*
  He staggered—and, terrible-eyed,
He brushed past the palms on the staircase
  And was helped to a hansom[5a] outside.

1937

2. Beeswing is a gauzy film that forms in old wine.
3. Robert Ross, Wilde's best friend.
4. The *Yellow Book* (1894–7) was the periodical of the Aesthetic movement of which Wilde was the most famous member, though he had no direct connection with the magazine. John Buchan (1875–1940), later famous for his adventure novels, published two stories in *Yellow Book* in 1896.
5. Wilde had an apartment at the Savoy Hotel, and often took his friends to dinner there and at Willis's Rooms. *Morocco portmanteau:* leather suitcase.
5a. Horse-drawn cab.

An Incident in the Early Life of Ebenezer Jones, Poet, 1828[6]

The lumber of a London-going dray,
The still-new stucco on the London clay,
Hot summer silence over Holloway.[7]

Dissenting chapels,[8] tea-bowers, lovers' lairs,
Neat new-built villas, ample Grecian squares,[8a]
Remaining orchards ripening Windsor pears.

Hot silence where the older mansions hide
On Highgate Hill's thick elm-encrusted side,
And Pancras, Hornsey, Islington[9] divide.

June's hottest silence where the hard rays strike
Yon hill-foot house, window and wall alike,
School of the Reverend Mr. Bickerdike,

For sons of Saints, blest with this world's possessions
(Seceders from the Protestant Secessions),[1]
Good grounding in the more genteel professions.

A lurcher[2] dog ,which draymen kick and pass,
Tongue lolling, thirsty over shadeless grass,
Leapt up the playground ladder to the class.

The godly usher[3] left his godly seat,
His skin was prickly in the ungodly heat,
The dog lay panting at his godly feet.

6. Ebenezer Jones (1820–1860) was a very minor poet whose one book, *Studies of Sensation and Event* (1843), was so badly received that he published no other poems. Betjeman prefaces this poem with an account of its central incident given by Jones's brother in an 1879 reissue of the book. "We were together at a well-known boarding-school of that day . . . on a hot summer afternoon. . . . Up the ladder-like stairs from the playground a lurcher dog had strayed into the schoolroom, panting with the heat, his tongue lolling out with thirst. The choleric usher who presided, and was detested by us for his tyranny, seeing this, advanced down the room. Enraged at our attention being distracted from our tasks, he dragged the dog to the top of the stairs, and there lifted him bodily up with the evident intention—and we had known him to do similar things—of hurling the poor creature to the bottom. 'YOU SHALL NOT!' rang through the room, as little Ebby, so exclaiming at the top of his voice, rushed with kindling face to the spot from among all the boys—some of them twice his age. But even while the words passed his lips, the heavy fall was heard, and the sound seemed to travel through his listening form and face, as, with a strange look of anguish in one so young, he stood still, threw up his arms, and burst into an uncontrollable passion of tears. With a coarse laugh at this, the usher led him back by his ear to the form; and there he sat long after his sobbing had subsided, like one dazed and stunned."

7. A district of North London.

8. Jones's parents were adherents of Calvinism, an especially strict Protestant sect; like all other Protestants who refused integration into the official Church of England, they were called "dissenters" or "nonconformists," and because of discriminatory laws against them tended to live together in areas such as Holloway.

8a. Surrounded by houses whose architecture was inspired by that of classical Greece.

9. London districts surrounding Holloway.

1. The Church of England seceded from the Roman Catholic Church in the reign of Henry VIII; the Puritans (who were in the habit of calling themselves Saints) considered the Church of England too little reformed and seceded from it.

2. Crossbred.

3. Assistant teacher (English usage).

The milkman on the road stood staring in,
The playground nettles nodded "Now begin"—
And Evil waited, quivering, for sin.

He lifted it and not a word he spoke,
His big hand tightened. Could he make it choke?
He trembled, sweated, and his temper broke.

"YOU SHALL NOT!" clear across to Highgate Hill
A boy's voice sounded. Creaking forms were still.
The cat jumped slowly from the window sill.

"YOU SHALL NOT!" flat against the summer sun,
Hard as the hard sky frowning over one,
Gloat, little boys! enjoy the coming fun!

"GOD DAMNS A CUR. I AM, I AM HIS WORD!"
He flung it, flung it and it never stirred,
"You shall not!—shall not!" ringing on unheard.

Blind desolation! bleeding, burning rod!
Big, bull-necked Minister of Calvin's God!
Exulting milkman, redfaced, shameless clod,

Look on and jeer! Not Satan's thunder-quake
Can cause the mighty walls of Heaven to shake
As now they do, to hear a boy's heart break.

1940

WILLIAM EMPSON
(*1906–*)

William Empson was born on September 27, 1906, near Howden, Yorkshire. He was educated at Winchester School and at Magdalene College, Cambridge, where he moved from the study of mathematics to literature. In 1930 he published *Seven Types of Ambiguity,* a consideration of the ways in which poems exploit the full range of a word's senses. From 1931–34 he was Professor of English Literature at Tokyo National University. Three years later he went to China and taught English at the National University in Peking; his work there was interrupted by the beginning of the Sino-Japanese War. In 1939, when the Second World War was certain, Empson returned to England, where he worked for the BBC. When the was was over, he returned with his wife and two sons to a teaching post in Peking. In 1952 he came back to England, and in 1953 he became Professor of English at Sheffield University, teaching there until his retirement in 1971.

Villanelle

It is the pain, it is the pain, endures.
Your chemic beauty burned my muscles through.
Poise of my hands reminded me of yours.

What later purge from this deep toxin cures?
What kindness now could the old salve renew?
It is the pain, it is the pain, endures.

The infection slept (custom or change inures)
And when pain's secondary phase was due
Poise of my hands reminded me of yours.

How safe I felt, whom memory assures,
Rich that your grace safely by heart I knew.
It is the pain, it is the pain, endures.

My stare drank deep beauty that still allures.
My heart pumps yet the poison draught of you.
Poise of my hands reminded me of yours.

You are still kind whom the same shape immures.[5]
Kind and beyond adieu. We miss our cue.
It is the pain, it is the pain, endures.
Poise of my hands reminded me of yours.

1935

Legal Fiction[6]

Law makes long spokes of the short stakes of men.
Your well fenced out real estate of mind
No high flat[7] of the nomad citizen
Looks over, or train leaves behind.

Your rights extend under and above your claim
Without bound; you own land in Heaven and Hell;
Your part of earth's surface and mass the same,
Of all cosmos' volume, and all stars as well.

Your rights reach down where all owners meet, in Hell's
Pointed exclusive conclave, at earth's centre
(Your spun farm's root still on that axis dwells);
And up, through galaxies, a growing sector.

5. Walls in.

6. A rule of law which assumes as true, and will not allow to be disproved, something which is unproven but not impossible and which is useful in settling a dispute. The poem is said to have been inspired by an English gentleman who assumed that his property rights extended to the air above his land, and shot at airplanes flying over it.

7. Apartment.

You are nomad yet; the lighthouse beam you own
Flashes, like Lucifer, through the firmament.
Earth's axis varies; your dark central cone
Wavers, a candle's shadow, at the end.

1935

Missing Dates

Slowly the poison the whole blood stream fills.
It is not the effort nor the failure tires.
The waste remains, the waste remains and kills.

It is not your system or clear sight that mills
Down small to the consequence a life requires;
Slowly the poison the whole blood stream fills.

They bled an old dog dry yet the exchange rills
Of young dog blood gave but a month's desires.
The waste remains, the waste remains and kills.

It is the Chinese tombs and the slag hills
Usurp the soil,[8] and not the soil retires.
Slowly the poison the whole blood stream fills.

Not to have fire is to be a skin that shrills.
The complete fire is death. From partial fires
The waste remains, the waste remains and kills.

It is the poems you have lost, the ills
From missing dates, at which the heart expires.
Slowly the poison the whole blood stream fills.
The waste remains, the waste remains and kills.

1940

8. "It is true about the old dog, at least I saw it reported somewhere, but the legend that a fifth or some such part of the soil of China is given up to ancestral tombs is (by the way) not true" (Empson's note).

W. H. AUDEN
(1907–1973)

Wystan Hugh Auden was born in 1907 in York, England, the third son of a physician. In 1908 his father became Medical Officer and Professor of Public Health at the University of Birmingham. Auden attended private schools and then Oxford, taking his degree in 1928.

During the Thirties Auden became by common consent the principal poet of his generation, and other writers such as Louis MacNeice, Cecil Day Lewis, and Stephen Spender, in spite of their considerable differences from him, were assumed to be writing under his banner. He supported himself at first by teaching, and was to do this sporadically for much of his life. But his urge to travel became conspicuous. In 1937 he and MacNeice published their *Letters from Iceland,* after making a trip to that country at their publisher's expense. The same year Auden went to Spain in support of the Loyalists. A year later he and Christopher Isherwood went to China, and Auden wrote *Journal to a War.* In January 1939 Auden and Isherwood left England with the intention of residing permanently in the United States. He became an American citizen in 1946. Most of his time in later years was shared equally between two residences, one in Greenwich Village (New York City) and the other in Kirchstetten, Lower Austria. But in 1972 he was invited to take up lodgings at his old college, Christ Church, Oxford, and consented to do so. In Vienna, where he had been invited to lecture on his poetry, he died suddenly on September 28, 1973.

The Letter[1]

From the very first coming down
Into a new valley with a frown
Because of the sun and a lost way,
You certainly remain: to-day
I, crouching behind a sheep-pen, heard
Travel across a sudden bird,
Cry out against the storm, and found
The year's arc a completed round
And love's worn circuit re-begun,
Endless with no dissenting turn.
Shall see, shall pass, as we have seen
The swallow on the tile, spring's green
Preliminary shiver, passed
A solitary truck, the last
Of shunting in the Autumn. But now,
To interrupt the homely brow,
Thought warmed to evening through and through
Your letter comes, speaking as you,
Speaking of much but not to come.

Nor speech is close nor fingers numb,
If love not seldom has received
An unjust answer, was deceived.
I, decent with the seasons, move
Different or with a different love,
Nor question overmuch the nod,
The stone smile of this country god[2]
That never was more reticent,
Always afraid to say more than it meant.

1928

1. This poem was first published with the title "The Love Letter."

2. Love.

Prologue[3]

By landscape reminded once of his mother's figure
The mountain heights he remembers get bigger and bigger:
With the finest of mapping pens he fondly traces
All the family names on the familiar places.

Among green pastures straying he walks by still waters;[4]
Surely a swan he seems to earth's unwise daughters,
Bending a beautiful head, worshipping not lying,
'Dear' the dear beak in the dear concha[5] crying.

Under the trees the summer bands were playing;
'Dear boy, be brave as these roots', he heard them saying:
Carries the good news gladly to a world in danger,
Is ready to argue, he smiles, with any stranger.

And yet this prophet, homing the day is ended,
Receives odd welcome from the country he so defended:
The band roars 'Coward, Coward', in his human fever.
The giantess shuffles nearer, cries 'Deceiver'.

1932

The Wanderer[7]

Doom is dark and deeper than any sea-dingle.[8]
Upon what man it fall
In spring, day-wishing flowers appearing,
Avalanche sliding, white snow from rock-face,
That he should leave his house,
No cloud-soft hand can hold him, restraint by women;
But ever that man goes
Through place-keepers, through forest trees,
A stranger to strangers over undried sea,
Houses for fishes, suffocating water,

3. Auden wrote this poem as prologue to *The Orators: An English Study*. He reprinted it later by itself with the title "Adolescence."

4. *Psalms* 23:2—"He maketh me to lie down in green pastures; He leadeth me beside the still waters."

5. The central concavity in the external ear.

7. This poem was first published with the title, "Something Is Bound to Happen."

8. Adapted from a Middle English West Midland homily, "Sawles Warde " probably written in the thirteenth century, where there is reference to God's judgments as "his dooms that are secret and deeper than any sea dingle." A dingle is an abyss. The rest of the poem owes something to an Old English poem also entitled "The Wanderer," from which Richard Hoggart translates these relevant lines: "Often the solitary man prays for favor, for the mercy of the Lord, though, sad at heart, he must needs stir with his hands for a weary while the icy sea across the watery wastes, must journey the paths of exile; settled in truth is fate! So spoke the wanderer, mindful of hardships. . . . He knows who puts it to the test how cruel a comrade is sorrow for him who has few dear protectors; his is the path of exile, in no wise the twisted gold; a chill body, in no wise the riches of the earth; he thinks of retainers in hall and the receiving of treasure, of how in his youth his gold-friend was kind to him at the feast. The joy has all perished. . . . Then the friendless man wakes again, sees before him the dark waves, the sea-birds bathing, spreading their feathers; frost and snow falling mingles with hail. Then heavier are the wounds in his heart, sore for his beloved; sorrow is renewed."

Or lonely on fell as chat,[9]
By pot-holed becks[1]
A bird stone-haunting, an unquiet bird.

There head falls forward, fatigued at evening,
And dreams of home,
Waving from window, spread of welcome,
Kissing of wife under single sheet;
But waking sees
Bird-flocks nameless to him, through doorway voices
Of new men making another love.

Save him from hostile capture,
From sudden tiger's spring at corner;
Protect his house,
His anxious house where days are counted
From thunderbolt protect,
From gradual ruin spreading like a stain;
Converting number from vague to certain,
Bring joy, bring day of his returning,
Lucky with day approaching, with leaning dawn.

1933

Our Hunting Fathers[2]

Our hunting fathers[3] told the story
 Of the sadness of the creatures,
Pitied the limits and the lack
 Set in their finished features;
Saw in the lion's intolerant look,
Behind the quarry's dying glare,
Love raging for the personal glory
 That reason's gift would add,
The liberal appetite and power,
 The rightness of a god.

Who, nurtured in that fine tradition,
 Predicted the result,
Guessed Love by nature suited to
 The intricate ways of guilt,
That human ligaments could so
His southern gestures modify
And make it his mature ambition
 To think no thought but ours,

9. A kind of bird, a warbler. A fell is a moorland ridge.
1. Stony brooks.
2. This poem was originally published with the title, "In Father's Footsteps."
3. Auden refers to the period, presumably in the late nineteenth-century, when "our hunting fathers" could complacently pity the lower animals, who showed passions comparable to human ones, but lacked that quality of reason which enables men to become individual and godlike.

To hunger, work illegally,
  And be anonymous?[4]

1935

Who's Who

A shilling life[5] will give you all the facts:
How Father beat him, how he ran away,
What were the struggles of his youth, what acts
Made him the greatest figure of his day:
Of how he fought, fished, hunted, worked all night,
Though giddy, climbed new mountains; named a sea:
Some of the last researchers even write
Love made him weep his pints like you and me.
With all his honours on, he sighed for one
Who, say astonished critics, lived at home;
Did little jobs about the house with skill
And nothing else; could whistle; would sit still
Or potter round the garden; answered some
Of his long marvellous letters but kept none.

1936

[Fish in the Unruffled Lakes]

Fish in the unruffled lakes
The swarming colours wear,
Swans in the winter air
A white perfection have,
And the great lion walks
Through his innocent grove;
Lion, fish, and swan
Act, and are gone
Upon Time's toppling wave.

We till shadowed days are done,
We must weep and sing
Duty's conscious wrong,
The Devil in the clock,
The Goodness carefully worn
For atonement or for luck;
We must lose our loves,
On each beast and bird that moves
Turn an envious look.

Sighs for folly said and done
Twist our narrow days;
But I must bless, I must praise
That you, my swan, who have
All gifts that to the swan

4. In our time human love, instead of making us pretend to be lords of the universe, finds expression in revolutionary activity which brings us to behave like those very beasts whom our fathers patronized.

5. A cheap biographical pamphlet.

Impulsive Nature gave,
The majesty and pride,
Last night should add
Your voluntary love.

1936

Lullaby

Lay your sleeping head, my love,
Human on my faithless arm;
Time and fevers burn away
Individual beauty from
Thoughtful children, and the grave
Proves the child ephemeral:
But in my arms till break of day
Let the living creature lie,
Mortal, guilty, but to me
The entirely beautiful.

Soul and body have no bounds:
To lovers as they lie upon
Her tolerant enchanted slope
In their ordinary swoon,
Grave the vision Venus[6] sends
Of supernatural sympathy,
Universal love and hope;
While an abstract insight wakes
Among the glaciers and the rocks
The hermit's carnal ecstasy.

Certainty, fidelity
On the stroke of midnight pass
Like vibrations of a bell
And fashionable madmen raise
Their pedantic boring cry:
Every farthing[7] of the cost,
All the dreaded cards foretell,
Shall be paid, but from this night
Not a whisper, not a thought,
Not a kiss nor look be lost.

Beauty, midnight, vision dies:
Let the winds of dawn that blow
Softly round your dreaming head
Such a day of welcome show

6. Venus is the Roman goddess of love.

7. A coin, no longer in use, worth one quarter of a penny.

Eye and knocking heart may bless,
Find our mortal world enough;
Noons of dryness find you fed
By the involuntary powers,
Nights of insult let you pass
Watched by every human love.

1940

Musée des Beaux Arts[8]

About suffering they were never wrong,
The Old Masters: how well they understood
Its human position; how it takes place
While someone else is eating or opening a window or just walking dully along;
How, when the aged are reverently, passionately waiting
For the miraculous birth, there always must be
Children who did not specially want it to happen, skating
On a pond at the edge of the wood:
They never forgot
That even the dreadful martyrdom must run its course
Anyhow in a corner, some untidy spot
Where the dogs go on with their doggy life and the torturer's horse
Scratches its innocent behind on a tree.

In Brueghel's *Icarus*,[9] for instance: how everything turns away
Quite leisurely from the disaster; the ploughman may
Have heard the splash, the forsaken cry,
But for him it was not an important failure; the sun shone
As it had to on the white legs disappearing into the green
Water; and the expensive delicate ship that must have seen
Something amazing, a boy falling out of the sky,
Had somewhere to get to and sailed calmly on.

1940

Our Bias

The hour-glass whispers to the lion's roar,
The clock-towers tell the gardens day and night
How many errors Time has patience for,
How wrong they are in being always right.

Yet Time, however loud its chimes or deep,
However fast its falling torrent flows,
Has never put one lion off his leap
Nor shaken the assurance of a rose.

8. Museum of Fine Arts (Fr).

9. Pieter Brueghel's painting, "The Fall of Icarus," hangs in the Palace of the Royal Museums of Painting and Sculpture in Brussels. Auden borrows the detail of the horse scratching its behind from another Brueghel painting, "The Massacre of the Innocents." Icarus flew using the wings his father Daedalus had made of feathers and wax, but recklessly went too close to the sun; the wax melted and he fell into the sea.

For they, it seems, care only for success:
While we choose words according to their sound
And judge a problem by its awkwardness;

And Time with us was always popular.
When have we not preferred some going round
To going straight to where we are?

1940

In Memory of W. B. Yeats

(d. Jan. 1939)

I

He disappeared in the dead of winter:[1]
The brooks were frozen, the airports almost deserted,
And snow disfigured the public statues;
The mercury sank in the mouth of the dying day.
What instruments we have agree
The day of his death was a dark cold day.

Far from his illness
The wolves ran on through the evergreen forests,
The peasant river was untempted by the fashionable quays;
By mourning tongues
The death of the poet was kept from his poems.

But for him it was his last afternoon as himself,
An afternoon of nurses and rumours;
The provinces of his body revolted,
The squares of his mind were empty,
Silence invaded the suburbs,
The current of his feeling failed; he became his admirers.

Now he is scattered among a hundred cities
And wholly given over to unfamiliar affections,
To find his happiness in another kind of wood[2]
And be punished under a foreign code of conscience.[3]
The words of a dead man
Are modified in the guts of the living.

But in the importance and noise of to-morrow
When the brokers are roaring like beasts on the floor of the Bourse,[4]
And the poor have the sufferings to which they are fairly accustomed,
And each in the cell of himself is almost convinced of his freedom,
A few thousand will think of this day

1. Yeats died on January 28, 1939, in Roquebrune in southern France.

2. An allusion to the beginning of the *Inferno*, where Dante finds himself, in middle life, "in a dark wood." Yeats, by dying, enters a realm of being where poets survive only in their poems.

3. A glance at Yeats's Irish nationalism. The foreign code to which he must now submit is the judgment of the living.

4. Stock exchange (Fr).

As one thinks of a day when one did something slightly unusual.
What instruments we have agree
The day of his death was a dark cold day.

II

You were silly like us;[5] your gift survived it all:
The parish of rich women,[6] physical decay,
Yourself. Mad Ireland hurt you into poetry.
Now Ireland has her madness and her weather still,
For poetry makes nothing happen: it survives
In the valley of its making where executives
Would never want to tamper, flows on south
From ranches of isolation and the busy griefs,
Raw towns that we believe and die in; it survives,
A way of happening, a mouth.

III

Earth, receive an honoured guest:
William Yeats is laid to rest.
Let the Irish vessel lie
Emptied of its poetry.[7]

In the nightmare of the dark
All the dogs of Europe bark,[8]
And the living nations wait,
Each sequestered in its hate;

Intellectual disgrace
Stares from every human face,
And the seas of pity lie
Locked and frozen in each eye.

Follow, poet, follow right
To the bottom of the night,
With your unconstraining voice
Still persuade us to rejoice;

With the farming of a verse
Make a vineyard of the curse,
Sing of human unsuccess
In a rapture of distress;

5. In prose writings, Auden has registered various objections to Yeats's thought, especially to his occultism.

6. Yeats as a young man accepted some financial help, later repaid, from Lady Gregory. He was friendly with other wealthy women later.

7. Following this line Auden originally included three stanzas in which Time, which is said to worship language and forgive "everyone by whom [language] lives," is expected to pardon "Kipling and his [imperialistic] views / And will pardon Paul Claudel [a French writer of extreme political conservatism], / Pardons him [Yeats, whose antidemocratic stance was antipathetic to Auden's own] for writing well." These stanzas were deleted in the 1966 edition of *Collected Shorter Poems*.

8. The Second World War was to begin in September 1939.

In the deserts of the heart
Let the healing fountain start,
In the prison of his days
Teach the free man how to praise.

1940

New Year Letter[9]

O Unicorn among the cedars,
To whom no magic charm can lead us,
White childhood moving like a sigh
Through the green woods unharmed in thy
Sophisticated innocence,
To call thy true love to the dance,[1]
O Dove of science and of light,[2]
Upon the branches of the night,
O Ichthus playful in the deep
Sea-lodges that forever keep
Their secret of excitement hidden,
O sudden Wind that blows unbidden,
Parting the quiet reeds, O Voice
Within the labyrinth of choice
Only the passive listener hears,
O Clock and Keeper of the years,
O Source of equity and rest,
Quando non fuerit, non est,[3]
It without image, paradigm
Of matter, motion, number, time,
The grinning gap of Hell, the hill
Of Venus and the stairs of Will,
Disturb our negligence and chill,
Convict our pride of its offence
In all things, even penitence,
Instruct us in the civil art
Of making from the muddled heart
A desert and a city where

9. This long poem is dated January 1, 1940, and was written in the United States, to which Auden had emigrated in 1939. The poem's closing lines are an invocation to the Holy Trinity, the members of which are addressed as traditional Christian symbols; thus Christ is the Unicorn and Ichthus (the fish), the Holy Ghost is the Wind and the Dove, and God is the Voice. Soon after its composition Auden joined the Church of England.

1. "Tomorrow shall be my dancing day / I would my true love did so chance / To see the legend of my play / To call my true love to the dance. / Sing O my love, O my love, my love, my love, / This have I done for my true love. (English Carol.)" (Auden's note). Edward Callan has pointed out that in this medieval lyric the speaker is Christ.

2. "O God of science and of light, / Apollo, by thy greate myght / This litel laste book thou gye (Chaucer. *The House of Fame.*)" (Auden's note).

3. The source of this quotation is Chapter 2, "About Christ," from *First Principles* by Origen (c.185–c.253), a great early writer on Christianity. It is translated, "There is not [a time] when he was not"—"he" being Christ, and the statement means that the Son of God is coeternal with God. Auden likely found this phrase and its explication in *The Descent of the Dove* (1939), by Charles Williams; he knew the book and its author well and has acknowledged the strong influence of Williams' thought on his.

The thoughts that have to labour there
May find locality and peace,
And pent-up feelings their release,
Send strength sufficient for our day,
And point out knowledge on its way,[4]
O da quod jubes, Domine.[5]

* * *

1941

In Praise of Limestone

If it form the one landscape that we, the inconstant ones,
Are consistently homesick for, this is chiefly
Because it dissolves in water. Mark these rounded slopes
With their surface fragrance of thyme and, beneath,
A secret system of caves and conduits; hear the springs
That spurt out everywhere with a chuckle,
Each filling a private pool for its fish and carving
Its own little ravine whose cliffs entertain
The butterfly and the lizard; examine this region
Of short distances and definite places:
What could be more like Mother or a fitter background
For her son, the flirtatious male who lounges
Against a rock in the sunlight, never doubting
That for all his faults he is loved; whose works are but
Extensions of his power to charm? From weathered outcrop
To hill-top temple, from appearing waters to
Conspicuous fountains, from a wild to a formal vineyard,
Are ingenious but short steps that a child's wish
To receive more attention than his brothers, whether
By pleasing or teasing, can easily take.

Watch, then, the band of rivals as they climb up and down
Their steep stone gennels[6] in twos and threes, at times
Arm in arm, but never, thank God, in step; or engaged
On the shady side of a square at midday in
Voluble discourse, knowing each other too well to think
There are any important secrets, unable
To conceive a god whose temper-tantrums are moral
And not to be pacified by a clever line
Or a good lay: for, accustomed to a stone that responds,
They have never had to veil their faces in awe

4. Auden's note gives a passage from John Donne's "The Litany" as a parallel prayer to God to give direction to human knowledge: "That learning, thine Ambassador, / From thine allegeance wee never tempt, / That beauty, paradises flower / For physicke [medicine] made, from poyson be exempt, / That wit, borne apt high good to doe, / By dwelling lazily / On Natures nothing, be not nothing too, / That our affections kill us not, nor dye, / Heare us, weak ecchoes, O thou eare, and cry."

5. "v. St. Augustine *Confessions.* Book X" (Auden's note). Charles Williams translates this, "Give what thou commandest, Lord." The full phrase asks, "Give (me) what you command; command (of me) what you will."

6. A narrow passage between houses or, as here, rocks.

Of a crater whose blazing fury could not be fixed;
  Adjusted to the local needs of valleys
Where everything can be touched or reached by walking,
  Their eyes have never looked into infinite space
Through the lattice-work of a nomad's comb; born lucky,
  Their legs have never encountered the fungi
And insects of the jungle, the monstrous forms and lives
  With which we have nothing, we like to hope, in common.
So, when one of them goes to the bad, the way his mind works
  Remains comprehensible: to become a pimp
Or deal in fake jewellery or ruin a fine tenor voice
  For effects that bring down the house, could happen to all
But the best and the worst of us . . .
                                        That is why, I suppose,
  The best and worst never stayed here long but sought
Immoderate soils where the beauty was not so external,
  The light less public and the meaning of life
Something more than a mad camp. 'Come!' cried the granite wastes,
  'How evasive is your humour, how accidental
Your kindest kiss, how permanent is death.' (Saints-to-be
  Slipped away sighing.) 'Come!' purred the clays and gravels.
'On our plains there is room for armies to drill; rivers
  Wait to be tamed and slaves to construct you a tomb
In the grand manner: soft as the earth is mankind and both
  Need to be altered.' (Intendant Caesars rose and
Left, slamming the door.)[7] But the really reckless were fetched
  By an older colder voice, the oceanic whisper:
'I am the solitude that asks and promises nothing;
  That is how I shall set you free. There is no love;
There are only the various envies, all of them sad.'
  They were right, my dear, all those voices were right
And still are; this land is not the sweet home that it looks,
  Nor its peace the historical calm of a site
Where something was settled once and for all: A backward
  And dilapidated province, connected
To the big busy world by a tunnel, with a certain
  Seedy appeal, is that all it is now? Not quite:
It has a worldly duty which in spite of itself
  It does not neglect, but calls into question
All the Great Powers assume; it disturbs our rights. The poet,
  Admired for his earnest habit of calling
The sun the sun, his mind Puzzle, is made uneasy
  By these marble statues which so obviously doubt
His antimythological myth; and these gamins,[8]
  Pursuing the scientist down the tiled colonnade
With such lively offers, rebuke his concern for Nature's

7. John Fuller suggests that this is an allusion to a remark by Joseph Goebbels, Hitler's propaganda minister and, in 1945, his successor: "If we are defeated, we shall slam the doors of history behind us."

8. Urchins.

Remotest aspects: I, too, am reproached, for what
And how much you know. Not to lose time, not to get caught,
Not to be left behind, not, please! to resemble
The beasts who repeat themselves, or a thing like water
Or stone whose conduct can be predicted, these
Are our Common Prayer,[9] whose greatest comfort is music
Which can be made anywhere, is invisible,
And does not smell. In so far as we have to look forward
To death as a fact, no doubt we are right: But if
Sins can be forgiven, if bodies rise from the dead,
These modifications of matter into
Innocent athletes and gesticulating fountains,
Made solely for pleasure, make a further point:
The blessed will not care what angle they are regarded from,
Having nothing to hide. Dear, I know nothing of
Either, but when I try to imagine a faultless love
Or the life to come, what I hear is the murmur
Of underground streams, what I see is a limestone landscape.

1951

9. The Book of Common Prayer is a collection of prayers in English; assembled during the 16th century, it standardizes the devotions of the Church of England.

LINCOLN KIRSTEIN
(1907–)

Lincoln Kirstein was born in Rochester, New York, on May 4, 1907. He went to school in Cambridge, Massachusetts, and entered Harvard in 1926. While still an undergraduate he helped to found a literary review, *Hound and Horn,* and by the time he graduated in 1930 it was widely regarded as one of the most serious and influential periodicals of its kind. He has since made a variety of contributions to American cultural life, particularly in the area of the ballet. He joined the Army in 1943; for a time he was stationed at Fort Belvoir with the Corps of Engineers; he was eventually sent overseas and attached to the Arts, Monuments, and Archives section of General George Patton's Third Army. Since the War, Kirstein has written extensively on the dance; he is Director of the New York City Ballet Company.

Fall In

My mother's brother hauled me to the big-boys' club,
Where they swam nude, drank beer, shared secrecy.
Males young and old held mystic privilege.
I was condemned to join their mystery.

These men were hairy on belly and groin;
The boys were hairier at least than me,

No boy, no man, a neuter in-between,
   One hairless silly, neither he nor she.

In locker room my uncle stripped me raw.
   My shyness shivered at his shameless, bare,
Terrible body. Off he tore my drawers
   And shoved me naked to the brink of where

In a tiled cage they'd sunk their sacred pool,
   Clean as a toilet bowl, its water poison-green;
No mama near to save or cry "Forbear!"
   The taste of infamy is sweet chlorine.

I knew that death swam near but hated uncle more.
   If I were doomed, then uncle, he must pay.
I'd scream, I'd make a scene, or the extreme:
   I'd plummet to bottom, midget martyr play

Profoundly drowned, which simply took despair
   (Distinct from courage since it involved caprice),
Hold my breath to bursting waiting The End.
   In suicide is blackmail and release.

He tugged me out with terror, even awe.
   I felt my fright infect his grizzled chest;
Palpating this drowned rat to retch and drain,
   He knew I knew who'd flunked his foolish test.

Thus one bears fear in action, guilt in pride.
   I was his sister's son, yet still no male.
The spineless kin he'd vowed to make a man
   Confounded polity[1] and saw him fail.

The rage of armies is the shame of boys;
   A hero's panic or a coward's whim
Is triggered by nerve or nervousness.
   We wish to sink. We do not choose to swim.

1964

Vaudeville

Pete Petersen, before this bit, a professional entertainer;
He and a partner tossed two girls on the Two-a-Day,
Swung them by their heels and snatched them in mid-air,
Billed as "Pete's Meteors: Acrobatic Adagio[2] & Classical Ballet."

1. Political or social order.
2. Adagio dancing; an acrobatic ballet by a man and woman, often in slow tempo.

His vulnerable grin, efficiency, or bland physique
Lands him in Graves' Registration, a slot few strive to seek.
He follows death around picking up pieces,
Recovering men and portions of men so that by dawn
Only the landscape bares its wounds, the dead are gone.

Near Echternach,[3] after the last stand they had the heart to make
With much personal slaughter by small arms at close range,
I drive for an officer sent down to look things over.
There is Pete slouched on a stump, catching his wind.

On your feet: salute. "Yes, sir?"
"Bad here, what?" "Yes, sir."

Good manners or knowing no word can ever condone
What happened, what he had to do, has done,
Spares further grief. Pete sits down.
A shimmering pulsation of exhaustion fixes him
In its throbbing aura like footlights when the curtain rises.

His act is over. Nothing now till the next show.

He takes his break while stagehands move the scenery,
And the performing dogs are led up from below.

1964

3. A town in Luxembourg.

THEODORE ROETHKE
(*1908–1963*)

Theodore Roethke was born on May 23, 1908, in Saginaw, Michigan. His grandfather, once Bismarck's chief forester, had emigrated from Prussia in 1870 and then, with his sons, had started some greenhouses there. Roethke went to the University of Michigan and afterwards took some graduate courses at Harvard. Subsequently he taught at several colleges and universities, lending himself generously to his students and even, at one time, coaching tennis. He was a tormented man, frantic for fame, a prey to breakdowns and a victim of alcoholism. His longest and last post was at the University of Washington, where his sporadic breakdowns were tolerated. He wrote little, but with great care. His collected poems, still a slender output, appeared under the title *Words for the Wind* in 1959. By 1963 he was dead.

Cuttings

Sticks-in-a-drowse droop over sugary loam,
Their intricate stem-fur dries;

But still the delicate slips keep coaxing up water;
The small cells bulge;

One nub of growth
Nudges a sand-crumb loose,
Pokes through a musty sheath
Its pale tendrilous horn.

1948

Cuttings

(later)

This urge, wrestle, resurrection of dry sticks,
Cut stems struggling to put down feet,
What saint strained so much,
Rose on such lopped limbs to a new life?

I can hear, underground, that sucking and sobbing,
In my veins, in my bones I feel it,—
The small waters seeping upward,
The tight grains parting at last.
When sprouts break out,
Slippery as fish,
I quail, lean to beginnings, sheath-wet.

1948

My Papa's Waltz

The whiskey on your breath
Could make a small boy dizzy;
But I hung on like death:
Such waltzing was not easy.

We romped until the pans
Slid from the kitchen shelf;
My mother's countenance
Could not unfrown itself.

The hand that held my wrist
Was battered on one knuckle;
At every step you missed
My right ear scraped a buckle.

You beat time on my head
With a palm caked hard by dirt,
Then waltzed me off to bed
Still clinging to your shirt.

1948

Dolor[3]

I have known the inexorable sadness of pencils,
Neat in their boxes, dolor of pad and paper-weight,
All the misery of manilla folders and mucilage,
Desolation in immaculate public places,
Lonely reception room, lavatory, switchboard,
The unalterable pathos of basin and pitcher,
Ritual of multigraph, paper-clip, comma,
Endless duplication of lives and objects.
And I have seen dust from the walls of institutions,
Finer than flour, alive, more dangerous than silica,
Sift, almost invisible, through long afternoons of tedium,
Dropping a fine film on nails and delicate eyebrows,
Glazing the pale hair, the duplicate grey standard faces.

1948

The Minimal

I study the lives on a leaf: the little
Sleepers, numb nudgers in cold dimensions,
Beetles in caves, newts, stone-deaf fishes,
Lice tethered to long limp subterranean weeds,
Squirmers in bogs,
And bacterial creepers
Wriggling through wounds
Like elvers[4] in ponds,
Their wan mouths kissing the warm sutures,
Cleaning and caressing,
Creeping and healing.

1948

The Waking

I wake to sleep, and take my waking slow.
I feel my fate in what I cannot fear.
I learn by going where I have to go.

We think by feeling. What is there to know?
I hear my being dance from ear to ear.
I wake to sleep, and take my waking slow.

Of those so close beside me, which are you?
God bless the Ground! I shall walk softly there,
And learn by going where I have to go.

Light takes the Tree; but who can tell us how?
The lowly worm climbs up a winding stair;
I wake to sleep, and take my waking slow.

3. Sadness.

4. Young eels.

Great Nature has another thing to do
To you and me; so take the lively air,
And, lovely, learn by going where to go.

This shaking keeps me steady. I should know.
What falls away is always. And is near.
I wake to sleep, and take my waking slow.
I learn by going where I have to go.

1953

Frau Bauman, Frau Schmidt, and Frau Schwartze[8]

Gone the three ancient ladies
Who creaked on the greenhouse ladders,
Reaching up white strings
To wind, to wind
The sweet-pea tendrils, the smilax,
Nasturtiums, the climbing
Roses, to straighten
Carnations, red
Chrysanthemums; the stiff
Stems, jointed like corn,
They tied and tucked,—
These nurses of nobody else.
Quicker than birds, they dipped
Up and sifted the dirt;
They sprinkled and shook;
They stood astride pipes,
Their skirts billowing out wide into tents,
Their hands twinkling with wet;
Like witches they flew along rows
Keeping creation at ease;
With a tendril for needle
They sewed up the air with a stem;
They teased out the seed that the cold kept asleep,—
All the coils, loops, and whorls.
They trellised the sun; they plotted for more than themselves.

I remember how they picked me up, a spindly kid,
Pinching and poking my thin ribs
Till I lay in their laps, laughing,
Weak as a whiffet[9];
Now, when I'm alone and cold in my bed,
They still hover over me,
These ancient leathery crones,
With their bandannas stiffened with sweat,

8. Roethke's father was a prominent florist in Saginaw, Michigan, and as a boy the poet played around the greenhouses. The employees included the three women of the title.

9. A very small dog.

And their thorn-bitten wrists,
And their snuff-laden breath blowing lightly over me in my first sleep.

1953

I Knew a Woman

I knew a woman, lovely in her bones,
When small birds sighed, she would sigh back at them;
Ah, when she moved, she moved more ways than one:
The shapes a bright container can contain!
Of her choice virtues only gods should speak,
Or English poets who grew up on Greek
(I'd have them sing in chorus, cheek to cheek).

How well her wishes went! She stroked my chin,
She taught me Turn, and Counter-turn, and Stand;[1]
She taught me Touch, that undulant white skin;
I nibbled meekly from her proffered hand;
She was the sickle; I, poor I, the rake,
Coming behind her for her pretty sake
(But what prodigious mowing we did make).

Love likes a gander, and adores a goose:
Her full lips pursed, the errant note to seize;
She played it quick, she played it light and loose;
My eyes, they dazzled at her flowing knees;
Her several parts could keep a pure repose,
Or one hip quiver with a mobile nose
(She moved in circles, and those circles moved).

Let seed be grass, and grass turn into hay:
I'm martyr to a motion not my own;
What's freedom for? To know eternity.
I swear she cast a shadow white as stone.
But who would count eternity in days?
These old bones live to learn her wanton ways:
(I measure time by how a body sways).

1958

Wish for a Young Wife

My lizard, my lively writher,
May your limbs never wither,
May the eyes in your face
Survive the green ice
Of envy's mean gaze;

1. The divisions of a classical Grecian ode, named for the movements of the chorus by which it was sung.

May you live out your life
Without hate, without grief,
And your hair ever blaze,
In the sun, in the sun,
When I am undone,
When I am no one.

1964

In a Dark Time[4]

In a dark time, the eye begins to see,
I meet my shadow in the deepening shade;[5]
I hear my echo in the echoing wood—
A lord of nature[6] weeping to a tree.
I live between the heron and the wren,[7]
Beasts of the hill and serpents of the den.

What's madness but nobility of soul
At odds with circumstance? The day's on fire!
I know the purity of pure despair,
My shadow[8] pinned against a sweating wall.
That place among the rocks—is it a cave,
Or winding path? The edge is what I have.

A steady storm of correspondences!
A night flowing with birds, a ragged moon,
And in broad day the midnight come again!
A man goes far to find out what he is—
Death of the self in a long, tearless night,
All natural shapes blazing unnatural light.

Dark, dark my light, and darker my desire.
My soul, like some heat-maddened summer fly,
Keeps buzzing at the sill. Which I is *I*?
A fallen man,[9] I climb out of my fear.
The mind enters itself, and God the mind,
And one is One,[1] free in the tearing wind.[2]

1964

4. Roethke has said that the title refers to a dark night of the soul.

5. "Deepening despair, with a hint of approaching death" (Roethke's note).

6. "A derisive epithet at this point in the poem" (Roethke's note).

7. The heron is solitary, the wren sociable, among other differences.

8. That part of the poet which is in darkness; the other part, which searches to find light, is distinguished from it.

9. Within time and therefore fallen, he may yet emerge from the dark. Roethke may also be referring to the Fall of man and God's promise of Redemption.

1. Ecstatic sense of single identity, and of union with God.

2. Roethke suggests that "tearing" (in contrast to the earlier "tearless") implies pity on the part of natural forces.

A. D. HOPE
(*1907–*)

Alec Derwent Hope was born in Coomo, New South Wales, on July 21, 1907. He attended high schools in Sydney and then went on to Sydney University, where he received a B.A. in 1928. He then went over to Oxford, receiving the same degree there in 1931. He became a teacher and vocational psychologist. He lectured in English at Sydney Teachers' College and Melbourne University before becoming a professor of English at the Australian National University in Canberra.

Observation Car

To be put on the train and kissed and given my ticket,
Then the station slid backward, the shops and the neon lighting,
Reeling off in a drunken blur, with a whole pound note in my pocket
And the holiday packed with Perhaps. It used to be very exciting.

The present and past were enough. I did not mind having my back
To the engine. I sat like a spider and spun
Time backward out of my guts—or rather my eyes—and the track
Was a Now dwindling off to oblivion. I thought it was fun:

The telegraph poles slithered up in a sudden crescendo
As we sliced the hill and scattered its grazing sheep;
The days were a wheeling delirium that led without end to
Nights when we plunged into roaring tunnels of sleep.

But now I am tired of the train. I have learned that one tree
Is much like another, one hill the dead spit of the next
I have seen tailing off behind all the various types of country
Like a clock running down. I am bored and a little perplexed;

And weak with the effort of endless evacuation
Of the long monotonous Now, the repetitive, tidy
Officialdom of each siding, of each little station
Labelled Monday, Tuesday—and goodness! what happened to Friday?

And the maddening way the other passengers alter:
The schoolgirl who goes to the Ladies' comes back to her seat
A lollipop blonde who leads you on to assault her,
And you've just got her skirts round her waist and her pants round her
feet

When you find yourself fumbling about the nightmare knees
Of a pink hippopotamus with a permanent wave

Who sends you for sandwiches and a couple of teas,
But by then she has whiskers, no teeth and one foot in the grave.

I have lost my faith that the ticket tells where we are going.
There are rumours the driver is mad—we are all being trucked
To the abattoirs [1] somewhere—the signals are jammed and unknowing
We aim through the night full speed at a wrecked viaduct.

But I do not believe them. The future is rumour and drivel;
Only the past is assured. From the observation car
I stand looking back and watching the landscape shrivel,
Wondering where we are going and just where the hell we are,

Remembering how I planned to break the journey, to drive
My own car one day, to have choice in my hands and my foot upon
    power,
To see through the trumpet throat of vertiginous perspective
My urgent Now explode continually into flower,

To be the Eater of Time, a poet and not that sly
Anus of mind the historian. It was so simple and plain
To live by the sole, insatiable influx of the eye.
But something went wrong with the plan: I am still on the train.

1955

1. Slaughterhouses.

LOUIS MACNEICE
(*1907–1963*)

Louis MacNeice was born in Belfast on September 12, 1907. His father was a clergyman, eventually a bishop, in the Church of Ireland. Although he spent most of his adult life in London, MacNeice took great pride in his Irishness. His mother, troubled by mental illness, died when he was a boy; his father was a kindly, cultivated man, capable of allegiances to unpopular causes, and MacNeice's references to him are affectionate. MacNeice was educated at Marlborough, a public school, and at Oxford, where he took a degree with distinction in philosophy.

MacNeice lectured on Classics at Birmingham and then at Bedford College, part of the University of London. Just before the outbreak of the Second World War, he visited the United States and taught at Cornell University. In 1940 he returned to England and married the singer Hedli Anderson. He gave up teaching to become a writer and producer for the BBC. In August 1963, while on location with a BBC team, MacNeice insisted on going down into a mine to check personally on sound effects and caught a chill which was diagnosed too late as pneumonia. He died on September 3, just before the publication of his twentieth book of poems, *The Burning Perch.*

Snow

The room was suddenly rich and the great bay-window was
Spawning snow and pink roses against it
Soundlessly collateral and incompatible:
World is suddener than we fancy it.

World is crazier and more of it than we think,
Incorrigibly plural. I peel and portion
A tangerine and spit the pips and feel
The drunkenness of things being various.

And the fire flames with a bubbling sound for world
Is more spiteful and gay than one supposes—
On the tongue on the eyes on the ears in the palms of one's hands—
There is more than glass between the snow and the huge roses.

1935

Bagpipe Music

It's no go the merrygoround, it's no go the rickshaw,
All we want is a limousine and a ticket for the peepshow.
Their knickers are made of crêpe-de-chine,[9] their shoes are made of python,
Their halls are lined with tiger rugs and their walls with heads of bison.

John MacDonald found a corpse, put it under the sofa,
Waited till it came to life and hit it with a poker,
Sold its eyes for souvenirs, sold its blood for whisky,
Kept its bones for dumb-bells to use when he was fifty.

It's no go the Yogi-Man, it's no go Blavatsky,[1]
All we want is a bank balance and a bit of skirt in a taxi.

Annie MacDougall went to milk, caught her foot in the heather,
Woke to hear a dance record playing of Old Vienna.
It's no go your maidenheads, it's no go your culture,
All we want is a Dunlop tyre and the devil mend the puncture.

The Laird o' Phelps spent Hogmanay[2] declaring he was sober,
Counted his feet to prove the fact and found he had one foot over.
Mrs. Carmichael had her fifth, looked at the job with repulsion,
Said to the midwife 'Take it away; I'm through with over production'.

It's no go the gossip column, it's no go the ceilidh,[3]
All we want is a mother's help and a sugar-stick for the baby.

9. A rayon or silk fabric.
1. Madame Helena Petrovna Blavatsky (1831–1891), a Russian occultist, founded the Theosophical Society.
2. New Year's Eve (Scots).
3. A sociable evening of singing and story-telling; pronounced *kaley*.

Willie Murray cut his thumb, couldn't count the damage,
Took the hide of an Ayrshire cow and used it for a bandage.
His brother caught three hundred cran[4] when the seas were lavish,
Threw the bleeders back in the sea and went upon the parish.[5]

It's no go the Herring Board,[6] it's no go the Bible,
All we want is a packet of fags[7] when our hands are idle.

It's no go the picture palace, it's no go the stadium,
It's no go the country cot with a pot of pink geraniums,
It's no go the Government grants, it's no go the elections,
Sit on your arse for fifty years and hang your hat on a pension.

It's no go my honey love, it's no go my poppet;
Work your hands from day to day, the winds will blow the profit.
The glass is falling hour by hour, the glass will fall for ever,
But if you break the bloody glass[8] you won't hold up the weather.

1937

Brother Fire[3]

When our brother Fire was having his dog's day
Jumping the London streets with millions of tin cans
Clanking at his tail, we heard some shadow say
'Give the dog a bone'—and so we gave him ours;
Night after night we watched him slaver and crunch away
The beams of human life, the tops of topless towers.[4]

Which gluttony of his for us was Lenten fare
Who mother-naked, suckled with sparks, were chill
Though cotted in a grille of sizzling air
Striped like a convict—black, yellow and red;
Thus were we weaned to knowledge of the Will
That wills the natural world but wills us dead.

O delicate walker, babbler, dialectician Fire,
O enemy and image of ourselves,
Did we not on those mornings after the All Clear,
When you were looting shops in elemental joy
And singing as you swarmed up city block and spire,
Echo your thought in ours? 'Destroy! Destroy!'

1944

4. A measure of fish.
5. Went on relief.
6. A government agency which in the Thirties unsuccessfully tried to save the failing British herring trade.
7. Cigarettes.
8. Barometer.
3. "Praise to Thee, my Lord, for Brother Fire, by whom Thou lightest the night; He is lovely and pleasant, mighty and strong." (St. Francis of Assisi, "The Song of Brother Sun and of All Creatures.") The occasion for the poem is the German bombing raids on London during the Second World War.
4. An allusion to the destruction of Troy, from Christopher Marlowe's *Doctor Faustus*: "Topless towers of Ilium."

The Libertine

In the old days with married women's stockings
Twisted round his bedpost he felt himself a gay
Dog but now his liver has begun to groan,
Now that pick-ups are the order of the day:
O leave me easy, leave me alone.

Voluptuary in his 'teens and cynic in his twenties,
He ran through women like a child through growing hay
Looking for a lost toy whose capture might atone
For his own guilt and the cosmic disarray:
O leave me easy, leave me alone.

He never found the toy and has forgotten the faces,
Only remembers the props . . . a scent-spray
Beside the bed or a milk-white telephone
Or through the triple ninon[5] the acrid trickle of day:
O leave me easy, leave me alone.

Long fingers over the gunwale,[6] hair in a hair-net,
Furs in January, cartwheel hats in May,
And after the event the wish to be alone—
Angels, goddesses, bitches, all have edged away:
O leave me easy, leave me alone.

So now, in middle age, his erotic programme
Torn in two, if after such a delay
An accident should offer him his own
Fulfilment in a woman, still he would say:
O leave me easy, leave me alone.

1944

Variation on Heraclitus[7]

Even the walls are flowing, even the ceiling,
Nor only in terms of physics; the pictures
Bob on each picture rail like floats on a line
While the books on the shelves keep reeling
Their titles out into space and the carpet
Keeps flying away to Arabia nor can this be where I stood—
Where I shot the rapids I mean—when I signed
On a line that rippled away with a pen that melted
Nor can this now be the chair—the chairoplane of a chair—
That I sat in the day that I thought I had made up my mind

5. Light, semi-transparent silk.

6. The top of a boat's side.

7. Heraclitus (c. 540–c. 480 B.C.), the Greek philosopher, is known for a number of apothegms on mutability, three of which are relevant to this poem: "All is flux; nothing stands still"; "It is not possible to step twice into the same river"; "Nothing endures but change."

And as for that standard lamp[8] it too keeps waltzing away
Down an unbridgeable Ganges[9] where nothing is standard
And lights are but lit to be drowned in honour and spite of some dark
And vanishing goddess. No, whatever you say,
Reappearance presumes disappearance, it may not be nice
Or proper or easily analysed not to be static
But none of your slide snide rules can catch what is sliding so fast
And, all you advisers on this by the time it is that,
I just do not want your advice
Nor need you be troubled to pin me down in my room
Since the room and I will escape for I tell you flat:
One cannot live in the same room twice.

1961

8. Floor lamp.

9. The holy river of Indian religion.

RICHARD WRIGHT
(*1908–1960*)

Richard Wright was born on a plantation near Natchez, Mississippi, on September 4, 1908. When he was five his father, a sharecropper, deserted his family; his mother was chronically ill, and the child was passed from one relative to another. At 16 Wright graduated from the ninth grade. He took a job in Memphis, where he discovered the books of H. L. Mencken and was inspired to begin the process of self-education so movingly described in his autobiography, *Black Boy*. In 1927 Wright and his family migrated to Chicago where he remained for ten years. He got a job on the Federal Writers' Project and won an award for his short novel *Uncle Tom's Children*, which, with three other stories, was published in 1938. The following year he wrote his very successful novel *Native Son*. During the Thirties Wright joined the Communist Party, and he remained a member until 1944. After the Second World War, with the encouragement of Gertrude Stein, Wright moved to Paris. He died there on November 28, 1960.

Between the World and Me

And one morning while in the woods I stumbled suddenly upon the thing,
Stumbled upon it in a grassy clearing guarded by scaly oaks and elms.
And the sooty details of the scene rose, thrusting themselves between the world and me. . . .
There was a design of white bones slumbering forgottenly upon a cushion of ashes.
There was a charred stump of a sapling pointing a blunt finger accusingly at the sky.
There were torn tree limbs, tiny veins of burnt leaves, and a scorched coil of greasy hemp;

A vacant shoe, an empty tie, a ripped shirt, a lonely hat, and a pair of trousers stiff with black blood.
And upon the trampled grass were buttons, dead matches, butt-ends of cigars and cigarettes, peanut shells, a drained gin-flask, and a whore's lipstick;
Scattered traces of tar, restless arrays of feathers, and the lingering smell of gasoline.
And through the morning air the sun poured yellow surprise into the eye sockets of a stony skull. . . .
And while I stood my mind was frozen with a cold pity for the life that was gone.
The ground gripped my feet and my heart was circled by icy walls of fear—
The sun died in the sky; a night wind muttered in the grass and fumbled the leaves in the trees; the woods poured forth the hungry yelping of hounds; the darkness screamed with thirsty voices; and the witnesses rose and lived:
The dry bones stirred, rattled, lifted, melting themselves into my bones.
The grey ashes formed flesh firm and black, entering into my flesh.
The gin-flask passed from mouth to mouth; cigars and cigarettes glowed, the whore smeared the lipstick red upon her lips,
And a thousand faces swirled around me, clamoring that my life be burned. . . .

And then they had me, stripped me, battering my teeth into my throat till I swallowed my own blood.
My voice was drowned in the roar of their voices, and my black wet body slipped and rolled in their hands as they bound me to the sapling.
And my skin clung to the bubbling hot tar, falling from me in limp patches.
And the down and quills of the white feathers sank into my raw flesh, and I moaned in my agony.
Then my blood was cooled mercifully, cooled by a baptism of gasoline.
And in a blaze of red I leaped to the sky as pain rose like water, boiling my limbs.
Panting, begging I clutched childlike, clutched to the hot sides of death.
Now I am dry bones and my face a stony skull staring in yellow surprise at the sun. . . .

1963

STEPHEN SPENDER
(*1909–*)

Stephen Spender was born in London on February 28, 1909. He began to write poems early, and when he came up to Oxford took his courage in his hands and showed the work to W. H. Auden, who was a little his senior. Later Spender published both Auden's first book and his own on a small handpress. After leaving Oxford he traveled in Germany for a time, and was later to translate various German poets, notably Rainer Maria Rilke. During the Thirties Spender and his friends worked for the Loyalists in Spain, though he became somewhat disillusioned about his efforts there. From 1939 to 1941 he was co-editor with Cyril Connolly of the important review *Horizon*, and from 1953 to 1967 he was co-editor with Melvin J. Lasky of *Encounter*. Spender has lectured a good deal, and for some years taught at American universities before accepting a chair in English Literature at University College in the University of London. He retired in 1975.

Icarus[1]

He will watch the hawk with an indifferent eye
    Or pitifully;
Nor on those eagles that so feared him, now
    Will strain his brow;
Weapons men use, stone, sling and strong-thewed bow
    He will not know.

This aristocrat, superb of all instinct,
    With death close linked
Had paced the enormous cloud, almost had won
    War on the sun;
Till now, like Icarus mid-ocean-drowned,
    Hands, wings, are found.

1933

The Express

After the first powerful, plain manifesto
The black statement of pistons, without more fuss
But gliding like a queen, she leaves the station.
Without bowing and with restrained unconcern
She passes the houses which humbly crowd outside,
The gasworks,[2] and at last the heavy page
Of death, printed by gravestones in the cemetery.
Beyond the town, there lies the open country
Where, gathering speed, she acquires mystery,
The luminous self-possession of ships on ocean.
It is now she begins to sing—at first quite low
Then loud, and at last with a jazzy madness—
The song of her whistle screaming at curves,
Of deafening tunnels, brakes, innumerable bolts.
And always light, aerial, underneath,
Retreats the elate metre of her wheels.

1. Icarus flew on wings of feathers and wax made by his father Daedalus; when he recklessly climbed too near the sun, the wax melted and he plunged into the sea.

2. The incorporation of the gasworks and other aspects of the urban landscape into poetry was a point which Spender learned from Auden.

Steaming through metal landscape on her lines,
She plunges new eras of white happiness,
Where speed throws up strange shapes, broad curves
And parallels clean like trajectories from guns.
At last, further than Edinburgh or Rome,
Beyond the crest of the world, she reaches night
Where only a low stream-line brightness
Of phosphorus on the tossing hills is light.
Ah, like a comet through flame, she moves entranced,
Wrapt in her music no bird song, no, nor bough
Breaking with honey buds, shall ever equal.

1933

CHARLES OLSON
(*1910–1970*)

Charles Olson was born on December 27, 1910, in Worcester, Massachusetts. His father was from Sweden, his mother an Irish-American. Up to 1947, by which time he was thirty-seven, his life is somewhat obscured by his own random accounts of it. He was "uneducated" at Wesleyan, Yale, and Harvard. From Wesleyan he received a B.A. in 1932 and an M.A. the following year. He taught first at Clark University in Worcester, then, from 1936 to 1939, at Harvard. For the next nine years he had various occupations, which came to a focus in the publication of a book on Melville. The following year, 1948, he took the place of his friend, the novelist Edward Dahlberg, at Black Mountain College, a highly influential experimental college of the arts. Many of its teachers and students have since been important in painting, music, and the dance as well as in literature. In 1951 Olson became rector (head) of the college, and stayed in this position until 1956. He was to teach later, in his own dynamic, unpredictable fashion, at the State University of New York at Buffalo, and then (briefly) at the University of Connecticut. He died on January 10, 1970.

A Newly Discovered 'Homeric' Hymn[5]

(FOR JANE HARRISON,[6] IF SHE WERE ALIVE)

Hail and beware the dead who will talk life until you are blue
in the face. And you will not understand what is wrong,
they will not be blue, they will have tears in their eyes,
they will seem to you so much more full of life
than the rest of us, and they will ask so much, not of you no

5. The so-called "Homeric Hymns" were preludes to Greek epic poems and invoked various divinities, often telling of their exploits. The hymns are of unknown authorship and various dates, and are written in hexameter.

6. (1850–1928), English classical scholar, author of important studies of Greek myth and religion.

but of life, they will cry, isn't it this way, if it isn't
I don't care for it, and you will feel the blackmail, you will not know
what to answer, it will all have become one mass

Hail and beware them, for they come from where you have not been,
they come from where you cannot have come, they come into life
by a different gate. They come from a place which is not easily known,
it is known only to those who have died. They carry seeds
you must not touch, you must not touch the pot they taste of,
no one must touch the pot, no one must, in their season.

Hail and beware them, in their season. Take care. Prepare
to receive them, they carry what the living cannot do without,
but take the proper precautions, do the prescribed things, let
down the thread from the right shoulder. And from the forehead.
And listen to what they say, listen to the talk, hear
every word of it—they are drunk from the pot, they speak
like no living man may speak, they have the seeds in their mouth—
listen, and beware

Hail them solely that they have the seeds in their mouth, they
are drunk, you cannot do without a drunkenness, seeds can't,
they must be soaked in the contents of the pot, they must be all one
mass.
But you who live cannot know what else the seeds must be. Hail
and beware the earth, where the dead come from. Life
is not of the earth. The dead are of the earth. Hail and beware
the earth, where the pot is buried.

Greet the dead in the dead man's time. He is drunk of the pot.
He speaks like spring does. He will deceive you. You are meant
to be deceived. You must observe the drunkenness. You are not to
drink. But you must hear, and see. You must beware.

Hail them, and fall off. Fall off! The drink is not yours,
it is not yours! You do not come
from the same place, you do not suffer as the dead do,
they do not suffer, they need, because they have drunk of the pot,
they need. Do not drink of the pot, do not touch it. Do not touch
them.

Beware the dead. And hail them. They teach you drunkenness.
You have your own place to drink. Hail and beware them, when they
come.

1960

ELIZABETH BISHOP
(*1911–*)

Elizabeth Bishop was born on February 8, 1911, in Worcester, Massachusetts. She grew up in New England and Nova Scotia, and attended Vassar, where she received her B.A. in 1934. Since then she has lived for long periods in Key West and, more recently, Brazil. She was Consultant in Poetry to the Library of Congress in 1949 and 1950. Her *Poems—North and South* won the Pulitzer Prize in 1956. She presently teaches creative writing at Harvard University.

The Man-Moth[1]

Here, above,
cracks in the buildings are filled with battered moonlight.
The whole shadow of Man is only as big as his hat.
It lies at his feet like a circle for a doll to stand on,
and he makes an inverted pin, the point magnetized to the moon.
He does not see the moon; he observes only her vast properties,
feeling the queer light on his hands, neither warm nor cold,
of a temperature impossible to record in thermometers.

But when the Man-Moth
pays his rare, although occasional, visits to the surface,
the moon looks rather different to him. He emerges
from an opening under the edge of one of the sidewalks
and nervously begins to scale the faces of the buildings.
He thinks the moon is a small hole at the top of the sky,
proving the sky quite useless for protection.
He trembles, but must investigate as high as he can climb.

Up the façades,
his shadow dragging like a photographer's cloth behind him,
he climbs fearfully, thinking that this time he will manage
to push his small head through that round clean opening
and be forced through, as from a tube, in black scrolls on the light.
(Man, standing below him, has no such illusions.)
But what the Man-Moth fears most he must do, although
he fails, of course, and falls back scared but quite unhurt.

Then he returns
to the pale subways of cement he calls his home. He flits,
he flutters, and cannot get aboard the silent trains
fast enough to suit him. The doors close swiftly.
The Man-Moth always seats himself facing the wrong way

1. "Newspaper misprint for 'mammoth' " (Bishop's note).

and the train starts at once at its full, terrible speed,
without a shift in gears or a gradation of any sort.
He cannot tell the rate at which he travels backwards.

Each night he must
be carried through artificial tunnels and dream recurrent dreams.
Just as the ties recur beneath his train, these underlie
his rushing brain. He does not dare look out the window,
for the third rail, the unbroken draught of poison,
runs there beside him. He regards it as a disease
he has inherited the susceptibility to. He has to keep
his hands in his pockets, as others must wear mufflers.

If you catch him,
hold up a flashlight to his eye. It's all dark pupil,
an entire night itself, whose haired horizon tightens
as he stares back, and closes up the eye. Then from the lids
one tear, his only possession, like the bee's sting, slips.
Slyly he palms it, and if you're not paying attention
he'll swallow it. However, if you watch, he'll hand it over,
cool as from underground springs and pure enough to drink.

1946

The Fish

I caught a tremendous fish
and held him beside the boat
half out of water, with my hook
fast in a corner of his mouth.
He didn't fight.
He hadn't fought at all.
He hung a grunting weight,
battered and venerable
and homely. Here and there
his brown skin hung in strips
like ancient wallpaper,
and its pattern of darker brown
was like wallpaper:
shapes like full-blown roses
stained and lost through age.
He was speckled with barnacles,
fine rosettes of lime,
and infested
with tiny white sea-lice,
and underneath two or three
rags of green weed hung down.
While his gills were breathing in
the terrible oxygen
—the frightening gills,

fresh and crisp with blood,
that can cut so badly—
I thought of the coarse white flesh
packed in like feathers,
the big bones and the little bones,
the dramatic reds and blacks
of his shiny entrails,
and the pink swim-bladder
like a big peony.
I looked into his eyes
which were far larger than mine
but shallower, and yellowed,
the irises backed and packed
with tarnished tinfoil
seen through the lenses
of old scratched isinglass.[2]
They shifted a little, but not
to return my stare.
—It was more like the tipping
of an object toward the light.
I admired his sullen face,
the mechanism of his jaw,
and then I saw
that from his lower lip
—if you could call it a lip—
grim, wet, and weaponlike,
hung five old pieces of fish-line,
or four and a wire leader
with the swivel still attached,
with all their five big hooks
grown firmly in his mouth.
A green line, frayed at the end
where he broke it, two heavier lines,
and a fine black thread
still crimped from the strain and snap
when it broke and he got away.
Like medals with their ribbons
frayed and wavering,
a five-haired beard of wisdom
trailing from his aching jaw.
I stared and stared
and victory filled up
the little rented boat,
from the pool of bilge
where oil had spread a rainbow
around the rusted engine
to the bailer rusted orange,
the sun-cracked thwarts,[3]

2. A semitransparent substance, either mica or fish gelatin, used for windows.

3. Seats. *Gunnels* (line 74): or gunwales, the tops of the boat's sides.

the oarlocks on their strings,
the gunnels—until everything
was rainbow, rainbow, rainbow!
And I let the fish go.

1946

The Armadillo

FOR ROBERT LOWELL

This is the time of year
when almost every night
the frail, illegal fire balloons[4] appear.
Climbing the mountain height,

rising toward a saint
still honored in these parts,[5]
the paper chambers flush and fill with light
that comes and goes, like hearts.

Once up against the sky it's hard
to tell them from the stars—
planets, that is—the tinted ones:
Venus going down, or Mars,

or the pale green one. With a wind,
they flare and falter, wobble and toss;
but if it's still they steer between
the kite sticks of the Southern Cross,[6]

receding, dwindling, solemnly
and steadily forsaking us,
or, in the downdraft from a peak,
suddenly turning dangerous.

Last night another big one fell.
It splattered like an egg of fire
against the cliff behind the house.
The flame ran down. We saw the pair

of owls who nest there flying up
and up, their whirling black-and-white
stained bright pink underneath, until
they shrieked up out of sight.

The ancient owls' nest must have burned.
Hastily, all alone,

4. Paper balloons, which rise because of heat from candles attached below them.

5. Brazil. The mountain may be Corcovado, near Rio de Janeiro; the "time of year" (line 1) may be Carnival.

6. A constellation visible only from the southern hemisphere.

a glistening armadillo left the scene,
rose-flecked, head down, tail down,

and then a baby rabbit jumped out,
short-eared, to our surprise.
So soft!—a handful of intangible ash
with fixed, ignited eyes.

Too pretty, dreamlike mimicry!
O falling fire and piercing cry
and panic, and a weak mailed fist
clenched ignorant against the sky!

1965

JOSEPHINE MILES
(*1911–*)

Josephine Miles was born on June 11, 1911, in Chicago. Her family moved to California five years later, and except for two years in Michigan she has lived there ever since. She took her B.A. at the University of California at Los Angeles, then did graduate work at Berkeley, where she has remained as a teacher. Besides writing poetry, she has made a systematic analysis and comparison of poetic grammars and vocabularies used in different periods of English literature.

Preliminary to Classroom Lecture

My quiet kin, must I affront you
With a telling tongue?
Will not a mission or request content you
To move as you belong
The fields of doubt among?

The voice to burden down a tale upon you
Were indolent with din.
Would better ask and have the answer from you.
And would you then begin
Querying too, querying, my quiet kin?

1941

Gypsy

The entire country is overrun with private property, the gypsy king said.
I don't know if this is true,
I believe in the gypsy kingship though.

The lost tribes of my own nation
Rove and rove.
In red and yellow rough and silent move.

I believe
The majesty pot mending, copper smith
On the hundred highways, nothing to do with.

And black eyes, black I never saw,
Searching out the pocket lines of cloth
The face lines and the furrows of belief.

It's a curious fact, Stephan, King, if you are made to doubt
Aegyptian[1] vision on the Jersey shore.
Property's private as ever, ever.

1946

Belief

Mother said to call her if the H bomb exploded
And I said I would, and it about did
When Louis my brother robbed a service station
And lay cursing on the oily cement in handcuffs.

But by that time it was too late to tell Mother,
She was too sick to worry the life out of her
Over *why why*. Causation is sequence
And everything is one thing after another.

Besides, my other brother, Eddie, had got to be President,
And you can't ask too much of one family.
The chances were as good for a good future
As bad for a bad one.

Therefore it was surprising that, as we kept the newspapers from
Mother,
She died feeling responsible for a disaster unverified,
Murmuring, in her sleep as it seemed, the ancient slogan
Noblesse oblige.[2]

1955

Reason[4]

Said, Pull her up a bit will you, Mac, I want to unload there.
Said, Pull her up my rear end, first come first serve.

1. The gypsies, though they actually came from India, were believed to have originated in Egypt, hence their name, and the frequent reference to them as "Little Egypt."
2. Noble birth entails obligations.

4. " 'Reason' is a favorite one of my poems because I like the idea of speech—not images, not ideas, not music, but people talking—as the material from which poetry is made" (Miles's note).

Said, Give her the gun, Bud, he needs a taste of his own bumper.
Then the usher came out and got into the act:

Said, Pull her up, pull her up a bit, we need this space, sir.
Said, For God's sake, is this still a free country or what?
You go back and take care of Gary Cooper's horse
And leave me handle my own car.

Saw them unloading the lame old lady,
Ducked out under the wheel and gave her an elbow,
Said, All you needed to do was just explain;
Reason, Reason is my middle name.

1955

[The Entrepreneur Chicken Shed His Tail Feathers, Surplus]

The entrepreneur chicken shed his tail feathers, surplus
Fat, his comb, wing weight, down to a mere
Shadow, like a Graves bird[5] ready to sing.
For him every morning
Paradise Merchant Mart reopened its doors
With regular fire sales, Shoe Parlor
Blackened its aroma, Professional
Building ran its elevators up and down
So fast that pulled teeth turned up in other mouths.

Activity. The tax base broadened in the sunlight
As gradually sun spreads wider after coffee.
It was a busy world on that side of the road,
For which the entrepreneur chicken was in his able
Way responsible.
At noon, loans, mortgages, personal interest,
At night notarized after-images, as if by sundown
The elevator had turned to moving sidewise
Frames and phrases to be read and reread.

He was not boss or mayor, but he certainly was
Right on that spinning wheel which spun the public
In and out of his stores, and his pleasantries
Began to spin the flesh right off his bones.
That is why the chicken began to sing
High, not loud, and why transparencies
Of pipestems were his legs, his beak aloft,
His feathers lean, drawing the busy air,
And why he crossed the road.

1967

5. Morris Graves (1910–), the American artist, painted a picture ("Guardian") of a ghostlike, transparent bird.

ROY FULLER
(*1912–*)

Roy Fuller was born on February 11, 1912, at Failsworth, England, near Manchester. At sixteen he left school and was articled to a solicitor; five years later he qualified as a lawyer. Fuller's military experience during the Second World War, part of it spent in East Africa, provided him with the material for poetry and, equally important, the time to write it. In 1946 he left the Navy and resumed his law practice until his retirement in 1969. In 1968 he was elected Professor of Poetry at Oxford University.

Autobiography of a Lungworm

My normal dwelling is the lungs of swine,
  My normal shape a worm,
But other dwellings, other shapes, are mine
  Within my natural term.
Dimly I see my life, of all, the sign,
  Of better lives the germ.

The pig, though I am inoffensive, coughs,
  Finding me irritant:
My eggs go with the contents of the troughs
  From mouth to excrement—
The pig thus thinks, perhaps, he forever doffs
  His niggling resident.

The eggs lie unconsidered in the dung
  Upon the farmyard floor,
Far from the scarlet and sustaining lung:
  But happily a poor
And humble denizen provides a rung
  To make ascension sure.

The earthworm eats the eggs; inside the warm
  Cylinder larvae hatch:
For years, if necessary, in this form
  I wait the lucky match
That will return me to my cherished norm,
  My ugly pelt dispatch.

Strangely, it is the pig himself becomes
  The god inside the car:[5]
His greed devours the earthworms; so the slums

5. The *deus ex machina* is a device of the classical stage; at the last moment a god arrives, often in a chariot, and saves the situation.

Of his intestines are
The setting for the act when clay succumbs
And force steers for its star.

The larvae burrow through the bowel wall
And, having to the dregs
Drained ignominy, gain the lung's great hall.
They change. Once more, like pegs,
Lungworms are anchored to the rise and fall
—And start to lay their eggs.

What does this mean? The individual,
Nature, mutation, strife?
I feel, though I am simple, still the whole
Is complex; and that life—
A huge, doomed throbbing—has a wiry soul
That must escape the knife.

1957

BROTHER ANTONINUS (William Everson) (*1912–*)

William Everson was born in Sacramento, California, on September 10, 1912. Brought up by his parents as a Christian Scientist, he became an agnostic during his teens. He attended Fresno College but dropped out to write poetry and to marry. Drafted as a conscientious objector in 1943, Everson spent the war years in a succession of work camps in the Pacific Northwest. After the war he went to San Francisco and was one of what he calls "the anarchists and poets around Kenneth Rexroth." He had divorced and remarried, and his new wife introduced him to Catholicism. In 1949 they separated to enter the Catholic Church, and after a year on a Guggenheim Fellowship and another doing work in the slums of Oakland Everson entered the Dominican Order of Preachers as Brother Antoninus. After six years of self-study and searching he rejoined the literary scene in California. In 1969 he reported that he had left the Order, but he is still identified by the Church and among poets as Brother Antoninus.

Year's End

The year dies fiercely: out of the north the beating storms,
And wind at the roof's edge, lightning swording the low sky:
This year dying like some traitored Norse stumbling under the deep wounds,
The furious steel, smashing and swinging.

From the northern room I watch in the dusk,
And being unsocial regard the coming year coldly,
Suspicious of strangers, distrustful of innovations,

Reluctant to chance one way or another the unknown.
I leave this year as a man leaves wine,
Remembering the summer, bountiful, the good fall, the months mellow
and full.
I sit in the northern room, in the dusk, the death of a year,
And watch it go down in thunder.

1948

The Raid

They came out of the sun undetected,
Who had lain in the thin ships
All night long on the cold ocean,
Watched Vega down, the Wain hover,[1]
Drank in the weakening dawn their brew,
And sent the lumbering death-laden birds
Level along the decks.

They came out of the sun with their guns geared,
Saw the soft and easy shape of that island
Laid on the sea,
An unwakening woman,
Its deep hollows and its flowing folds
Veiled in the garlands of its morning mists.
Each of them held in his aching eyes the erotic image,
And then tipped down,
In the target's trance,
In the ageless instant of the long descent,
And saw sweet chaos blossom below,
And felt in that flower the years release.

The perfect achievement.
They went back toward the sun crazy with joy,
Like wild birds weaving,
Drunkenly stunting;
Passed out over edge of that injured island,
Sought the rendezvous on the open sea
Where the ships would be waiting.

None were there.
Neither smoke nor smudge;
Neither spar nor splice nor rolling raft.
Only the wide waiting waste,
That each of them saw with intenser sight
Than he ever had spared it,
Who circled that spot,
The spent gauge caught in its final flutter,
And straggled down on their wavering wings

1. The former is a star, and the latter a constellation, visible in the northern hemisphere.

From the vast sky,
From the endless spaces,
Down at last for the low hover,
And the short quick quench of the sea.

1948

KARL SHAPIRO
(*1913–*)

Karl Shapiro was born in Baltimore, Maryland, on November 10, 1913. After graduating from high school there, he enrolled at the University of Virginia but found that he was more interested in writing than studying and soon withdrew. While working at various jobs in Baltimore and studying on his own, Shapiro wrote "many long poems and plays in verse, nearly all of which I later destroyed"; the collection of shorter poems that he published in 1935 went largely unnoticed. He resumed his formal education at Johns Hopkins University but was inducted into the Army before receiving his degree and served in the South Pacific until the Second World War was over. While overseas, Shapiro continued to write poetry, while his fiancée Evelyn Katz (whom he married in 1945) sought successfully to get it published. His book, *V-Letter*, won the Pulitzer Prize for poetry in 1945. When he returned to civilian life, he was well known in American letters and served for a year as poetry consultant to the Library of Congress; he then taught at Johns Hopkins. In 1950 he succeeded Hayden Carruth as editor of *Poetry* magazine, a post he held until 1956, when he joined the faculty of the University of Nebraska and became editor of *Prairie Schooner*. He presently teaches at the University of California at Davis.

The Fly

O hideous little bat, the size of snot,
With polyhedral eye and shabby clothes,
To populate the stinking cat you walk
The promontory of the dead man's nose,
Climb with the fine leg of a Duncan-Phyfe[1]
  The smoking mountains of my food
    And in a comic mood
  In mid-air take to bed a wife.

Riding and riding with your filth of hair
On gluey foot or wing, forever coy,
Hot from the compost and green sweet decay,
Sounding your buzzer like an urchin toy—
You dot all whiteness with diminutive stool,
  In the tight belly of the dead
    Burrow with hungry head
  And inlay maggots like a jewel.

1. Duncan Phyfe (c. 1768–1854), U.S. cabinetmaker, whose early style was delicate.

At your approach the great horse stomps and paws
Bringing the hurricane of his heavy tail;
Shod in disease you dare to kiss my hand
Which sweeps against you like an angry flail;
Still you return, return, trusting your wing
To draw you from the hunter's reach
That learns to kill to teach
Disorder to the tinier thing.

My peace is your disaster. For your death
Children like spiders cup their pretty hands
And wives resort to chemistry of war.
In fens of sticky paper and quicksands
You glue yourself to death. Where you are stuck
You struggle hideously and beg
You amputate your leg
Imbedded in the amber muck.

But I, a man, must swat you with my hate,
Slap you across the air and crush your flight,
Must mangle with my shoe and smear your blood,
Expose your little guts pasty and white,
Knock your head sidewise like a drunkard's hat,
Pin your wings under like a crow's,
Tear off your flimsy clothes
And beat you as one beats a rat.

Then like Gargantua[2] I stride among
The corpses strewn like raisins in the dust,
The broken bodies of the narrow dead
That catch the throat with fingers of disgust.
I sweep. One gyrates like a top and falls
And stunned, stone blind, and deaf
Buzzes its frightful F
And dies between three cannibals.

1942

Lower the Standard: That's My Motto

Lower the standard: that's my motto. Somebody is always putting the food out of reach. We're tired of falling off ladders. Who says a child can't paint? A pro is somebody who does it for money. Lower the standards. Let's all play poetry. Down with ideals, flags, convention buttons, morals, the scrambled eggs on the admiral's hat. I'm talking sense. Lower the standards. Sabotage the stylistic approach. Let weeds grow in the subdivision. Putty up the incisions in the library façade, those names that frighten grade-school teachers, those names whose U's are cut like V's.

2. Giant of medieval legend adopted by Rabelais in *Gargantua and Pantagruel* (1532). One of his exploits was to swallow five pilgrims, with their staves, in a salad.

Burn the *Syntopicon* and *The Harvard Classics.*[3] Lower the standard on classics, battleships, Russian ballet, national anthems (but they're low enough). Break through to the bottom. Be natural as an American abroad who knows no language, not even American. Keelhaul the poets in the vestry[4] chairs. Renovate the Abbey of cold-storage dreamers.[5] Get off the Culture Wagon. Learn how to walk the way you want. Slump your shoulders, stick your belly out, arms all over the table. How many generations will this take? Don't think about it, just make a start. (You have made a start.) Don't break anything you can step around, *but don't pick it up.* The law of gravity is the law of art. You first, poetry second, the good, the beautiful, the true come last. As the lad said: We must love one another or die.[6]

1964

3. A selection from the "great books" of literature, philosophy, and science, edited by Harvard president Charles William Eliot (1834–1926), was called the *Harvard Classics*, and a similar selection edited by Robert Hutchins had a topical index, prepared by Mortimer J. Adler, called the *Syntopicon;* these were intended as tools for self-education.

4. Lay governors of a church.

5. The "poets' corner" in Westminster Abbey, in London, is where many important English poets, from Chaucer to the present, are buried.

6. Quoted from Auden, "September 1939" (first version), urging mutual love as an antidote to war.

ROBERT HAYDEN
(*1913–*)

Robert Hayden was born in Detroit, Michigan, on August 4, 1913. He went to Wayne State University; after graduate studies and some teaching at the University of Michigan, he moved south to Nashville, Tennessee, to join the faculty of Fisk University. In 1954 he went to Mexico on a grant and wrote poems with Mexican settings and themes. He twice won the Hopwood Award for poetry, and in 1966 he won the Grand Prize for Poetry at the Dakar (Senegal) World Festival of the Arts. He now teaches at the University of Michigan.

Those Winter Sundays

Sundays too my father got up early
and put his clothes on in the blueblack cold,
then with cracked hands that ached
from labor in the weekday weather made
banked fires blaze. No one ever thanked him.

I'd wake and hear the cold splintering, breaking.
When the rooms were warm, he'd call,
and slowly I would rise and dress,
fearing the chronic angers of that house,

Speaking indifferently to him,
who had driven out the cold
and polished my good shoes as well.
What did I know, what did I know
of love's austere and lonely offices?

1962

DELMORE SCHWARTZ
(*1913–1966*)

Delmore Schwartz was born in Brooklyn, New York, on December 8, 1913, and grew up in a middle-class Jewish family there. After brief periods at three universities, among them Harvard, where he studied philosophy, he was graduated from New York University in 1935. Schwartz taught writing at six colleges and selected poetry for the *Partisan Review* and the *New Republic.*

For his *Selected Poems: Summer Knowledge* Schwartz was awarded the Bollingen Poetry Prize for 1959; he was the youngest poet to have received this impressive award. Instead of being encouraged, Schwartz grew increasingly dissatisfied with the quality of his work and published only a handful of poems during the rest of his life—nothing at all after 1963—though he continued to write copiously. One reason may have been the depredations of mental illness; since the late Forties he had been in and out of sanatoriums, and in the grip of paranoid obsessions Schwartz denounced all his old friends, resigned as visiting professor at Syracuse University in 1965, and dropped out of sight for over a year. His last months were spent alone in a Times Square hotel, still writing; it was not until three days after his fatal heart attack, on July 11, 1966, that someone was found to claim his body.

The Heavy Bear Who Goes with Me

"the withness of the body"

The heavy bear who goes with me,
A manifold honey to smear his face,
Clumsy and lumbering here and there,
The central ton of every place,
The hungry beating brutish one
In love with candy, anger, and sleep,
Crazy factotum,[1] dishevelling all,
Climbs the building, kicks the football,
Boxes his brother in the hate-ridden city.

Breathing at my side, that heavy animal,
That heavy bear who sleeps with me,
Howls in his sleep for a world of sugar,
A sweetness intimate as the water's clasp,

1. A general servant; jack of all trades.

Howls in his sleep because the tight-rope
Trembles and shows the darkness beneath.
—The strutting show-off is terrified,
Dressed in his dress-suit, bulging his pants,
Trembles to think that his quivering meat
Must finally wince to nothing at all.

That inescapable animal walks with me,
Has followed me since the black womb held,
Moves where I move, distorting my gesture,
A caricature, a swollen shadow,
A stupid clown of the spirit's motive,
Perplexes and affronts with his own darkness,
The secret life of belly and bone,
Opaque, too near, my private, yet unknown,
Stretches to embrace the very dear
With whom I would walk without him near,
Touches her grossly, although a word
Would bare my heart and make me clear,
Stumbles, flounders, and strives to be fed
Dragging me with him in his mouthing care,
Amid the hundred million of his kind,
The scrimmage of appetite everywhere.

1938

DUDLEY RANDALL
(*1914–*)

Born in Washington, D.C. on January 14, 1914, Dudley Randall has spent most of his life in Detroit. He was a foundry worker at the Ford Motor Company, and then became a letter carrier and clerk for the post office. He served with the Army in the South Pacific during the Second World War, then resumed his job with the post office and enrolled at Detroit's Wayne State University, where he received a B.A. in 1949. He studied library science at the University of Michigan and, armed with an M.A., worked as a librarian at Lincoln University in Missouri and Morgan State College in Baltimore before returning to Detroit, where he assumed increasingly important positions in the city's public library system. In 1965 he founded the Broadside Press, an event of crucial importance in the development of postwar black American poetry. He started with a capital of $12.00, which paid the bill for printing the first "broadside"—his poem "Ballad of Birmingham"—on a single sheet of paper. From these beginnings Broadside Press has become one of the most influential publishers of contemporary black poetry; its titles include the work of young writers as well as recent books by established poets. Since 1969 he has been reference librarian and poet-in-residence at the University of Detroit and has taught at the University of Michigan; he continues to operate the Broadside Press out of his Detroit home.

Ballad of Birmingham

(On the bombing of a church in Birmingham, Alabama, 1963)

"Mother dear, may I go downtown
Instead of out to play,
And march the streets of Birmingham
In a Freedom March today?"

"No, baby, no, you may not go,
For the dogs are fierce and wild,
And clubs and hoses, guns and jails
Aren't good for a little child."

"But, mother, I won't be alone.
Other children will go with me,
And march the streets of Birmingham
To make our country free."

"No, baby, no, you may not go,
For I fear those guns will fire.
But you may go to church instead
And sing in the children's choir."

She has combed and brushed her night-dark hair,
And bathed rose petal sweet,
And drawn white gloves on her small brown hands,
And white shoes on her feet.

The mother smiled to know her child
Was in the sacred place,
But that smile was the last smile
To come upon her face.

For when she heard the explosion,
Her eyes grew wet and wild.
She raced through the streets of Birmingham
Calling for her child.

She clawed through bits of glass and brick,
Then lifted out a shoe.
"O, here's the shoe my baby wore,
But, baby, where are you?"

1969

Booker T. and W. E. B.

(Booker T. Washington and W. E. B. Du Bois)

"It seems to me," said Booker T.,
"It shows a mighty lot of cheek

To study chemistry and Greek
When Mister Charlie needs a hand
To hoe the cotton on his land,
And when Miss Ann looks for a cook,
Why stick your nose inside a book?"

"I don't agree," said W. E. B.
"If I should have the drive to seek
Knowledge of chemistry or Greek,
I'll do it. Charles and Miss can look
Another place for hand or cook.
Some men rejoice in skill of hand,
And some in cultivating land,
But there are others who maintain
The right to cultivate the brain."

"It seems to me," said Booker T.,
"That all you folks have missed the boat
Who shout about the right to vote,
And spend vain days and sleepless nights
In uproar over civil rights.
Just keep your mouths shut, do not grouse,
But work, and save, and buy a house."

"I don't agree," said W. E. B.,
"For what can property avail
If dignity and justice fail?
Unless you help to make the laws,
They'll steal your house with trumped-up clause.
A rope's as tight, a fire as hot,
No matter how much cash you've got.
Speak soft, and try your little plan,
But as for me, I'll be a man."

"It seems to me," said Booker T.—

"I don't agree,"
Said W. E. B.

1969

Pacific Epitaphs[3]

New Georgia

I loved to talk of home.
Now I lie silent here.

* * *

3. New Georgia, Bougainville, and Vella Lavella are three of the Solomon Islands; Borneo is the largest island in the East Indies; and Palawan is one of the Philippine Islands. All were captured by U.S. forces during the Second World War. Espiritu Santo, in the New Hebrides, was the site of an important American air base.

Palawan

Always the peacemaker,
I stepped between
One buddy armed with an automatic
And another with a submachine gun.

* * *

Espiritu Santu

I hated guns,
Was a poor marksman,
But struck one target.

* * *

Bougainville

A spent bullet
Entered the abdominal cavity
At an angle of thirty-five degrees,
Penetrated the *pars pylorica,*
Was deflected by the *sternum,*
Pierced the *auricula dextra,*
And severed my medical career.

* * *

Vella Vella

The rope hugged tighter
Than the girl I raped.

* * *

Borneo

Kilroy
Is
Here.

1971

WELDON KEES
(*1914–1955*)

Weldon Kees was born in Beatrice, Nebraska, in 1914. A versatile man, he was not only a poet but a painter in the abstract expressionist style, a jazz pianist, a composer, a photographer, and a documentary film maker. He disappeared on July 18, 1955, under circumstances which suggested that he had taken his own life.

Robinson

The dog stops barking after Robinson has gone.
His act is over. The world is a gray world,
Not without violence, and he kicks under the grand piano,
The nightmare chase well under way.

The mirror from Mexico, stuck to the wall,
Reflects nothing at all. The glass is black.
Robinson alone provides the image Robinsonian.

Which is all of the room—walls, curtains,
Shelves, bed, the tinted photograph of Robinson's first wife,
Rugs, vases, panatellas in a humidor.
They would fill the room if Robinson came in.

The pages in the books are blank,
The books that Robinson has read. That is his favorite chair,
Or where the chair would be if Robinson were here.

All day the phone rings. It could be Robinson
Calling. It never rings when he is here.

Outside, white buildings yellow in the sun.
Outside, the birds circle continuously
Where trees are actual and take no holiday.

1947

RANDALL JARRELL
(*1914–1965*)

Randall Jarrell was born in Nashville, Tennessee, on May 16, 1914. His family soon moved to California, his parents were divorced, and he spent a year or so in Hollywood with grandparents and a great-grandmother. He then returned to Nashville, where he spent a somewhat drab Depression childhood. His refuge was books and the local public library.

Jarrell studied at Vanderbilt University, moving from psychology to English. In 1937–39 he taught at Kenyon College, and his friends there—John Crowe Ransom, Robert Lowell, and the novelist Peter Taylor—have all written of his gaiety, learning, and bright assurance. In 1942 he enlisted in the Army Air Corps. He washed out as a pilot, then served as a control tower operator working with B-29 crews.

After the war in 1946 Jarrell taught at Sarah Lawrence and served as acting literary editor of the *Nation*; from 1947 until his death he taught at the Women's College of the University of North Carolina at Greensboro, and occasionally visited other colleges and universities. In 1965 he was struck by a car and died.

The Death of the Ball Turret Gunner[1]

From my mother's sleep I fell into the State,
And I hunched in its belly till my wet fur froze.
Six miles from earth, loosed from its dream of life,
I woke to black flak and the nightmare fighters.
When I died they washed me out of the turret with a hose.

1945

Eighth Air Force[2]

If, in an odd angle of the hutment,
A puppy laps the water from a can
Of flowers, and the drunk sergeant shaving
Whistles *O Paradiso!*[3]—shall I say that man
Is not as men have said: a wolf to man?[4]

The other murderers troop in yawning;
Three of them play Pitch,[5] one sleeps, and one
Lies counting missions, lies there sweating
Till even his heart beats: One; One; One.
O murderers! . . . Still, this is how it's done:

This is a war. . . . But since these play, before they die,
Like puppies with their puppy; since, a man,
I did as these have done, but did not die—
I will content the people as I can
And give up these to them: Behold the man![6]

I have suffered, in a dream, because of him,
Many things;[7] for this last saviour, man,
I have lied as I lie now. But what is lying?
Men wash their hands, in blood, as best they can:
I find no fault in this just man.

1948

1. "A ball turret was a plexiglass sphere set into the belly of a B-17 or B-24, and inhabited by two .50 caliber machine-guns and one man, a short small man. When this gunner tracked with his machine guns a fighter attacking his bomber from below, he revolved with the turret; hunched upside-down in his little sphere, he looked like the foetus in the womb. The fighters which attacked him were armed with cannon firing explosive shells. The hose was a steam hose" (Jarrell's note).

2. " 'Eighth Air Force' is a poem about the air force which bombed the continent from England. The man who lies counting missions has one to go before being sent home. The phrases from the Gospels compare such criminals and scapegoats as these with that earlier criminal and scapegoat about whom the Gospels were written" (Jarrell's note). And, later, Jarrell remarked: " 'Eighth Air Force' expresses better than any other of the poems I wrote about the war what I felt about the war."

3. An operatic aria.

4. An often quoted phrase from the Roman poet Plautus (ca. 254–184 B.C.), *Asinaria*, II, iv, 88. In particular, Jarrell may be alluding to Bartolomeo Vanzetti's (1888–1927) speech in the court where he and Nicola Sacco had been convicted of murder and sentenced to death in what amounted to a trial of their Anarchistic political beliefs.

5. A card game.

6. Pilate offered the Jews their choice whether Jesus or Barabbas should be released, and the people chose Barabbas. "Pilate therefore went forth again, and said to them, Behold, I bring him forth to you, that you may know that I find no fault in him. Then came Jesus forth, wearing the crown of thorns, and the purple robe. And Pilate said unto them, Behold the man!" (*John* 19:4–5.)

7. Just before calling on the Jews to decide between Jesus and Barabbas, Pilate received a message from his wife: "Have nothing to do with that just man: for I have suffered many things this day in a dream because of him." (*Matthew* 27:19.)

A Girl in a Library[8]

An object among dreams, you sit here with your shoes off
And curl your legs up under you; your eyes
Close for a moment, your face moves toward sleep . . .
You are very human.
But my mind, gone out in tenderness,
Shrinks from its object with a thoughtful sigh.
This is a waist the spirit breaks its arm on.
The gods themselves, against you, struggle in vain.[8a]
This broad low strong-boned brow; these heavy eyes;
These calves, grown muscular with certainties;
This nose, three medium-sized pink strawberries
—But I exaggerate. In a little you will leave:
I'll hear, half squeal, half shriek, your laugh of greeting—
Then, *decrescendo,*[9] bars of that strange speech
In which each sound sets out to seek each other,
Murders its own father, marries its own mother,
And ends as one grand transcendental vowel.

(Yet for all I know, the Egyptian Helen spoke so.)
As I look, the world contracts around you:
I see Brünnhilde had brown braids and glasses
She used for studying; Salome straight brown bangs,
A calf's brown eyes, and sturdy light-brown limbs
Dusted with cinnamon, an apple-dumpling's . . .
Many a beast has gnawn a leg off and got free,
Many a dolphin curved up from Necessity—
The trap has closed about you, and you sleep.
If someone questioned you, *What doest thou here?*
You'd knit your brows like an orangoutang
(But not so sadly; not so thoughtfully)
And answer with a pure heart, guilelessly:
I'm studying. . . .
If only you were not!

Assignments,
recipes,
the *Official Rulebook*
Of Basketball—ah, let them go; you needn't mind.
The soul has no assignments, neither cooks
Nor referees: it wastes its time.
It wastes its time.
Here in this enclave there are centuries
For you to waste: the short and narrow stream
Of Life meanders into a thousand valleys

8. " 'A Girl in a Library' is a poem about the New World and the Old: about a girl, a student of Home Economics and Physical Education, who has fallen asleep in the library of a Southern college; about a woman who looks out of one book, Pushkin's *Eugen Onegin,* at this girl asleep among so many; and about the *I* of the poem, a man somewhere between the two" (Jarrell's note).

8a. From *The Maid of Orleans,* a play by Friedrich Schiller (1759–1805): "With stupidity the gods themselves struggle in vain."

9. In music, growing softer.

Of all that was, or might have been, or is to be.
The books, just leafed through, whisper endlessly . . .
Yet it is hard. One sees in your blurred eyes
The "uneasy half-soul" Kipling saw in dogs'.[1]
One sees it, in the glass, in one's own eyes.
In rooms alone, in galleries, in libraries,
In tears, in searchings of the heart, in staggering joys
We memorize once more our old creation,
Humanity: with what yawns the unwilling
Flesh puts on its spirit, O my sister!

So many dreams! And not one troubles
Your sleep of life? no self stares shadowily
From these worn hexahedrons, beckoning
With false smiles, tears? . . .
                                        Meanwhile Tatyana
Larina[2] (gray eyes nickel with the moonlight
That falls through the willows onto Lensky's tomb;
Now young and shy, now old and cold and sure)
Asks, smiling: "But what is she dreaming of, fat thing?"
I answer: She's not fat. She isn't dreaming.
She purrs or laps or runs, all in her sleep;
Believes, awake, that she is beautiful;
She never dreams.
                              Those sunrise-colored clouds
Around man's head[3]—that inconceivable enchantment
From which, at sunset, we come back to life
To find our graves dug, families dead, selves dying:
Of all this, Tanya, she is innocent.
For nineteen years she's faced reality:
They look alike already.
                                        They say, man wouldn't be
The best thing in this world—and isn't he?—
If he were not too good for it.[4] But she
—She's good enough for it.
                                        And yet sometimes
Her sturdy form, in its pink strapless formal,
Is as if bathed in moonlight—modulated
Into a form of joy, a Lydian mode;[5]

1. Alludes to Rudyard Kipling's poem, "Supplication of the Black Aberdeen," in which the dog prays to his master not to leave him, and attributes to him the godlike power of having made "This dim, distressed half-soul that hurts me so."

2. The heroine of Pushkin's *Eugen Onegin,* Tatyana (or Tanya) Larina is a naïve country girl who is infatuated with the melancholy, cynical Onegin, but is rejected by him. He provokes a duel with Lensky, her sister's lover and his own best friend, in which Lensky is killed. Remorseful, Onegin travels abroad. Several years later he returns to find that Tatyana, now the wife of a prince, has become a sophisticated beauty, and he falls in love with her. Though she still loves Onegin, she refuses to betray her husband.

3. From Wordsworth's *Ode: Intimations of Immortality:* "But trailing clouds of glory do we come / From God, who is our home." He believed that children are endowed with a special awareness of nature that dims and dies after they are born and grow to adulthood.

4. Jarrell says in his notes that this is a quotation but declines to identify it.

5. A variant of the major scale in music, whose softer tone has been used by many composers to express a subdued, religious joy.

This Wooden Mean's a kind, furred animal
That speaks, in the Wild of things, delighting riddles
To the soul that listens, trusting . . .
Poor senseless Life:
When, in the last light sleep of dawn, the messenger
Comes with his message, you will not awake.
He'll give his feathery whistle, shake you hard,
You'll look with wide eyes at the dewy yard
And dream, with calm slow factuality:
"Today's Commencement. My bachelor's degree
In Home Ec., my doctorate of philosophy
In Phys. Ed.
[Tanya, they won't even *scan*]
Are waiting for me. . . ."
Oh, Tatyana,
The Angel comes: better to squawk like a chicken
Than to say with truth, "But I'm a *good* girl,"
And Meet his Challenge with a last firm strange
Uncomprehending smile; and—then, then!—see
The blind date that has stood you up: your life.
(For all this, if it isn't, perhaps, life,
Has yet, at least, a language of its own
Different from the books'; worse than the books'.)
And yet, the ways we miss our lives are life.
Yet . . . yet . . .
to have one's life add up to *yet!*

You sigh a shuddering sigh. Tatyana murmurs,
"Don't cry, little peasant"; leaves us with a swift
"Good-bye, good-bye . . . Ah, don't think ill of me . . ."
Your eyes open: you sit here thoughtlessly.

I love you—and yet—and yet—I love you.

Don't cry, little peasant. Sit and dream.
One comes, a finger's width beneath your skin,
To the braided maidens singing as they spin;
There sound the shepherd's pipe, the watchman's rattle[6]
Across the short dark distance of the years.
I am a thought of yours: and yet, you do not think . . .
The firelight of a long, blind, dreaming story
Lingers upon your lips; and I have seen
Firm, fixed forever in your closing eyes,
The Corn King beckoning to his Spring Queen.[7]

1951

6. The "braided maidens," shepherd, and watchman are minor characters in Richard Wagner's operas who have good tunes to sing but are utterly unaware of the significance of the events which transpire around them.

7. "The Corn King and the Spring Queen went by many names; in the beginning they were the man and woman who, after ruling for a time, were torn to pieces and scattered over the fields in order that the grain might grow" (Jarrell's note).

Next Day

Moving from Cheer to Joy, from Joy to All,
I take a box
And add it to my wild rice, my Cornish game hens.
The slacked or shorted, basketed, identical
Food-gathering flocks
Are selves I overlook. Wisdom, said William James,

Is learning what to overlook.[8] And I am wise
If that is wisdom.
Yet somehow, as I buy All from these shelves
And the boy takes it to my station wagon,
What I've become
Troubles me even if I shut my eyes.

When I was young and miserable and pretty
And poor, I'd wish
What all girls wish: to have a husband,
A house and children. Now that I'm old, my wish
Is womanish:
That the boy putting groceries in my car

See me. It bewilders me he doesn't see me.
For so many years
I was good enough to eat: the world looked at me
And its mouth watered. How often they have undressed me,
The eyes of strangers!
And, holding their flesh within my flesh, their vile

Imaginings within my imagining,
I too have taken
The chance of life. Now the boy pats my dog
And we start home. Now I am good.
The last mistaken,
Ecstatic, accidental bliss, the blind

Happiness that, bursting, leaves upon the palm
Some soap and water—
It was so long ago, back in some Gay
Twenties, Nineties, I don't know . . . Today I miss
My lovely daughter
Away at school, my sons away at school,

My husband away at work—I wish for them.
The dog, the maid,
And I go through the sure unvarying days
At home in them. As I look at my life,

8. William James (1842–1910) was an American philosopher and psychologist; the quotation, slightly paraphrased is from *The Principles of Psychology* (1890).

I am afraid
Only that it will change, as I am changing:

I am afraid, this morning, of my face.
It looks at me
From the rear-view mirror, with the eyes I hate,
The smile I hate. Its plain, lined look
Of gray discovery
Repeats to me: "You're old." That's all, I'm old.

And yet I'm afraid, as I was at the funeral
I went to yesterday.
My friend's cold made-up face, granite among its flowers,
Her undressed, operated-on, dressed body
Were my face and body.
As I think of her I hear her telling me

How young I seem; I *am* exceptional;
I think of all I have.
But really no one is exceptional,
No one has anything, I'm anybody,
I stand beside my grave
Confused with my life, that is commonplace and solitary.

1965

JOHN BERRYMAN
(*1914–1972*)

John Berryman was born John Smith on October 25, 1914, in McAlester, Oklahoma. He lived till the age of ten in Anadarko, a nearby town where his father, also named John Smith, was a banker and his mother a schoolteacher. Then the family moved to Tampa, Florida. It was here that his parents' quarrels, furious for years, ended when his father shot himself outside his son's window. The widow brought John and a younger son to Gloucester, Massachusetts, and then to New York City. Here she married another banker, John Berryman, whose name the children took. The stepfather was soon to divorce his wife, but he remained kind to the children. He sent John to a private school in Connecticut (South Kent School), and then to Columbia College. John Berryman received a B.A. in 1936, and then attended Clare College, Cambridge, on a fellowship. When he returned to the United States he taught for a year at Wayne State, then from 1940 to 1943 at Harvard, and following that, for eight years, off and on, at Princeton. From 1955 until his death he taught at the University of Minnesota. A nervous, tense man prone to overdrinking, Berryman lived turbulently. He was married three times. In later life, he was received into Roman Catholicism, the faith of his childhood. On January 7, 1972, he threw himself from a bridge in Minneapolis to end his life at the age of fifty-seven.

A Professor's Song

(. . rabid or dog-dull.) Let me tell you how
The Eighteenth Century couplet ended. Now
Tell me. Troll me the sources of that Song—
Assigned last week—by Blake. Come, come along,
Gentlemen. (Fidget and huddle, do. Squint soon.)
I want to end these fellows all by noon.

'That deep romantic chasm'[8]—an early use;
The word is from the French, by our abuse
Fished out a bit. (Red all your eyes. O when?)
'A poet is a man speaking to men':[9]
But I am then a poet, am I not?—
Ha ha. The radiator, please. Well, what?

Alive now—no—Blake would have written prose,
But movement following movement crisply flows,
So much the better, better the much so,
As burbleth Mozart. Twelve. The class can go.
Until I meet you, then, in Upper Hell
Convulsed, foaming immortal blood: farewell.

1958

The Dream Songs [1]

14

Life, friends, is boring. We must not say so.
After all, the sky flashes, the great sea yearns,
we ourselves flash and yearn,
and moreover my mother told me as a boy
(repeatingly) 'Ever to confess you're bored
means you have no

Inner Resources.' I conclude now I have no
inner resources, because I am heavy bored.
Peoples bore me,
literature bores me, especially great literature,
Henry bores me, with his plights & gripes
as bad as achilles,[1a]

8. Quoted from Coleridge's "Kubla Khan," line 12.

9. Quoted from Wordsworth's preface to the second edition of *Lyrical Ballads*.

1. "[*The Dream Songs* are] essentially about an imaginary character (not the poet, not me) named Henry, a white American in early middle age sometimes in blackface, who has suffered an irreversible loss and talks about himself sometimes in the first person, sometimes in the third, sometimes even in the second; he has a friend, never named, who addresses him as Mr. Bones and variants thereof" (Berryman's note).

1a. Achilles, the Greek warrior whose strength was needed if the Trojans were to be defeated, withdrew from fighting over a slight from the Greeks' general, King Agamemnon.

who loves people and valiant art, which bores me.
And the tranquil hills, & gin, look like a drag
and somehow a dog
has taken itself & its tail considerably away
into mountains or sea or sky, leaving
behind: me, wag.

1964

16

Henry's pelt was put on sundry walls
where it did much resemble Henry and
them persons was delighted.
Especially his long & glowing tail
by all them was admired, and visitors.
They whistled: This is *it*!

Golden, whilst your frozen daiquiris
whir at midnight, gleams on you his fur
& silky & black.
Mission accomplished, pal.
My molten yellow & moonless bag,
drained, hangs at rest.

Collect in the cold depths barracuda. Ay,
in Sealdah Station some possessionless
children survive to die.
The Chinese communes hum. Two daiquiris
withdrew into a corner of the gorgeous room
and one told the other a lie.

1964

75[2]

Turning it over, considering, like a madman
Henry put forth a book.
No harm resulted from this.
Neither the menstruating stars (nor man) was moved
at once.
Bare dogs drew closer for a second look

and performed their friendly operations there.
Refreshed, the bark rejoiced.
Seasons went and came.
Leaves fell, but only a few.
Something remarkable about this
unshedding bulky bole-proud blue-green moist

2. This Dream Song is dedicated to Berryman's close friend Saul Bellow, the American novelist.

thing made by savage & thoughtful
surviving Henry
began to strike the passers from despair
so that sore on their shoulders old men hoisted
six-foot sons and polished women called
small girls to dream awhile toward the flashing & bursting tree!

1964

76

Henry's Confession

Nothin very bad happen to me lately.
How you explain that? —I explain that, Mr Bones,
terms o' your bafflin odd sobriety.
Sober as man can get, no girls, no telephones,
what could happen bad to Mr Bones?
—*If* life is a handkerchief sandwich,

in a modesty of death I join my father
who dared so long agone leave me.
A bullet on a concrete stoop
close by a smothering southern sea
spreadeagled on an island, by my knee.
—You is from hunger, Mr Bones,

I offers you this handkerchief, now set
your left foot by my right foot,
shoulder to shoulder, all that jazz,
arm in arm, by the beautiful sea,[3]
hum a little, Mr Bones.
—I saw nobody coming, so I went instead.

1964

149

This world is gradually becoming a place
where I do not care to be any more. Can Delmore die?[4]
I don't suppose
in all them years a day went ever by
without a loving thought for him. Welladay.
In the brightness of his promise,

unstained, I saw him thro' the mist of the actual
blazing with insight, warm with gossip

3. A popular song of 1914.

4. Delmore Schwartz (see p. 319) was a close friend of Berryman's and in 1940 helped to get him his first teaching job, at Harvard. *His Toy, His Dream, His Rest,* the second book of Berryman's *Dream Songs* (in which this poem appears), is in part dedicated "to the sacred memory of Delmore Schwartz."

thro' all our Harvard years
when both of us were just becoming known
I got him out of a police-station once, in Washington, the world is *tref*[5]
and grief too astray for tears.

I imagine you have heard the terrible news,
that Delmore Schwartz is dead, miserably & alone,
in New York: he sang me a song
'I am the Brooklyn poet Delmore Schwartz
Harms & the child I sing,[6] two parents' torts'
when he was young & gift-strong.

1968

312

I have moved to Dublin to have it out with you,
majestic Shade,[7] You whom I read so well
so many years ago,
did I read your lesson right? did I see through
your phases to the real? your heaven, your hell
did I enquire properly into?

For years then I forgot you, I put you down,
ingratitude is the necessary curse
of making things new:[8]
I brought my family to see me through,
I brought my homage & my soft remorse,
I brought a book or two

only, including in the end your last
strange poems made under the shadow of death
Your high figures float
again across my mind and all your past
fills my walled garden with your honey breath
wherein I move, a mote.

1968

Henry's Understanding

He was reading late, at Richard's, down in Maine,
aged 32? Richard & Helen long in bed,
my good wife long in bed.
All I had to do was strip & get into my bed,
putting the marker in the book, & sleep,
& wake to a hot breakfast.

5. Ritually unclean, according to Jewish law.

6. A parody of the opening words of Virgil's *Aeneid*, "Arms and the man I sing." *Torts:* wrongs.

7. W. B. Yeats, whom Berryman called his first and last influence, whom he met in 1936. Berryman was a student at Clare College, Cambridge University.

8. An adaptation of Ezra Pound's famous slogan, "Make it new."

Off the coast was an island, P'tit Manaan,
the bluff from Richard's lawn was almost sheer.
A chill at four o'clock.
It only takes a few minutes to make a man.
A concentration upon now & here.
Suddenly, unlike Bach,

& horribly, unlike Bach, it occurred to me
that *one* night, instead of warm pajamas,
I'd take off all my clothes
& cross the damp cold lawn & down the bluff
into the terrible water & walk forever
under it out toward the island.

1972

DYLAN THOMAS
(*1914–1953*)

Dylan Thomas was born October 27, 1914, in Swansea, Wales, which he described bitterly as "the smug darkness of a provincial town." Thomas was educated at the Swansea Grammar School, which he left in 1931. His father, a schoolteacher, urged him to go to a university, but Thomas adduced the example of Bernard Shaw to justify his attempting to become a writer at once. His style, in fact, was formed by the time he was seventeen. In 1934 he published, at twenty, his first book, 18 *Poems*, and went to live in London in that year. In 1936 he met Caitlin Macnamara, a young Irishwoman whose temperament was as turbulent as his own; they married the following year, and subsequently had three children. Thomas supported himself in his last years in part by long lecture tours in the United States, during which—drunk or sober—he gave magnificent readings of poems (mostly by other writers) on dozens of college campuses. His extravagant drinking gradually usurped most of his time, and chronic alcoholism helped bring about his early death on November 9, 1953, in New York City.

The Force That Through the Green Fuse Drives the Flower

The force that through the green fuse drives the flower
Drives my green age; that blasts the roots of trees
Is my destroyer.
And I am dumb to tell the crooked rose
My youth is bent by the same wintry fever.

The force that drives the water through the rocks
Drives my red blood; that dries the mouthing streams
Turns mine to wax.

And I am dumb to mouth unto my veins
How at the mountain spring the same mouth sucks.

The hand that whirls the water in the pool
Stirs the quicksand; that ropes the blowing wind
Hauls my shroud[1] sail.
And I am dumb to tell the hanging man
How of my clay is made the hangman's lime.

The lips of time leech to the fountain head;
Love drips and gathers, but the fallen blood
Shall calm her sores.
And I am dumb to tell a weather's wind
How time has ticked a heaven round the stars.

And I am dumb to tell the lover's tomb
How at my sheet goes the same crooked worm.

1934

The Hand That Signed the Paper

The hand that signed the paper felled a city;
Five sovereign fingers taxed the breath,
Doubled the globe of dead and halved a country;
These five kings did a king to death.

The mighty hand leads to a sloping shoulder,
The finger joints are cramped with chalk;
A goose's quill has put an end to murder
That put an end to talk.

The hand that signed the treaty bred a fever,
And famine grew, and locusts came;
Great is the hand that holds dominion over
Man by a scribbled name.

The five kings count the dead but do not soften
The crusted wound nor stroke the brow;
A hand rules pity as a hand rules heaven;
Hands have no tears to flow.

1936

A Refusal to Mourn the Death, by Fire, of a Child in London

Never until the mankind making
Bird beast and flower
Fathering and all humbling darkness

1. Burial garment; also, the ropes that run from a boat's sides to the top of its mast, bracing it against sidewards movement.

Tells with silence the last light breaking
And the still hour
Is come of the sea tumbling in harness

And I must enter again the round
Zion[2] of the water bead
And the synagogue of the ear of corn
Shall I let pray the shadow of a sound
Or sow my salt seed
In the least valley of sackcloth to mourn

The majesty and burning of the child's death.
I shall not murder
The mankind of her going with a grave truth
Nor blaspheme down the stations of the breath[3]
With any further
Elegy of innocence and youth.

Deep with the first dead lies London's daughter,
Robed in the long friends,
The grains beyond age, the dark veins of her mother,
Secret by the unmourning water
Of the riding Thames.
After the first death, there is no other.

1946

In My Craft or Sullen Art

In my craft or sullen art
Exercised in the still night
When only the moon rages
And the lovers lie abed
With all their griefs in their arms,
I labour by singing light
Not for ambition or bread
Or the strut and trade of charms
On the ivory stages
But for the common wages
Of their most secret heart.

Not for the proud man apart
From the raging moon I write
On these spindrift[4] pages
Nor for the towering dead
With their nightingales and psalms
But for the lovers, their arms
Round the griefs of the ages,

2. In the Biblical book of Exodus, the promised land of the Hebrews; hence, the City of God.

3. By analogy with the "stations of the Cross," images of the events of Christ's passion, and the appropriate devotions for each.

4. Sea spray.

Who pay no praise or wages
Nor heed my craft or art.

1946

Fern Hill[5]

Now as I was young and easy under the apple boughs
About the lilting house and happy as the grass was green,
The night above the dingle[6] starry,
Time let me hail and climb
Golden in the heydays of his eyes,
And honoured among wagons I was prince of the apple towns
And once below a time I lordly had the trees and leaves
Trail with daisies and barley
Down the rivers of the windfall light.

And as I was green and carefree, famous among the barns
About the happy yard and singing as the farm was home,
In the sun that is young once only,
Time let me play and be
Golden in the mercy of his means,
And green and golden I was huntsman and herdsman, the calves
Sang to my horn, the foxes on the hills barked clear and cold,
And the sabbath rang slowly
In the pebbles of the holy streams.

All the sun long it was running, it was lovely, the hay
Fields high as the house, the tunes from the chimneys, it was air
And playing, lovely and watery
And fire green as grass.
And nightly under the simple stars
As I rode to sleep the owls were bearing the farm away,
All the moon long I heard, blessed among stables, the night-jars
Flying with the ricks,[7] and the horses
Flashing into the dark.

And then to awake, and the farm, like a wanderer white
With the dew, come back, the cock on his shoulder: it was all
Shining, it was Adam and maiden,
The sky gathered again
And the sun grew round that very day.
So it must have been after the birth of the simple light
In the first, spinning place,[8] the spellbound horses walking warm
Out of the whinnying green stable
On to the fields of praise.

5. A country house where the poet's aunt lived, and where he spent summer holidays as a boy.

6. Valley, dale.

7. Piles of hay.

8. Refers to the story of the Creation in the Biblical book of Genesis.

And honoured among foxes and pheasants by the gay house
Under the new made clouds and happy as the heart was long,
In the sun born over and over,
I ran my heedless ways,
My wishes raced through the house high hay
And nothing I cared, at my sky blue trades, that time allows
In all his tuneful turning so few and such morning songs
Before the children green and golden
Follow him out of grace,

Nothing I cared, in the lamb white days, that time would take me
Up to the swallow thronged loft by the shadow of my hand,
In the moon that is always rising,
Nor that riding to sleep
I should hear him fly with the high fields
And wake to the farm forever fled from the childless land.
Oh as I was young and easy in the mercy of his means,
Time held me green and dying
Though I sang in my chains like the sea.

1946

Do Not Go Gentle into That Good Night[9]

Do not go gentle into that good night,
Old age should burn and rave at close of day;
Rage, rage against the dying of the light.

Though wise men at their end know dark is right,
Because their words had forked no lightning they
Do not go gentle into that good night.

Good men, the last wave by, crying how bright
Their frail deeds might have danced in a green bay,
Rage, rage against the dying of the light.

Wild men who caught and sang the sun in flight,
And learn, too late, they grieved it on its way,
Do not go gentle into that good night.

Grave men, near death, who see with blinding sight
Blind eyes could blaze like meteors and be gay,
Rage, rage against the dying of the light.

And you, my father, there on the sad height,
Curse, bless, me now with your fierce tears, I pray.

9. This poem was written during the final illness of Thomas' father.

Do not go gentle into that good night.
Rage, rage against the dying of the light.

1952

ROBERT LOWELL
(*1917–*)

Robert Lowell was born March 1, 1917, in Boston, a member of a patrician New England family, with James Russell Lowell for great-great-uncle and Amy Lowell for distant cousin. He spent his early years in Boston except for several periods in Washington and Philadelphia, where his father, a naval officer, was stationed. He attended St. Mark's School and came to know the poet Richard Eberhart, who was teaching there. Then, or soon after, Lowell began to prepare himself with uncanny deliberateness for the life of a poet. He enrolled at Harvard and immersed himself in courses in English literature; but after two years he abruptly transferred to Kenyon College so he could study with John Crowe Ransom. Under Ransom's guidance he studied the classics, logic, and philosophy. After graduation in 1940, Lowell attended Louisiana State University, where he studied with Robert Penn Warren and Cleanth Brooks. At the same time he formed a close friendship with Allen Tate, so that he was immersed in the school of New Criticism and in their predilection for "formal, difficult poems."

In 1940, the year he was graduated from Kenyon College, Lowell married the novelist Jean Stafford. (They were divorced in 1948.) He also was converted to Catholicism. Lowell was greatly disturbed by the advent of the Second World War. At first he tried, unsuccessfully, to enlist. Then in 1943, as his apocalyptic view sharpened, he grew horrified, particularly by the bombing of civilians, and declared himself a conscientious objector. He was given a year's jail sentence but was released after six months, and afterwards lived for a time in Black Rock, near Bridgeport, Connecticut.

Lowell has confronted recent events with courage and conviction. He has been at the center of things, especially in opposition to the Vietnam War, both through poems and by public action. In temporary withdrawal from the political scene, he lived in England from 1970 to 1974. He now teaches creative writing at Harvard.

The Quaker Graveyard in Nantucket[8]

(FOR WARREN WINSLOW, DEAD AT SEA)

Let man have dominion over the fishes of the sea and the fowls of the air and the beasts and the whole earth, and every creeping creature that moveth upon the earth.[9]

I

A brackish reach of shoal off Madaket,—[1]
The sea was still breaking violently and night

8. An island south of the Massachusetts coast, famous as the home port for whaling ships in the nineteenth century. Many of these were owned and manned by Quakers. Warren Winslow, a cousin of Lowell, died at sea when his naval vessel went down.

9. The epigraph is slightly paraphrased from *Genesis* 1:26.

1. A place on the west of Nantucket Island.

Had steamed into our North Atlantic Fleet,
When the drowned sailor clutched the drag-net. Light
Flashed from his matted head and marble feet,
He grappled at the net
With the coiled, hurdling muscles of his thighs:
The corpse was bloodless, a botch of reds and whites,
Its open, staring eyes
Were lustreless dead-lights[2]
Or cabin-windows on a stranded hulk
Heavy with sand.[3] We weight the body, close
Its eyes and heave it seaward whence it came,[4]
Where the heel-headed dogfish[5] barks its nose
On Ahab's void and forehead;[6] and the name
Is blocked in yellow chalk.
Sailors, who pitch this portent at the sea
Where dreadnaughts[7] shall confess
Its hell-bent deity,
When you are powerless
To sand-bag this Atlantic bulwark, faced
By the earth-shaker, green, unwearied, chaste
In his steel scales: ask for no Orphean lute
To pluck life back.[8] The guns of the steeled fleet
Recoil and then repeat
The hoarse salute.

II

Whenever winds are moving and their breath
Heaves at the roped-in bulwarks of this pier,
The terns and sea-gulls tremble at your death
In these home waters. Sailor, can you hear
The Pequod's[1] sea wings, beating landward, fall
Headlong and break on our Atlantic wall
Off 'Sconset,[2] where the yawing S-boats splash
The bellbuoy, with ballooning spinnakers,[3]
As the entangled, screeching mainsheet[4] clears
The blocks: off Madaket, where lubbers[5] lash

2. Metal covers that close over portholes and ventilators to keep out light and water.

3. The imagery of these lines is largely borrowed from Henry David Thoreau, *Cape Cod* (Boston, 1898, pp. 5–6), as Hugh B. Staples has pointed out:

"The brig *St. John*, from Galway, Ireland, laden with emigrants, was wrecked on Sunday morning; it was now Tuesday morning, and the sea was still breaking violently on the rocks. . . . I saw many marble feet and matted heads as the clothes were raised, and one livid, swollen, and mangled body of a drowned girl . . . ; the coiled-up wreck of a human hulk, gashed by the rocks or fishes, so that the bone and muscle were exposed, but quite bloodless, —merely red and white,— with wide-open and staring eyes, yet lustreless, dead-lights; or like the cabin windows of a stranded vessel, filled with sand . . ."

4. The origin of life.

5. A small shark.

6. Ahab is the monomaniacal hunter of the white whale in Herman Melville's *Moby Dick*. This phrase, used for "heart and head," implies the emptiness of Ahab's heart and the strength of his will.

7. Battleships.

8. Orpheus went to Hades and by his music persuaded Persephone to let his wife, Eurydice, return to earth.

1. Ahab's ship, which the whale Moby Dick destroyed.

2. Siasconset, on eastern Nantucket. S-boats are large racing sailboats once popular in New England.

3. Large, parachute-like racing sails designed to catch the wind.

4. The rope by which a sailboat's main sails is angled to the wind. *Clears the blocks:* is disentangled from the pulleys through which it runs.

5. Landlubbers.

The heavy surf and throw their long lead squids
For blue-fish? Sea-gulls blink their heavy lids
Seaward. The winds' wings beat upon the stones,
Cousin, and scream for you and the claws rush
At the sea's throat and wring it in the slush
Of this old Quaker graveyard where the bones
Cry out in the long night for the hurt beast[6]
Bobbing by Ahab's whaleboats in the East.

III

All you recovered from Poseidon[7] died
With you, my cousin, and the harrowed brine
Is fruitless on the blue beard of the god,
Stretching beyond us to the castles in Spain,
Nantucket's[8] westward haven. To Cape Cod
Guns, cradled on the tide,
Blast the eelgrass about a waterclock
Of bilge and backwash, roil the salt and sand
Lashing earth's scaffold, rock
Our warships in the hand
Of the great God, where time's contrition blues
Whatever it was these Quaker sailors lost
In the mad scramble of their lives. They died
When time was open-eyed,
Wooden and childish; only bones abide
There, in the nowhere, where their boats were tossed
Sky-high, where mariners had fabled news
Of IS,[9] the whited monster. What it cost
Them is their secret. In the sperm-whale's slick
I see the Quakers drown and hear their cry:
"If God himself had not been on our side,
If God himself had not been on our side,
When the Atlantic rose against us, why,
Then it had swallowed us up quick."[1]

IV

This is the end of the whaleroad[2] and the whale
Who spewed Nantucket bones on the thrashed swell
And stirred the troubled waters to whirlpools
To send the Pequod packing off to hell:
This is the end of them, three-quarters fools,
Snatching at straws to sail
Seaward and seaward on the turntail whale,
Spouting out blood and water as it rolls,
Sick as a dog to these Atlantic shoals:
Clamavimus,[3] O depths. Let the sea-gulls wail

6. Moby Dick.

7. Greek god of the sea.

8. From this island, off the coast of Massachusetts, the whalers put to sea. Many of them were Quakers.

9. Moby Dick, here identified with God, who told Moses, "I AM THAT I AM" and instructed him to say to the Israelites, "I AM hath sent me to you." (*Exodus* 3:14.) "Whited monster" is adapted from "whited sepulchre" (*Matthew* 23:27).

1. Alive.

2. An Old English kenning (or epithet) for the sea.

3. "We have cried" (Lat). Compare *Psalms* 130:1—"Out of the depths have I cried unto thee, O Lord."

For water, for the deep where the high tide
Mutters to its hurt self, mutters and ebbs.
Waves wallow in their wash, go out and out,
Leave only the death-rattle of the crabs,
The beach increasing, its enormous snout
Sucking the ocean's side.
This is the end of running on the waves;
We are poured out like water. Who will dance
The mast-lashed master of Leviathans[4]
Up from this field of Quakers in their unstoned graves?

V

When the whale's viscera go and the roll
Of its corruption overruns this world
Beyond tree-swept Nantucket and Wood's Hole[5]
And Martha's Vineyard, Sailor, will your sword
Whistle and fall and sink into the fat?
In the great ash-pit of Jehoshaphat[6]
The bones cry for the blood of the white whale,
The fat flukes arch and whack about its ears,
The death-lance churns into the sanctuary, tears
The gun-blue swingle, heaving like a flail,
And hacks the coiling life out: it works and drags
And rips the sperm-whale's midriff into rags,
Gobbets of blubber spill to wind and weather,
Sailor, and gulls go round the stoven[7] timbers
Where the morning stars sing out together[8]
And thunder shakes the white surf and dismembers
The red flag hammered in the mast-head.[9] Hide,
Our steel, Jonas Messias,[1] in Thy side.

VI

Our Lady of Walsingham[2]

There once the penitents took off their shoes
And then walked barefoot the remaining mile;
And the small trees, a stream and hedgerows file

4. Leviathan is a great water animal, mentioned in the Old Testament, here identified with the whale.

5. The closest point on the mainland of Massachusetts to Martha's Vineyard, an island near Nantucket.

6. "The valley of judgment. The world, according to some prophets and scientists, will end in fire" (Lowell, writing to Kimon Friar and John Malcolm Brinnin). Compare: "Let the heathen we wakened, and come unto the valley of Jehosophat; for there will I sit to judge all the heathen round about." (*Joel* 3:12).

7. Broken inwards.

8. From *Job* 38:7, "The morning stars sang together, and all the sons of God shouted for joy."

9. At the end of *Moby Dick,* as the Pequod is sinking, the Indian Tashtego's arm rises from the water to nail Ahab's flag to the sinking mast. A sky-hawk is caught between hammer and flag, and Melville says that the "bird of heaven" is dragged down with the satanic ship.

1. Jonah (in the New Testament, Jonas) is identified with the Messiah or Christ because Lowell imagines the whaler's harpoon penetrating the whale, and Jonah within it, just as the centurion's spear pierced the side of Christ, and also because Jonah, like Christ, emerged after a three-day "burial."

2. Adapted, Lowell has said, from E. I. Watkins, *Catholic Art and Culture,* London, 1947, p. 177: "For centuries the shrine of Our Lady of Walsingham has been an historical memory. Now once again pilgrims visit her image erected in a mediaeval chapel, where, it is said, they took off their shoes to walk barefoot the remaining mile to the shrine. . . . The road to the chapel is a quiet country lane shaded with trees, and lined on one side by a hedgerow. On the other, a stream flows beneath the

Slowly along the munching English lane,
Like cows to the old shrine, until you lose
Track of your dragging pain.
The stream flows down under the druid tree,
Shiloah's whirlpools gurgle and make glad
The castle of God. Sailor, you were glad
And whistled Sion[3] by that stream. But see:

Our Lady, too small for her canopy,
Sits near the altar. There's no comeliness
At all or charm in that expressionless
Face with its heavy eyelids. As before,
This face, for centuries a memory,
Non est species, neque decor,
Expressionless, expresses God: it goes
Past castled Sion. She knows what God knows,
Not Calvary's Cross nor crib at Bethlehem
Now, and the world shall come to Walsingham.

VII

The empty winds are creaking and the oak
Splatters and splatters on the cenotaph,[4]
The boughs are trembling and a gaff[5]
Bobs on the untimely stroke
Of the greased wash exploding on a shoal-bell[6]
In the old mouth of the Atlantic. It's well;
Atlantic, you are fouled with the blue sailors,
Sea-monsters, upward angel, downward fish:
Unmarried and corroding, spare of flesh
Mart once of supercilious, wing'd clippers,
Atlantic, where your bell-trap guts its spoil
You could cut the brackish winds with a knife
Here in Nantucket, and cast up the time
When the Lord God formed man from the sea's slime
And breathed into his face the breath of life,
And blue-lung'd combers lumbered to the kill.
The Lord survives the rainbow of His will.

1946

---

trees, the water symbol of the Holy Spirit, 'the waters of Shiloah that go softly,' the 'flow of the river making glad the city of God.' Within the chapel, an attractive example of Decorated architecture, near an altar of mediaeval fashion, is seated Our Lady's image. It is too small for its canopy, and is not superficially beautiful. 'Non est species neque decor,' there is no comeliness or charm in that expressionless face with heavy eyelids. But let us look carefully. . . . We become aware of an inner beauty more impressive than outward grace. That expressionless countenance expresses what is beyond expression. . . . Mary is beyond joy and sorrow. . . . No longer the Mother of Sorrows nor yet of the human joy of the crib, she understands the secret counsel of God to whose accomplishment Calvary and Bethlehem alike ministered."

3. Or Zion. Compare *Isaiah* 51:11: "Therefore the redeemed of the Lord shall return, and come with singing unto Zion."

4. A tomb for a person whose body is not buried there.

5. A wooden spar, part of the rigging of a sailboat.

4. A bell buoy marking shallow waters.

"To Speak of Woe That Is in Marriage"

"It is the future generation that presses into being by means of these exuberant feelings and supersensible soap bubbles of ours."

SCHOPENHAUER[4]

"The hot night makes us keep our bedroom windows open.
Our magnolia blossoms. Life begins to happen.
My hopped up husband drops his home disputes,
and hits the streets to cruise for prostitutes,
free-lancing out along the razor's edge.
This screwball might kill his wife, then take the pledge.
Oh the monotonous meanness of his lust. . . .
It's the injustice . . . he is so unjust—
whiskey-blind, swaggering home at five.
My only thought is how to keep alive.
What makes him tick? Each night now I tie
ten dollars and his car key to my thigh. . . .
Gored by the climacteric [4a] of his want,
he stalls above me like an elephant."

1959

Skunk Hour[5]

(FOR ELIZABETH BISHOP)[6]

Nautilus Island's hermit
heiress still lives through winter in her Spartan cottage;
her sheep still graze above the sea.
Her son's a bishop. Her farmer
is first selectman in our village;
she's in her dotage.

Thirsting for
the hierarchic privacy
of Queen Victoria's century,
she buys up all
the eyesores facing her shore,
and lets them fall.

The season's ill—
we've lost our summer millionaire,
who seemed to leap from an L. L. Bean[7]

4. Arthur Schopenhauer (1788–1860), pessimistic German philosopher.

4a. Also called the male menopause.

5. The scene is Castine, Maine, where Lowell had a summer house. As he has written, "The first four stanzas are meant to give a dawdling more or less amiable picture of a declining Maine sea town. I move from the ocean inland. Sterility howls through the scenery, but I try to give a tone of tolerance, humor, and randomness to the sad prospect." *The Contemporary Poet as Artist and Critic,* ed. Anthony Ostroff, p. 107.

6. "The dedication is to Elizabeth Bishop, because re-reading her suggested a way of breaking through the shell of my old manner. . . . 'Skunk Hour' is modelled on Miss Bishop's 'The Armadillo' [p. 309]. . . . Both . . . use short line stanzas, start with drifting description and end with a single animal" (Lowell's note).

7. A Maine mail order house that deals in sporting goods, including clothes for the outdoors.

catalogue. His nine-knot yawl [7a]
was auctioned off to lobstermen.
A red fox stain covers Blue Hill.[8]

And now our fairy
decorator brightens his shop for fall;
his fishnet's filled with orange cork,
orange, his cobbler's bench and awl;
there is no money in his work,
he'd rather marry.

One dark night,[9]
my Tudor Ford climbed the hill's skull;
I watched for love-cars. Lights turned down,
they lay together, hull to hull,
where the graveyard shelves on the town. . . .
My mind's not right.

A car radio bleats,
"Love, O careless Love. . . ."[1] I hear
my ill-spirit sob in each blood cell,
as if my hand were at its throat. . . .
I myself am hell;[2]
nobody's here—

only skunks, that search
in the moonlight for a bite to eat.
They march on their soles up Main Street:
white stripes, moonstruck eyes' red fire
under the chalk-dry and spar spire
of the Trinitarian Church.

I stand on top
of our back steps and breathe the rich air—
a mother skunk with her column of kittens swills the garbage pail.
She jabs her wedge-head in a cup
of sour cream, drops her ostrich tail,
and will not scare.[3]

1959

7a. Nine nautical miles an hour (about 10 mph) is fast for a sailboat, and indicates that the millionaire's two-masted yacht was fairly large—about 40 feet long.

8. "Meant to describe the rusty reddish color of autumn on Blue Hill, a Maine mountain near where we were living" (Lowell's note).

9. A reference, Lowell says, to *The Dark Night of the Soul* of St. John of the Cross.

1. A popular song of the time, entitled "Careless Love," which contains the two lines: "Now you see what careless love will do . . . / Make you kill yourself and your sweetheart too."

2. An adaptation of Lucifer's line, "Which way I fly is Hell; myself am Hell," in *Paradise Lost*, IV:75.

3. "The skunks," says Lowell, "are both quixotic and barbarously absurd, hence the tone of amusement and defiance." Their "affirmation" is therefore "ambiguous."

For the Union Dead[4]

"Relinquunt Omnia Servare Rem Publicam."[5]

The old South Boston Aquarium stands
in a Sahara of snow now. Its broken windows are boarded.
The bronze weathervane cod has lost half its scales.
The airy tanks are dry.

Once my nose crawled like a snail on the glass;
my hand tingled
to burst the bubbles
drifting from the noses of the cowed, compliant fish.

My hand draws back. I often sigh still
for the dark downward and vegetating kingdom
of the fish and reptile. One morning last March,
I pressed against the new barbed and galvanized

fence on the Boston Common. Behind their cage,
yellow dinosaur steamshovels were grunting
as they cropped up tons of mush and grass
to gouge their underworld garage.

Parking spaces luxuriate like civic
sandpiles in the heart of Boston.
A girdle of orange, Puritan-pumpkin colored girders
braces the tingling Statehouse,

shaking over the excavations, as it faces Colonel Shaw
and his bell-cheeked Negro infantry
on St. Gaudens' shaking Civil War relief,
propped by a plank splint against the garage's earthquake.

Two months after marching through Boston,
half the regiment was dead;
at the dedication,
William James[6] could almost hear the bronze Negroes breathe.

Their monument sticks like a fishbone
in the city's throat.
Its Colonel is as lean
as a compass-needle.

He has an angry wrenlike vigilance,
a greyhound's gentle tautness;

4. The poem was first published with the title, "Colonel Shaw and the Massachusetts 54th." The monument it describes is a bronze relief by Augustus Saint-Gaudens (1848–1907) depicting Robert Gould Shaw (1837–1863), commander of the first Negro regiment organized in a free state, who was killed in the assault his troops led against Fort Wagner, South Carolina. The relief, dedicated in 1897, stands on Boston Common opposite the Massachusetts State House.

5. "They give up everything to serve the Republic" (Lat).

6. (1842–1910), American philosopher and psychologist, who taught at Harvard.

he seems to wince at pleasure,
and suffocate for privacy.

He is out of bounds now. He rejoices in man's lovely,
peculiar power to choose life and die—
when he leads his black soldiers to death,
he cannot bend his back.

On a thousand small town New England greens,
the old white churches hold their air
of sparse, sincere rebellion; frayed flags
quilt the graveyards of the Grand Army of the Republic.[7]

The stone statues of the abstract Union Soldier
grow slimmer and younger each year—
wasp-wasted, they doze over muskets
and muse through their sideburns . . .

Shaw's father wanted no monument
except the ditch,
where his son's body was thrown [8]
and lost with his "niggers."

The ditch is nearer.
There are no statues for the last war[9] here;
on Boylston Street,[1] a commercial photograph
shows Hiroshima boiling

over a Mosler Safe, the "Rock of Ages"
that survived the blast. Space is nearer.
When I crouch to my television set,
the drained faces of Negro school-children[2] rise like balloons.

Colonel Shaw
is riding on his bubble,
he waits
for the blessèd break.

The Aquarium is gone. Everywhere,
giant finned cars nose forward like fish;
a savage servility
slides by on grease.

1959

7. The Union forces in the Civil War.

8. By the Confederate soldiers at Fort Wagner.

9. That is, the Second World War.

1. A street in downtown Boston.

2. Such as those who were conducted to the public schools of Little Rock, Arkansas, by Federal troops in 1957, enforcing the Supreme Court's demand for integrated schools.

Ezra Pound

Horizontal in a deckchair on the bleak ward,[6]
some feeble-minded felon in pajamas, clawing
a Social Credit[7] broadside from your table, you saying,
". . . here with a black suit and black briefcase; in the briefcase,
an abomination, Possum's[8] *hommage* to Milton."
Then sprung; Rapallo,[9] and then the decade gone;
then three years, then Eliot dead, you saying,
"And who is left to understand my jokes?
My old Brother in the arts . . . and besides, he was a smash of a poet."
He showed us his blotched, bent hands, saying, "Worms.
When I talked that nonsense about Jews on the Rome
wireless,[1] she knew it was shit, and still loved me."
And I, "Who else has been in Purgatory?"
And he, "To begin with a swelled head and end with swelled feet."

1969

Robert Frost

Robert Frost at midnight, the audience gone
to vapor, the great act laid on the shelf in mothballs,
his voice musical, raw and raw—he writes in the flyleaf:
"Robert Lowell from Robert Frost, his friend in the art."
"Sometimes I feel too full of myself," I say.
And he, misunderstanding, "When I am low,
I stray away. My son[2] wasn't your kind. The night
we told him Merrill Moore[3] would come to treat him,
he said, 'I'll kill him first.' One of my daughters thought things,
knew every male she met was out to make her;
the way she dresses, she couldn't make a whorehouse."
And I, "Sometimes I'm so happy I can't stand myself."
And he, "When I am too full of joy, I think
how little good my health did anyone near me."

1969

6. Lowell visited Pound when the latter was in St. Elizabeth's Hospital for the criminally insane, in Washington.
7. A dubious economic program which Pound fanatically supported.
8. Eliot, who originally denounced Milton, as Pound did, and then later recanted.
9. Released from the hospital, Pound went back to Rapallo, Italy, to live.
1. Pound talked several times on the Italian radio during the Second World War. "She" is Olga Rudge, Pound's companion.
2. Frost's son committed suicide.
3. A poet and psychoanalyst.

GWENDOLYN BROOKS
(1917–)

Gwendolyn Brooks was born June 7, 1917, in Topeka, Kansas. But she grew up in Chicago, was educated at the Englewood High School and Wilson Junior College there, and identifies herself with that city. After her graduation she worked for a quack "spiritual advisor," her job being to write hundreds of letters to prospective patients. Her office was in the Mecca Building on South State Street, where many poor families and derelicts lived. When she refused to take on the duties of "Assistant Pastor," she was honorably fired from her job.

Miss Brooks then attended art school at the South Side Community Center. Her main interest, however, was poetry, and she began to demonstrate her talent. She won contests sponsored by *Poetry* magazine and various organizations, and was able to publish her first book in 1945. She later won a Pulitzer prize for her book *Annie Allen*. Another honor was her appointment as Poet Laureate of Illinois, a post in which she succeeded Carl Sandburg. Miss Brooks now teaches at several colleges in the Chicago area. She is married to Henry Blakely and they have a son and a daughter.

Sadie and Maud

Maud went to college.
Sadie stayed at home.
Sadie scraped life
With a fine-tooth comb.

She didn't leave a tangle in.
Her comb found every strand.
Sadie was one of the livingest chits
In all the land.

Sadie bore two babies
Under her maiden name.
Maud and Ma and Papa
Nearly died of shame.

When Sadie said her last so-long
Her girls struck out from home.
(Sadie had left as heritage
Her fine-tooth comb.)

Maud, who went to college,
Is a thin brown mouse.
She is living all alone
In this old house.

1945

The Lovers of the Poor

arrive. The Ladies from the Ladies' Betterment League
Arrive in the afternoon, the late light slanting
In diluted gold bars across the boulevard brag
Of proud, seamed faces with mercy and murder hinting

Here, there, interrupting, all deep and debonair,
The pink paint on the innocence of fear;
Walk in a gingerly manner up the hall.
Cutting with knives served by their softest care,
Served by their love, so barbarously fair.
Whose mothers taught: You'd better not be cruel!
You had better not throw stones upon the wrens!
Herein they kiss and coddle and assault
Anew and dearly in the innocence
With which they baffle nature. Who are full,
Sleek, tender-clad, fit, fiftyish, a-glow, all
Sweetly abortive, hinting at fat fruit,
Judge it high time that fiftyish fingers felt
Beneath the lovelier planes of enterprise.
To resurrect. To moisten with milky chill.
To be a random hitching-post or plush.
To be, for wet eyes, random and handy hem.
                                        Their guild is giving money to the poor.
The worthy poor. The very very worthy
And beautiful poor. Perhaps just not too swarthy?
Perhaps just not too dirty nor too dim
Nor—passionate. In truth, what they could wish
Is—something less than derelict or dull.
Not staunch enough to stab, though, gaze for gaze!
God shield them sharply from the beggar-bold!
The noxious needy ones whose battle's bald
Nonetheless for being voiceless, hits one down.
                                        But it's all so bad! and entirely too much for them.
The stench; the urine, cabbage, and dead beans,
Dead porridges of assorted dusty grains,
The old smoke, *heavy* diapers, and, they're told,
Something called chitterlings. The darkness. Drawn
Darkness, or dirty light. The soil that stirs.
The soil that looks the soil of centuries.
And for that matter the *general* oldness. Old
Wood. Old marble. Old tile. Old old old.
Not homekind Oldness! Not Lake Forest, Glencoe.[4]
Nothing is sturdy, nothing is majestic,
There is no quiet drama, no rubbed glaze, no
Unkillable infirmity of such
A tasteful turn as lately they have left,
Glencoe, Lake Forest, and to which their cars
Must presently restore them. When they're done
With dullards and distortions of this fistic
Patience of the poor and put-upon.
                                        They've never seen such a make-do-ness as
Newspaper rugs before! In this, this "flat,"
Their hostess is gathering up the oozed, the rich
Rugs of the morning (tattered! the bespattered. . . .)

4. Prosperous suburbs north of Chicago.

Readies to spread clean rugs for afternoon.
Here is a scene for you. The Ladies look,
In horror, behind a substantial citizeness
Whose trains clank out across her swollen heart.
Who, arms akimbo, almost fills a door.
All tumbling children, quilts dragged to the floor
And tortured thereover, potato peelings, soft-
Eyed kitten, hunched-up, haggard, to-be-hurt.
Their League is allotting largesse to the Lost.
But to put their clean, their pretty money, to put
Their money collected from delicate rose-fingers
Tipped with their hundred flawless rose-nails seems . . .
They own Spode, Lowestoft,[5] candelabra,
Mantels, and hostess gowns, and sunburst clocks,
Turtle soup, Chippendale,[6] red satin "hangings,"
Aubussons and Hattie Carnegie.[7] They Winter
In Palm Beach; cross the Water in June; attend,
When suitable, the nice Art Institute;
Buy the right books in the best bindings; saunter
On Michigan,[8] Easter mornings, in sun or wind.
Oh Squalor! This sick four-story hulk, this fibre
With fissures everywhere! Why, what are bringings
Of loathe-love largesse? What shall peril hungers
So old old, what shall flatter the desolate?
Tin can, blocked fire escape and chitterling
And swaggering seeking youth and the puzzled wreckage
Of the middle passage,[9] and urine and stale shames
And, again, the porridges of the underslung
And children children children. Heavens! That
Was a rat, surely, off there, in the shadows? Long
And long-tailed? Gray? The Ladies from the Ladies'
Betterment League agree it will be better
To achieve the outer air that rights and steadies,
To hie[1] to a house that does not holler, to ring
Bells elsetime, better presently to cater
To no more Possibilities, to get
Away. Perhaps the money can be posted.
Perhaps they two may choose another Slum!
Some serious sooty half-unhappy home!—
Where loathe-love likelier may be invested.
Keeping their scented bodies in the center
Of the hall as they walk down the hysterical hall,
They allow their lovely skirts to graze no wall,
Are off at what they manage of a canter,
And, resuming all the clues of what they were,
Try to avoid inhaling the laden air.

1960

5. English chinaware.
6. English furniture.
7. Aubussons are medieval tapestries; Hattie Carnegie is a fashionable American dress designer.
8. Michigan Avenue, known as the "Magnificent Mile."
9. The route across the Atlantic Ocean by which slaves were brought from Africa to the western hemisphere.
1. Hasten.

Of Robert Frost

There is a little lightning in his eyes.
Iron at the mouth.
His brows ride neither too far up nor down.

He is splendid. With a place to stand.

Some glowing in the common blood.
Some specialness within.

1963

Boy Breaking Glass

TO MARC CRAWFORD
FROM WHOM THE COMMISSION

Whose broken window is a cry of art
(success, that winks aware
as elegance, as a treasonable faith)
is raw: is sonic: is old-eyed première.
Our beautiful flaw and terrible ornament.
Our barbarous and metal little man.

"I shall create! If not a note, a hole.
If not an overture, a desecration."

Full of pepper and light
and Salt and night and cargoes.

"Don't go down the plank
if you see there's no extension.
Each to his grief, each to
his loneliness and fidgety revenge.

Nobody knew where I was and now I am no longer there."

The only sanity is a cup of tea.
The music is in minors.[2]

Each one other
is having different weather.
"It was you, it was you who threw away my name!
And this is everything I have for me."

Who has not Congress, lobster, love, luau,
the Regency Room, the Statue of Liberty,

2. Children, but also the minor keys in music.

runs. A sloppy amalgamation.
A mistake.
A cliff.
A hymn, a snare, and an exceeding sun.

1968

ROBERT CONQUEST
(*1917–*)

Robert Conquest was born in Malvern, England, on July 15, 1917. He was educated at Winchester College, at the University of Grenoble, and at Oxford, where in 1939 he tooked a degree in Philosophy, Politics, and Economics. He served in the Second World War, then began a ten-year career in the diplomatic service. In 1956, in collaboration with Kingsley Amis, he edited the first *New Lines* anthology, a collection of poems by men who shared Conquest's distrust of modernism. Though Conquest disclaimed any intention of speaking for a coterie, the poets represented in *New Lines* came to be known as "The Movement." Since 1956 Conquest has divided his time between teaching and writing. He has published numerous books on Soviet affairs, including an eight-volume series on Soviet institutions and policies.

The Rokeby Venus[1]

Life pours out images, the accidental
At once deleted when the purging mind
Detects their resonance as inessential:
Yet these may leave some fruitful trace behind.

Thus on this painted mirror is projected
The shield that rendered safe the Gorgon's head.[2]
A travesty.—Yet even as reflected
The young face seems to strike us, if not dead,

At least into an instantaneous winter
Which life and reason can do nothing with,
Freezing the watcher and the painting into
A single immobility of myth.

But underneath the pigments' changeless weather
The artist only wanted to devise
A posture that could show him, all together,
Face, shoulders, waist, delectable smooth thighs.

1. "The Toilet of Venus," also known as the "Rokeby Venus," is a painting by Velasquez which hangs in the National Gallery in London. It shows the reclining nude figure of a beautiful young woman; her head is turned away from the viewer, but she is gazing into a mirror held by a winged Cupid, so that we can see her face.

2. In Greek mythology, the head of a monster which turned to stone anyone who looked at it; it could, however, be safely seen reflected in a mirror, and the Greek hero Perseus polished his shield to a mirror-like surface before cutting the monster's head off.

So with the faulty image as a start
We come at length to analyse and name
The luminous darkness in the depths of art:
The timelessness that holds us is the same

As that of the transcendent sexual glance
And art grows brilliant in the light it sheds,
Direct or not, on the inhabitants
Of our imaginations and our beds.

1955

MARGARET AVISON
(*1918–*)

Margaret Avison was born in Galt, Ontario, on April 23, 1918, a clergyman's daughter (though a convert to Christianity as recently as 1963). She took a degree at the University of Toronto in 1940, and while at college began to write and publish her poems. Since then she has lived in Toronto, and until recently she was a social worker in a storefront mission there; her interest in social work extended also to preparing abstracts of graduate dissertations and papers on the subject presented at the University of Toronto (where she took an M.A. in 1964) and to editing a compendium of these abstracts for the University's press. Her first book of poems, *Winter Sun* (1960), won Canada's Governor-General's award.

Tennis

Service is joy, to see or swing. Allow
All tumult to subside. Then tensest winds
Buffet, brace, viol[1] and sweeping bow.
Courts are for love and volley. No one minds
The cruel ellipse of service and return,
Dancing white galliardes[2] at tape or net
Till point, on the wire's tip, or the long burn-
ing arc to nethercourt marks game and set.
Purpose apart, perched like an umpire, dozes,
Dreams golden balls whirring through indigo.
Clay blurs the whitewash but day still encloses
The albinos, bonded in their flick and flow.
Playing in musicked gravity, the pair
Score liquid Euclids in foolscaps[3] of air.

1960

1. Early stringed instrument, in use until the 18th century.

2. A medieval dance, notable for leaping.

3. Euclid (fl. c. 300 B.C.) formulated and compiled the first comprehensive plane geometry. A foolscap is a large, strong piece of paper, often used in architectural drawing.

The Two Selves

All the cages are empty
and crusted dry.
Why do they hang from
your lintel and ceiling?

The birds in the sky
left this to me.

But your room is bare
as a customs shed,
and the cages at head-
level swivel, and there
is no *escritoire*. . . .[4]

No, only a linen sky
and a bicycle-tree
somewhere, for me.

Your Philip Sparrow[5]
scribbles his tracks
in the waterfront soot at
a warehouse door.

That one? Maybe—
there were many
who flickered away.

And you *wait* for them here?

Oh no. It is more
like knowing the sound of the sea when you
live under the sea.

1966

4. Desk (Fr).
5. "Philip Sparrow," by John Skelton (1460–1529), is a long elegy for a child's pet bird.

A. W. PURDY
(*1918–*)

Alfred Wellington Purdy was born in Wooller, Ontario, on December 30, 1918. He was educated at Albert College, Belleville, and during World War II he served in the Royal Canadian Air Force. Before 1960, when he settled in southeastern Ontario, he worked at a number of jobs, "factory and otherwise, too numerous to mention." In 1965 he spent a summer among the Eskimos of Baffin Island. *The Cariboo Horses* won the Governor-General's Award for Poetry in 1966.

Dead Seal

He looks like a fat little old man
an 'Old Bill'[2]   sort of face
both wise and senile   at the same time
with an anxious to please expression
                in fact a clown
which is belied on account of the dark slow worm
of blood crawling down his forehead
that precludes laughter
or being anything   but a dead animal
tho perhaps part of a fur coat

Often I want to pet something
that looks like this
(and been warned the Eskimo dogs are dangerous)
which appeals to me on common ground i.e.
they unsure of what being an animal consists of
I equally unsure of what a human being is supposed to be
(despite the legal and moral injunctions that say
                        "Thou Shalt Not"
nobody says or is likely to say with real conviction
                        "Thou Shalt—go ahead and Shalt"
                         or 'shall' as the case may be)
On the other hand it would be ridiculous
to pat the head of a dead seal
touch the wet blood that streams back from the boat
a feather of smoky brown in the water widening
into a crude trailing isosceles triangle
with mathematically impossible fish
re-tracing the seal's ghost past not
knowing they're involved in anything
And here he is now
                          casually taking a nap
with flippers like futile baby hands
and clown look   of just pretending
                I shan't wake him
for it would be disgusting to touch the blood
and it's unnecessary to prove anything
even to myself
                    Then change my mind
                "I (damn well) Shalt"
—reach out as if the head were electric
with a death-taboo invisibly attached
dark and dank-cold with the hair on it
sticky where the bullet touched
                                    less gently

2. "Old Bill" was an old British soldier with walrus mustaches in Bruce Bairnsfather's cartoons of the First World War.

smooth elsewhere like an intimate part
                    of the human body
that must be touched with delight in living
not curiosity and defiance of breaking rules
—But I am no hunter
                    of any kind
go back to the tent
                    to sit for a few minutes
inside the white canvas blindfold and wonder
what got into me?

1967

ROBERT DUNCAN
(*1919–*)

Robert Duncan was born January 7, 1919, in Oakland, California. At the age of one year, he was adopted by a family named Symmes, and his early poetry was signed with that name. His homoerotic direction has been important in his life and in his work: of it he writes, "Perhaps the sexual irregularity underlay and led to the poetic; neither as homosexual nor as poet could one take over readily the accepted paradigms of the Protestant ethic." His education at the University of California at Berkeley, which began in 1936, was interrupted by a love affair; during his sophomore year he dropped out and followed his lover east. Subsequently he spent some time in the Army but was granted a psychiatric discharge in 1941. He had meanwhile edited two magazines, the first, with Sanders Russell, the *Experimental Review* (1938–40), the second, *Phoenix*. He returned to the university at Berkeley from 1948 to 1950 and edited then the *Berkeley Miscellany* (1948–49). He has taught sporadically at universities, notably with Olson at Black Mountain College in 1956.

The Ballad of Mrs Noah

Mrs Noah in the Ark
wove a great nightgown out of the dark,
did Mrs Noah,

had her own hearth in the Holy Boat,
two cats, two books, two cooking pots,
had Mrs Noah,

two pints of porter, two pecks of peas,
and a stir in her stew of memories.

Oh, that was a town, said Mrs Noah,
that the Lord in His wrath
did up and drown!

I liked its windows and I liked its trees.
Save me a little, Lord, I prayd on my knees.
And now, Lord save me, I've two of each!
apple, apricot, cherry and peach.

How shall I manage it? I've two of them all—
hairy, scaly, leathery, slick,
fluttery, buttery, thin and thick,
shaped like a stick, shaped like a ball,
too tiny to see, and much too tall.

I've all that I askd for and more and more,
windows and chimneys, and a great store
of needles and pins, of outs and ins,
and a regular forgive-us for some of my sins.

She wove a great nightgown out of the dark
decorated like a Sunday Park
with clouds of black thread to remember her grief
sewn about with bright flowers to give relief,

and, in a grim humor, a border all round
with the little white bones of the wicked drownd.

Tell me, Brother, what do you see?
said Mrs Noah to the Lowly Worm.

O Mother, the Earth is black, black.
To my crawlly bride and lowly me
the Earth is bitter as can be
where the Dead lie down and never come back,
said the blind Worm.

Tell me, Brother, what do *you* see?
said Mrs Noah to the sleeping Cat.

O Mother, the weather is dreadful wet.
I'll keep house for you wherever you'll be.
I'll sit by the fireside and be your pet.
And as long as I'm dry I'll purr for free,
said snug-loving Cat.

Tell me, Brother, has the Flood gone?
said Mrs Noah to the searching Crow.

No. No. No home in sight.
I fly thru the frightful waste alone,
said the carrion Crow.
The World is an everlasting Night.

Now that can't be true, Noah, Old Noah,
said the good Housewife to her good Spouse.
How long must we go in this floating House?
growing old and hope cold,
Husband, without new land?

And then Glory-Be with a Rainbow to-boot!
the Dove returnd with an Olive Shoot.

Tell me, Brother, what have we here,
my Love? to the Dove said Mrs Noah.

It's a Branch of All-Cheer
you may wear on your nightgown all the long year
as a boa. Mrs Noah, said the Dove,
with God's Love!

Then out from the Ark
in her nightgown all dark
with only her smile to betoken the Day
and a wreath-round of olive leaves

Mrs Noah steppd down
into the same old wicked repenting
Lord-Will-We-Ever recently recoverd
comfortable World-Town.

O where have you been, Mother Noah, Mother Noah?

I've had a great Promise for only Tomorrow.
In the Ark of Sleep I've been on a sail
over the wastes of the world's sorrow.

And the Promise? the Tomorrow? Mother Noah, Mother Noah?

Ah! the Rainbow's awake
and we will not fail!

1960

LAWRENCE FERLINGHETTI
(*1919*(?)–)

Lawrence Ferlinghetti says that he was born in either 1919 or 1920, on March 24. Probably it was 1919, in Yonkers, New York. He was the fifth son of an Italian immigrant father and a Portuguese mother. His father found it expedient as an auctioneer to change his name to Ferling, but the son practiced a higher expediency later in changing it back to Ferlinghetti.

While the boy was still small, his father died suddenly; his mother went insane and was placed in an asylum. It seems that Ferlinghetti was sent to an orphanage in Chappaqua, New York. He was apparently rescued by a relative of his mother, Emily Monsanto; she took him with her to France for several years. On their return his "aunt" took a job as French governess in a family named Lawrence, and after she too went insane, Ferlinghetti remained with them. It may have been from them that he derived his first name; what it had been originally has not been disclosed.

Presumably with the help of this family, he attended the University of North Carolina and took a bachelor's degree. When war broke out he entered the Navy and was given assignments to the Free French and the Norwegian underground. He eventually became a lieutenant commander. Following his release he worked for *Time* magazine. Then he resumed his education, first with an M.A. at Columbia in 1948, then with a *Doctorat de l'Université* at the Sorbonne in 1951.

The year 1952 was momentous for Beat poetry, and Ferlinghetti played a major role. With Peter D. Martin he founded in San Francisco the first all-paperback bookstore in the United States, City Lights. The two men began to publish City Lights Books and the Pocket Poets Series, and Ferlinghetti also issued a mimeographed magazine which he called "Beatitude." Though Ferlinghetti continues to share some of the Beats' intellectual questing and their antiestablishment stance—his books include *Back Roads to Far Places* (1971), a prose work in the style of the Japanese travel journal, and *Where Is Vietnam?* (1965)—he has not found necessary the prolonged travels abroad of a Ginsberg or a Snyder. His base is still the City Lights Bookstore in San Francisco, and the series of books under that imprint which launched Ginsberg and Corso continues under his editorship.

[In Goya's Greatest Scenes We Seem to See]

In Goya's greatest scenes[1] we seem to see
the people of the world
exactly at the moment when
they first attained the title of
'suffering humanity'
They writhe upon the page
in a veritable rage
of adversity
Heaped up
groaning with babies and bayonets
under cement skies
in an abstract landscape of blasted trees
bent statues bats wings and beaks
slippery gibbets [2]
cadavers and carnivorous cocks
and all the final hollering monsters

1. Francisco Goya y Lucientes (1746–1828), Spanish painter and etcher, did a series of etchings, the "Disasters of War" (1810–13), which express his outrage at a world at war.

2. Gallows, or gallows-like posts on which the bodies of executed men were hung in irons as a warning.

of the
'imagination of disaster'
they are so bloody real
it is as if they really still existed

And they do

Only the landscape is changed

They still are ranged along the roads
plagued by legionaires
false windmills and demented roosters

They are the same people
only further from home
on freeways fifty lanes wide
on a concrete continent
spaced with bland billboards
illustrating imbecile illusions of happiness

The scene shows fewer tumbrils
but more maimed citizens
in painted cars
and they have strange license plates
and engines
that devour America

1958

DAVID WRIGHT
(*1920–*)

David Wright was born in Johannesburg, South Africa, on February 23, 1920. At the age of seven he became deaf. He was then sent to England to attend the Northampton School for the Deaf. From there he proceeded to Oriel College, Oxford, where he took a B.A. in 1942. He has published numerous anthologies of nineteenth- and twentieth-century poetry, translations of the *Beowulf* and Chaucer's *Canterbury Tales*, and the autobiographical *Deafness: A Personal Account*. He also edited *X*, a literary journal which sponsored the work of MacDiarmid, Kavanagh, and other poets.

Kleomedes

Both Plutarch and Pausanius tell a story [1]
That is a worry to imagination.

1. The sources of this story are the "Life of Romulus," by the Greek biographer and philosopher Plutarch (c. 350–430), and *Description of Hellas*, by Pausanias (fl. 2nd century A.D.), a Greek author of travel books.

It's of the athlete Kleomedes, a moody
Instrument for a theophanic[2] anger
And for an outrageous justice not our own.

Plutarch reports the tale in the barest outline,
Evidently having no comment to offer,
And certainly no word of explanation
To throw light upon what happened to Kleomedes
Or the subsequent oracular non sequitur.

As for Kleomedes: at the Olympic Games he
Killed his opponent in the boxing-contest.
The ox-felling blow was not his, so he claimed; the
Fury[3] struck through him, it was not his own strength.
He'd won, but they withheld the palm nevertheless.

The injustice of it. Nursing rage like a pot-plant,
Watering it with his thoughts, which were few and stupid,
When he drank with others he drank with his back turned
To cherish that shrub till one more bud had sprouted.
It was growing to be a beauty and he loved it.

The palm of victory, his by rights, denied him.
Well, he would go home to Astypalaea.[4]
There they would understand; were they not his own kin?
Anger. His heart fed an ulcer. Would it disappear
At sight of the headland of his own dear island?

So Kleomedes went away; his rage didn't.
It's hard being done by foreigners, but far worse
When the people one grew up with see no harm in it.
Even the light of the noonday sun seemed altered
In the familiar market-place where fools chaffered.

Wrath. Wrath. In an access of it he stood up.
May God damn the lot of you, he said, seizing the first
Thing his eye fell on: it was a marble column.
Ah, and he tugged. Tugged. And his brow pimpled with sweat.
Possessed, he exerted more than his might. It tumbled.

Slowly a coping-stone[5] slid. Then the whole roof
Collapsed with a roar. Thunder. A pall of dust
Stood like a rose where had been a schoolroom of children.
Kleomedes saw their blood lapped up by the earth.
There was silence and grief. Then a cry, Murderer!

2. Manifesting the gods.

3. One of the Greek goddesses of revenge.

4. A Greek island near the Turkish coast.

5. One of the stones, often large and heavy, which tops a wall.

Murderer! Murderer! He was among strangers.
Hatred and anger in that man's, that woman's eye.
And now they were one eye. The eye of an animal,
Hackles up, about to rend. Its name Mob, hairy
Gorgon.[6] Brute, it is a beast made up of us all;

May none of us ever be or see it! He saw,
Miserable quarry, lust ripple its muscles.
Act now or die! He acted. Ran for sanctuary
To the holy temple, the temple of Pallas Athena:[7]
Mob may respect the precinct of the armed goddess.

But what does a beast know of gods? He heard baying
Hard at his heels. Saw a chest there in the forecourt.
Prayed it be empty. He lifted the lid. Stepped in
Pulling the lid behind him, and held it fast shut.
More strength than his own held it against all efforts.

I don't understand the story from this point on.
Here enters mystery. Levering a crowbar
They heaved at hinges; the wood groaned and a hasp cracked.
Now for the fellow. Kleomedes did not appear.
They looked; but the chest was empty; the man was gone.

It was anticlimax. Fear fluttered from dismay.
They were people again. The sun continued to shine
As it had done. There were the children to bury.
Catastrophe and the violated shrine
Remained; and, before them, a vacant box grinning.

Astypalaea sent to Delphi[8] embassies
To ask the pythoness what these events forbode;
What might be their significance; where the guilt lay.
The oracle kept silence. Then vouchsafed its word.
'The last of the heroes was Kleomedes.'

1965

6. A mythical monster whose gaze turned those who met it to stone.

7. Greek goddess who presides over the moral and intellectual aspects of human life; she is usually shown in armor.

8. Site of the temple of the god Apollo, whose priestess (or pythoness) spoke prophetically, though often obscurely or ambiguously, in response to questions.

HOWARD NEMEROV
(1920–)

Howard Nemerov was born in New York City on March 1, 1920. He received his B.A. from Harvard in 1941, then enlisted in the Canadian Air Force during the Second World War and became a pilot, flying combat missions against German shipping in the North Sea; he joined the U.S. Army Air Corps for the last two years of the war. Married in 1944, Nemerov returned to New York after leaving the service and lived there for a year, working as an editor of the literary periodical *Furioso*. Since then he has been a college teacher at several campuses, most recently at Washington University in St. Louis. In 1963–64 Nemerov served as Consultant in Poetry to the Library of Congress.

The Sparrow in the Zoo[3]

No bars are set too close, no mesh too fine
To keep me from the eagle and the lion,
Whom keepers feed that I may freely dine.
This goes to show that if you have the wit
To be small, common, cute, and live on shit,
Though the cage fret kings, you may make free with it.

1958

The Icehouse in Summer

see Amos, 3:15[4]

A door sunk in a hillside, with a bolt
thick as the boy's arm, and behind that door
the walls of ice, melting a blue, faint light,
an air of cedar branches, sawdust, fern:
decaying seasons keeping from decay.

A summer guest, the boy had never seen
(a servant told him of it) how the lake
froze three foot thick, how farmers came with teams,
with axe and saw, to cut great blocks of ice,
translucid, marbled, glittering in the sun,
load them on sleds and drag them up the hill
to be manhandled down the narrow path
and set in courses for the summer's keeping,
the kitchen uses and luxuriousness
of the great houses. And he heard how once
a team and driver drowned in the break of spring:
the man's cry melting from the ice that summer
frightened the sherbet-eaters off the terrace.

Dust of the cedar, lost and evergreen
among the slowly blunting water walls

3. This poem was first entitled "Political Reflexion."

4. " 'I will smite the winter house with the summer house; and the houses of ivory shall perish, and the great houses shall come to an end,' says the Lord." Amos, a shepherd and prophet, was warning the Israelites of God's retribution for their transgressions.

where the blade edge melted and the steel saw's bite
was rounded out, and the horse and rider drowned
in the red sea's blood,[5] I was the silly child
who dreamed that riderless cry, and saw the guests
run from a ghostly wall, so long before
the winter house fell with the summer house,
and the houses, Egypt, the great houses, had an end.[6]

1960

5. Alludes to the Israelites' escape from Egypt through the miraculously parted Red Sea, which then rejoined destroying the Pharaoh's horsemen.

6. Perhaps an echo of Shakespeare's *Antony and Cleopatra*, IV.xv. 41: "I am dying, Egypt, dying."

RICHARD WILBUR
(*1921–*)

Richard Wilbur was born March 1, 1921, in New York City. His father, Lawrence Wilbur, was an artist; his mother came from a family prominent in journalism, a direction which he was to follow briefly later. Two years after his birth, the family took a very old house in North Caldwell, New Jersey, and he developed there, he has said, a taste for country things. He worked on student newspapers at his high school and then at Amherst College. During the Second World War he served at Cassino, Anzio, and the Siegfried Line. After the war he took an M.A. at Harvard and was elected a member of the Society of Fellows, where for three years he devoted himself to verse. He then taught at Harvard (1950–54), Wellesley (1955–57), and finally at Wesleyan. Wilbur has made splendid translations of Molière's *The Misanthrope* and *Tartuffe*, and with Lillian Hellman he wrote lyrics for a comic opera, *Candide*, based on Voltaire's novel.

The Pardon

My dog lay dead five days without a grave
In the thick of summer, hid in a clump of pine
And a jungle of grass and honeysuckle-vine.
I who had loved him while he kept alive

Went only close enough to where he was
To sniff the heavy honeysuckle-smell
Twined with another odor heavier still
And hear the flies' intolerable buzz.

Well, I was ten and very much afraid.
In my kind world the dead were out of range
And I could not forgive the sad or strange
In beast or man. My father took the spade

And buried him. Last night I saw the grass
Slowly divide (it was the same scene
But now it glowed a fierce and mortal green)
And saw the dog emerging. I confess

I felt afraid again, but still he came
In the carnal sun, clothed in a hymn of flies,
And death was breeding in his lively eyes.
I started in to cry and call his name,

Asking forgiveness of his tongueless head.
. . . I dreamt the past was never past redeeming:
But whether this was false or honest dreaming
I beg death's pardon now. And mourn the dead.

1950

Still, Citizen Sparrow

Still, citizen sparrow, this vulture which you call
Unnatural, let him but lumber again to air
Over the rotten office, let him bear
The carrion ballast up, and at the tall

Tip of the sky lie cruising. Then you'll see
That no more beautiful bird is in heaven's height,
No wider more placid wings, no watchfuller flight;
He shoulders nature there, the frightfully free,

The naked-headed one. Pardon him, you
Who dart in the orchard aisles, for it is he
Devours death, mocks mutability,
Has heart to make an end, keeps nature new.

Thinking of Noah, childheart, try to forget
How for so many bedlam[4] hours his saw
Soured the song of birds with its wheezy gnaw,
And the slam of his hammer all the day beset

The people's ears. Forget that he could bear
To see the towns like coral under the keel,
And the fields so dismal deep. Try rather to feel
How high and weary it was, on the waters where

He rocked his only world, and everyone's.
Forgive the hero, you who would have died
Gladly with all you knew; he rode that tide
To Ararat;[5] all men are Noah's sons.

1950

4. Noisy, as in a madhouse.

5. A mountain in the Caucasus where Noah's ark came to rest.

The Death of a Toad[6]

A toad the power mower caught,
Chewed and clipped of a leg, with a hobbling hop has got
To the garden verge, and sanctuaried him
Under the cineraria leaves, in the shade
Of the ashen heartshaped leaves, in a dim,
Low, and a final glade.

The rare original heartsblood goes,
Spends on the earthen hide, in the folds and wizenings, flows
In the gutters of the banked and staring eyes. He lies
As still as if he would return to stone,
And soundlessly attending, dies
Toward some deep monotone,

Toward misted and ebullient seas
And cooling shores, toward lost Amphibia's emperies.[7]
Day dwindles, drowning, and at length is gone
In the wide and antique eyes, which still appear
To watch, across the castrate lawn,
The haggard daylight steer.

1950

Ceremony

A striped blouse in a clearing by Bazille[8]
Is, you may say, a patroness of boughs
Too queenly kind toward nature to be kin.
But ceremony never did conceal,
Save to the silly eye, which all allows,
How much we are the woods we wander in.

Let her be some Sabrina[9] fresh from stream,
Lucent as shallows slowed by wading sun,
Bedded on fern, the flowers' cynosure:[9a]
Then nymph and wood must nod and strive to dream
That she is airy earth, the trees, undone,
Must ape her languor natural and pure.

Ho-hum. I am for wit and wakefulness,
And love this feigning lady by Bazille.
What's lightly hid is deepest understood,

6. This poem, according to Wilbur, is "the only instance in which I went straight from something that happened to me to writing a poem about it, with very little violation of the actual circumstances, though I put more into it before I was through than I'd felt at the time."

7. Wilbur, asked about this word, replied: "I may have found it in John Donne in the first place, but I think I wanted to use it here as a kind of confession that I'm doing rather a lot with that toad. I'm turning him into the primal energies of the world in the course of this poem. And so I get a little bombastic as a way of acknowledging that I'm going rather far." Amphibia is imagined as the presiding spirit of the toad's (and of all amphibians') universe. *Emperies:* dominions (archaic usage).

8. Frédéric Bazille (1841–1871), French painter associated with the Impressionists. Most of his paintings show figures in close association with a landscape.

9. The nymph of the river Severn, in Milton's *Comus.* But here identified with thoughtless, unceremonious nature, and contrasted with Bazille's lady.

9a. Center of attention.

And when with social smile and formal dress
She teaches leaves to curtsey and quadrille,[1]
I think there are most tigers in the wood.

1950

"A World Without Objects Is a Sensible Emptiness"[2]

The tall camels of the spirit
Steer for their deserts, passing the last groves loud
With the sawmill shrill of the locust, to the whole honey of the arid
Sun. They are slow, proud,

And move with a stilted stride
To the land of sheer horizon, hunting Traherne's
Sensible emptiness, there where the brain's lantern-slide
Revels in vast returns.

O connoisseurs of thirst,
Beasts of my soul who long to learn to drink
Of pure mirage, those prosperous islands are accurst
That shimmer on the brink

Of absence; auras, lustres,
And all shinings need to be shaped and borne.
Think of those painted saints, capped by the early masters
With bright, jauntily-worn

Aureate[3] plates, or even
Merry-go-round rings. Turn, O turn
From the fine sleights[4] of the sand, from the long empty oven
Where flames in flamings burn

Back to the trees arrayed
In bursts of glare, to the halo-dialing[5] run
Of the country creeks, and the hills' bracken tiaras made
Gold in the sunken sun,

Wisely watch for the sight
Of the supernova[6] burgeoning over the barn,
Lampshine blurred in the steam of beasts, the spirit's right
Oasis, light incarnate.

1950

1. To dance a quadrille, a kind of square dance.

2. The title comes from Thomas Traherne (c. 1638–1674), *Second Century,* Meditation 65: "You are as prone to love as the sun is to shine; it being the most delightful and natural employment of the soul of man, without which you are dark and miserable. . . . For certainly he that delights not in love makes vain the universe. . . . The whole world ministers to you as the theatre of your love. It sustains you and all objects that you may continue to love them. Without which it were better for you to have no being. Life without objects is sensible emptiness, and that is a greater misery than death or nothing."

3. Golden.

4. Mirages.

5. Like a sundial, the light on the creeks forms a halo-dial which reflects the solar changes.

6. Astronomers now believe that the star of Bethlehem, a symbol of Christ's birth, was a supernova, an exploding star.

Pangloss's Song[7]

I

Dear boy, you will not hear me speak
With sorrow or with rancor
Of what has paled my rosy cheek
And blasted it with canker;
'Twas Love, great Love, that did the deed
Through Nature's gentle laws,
And how should ill effects proceed
From so divine a cause?

Sweet honey comes from bees that sting,
As you are well aware;
To one adept in reasoning,
Whatever pains disease may bring
Are but the tangy seasoning
To Love's delicious fare.

II

Columbus and his men, they say,
Conveyed the virus hither
Whereby my features rot away
And vital powers wither;
Yet had they not traversed the seas
And come infected back,
Why, think of all the luxuries
That modern life would lack!

All bitter things conduce to sweet,
As this example shows;
Without the little spirochete
We'd have no chocolate to eat,
Nor would tobacco's fragrance greet
The European nose.

III

Each nation guards its native land
With cannon and with sentry,
Inspectors look for contraband
At every port of entry,
Yet nothing can prevent the spread
Of Love's divine disease:
It rounds the world from bed to bed
As pretty as you please.

7. A lyric written for the comic operetta based on Voltaire's *Candide*, produced in New York in 1956. Dr. Pangloss is the optimistic philosopher who assures his friend, the ingenuous Candide, that all evils, even syphilis, are for the best, and that this is the best of all possible worlds.

Men worship Venus everywhere,
As plainly may be seen;
The decorations which I bear
Are nobler than the Croix de Guerre,
And gained in service of our fair
And universal Queen.

1961

Playboy

High on his stockroom ladder like a dunce
The stock-boy sits, and studies like a sage
The subject matter of one glossy page,
As lost in curves as Archimedes[8] once.

Sometimes, without a glance, he feeds himself.
The left hand, like a mother-bird in flight,
Brings him a sandwich for a sidelong bite,
And then returns it to a dusty shelf.

What so engrosses him? The wild décor
Of this pink-papered alcove into which
A naked girl has stumbled, with its rich
Welter of pelts and pillows on the floor,

Amidst which, kneeling in a supple pose,
She lifts a goblet in her farther hand,
As if about to toast a flower-stand
Above which hovers an exploding rose

Fired from a long-necked crystal vase that rests
Upon a tasseled and vermilion cloth
One taste of which would shrivel up a moth?
Or is he pondering her perfect breasts?

Nothing escapes him of her body's grace
Or of her floodlit skin, so sleek and warm
And yet so strangely like a uniform,
But what now grips his fancy is her face,

And how the cunning picture holds her still
At just that smiling instant when her soul,
Grown sweetly faint, and swept beyond control,
Consents to his inexorable will.

1969

8. (c. 287–212 B.C.), Greek mathematician and inventor, known for his invention of a tubular helix, or screw, used to lift water from the hold of a ship.

KINGSLEY AMIS
(*1922–*)

Kingsley Amis was born in a lower middle-class family in London on April 16, 1922. He attended the City of London School, then served in the Army from 1942 to 1945. After the war he went up to Oxford and took a brilliant degree in English literature. At first an academic career seemed expedient: he taught at University College, Swansea, for several years, long enough to gather the material for his satirical novel, *Lucky Jim* (1954). He then went to teach at Cambridge University, but had little stomach for it and was happy to extricate himself by writing fiction, for which he is now best known.

An Ever-Fixed Mark[4]

Years ago, at a private school
Run on traditional lines,
One fellow used to perform
Prodigious feats in the dorm;
His quite undevious designs
Found many a willing tool.

On the rugger[5] field, in the gym,
Buck marked down at his leisure
The likeliest bits of stuff;
The notion, familiar enough,
Of 'using somebody for pleasure'
Seemed handy and harmless to him.

But another chap was above
The diversions of such a lout;
Seven years in the place
And he never got to first base
With the kid he followed about:
What interested Ralph was love.

He did the whole thing in style—
Letters three times a week,
Sonnet-sequences, Sunday walks;
Then, during one of their talks,
The youngster caressed his cheek,
And that made it all worth while.

4. The title is taken from Shakespeare's Sonnet CXVI: "Love is not love / Which alters when it alteration finds, / Or bends with the remover to remove: / O no! it is an ever-fixed mark, / That looks on tempests and is never shaken."

5. Colloquial for Rugby football, a common English schoolboy sport.

These days, for a quid pro quo,[6]
Ralph's chum is all for romance;
Buck's playmates, family men,
Eye a Boy Scout now and then.
Sex stops when you pull up your pants,
Love never lets you go.

1967

6. This for that (Lat), something offered in return.

PHILIP LARKIN
(*1922–*)

Philip Larkin was born on August 9, 1922, in Coventry, Warwickshire. His miseries as a student at Oxford are depicted in *Jill*, the first of his two novels. As an undergraduate, Larkin belonged to a group that came to be known as "The Movement." They revolted against poetry of excess, whether rhetorical excess, which they attributed to Dylan Thomas, or cosmic portentousness, which they thought they saw in Eliot or Pound. Since taking his Oxford degree in 1943, he has been a librarian, most recently at the University of Hull.

Church Going

Once I am sure there's nothing going on
I step inside, letting the door thud shut.
Another church: matting, seats, and stone,
And little books; sprawlings of flowers, cut
For Sunday, brownish now; some brass and stuff
Up at the holy end; the small neat organ;
And a tense, musty, unignorable silence,
Brewed God knows how long. Hatless, I take off
My cycle-clips in awkward reverence,

Move forward, run my hand around the font.
From where I stand, the roof looks almost new—
Cleaned, or restored? Someone would know: I don't.
Mounting the lectern, I peruse a few
Hectoring large-scale verses, and pronounce
'Here endeth' much more loudly than I'd meant.
The echoes snigger briefly. Back at the door
I sign the book, donate an Irish sixpence,
Reflect the place was not worth stopping for.

Yet stop I did: in fact I often do,
And always end much at a loss like this,
Wondering what to look for; wondering, too,
When churches fall completely out of use
What we shall turn them into, if we shall keep

A few cathedrals chronically on show,
Their parchment, plate and pyx[1] in locked cases,
And let the rest rent-free to rain and sheep.
Shall we avoid them as unlucky places?

Or, after dark, will dubious women come
To make their children touch a particular stone;
Pick simples[2] for a cancer; or on some
Advised night see walking a dead one?
Power of some sort or other will go on
In games, in riddles, seemingly at random;
But superstition, like belief, must die,
And what remains when disbelief has gone?
Grass, weedy pavement, brambles, buttress, sky,

A shape less recognisable each week,
A purpose more obscure. I wonder who
Will be the last, the very last, to seek
This place for what it was; one of the crew
That tap and jot and know what rood-lofts[3] were?
Some ruin-bibber, randy for antique,
Or Christmas-addict, counting on a whiff
Of gown-and-bands and organ-pipes and myrrh?
Or will he be my representative,

Bored, uninformed, knowing the ghostly silt
Dispersed, yet tending to this cross of ground
Through suburb scrub because it held unspilt
So long and equably what since is found
Only in separation—marriage, and birth,
And death, and thoughts of these—for whom was built
This special shell? For, though I've no idea
What this accoutred frowsty barn is worth,
It pleases me to stand in silence here;

A serious house on serious earth it is,
In whose blent air all our compulsions meet,
Are recognised, and robed as destinies.
And that much never can be obsolete,
Since someone will forever be surprising
A hunger in himself to be more serious,
And gravitating with it to this ground,
Which, he once heard, was proper to grow wise in,
If only that so many dead lie round.

1955

1. The box, often made of gold or silver, in which the communion wafers are kept.
2. Medicinal herbs.
3. Lofts or galleries above the screen that in medieval churches often separates the altar and pulpit from the congregation. Loft and screen both displayed the rood (or Cross).

Myxomatosis[4]

Caught in the centre of a soundless field
While hot inexplicable hours go by
What trap is this? Where were its teeth concealed?
You seem to ask.
                I make a sharp reply,
Then clean my stick. I'm glad I can't explain
Just in what jaws you were to suppurate:
You may have thought things would come right again
If you could only keep quite still and wait.

1955

The Whitsun[5] Weddings

That Whitsun, I was late getting away:
  Not till about
One-twenty on the sunlit Saturday
Did my three-quarters-empty train pull out,
All windows down, all cushions hot, all sense
Of being in a hurry gone. We ran
Behind the backs of houses, crossed a street
Of blinding windscreens,[6] smelt the fish-dock; thence
The river's level drifting breadth began,
Where sky and Lincolnshire and water meet.

All afternoon, through the tall heat that slept
  For miles inland,
A slow and stopping curve southwards we kept.
Wide farms went by, short-shadowed cattle, and
Canals with floatings of industrial froth;
A hothouse flashed uniquely: hedges dipped
And rose: and now and then a smell of grass
Displaced the reek of buttoned carriage-cloth
Until the next town, new and nondescript,
Approached with acres of dismantled cars.

At first, I didn't notice what a noise
  The weddings made
Each station that we stopped at: sun destroys
The interest of what's happening in the shade,
And down the long cool platforms whoops and skirls
I took for porters larking with the mails,
And went on reading. Once we started, though,
We passed them, grinning and pomaded, girls
In parodies of fashion, heels and veils,
All posed irresolutely, watching us go,

4. A disease of rabbits, often fatal; an English epidemic of myxomatosis killed millions of rabbits in 1953.

5. Or Whitsunday, the seventh Sunday after Easter, and one of the six British bank-holidays (legal holidays), or long weekends.

6. Windshields of cars.

As if out on the end of an event
   Waving goodbye
To something that survived it. Struck, I leant
More promptly out next time, more curiously,
And saw it all again in different terms:
The fathers with broad belts under their suits
And seamy foreheads; mothers loud and fat;
An uncle shouting smut; and then the perms,
The nylon gloves and jewellery-substitutes,
The lemons, mauves, and olive-ochres that

Marked off the girls unreally from the rest.
   Yes, from cafés
And banquet-halls up yards, and bunting-dressed
Coach-party annexes, the wedding-days
Were coming to an end. All down the line
Fresh couples climbed aboard: the rest stood round;
The last confetti and advice were thrown,
And, as we moved, each face seemed to define
Just what it saw departing: children frowned
At something dull; fathers had never known

Success so huge and wholly farcical;
   The women shared
The secret like a happy funeral;
While girls, gripping their handbags tighter, stared
At a religious wounding. Free at last,
And loaded with the sum of all they saw,
We hurried towards London, shuffling gouts of steam.
Now fields were building-plots, and poplars cast
Long shadows over major roads, and for
Some fifty minutes, that in time would seem

Just long enough to settle hats and say
   I nearly died,
A dozen marriages got under way.
They watched the landscape, sitting side by side
—An Odeon[7] went past, a cooling tower,
And someone running up to bowl[8]—and none
Thought of the others they would never meet
Or how their lives would all contain this hour.
I thought of London spread out in the sun,
Its postal districts packed like squares of wheat:

There we were aimed. And as we raced across
   Bright knots of rail
Past standing Pullmans, walls of blackened moss
Came close, and it was nearly done, this frail

7. One of a chain of English movie houses.

8. In the sport of cricket, to pitch the ball to the batsman.

Travelling coincidence; and what it held
Stood ready to be loosed with all the power
That being changed can give. We slowed again,
And as the tightened brakes took hold, there swelled
A sense of falling, like an arrow-shower
Sent out of sight, somewhere becoming rain.

1964

JAMES DICKEY
(1923–)

James Dickey was born in a suburb of Atlanta on February 2, 1923. Already tall—six feet three—as a boy, he became a high school football star. His interest in poetry had been awakened by his father, a lawyer, who delighted in oratory and used to read to him famous speeches to the jury and also speeches by Robert Ingersoll. Dickey went on to Clemson College in South Carolina in 1942, but left after a year to enlist in the Air Force, and flew a hundred combat missions in the Pacific.

On his return from the war Dickey went to Vanderbilt, where he worked with an older student's zeal to learn about anthropology, astronomy, philosophy, and to study foreign languages as well as English literature. A friendly professor, Monroe K. Spears, encouraged him to write more poetry. He took his B.A. there in 1949, and his M.A. a year later. The Air Force recalled him to active service for the Korean War, during which he spent two years as a training officer. On his return he went, after a year in Europe, to the University of Florida, nominally to assist the novelist Andrew Lytle, but chiefly to teach. A dispute arose over the propriety of a poem he read to a group; he abruptly resigned in April 1956 and went to New York at the age of thirty-three. McCann-Ericson took him on as a writer of advertising copy. He stayed there for a time, then shifted to Atlanta agencies; in between writing advertisements for Coca-Cola he composed some of his best poems, and the same secretary typed both products. He finally gave up this work in 1961 to accept a Guggenheim Fellowship and spend a year in Italy with his family. Since that time he has taught, lectured, and written. His book, *Buckdancer's Choice*, won the National Book Award for Poetry in 1966. For two years (from 1966 to 1968) he was Poetry Consultant to the Library of Congress.

The Performance

The last time I saw Donald Armstrong
He was staggering oddly off into the sun,
Going down, of the Philippine Islands.
I let my shovel fall, and put that hand
Above my eyes, and moved some way to one side
That his body might pass through the sun,

And I saw how well he was not
Standing there on his hands,
On his spindle-shanked forearms balanced,
Unbalanced, with his big feet looming and waving
In the great, untrustworthy air
He flew in each night, when it darkened.

Dust fanned in scraped puffs from the earth
Between his arms, and blood turned his face inside out,
To demonstrate its suppleness
Of veins, as he perfected his role.
Next day, he toppled his head off
On an island beach to the south,

And the enemy's two-handed sword[1]
Did not fall from anyone's hands
At that miraculous sight,
As the head rolled over upon
Its wide-eyed face, and fell
Into the inadequate grave

He had dug for himself, under pressure.
Yet I put my flat hand to my eyebrows
Months later, to see him again
In the sun, when I learned how he died,
And imagined him, there,
Come, judged, before his small captors,

Doing all his lean tricks to amaze them—
The back somersault, the kip-up—
And at last, the stand on his hands,
Perfect, with his feet together,
His head down, evenly breathing,
As the sun poured up from the sea

And the headsman broke down
In a blaze of tears, in that light
Of the thin, long human frame
Upside down in its own strange joy,
And, if some other one had not told him,
Would have cut off the feet

Instead of the head,
And if Armstrong had not presently risen
In kingly, round-shouldered attendance,
And then knelt down in himself
Beside his hacked, glittering grave, having done
All things in this life that he could.

1957

1. An execution by Japanese soldiers during the Second World War is described.

The Sheep Child

Farm boys wild to couple
With anything   with soft-wooded trees
With mounds of earth   mounds
Of pinestraw   will keep themselves off
Animals by legends of their own:
In the hay-tunnel dark
And dung of barns, they will
Say   I have heard tell

That in a museum in Atlanta
Way back in a corner somewhere
There's this thing that's only half
Sheep   like a woolly baby
Pickled in alcohol   because
Those things can't live   his eyes
Are open   but you can't stand to look
I heard from somebody who . . .

But this is now almost all
Gone. The boys have taken
Their own true wives in the city,
The sheep are safe in the west hill
Pasture   but we who were born there
Still are not sure. Are we,
Because we remember, remembered
In the terrible dust of museums?

Merely with his eyes, the sheep-child may

Be saying   saying

I am here, in my father's house.
I who am half of your world, came deeply
To my mother in the long grass
Of the west pasture, where she stood like moonlight
Listening for foxes. It was something like love
From another world that seized her
From behind, and she gave, not lifting her head
Out of dew, without ever looking, her best
Self to that great need. Turned loose, she dipped her face
Farther into the chill of the earth, and in a sound
Of sobbing   of something stumbling
Away, began, as she must do,
To carry me. I woke, dying,

In the summer sun of the hillside, with my eyes
Far more than human. I saw for a blazing moment
The great grassy world from both sides,
Man and beast in the round of their need,

And the hill wind stirred in my wool,
My hoof and my hand clasped each other,
I ate my one meal
Of milk, and died
Staring. From dark grass I came straight

To my father's house, whose dust
Whirls up in the halls for no reason
When no one comes   piling deep in a hellish mild corner,
And, through my immortal waters,
I meet the sun's grains eye
To eye, and they fail at my closet of glass.
Dead, I am most surely living
In the minds of farm boys: I am he who drives
Them like wolves from the hound bitch and calf
And from the chaste ewe in the wind.
They go into woods   into bean fields   they go
Deep into their known right hands. Dreaming of me,
They groan   they wait   they suffer
Themselves, they marry, they raise their kind.

1967

ALAN DUGAN
(1923–   )

Alan Dugan was born on February 12, 1923. In the absence of much biographical information, a kind of life can be pieced together out of poems and random materials. He was probably brought up in a Catholic family, uncomfortably situated. He took part in the Second World War. After it, he became a handicraftsman, making models in plastics. He received a B.A. from Mexico City College. He had published very little poetry until his first book was accepted for the Yale Series of Younger Poets and published in 1961. The resultant praise, and two prizes he won later, the Pulitzer Prize and the National Book Award, led him to devote himself to writing. He lives in New York and teaches at Sarah Lawrence College.

Love Song: I and Thou

Nothing is plumb, level or square:
  the studs are bowed, the joists
are shaky by nature, no piece fits
  any other piece without a gap
or pinch, and bent nails
  dance all over the surfacing
like maggots. By Christ
  I am no carpenter. I built
the roof for myself, the walls
  for myself, the floors

for myself, and got
  hung up in it myself. I
danced with a purple thumb
  at this house-warming, drunk
with my prime whiskey: rage.
  Oh I spat rage's nails
into the frame-up of my work:
  it held. It settled plumb,
level, solid, square and true
  for that great moment. Then
it screamed and went on through,
  skewing as wrong the other way.
God damned it. This is hell,
  but I planned it, I sawed it,
I nailed it, and I
  will live in it until it kills me.
I can nail my left palm
  to the left-hand cross-piece but
I can't do everything myself.
  I need a hand to nail the right,
a help, a love, a you, a wife.

1961

LOUIS SIMPSON
(*1923–*)

Louis Simpson was born in Jamaica, British West Indies, on March 27, 1923. His father was a second-generation Jamaican of Scots descent, and his mother a Russian Jewess. "I most of all wanted to be an American," he said. In 1943 he left Columbia to join the American Army, and served first with a tank corps, then as a combat infantryman with the 101st Airborne Division. It was in Germany that he obtained American citizenship. His health broke down late in the war; after his recovery he returned to Columbia University. There, after his undergraduate course, he took a Master of Arts degree. While completing his doctorate, Simpson taught for a time at Columbia and tried himself also in publishing and in export trade. But he reverted to teaching, first at the University of California at Berkeley and then at the State University of New York at Stony Brook.

The Man Who Married Magdalene[1]

The man who married Magdalene
Had not forgiven her.
God might pardon every sin . . .
Love is no pardoner.

1. Mary Magdalene is the repentant sinner of *Luke* 7:44–50 whom Christ forgave, and who was one of the first to learn of his resurrection. The nature of her sin is not given, but "Magdalene" may be derived from a Talmudic allusion to an adulteress.

Her hands were hollow, pale and blue,
Her mouth like watered wine.
He watched to see if she were true
And waited for a sign.

It was old harlotry, he guessed,
That drained her strength away,
So gladly for the dark she dressed,
So sadly for the day.

Their quarrels made her dull and weak
And soon a man might fit
A penny in the hollow cheek
And never notice it.

At last, as they exhausted slept,
Death granted the divorce,
And nakedly the woman leapt
Upon that narrow horse.

But when he woke and woke alone
He wept and would deny
The loose behavior of the bone
And the immodest thigh.

1955

American Poetry

Whatever it is, it must have
A stomach that can digest
Rubber, coal, uranium, moons, poems.

Like the shark, it contains a shoe.
It must swim for miles through the desert
Uttering cries that are almost human.

1963

DENISE LEVERTOV
(1923–   )

Denise Levertov was born at Ilford, Essex, on October 24, 1923. Her father's Jewish ancestry and her mother's Welsh forebears are celebrated in the poem "Illustrious Ancestors." Her parents sent her neither to school nor to college, preferring to educate her at home. In early youth she took ballet lessons, and during the war she served as a nurse. She was married in 1947 to the writer Mitchell Goodman, with whom she lives in New York. In the late Sixties, when his indignation with the Vietnam War resulted in his being arraigned with other notable persons for "conspiracy," Miss Levertov wrote a number of poems about the war, expressions of her sympathy with the mistreated Vietnamese.

The Dog of Art

That dog with daisies for eyes
who flashes forth
flame of his very self at every bark
is the Dog of Art.
Worked in wool, his blind eyes
look inward to caverns and jewels
which they see perfectly,
and his voice
measures forth the treasure
in music sharp and loud,
sharp and bright,
bright flaming barks,
and growling smoky soft, the Dog
of Art turns to the world
the quietness of his eyes.

1959

Illustrious Ancestors

The Rav[9]
of Northern White Russia declined,
in his youth, to learn the
language of birds, because
the extraneous did not interest him; nevertheless
when he grew old it was found
he understood them anyway, having
listened well, and as it is said, 'prayed
with the bench and the floor.' He used
what was at hand—as did
Angel Jones of Mold,[1] whose meditations
were sewn into coats and britches.
Well, I would like to make,
thinking some line still taut between me and them,
poems direct as what the birds said,
hard as a floor, sound as a bench,
mysterious as the silence when the tailor
would pause with his needle in the air.

1958

Matins[2]

i

The authentic! Shadows of it
sweep past in dreams, one could say imprecisely,
evoking the almost-silent
ripping apart of giant
sheets of cellophane. No.

9. Rabbi.
1. A town in Wales.
2. Prayers offered at dawn; in the Roman Catholic church, this is the most important office of the day.

It thrusts up close. Exactly in dreams
it has you off-guard, you
recognize it before you have time.
For a second before waking
the alarm bell is a red conical hat, it
takes form.

ii

The authentic! I said
rising from the toilet seat.
The radiator in rhythmic knockings
spoke of the rising steam.
The authentic, I said
breaking the handle of my hairbrush as I
brushed my hair in
rhythmic strokes: That's it,
that's joy, it's always
a recognition, the known
appearing fully itself, and
more itself than one knew.

iii

The new day rises
as heat rises,
knocking in the pipes
with rhythms it seizes for its own
to speak of its invention—
the real, the new-laid
egg whose speckled shell
the poet fondles and must break
if he will be nourished.

iv

A shadow painted where
yes, a shadow must fall.
The cow's breath
not forgotten in the mist, in the
words. Yes,
verisimilitude draws up
heat in us, zest
to follow through,
follow through,
follow
transformations of day
in its turning, in its becoming.

v

Stir the holy grains, set
the bowls on the table and
call the child to eat.

While we eat we think,
as we think an undercurrent
of dream runs through us
faster than thought
towards recognition.

Call the child to eat,
send him off, his mouth
tasting of toothpaste, to go down
into the ground, into a roaring train
and to school.

His cheeks are pink
his black eyes hold his dreams, he has left
forgetting his glasses.

Follow down the stairs at a clatter
to give them to him and save
his clear sight.

Cold air
comes in at the street door.

vi

The authentic! It rolls
just out of reach, beyond
running feet and
stretching fingers, down
the green slope and into
the black waves of the sea.
Speak to me, little horse, beloved,
tell me
how to follow the iron ball,
how to follow through to the country
beneath the waves
to the place where I must kill you and you step out
of your bones and flystrewn meat
tall, smiling, renewed,
formed in your own likeness.[3]

vii

Marvelous Truth, confront us
at every turn,
in every guise, iron ball,
egg, dark horse, shadow,

3. "In section vi of these meditations on the idea of 'the authentic,' the Irish tale of Conn-Edda is summarized, as it were, and in section vii referred to, though the name of Conn-Edda is never mentioned" (Levertov's note). In the folktale Conn-Edda, a prince in danger of losing his kingdom, is magically drawn to ride in pursuit of a seemingly wayward iron ball. His last trial is to kill his beloved horse, which is immediately transformed into a handsome young man who helps Conn-Edda achieve his inheritance.

cloud
of breath on the air,

dwell
in our crowded hearts
our steaming bathrooms, kitchens full of
things to be done, the
ordinary streets.

Thrust close your smile
that we know you, terrible joy.

1962

Song for Ishtar[4]

The moon is a sow
and grunts in my throat
Her great shining shines through me
so the mud of my hollow gleams
and breaks in silver bubbles

She is a sow
and I a pig and a poet

When she opens her white
lips to devour me I bite back
and laughter rocks the moon

In the black of desire
we rock and grunt, grunt and
shine

1964

Losing Track

Long after you have swung back
away from me
I think you are still with me:

you come in close to the shore
on the tide
and nudge me awake the way

a boat adrift nudges the pier:
am I a pier
half-in half-out of the water?

4. Life giving mother-goddess of the ancient Babylonians. The pig is sacred to her.

and in the pleasure of that communion
I lose track,
the moon I watch goes down, the

tide swings you away before
I know I'm
alone again long since,

mud sucking at gray and black
timbers of me,
a light growth of green dreams drying.

1964

KENNETH KOCH
(1925–)

Kenneth Koch was born in Cincinnati, Ohio, on February 27, 1925. At eighteen he went into the army for three years and served in the Pacific theater as a rifleman. On his return he took a B.A. (in 1948) at Harvard, and there became friends with the poet John Ashbery. In 1959 he took his doctorate at Columbia. More important were his three years in France and Italy. It was then that he discovered the humorous, surrealist verse of Jacques Prévert, with whom he has affinities. Koch has taught at several colleges and is now established at Columbia University, as befits his metropolitan muse. He has also taught the reading and writing of poetry to children in the New York public schools.

Mending Sump[1]

"Hiram, I think the sump is backing up.
The bathroom floor boards for above two weeks
Have seemed soaked through. A little bird, I think
Has wandered in the pipes, and all's gone wrong."
"Something there is that doesn't hump a sump,"
He said; and through his head she saw a cloud
That seemed to twinkle. "Hiram, well," she said,
"Smith is come home! I saw his face just now
While looking through your head. He's come to die
Or else to laugh, for hay is dried-up grass
When you're alone." He rose, and sniffed the air.
"We'd better leave him in the sump," he said.

1960

1. Compare Frost, "Mending Wall."

You Were Wearing

You were wearing your Edgar Allan Poe printed cotton blouse.
In each divided up square of the blouse was a picture of Edgar Allan Poe.
Your hair was blonde and you were cute. You asked me, "Do most boys think that most girls are bad?"
I smelled the mould of your seaside resort hotel bedroom on your hair held in place by a John Greenleaf Whittier clip.
"No," I said, "it's girls who think that boys are bad." Then we read *Snowbound* [2] together
And ran around in an attic, so that a little of the blue enamel was scraped off my George Washington, Father of His Country, shoes.

Mother was walking in the living room, her Strauss Waltzes comb in her hair.
We waited for a time and then joined her, only to be served tea in cups painted with pictures of Herman Melville
As well as with illustrations from his book *Moby Dick* and from his novella, *Benito Cereno.*
Father came in wearing his Dick Tracy necktie: "How about a drink, everyone?"
I said, "Let's go outside a while." Then we went onto the porch and sat on the Abraham Lincoln swing.
You sat on the eyes, mouth, and beard part, and I sat on the knees.
In the yard across the street we saw a snowman holding a garbage can lid smashed into a likeness of the mad English king, George the Third.

1962

2. A poem by Whittier, long a favorite in schools.

W. D. SNODGRASS
(*1926–*)

William Dewitt Snodgrass was born on January 5, 1926, in Wilkinsburg, Pennsylvania. He grew up in Beaver Falls, Pennsylvania, where he graduated from high school and attended Geneva College. His studies there were interrupted by service in the Navy during the Second World War. In 1947 he went to the State University of Iowa, and at the famous writers' workshop there he studied under Robert Lowell. He and Lowell taught each other a new autobiographical, "confessional" mode for modern poetry. In 1959 he published his first book, *Heart's Needle*, which was showered with awards, including a Pulitzer Prize. Snodgrass has held a number of academic appointments, most recently at the University of Syracuse.

These Trees Stand . . .

These trees stand very tall under the heavens.
While *they* stand, if I walk, all stars traverse
This steep celestial gulf their branches chart.
Though lovers stand at sixes and at sevens
While civilizations come down with the curse,[1]
Snodgrass is walking through the universe.

I can't make any world go around *your* house.
But note this moon. Recall how the night nurse
Goes ward-rounds, by the mild, reflective art
Of focusing her flashlight on her blouse.
Your name's safe conduct into love or verse;
Snodgrass is walking through the universe.

Your name's absurd, miraculous as sperm
And as decisive. If you can't coerce
One thing outside yourself, why you're the poet!
What irrefrangible[2] atoms whirl, affirm
Their destiny and form Lucinda's skirts!
She can't make up your mind. Soon as you know it,
Your firmament grows touchable and firm.
If all this world runs battlefield or worse,
Come, let us wipe our glasses on our shirts:
Snodgrass is walking through the universe.

1959

1. Menstruation; hence bloodshed.

2. Indestructible.

A. R. AMMONS
(*1926–*)

A. R. Ammons was born in Whiteville, North Carolina on February 18, 1926. His early interests were scientific, and he took a Bachelor of Science degree at Wake Forest College in 1949. Afterwards he attended the University of California at Berkeley for two years. Still uncertain of his direction, he became principal of an elementary school in his home state, and later an executive in the biological glass industry. But in 1964 he accepted a teaching position at Cornell, and in seven years went from instructor to full professor. In 1973 his *Collected Poems: 1951–1971* won the National Book Award for poetry, and *Sphere* won the Bollingen Prize in 1975.

Coon Song

I got one good look
    in the raccoon's eyes
        when he fell from the tree

came to his feet
and perfectly still
seized the baying hounds
in his dull fierce stare,
in that recognition all
decision lost,
choice irrelevant, before the
battle fell
and the unwinding
of his little knot of time began:

Dostoevsky would think
it important if the coon
could choose to
be back up the tree:
or if he could choose to be
wagging by a swamp pond,
dabbling at scuttling
crawdads: the coon may have
dreamed in fact of curling
into the holed-out gall
of a fallen oak some squirrel
had once brought
high into the air
clean leaves to: but

reality can go to hell
is what the coon's eyes said to me:
and said how simple
the solution to my
problem is: it needs only
not to be: I thought the raccoon
felt no anger,
saw none; cared nothing for cowardice,
bravery; was in fact
bored at
knowing what would ensue:
the unwinding, the whirling growls,
exposed tenders,
the wet teeth—a problem to be
solved, the taut-coiled vigor
of the hunt
ready to snap loose:

you want to know what happened,
you want to hear me describe it,
to placate the hound's-mouth
slobbering in your own heart:
I will not tell you: actually the coon
possessing secret knowledge

pawed dust on the dogs
and they disappeared, yapping into
nothingness, and the coon went
down to the pond
and washed his face and hands and beheld
the world: maybe he didn't:
I am no slave that I
should entertain you, say what you want
to hear, let you wallow in
your silt: one two three four five:
one two three four five six seven eight nine ten:

(all this time I've been
counting spaces
while you were thinking of something else)
mess in your own sloppy silt:
the hounds disappeared
yelping (the way you would at extinction)
into—the order
breaks up here—immortality:
I know that's where you think the brave
little victims should go:
I do not care what
you think: I do not care what you think:
I do not care what you
think: one two three four five
six seven eight nine ten: here we go
round the here-we-go-round, the
here-we-go-round, the here-we-
go-round: coon will end in disorder at the
teeth of hounds: the situation
will get him:
spheres roll, cubes stay put: now there
one two three four five
are two philosophies:
here we go round the mouth-wet of hounds:

what I choose
is youse:
baby

1965

Corsons Inlet[1]

I went for a walk over the dunes again this morning
to the sea,
then turned right along
the surf

1. Located in southeast New Jersey.

rounded a naked headland
and returned

along the inlet shore:

it was muggy sunny, the wind from the sea steady and high,
crisp in the running sand,
some breakthroughs of sun
but after a bit

continuous overcast:

the walk liberating, I was released from forms,
from the perpendiculars,
straight lines, blocks, boxes, binds
of thought
into the hues, shadings, rises, flowing bends and blends
of sight:

I allow myself eddies of meaning:
yield to a direction of significance
running
like a stream through the geography of my work:
you can find
in my sayings
swerves of action
like the inlet's cutting edge:
there are dunes of motion,
organizations of grass, white sandy paths of remembrance
in the overall wandering of mirroring mind:

but Overall is beyond me: is the sum of these events
I cannot draw, the ledger I cannot keep, the accounting
beyond the account:

in nature there are few sharp lines: there are areas of
primrose
more or less dispersed;
disorderly orders of bayberry; between the rows
of dunes,
irregular swamps of reeds,
though not reeds alone, but grass, bayberry, yarrow,[2] all . . .
predominantly reeds:

I have reached no conclusions, have erected no boundaries,
shutting out and shutting in, separating inside
from outside: I have
drawn no lines:
as

2. An herb with small white flowers.

manifold events of sand
change the dune's shape that will not be the same shape
tomorrow,

so I am willing to go along, to accept
the becoming
thought, to stake off no beginnings or ends, establish
    no walls:

by transitions the land falls from grassy dunes to creek
to undercreek: but there are no lines, though
  change in that transition is clear
  as any sharpness: but "sharpness" spread out,
allowed to occur over a wider range
than mental lines can keep:

the moon was full last night: today, low tide was low:
black shoals of mussels exposed to the risk
of air
and, earlier, of sun,
waved in and out with the waterline, waterline inexact,
caught always in the event of change:
  a young mottled gull stood free on the shoals
  and ate
to vomiting: another gull, squawking possession, cracked a crab,
picked out the entrails, swallowed the soft-shelled legs, a ruddy
turnstone[3] running in to snatch leftover bits:

risk is full: every living thing in
siege: the demand is life, to keep life: the small
white blacklegged egret, how beautiful, quietly stalks and spears
    the shallows, darts to shore
        to stab—what? I couldn't
  see against the black mudflats—a frightened
  fiddler crab?

    the news to my left over the dunes and
reeds and bayberry clumps was
    fall: thousands of tree swallows
    gathering for flight:
    an order held
    in constant change: a congregation
rich with entropy:[4] nevertheless, separable, noticeable
   as one event,
      not chaos: preparations for
flight from winter,
cheet, cheet, cheet, cheet, wings rifling the green clumps,
beaks
at the bayberries

3. A shore bird like the sandpiper.
4. The process by which energy and physical order are reduced to inertia and chaos.

a perception full of wind, flight, curve,
sound:
the possibility of rule as the sum of rulelessness:
the "field" of action
with moving, incalculable center:

in the smaller view, order tight with shape:
blue tiny flowers on a leafless weed: carapace[5] of crab:
snail shell:
pulsations of order
in the bellies of minnows: orders swallowed,
broken down, transferred through membranes
to strengthen larger orders: but in the large view, no
lines or changeless shapes: the working in and out, together
and against, of millions of events: this,
so that I make
no form
formlessness:

orders as summaries, as outcomes of actions override
or in some way result, not predictably (seeing me gain
the top of a dune,
the swallows
could take flight—some other fields of bayberry
could enter fall
berryless) and there is serenity:

no arranged terror: no forcing of image, plan,
or thought:
no propaganda, no humbling of reality to precept:

terror pervades but is not arranged, all possibilities
of escape open: no route shut, except in
the sudden loss of all routes:

I see narrow orders, limited tightness, but will
not run to that easy victory:
still around the looser, wider forces work:
I will try
to fasten into order enlarging grasps of disorder, widening
scope, but enjoying the freedom that
Scope eludes my grasp, that there is no finality of vision,
that I have perceived nothing completely,
that tomorrow a new walk is a new walk.

1965

5. Shell.

The City Limits

When you consider the radiance, that it does not withhold
itself but pours its abundance without selection into every
nook and cranny not overhung or hidden; when you consider

that birds' bones make no awful noise against the light but
lie low in the light as in a high testimony; when you consider
the radiance, that it will look into the guiltiest

swervings of the weaving heart and bear itself upon them,
not flinching into disguise or darkening; when you consider
the abundance of such resource as illuminates the glow-blue

bodies and gold-skeined wings of flies swarming the dumped
guts of a natural slaughter or the coil of shit and in no
way winces from its storms of generosity; when you consider

that air or vacuum, snow or shale, squid or wolf, rose or lichen,
each is accepted into as much light as it will take, then
the heart moves roomier, the man stands and looks about, the

leaf does not increase itself above the grass, and the dark
work of the deepest cells is of a tune with May bushes
and fear lit by the breadth of such calmly turns to praise.

1971

JAMES MERRILL
(*1926–*)

James Merrill was born March 3, 1926, in New York City. His father was a founder of an enormously successful investment firm. Merrill's education at Amherst College was interrupted by Army service in the last months of the Second World War; he received his B.A. from Amherst in 1947. Of his books of poetry, *Nights and Days* (1966) won the National Book Award and *Braving the Elements* (1972) the Bollingen Prize. Merrill lives in Connecticut and has taught sporadically at Amherst and other colleges.

The Broken Home

Crossing the street,
I saw the parents and the child
At their window, gleaming like fruit
With evening's mild gold leaf.

In a room on the floor below,
Sunless, cooler—a brimming

Saucer of wax, marbly and dim—
I have lit what's left of my life.

I have thrown out yesterday's milk
And opened a book of maxims.
The flame quickens. The word stirs.

Tell me, tongue of fire,
That you and I are as real
At least as the people upstairs.

My father,[1] who had flown in World War I,
Might have continued to invest his life
In cloud banks well above Wall Street and wife.
But the race was run below, and the point was to win.

Too late now, I make out in his blue gaze
(Through the smoked glass of being thirty-six)
The soul eclipsed by twin black pupils, sex
And business; time was money in those days.

Each thirteenth year he married. When he died
There were already several chilled wives
In sable orbit—rings, cars, permanent waves.
We'd felt him warming up for a green bride.

He could afford it. He was "in his prime"
At three score ten. But money was not time.

When my parents were younger this was a popular act:
A veiled woman would leap from an electric, wine-dark car
To the steps of no matter what—the Senate or the Ritz Bar—
And bodily, at newsreel speed, attack

No matter whom—Al Smith or José Maria Sert
Or Clemenceau[2]—veins standing out on her throat
As she yelled *War mongerer! Pig! Give us the vote!*,
And would have to be hauled away in her hobble skirt.

What had the man done? Oh, made history.
Her business (he had implied) was giving birth,
Tending the house, mending the socks.

1. Charles E. Merrill, who was a founding partner of the investment firm of Merrill Lynch Pierce Fenner & Beane.

2. Alfred E. Smith (1873–1944) was governor of New York and in 1928 a candidate for the Presidency; José María Sert (1876–1945), the Spanish painter of murals, decorated the lobby of New York's Waldorf Astoria Hotel in 1930; and Georges Clemenceau (1841–1929), premier of France during the First World War, visited the United States in 1922.

Always that same old story—
Father Time and Mother Earth,
A marriage on the rocks.

One afternoon, red, satyr-thighed[3]
Michael, the Irish setter, head
Passionately lowered, led
The child I was to a shut door. Inside,

Blinds beat sun from the bed.
The green-gold room throbbed like a bruise.
Under a sheet, clad in taboos
Lay whom we sought, her hair undone, outspread,

And of a blackness found, if ever now, in old
Engravings where the acid bit.
I must have needed to touch it
Or the whiteness—was she dead?
Her eyes flew open, startled strange and cold.
The dog slumped to the floor. She reached for me. I fled.

Tonight they have stepped out onto the gravel.
The party is over.[4] It's the fall
Of 1931. They love each other still.

She: Charlie, I can't stand the pace.
He: Come on, honey—why, you'll bury us all!

A lead soldier guards my windowsill:
Khaki rifle, uniform, and face.
Something in me grows heavy, silvery, pliable.

How intensely people used to feel!
Like metal poured at the close of a proletarian novel,[5]
Refined and glowing from the crucible,
I see those two hearts, I'm afraid,
Still. Cool here in the graveyard of good and evil,
They are even so to be honored and obeyed.

. . . Obeyed, at least, inversely. Thus
I rarely buy a newspaper, or vote.
To do so, I have learned, is to invite
The tread of a stone guest[7] within my house.

3. The satyr, a forest deity of Greek myth, usually depicted as human from the waist up and goatlike from the haunches down.

4. Alludes to the stock market crash of 1929 and the Great Depression that followed it.

5. A kind of novel, popular in the Thirties which, instead of depicting upper or middle class society, was concerned with the lives of workers.

7. Such as the stone statue of the commander of Seville which, in Molière's play *The Stone Feast*, visits his murderer Don Juan and drags him off to Hell.

Shooting this rusted bolt, though, against him,
I trust I am no less time's child than some
Who on the heath impersonate Poor Tom[8]
Or on the barricades risk life and limb.

Nor do I try to keep a garden, only
An avocado in a glass of water—
Roots pallid, gemmed with air. And later,

When the small gilt leaves have grown
Fleshy and green, I let them die, yes, yes,
And start another. I am earth's no less.

A child, a red dog roam the corridors,
Still, of the broken home. No sound. The brilliant
Rag runners[9] halt before wide-open doors.
My old room! Its wallpaper—cream, medallioned
With pink and brown—brings back the first nightmares,
Long summer colds, and Emma, sepia-faced,
Perspiring over broth carried upstairs
Aswim with golden fats I could not taste.

The real house became a boarding-school.
Under the ballroom ceiling's allegory
Someone at last may actually be allowed
To learn something; or, from my window, cool
With the unstiflement of the entire story,
Watch a red setter stretch and sink in cloud.

1966

8. In Shakespeare's *King Lear*, Edgar, disowned by his father, wanders over the heath disguised as a madman and calling himself "Poor Tom."

9. A narrow rug designed for corridors and stairs, made cushiony by a filling of cloth strips or rags.

ROBERT CREELEY
(*1926–*)

Robert Creeley was born in Arlington, Massachusetts, on May 21, 1926. His father, a doctor, died when Robert was very young. After attending Holderness School in Plymouth, New Hampshire, Creeley entered Harvard but left in 1945 to join the American Field Service in India and Burma. He came back to Harvard a year later, and while a student was married, in 1946. A year later, just in time to avoid receiving a degree (he had one term left), Creeley dropped out again. He and his wife lived on Cape Cod, then spent three years on a farm in New Hampshire; from there they went to Aix-en-Provence and then to Majorca, where Creeley started the Divers Press. In 1954 Charles Olson invited him to join the faculty of Black

Mountain College, and he founded and edited the *Black Mountain Review*. In 1956 he suffered another crisis when his marriage collapsed and he left the college. For a time he taught in New Mexico, and he obtained an M.A. degree from the University of New Mexico in 1960. He then went to Guatemala and taught on a coffee plantation. Since 1966 he has been on the faculty of the State University of New York at Buffalo.

The Whip

I spent a night turning in bed,
my love was a feather, a flat

sleeping thing. She was
very white

and quiet, and above us on
the roof, there was another woman I

also loved, had
addressed myself to in

a fit she
returned. That

encompasses it. But now I was
lonely, I yelled,

but what is that? Ugh,
she said, beside me, she put

her hand on
my back, for which act

I think to say this
wrongly.

1957

A Wicker Basket

Comes the time when it's later
and onto your table the headwaiter
puts the bill, and very soon after
rings out the sound of lively laughter—

Picking up change, hands like a walrus,
and a face like a barndoor's,
and a head without any apparent size,
nothing but two eyes—

So that's you, man,
or me. I make it as I can,
I pick up, I go
faster than they know—

Out the door, the street like a night,
any night, and no one in sight,
but then, well, there she is,
old friend Liz—

And she opens the door of her cadillac,
I step in back,
and we're gone.
She turns me on—

There are very huge stars, man, in the sky,
and from somewhere very far off someone hands me a slice of apple pie,
with a gob of white, white ice cream on top of it,
and I eat it—

Slowly. And while certainly
they are laughing at me, and all around me is racket
of these cats not making it, I make it

in my wicker basket.

1959

If You

If you were going to get a pet
what kind of animal would you get.

A soft bodied dog, a hen—
feathers and fur to begin it again.

When the sun goes down and it gets dark
I saw an animal in a park.

Bring it home, to give it to you.
I have seen animals break in two.

You were hoping for something soft
and loyal and clean and wondrously careful—

a form of otherwise vicious habit
can have long ears and be called a rabbit.

Dead. Died. Will die. Want.
Morning, midnight. I asked you

if you were going to get a pet
what kind of animal would you get.

1959

The World

I wanted so ably
to reassure you, I wanted
the man you took to be me,

to comfort you, and got
up, and went to the window,
pushed back, as you asked me to,

the curtain, to see
the outline of the trees
in the night outside.

The light, love,
the light we felt then,
greyly, was it, that

came in, on us, not
merely my hands or yours,
or a wetness so comfortable,

but in the dark then
as you slept, the grey
figure came so close

and leaned over,
between us, as you
slept, restless, and

my own face had to
see it, and be seen by it,
the man it was, your

grey lost tired bewildered
brother, unused, untaken—
hated by love, and dead,

but not dead, for an
instant, saw me, myself
the intruder, as he was not.

I tried to say, it is
all right, she is
happy, you are no longer

needed. I said,
he is dead, and he
went as you shifted

and woke, at first afraid,
then knew by my own knowing
what had happened—

and the light then
of the sun coming
for another morning
in the world.

1969

ALLEN GINSBERG

(*1926–*)

Allen Ginsberg was born in Newark, New Jersey, on June 3, 1926. His father, Louis Ginsberg, once a high school teacher, is also a poet; his mother Naomi was a Communist, and she may have encouraged her son in his more anarchic radical bias. She spent her last years in a mental institution, and her death in 1956 is the occasion for Ginsberg's long elegiac poem *Kaddish* (1961). Ginsburg was educated in the public schools of Paterson, New Jersey. One of his earliest friends in the arts was Paterson's most famous man of letters, William Carlos Williams.

From Paterson, Ginsberg went to Columbia University. In 1945 he was temporarily suspended, and William Burroughs, whose experiments with drugs are recorded in such frankly disorganized novels as *Naked Lunch,* took over Ginsberg's literary education. He received a B.A. from Columbia in 1948, and in the summer of that year he underwent an extraordinary experience which he always mentions in accounts of his spiritual development. He was alone in New York, feeling cut off from his friends and uncertain as to his vocation, when one day he heard a voice, which he took to be that of the poet himself, reciting William Blake's "Ah! Sun-Flower" and several other lyrics. The auditory hallucination was accompanied by a feeling of participation in a universal harmony. Although Ginsberg eventually had to free himself from his dependence on this remembered moment, he continues to treasure it as a personal revelation.

In 1953 Ginsberg went to San Francisco. He already knew Burroughs, Jack Kerouac, and Gregory Corso, all writers who would be identified with the Beat movement. Another friend was Neal Cassady, a railway brakeman with literary interests, who inspired the figure of Dean Moriarty in Kerouac's novel *On the Road.* Having settled around the corner from Lawrence Ferlinghetti's City Lights Bookstore, which would become the publisher of *Howl* and other Beat poems, Ginsberg worked for a time as a market researcher; he was dissatisfied and eager to change his life. In talks with a psychiatrist he found the courage to give up his job and to follow his own sexual bent. He met Peter Orlovsky, who has been his companion ever since, and he finished the first part of *Howl.*

The first edition of *Howl* was printed in England and published at the City Lights Bookstore in October 1956. In March 1957, the U.S. Customs intercepted a second printing. There was a long trial, and after hearing expert testimony from writers and critics, Judge Clayton Horn decided that *Howl* was not without "redeeming social importance." The effect of the trial was to make *Howl* an extraordinary popular success—in 1967 there were 146,000 copies in print—and to draw public attention to Ginsberg and his friends.

Ginsberg spent the early Sixties traveling, for the most part in the East, speaking with wise men of all persuasions. In 1965 he returned from the East. He was crowned King of the May in Prague and then thrown out of the country as a subversive. He went to England, where he examined Blake manuscripts, visited literary shrines, and starred in a poetry reading marathon in the Albert Hall. Back in the States, he began a tour of American colleges and universities, chanting his poems to students, talking with them endlessly and patiently, giving sound practical advice; eventually the institutions he visited gratefully supplied him with classrooms and office space. When not on the road, Ginsberg lives on a communal farm he founded in upstate New York. In 1974 his book, *The Fall of America,* won the National Book Award for poetry.

Howl[1]

FOR CARL SOLOMON

I

I saw the best minds of my generation destroyed by madness, starving hysterical naked,
dragging themselves through the negro streets at dawn looking for an angry fix,
angelheaded hipsters burning for the ancient heavenly connection to the starry dynamo in the machinery of night,
who poverty and tatters and hollow-eyed and high sat up smoking in the supernatural darkness of cold-water flats floating across the tops of cities contemplating jazz,

1. This poem is a chronicle, and also one of the most famous artifacts, of the Beat counterculture of the Fifties. It alludes to the experiences of the Beats, especially Carl Solomon (1928–), to whom it is dedicated, and Ginsberg himself; they met as patients at the Columbia Psychiatric Institute in 1949, and Solomon, whom Ginsberg calls an "intuitive Bronx dadaist and prose-poet", was an inmate of various mental hospitals, undergoing insulin and electroshock therapy, during the Fifties. Others mentioned but not named are William S. Burroughs (1914–), whose first book, *Junkie* (1953), was published through Solomon's efforts; Herbert E. Huncke (1922–), a down-and-out intellectual, Times Square con artist, petty thief, and hipster who, like his friend Burroughs, was a drug addict, and who appears in *Junkie;* and Neal Cassady (1926–1968), a hipster from Denver, whose travels around the country with Jack Kerouac (1922–1969) were recorded by the latter in *On the Road* (1957), in which the two appear as Dean Moriarty and Sal Paradise. Line 66 and much else in "Howl" evidently derives from Solomon's "apocryphal history of my adventures," which he told to Ginsberg in 1949 and later, but in *More Mishaps* (1968) he describes this account as "compounded partly of truth, but for the most raving self-justification, crypto-bohemian boasting . . . effeminate prancing and esoteric aphorisms." Line 7 doubtless refers to Ginsberg's two suspensions from Columbia, in 1945 for scraping obscene pictures and phrases on the grimy windows of his dormitory room to provoke the cleaning-woman into cleaning it, and in 1948 when, in danger of conviction as an accessory to Huncke's burglaries, he volunteered for psychiatric treatment; line 45 describes Huncke's arrival, fresh from jail, at Ginsberg's lower East Side apartment in 1948. A number of the incidents recalled in the poem happened to more than one of the Beats.

who bared their brains to Heaven under the El[2] and saw Mohammedan angels staggering on tenement roofs illuminated,
who passed through universities with radiant cool eyes hallucinating Arkansas and Blake-light tragedy[3] among the scholars of war,
who were expelled from the academies for crazy & publishing obscene odes on the windows of the skull,
who cowered in unshaven rooms in underwear, burning their money in wastebaskets and listening to the Terror through the wall,
who got busted in their pubic beards returning through Laredo[4] with a belt of marijuana for New York,
who ate fire in paint hotels or drank turpentine in Paradise Alley,[5] death, or purgatoried their torsos night after night
with dreams, with drugs, with waking nightmares, alcohol and cock and endless balls,
incomparable blind streets of shuddering cloud and lightning in the mind leaping toward poles of Canada & Paterson,[6] illuminating all the motionless world of Time between,
Peyote solidities of halls, backyard green tree cemetery dawns, wine drunkenness over the rooftops, storefront boroughs of teahead joyride neon blinking traffic light, sun and moon and tree vibrations in the roaring winter dusks of Brooklyn, ashcan rantings and kind king light of mind,
who chained themselves to subways for the endless ride from Battery to holy Bronx[7] on benzedrine until the noise of wheels and children brought them down shuddering mouth-wracked and battered bleak of brain all drained of brilliance in the drear light of Zoo,[8]
who sank all night in submarine light of Bickford's[9] floated out and sat through the stale beer afternoon in desolate Fugazzi's,[1] listening to the crack of doom on the hydrogen jukebox,
who talked continuously seventy hours from park to pad to bar to Bellevue[2] to museum to the Brooklyn Bridge,
a lost battalion of platonic conversationalists jumping down the stoops off fire escapes off windowsills off Empire State out of the moon,
yacketayakking screaming vomiting whispering facts and memories and anecdotes and eyeball kicks and shocks of hospitals and jails and wars,
whole intellects disgorged in total recall for seven days and nights with brilliant eyes, meat for the Synagogue cast on the pavement,
who vanished into nowhere Zen New Jersey leaving a trail of ambiguous picture postcards of Atlantic City Hall,
suffering Eastern sweats and Tangerian bone-grindings and migraines

2. The elevated railway.

3. Perhaps an allusion to Ginsberg's auditory hallucination in 1948 of the voice of William Blake reciting "Ah, Sun-flower" and "The Sick Rose."

4. A city in Texas, on the Mexican border.

5. A slum courtyard in New York's lower East Side, the setting of Jack Kerouac's novel, *The Subterraneans* (1958).

6. In New Jersey, where Ginsberg grew up.

7. The southern and northern ends of a New York subway line.

8. The Bronx Zoo.

9. One of a chain of all-night cafeterias, where Ginsberg mopped floors and washed dishes during his college years.

1. A bar north of New York City's bohemian district, Greenwich Village.

2. The public hospital in New York City which is a receiving center for the mentally disturbed.

of China under junk-withdrawal in Newark's bleak furnished room,
who wandered around and around at midnight in the railroad yard wondering where to go, and went, leaving no broken hearts,
who lit cigarettes in boxcars boxcars boxcars racketing through snow toward lonesome farms in grandfather night,
who studied Plotinus Poe St. John of the Cross[3] telepathy and bop kaballa[4] because the cosmos instinctively vibrated at their feet in Kansas,
who loned it through the streets of Idaho seeking visionary indian angels who were visionary indian angels,
who thought they were only mad when Baltimore gleamed in supernatural ecstasy,
who jumped in limousines with the Chinaman of Oklahoma on the impulse of winter midnight streetlight smalltown rain,
who lounged hungry and lonesome through Houston seeking jazz or sex or soup, and followed the brilliant Spaniard to converse about America and Eternity, a hopeless task, and so took ship to Africa,
who disappeared into the volcanoes of Mexico leaving behind nothing but the shadow of dungarees and the lava and ash of poetry scattered in fireplace Chicago,
who reappeared on the West Coast investigating the F.B.I. in beards and shorts with big pacifist eyes sexy in their dark skin passing out incomprehensible leaflets,
who burned cigarette holes in their arms protesting the narcotic tobacco haze of Capitalism,
who distributed Supercommunist pamphlets in Union Square[5] weeping and undressing while the sirens of Los Alamos[6] wailed them down, and wailed down Wall,[7] and the Staten Island ferry also wailed,
who broke down crying in white gymnasiums naked and trembling before the machinery of other skeletons,
who bit detectives in the neck and shrieked with delight in policecars for committing no crime but their own wild cooking pederasty and intoxication,
who howled on their knees in the subway and were dragged off the roof waving genitals and manuscripts,
who let themselves be fucked in the ass by saintly motorcyclists, and screamed with joy,
who blew and were blown by those human seraphim, the sailors, caresses of Atlantic and Caribbean love,

3. Ginsberg had studied these writers while in college, and perhaps treasured them for their visionary insights into the mystical and symbolic significances of the apparent real world. After his vision of Blake, he immediately reread passages from St. John of the Cross and Plotinus to help him interpret the experience.

4. "Bop" is a style of modern jazz especially influential during the Forties and Fifties; the Kaballa is a Hebraic system of mystical interpretation of the scriptures, which asserts the supremacy of the spirit over bodily desires.

5. In New York City; it was a center for radical speeches and demonstrations during the Thirties.

6. In New Mexico, the site of the laboratory at which the development of the atomic bomb was completed.

7. Wall Street, in New York, but perhaps also the Wailing Wall in Jerusalem where Jews lament their losses and seek consolation.

who balled in the morning in the evenings in rosegardens and the grass of public parks and cemeteries scattering their semen freely to whomever come who may,
who hiccupped endlessly trying to giggle but wound up with a sob behind a partition in a Turkish Bath when the blonde & naked angel came to pierce them with a sword,
who lost their loveboys to the three old shrews of fate the one eyed shrew of the heterosexual dollar the one eyed shrew that winks out of the womb and the one eyed shrew that does nothing but sit on her ass and snip the intellectual golden threads of the craftsman's loom,
who copulated ecstatic and insatiate with a bottle of beer a sweetheart a package of cigarettes a candle and fell off the bed, and continued along the floor and down the hall and ended fainting on the wall with a vision of ultimate cunt and come eluding the last gyzym of consciousness,
who sweetened the snatches of a million girls trembling in the sunset, and were red eyed in the morning but prepared to sweeten the snatch of the sunrise, flashing buttocks under barns and naked in the lake,
who went out whoring through Colorado in myriad stolen night-cars, N.C.,[8] secret hero of these poems, cocksman and Adonis of Denver—joy to the memory of his innumerable lays of girls in empty lots & diner backyards, moviehouses' rickety rows, on mountaintops in caves or with gaunt waitresses in familiar roadside lonely petticoat upliftings & especially secret gas-station solipsisms of johns, & hometown alleys too,
who faded out in vast sordid movies, were shifted in dreams, woke on a sudden Manhattan, and picked themselves up out of basements hungover with heartless Tokay and horrors of Third Avenue iron dreams & stumbled to unemployment offices,
who walked all night with their shoes full of blood on the snowbank docks waiting for a door in the East River to open to a room full of steamheat and opium,
who created great suicidal dramas on the apartment cliff-banks of the Hudson under the wartime blue floodlight of the moon & their heads shall be crowned with laurel in oblivion,
who ate the lamb stew of the imagination or digested the crab at the muddy bottom of the rivers of Bowery,[9]
who wept at the romance of the streets with their pushcarts full of onions and bad music,
who sat in boxes breathing in the darkness under the bridge, and rose up to build harpsichords in their lofts,
who coughed on the sixth floor of Harlem crowned with flame under the tubercular sky surrounded by orange crates of theology,
who scribbled all night rocking and rolling over lofty incantations which in the yellow morning were stanzas of gibberish,

8. Neal Cassady.

9. The avenue in New York famous as the haunt of alcoholics and derelicts.

who cooked rotten animals lung heart feet tail borsht & tortillas dreaming of the pure vegetable kingdom,
who plunged themselves under meat trucks looking for an egg,
who threw their watches off the roof to cast their ballot for Eternity outside of Time, & alarm clocks fell on their heads every day for the next decade,
who cut their wrists three times successively unsuccessfully, gave up and were forced to open antique stores where they thought they were growing old and cried,
who were burned alive in their innocent flannel suits on Madison Avenue[1] amid blasts of leaden verse & the tanked-up clatter of the iron regiments of fashion & the nitroglycerine shrieks of the fairies of advertising & the mustard gas of sinister intelligent editors, or were run down by the drunken taxicabs of Absolute Reality,
who jumped off the Brooklyn Bridge this actually happened and walked away unknown and forgotten into the ghostly daze of Chinatown soup alleyways & firetrucks, not even one free beer,
who sang out of their windows in despair, fell out of the subway window, jumped in the filthy Passaic,[2] leaped on negroes, cried all over the street, danced on broken wineglasses barefoot smashed phonograph records of nostalgic European 1930's German jazz finished the whiskey and threw up groaning into the bloody toilet, moans in their ears and the blast of colossal steamwhistles,
who barreled down the highways of the past journeying to each other's hotrod-Golgotha[3] jail-solitude watch or Birmingham jazz incarnation,
who drove crosscountry seventytwo hours to find out if I had a vision or you had a vision or he had a vision to find out Eternity,
who journeyed to Denver, who died in Denver, who came back to Denver & waited in vain, who watched over Denver & brooded & loned in Denver and finally went away to find out the Time, & now Denver is lonesome for her heroes,
who fell on their knees in hopeless cathedrals praying for each other's salvation and light and breasts, until the soul illuminated its hair for a second,
who crashed through their minds in jail waiting for impossible criminals with golden heads and the charm of reality in their hearts who sang sweet blues to Alcatraz,
who retired to Mexico to cultivate a habit,[4] or Rocky Mount to tender Buddha[5] or Tangiers[6] to boys or Southern Pacific to the black locomotive[7] or Harvard to Narcissus to Woodlawn[8] to the daisychain or grave,

1. The avenue in New York which is the center of the advertising industry, in which Burroughs had worked for a year as a copy writer during the Thirties. The conventional, middle-class New York businessman was satirized by Sloan Wilson in his novel, *The Man in the Grey Flannel Suit* (1955).
2. The river that flows past Paterson, New Jersey.
3. Golgotha, or "the place of skulls," is the hill near Jerusalem where Christ was crucified.
4. Burroughs.
5. Kerouac, who was then living in Rocky Mount, North Carolina.
6. Both Burroughs and Ginsberg lived in Tangiers for a time.
7. Neal Cassady, who worked as a brakeman for the Southern Pacific Railroad.
8. A cemetery in the Bronx.

who demanded sanity trials accusing the radio of hypnotism & were left with their insanity & their hands & a hung jury,
who threw potato salad at CCNY lecturers on Dadaism[9] and subsequently presented themselves on the granite steps of the madhouse with shaven heads and harlequin speech of suicide, demanding instantaneous lobotomy,
and who were given instead the concrete void of insulin metrasol electricity hydrotherapy psychotherapy occupational therapy pingpong & amnesia,
who in humorless protest overturned only one symbolic pingpong table, resting briefly in catatonia,
returning years later truly bald except for a wig of blood, and tears and fingers, to the visible madman doom of the wards of the madtowns of the East,
Pilgrim State's Rockland's and Greystone's[1] foetid halls, bickering with the echoes of the soul, rocking and rolling in the midnight solitude-bench dolmen-realms of love, dream of life a nightmare, bodies turned to stone as heavy as the moon,
with mother finally ******,[2] and the last fantastic book flung out of the tenement window, and the last door closed at 4 AM and the last telephone slammed at the wall in reply and the last furnished room emptied down to the last piece of mental furniture, a yellow paper rose twisted on a wire hanger in the closet, and even that imaginary, nothing but a hopeful little bit of hallucination—
ah, Carl, while you are not safe I am not safe, and now you're really in the total animal soup of time—
and who therefore ran through the icy streets obsessed with a sudden flash of the alchemy of the use of the ellipse the catalog the meter & the vibrating plane,
who dreamt and made incarnate gaps in Time & Space through images juxtaposed, and trapped the archangel of the soul between 2 visual images and joined the elemental verbs and set the noun and dash of consciousness together jumping with sensation of Pater Omnipotens Aeterna Deus[3]

9. An artistic movement (c. 1916–1920) based on absurdity and accident. CCNY is the City College of New York.

1. Three mental hospitals near New York. Carl Solomon was an inmate at Pilgrim State and Rockland hospitals, while Ginsberg's mother was a patient at Greystone Hospital.

2. Naomi Ginsberg, who for many years suffered from aggravated paranoia and was hospitalized for it several times, was permanently institutionalized shortly after Ginsberg graduated from Columbia. She died in 1956, the year after "Howl" was written, and is memorialized in Ginsberg's long poem, "Kaddish."

3. All-powerful Father, Eternal God (Lat). The phrase was used by Paul Cézanne (1839–1906), the French Impressionist painter, in a letter of 1904 to Emile Bernard, to describe the sensations he received from observing and registering the appearance of the natural world. "The last part of 'Howl' was really an homage to art but also in specific terms an homage to Cézanne's method. . . . Just as Cézanne doesn't use perspective lines to create space, but it's a juxtaposition of one color against another color (that's one element of his space), so, I had the idea, perhaps overrefined, that by the unexplainable, unexplained nonperspective line, that is, juxtaposition of one *word* against another, . . . there'd be a *gap* between the two words which the mind would fill in with the sensation of existence. . . . So, I was trying to do similar things with juxtapositions like 'hydrogen jukebox' or 'winter midnight smalltown streetlight rain'. . . . like: jazz, jukebox, and all that, and we have the jukebox from that; politics, hydrogen bomb, and we have the hydrogen of that, you see 'hydrogen jukebox.' [line 15] And that actually compresses in one instant like a whole series of things." (*Writers at Work: Third Series,* New York, 1967, pp. 295–6.)

to recreate the syntax and measure of poor human prose and stand before you speechless and intelligent and shaking with shame, rejected yet confessing out the soul to conform to the rhythm of thought in his naked and endless head,
the madman bum and angel beat in Time, unknown, yet putting down here what might be left to say in time come after death,
and rose reincarnate in the ghostly clothes of jazz in the goldhorn shadow of the band and blew the suffering of America's naked mind for love into an eli eli lamma lamma sabacthani[4] saxophone cry that shivered the cities down to the last radio
with the absolute heart of the poem of life butchered out of their own bodies good to eat a thousand years.

1956

Death News

Visit to W.C.W.[5] circa 1957, poets Kerouac Corso Orlovsky on sofa in living room inquired wise words, stricken Williams pointed thru window curtained on Main Street, "There's a lot of bastards out there!"

Walking at night on asphalt campus
road by the German Instructor with Glasses
W.C. Williams is dead he said in accent
under the trees in Benares;[6] I stopped and asked
Williams is Dead? Enthusiastic and wide-eyed
under the Big Dipper. Stood on the Porch
of the International House Annex bungalow
insects buzzing round the electric light
reading the Medical obituary in *Time.*
"out among the sparrows behind the shutters"
Williams is in the Big Dipper.[7] He isn't dead
as the many pages of words arranged thrill
with his intonations the mouths of meek kids
becoming subtle even in Bengal. Thus
there's a life moving out of his pages; Blake
also "alive" thru his experienced machines.
Were his last words anything Black out there
in the carpeted bedroom of the gabled wood house
in Rutherford?[8] Wonder what he said,
or was there anything left in realms of speech
after the stroke & brain-thrill doom entered

4. Christ's last words from the Cross (*Matthew* 26:46, *Mark* 15:33): "My God, my God, why have you forsaken me?"

5. William Carlos Williams. The visitors are Jack Kerouac (1922–1969), Gregory Corso (see p. 442), and Ginsberg's friend Peter Orlovsky (1933–). Williams was a fatherly friend and advisor to Ginsberg; he wrote introductions for *Howl* and *Empty Mirror* and incorporated three Ginsberg letters into his long poem, *Paterson.* News of Williams' death reached Ginsberg in India; the setting of this poem is the campus of the Benares Hindu University.

6. Holy city of the Hindus.

7. In Lamaism (Tibetan Buddhism), the souls of the dead pass through an astral state called "Bardo" (line 22) during transmigration to a new body or form of life.

8. Williams' home was in Rutherford, N.J.

his thoughts? If I pray to his soul in Bardo Thodol[8a]
he may hear the unexpected vibration of foreign mercy.
Quietly unknown for three weeks; now I saw Passaic
and Ganges one,[9] consenting his devotion,
because he walked on the steeley bank & prayed
to a Goddess in the river, that he only invented,
another Ganga-Ma.[1] Riding on the old
rusty Holland submarine[2] on the ground floor
Paterson Museum instead of a celestial crockodile.
Mourn O Ye Angels of the Left Wing! that the poet
of the streets is a skeleton under the pavement now
and there's no other old soul so kind and meek
and feminine jawed and him-eyed can see you
What you wanted to be among the bastards out there.

1968

8a. "Liberation by Hearing from the Astral State," a collection of prayers to be read to the soul of a dead person by a guru or a friend.

9. The Passaic River flows past Paterson and Rutherford, and figures importantly in Williams' poem, *Paterson;* the Ganges is the holy river in India.

1. A river-goddess of the Ganges.

2. John Philip Holland (1840–1914), who spent his last years in New Jersey, invented a practical submarine in 1898.

FRANK O'HARA
(*1926–1966*)

Frank O'Hara was born in Baltimore on June 27, 1926, and grew up in Worcester, Massachusetts. After serving in the Navy during the Second World War, he studied at Harvard, where he helped to found the Poets' Theatre. Later he attended graduate school at the University of Michigan. In 1951 he settled in New York, where he worked for *Art News* and joined the staff of the Museum of Modern Art, eventually becoming associate curator of exhibitions of painting and sculpture. During the Sixties he was a leading figure in a group of young writers (Ashbery and Koch among them) who came to be known as the New York poets. O'Hara wrote many of his poems in spare moments snatched from an increasingly busy life in the art world; most were left around his apartment or sent in letters to friends, and the books he published gave little idea of his abundance. After O'Hara's death in 1966 (he was run down by a dune buggy on Fire Island), Donald Allen assembled hundreds of manuscripts for a posthumous collection, and there are doubtless still more to be found.

The Day Lady Died

It is 12:20 in New York a Friday
three days after Bastille day,[4] yes
it is 1959 and I go get a shoeshine

4. July 14, a French national holiday celebrating the first great event of the French Revolution.

because I will get off the 4:19 in Easthampton[5]
at 7:15 and then go straight to dinner
and I don't know the people who will feed me

I walk up the muggy street beginning to sun
and have a hamburger and a malted and buy
an ugly NEW WORLD WRITING to see what the poets
in Ghana are doing these days
I go on to the bank
and Miss Stillwagon (first name Linda I once heard)
doesn't even look up my balance for once in her life
and in the GOLDEN GRIFFIN I get a little Verlaine
for Patsy with drawings by Bonnard[6] although I do
think of Hesiod,[7] trans. Richmond Lattimore or
Brendan Behan's new play[8] or *Le Balcon* or *Les Nègres*
of Genet,[9] but I don't, I stick with Verlaine
after practically going to sleep with quandariness

and for Mike I just stroll into the PARK LANE
Liquor Store and ask for a bottle of Strega[1] and
then I go back where I came from to 6th Avenue
and the tobacconist in the Ziegfeld Theatre and
casually ask for a carton of Gauloises[2] and a carton
of Picayunes, and a NEW YORK POST with her[3] face on it

and I am sweating a lot by now and thinking of
leaning on the john door in the 5 SPOT
while she whispered a song along the keyboard
to Mal Waldron[4] and everyone and I stopped breathing

1964

Why I Am Not a Painter

I am not a painter, I am a poet.
Why? I think I would rather be
a painter, but I am not. Well,

for instance, Mike Goldberg[5]
is starting a painting. I drop in.
"Sit down and have a drink" he
says. I drink; we drink. I look

5. A town on eastern Long Island.

6. An edition of the poems of Paul Verlaine (1844–1896), the French poet, with illustrations by Pierre Bonnard (1867–1947).

7. (8th century B.C.), Greek poet, author of *Works and Days*.

8. Probably *The Quare Fellow* (1956) or *The Hostage* (1958).

9. Jean Genet (1910–), French writer, author of the plays *The Balcony* (1956) and *The Blacks* (1958).

1. A yellow Italian liqueur.

2. A French brand of cigarettes. Picayunes are an American brand.

3. Billie Holiday (1915–1959), or "Lady Day," the Blues singer.

4. (1925–), pianist, Billie Holiday's accompanist from 1957 until her death.

5. (1924–), a New York artist who provided silk screen prints for O'Hara's *Odes* (1960).

up. "You have SARDINES in it."
"Yes, it needed something there."
"Oh." I go and the days go by
and I drop in again. The painting
is going on, and I go, and the days
go by. I drop in. The painting is
finished. "Where's SARDINES?"
All that's left is just
letters, "It was too much," Mike says.

But me? One day I am thinking of
a color: orange. I write a line
about orange. Pretty soon it is a
whole page of words, not lines.
Then another page. There should be
so much more, not of orange, of
words, of how terrible orange is
and life. Days go by. It is even in
prose, I am a real poet. My poem
is finished and I haven't mentioned
orange yet. It's twelve poems, I call
it ORANGES. And one day in a gallery
I see Mike's painting, called SARDINES.

1971

PAUL BLACKBURN
(*1926–1971*)

Paul Blackburn was born in St. Albans, Vermont, on November 24, 1926. His mother was Frances Frost, a poet and novelist. He attended New York University, then served in the Army from 1945 to 1947, after which he completed his undergraduate work at the University of Wisconsin in 1950. In 1954 he went to France on a Fulbright Fellowship to study at the University of Toulouse, and served as *lecteur américain* there during the following year. He then lived in Spain and Morocco until his return to the United States in 1958. He worked for two encyclopedias and was briefly poetry editor for *The Nation*. After 1968 he taught at the City University of New York. He died of cancer on September 13, 1971.

Clickety-Clack

FOR LAWRENCE FERLINGHETTI[3]

I took
    a coney island of the mind

3. See p. 360. *A Coney Island of the Mind* (1958) is his best-known book of poems.

to the coney
island of the flesh
    the brighton local[4]
    riding
past church avenue, beverly, cortelyou, past
    avenues h & j
king's highway, neck road, sheepshead bay,
brighton, all the way to stillwell
avenue
    that hotbed of assignation
clickety-clack

I had started reading when I got on
and somewhere down past newkirk reached
number 29[5] and read aloud

                    The crowd
in the train
looked startled at first but settled down
to enjoy the bit even if they did think I
was insane or something
and when I reached the line : "the cock
of flesh at last cries out and has his glory
                    moment God"
some girl sitting opposite me with golden hair
fresh from the bottle began to stare dis-
approvingly and wiggle as tho she had ants
somewhere where it counted
                    And sorry to say
5 lines later the poem finished and I
started to laugh like hell Aware
of the dirty look I was getting I
stared back at her thighs imagining
what she had inside those toreador pants besides
              her bathing suit and, well
              we both got off at stillwell

Watching her high backside sway and swish down that
street of tattoo artists, franks 12 inches long, past
              the wax museum and a soft
drink stand with its white inside,
I stepped beside her and said: "Let's
fling that old garment of repentance, baby!"[6]

4. A New York subway line through Brooklyn to Coney Island.

5. The last poem of Ferlinghetti's sequence, which is in imitation of the erotic stream-of-consciousness monologue by Molly Bloom which closes James Joyce's *Ulysses*. Blackburn quotes from the poem in lines 22–24.

6. A reference to Edward Fitzgerald's translation of the *Rubaiyat of Omar Khayyam:* "Come, fill the Cup, and in the Fire of Spring / The Winter Garment of Repentance fling; / The Bird of Time has but a little way / To flutter—and the Bird is on the Wing."

smitten, I
hadn't noticed her 2 brothers were behind me

clickety-clack
Horseman, pass by[7]

1967

7. From W. B. Yeats's epitaph for himself in "Under Ben Bulben."

ROBERT BLY
(*1926–*)

Robert Bly was born in Madison, Minnesota, on December 23, 1926. He served in the Navy during the Second World War and then entered St. Olaf's College in Minnesota. After a year there he transferred to Harvard, from which he graduated in 1950. For several years he lived in New York, and spent one year in Norway. Then he returned to Minnesota. Bly now lives on a farm in the western part of the state, with his wife and three children. In 1958 he founded and edited a magazine called *The Fifties* and a press of the same name in Madison, Minnesota established to publish translations of South American and European verse. Bly has himself done a good deal of translating. In 1966 he founded, with David Ray, American Writers against the Vietnam War, and he several times returned literary prizes to protest American involvement there.

Johnson's Cabinet Watched by Ants

1

It is a clearing deep in a forest: overhanging boughs
Make a low place. Here the citizens we know during the day,
The ministers, the department heads,
Appear changed: the stockholders of large steel companies
In small wooden shoes: here are the generals dressed as gamboling lambs.

2

Tonight they burn the rice-supplies; tomorrow
They lecture on Thoreau; tonight they move around the trees,
Tomorrow they pick the twigs from their clothes;
Tonight they throw the fire-bombs, tomorrow
They read the Declaration of Independence; tomorrow they are in church.

3

Ants are gathered around an old tree.
In a choir they sing, in harsh and gravelly voices,
Old Etruscan[1] songs on tyranny.

1. Of the ancient north Italian kingdom of Etruria, conquered and absorbed into the Roman empire.

Toads nearby clap their small hands, and join
The fiery songs, their five long toes trembling in the soaked earth.

1967

Evolution from the Fish

This grandson of fishes holds inside him
A hundred thousand small black stones.
This nephew of snails, six feet long, lies naked on a bed
With a smiling woman, his head throws off light
Under marble, he is moving toward his own life
Like fur, walking. And when the frost comes, he is
Fur, mammoth fur, growing longer
And silkier, passing the woman's dormitory,
Kissing a stomach, leaning against a pillar,
He moves toward the animal, the animal with furry head!

What a joy to smell the flesh of a new child!
Like new grass! And this long man with the student girl,
Coffee cups, her pale waist, the spirit moving around them,
Moves, dragging a great tail into the darkness.
In the dark we blaze up, drawing pictures
Of spiny fish, we throw off the white stones!
Serpents rise from the ocean floor with spiral motions,
A man goes inside a jewel, and sleeps. Do
Not hold my hands down! Let me raise them!
A fire is passing up through the soles of my feet!

1967

CHARLES TOMLINSON
(*1927–*)

Charles Tomlinson was born in Stoke-on-Trent, England, on January 8, 1927, and received a B.A. from Queen's College, Cambridge, in 1948. During the next few years he taught in a London elementary school and was a private secretary in northern Italy; he then resumed his studies at the University of London, from which he received an M.A. in 1955, and since 1956 he has taught English literature at the University of Bristol. He visited the United States in 1959, again in 1962 to teach at the University of New Mexico, and most recently in 1967 as O'Connor Professor of Literature at Colgate University.

Mr. Brodsky

I had heard
before, of an
American who would have preferred
to be an Indian;

but not
until Mr. Brodsky, of one
whose professed and long
pondered-on passion
was to become a Scot,
who even sent for haggis and oatcakes[5]
across continent.
Having read him
in Cambridge English
a verse or two
from MacDiarmid,[6]
I was invited
to repeat the reading
before a Burns Night Gathering[7]
where the Balmoral Pipers
of Albuquerque would
play in the haggis
out of its New York tin.
Of course, I said
No. No. I could *not* go
and then
half-regretted I had not been.
But to console
and cure the wish, came
Mr. Brodsky, bringing
his pipes and played
until the immense, distended
bladder of leather seemed
it could barely contain its water—
tears (idle
tears)[8] for the bridal of Annie Laurie
and Morton J. Brodsky.
A bagpipe in a dwelling is
a resonant instrument
and there he stood
lost in the gorse
the heather or whatever
six thousand
miles and more
from the infection's source,
in our neo-New Mexican parlour
where I had heard
before of an
American who would have preferred
to be merely an Indian.

1966

5. Scottish foods, the former a mixture of herbs, oatmeal and a sheep's internal organs cooked in its stomach, the latter a kind of pancake. At a Scottish banquet the haggis was ceremonially brought to the table to the accompaniment of bagpipes (line 19–22).

6. Hugh MacDiarmid; see p. 504.

7. Meetings of devotees of Scottish culture were often called Burns Nights, after the Scottish poet Robert Burns (1759–1796).

8. The first words of a song from Tennyson's narrative poem, *The Princess*.

At Barstow[9]

Nervy with neons, the main drag
was all there was. A placeless place.
A faint flavour of Mexico in the tacos
tasting of gasoline. Trucks refuelled
before taking off through space. Someone lived
in the houses with their houseyards wired
like tiny Belsens.[1] The Götterdämmerung[2]
would be like this. No funeral pyres, no choirs
of lost trombones. An Untergang [3]
without a clang, without
a glimmer of gone glory
however dimmed. At the motel desk
was a photograph of Roy Rogers
signed. It was here
he made a stay. He did not
ride away on Trigger
through the high night, the tilted
Pleiades[4] overhead, the polestar low, no
going off until
the eyes of beer-cans
had ceased to glint at him
and the desert darknesses
had quenched the neons. He was spent.
He was content. Down he lay.
The passing trucks patrolled his sleep,
the shifted gears contrived
a muffled fugue against the fading of his day
and his dustless, undishonoured stetson rode
beside the bed,
glowed in the pulsating, never-final twilight
there, at that execrable conjunction
of gasoline and desert air.

1966

Swimming Chenango Lake[1]

Winter will bar the swimmer soon.
He reads the water's autumnal hesitations
A wealth of ways: it is jarred,

9. A city in southern California.

1. Belsen was one of the most infamous of the Nazi concentration camps.

2. *The Twilight of the Gods* (Ger), an opera by Richard Wagner, concludes with a scene in which the hero's funeral pyre ignites the gods' great fortress Valhalla, bringing the corrupt but heroic old order to a spectacular end.

3. End of the world; literally, going under (Ger).

4. The seven most brilliant stars in the constellation Taurus (the bull).

1. A lake near the campus of Colgate University, where Tomlinson taught in 1967. In his discussion of this poem, Tomlinson cites Claude Levi-Strauss' anthropological study, *The Savage Mind:* "Now, the Pawnee Indians have a ceremony called the Hako, for the crossing of a stream. A poetic invocation is the essence of this ceremony. The invocation is divided, we are told, 'into several parts which correspond respectively to the moment when the travelers put their feet in water, the moment when they move them and the moment when the water completely

It is astir already despite its steadiness,
Where the first leaves at the first
Tremor of the morning air have dropped
Anticipating him, launching their imprints
Outwards in eccentric, overlapping circles.
There is a geometry of water, for this
Squares off the clouds' redundances
And sets them floating in a nether atmosphere
All angles and elongations: every tree
Appears a cypress as it stretches there
And every bush that shows the season,
A shaft of fire. It is a geometry and not
A fantasia of distorting forms, but each
Liquid variation answerable to the theme
It makes away from, plays before:
It is a consistency, the grain of the pulsating flow.
But he has looked long enough, and now
Body must recall the eye to its dependence
As he scissors the waterscape apart
And sways it to tatters. Its coldness
Holding him to itself, he grants the grasp,
For to swim is also to take hold
On water's meaning, to move in its embrace
And to be, between grasp and grasping free.
He reaches in-and-through to that space
The body is heir to, making a where
In water, a possession to be relinquished
Willingly at each stroke. The image he has torn
Flows-to behind him, healing itself,
Lifting and lengthening, splayed like the feathers
Down an immense wing whose darkening spread
Shadows his solitariness: alone, he is unnamed
By this baptism, where only Chenango bears a name
In a lost language he begins to construe—
A speech of densities and derisions, of half-
Replies to the questions his body must frame
Frogwise across the all but penetrable element.[2]
Human, he fronts it and, human, he draws back
From the interior cold, the mercilessness

covers their feet.' All these stages are celebrated and differentiated. I borrow this instance of the crossing of the water because it seems to correspond with the way of working of a poem like 'Swimming Chenango Lake.'" (*The Poem as Initiation*, Hamilton, N.Y., 1968.)

2. "But having defended ceremony, let me also speak of its limits. . . . In the Hopi ceremonials, the tribal spirits are impersonated by clansmen who wear masks. Hopi children are brought up to believe that these masked figures are truly the tribal spirits. . . . Then comes the central moment, when the child is initiated into youth by these spirits, and . . . the spirits remove their masks and the child sees that those he had taken for gods are only metaphors for gods: they are his uncles and kinsmen. . . . The end of 'Swimming Chenango Lake' tries to do something similar: when the naked reality, the spreading, pulsating water takes over from the swimmer, the mask of the poem (so to speak) is being put by, and the elusive reality of the lake, or of life, is admitted back into its own. We can never *know* all that reality, but the rite of the poem has, so one hopes, brought us into closer relation with it" (Tomlinson's note).

That yet shows a kind of mercy sustaining him.
  The last sun of the year is drying his skin
Above a surface a mere mosaic of tiny shatterings,
  Where a wind is unscaping all images in the flowing obsidian,
The going-elsewhere of ripples incessantly shaping.

1968

JOHN ASHBERY
(1927–)

John Ashbery was born on July 28, 1927, in Rochester, New York, and grew up on a farm near Lake Ontario. After receiving his B.A. at Harvard in 1949, he took an M.A. at Columbia University. He held jobs as a copywriter with two New York publishers. In 1956 Ashbery went to France as a Fulbright Scholar. He stayed in Paris for ten years, writing art criticism for the overseas edition of the *New York Herald Tribune*, as he would later for *Art News*. His first book, *Some Trees*, was published in the Yale Series of Younger Poets in 1956, with a preface by W. H. Auden. His plays include *The Heroes*, produced by the Living Theatre in 1953, and *The Compromise, or Queen of the Caribou*, produced at the Poets' Theatre in Cambridge, Massachusetts, in 1956. Upon his return from Paris he was appointed executive editor of *Art News*, a post he held until 1972.

The Instruction Manual

As I sit looking out of a window of the building
I wish I did not have to write the instruction manual on the uses of a new metal.
I look down into the street and see people, each walking with an inner peace,
And envy them—they are so far away from me!
Not one of them has to worry about getting out this manual on schedule.
And, as my way is, I begin to dream, resting my elbows on the desk and leaning out of the window a little,
Of dim Guadalajara! City of rose-colored flowers!
City I wanted most to see, and most did not see, in Mexico!
But I fancy I see, under the press of having to write the instruction manual,
Your public square, city, with its elaborate little bandstand!
The band is playing *Scheherazade* by Rimsky-Korsakov.
Around stand the flower girls, handing out rose- and lemon-colored flowers,
Each attractive in her rose-and-blue striped dress (Oh! such shades of rose and blue),
And nearby is the little white booth where women in green serve you green and yellow fruit.

The couples are parading; everyone is in a holiday mood.
First, leading the parade, is a dapper fellow
Clothed in deep blue. On his head sits a white hat
And he wears a mustache, which has been trimmed for the occasion.
His dear one, his wife, is young and pretty; her shawl is rose, pink, and white.
Her slippers are patent leather, in the American fashion,
And she carries a fan, for she is modest, and does not want the crowd to see her face too often.
But everybody is so busy with his wife or loved one
I doubt they would notice the mustachioed man's wife.
Here come the boys! They are skipping and throwing little things on the sidewalk
Which is made of gray tile. One of them, a little older, has a toothpick in his teeth.
He is silenter than the rest, and affects not to notice the pretty young girls in white.
But his friends notice them, and shout their jeers at the laughing girls.
Yet soon all this will cease, with the deepening of their years,
And love bring each to the parade grounds for another reason.
But I have lost sight of the young fellow with the toothpick.
Wait—there he is—on the other side of the bandstand,
Secluded from his friends, in earnest talk with a young girl
Of fourteen or fifteen. I try to hear what they are saying
But it seems they are just mumbling something—shy words of love, probably.
She is slightly taller than he, and looks quietly down into his sincere eyes.
She is wearing white. The breeze ruffles her long fine black hair against her olive cheek.
Obviously she is in love. The boy, the young boy with the toothpick, he is in love too;
His eyes show it. Turning from this couple,
I see there is an intermission in the concert.
The paraders are resting and sipping drinks through straws
(The drinks are dispensed from a large glass crock by a lady in dark blue),
And the musicians mingle among them, in their creamy white uniforms, and talk
About the weather, perhaps, or how their kids are doing at school.
Let us take this opportunity to tiptoe into one of the side streets.
Here you may see one of those white houses with green trim
That are so popular here. Look—I told you!
It is cool and dim inside, but the patio is sunny.
An old woman in gray sits there, fanning herself with a palm leaf fan.
She welcomes us to her patio, and offers us a cooling drink.
"My son is in Mexico City," she says. "He would welcome you too
If he were here. But his job is with a bank there.
Look, here is a photograph of him."
And a dark-skinned lad with pearly teeth grins out at us from the worn leather frame.

We thank her for her hospitality, for it is getting late
And we must catch a view of the city, before we leave, from a good high place.
That church tower will do—the faded pink one, there against the fierce blue of the sky. Slowly we enter.
The caretaker, an old man dressed in brown and gray, asks us how long we have been in the city, and how we like it here.
His daughter is scrubbing the steps—she nods to us as we pass into the tower.
Soon we have reached the top, and the whole network of the city extends before us.
There is the rich quarter, with its houses of pink and white, and its crumbling, leafy terraces.
There is the poorer quarter, its homes a deep blue.
There is the market, where men are selling hats and swatting flies
And there is the public library, painted several shades of pale green and beige.
Look! There is the square we just came from, with the promenaders.
There are fewer of them, now that the heat of the day has increased,
But the young boy and girl still lurk in the shadows of the bandstand.
And there is the home of the little old lady—
She is still sitting in the patio, fanning herself.
How limited, but how complete withal, has been our experience of Guadalajara!
We have seen young love, married love, and the love of an aged mother for her son.
We have heard the music, tasted the drinks, and looked at colored houses.
What more is there to do, except stay? And that we cannot do.
And as a last breeze freshens the top of the weathered old tower, I turn my gaze
Back to the instruction manual which has made me dream of Guadalajara.

1956

W. S. MERWIN
(*1927–*)

W. S. Merwin was born in New York City on September 30, 1927, and grew up in Union, New Jersey, and Scranton, Pennsylvania; his father was a Presbyterian minister, and Merwin recalls, "I started writing hymns for my father almost as soon as I could write at all." He received his B.A. from Princeton University, where he encountered John Berryman (who taught creative writing) and the poet and critic R. P. Blackmur, to whom *The Moving Target* (1963) was dedicated. During a year of graduate work there he continued the study of foreign languages which was to equip him to prepare excellent translations from Latin, Spanish, and French. He then left the United States and for many years lived mainly in England and France. In 1950 he tutored Robert Graves's son on Majorca. From 1951 to 1954 he was in London, supporting himself primarily by making translations of French and Spanish literature for broadcast by the BBC, while his first two books of poetry were published in the United States. In 1956 Merwin was playwright-in-residence at the Poets' Theater in Cambridge, Massachusetts, and in the next few years he wrote four plays, one produced in Cambridge and the others in England. During another brief return to the United States, from 1961 to 1963, he was poetry editor of *The Nation.* Since 1968 he has lived in the United States. His fifth book of poems, *The Moving Target*, won the National Book Award, and in 1971 Merwin was awarded the Pulitzer Prize for *A Carrier of Ladders.*

Leviathan[9]

This is the black sea-brute bulling through wave-wrack,
Ancient as ocean's shifting hills, who in sea-toils
Travelling, who furrowing the salt acres
Heavily, his wake hoary behind him,[1]
Shoulders spouting, the fist of his forehead
Over wastes gray-green crashing, among horses unbroken
From bellowing fields, past bone-wreck of vessels,
Tide-ruin, wash of lost bodies bobbing
No longer sought for, and islands of ice gleaming,
Who ravening the rank flood, wave-marshalling,
Overmastering the dark sea-marches,[1a] finds home
And harvest. Frightening to foolhardiest
Mariners, his size were difficult to describe:
The hulk of him is like hills heaving,
Dark, yet as crags of drift-ice, crowns cracking in thunder,
Like land's self by night black-looming, surf churning and trailing
Along his shores' rushing, shoal-water boding
About the dark of his jaws; and who should moor at his edge
And fare on afoot would find gates of no gardens,
But the hill of dark underfoot diving,
Closing overhead, the cold deep, and drowning.[2]
He is called Leviathan, and named for rolling,[3]
First created he was of all creatures,[4]
He has held Jonah three days and nights,
He is that curling serpent that in ocean is,[5]
Sea-fright he is, and the shadow under the earth.
Days there are, nonetheless, when he lies

9. "Leviathan" comes from a Hebrew word meaning "great water animal," and is traditionally associated with the whale.

1. Compare the description of the whale in *Job* 41:32: "Behind him he leaves a shining wake; one would think the deep to be hoary."

1a. Marches are frontier regions or boundaries.

2. This description is adapted from a more elaborate one in the bestiary included in the important Old English compendium, *The Exeter Book.*

3. In the "Etymology" at the beginning of *Moby-Dick*, Melville quotes "Webster's Dictionary": "WHALE. * * * Sw. and Dan. *hval.* This animal is named from roundness or rolling; for in Dan. *hvalt* is arched or vaulted."

4. According to *Genesis* 1:21.

5. "In that day the Lord, with his sore, and great, and strong sword, shall punish leviathan the piercing serpent, even leviathan the crooked serpent; and he shall slay the dragon that is in the sea." (*Isaiah* 27:1)

Like an angel, although a lost angel
On the waste's unease, no eye of man moving,
Bird hovering, fish flashing, creature whatever
Who after him came to herit earth's emptiness.
Froth at flanks seething soothes to stillness,
Waits; with one eye he watches
Dark of night sinking last, with one eye dayrise
As at first over foaming pastures. He makes no cry
Though that light is a breath. The sea curling,
Star-climbed, wind-combed, cumbered with itself still
As at first it was, is the hand not yet contented
Of the Creator. And he waits for the world to begin.

1956

The Drunk in the Furnace

For a good decade
The furnace stood in the naked gully, fireless
And vacant as any hat. Then when it was
No more to them than a hulking black fossil
To erode unnoticed with the rest of the junk-hill
By the poisonous creek, and rapidly to be added
To their ignorance.

They were afterwards astonished
To confirm, one morning, a twist of smoke like a pale
Resurrection, staggering out of its chewed hole,
And to remark then other tokens that someone,
Cosily bolted behind the eye-holed iron
Door of the drafty burner, had there established
His bad castle.

Where he gets his spirits
It's a mystery. But the stuff keeps him musical:
Hammer-and-anvilling with poker and bottle
To his jugged bellowings, till the last groaning clang
As he collapses onto the rioting
Springs of a litter of car-seats ranged on the grates,
To sleep like an iron pig.

In their tar-paper church
On a text about stoke-holes that are sated never
Their Reverend lingers. They nod and hate trespassers.[6]
When the furnace wakes, though, all afternoon
Their witless offspring flock like piped rats to its siren
Crescendo,[7] and agape on the crumbling ridge
Stand in a row and learn.

1960

6. Contraveners of God's laws.

7. In music, growing in volume. The Sirens (line 24) sang irresistibly, so as to lure men to destruction. "Piped rats" alludes to the tale of the Pied Piper of Hamelin, whose flute playing lured first the rats and then the children of Hamelin away from the town.

Footprints on the Glacier

Where the wind
year round out of the gap
polishes everything
here this day are footprints like my own
the first ever
frozen
pointing up into the cold

and last night someone
marched and marched on the candle flame
hurrying
a painful road
and I heard the echo a long time afterwards
gone and some connection of mine

I scan the high slopes for a dark speck
that was lately here
I pass my hands
over the melted wax
like a blind man
they are all
moving into their seasons at last
my bones face each other trying
to remember a question

nothing moves while I watch
but here the black trees
are the cemetery of a great battle
and behind me as I turn
I hear names leaving the bark
in growing numbers and flying north

1970

JAMES WRIGHT
(*1927–*)

James Wright was born December 13, 1927, at Martin's Ferry, Ohio. He attended Kenyon College and received a B.A. He served with the United States Army in Japan during the American occupation. He resumed his studies at the University of Washington, where he received the M.S. and Ph.D.; then he won a Fulbright scholarship for study at the University of Vienna. He has taught at several colleges, most recently Hunter College in New York City. His *Collected Poems* received the Pulitzer Prize for poetry in 1972.

Two Poems About President Harding

One: His Death

In Marion,[1] the honey locust trees are falling.
Everybody in town remembers the white hair,
The campaign of a lost summer, the front porch
Open to the public, and the vaguely stunned smile
Of a lucky man.[2]

"Neighbor, I want to be helpful," he said once.
Later, "You think I'm honest, don't you?"[3]
Weeping drunk.

I am drunk this evening in 1961,
In a jag for my countryman,
Who died of crab meat on the way back from Alaska.[4]
Everyone knows that joke.

How many honey locusts have fallen,
Pitched rootlong into the open graves of strip mines,
Since the First World War ended
And Wilson the gaunt deacon jogged sullenly
Into silence?[5]
Tonight,
The cancerous ghosts of old con men
Shed their leaves.
For a proud man,
Lost between the turnpike near Cleveland
And the chiropractors' signs looming among dead mulberry trees,
There is no place left to go
But home.

"Warren lacks mentality," one of his friends said.
Yet he was beautiful, he was the snowfall
Turned to white stallions standing still
Under dark elm trees.

He died in public. He claimed the secret right
To be ashamed.

1. Marion, Ohio, the home of Warren G. Harding (1865–1923), President of the United States from 1921 to 1923.

2. Harding, after an unremarkable career as a newspaper editor and Republican politician, was his party's dark-horse nominee for the Presidency in 1920; he conducted his campaign from the front porch of his home in Marion, and won the election more because of popular disaffection with the Democrats and Woodrow Wilson than from his own personal force or magnetism.

3. During Harding's administration, corruption and incompetence in the federal government became appallingly widespread, but the President himself was probably unaware of its extent and was not implicated in it.

4. In 1923, Harding undertook a national tour, ending in Alaska, trying to restore confidence in the Republican party. On his return, he received a message informing him of the scandals which were about to break, and he died soon thereafter.

5. Woodrow Wilson suffered a physical collapse in 1919, after which he was generally unable to make public appearances or to perform his official duties.

Two: His Tomb in Ohio

"... he died of a busted gut."
—MENCKEN, on BRYAN.[6]

A hundred slag piles north of us,
At the mercy of the moon and rain,
He lies in his ridiculous
Tomb[6a], our fellow citizen.
No, I have never seen that place,
Where many shadows of faceless thieves
Chuckle and stumble and embrace
On beer cans, stogie butts, and graves.

One holiday, one rainy week
After the country fell apart,
Hoover and Coolidge[7] came to speak
And snivel about his broken heart.
His grave, a huge absurdity,
Embarrassed cops and visitors.
Hoover and Coolidge crept away
By night, and women closed their doors.

Now junkmen call their children in
Before they catch their death of cold;
Young lovers let the moon begin
Its quick spring; and the day grows old;
The mean one-legger who rakes up leaves
Has chased the loafers out of the park;
Minnegan Leonard half-believes
In God, and the poolroom goes dark;

America goes on, goes on
Laughing, and Harding was a fool.
Even his big pretentious stone
Lays him bare to ridicule.
I know it. But don't look at me.
By God, I didn't start this mess.
Whatever moon and rain may be,
The hearts of men are merciless.

1963

6. H. L. Mencken (1880–1956), American editor and social commentator, on William Jennings Bryan (1860–1925), twice Democratic Presidential candidate. Bryan died soon after serving as a prosecuting attorney in the trial of John Scopes, who was fined $100 for teaching the theory of evolution in a Tennessee school; because of his humiliation by the defense attorney, Clarence Darrow, it was said by many that Bryan had died of a broken heart.

6a. A large monument in imitation of classical Greek architecture.

7. Calvin Coolidge (1872–1933), Harding's Vice-President, succeeded him in 1923; Herbert Hoover (1874–1964), Coolidge's Vice-President from 1924 to 1928 and then President for the next four years, had been Harding's Secretary of Commerce.

PHILIP LEVINE
(*1928–*)

Philip Levine was born on January 10, 1928. He studied with John Berryman at Wayne State University. In 1958 he received a Fellowship in Poetry at Stanford University and still lives in California, though he travels much, particularly in Spain; he acknowledges the importance to him of the Spanish-American surrealist poets and of their advocate, Robert Bly, as well as the influence of Rexroth and the San Francisco poets, who "opened me up." Though he has published in magazines since the mid-Fifties, his first book did not appear until 1963.

To a Child Trapped in a Barber Shop

You've gotten in through the transom
and you can't get out
till Monday morning or, worse,
till the cops come.

That six-year-old red face
calling for mama
is yours; it won't help you
because your case

is closed forever, hopeless.
So don't drink
the Lucky Tiger,[1] don't
fill up on grease

because that makes it a lot worse,
that makes it a crime
against property and the state
and that costs time.

We've all been here before,
we took our turn
under the electric storm
of the vibrator

and stiffened our wills to meet
the close clippers
and heard the true blade mowing
back and forth

on a strip of dead skin,
and we stopped crying.
You think your life is over?
It's just begun.

1968

1. A brand of hair tonic.

They Feed They Lion

Out of burlap sacks, out of bearing butter,
Out of black bean and wet slate bread,
Out of the acids of rage, the candor of tar,
Out of creosote, gasoline, drive shafts, wooden dollies,
They Lion grow.

Out of the grey hills
Of industrial barns, out of rain, out of bus ride,
West Virginia to Kiss My Ass, out of buried aunties,
Mothers hardening like pounded stumps, out of stumps,
Out of the bones' need to sharpen and the muscles' to stretch,
They Lion grow.

Earth is eating trees, fence posts,
Gutted cars, earth is calling her little ones,
"Come home, Come home!" From pig balls,
From the ferocity of pig driven to holiness,
From the furred ear and the full jowl come
The repose of the hung belly, from the purpose
They Lion grow.

From the sweet glues of the trotters
Come the sweet kinks of the fist, from the full flower
Of the hams the thorax of caves,
From "Bow Down" come "Rise Up,"
Come they Lion from the reeds of shovels,
The grained arm that pulls the hands,
They Lion grow.

From my five arms and all my hands,
From all my white sins forgiven, they feed,
From my car passing under the stars,
They Lion, from my children inherit,
From the oak turned to a wall, they Lion,
From they sack and they belly opened
And all that was hidden burning on the oil-stained earth
They feed they Lion and he comes.

1970

THOMAS KINSELLA
(*1928–*)

Thomas Kinsella was born in Dublin on May 4, 1928. At 18 he joined the Irish Civil Service, with which he served until 1965, eventually becoming the assistant principal officer in the Department of Finance. In 1956 he published his first book, *Poems*, with the Dolmen Press, of which he later became a director; two years later his second book, *Another September*, won the Guinness Poetry Award. In 1965 he left Ireland to become Writer in Residence at Southern Illinois University, and two years later he became a Professor of English there; in 1963 he was awarded a Guggenheim fellowship. Although he lives much in the United States, he continues to write as an Irishman.

Westland Row[1]

We came to the outer light down a ramp in the dark
Through eddying cold gusts and grit, our ears
Stopped with noise. The hands of the station clock
Stopped, or another day vanished exactly.
The engine departing hammered slowly overhead.
Dust blowing under the bridge, we stooped slightly
With briefcases and books and entered the wind.

The savour of our days restored, dead
On nostril and tongue. Drowned in air,
We stepped on our own traces, not on stone,
Nodded and smiled distantly and followed
Our scattering paths, not stumbling, not touching.

Until, in a breath of benzine[2] from a garage-mouth,
By the Academy of Music coming against us
She stopped an instant in her wrinkled coat
And ducked her childish cheek in the coat-collar
To light a cigarette: seeing nothing,
Thick-lipped, in her grim composure.

Daughterwife, look upon me.

1967

Je t'adore[3]

The other props are gone.
Sighing in one another's
Iron arms, propped above nothing,
We praise Love the limiter.

1967

1. A street in Dublin.
2. Gasoline.
3. I adore you (Fr).

ANNE SEXTON
(1928–1974)

Anne (Harvey) Sexton was born November 9, 1928 in Newton, Massachusetts. She was educated at Garland Junior College (though she later deprecated her schooling), and she married in 1948. Eleven years later she became a member of Robert Lowell's creative writing class at Boston University; one of her classmates was the 27-year-old Sylvia Plath. By 1960 her first book of poems, *To Bedlam and Part Way Back*, had appeared, and recognition was not long in coming: in 1961 she was invited to join the Radcliffe Institute for Independent Study; *Live or Die* (1966) won the Pulitzer Prize for poetry; and in 1968 she was elected a Fellow of the Royal Society of Literature in London.

Anne Sexton believed that her career as a poet and her life itself fatefully resembled Sylvia Plath's. "Wanting to Die," written not long after Plath's suicide, now seems to look forward as well as back, for on October 4, 1974, at her home in Weston, Massachusetts, she took her own life.

Unknown Girl in the Maternity Ward

Child, the current of your breath is six days long.
You lie, a small knuckle on my white bed;
lie, fisted like a snail, so small and strong
at my breast. Your lips are animals; you are fed
with love. At first hunger is not wrong.
The nurses nod their caps; you are shepherded
down starch halls with the other unnested throng
in wheeling baskets. You tip like a cup; your head
moving to my touch. You sense the way we belong.
But this is an institution bed.
You will not know me very long.

The doctors are enamel. They want to know
the facts. They guess about the man who left me,
some pendulum soul, going the way men go
and leave you full of child. But our case history
stays blank. All I did was let you grow.
Now we are here for all the ward to see.
They thought I was strange, although
I never spoke a word. I burst empty
of you, letting you learn how the air is so.
The doctors chart the riddle they ask of me
and I turn my head away. I do not know.

Yours is the only face I recognize.
Bone at my bone, you drink my answers in.
Six times a day I prize
your need, the animals of your lips, your skin
growing warm and plump. I see your eyes
lifting their tents. They are blue stones, they begin
to outgrow their moss. You blink in surprise
and I wonder what you can see, my funny kin,
as you trouble my silence. I am a shelter of lies
Should I learn to speak again, or hopeless in
such sanity will I touch some face I recognize?

Down the hall the baskets start back. My arms
fit you like a sleeve, they hold
catkins of your willows, the wild bee farms
of your nerves, each muscle and fold
of your first days. Your old man's face disarms
the nurses. But the doctors return to scold
me. I speak. It is you my silence harms.
I should have known; I should have told
them something to write down. My voice alarms
my throat. 'Name of father—none.' I hold
you and name you bastard in my arms.

And now that's that. There is nothing more
that I can say or lose.
Others have traded life before
and could not speak. I tighten to refuse
your owling eyes, my fragile visitor.
I touch your cheeks, like flowers. You bruise
against me. We unlearn. I am a shore
rocking you off. You break from me. I choose
your only way, my small inheritor
and hand you off, trembling the selves we lose.
Go child, who is my sin and nothing more.

1960

Wanting to Die

Since you ask, most days I cannot remember.
I walk in my clothing, unmarked by that voyage.
Then the almost unnameable lust returns.

Even then I have nothing against life.
I know well the grass blades you mention,
the furniture you have placed under the sun.

But suicides have a special language.
Like carpenters they want to know *which tools.*
They never ask *why build.*

Twice I have so simply declared myself,
have possessed the enemy, eaten the enemy,
have taken on his craft, his magic.

In this way, heavy and thoughtful,
warmer than oil or water,
I have rested, drooling at the mouth-hole.

I did not think of my body at needle point.
Even the cornea and the leftover urine were gone.
Suicides have already betrayed the body.

Still-born, they don't always die,
but dazzled, they can't forget a drug so sweet
that even children would look on and smile.

To thrust all that life under your tongue!—
that, all by itself, becomes a passion.
Death's a sad bone; bruised, you'd say,

and yet she waits for me, year after year,
to so delicately undo an old wound,
to empty my breath from its bad prison.

Balanced there, suicides sometimes meet,
raging at the fruit, a pumped-up moon,
leaving the bread they mistook for a kiss,

leaving the page of the book carelessly open,
something unsaid, the phone off the hook
and the love, whatever it was, an infection.

1966

ADRIENNE RICH
(*1929–*)

Adrienne Rich was born, the elder of two sisters, in Baltimore, Maryland, on May 16, 1929. She graduated from Radcliffe College in 1951, and in the same year W. H. Auden chose her first book, *A Change of World*, for the Yale Younger Poets series. She married in her twenties and bore three children before she was thirty.

After 1966, when her husband accepted a teaching post at the City College of New York, they became deeply involved in antiwar activities. She also began to teach impoverished young people, and teaching has since then become an increasingly important vocation for her. Her husband died suddenly in 1970. In 1974 she received the National Book Award for *Diving into the Wreck.*

Orion[4]

Far back when I went zig-zagging
through tamarack[5] pastures
you were my genius, you
my cast-iron Viking, my helmed

4. A constellation named for the giant hunter of Greek mythology, who at his death was placed among the stars by the gods.

5. Larch tree.

lion-heart king in prison.[6]
Years later now you're young

my fierce half-brother, staring
down from that simplified west
your breast open, your belt dragged down
by an oldfashioned thing, a sword
the last bravado you won't give over
though it weighs you down as you stride

and the stars in it are dim
and maybe have stopped burning.
But you burn, and I know it;
as I throw back my head to take you in
an old transfusion happens again:
divine astronomy is nothing to it.

Indoors I bruise and blunder,
break faith, leave ill enough
alone, a dead child born in the dark.
Night cracks up over the chimney,
pieces of time, frozen geodes[7]
come showering down in the grate.

A man reaches behind my eyes
and finds them empty
a woman's head turns away
from my head in the mirror
children are dying my death
and eating crumbs of my life.

Pity is not your forte.
Calmly you ache up there
pinned aloft in your crow's nest,
my speechless pirate!
You take it all for granted
and when I look you back

it's with a starlike eye
shooting its cold and egotistical spear
where it can do least damage.
Breathe deep! No hurt, no pardon
out here in the cold with you
you with your back to the wall.

1969

6. Like Richard I of England (1157–1199), called "the lion-hearted," who on his return from a crusade was briefly imprisoned in Austria.

7. Hollow, spherical rocks hurled from volcanoes; the center of each rock is lined with quartz crystals.

Planetarium

(Thinking of Caroline Herschel, 1750–1848, astronomer, sister of William;[2] *and others)*

A woman in the shape of a monster
a monster in the shape of a woman
the skies are full of them

a woman   'in the snow
among the Clocks and instruments
or measuring the ground with poles'

in her 98 years to discover
8 comets

she whom the moon ruled
like us
levitating into the night sky
riding the polished lenses

Galaxies of women, there
doing penance for impetuousness
ribs chilled
in those spaces   of the mind

An eye,
    'virile, precise and absolutely certain'
    from the mad webs of Uranisborg[3]
                encountering the NOVA[4]

every impulse of light exploding
from the core
as life flies out of us

    Tycho whispering at last
    'Let me not seem to have lived in vain'

What we see, we see
and seeing is changing

the light that shrivels a mountain
and leaves a man alive

Heartbeat of the pulsar[5]
heart sweating through my body

2. (1738–1822), astronomer to King George III; he discovered the planet Uranus.

3. The castle of the heavens (Dutch), the name of the great observatory built by Tycho Brahe (1546–1601), the Dutch astronomer, famous for his studies of comets.

4. An exploding star.

5. A star that emits powerful radio pulses at regular intervals.

The radio impulse
pouring in from Taurus[6]

I am bombarded yet I stand

I have been standing all my life in the
direct path of a battery of signals
the most accurately transmitted most
untranslateable language in the universe
I am a galactic cloud so deep so invo-
luted that a light wave could take 15
years to travel through me And has
taken I am an instrument in the shape
of a woman trying to translate pulsations
into images for the relief of the body
and the reconstruction of the mind.

1971

Diving into the Wreck

First having read the book of myths,
and loaded the camera,
and checked the edge of the knife-blade,
I put on
the body-armor of black rubber
the absurd flippers
the grave and awkward mask.
I am having to do this
not like Cousteau with his
assiduous team
aboard the sun-flooded schooner
but here alone.

There is a ladder.
The ladder is always there
hanging innocently
close to the side of the schooner.
We know what it is for,
we who have used it.
Otherwise
it is a piece of maritime floss
some sundry equipment.

I go down.
Rung after rung and still
the oxygen immerses me
the blue light
the clear atoms
of our human air.

6. The constellation "the Bull."

I go down.
My flippers cripple me,
I crawl like an insect down the ladder
and there is no one
to tell me when the ocean
will begin.

First the air is blue and then
it is bluer and then green and then
black I am blacking out and yet
my mask is powerful
it pumps my blood with power
the sea is another story
the sea is not a question of power
I have to learn alone
to turn my body without force
in the deep element.

And now: it is easy to forget
what I came for
among so many who have always
lived here
swaying their crenellated[7] fans
between the reefs
and besides
you breathe differently down here.

I came to explore the wreck.
The words are purposes.
The words are maps.
I came to see the damage that was done
and the treasures that prevail.
I stroke the beam of my lamp
slowly along the flank
of something more permanent
than fish or weed

the thing I came for:
the wreck and not the story of the wreck
the thing itself and not the myth
the drowned face always staring
toward the sun
the evidence of damage
worn by salt and sway into this threadbare beauty
the ribs of the disaster
curving their assertion
among the tentative haunters.

This is the place.
And I am here, the mermaid whose dark hair

7. Regularly indented, like the top of a castle wall.

streams black, the merman in his armored body.
We circle silently
about the wreck
we dive into the hold.
I am she: I am he

whose drowned face sleeps with open eyes
whose breasts still bear the stress
whose silver, copper, vermeil[8] cargo lies
obscurely inside barrels
half-wedged and left to rot
we are the half-destroyed instruments
that once held to a course
the water-eaten log
the fouled compass

We are, I am, you are
by cowardice or courage
the one who find our way
back to this scene
carrying a knife, a camera
a book of myths
in which
our names do not appear.

1973

8. Vermillion.

THOM GUNN
(1929–)

Thom Gunn was born in Gravesend, England, on August 29, 1929. During his first years his family moved often, for his father, a journalist, worked for several different newspapers. Gunn served for two years in the British Army, and then went to Paris, where for several months he worked in the offices of the Métro (the Paris subway) while trying to write a novel. He then entered Trinity College, Cambridge University, where he wrote his first published poems. In 1953 he received his B.A. and went to Rome for six months before entering Stanford University as a graduate student.

Gunn was associated with the young English poets who began to publish during the early Fifties, and who were called "The Movement." He was one of the youngest members, and was already living in California when the first Movement anthology appeared. Except for a year teaching in San Antonio, Texas, and occasional visits to England, Gunn has remained in San Francisco ever since. From 1958 to 1966 he taught at the University of California at Berkeley. Since then he has taught or taken other jobs only as needed, most often at Berkeley, so as to have most of his time free for writing.

The Byrnies[1]

The heroes paused upon the plain.
When one of them but swayed, ring mashed on ring:
Sound of the byrnie's knitted chain,
Vague evocations of the constant Thing.

They viewed beyond a salty hill
Barbaric forest, mesh of branch and root
—A huge obstruction growing still,
Darkening the land, in quietness absolute.

That dark was fearful—lack of presence—
Unless some man could chance upon or win
Magical signs to stay the essence
Of the broad light that they adventured in.

Elusive light of light that went
Flashing on water, edging round a mass,
Inching across fat stems, or spent
Lay thin and shrunk among the bristling grass.

Creeping from sense to craftier sense,
Acquisitive, and loss their only fear,
These men had fashioned a defence
Against the nicker's snap, and hostile spear.

Byrnie on byrnie! as they turned
They saw light trapped between the man-made joints,
Central in every link it burned,
Reduced and steadied to a thousand points.

Thus for each blunt-faced ignorant one
The great grey rigid uniform combined
Safety with virtue of the sun.
Thus concepts linked like chainmail in the mind.

Reminded, by the grinding sound,
Of what they sought, and partly understood,
They paused upon that open ground,
A little group above the foreign wood.

1961

Moly[2]

Nightmare of beasthood, snorting, how to wake.
I woke. What beasthood skin she made me take?

1. Coats of mail (Middle Eng).

2. A magic herb of Greek mythology. The enchantress Circe transformed Odysseus' shipmates into swine; Odysseus, protected by the herb moly, which he had been given by the gods' messenger Hermes, compelled her to restore them to human shape.

Leathery toad that ruts for days on end,
Or cringing dribbling dog, man's servile friend,

Or cat that prettily pounces on its meat,
Tortures it hours, then does not care to eat:

Parrot, moth, shark, wolf, crocodile, ass, flea.
What germs, what jostling mobs there were in me.

These seem like bristles, and the hide is tough.
No claw or web here: each foot ends in hoof.

Into what bulk has method disappeared?
Like ham, streaked. I am gross—grey, gross, flap-eared.

The pale-lashed eyes my only human feature.
My teeth tear, tear. I am the snouted creature

That bites through anything, root, wire, or can.
If I was not afraid I'd eat a man.

Oh a man's flesh already is in mine.
Hand and foot poised for risk. Buried in swine.

I root and root, you think that it is greed,
It is, but I seek out a plant I need.

Direct me gods, whose changes are all holy,
To where it flickers deep in grass, the moly:

Cool flesh of magic in each leaf and shoot,
From milk flower to the black forked root.

From this fat dungeon I could rise to skin
And human title, putting pig within.

I push my big grey wet snout through the green,
Dreaming the flower I have never seen.

1971

DEREK WALCOTT
(*1930–*)

Derek Walcott was born on the island of St. Lucia in the British West Indies on January 23, 1930. Within a year his father died, leaving him and his twin brother Roderick to be brought up by their mother. Walcott was fourteen when one of his poems was published in a newspaper, and four years later he published a booklet of twenty-five poems. The money for this project came from his mother, who could little spare it; he hawked the pamphlet throughout the island and was able to pay the money back. The next year his play *Henry Christophe* was produced. In 1950 he left St. Lucia and entered the University of the West Indies in Jamaica, where he took a B.A. in 1953. He then moved to Trinidad, where he has worked as a book reviewer, art critic, and playwright as well as a poet, and for ten years has been artistic director of a theater workshop. His poetry began to attract international attention when *In a Green Night* (1962) was published in England, and he has achieved growing success as a dramatist. Several of Walcott's plays have received performances in New York and London; many are concerned with the history and culture of the West Indies and are written in the native Creole dialect. Recently he has spent much time in the United States, and was poet-in-residence at Lake Forest College in 1972.

A Far Cry from Africa

A wind is ruffling the tawny pelt
Of Africa. Kikuyu,[1] quick as flies,
Batten upon the bloodstreams of the veldt.[1a]
Corpses are scattered through a paradise.
Only the worm, colonel of carrion, cries:
'Waste no compassion on these separate dead!'
Statistics justify and scholars seize
The salients of colonial policy.
What is that to the white child hacked in bed?
To savages, expendable as Jews?

Threshed out by beaters,[2] the long rushes break
In a white dust of ibises whose cries
Have wheeled since civilization's dawn
From the parched river or beast-teeming plain.
The violence of beast on beast is read
As natural law, but upright man
Seeks his divinity by inflicting pain.
Delirious as these worried beasts, his wars
Dance to the tightened carcass of a drum,
While he calls courage still that native dread
Of the white peace contracted by the dead.

Again brutish necessity wipes its hands
Upon the napkin of a dirty cause, again
A waste of our compassion, as with Spain,[3]
The gorilla wrestles with the superman.

I who am poisoned with the blood of both,
Where shall I turn, divided to the vein?

1. An African tribe whose members, as Mau Mau fighters, conducted an eight-year campaign of terrorism against British colonial settlers in Kenya.

1a. The central and south African plains.

2. In African game hunting, natives are hired to beat the brush, chasing birds and animals from their hiding places.

3. Perhaps a reference to the massacres inflicted on both sides during the Spanish Civil War of 1936–9.

I who have cursed
The drunken officer of British rule, how choose
Between this Africa and the English tongue I love?
Betray them both, or give back what they give?
How can I face such slaughter and be cool?
How can I turn from Africa and live?

1962

Codicil[4]

Schizophrenic, wrenched by two styles,
one a hack's hired prose, I earn
my exile. I trudge this sickle, moonlit beach for miles,

tan, burn
to slough off
this love of ocean that's self-love.

To change your language you must change your life.

I cannot right old wrongs.
Waves tire of horizon and return.
Gulls screech with rusty tongues

Above the beached, rotting pirogues,[4a]
they were a venomous beaked cloud at Charlotteville.[5]

Once I thought love of country was enough,
now, even I chose, there's no room at the trough.

I watch the best minds root like dogs
for scraps of favour.
I am nearing middle-

age, burnt skin
peels from my hand like paper, onion-thin,
like Peer Gynt's riddle.[6]

At heart there's nothing, not the dread
of death. I know too many dead.
They're all familiar, all in character,

even how they died. On fire,
the flesh no longer fears that furnace mouth
of earth,

4. An addition to a will.
4a. Dugout canoes.
5. A town on the West Indian island of Tobago.
6. In Ibsen's play, Peer Gynt peels an onion, likening each layer to an aspect of his own character, but discovers that there is nothing at its core.

that kiln or ashpit of the sun,
nor this clouding, unclouding sickle moon
whitening this beach again like a blank page.

All its indifference is a different rage.

1965

Moon

Resisting poetry I am becoming a poem.
O lolling Orphic head[7] silently howling,
my own head rises from its surf of cloud.

Slowly my body grows a single sound,
slowly I become
a bell,
an oval, disembodied vowel,
I grow, an owl,
an aureole, white fire.

I watch the moonstruck image of the moon burn,
a candle mesmerised by its own aura,
and turn
my hot, congealing face, towards that forked mountain
which wedges the drowned singer.

That frozen glare,
that morsured,[8] classic petrifaction.
Haven't you sworn off such poems for this year,
and no more on the moon?

Why are you gripped by demons of inaction?
Whose silence shrieks so soon?

1970

7. Orpheus, the mythical Greek musician and poet, was dismembered by the worshippers of Bacchus, god of wine; his head fell into a river and was carried across the sea to the island of Lesbos.

8. Bitten (archaic usage).

GREGORY CORSO
(*1930–*)

Gregory Corso was born on March 26, 1930, in Greenwich Village, New York City. His Italian parents were extremely young, his father seventeen, his mother sixteen. When Corso was a year old his mother went back to Milan, and he was consigned to orphanages and four or five sets of foster parents. Ten years later his father remarried and took him back, but at twelve Corso ran off again. This time he was sent to a boys' home. He stole a radio and was remanded for five months to the Tombs (a New York prison) as a material witness against the receiver of the goods. These months were devastating: the other convicts stole his food and beat him up. A year later he went back home, then ran away again, and this time was sent to Bellevue for three months of mental tests. Released once more, he repeated his cycle of going home and running away. At the age of seventeen he was sent to prison for three years for theft.

Somewhere along this stumbling way, Corso had formed an idea of writing poetry, and did not give it up when his father tried to discourage him. In prison, however, he wrote poems, and on his release in 1950 he met Allen Ginsberg one night when he had the poems with him. The meeting was pivotal. Ginsberg taught Corso about contemporary poetry, and about means of survival outside prison walls. Corso took what work he could find, while continuing to write; then he quit his job to live "in Village with kind girl until 1952." After this, restive as ever, he traveled to Los Angeles and found a job as a cub reporter on the Los Angeles *Examiner.* Seven months later he was off to South America and Africa, and then back to the Village, drinking and sleeping on rooftops. In 1954 all this was changed: "beautiful now dead Violet Lang brought me to Harvard where I wrote and wrote and met lots of wild young brilliant people who were talking about Hegel and Kierkegaard." Fifty students at Harvard and Radcliffe shared the costs of printing *The Vestal Lady on Brattle* (1955).

In 1956 he went to San Francisco and joined Ginsberg. Together they traveled to Mexico, and from there they went to Paris in October 1957. Corso has since returned to the States. He married in 1963.

Marriage

Should I get married? Should I be good?
Astound the girl next door with my velvet suit and faustus[8] hood?
Don't take her to movies but to cemeteries
tell all about werewolf bathtubs and forked clarinets
then desire her and kiss her and all the preliminaries
and she going just so far and I understanding why
not getting angry saying You must feel! It's beautiful to feel!
Instead take her in my arms lean against an old crooked tombstone
and woo her the entire night the constellations in the sky—

When she introduces me to her parents
back straightened, hair finally combed, strangled by a tie,
should I sit knees together on their 3rd degree sofa
and not ask Where's the bathroom?
How else to feel other than I am,
often thinking Flash Gordon soap—
O how terrible it must be for a young man
seated before a family and the family thinking
We never saw him before! He wants our Mary Lou!
After tea and homemade cookies they ask What do you do for a living?
Should I tell them? Would they like me then?

8. Dr. Faustus is the medieval alchemist who, in the play by Christopher Marlowe, sells his soul to the Devil in exchange for renewed youth and supernatural powers.

Say All right get married, we're losing a daughter
but we're gaining a son—
And should I then ask Where's the bathroom?

O God, and the wedding! All her family and her friends
and only a handful of mine all scroungy and bearded
just wait to get at the drinks and food—
And the priest! he looking at me as if I masturbated
asking me Do you take this woman for your lawful wedded wife?
And I trembling what to say say Pie Glue!
I kiss the bride all those corny men slapping me on the back
She's all yours, boy! Ha-ha-ha!
And in their eyes you could see some obscene honeymoon going on—
Then all that absurd rice and clanky cans and shoes
Niagara Falls! Hordes of us! Husbands! Wives! Flowers! Chocolates!
All streaming into cozy hotels
All going to do the same thing tonight
The indifferent clerk he knowing what was going to happen
The lobby zombies they knowing what
The whistling elevator man he knowing
The winking bellboy knowing
Everybody knowing! I'd be almost inclined not to do anything!
Stay up all night! Stare that hotel clerk in the eye!
Screaming: I deny honeymoon! I deny honeymoon!
running rampant into those almost climactic suites
yelling Radio belly! Cat shovel!
O I'd live in Niagara forever! in a dark cave beneath the Falls
I'd sit there the Mad Honeymooner
devising ways to break marriages, a scourge of bigamy
a saint of divorce—

But I should get married I should be good
How nice it'd be to come home to her
and sit by the fireplace and she in the kitchen
aproned young and lovely wanting my baby
and so happy about me she burns the roast beef
and comes crying to me and I get up from my big papa chair
saying Christmas teeth! Radiant brains! Apple deaf!
God what a husband I'd make! Yes, I should get married!
So much to do! like sneaking into Mr Jones' house late at night
and cover his golf clubs with 1920 Norwegian books
Like hanging a picture of Rimbaud[9] on the lawnmower
like pasting Tannu Tuva[1] postage stamps all over the picket fence
like when Mrs Kindhead comes to collect for the Community Chest
grab her and tell her There are unfavorable omens in the sky!
And when the mayor comes to get my vote tell him
When are you going to stop people killing whales!
And when the milkman comes leave him a note in the bottle
Penguin dust, bring me penguin dust, I want penguin dust—

9. Arthur Rimbaud (1854–1891), French poet.

1. A remote Asian district of the U.S.S.R.

Yet if I should get married and it's Connecticut and snow
and she gives birth to a child and I am sleepless, worn,
up for nights, head bowed against a quiet window, the past behind me,
finding myself in the most common of situations a trembling man
knowledged with responsibility not twig-smear nor Roman coin soup—
O what would that be like!
Surely I'd give it for a nipple a rubber Tacitus[2]
For a rattle a bag of broken Bach records
Tack Della Francesca[3] all over its crib
Sew the Greek alphabet on its bib
And build for its playpen a roofless Parthenon

No, I doubt I'd be that kind of father
not rural not snow no quiet window
but hot smelly tight New York City
seven flights up roaches and rats in the walls
a fat Reichian[4] wife screeching over potatoes Get a job!
And five nose running brats in love with Batman
And the neighbors all toothless and dry haired
like those hag masses of the 18th century
all wanting to come in and watch TV
The landlord wants his rent
Grocery store Blue Cross Gas & Electric Knights of Columbus
Impossible to lie back and dream Telephone snow, ghost parking—
No! I should not get married I should never get married!
But—imagine If I were married to a beautiful sophisticated woman
tall and pale wearing an elegant black dress and long black gloves
holding a cigarette holder in one hand and a highball in the other
and we lived high up in a penthouse with a huge window
from which we could see all of New York and ever farther on clearer
days
No, can't imagine myself married to that pleasant prison dream—

O but what about love? I forget love
not that I am incapable of love
it's just that I see love as odd as wearing shoes—
I never wanted to marry a girl who was like my mother
And Ingrid Bergman was always impossible
And there's maybe a girl now but she's already married
And I don't like men and—
but there's got to be somebody!
Because what if I'm 60 years old and not married,
all alone in a furnished room with pee stains on my underwear
and everybody else is married! All the universe married but me!

Ah, yet well I know that were a woman possible as I am possible
then marriage would be possible—

2. (c. 55–c. 115), Roman historian.
3. Piero della Francesca (c. 1420–1492), Italian Renaissance painter.
4. Referring to Wilhelm Reich (1897–1957), Austrian psychiatrist and biophysicist, the founder of a highly controversial school of psychiatry.

Like SHE in her lonely alien gaud waiting her Egyptian lover[5]
so I wait—bereft of 2,000 years and the bath of life.

1960

5. The heroine of H. Rider Haggard's *She* (1887) achieves eternal youth by bathing in a pillar of flame only to wait thousands of years for the return of her Egyptian lover.

GARY SNYDER
(1930–)

Gary Snyder was born in San Francisco on May 8, 1930, and was brought up in Oregon and Washington. In the summer of 1948, after he had finished his freshman year at college, he shipped out of New York as an ordinary seaman. On his return, he took a B.A. in anthropology from Reed College in 1951. He worked as a logger and a Forest Service trail crew member in the Pacific Northwest; then he studied Oriental languages at Berkeley from 1953 to 1956. He also joined Allen Ginsberg, Jack Kerouac, and others in what turned into the Beat movement. (Kerouac used Snyder as the protagonist of his novel *The Dharma Bums.*) From 1956 until 1964 he lived mainly in Japan, though he visited India for a year and also worked as a hand on an American tanker in the Indian and South Pacific Oceans. In 1964 he taught at the University of California at Berkeley, then returned to Japan for four years to study Buddhism in the Mahayana-Vajrayana line; some of his experiences are recounted in the prose book *Earth House Hold* (1969), which is written in the Japanese form of the poetic travel journal. His many books of poems include a number of translations from ancient and modern Japanese poetry. Twice divorced, he now lives in the United States with his Japanese wife and their son Kai. His *Turtle Island* (1974) won the Pulitzer Prize for Poetry.

Four Poems for Robin

Siwashing It[2] Out Once in Siuslaw Forest

I slept under rhododendron
All night blossoms fell
Shivering on a sheet of cardboard
Feet stuck in my pack
Hands deep in my pockets
Barely able to sleep.
I remembered when we were in school
Sleeping together in a big warm bed
We were the youngest lovers
When we broke up we were still nineteen.
Now our friends are married

2. Camping or traveling with minimal equipment; roughing it. Siuslaw Forest is west of Eugene, Oregon.

You teach   school back east
I dont mind   living this way
Green hills   the long blue beach
But sometimes   sleeping in the open
I think back   when I had you.

A Spring Night in Shokoku-ji[3]

Eight years ago this May
We walked under cherry blossoms
At night in an orchard in Oregon.
All that I wanted then
Is forgotten now, but you.
Here in the night
In a garden of the old capital
I feel the trembling ghost of Yugao
I remember your cool body
Naked under a summer cotton dress.

An Autumn Morning in Shokoku-ji

Last night watching the Pleiades,[4]
Breath smoking in the moonlight,
Bitter memory like vomit
Choked my throat.
I unrolled a sleeping bag
On mats on the porch
Under thick autumn stars.
In dream you appeared
(Three times in nine years)
Wild, cold, and accusing.
I woke shamed and angry:
The pointless wars of the heart.
Almost dawn. Venus and Jupiter.
The first time I have
Ever seen them close.

December at Yase[5]

You said, that October,
In the tall dry grass by the orchard
When you chose to be free,
"Again someday, maybe ten years."

After college I saw you
One time. You were strange.
And I was obsessed with a plan.

3. A Zen monastery built in the fourteenth century in Kyoto, the ancient capital of Japan.
4. A group of seven brilliant stars in the constellation Taurus (the bull).
5. A subdistrict adjoining northeast Kyoto.

Now ten years and more have
Gone by: I've always known
where you were—
I might have gone to you
Hoping to win your love back.
You still are single.

I didn't.
I thought I must make it alone. I
Have done that.

Only in dream, like this dawn,
Does the grave, awed intensity
Of our young love
Return to my mind, to my flesh.

We had what the others
All crave and seek for;
We left it behind at nineteen.

I feel ancient, as though I had
Lived many lives.
And may never now know
If I am a fool
Or have done what my
karma[6] demands.

1968

6. In Buddhism, the force generated by one's actions that determines the nature of his next incarnation, and that prevents his liberation from the cycle of rebirth.

TED HUGHES
(1930–)

Ted Hughes was born in Mytholmroyd, Yorkshire, in 1930. For two years he was a ground radio mechanic in the Royal Air Force. Afterwards he took a B.A. at Cambridge, where he met the American poet Sylvia Plath, who was on a Fulbright fellowship. They were married in 1956. They lived at first in the United States, then settled in England. They had two children. But their marriage was troubled and they were living apart at the time of Sylvia Plath's suicide in 1963. More recently, in addition to writing poetry, Hughes has collaborated with the avant-garde theater director Peter Brook, notably on an adaptation of Seneca's *Oedipus* and a version of the Prometheus myth whose title (and the name of the synthetic language in which it is written) is *Orghast*.

The Thought-Fox

I imagine this midnight moment's forest:
Something else is alive
Beside the clock's loneliness
And this blank page where my fingers move.

Through the window I see no star:
Something more near
Though deeper within darkness
Is entering the loneliness:

Cold, delicately as the dark snow,
A fox's nose touches twig, leaf;
Two eyes serve a movement, that now
And again now, and now, and now

Sets neat prints into the snow
Between trees, and warily a lame
Shadow lags by stump and in hollow
Of a body that is bold to come

Across clearings, an eye,
A widening deepening greenness,
Brilliantly, concentratedly,
Coming about its own business

Till, with a sudden sharp hot stink of fox
It enters the dark hole of the head.
The window is starless still; the clock ticks,
The page is printed.

1957

An Otter

I

Underwater eyes, an eel's
Oil of water body, neither fish nor beast is the otter:
Four-legged yet water-gifted, to outfish fish;
With webbed feet and long ruddering tail
And a round head like an old tomcat.

Brings the legend of himself
From before wars or burials, in spite of hounds and vermin-poles;[1]
Does not take root like the badger. Wanders, cries;
Gallops along land he no longer belongs to;
Re-enters the water by melting.

1. Poles on which the carcasses of predators are hung to scare other predators.

Of neither water nor land. Seeking
Some world lost when first he dived, that he cannot come at since,
Takes his changed body into the holes of lakes;
As if blind, cleaves the stream's push till he licks
The pebbles of the source; from sea

To sea crosses in three nights
Like a king in hiding. Crying to the old shape of the starlit land,
Over sunken farms where the bats go round,
Without answer. Till light and birdsong come
Walloping up roads with the milk wagon.

II

The hunt's lost him. Pads on mud,
Among sedges, nostrils a surface bead,
The otter remains, hours. The air,
Circling the globe, tainted and necessary,

Mingling tobacco-smoke, hounds and parsley,
Comes carefully to the sunk lungs.
So the self under the eye lies,
Attendant and withdrawn. The otter belongs

In double robbery and concealment—
From water that nourishes and drowns, and from land
That gave him his length and the mouth of the hound.
He keeps fat in the limpid integument [2]

Reflections live on. The heart beats thick,
Big trout muscle out of the dead cold;
Blood is the belly of logic; he will lick
The fishbone bare. And can take stolen hold

On a bitch otter in a field full
Of nervous horses, but linger nowhere.
Yanked above hounds, reverts to nothing at all,
To this long pelt over the back of a chair.

1960

Wodwo[3]

What am I? Nosing here, turning leaves over
Following a faint stain on the air to the river's edge
I enter water. What am I to split
The glassy grain of water looking upward I see the bed

2. Covering; skin.

3. A Middle English word taken from line 721 of the anonymous poem, *Sir Gawain and the Green Knight*, and translated as "wild man of the woods" or "wood demon." The source, which is the epigraph for the book of which this is the title-poem, describes Gawain's difficult journey to the Green Knight's castle: "Now with serpents he wars, now with savage wolves, / Now with wild men of the woods, that watched from the rocks." (Translation by Marie Borroff.)

Of the river above me upside down very clear
What am I doing here in mid-air? Why do I find
this frog so interesting as I inspect its most secret
interior and make it my own? Do these weeds
know me and name me to each other have they
seen me before, do I fit in their world? I seem
separate from the ground and not rooted but dropped
out of nothing casually I've no threads
fastening me to anything I can go anywhere
I seem to have been given the freedom
of this place what am I then? And picking
bits of bark off this rotten stump gives me
no pleasure and it's no use so why do I do it
me and doing that have coincided very queerly
But what shall I be called am I the first
have I an owner what shape am I what
shape am I am I huge if I go
to the end on this way past these trees and past these trees
till I get tired that's touching one wall of me
for the moment if I sit still how everything
stops to watch me I suppose I am the exact centre
but there's all this what is it roots
roots roots roots and here's the water
again very queer but I'll go on looking

1967

Crow's First Lesson

God tried to teach Crow how to talk.
"Love," said God. "Say, Love."
Crow gaped, and the white shark crashed into the sea
And went rolling downwards, discovering its own depth.

"No, no," said God, "Say Love. Now try it. LOVE."
Crow gaped, and a bluefly, a tsetse, a mosquito
Zoomed out and down
To their sundry flesh-pots.

"A final try," said God. "Now, LOVE."
Crow convulsed, gaped, retched and
Man's bodiless prodigious head
Bulbed out onto the earth, with swivelling eyes,
Jabbering protest—

And Crow retched again, before God could stop him.
And woman's vulva dropped over man's neck and tightened.
The two struggled together on the grass.
God struggled to part them, cursed, wept—

Crow flew guiltily off.

1970

JON SILKIN
(*1930–*)

Jon Silkin was born in London on December 2, 1930. After attending Wycliff and Dulwich Colleges he was drafted into the Army in 1948 and spent two years in the Education Corps. After six years as a manual laborer in London and two years teaching English to foreign students, Silkin resumed his own studies at the University of Leeds, where he was Gregory Fellow in poetry and from which he received his B.A. in 1962. He lives in Newcastle-upon-Tyne, where he edits the literary quarterly *Stand*, which he founded in 1952, and helps to manage the publishing firm Northern House, of which he was the cofounder in 1964.

Death of a Son

(*who died in a mental hospital aged one*)

Something has ceased to come along with me.
Something like a person: something very like one.
And there was no nobility in it
Or anything like that.

Something was there like a one year
Old house, dumb as stone. While the near buildings
Sang like birds and laughed
Understanding the pact

They were to have with silence. But he
Neither sang nor laughed. He did not bless silence
Like bread, with words.
He did not forsake silence.

But rather, like a house in mourning
Kept the eye turned in to watch the silence while
The other houses like birds
Sang around him.

And the breathing silence neither
Moved nor was still.

I have seen stones: I have seen brick
But this house was made up of neither bricks nor stone
But a house of flesh and blood
With flesh of stone

And bricks for blood. A house
Of stones and blood in breathing silence with the other
Birds singing crazy on its chimneys.
But this was silence,

This was something else, this was
Hearing and speaking though he was a house drawn
Into silence, this was
Something religious in his silence,

Something shining in his quiet,
This was different this was altogether something else:
Though he never spoke, this
Was something to do with death.

And then slowly the eye stopped looking
Inward. The silence rose and became still.
The look turned to the outer place and stopped,
With the birds still shrilling around him.
And as if he could speak

He turned over on his side with his one year
Red as a wound
He turned over as if he could be sorry for this
And out of his eyes two great tears rolled, like stones,
and he died.

1954

GEORGE MACBETH
(*1932–*)

George Macbeth was born in the mining village of Shotts, in Scotland, on January 19, 1932. After winning first class honors at New College, Oxford, he became a producer of radio programs about literature and the arts for the British Broadcasting Corporation; he says that this work has made him particularly interested in writing poetry to be read aloud, and that he has written several dramatic monologues with this in mind. Macbeth was a member of "The Group," a number of young British poets who met to discuss poetry and criticize each other's work. Since 1963 he has continued his activities with the BBC.

Bedtime Story

Long long ago when the world was a wild place
Planted with bushes and peopled by apes, our
Mission Brigade was at work in the jungle.
Hard by the Congo

Once, when a foraging detail was active
Scouting for green-fly,[1] it came on a grey man, the
Last living man, in the branch of a baobab[2]
Stalking a monkey.

1. Aphids.

2. A huge Afro-Asian tree.

Earlier men had disposed of, for pleasure,
Creatures whose names we scarcely remember—
Zebra, rhinoceros, elephants, wart-hog,
    Lion, rats, deer. But

After the wars had extinguished the cities
Only the wild ones were left, half-naked
Near the Equator: and here was the last one,
    Starved for a monkey.

By then the Mission Brigade had encountered
Hundreds of such men: and their procedure,
History tells us, was only to feed them:
    Find them and feed them;

Those were the orders. And this was the last one.
Nobody knew that he was, but he was. Mud
Caked on his flat grey flanks. He was crouched, half-
    armed with a shaved spear

Glinting beneath broad leaves. When their jaws cut
Swathes through the bark and he saw fine teeth shine,
Round eyes roll round and forked arms waver
    Huge as the rough trunks

Over his head, he was frightened. Our workers
Marched through the Congo before he was born, but
This was the first time perhaps that he'd seen one.
    Staring in hot still

Silence, he crouched there: then jumped. With a long swing
Down from his branch, he had angled his spear too
Quickly, before they could hold him, and hurled it
    Hard at the soldier

Leading the detail. How could he know Queen's
Orders were only to help him? The soldier
Winced when the tipped spear pricked him. Unsheathing his
    Sting was a reflex.

Later the Queen was informed. There were no more
Men. An impetuous soldier had killed off,
Purely by chance, the penultimate primate.
    When she was certain,

Squadrons of workers were fanned through the Congo
Detailed to bring back the man's picked bones to be
Sealed in the archives in amber. I'm quite sure
    Nobody found them

After the most industrious search, though.
Where had the bones gone? Over the earth, dear,
Ground by the teeth of the termites, blown by the
Wind, like the dodo's.

1963

GEOFFREY HILL
(*1932–*)

Geoffrey Hill was born in Bromsgrove, Worcestershire, on June 18, 1932, and attended schools there before going up to Keble College, Oxford University. In 1952, while still an undergraduate, he published his first book of poems. He is a Lecturer in English Literature at the University of Leeds, and won its Gregory Award for Poetry in 1961.

In Memory of Jane Fraser

When snow like sheep lay in the fold
And winds went begging at each door
And the far hills were blue with cold,
And a cold shroud lay on the moor

She kept the siege. And every day
We watched her brooding over death
Like a strong bird above its prey.
The room filled with the kettle's breath.

Damp curtains glued against the pane
Sealed time away. Her body froze
As if to freeze us all and chain
Creation to a stunned repose.

She died before the world could stir.
In March the ice unloosed the brook
And water ruffled the sun's hair.
Dead cones upon the altar shook.

1959

SYLVIA PLATH
(*1932–1963*)

Sylvia Plath was born in Boston on October 27, 1932. Her father, Otto Plath, had come from Grabow in Poland to the United States when he was fifteen; as an adult he taught biology and German at Boston University and wrote a treatise on bees. After his death in 1940, she wrote her elegy, "Daddy." For a time, Sylvia Plath's history is ordinary, the events of her life innocuous, even hackneyed: report cards, scholarships at Smith College, prizes like a month's editing of a magazine, election to Phi Beta Kappa, a *summa cum laude* graduation. But her autobiographical novel, *The Bell Jar*, records a breakdown at the end of the junior year. She recovered and won a Fulbright year at Cambridge University, and it was extended through a second year.

In 1956 she married the English poet Ted Hughes. They came to America for more than a year, and she taught at Smith. But the reading of students' papers consumed all her energy, and after a short time in Boston the couple returned to England. They had two children. By the end of 1962, Sylvia Plath had moved back alone to London from the family home in Devon, and brought the children with her. She and Hughes became estranged. On February 11, 1963, at the age of thirty, she killed herself.

Lady Lazarus[2]

I have done it again.
One year in every ten
I manage it——

A sort of walking miracle, my skin
Bright as a Nazi lampshade,[3]
My right foot

A paperweight,
My face a featureless, fine
Jew linen.

Peel off the napkin
O my enemy.
Do I terrify?——

The nose, the eye pits, the full set of teeth?
The sour breath
Will vanish in a day.

Soon, soon the flesh
The grave cave ate will be
At home on me

And I a smiling woman.
I am only thirty.
And like the cat I have nine times to die.

This is Number Three.
What a trash
To annihilate each decade.

2. Lazarus was raised from the dead by Jesus Christ (*John* 11:44).

3. The skins of some Jewish victims of the Nazis were used to make lampshades.

What a million filaments.
The peanut-crunching crowd
Shoves in to see

Them unwrap me hand and foot——
The big strip tease.
Gentleman, ladies,

These are my hands,
My knees.
I may be skin and bone,

Nevertheless, I am the same, identical woman.
The first time it happened I was ten.
It was an accident.

The second time I meant
To last it out and not come back at all.
I rocked shut

As a seashell.
They had to call and call
And pick the worms off me like sticky pearls.

Dying
Is an art, like everything else.
I do it exceptionally well.

I do it so it feels like hell.
I do it so it feels real.
I guess you could say I've a call.

It's easy enough to do it in a cell.
It's easy enough to do it and stay put.
It's the theatrical

Comeback in broad day
To the same place, the same face, the same brute
Amused shout:

"A miracle!"
That knocks me out.
There is a charge

For the eyeing of my scars, there is a charge
For the hearing of my heart——
It really goes.

And there is a charge, a very large charge,
For a word or a touch
Or a bit of blood

Or a piece of my hair or my clothes.
So, so, Herr Doktor.
So, Herr Enemy.

I am your opus,
I am your valuable,
The pure gold baby

That melts to a shriek.
I turn and burn.
Do not think I underestimate your great concern.

Ash, ash—
You poke and stir.
Flesh, bone, there is nothing there——

A cake of soap,
A wedding ring,
A gold filling.

Herr God, Herr Lucifer,
Beware
Beware.

Out of the ash
I rise with my red hair
And I eat men like air.

1966

Ariel[4]

Stasis in darkness.
Then the substanceless blue
Pour of tor[5] and distances.

God's lioness,
How one we grow,
Pivot of heels and knees!—The furrow

Splits and passes, sister to
The brown arc
Of the neck I cannot catch,

Nigger-eye
Berries cast dark
Hooks——

Black sweet blood mouthfuls,
Shadows.
Something else

4. The airy spirit in Shakespeare's *The Tempest*; also, the name of Sylvia Plath's horse.

5. A rocky peak.

Hauls me through air——
Thighs, hair;
Flakes from my heels.

White
Godiva, I unpeel——
Dead hands, dead stringencies.

And now I
Foam to wheat, a glitter of seas.
The child's cry

Melts in the wall.
And I
Am the arrow,

The dew that flies
Suicidal, at one with the drive
Into the red

Eye, the cauldron of morning.

1966

Daddy

You do not do, you do not do
Any more, black shoe
In which I have lived like a foot
For thirty years, poor and white,
Barely daring to breathe or Achoo.

Daddy, I have had to kill you.
You died before I had time——
Marble-heavy, a bag full of God,
Ghastly statue with one grey toe
Big as a Frisco seal

And a head in the freakish Atlantic
Where it pours bean green over blue
In the waters off beautiful Nauset.
I used to pray to recover you.
Ach, du.[6]

In the German tongue, in the Polish town[7]
Scraped flat by the roller
Of wars, wars, wars.
But the name of the town is common.
My Polack friend

Says there are a dozen or two.
So I never could tell where you

6. Ah, you (Ger).

7. Grabów, Otto Plath's birthplace.

Put your foot, your root,
I never could talk to you.
The tongue stuck in my jaw.

It stuck in a barb wire snare.
Ich, ich, ich, ich,[8]
I could hardly speak.
I thought every German was you.
And the language obscene

An engine, an engine
Chuffing me off like a Jew.
A Jew to Dachau, Auschwitz, Belsen.
I began to talk like a Jew.
I think I may well be a Jew.

The snows of the Tyrol, the clear beer of Vienna
Are not very pure or true.
With my gypsy ancestress and my weird luck
And my Taroc pack[9] and my Taroc pack
I may be a bit of a Jew.

I have always been scared of *you,*
With your Luftwaffe,[1] your gobbledygoo.
And your neat moustache
And your Aryan eye, bright blue.
Panzer-man, panzer-man, O You——

Not God but a swastika
So black no sky could squeak through.
Every woman adores a Fascist,
The boot in the face, the brute
Brute heart of a brute like you.

You stand at the blackboard, daddy,
In the picture I have of you,
A cleft in your chin instead of your foot
But no less a devil for that, no not
Any less the black man who

Bit my pretty red heart in two.
I was ten when they buried you.
At twenty I tried to die
And get back, back, back to you.
I thought even the bones would do.

But they pulled me out of the sack,
And they stuck me together with glue.

8. I, I, I, I (Ger).
9. Or Tarot pack, used for telling fortunes.
1. Air Force (Ger).

And then I knew what to do.
I made a model of you,
A man in black with a Meinkampf[2] look

And a love of the rack and the screw.
And I said I do, I do.
So daddy, I'm finally through.
The black telephone's off at the root,
The voices just can't worm through.

If I've killed one man, I've killed two——
The vampire who said he was you
And drank my blood for a year,
Seven years, if you want to know.
Daddy, you can lie back now.

There's a stake in your fat black heart
And the villagers never liked you.
They are dancing and stamping on you.
They always *knew* it was you.
Daddy, daddy, you bastard, I'm through.

1966

2. *Mein Kampf* (My Battle) was the title of Adolf Hitler's political autobiography.

ETHERIDGE KNIGHT
(1933–)

Etheridge Knight was born in Corinth, Mississippi, on April 19, 1933. After two years of high school he was in the Army fighting in the Korean War, in which he was wounded. He reports a period of drug addition during the Fifties, followed by imprisonment in 1960 on a charge of robbery. Paroled in 1968, he lives in Indianapolis.

Hard Rock Returns to Prison from the Hospital for the Criminal Insane

Hard Rock was "known not to take no shit
From nobody," and he had the scars to prove it:
Split purple lips, lumped ears, welts above
His yellow eyes, and one long scar that cut
Across his temple and plowed through a thick
Canopy of kinky hair.

The WORD was that Hard Rock wasn't a mean nigger
Anymore, that the doctors had bored a hole in his head,
Cut out part of his brain, and shot electricity

Through the rest. When they brought Hard Rock back,
Handcuffed and chained, he was turned loose,
Like a freshly gelded stallion, to try his new status.
And we all waited and watched, like indians at a corral,
To see if the WORD was true.

As we waited we wrapped ourselves in the cloak
Of his exploits: "Man, the last time, it took eight
Screws to put him in the Hole." "Yeah, remember when he
Smacked the captain with his dinner tray?" "He set
The record for time in the Hole—67 straight days!"
"Ol Hard Rock! man, that's one crazy nigger."
And then the jewel of a myth that Hard Rock had once bit
A screw on the thumb and poisoned him with syphilitic spit.

The testing came, to see if Hard Rock was really tame.
A hillbilly called him a black son of a bitch
And didn't lose his teeth, a screw who knew Hard Rock
From before shook him down and barked in his face.
And Hard Rock did *nothing*. Just grinned and looked silly,
His eyes empty like knot holes in a fence.

And even after we discovered that it took Hard Rock
Exactly 3 minutes to tell you his first name,
We told ourselves that he had just wised up,
Was being cool; but we could not fool ourselves for long,
And we turned away, our eyes on the ground. Crushed.
He had been our Destroyer, the doer of things
We dreamed of doing but could not bring ourselves to do,
The fears of years, like a biting whip,
Had cut grooves too deeply across our backs.

1968

Haiku

1

Eastern guard tower
glints in sunset; convicts rest
like lizards on rocks.

2

The piano man
is sting at 3 am
his songs drop like plum.

3

Morning sun slants cell.
Drunks stagger like cripple flies
On Jailhouse floor.

4
To write a blues song
is to regiment riots
and pluck gems from graves.

5
A bare pecan tree
slips a pencil shadow down
a moonlit snow slope.

6
The falling snow flakes
Can not blunt the hard aches nor
Match the steel stillness.

7
Under moon shadows
A tall boy flashes knife and
Slices star bright ice.

8
In the August grass
Struck by the last rays of sun
The cracked teacup screams.

9
Making jazz swing in
Seventeen syllables AIN'T
No square poet's job.

1968

MARK STRAND
(*1934–*)

Mark Strand was born on Prince Edward Island, Canada, on April 11, 1934. He received his B.A. from Antioch College, then went to Yale for a B.F.A. He studied with the poet Donald Justice at the writer's workshop of the University of Iowa, spent a year in Italy on a Fulbright scholarship, then completed his M.A. in 1962 and stayed on at Iowa as an instructor for three years. In 1965 he went to Rio de Janeiro as Fulbright Lecturer at the University of Brazil; since then he has taught briefly at four universities. He has published an anthology of contemporary American poetry and has written a screenplay. He has also done translations from several European languages.

Eating Poetry

Ink runs from the corners of my mouth.
There is no happiness like mine.
I have been eating poetry.

The librarian does not believe what she sees.
Her eyes are sad
and she walks with her hands in her dress.

The poems are gone.
The light is dim.
The dogs are on the basement stairs and coming up.

Their eyeballs roll,
their blond legs burn like brush.
The poor librarian begins to stamp her feet and weep.

She does not understand.
When I get on my knees and lick her hand,
she screams.

I am a new man.
I snarl at her and bark.
I romp with joy in the bookish dark.

1968

LEONARD COHEN
(*1934–*)

Leonard Cohen was born in Montreal, Canada, on September 21, 1934. His father was a clothing merchant, and at one time Cohen halfheartedly tried the family business. But there were early signs of rebellion: at the age of fifteen he went to a socialist camp and there learned to play the guitar. The socialism was to fade, but the guitar, as he has said, underlies all his work, even his novels. He was soon playing it to accompany his own songs in a Montreal cafe. He attended McGill University and took a degree in 1955. In 1961 he was in Cuba at the time of the Bay of Pigs invasion but characteristically could not decide on which side to fight. Cohen attended graduate school at Columbia University for a time but eventually settled into a life that takes him from Canada to a small Greek island called Hydra, which he regards as suited to his temperament. In 1967 he began making records of his songs to his guitar accompaniment, which have brought him many listeners and readers. Besides his poetry, he has published two novels.

The Only Tourist in Havana Turns His Thoughts Homeward

Come, my brothers,
let us govern Canada,
let us find our serious heads,

let us dump asbestos on the White House,
let us make the French talk English,
  not only here but everywhere,
let us torture the Senate individually
  until they confess,
let us purge the New Party,
let us encourage the dark races
  so they'll be lenient
  when they take over,
let us make the CBC[1] talk English,
let us all lean in one direction
  and float down
  to the coast of Florida,
let us have tourism,
let us flirt with the enemy,
let us smelt pig-iron in our back yards,[2]
let us sell snow
  to under-developed nations,
(Is it true one of our national leaders
  was a Roman Catholic?)
let us terrorize Alaska,
let us unite
  Church and State,
let us not take it lying down,
let us have two Governor Generals[3]
  at the same time,
let us have another official language,
let us determine what it will be,
let us give a Canada Council Fellowship
  to the most original suggestion,
let us teach sex in the home
  to parents,
let us threaten to join the U.S.A.
  and pull out at the last moment,
my brothers, come,
our serious heads are waiting for us somewhere
  like Gladstone bags[4] abandoned
  after a *coup d'état*,
let us put them on very quickly,
let us maintain a stony silence
  on the St. Lawrence Seaway.

1964

1. The Canadian Broadcasting Corporation, which broadcasts in English and French.

2. A requirement of the Chinese government during the economic program for 1957–1962, called the "Great Leap Forward."

3. The Governor-General of Canada, the highest administrative officer, is appointed by the Queen of England on recommendation of the Canadian parliament.

4. A kind of suitcase, named for British prime minister William Ewart Gladstone (1809–1898).

IMAMU AMIRI BARAKA (LeRoi Jones) (1934–   )

LeRoi Jones was born in Newark, New Jersey, on October 7, 1934. As a child he made up his own comic strips and wrote science fiction. He graduated from high school two years ahead of schedule and took a B.A. at Howard University in 1954, then spent three years as a weatherman and gunner in the U.S. Air Force. As a graduate student at Columbia, he knew some of the writers identified with the Beat movement, writers with whom he was likely to feel some comradeship since they shared his interest in Americans who lived on the edge of American society. In the late Fifties he was an active figure in the New York literary underground. He and his first wife published *Yugen*, a poetry magazine; he was poetry editor for Corinth Books; he was coeditor of a literary newsletter called *Floating Bear*, and in 1961 he helped to found the American Theatre for Poets. Meanwhile he had two Master's degrees, at Columbia in philosophy and at the New School for Social Research in German literature, and he was for a time an instructor at the New School.

In the middle Sixties Jones began to make his reputation as a dramatist; his one-act play *Dutchman* had a long run off-Broadway. A visit to Cuba led Jones to conclude that most of American life was socially useless and that any attempt to create a multiracial society would not succeed. Eager to find a focus for a black community which would use the arts, Jones moved first to Harlem, where he founded the Black Arts Repertory Theater, and then in 1966 to the Newark slums, where he set up a community called Spirit House. During the riots in the summer of 1967 Jones was arrested and charged with carrying a concealed weapon; he was convicted, but eventually, in a retrial, the conviction was overturned. In 1968 he founded the Black Community Development and Defense Organization, a group then composed of 100 men and 50 women who wore traditional African dress, spoke Swahili as well as English, and practiced the Muslim religion. He chose to be known by a Muslim name, Imamu Amiri Baraka. In recent years he has played an increasingly important role in national black politics and in relations between the American black community and the nations of black Africa.

Political Poem

(FOR BASIL)

Luxury, then, is a way of
being ignorant, comfortably
An approach to the open market
of least information. Where theories
can thrive, under heavy tarpaulins
without being cracked by ideas.
(I have not seen the earth for years
and think now possibly "dirt" is
negative, positive, but clearly
social. I cannot plant a seed, cannot
recognize the root with clearer dent

than indifference. Though I eat
and shit as a natural man. (Getting up
from the desk to secure a turkey sandwich
and answer the phone: the poem undone
undone by my station, by my station,
and the bad words of Newark.[1]) Raised up
to the breech, we seek to fill for this
crumbling century. The darkness of love,
in whose sweating memory all error is forced.

Undone by the logic of any specific death. (Old gentlemen
who still follow fires, tho are quieter
and less punctual. It is a polite truth
we are left with. Who are you? What are you
saying? Something to be dealt with, as easily.
The noxious game of reason, saying, "No, No,
you cannot feel," like my dead lecturer
lamenting thru gipsies his fast suicide.

1964

Legacy

(FOR BLUES PEOPLE)

In the south, sleeping against
the drugstore, growling under
the trucks and stoves, stumbling
through and over the cluttered eyes
of early mysterious night. Frowning
drunk waving moving a hand or lash.
Dancing kneeling reaching out, letting
a hand rest in shadows. Squatting
to drink or pee. Stretching to climb
pulling themselves onto horses near
where there was sea (the old songs
lead you to believe). Riding out
from this town, to another, where
it is also black. Down a road
where people are asleep. Towards
the moon or the shadows of houses.
Towards the songs' pretended sea.

1969

Babylon Revisited

The gaunt thing
with no organs
creeps along the streets
of Europe, she will

1. Baraka's birthplace, and once again his home.

commute, in her feathered bat stomach-gown
with no organs
with sores on her insides
even her head
a vast puschamber
of pus(sy) memories
with no organs
nothing to make babies
she will be the great witch of euro-american legend
who sucked the life
from some unknown nigger
whose name will be known
but whose substance will not ever
not even by him
who is dead in a pile of dopeskin

This bitch killed a friend of mine named Bob Thompson
a black painter, a giant, once, she reduced
to a pitiful imitation faggot
full of American holes and a monkey on his back
slapped airplanes
from the empire state building

May this bitch and her sisters, all of them,
receive my words
in all their orifices like lye mixed with
cocola and alaga syrup

feel this shit, bitches, feel it, now laugh your
hysterectic laughs
while your flesh burns
and your eyes peel to red mud

1969

JON STALLWORTHY
(*1935–*)

Jon Stallworthy was born in London on January 18, 1935; his father is an obstetrician. He attended Rugby School and then went up to Magdalen College at Oxford University, from which he received a B.A. in 1958. In that year he also won the Newdigate Prize for Poetry. He received a B.Litt. degree from Oxford in 1961. Since then he has been an editor with the Oxford University Press, and he has taught modern poetry at the University; he has also published two critical studies of the making of Yeats's poems.

A Letter from Berlin

My dear,
Today a letter from Berlin
where snow—the first of '38[1]*—flew in,*
settled and shrivelled on the lamp last night,
broke moth wings mobbing the window. Light
woke me early, but the trams were late:
I had to run from the Brandenburg Gate[2]
skidding, groaning like a tram, and sodden
to the knees. Von Neumann operates at 10
and would do if the sky fell in. They lock
his theatre doors on the stroke of the clock—
but today I was lucky: found a gap
in the gallery next to a chap
I knew just as the doors were closing. Last,
as expected, on Von Showmann's list
the new vaginal hysterectomy
that brought me to Berlin.
Delicately
he went to work, making from right to left
a semi-circular incision. Deft
dissection of the fascia.[3] *The blood-*
blossoming arteries nipped in the bud.
Speculum, scissors, clamps—the uterus
cleanly delivered, the pouch of Douglas
stripped to the rectum, and the cavity
closed. Never have I seen such masterly
technique. 'And so little bleeding!' I said
half to myself, half to my neighbour.
'Dead',
came his whisper. 'Don't be a fool'
I said, for still below us in the pool
of light the marvellous unhurried hands
were stitching, tying the double strands
of catgut, stitching, tying. It was like
a concert, watching those hands unlock
the music from their score. And at the end
one half expected him to turn and bend
stiffly towards us. Stiffly he walked out
and his audience shuffled after. But
finishing my notes in the gallery
I saw them uncover the patient: she
was dead.
I met my neighbour in the street
waiting for the same tram, stamping his feet
on the pavement's broken snow, and said:

1. The year before Germany's invasion of Poland opened hostilities in the Second World War.
2. A grandiose monument in the center of Berlin.
3. A layer of tissue that holds the inner parts of the body together.

'I have to apologize. She was dead,
but how did you know?' Back came his voice
like a bullet '—saw it last month, twice.'
Returning your letter to an envelope
yellower by years than when you sealed it up,
darkly the omens emerge. A ritual wound
yellow at the lip yawns in my hand;
a turbulent crater; a trench, filled
not with snow only, east of Buchenwald.[4]

1969

4. A Nazi concentration camp where, a few years later, German doctors performed experimental surgery on prisoners, often killing them.

JUDITH JOHNSON SHERWIN
(*1936–*)

Judith Johnson Sherwin was born in New York City on October 3, 1936; she attended grade school and studied at the Juilliard School of Music simultaneously, and at eleven she was a finalist in the New York Philharmonic Young Composer's Contest. Two years later she wrote the libretto and music for an opera. She was already a published poet when a freshman at Radcliffe College. She married James T. Sherwin, a New York attorney, in 1955, and three years later completed her work for the B.A. at Barnard College, staying on for a year of graduate study at Columbia University as a Woodrow Wilson fellow. After 1960 her work began to attract attention: a one-act play was produced off-Broadway, her *Uranium Poems* (1969) won the Yale Younger Poets award, and a collection of her short stories was published.

Dr. Potatohead Talks to Mothers

when you put on the feet be sure
the claws are attached long
three-toed   when we landed
        on the wetgreen planet in libra[1]
        the *three-toed* chef broke out
        a gourmet spread frogs' legs
        that had made the hop frozen
        from baltimore / mushrooms
        champagne /
                            when you put on
the hands   that same day
the thumbs should not necessarily
oppose   the dominant life forms

1. The Lyre, a constellation.

great big black buck mushrooms
undulated their velvet
blackribbed mouths flowed open
closed on us sucked our juices
and the monster frogs big as tanks
ripped off our navigator's
legs sautéed them in melted
rumpfat /
when you put on
the arms push in the pegs
deep so they can't be ripped
off in alpha centauri[3] minced
frozen to fatten their giant
cats god we fought them
napalm and h-bomb blasted nine
planets and all the influences
out of the starry night
shivered
when you put on
the head when you put on
the head be very sure
the hat doesn't cover more
of them came when we landed we
landed half the universe
the hat should cover
the hair shelter the brain
from being baked powdered the ears
frozen we signed
treaties / what
to eat
but the eyes
uncovered
potatos we died
of boredom last week *but the eyes*
left open to spot what
we landed on x-37
in gemini[4] giant potatos rolled
out riding fantastic tractors
of an unmeltable alloy
peeled off *but the eyes*
bare, freezing, spied out
our jackets
of skin dropped us flayed
and the teeth should be firmly planted
in hot water and boiled
yesterday when the dust
had settled we signed the treaty

3. The nearest star to our sun.

4. The 37th planet of the star "x" in the constellation Gemini.

we looked for something legal
to eat
and the teeth
there the mouth
open

1969

DIANE WAKOSKI
(*1937–*)

Diane Wakoski was born in Whittier, California, on August 3, 1937. She attended the University of California at Berkeley, receiving her B.A. in 1960. She then moved to New York City, where she worked as a bookstore clerk and then taught English at Junior High School 22. While living in New York she went through what she describes as a "short marriage." She gives many readings of her poetry, and has taught at New York's New School for Social Research.

Sestina from the Home Gardener

These dried-out paint brushes which fell from my lips have been removed
with your departure; they are such minute losses
compared with the light bulb gone from my brain, the sections
of chicken wire from my liver, the precise
silver hammers in my ankles which delicately banged and pointed
magnetically to you. Love has become unfamiliar

and plenty of time to tend the paint brushes now. Once unfamiliar
with my processes. Once removed
from that sizzling sun, the ego, to burn my poet shadow to the wall, I pointed,
I suppose, only to your own losses
which made you hate that 200 pound fish called marriage. Precise
ly, I hate my life, hate its freedom, hate the sections

of fence stripped away, hate the time for endless painting, hate the sections
of my darkened brain that wait for children to snap on the light, the unfamiliar
corridors of my heart with strangers running in them, shouting. The precise
incisions in my hip to extract an image, a dripping pickaxe or palmtree removed
and each day my paint brushes get softer and cleaner—better tools, and losses
cease to mean loss. Beauty, to each eye, differently pointed.

I admire sign painters and carpenters. I like that black hand pointed
up a drive-way whispering to me, "The Washingtons live in those sections"
and I explain autobiographically that George Washington is sympathetic to my losses;
His face or name is everywhere. No one is unfamiliar
with the American dollar, and since you've been removed
from my life I can think of nothing else. A precise

replacement for love can't be found. But art and money are precise
ly for distraction. The stars popping out of my blood are pointed
nowhere. I have removed
my ankles so that I cannot travel. There are sections
of my brain growing teeth and unfamiliar
hands tie strings through my eyes. But there are losses

Of the spirit like vanished bicycle tires and losses
of the body, like the whole bike, every precise
bearing, spoke, gear, even the unfamiliar
handbrakes vanished. I have pointed
myself in every direction, tried sections
of every map. It's no use. The real body has been removed.

Removed by the ice tongs. If a puddle remains what losses
can those sections of glacier be? Perhaps a precise
count of drops will substitute the pointed mountain, far away, unfamiliar?

1968

You, Letting the Trees Stand as My Betrayer

You replaced the Douglas firs
that reached
like mechanics' hands
outside my windows

trying to understand the glass
with furry, needle-tipped noses

You,
who understood me
in the rain

or at least
accepted me.

The trees never left
my windows
even when they put on gloves

for age;
they had married the glass
with the thud of falling cones.
They remembered my name
on windy nights.

But you
are my betrayer
who tried to frighten me with trees one night.
Then chopped them down
outside my windows
the next day

You ride a motorcycle
past wintry trees
and summer trees
and never once
think of me.
But my friends are
the falling branches
that will tilt you
and snap your neck one day.
I dream of your thick body
uprooted
and torn by a storm
on a motorcycle track.

You chopped down my trees—
they were my legs—
and unlike George Washington you did tell
many lies.
You are my betrayer,
you woodsman,
the man who stomps into the heart of this
forest.

1971

ROGER McGOUGH
(*1937–*)

Roger McGough was born in Liverpool, England, on November 9, 1937. He has a B.A. in French and Geography and a Certificate in Education from Hull University, Yorkshire. He has lectured at the Liverpool College of Art, and is now a member of a group of Liverpool poets and musicians called "The Scaffold."

Goodbat Nightman

God bless all policemen
and fighters of crime,
May thieves go to jail
for a very long time.

They've had a hard day
helping clean up the town,
Now they hang from the mantelpiece
both upside down.

A glass of warm blood
and then straight up the stairs,
Batman and Robin
are saying their prayers.

. . . .

They've locked all the doors
and they've put out the bat,
Put on their batjamas
(They like doing that)

They've filled their batwater-bottles
made their batbeds,
With two springy battresses
for sleepy batheads.

They're closing red eyes
and they're counting black sheep,
Batman and Robin
are falling asleep.

1967

The Newly Pressed Suit

Here is a poem for the two of us to play.
Choose any part from the following:
The *hero*
The *heroine*
The *bed*
The *bedroom*
The *newly pressed suit*
(I will play the VILLAIN)

The poem begins late this evening
at a poetryreading
Where the *hero* and the *heroine*
Are sitting and drinking and thinking
of making love.

At 10.30 they leave the pub and hurryhome.
Once inside the flat they waste no time.
The hero quickly undresses the *heroine*,
carries her naked into the *bedroom*
and places her gently upon the *bed*
like a *newly pressed suit*.

Just then I step into the poem.
With a sharp left hook
I render unconscious the *hero*.
And with a cruel laugh
Rape the *heroine*
(The raping continues for several stanzas)

Thank you for playing.

When you go out tonight
I hope you have better luck in your poem
Than you had in mine.

1971

P.C.[1] Plod Versus the Dale St Dog Strangler

For several months
Liverpool was held in the grip of fear
by a dogstrangler most devilish,
who roamed the streets after dark
looking for strays. Finding one
he would tickle it seductively
about the body to gain its confidence,
then lead it down a deserted backstreet
where he would strangle the poor brute.
Hardly a night passed without somebody's
faithful fourlegged friend being dispatched
to that Golden Kennel in the sky.

The public were warned,
At the very first sign
of anything suspicious,
ring Canine-nine-nine.[2]

Nine o'clock on the evening of January 11th sees P.C. Plod
on the corner of Dale St and Sir Thomas St
disguised as a Welsh collie.
It is part of a daring plan to apprehend the strangler.
For though it is a wet and moonless night,
Plod is cheered in the knowledge

1. Police Constable; that is, a patrolman.
2. Everywhere in England, the emergency telephone number to report actual or potential crimes to the police is 999.

that the whole of the Liverpool City Constabulary
is on the beat that night disguised as dogs.
Not ten minutes earlier, a pekinese (Policewoman Hodges)
had scampered past on her way to Clayton Square.

For Plod, the night passed uneventfully
and so in the morning he was horrified to learn
that no less than fourteen policemen and policewomen
had been tickled and strangled during the night.

The public were horrified
The Commissioner aghast
Something had to be done
And fast.

P.C. Plod (wise as a brace of owls)
met the challenge magnificently
and submitted an idea so startling in its vision
so audacious in its conception
that the Commissioner gasped
before ordering all dogs in the city
to be thereinafter disguised as fuzz.
The plan worked
and the dogstrangler was heard of no more.

Cops and mongrels
like P.C.s in a pod
To a grateful public
Plod was God.

So next time you're up in Liverpool
take a closer look at that
policeman on pointduty, he might
well be a cocker spaniel.

1971

JIM HARRISON
(*1937–*)

Jim Harrison was born in Grayling, Michigan, on December 11, 1937, and spent his childhood in Osceola County, where his father was Agricultural Agent for the federal government. He received his B.A. from Michigan State University in 1960, and also spent two more years there, receiving his M.A. in comparative literature. He lived in San Francisco, Boston, and New York before joining the faculty of the State University of New York at Stony Brook, where he taught for several years. A grant from the National Endowment for the Arts and a Guggenheim Fellowship helped him to return to Michigan, where he lives on a farm with his wife and daughter.

Sketch for a Job Application Blank

My left eye is blind and jogs like
a milky sparrow in its socket;
my nose is large and never flares
in anger, the front teeth, bucked,
but not in lechery—I sucked
my thumb until the age of twelve.
O my youth was happy and I was never lonely
though my friends called me "pig eye"
and the teachers thought me loony.

(When I bruised, my psyche kept intact:
I fell from horses, and once a cow but never
pigs—A neighbor lost a hand to a sow.)

But I had some fears:
the salesman of eyes
his case was full of fishy baubles,
against black velvet, jeweled gore,
the great cocked hoof of a Belgian mare,
a nest of milk snakes by the water trough,
electric fences
my uncle's hounds,
the pump arm of an oil well,
the chop and whirr of a combine in the sun.

From my ancestors, the Swedes,
I suppose I inherit the love of rainy woods,
kegs of herring and neat whiskey—
I remember long nights of pinochle,
the bulge of Redman[1] in my grandpa's cheek;
the rug smelled of manure and kerosene.
They laughed loudly and didn't speak for days.

(But on the other side, from the German Mennonites,
their rag smoke prayers and porky daughters
I got intolerance, an aimless diligence.)

In '51 during a revival I was saved:
I prayed on a cold register for hours
and woke up lame. I was baptized
by immersion in the tank at Williamston—
the rusty water stung my eyes.
I left off the old things of the flesh
but not for long—one night beside a pond

she dried my feet with her yellow hair.
O actual event dead quotient

1. A brand of chewing tobacco.

cross become green
I still love Jubal but pity Hagar.[2]

(Now self is the first sacrament
who loves not the misery and taint
of the present tense is lost.
I strain for a lunar arrogance.
Light macerates[3]
the lamp infects
warmth, more warmth, I cry.)

1965

2. Jubal was the inventor of the lyre and flute (*Genesis* 4). Hagar, an Egyptian slave, had a child by Abraham when his wife Sarah proved unable to bear children; then, when God allowed old Abraham and Sarah to have a child of their own, Sarah ordered Hagar and her son sent away into the desert, where they would have died if not for divine intervention. (*Genesis* 16)

3. Softens, wastes away.

SEAMUS HEANEY
(1939–)

Seamus Heaney was born in County Derry, Ireland, on April 13, 1939, and studied at St. Columb's College before going on to Queen's University at Belfast, from which he earned a First Class Honors degree in English. He taught at a secondary school for a year, then lectured at St. Joseph's College of Education before returning to Queen's University in 1966 as a Lecturer in English. In that year he published his first book, *Death of a Naturalist,* which won three notable awards (the Eric Gregory award, the Cholmondeley Award, and the Geoffrey Faber Prize) and brought him recognition as a leading young poet. Though he recently spent a year visiting the United States, he presently lives in Belfast with his wife and two children.

Docker

There, in the corner, staring at his drink.
The cap juts like a gantry's crossbeam,
Cowling plated forehead and sledgehead jaw.
Speech is clamped in the lips' vice.

That fist would drop a hammer on a Catholic—
Oh yes, that kind of thing could start again;
The only Roman collar he tolerates
Smiles all round his sleek pint of porter.[1]

Mosaic imperatives bang home like rivets;
God is a foreman with certain definite views

1. **A strong, dark ale.**

Who orders life in shifts of work and leisure.
A factory horn will blare the Resurrection.

He sits, strong and blunt as a Celtic cross,[2]
Clearly used to silence and an armchair:
Tonight the wife and children will be quiet
At slammed door and smoker's cough in the hall.

1966

The Outlaw

Kelly's kept an unlicensed bull, well away
From the road: you risked fine but had to pay

The normal fee if cows were serviced there.
Once I dragged a nervous Friesian on a tether

Down a lane of alder, shaggy with catkin,
Down to the shed the bull was kept in.

I gave Old Kelly the clammy silver, though why
I could not guess. He grunted a curt 'Go by

Get up on that gate'. And from my lofty station
I watched the business-like conception.

The door, unbolted, whacked back against the wall.
The illegal sire fumbled from his stall

Unhurried as an old steam engine shunting.
He circled, snored and nosed. No hectic panting,

Just the unfussy ease of a good tradesman;
Then an awkward, unexpected jump, and

His knobbed forelegs straddling her flank,
He slammed life home, impassive as a tank,

Dropping off like a tipped-up load of sand.
'She'll do,' said Kelly and tapped his ash-plant [3]

Across her hindquarters. 'If not, bring her back.'
I walked ahead of her, the rope now slack

While Kelly whooped and prodded his outlaw
Who, in his own time, resumed the dark, the straw.

1969

2. A cross which has been imposed on a circle at the point of intersection.

3. A walking stick made from an ash sapling.

DON L. LEE
(*1942–*)

Don L. Lee was born on February 23, 1942, and grew up in the black ghetto that is the lower east side of Detroit. He had early ambitions to be a writer, even though, as he says, poetry was almost as strange in his home as money. He went to Wilson Junior College in Chicago, the same school attended by Gwendolyn Brooks a generation earlier, and then to Roosevelt University, where he later taught.

By 1965, Lee was writing the first of the poems in *Think Black*, which was privately printed in 1967 and published by Dudley Randall's Broadside Press the next year. The book was instantly popular, and it and its successors have made Lee one of the most widely read of the younger black poets. He has also taught at Northeast Illinois State College, Cornell University, Howard University, and the University of Illinois; in his home city of Chicago he helped to found the Writer's Workshop of the Organization of Black American Culture; he has been an editor of the journal *Black Expression*; and, following the examples of Dudley Randall and LeRoi Jones, he has started his own publishing house, Third World Press.

But He Was Cool
or: He Even Stopped for Green Lights

super-cool
ultrablack
a tan/purple
had a beautiful shade.

he had a double-natural
that wd put the sisters to shame.
his dashikis were tailor made
& his beads were imported sea shells
        (from some blk/country i never heard of)
he was triple-hip.

his tikis[4] were hand carved
out of ivory
& came express from the motherland.
he would greet u in swahili
& say good-by in yoruba.
wooooooooooooo-jim he bes so cool & ill tel li gent
                cool-cool is so cool he was un-cooled by other niggers' cool
                cool-cool ultracool was bop-cool/ice box cool so cool cold cool

4. A Maori image of an ancestor, worn as a pendant.

his wine didn't have to be cooled, him was air conditioned cool
cool-cool/real cool made me cool—now ain't that cool
cool-cool so cool him nick-named refrigerator.

cool-cool so cool
he didn't know,
after detroit, newark, chicago &c.,
we had to hip
cool-cool/ super-cool/ real cool
that
to be black
is
to be
very-hot.

1969

Man Thinking About Woman

some thing is lost in me,
like
the way you lose old thoughts that
somehow seemed unlost at the right time.

i've not known it or you many days;
we met as friends with an absence of strangeness.
it was the month
that my lines got longer & my metaphors softer.

it was the week that
i felt the city's narrow breezes rush about
me
looking for a place to disappear
as i walked the clearway,
sure footed in used sandals screaming to be replaced

your empty shoes (except for used stockings)
partially hidden beneath the dresser
looked at me,
as i sat thoughtlessly waiting
for your touch.

that day,
as your body rested upon my chest
i saw the shadow of the
window blinds beam
across the unpainted ceiling
going somewhere
like the somewhere i was going

when
the clearness of yr/teeth,
& the scars on yr/legs stopped me.

your beauty: un-noticed by regular eyes   is
like   a blackbird resting
on a telephone wire   that moves
quietly with the wind.

a southwind.

1970

NIKKI GIOVANNI
(*1943–*)

Nikki Giovanni was born in Knoxville, Tennessee, in 1943 and grew up in Lincoln Heights, Ohio, a black suburb of Cincinnati. She entered Fisk University at sixteen, was expelled, then was readmitted, worked at the University's Writers' Workshop, and finally completed her degree eight years later in 1967. Meanwhile, in Cincinnati, she organized the city's first Black Arts Festival. She studied briefly at the University of Pennsylvania graduate school while writing the poems collected in her first book, *Black Feeling, Black Talk* (1968), which was published by Dudley Randall's Broadside Press. She shares with many other poets, black and white, a vocation for teaching, and recently taught black literature and poetry at the Livingston campus of Rutgers University.

Nikki-Rosa

childhood remembrances are always a drag
if you're Black
you always remember things like living in Woodlawn[1]
with no inside toilet
and if you become famous or something
they never talk about how happy you were to have your mother
all to yourself and
how good the water felt when you got your bath from one of those
big tubs that folk in chicago barbecue in
and somehow when you talk about home
it never gets across how much you
understood their feelings
as the whole family attended meetings about Hollydale
and even though you remember
your biographers never understand
your father's pain as he sells his stock

1. A black suburb of Cincinnati.

and another dream goes
and though you're poor it isn't poverty that
concerns you
and though they fought a lot
it isn't your father's drinking that makes any difference
but only that everybody is together and you
and your sister have happy birthdays and very good christmasses
and I really hope no white person ever has cause to write about me
because they never understand Black love is Black wealth and they'll
probably talk about my hard childhood and never understand that
all the while I was quite happy

1969

Ego Tripping

(there may be a reason why)

I was born in the congo
I walked to the fertile crescent and built
the sphinx
I designed a pyramid so tough that a star
that only glows every one hundred years falls
into the center giving divine perfect light
I am bad

I sat on the throne
drinking nectar with allah
I got hot and sent an ice age to europe
to cool my thirst
My oldest daughter is nefertiti[2]
the tears from my birth pains
created the nile
I am a beautiful woman

I gazed on the forest and burned
out the sahara desert
with a packet of goat's meat
and a change of clothes
I crossed it in two hours
I am a gazelle so swift
so swift you can't catch me

For a birthday present when he was three
I gave my son hannibal an elephant
He gave me rome for mother's day[3]
My strength flows ever on

2. A beautiful Egyptian queen of the fourteenth century B.C.

3. Alludes to the Carthaginian prince Hannibal's unsuccessful campaign against Rome, during which his army, bringing with it a number of elephants, crossed the Alps into Italy.

My son noah built new/ark[4] and
I stood proudly at the helm
    as we sailed on a soft summer day
I turned myself into myself and was
    jesus
    men intone my loving name
    All praises All praises
I am the one who would save

I sowed diamonds in my back yard
My bowels deliver uranium
    the filings from my fingernails are
    semi-precious jewels
    On a trip north
I caught a cold and blew
My nose giving oil to the arab world
I am so hip even my errors are correct
I sailed west to reach east and had to round off
    the earth as I went
    The hair from my head thinned and gold was laid
    across three continents

I am so perfect so divine so ethereal so surreal
I cannot be comprehended
    except by my permission

I mean . . . I . . . can fly
    like a bird in the sky . . .

1970

4. Since the election of its first black mayor, the city of Newark is called New Ark by its black community.

Modern Poetry In English

A Brief History

Modern poetry is poetry written in this century, but the word "modern" (at least as it relates to poetry) signifies more than chronological recentness. Modernism is an enterprise of the mind in which many poets, over several generations and in different countries, sought to change most of the assumptions about what poets write and what poetry does. The best known of these writers were W. B. Yeats, Ezra Pound, and T. S. Eliot. The language they evolved, the themes they presented, the modes of consciousness they evoked, had an air of achieved innovation.

Because they conceived of their work as different from that of their predecessors, they often appeared to their first readers—readers trained on verse written in earlier times—as bewildering and even unintelligible. The modernists had no wish to imitate the nineteenth-century poets, and to some extent reacted against them. Yet, paradoxically, any search for the origins of modernism leads back to Romanticism, that combination of literary and philosophical attitudes which dominated European and American literature for most of the nineteenth century. Earlier poetry more often than not celebrated the ideals of the society to which the poet belonged, but Romanticism provided an opportunity for a fuller and more diversified expression of oneself, for more various relations between the poet and society. An element of subversion is probably present in all great poets. But in the early nineteenth century, after the American and French Revolutions, individuality rather than obedience to authority came to be seen as positive, rather than antisocial or eccentric, and the guerrilla poet—outcast, victim, misfit, radical, solitary—became a literary and popular model.

2. Precursors

There were modern poets before there was modern poetry. Walt Whitman stands monolithically at the threshold, as poets like William Carlos Williams and Hart Crane have eagerly attested, and as Ezra Pound more grudgingly conceded. Whitman expressed a new way of looking at the world: in *Leaves of Grass* (1855), he orchestrates the universe by finding and acknowledging the relationships among the most disparate things, and relating them to himself as poet and as archetypal man. This largeness of conception broke the bonds of conventional prosody. Whitman became the first major poet to write in free verse, a crucial innovation which Pound was to institutionalize fifty years later as a prime tenet of "modernism"—"To break the pentameter, that was the first heave." Beside Whitman a second poet, Emily Dickinson, may seem an incongruous as well as a diminutive figure. Like him she "wrote a letter to the world," but her world is one of minute examination of her surroundings, a microcosm as opposed to Whitman's macrocosm, expressed as shy confidences that seem to have been preserved almost accidentally. With short lines which seem the antitheses of Whitman's long ones, with her attentive inspection of domestic and natural objects while he is off to the city or the battlefield embracing farflung multitudes, she too draws all things into cohesion, for to her "the brain is wider than the sky" and can encompass and absorb sky, sea, and all. Her poetry seconds what Yeats and William Blake both asserted, that infinity may be represented by things infinitely small as well as infinitely large.

Gerard Manley Hopkins, a third precursor of the modern movement, was a devout student of Whitman, and remarked in a letter, "I may as well say . . . that I always knew in my heart Walt Whitman's mind to be more like my own than any other man's living. As he is a very great scoundrel this is not a very pleasant confession." Hopkins doubtless thought Whitman a scoundrel because of the latter's homosexual leanings, unChristian religion, and general bravado, but their poetic kinship is unmistakable. The sense of unity overcoming diversity is shared by the two poets, though where Whitman found the multitudinous world's coherence in his own sensibility, Hopkins found it in God. Like Whitman, Hopkins felt the need to transform the apparatus of poetry in the process of re-symbolizing the world. He did not desert rhyme or meter, but he pulled, twisted, and stretched them like nerve ends until they looked like nothing seen before in English verse. One of his affinities with Whitman is the way he confronts and even affronts the reader with new shapes, rhythms, and sounds. Something of this attitude is apparent also in Thomas Hardy, who like Whitman valued himself as "one of the roughs," and offers verse based upon tormented syntax and inelegant vocabulary, as if they, rather than suavities, might best contain the uncouth universe. That these poets were out of phase with their time is indicated by the fact that they were little understood while alive; neither Dickinson nor Hopkins was even known.

3. Symbolism

The term that is most frequently used to describe post-Romantic verse is "symbolism." The Symbolist movement was related to the nineteenth-century philosophical stance called Idealism, which argued that truth inheres in consciousness rather than in the outside world. Against materialism or naturalism—movements adversary to it—practitioners of symbolism in varying ways and degrees proclaimed the supremacy of idea over fact. They rejected the conception of objects uninfluenced by perceiving subjects, and found in seemingly disconnected things secret and unexpected links. Their poetry is an attempt to render organic what appears fragmentary.

The term symbolism became popular in France about 1886, and

after about ten years crossed the English Channel. Arthur Symons, the poet and critic, had begun writing about the new French poets as "The Decadent Movement in Literature," but eventually called his book, instead, *The Symbolist Movement in Literature*. His change of heart was largely caused by his friend W. B. Yeats, with whom he shared rooms for a time in the mid-Nineties. Yeats published in 1899 *The Wind Among the Reeds*, a book of poems which was the culmination of the early symbolist manner.

This book was made out of many disparate elements, including Irish nationalism and occult lore, but all were given a new unity in a kind of counter-universe of Yeats's own invention. He created a hierarchy of symbols and of moods attendant upon them. The four elements which he found in stars, sea, winds, and woods, became aspects of feeling; bird and beast alike were bent upon expressing human passion rather than retaining their own identity. The human figures too became archetypes: the lover was Christ suffering sacrificially for his love, his passion a confirmation of spiritual reality, and the beloved, often symbolized as a pale rose, was an ideal figure, dim and almost spectral. The book appeared in the same year as Freud's *The Interpretation of Dreams* (though that had the following year on its title page), a discussion of the symbols of the unconscious. In the same year there also appeared Arthur Symons' *The Symbolist Movement in Literature*, dedicated to Yeats. It was this book which introduced to T. S. Eliot the French symbolist poets who provided the models for his early verse. For these reasons the year 1899 is probably the aptest from which to date the beginning of the modernist movement.

Yeats may be said to have achieved his aims in *The Wind Among the Reeds* only too well. His task now was to make symbolism less lugubrious and less disembodied, to unlock the secrets of nature for a larger and different audience. He began work on a second system, or symbology, which should allow for the whole man thinking and feeling, rather than for a pilgrim amorist ecstatically languishing. Verse must be "athletic," with leaps instead of dying falls. He began the attempt to assemble in verse material eschewed earlier as imperfect and "unpoetic."

In this development, Yeats found unexpected company in an American, Ezra Pound. Pound arrived in London in 1908, at the age of twenty-three, convinced that Yeats was the best poet then writing in English and determined to learn from him. He did so, but Yeats also discovered how much this young man could tell him of new ideas and techniques. Pound's openness to modernism—his exhortation to "make it new"—and his generosity and gregariousness made his apartment in Kensington the headquarters of innovative verse for both England and America. He was set on this new course by the novelist Ford Madox Ford and the philosopher T. E. Hulme, both of whom encouraged him to renounce his earlier exuberant rhetoric in favor of a more epigrammatic and ironic mode. In 1912 Pound, with H. D. and others, founded the Imagist movement, demanding "direct treatment of the thing," whether the thing was inside or outside the mind. They warned against slackness and sentimentality and counselled that form, whether free verse or not, should not be determined by the metronome. These were useful rules, but rather bare, and Pound soon shifted from

Imagism to Vorticism. In his manifesto for the latter he emphasized not the do's and don'ts of style but the dynamism of content. Vorticism lasted only for a short time, and after it Pound left off founding movements, but he began to demonstrate in his verse what innovations were possible.

His closest confederate was T. S. Eliot, whom Pound may be said to have discovered. The two men met in 1914, when Eliot came to England to study philosophy at Oxford; Pound was astonished by the poems which Eliot showed him, among them "The Love Song of J. Alfred Prufrock," observing that Eliot had modernized himself on his own as, Pound felt, no one else had done. At first it seemed that they were moving in much the same direction. They both wrote about the modern world as a group of fragments, Pound in the first Cantos which he published in *Poetry* (the magazine which, through his efforts and those of its founder Harriet Monroe, became the American clearing-house for modern verse) and Eliot in *The Waste Land*, which Pound had helped him to complete. Only gradually did it become clear that these very poems embodied divergent views: for Eliot the fragmentariness of the world was intolerable, and he was determined to mend it (as his eventual conversion to Anglican Christianity helped him to do), but Pound preferred to accept and exploit this disjunctiveness. He saw how he might accept the fragments and make them material for a modern epic, *The Cantos*, which would achieve its paradise, as well as its hell and purgatory, intermittently.

As a result *The Waste Land*, with the poems by Eliot that became its sequels, and *The Cantos*, which Pound continued to write until his death, may be seen as rival eminences of modern verse. The fragments which Eliot wished to re-combine Pound was willing to keep unchanged. Although Pound wrote Eliot that he envied him his sense of form, he did not emulate it. Eliot's sifting and fusion ended in a surprisingly orthodox religious view which Pound regarded as based upon too limited a number of particulars. Pound preferred his own "ideogrammic method," as he called it, by which he meant the heaping up of the components of thought so that they would eventually converge almost without artistic intervention. *The Cantos* collate slices of time and space, fable and fact, examples from aboriginal tribes and effete cultures. There is no purification or evident exclusion; the poet achieves his effect by collocating diffuse materials. Eliot consolidated his innovations, while Pound restlessly extended his.

The Waste Land was published in 1922, and the first collection of *Cantos* in volume form appeared in 1925. In recent years Pound has probably exerted the greater influence on younger poets, but during the Twenties it was Eliot who had the cry. Yet the reaction to Eliot's poems was violently mixed.

William Carlos Williams found it necessary to campaign against the poem; its sinister merit was so powerful that it might well block the movement towards an indigenous American verse. For him it was "the great catastrophe" which by its genius (a quality he admitted) interrupted the "rediscovery of a primal impulse, the elementary principle of all art, in the local [as opposed to cosmopolitan] conditions." Williams considered that Eliot had imposed a shape upon material which should have been allowed to take its own shape. His own conception of poetry he expressed by the poem beginning, "So much depends upon / a red wheelbarrow," as if objects in the world should be allowed to retain their nature without being conceptualized into abstract schemas. When during the Thirties the term "Objectivism" was devised to enforce the primacy of the natural object in works of the imagination, Williams heartily endorsed it as a formulation of his own practice. "No ideas but in things," was his credo. Williams opposed "literature" as a phenomenon created by the "establishment"; he regarded language as the vital instrument which must be sharpened by keeping it local rather than cosmopolitan. His own poems, unlike Pound's or Eliot's, are all but devoid of "literary" English, and their unmistakable distinctiveness comes, as he insisted, from contact with native materials.

Wallace Stevens led a different revolt against the religious presuppositions of *The Waste Land.* In *Harmonium* (1923) and later books, he presented the death of the old gods as a liberation of the imagination. In contradistinction to Eliot's return to Christianity, Stevens asked for a new religion which should be closer to physical life and willing to encompass death, as well as life, in its conception of being. Its paradise must be within the world. The poet's task is to replace the satisfactions of belief once provided by religion with those of verse: "What makes the poet the potent figure that he is, or was, or ought to be, is that he creates the world to which we turn incessantly and without knowing it and that he gives to life the supreme fictions without which we are unable to conceive of it." The creation of these fictions, which he changed even as he affirmed, occupied Stevens steadily.

Hart Crane was moved by *The Waste Land,* and fascinated by its author's technical brilliance, but he thought Eliot's despair exaggerated and (like Williams) rejected his cosmopolitanism. In his own major work, *The Bridge,* Crane went back beyond Eliot to find affinities of theme and temperament with Walt Whitman. Brooklyn Bridge, like Whitman's Brooklyn Ferry, becomes a symbol spanning not only space but time; in *The Bridge* Crane sought to embrace America, its land, people, and history, with Whitmanesque exuberance. The poem can be seen as an answer to *The Waste Land,* as an attempt to redeem Eliot's fallen world.

Apart from Yeats, British poets have been less attracted to the problems raised by the symbolists than Americans, and those few who followed the lead of Eliot and Pound have made relatively little impact on their countrymen. An exception to this as to many other rules was Edith Sitwell, whose quirky sequence of poems, *Façade* (read to the music of her friend William Walton), produced a first-rate literary scandal of the Twenties. At about the same time, in the anthologies called *Wheels,* she was vigorously attacking poetry less lively than her own, and also brought to light the war poems of Wilfred Owen. Hugh MacDiarmid achieved both fame and notoriety in Scotland—fame for his lyric poems, written in a synthetic Scots dialect of his own invention, and notoriety for his activities on behalf of the Communist and Scottish Nationalist Parties. He aligned himself with Pound and especially with James Joyce, whose linguistic experiments in *Finnegans Wake* he praised and imitated. In England as in America, however, the influence of strongly programmatic poetry such as that by the poets from Yeats to Williams has been balanced by much more traditional modes of verse. These alternatives must be considered.

4. Elegant and Inelegant Variations

English poets of the early twentieth century declined to follow the examples of Yeats and Pound, and yet were also dissatisfied by much late Victorian verse. Some looked further back to the Romantics for a mode of literary survival. They were included in an anthology published soon after the accession of George V in 1910, entitled *Georgian Poetry*. Among those who trooped to this strange device, which appeared on four subsequent anthologies, were Rupert Brooke, Walter de la Mare, Robert Graves, Siegfried Sassoon, and even D. H. Lawrence. Curiously, because of the editor's taste, Edward Thomas was omitted, though he best epitomized Georgian ideals. At first these poets, with their celebration of the English countryside and its people, seemed to open a window into a more wholesome outdoors, and the movement was received enthusiastically by those who wished to preserve rural England in traditional prosody. Traces of Georgian tendencies can be found in the work of Thomas's friend Robert Frost, who lived in England from 1912 to 1915. Almost from the beginning the Georgians were under critical attack; they were the principal targets of Edith Sitwell in the *Wheels* anthologies, for she regarded them as insipid and pretentious. The movement succumbed to the First World War, during which Brooke and Thomas died. Walter de la Mare and Robert Graves lasted longer than the movement to which they had belonged. Graves's verse was renewed by his association with Laura Riding. Sassoon, who survived the war, and Owen, who was killed in its last week, became the most famous of the war poets; their experiences in the trenches withered away their conventional patriotism and stirred them to devise a bitter new rhetoric to express their disillusion and anger at martial inhumanity.

D. H. Lawrence was little more in place as a Georgian than as an Imagist, although both groups had sought to claim him. His praise for the Georgians was more for their potential than their actual accomplishments. He conceded that *Georgian Poetry* had not much concern with love—an understatement—but prophesied that the group were "just ripening to be love poets." He quickly imputed to them his own doctrine: "If I take my whole, passionate, spiritual and physical love to the woman who in return loves me, that is how I serve God. . . . All of which I read in the anthology of *Georgian Poetry*." As a statement of his own purpose this was accurate. Lawrence sought to break through the tinsel with his burning honesty and directness, and centered his own verse in the passions of tortoises and elephants as well as of men and women. Robinson Jeffers and Brother Antoninus in America, and Ted Hughes in England, were to pursue the same qualities, though in Jeffers and Hughes it often seems that more reality attaches to hate than to love. Unlike the Georgians, Lawrence worked often in free verse, but did not share Pound's interest in the minute technicalities of that freedom. He thought that an interest in form usually accompanied an interest in imitation, and preferred to let his subjects command their own shape. He remained an isolated figure, almost an outcast, beset during his short life by the public's unfounded notion that his writings were obscene. They were in fact the opposite.

In America, during the first two decades of the new century, poets explored their environment with little regard for the symbolist patterns being woven by their compatriots Pound, Eliot, and H. D. in England. Edwin Arlington Robinson exposed the life of his Tilbury Town, and Edgar Lee Masters of his Spoon River, so as to impart public lessons from private scandals. Robert Frost returned from England in 1915, bought a farm in New Hampshire, and consolidated his reputation as America's greatest pastoral poet. For many he was its greatest poet of the twentieth century. Frost brought a toughness to pastoralism; on the one hand he tapped the seasoned country wisdom of New England, on the other he converted his self-disgust and loneliness into verses of Horatian dignity phrased in the accents of New Hampshire and Vermont. The more brazen Carl Sandburg wrote of the brawling city of Chicago and its workers; his ebullient rhetoric constituted the most "modern" literature to gain much public acceptance in the United States. Many poets who wished a more radical break with tradition left the country to find it, while the early poems of others, such as William Carlos Williams, were printed either privately or abroad. In 1923 the Pulitzer Prize for poetry went not to *The Waste Land* but to three books by Edna St. Vincent Millay.

Some poets of less prominence were to outstay some of the more obvious reputations. In New York two poets, Marianne Moore in Brooklyn and E. E. Cummings in Greenwich Village, were proceeding with subtlety in ways more decisively modern. Marianne Moore, like her friend William Carlos Williams, was a sharp observer, and upholder, of the physical world, but hers was a world which few others knew, made up of rare birds and animals, insects, baseball players and steeplejacks, steamrollers and other creatures. Pretending that her lines were prose, she employed light rhymes and odd stanzaic patterns as if to conceal the finish of her work. Poetry, she alleged, was all "fiddle," and yet, she confided, it had in it "a place for the genuine." Cummings was a more flamboyant poet: he invented an astonishing number of typographical oddities, partly to tantalize and disconcert, partly to amuse, but mostly to indicate to his devotees how the poems might be best read aloud. With all his up-to-date pyrotechnics, he kept to the ancient themes of lyric poetry.

The black poets of the Harlem Renaissance, on the other hand, sought revitalization by content rather than form. They adopted the devices of nineteenth-century verse in expressing their new theme of black racial consciousness and culture. They rejected the "Uncle Remus" dialect and the exoticism of Paul Laurence Dunbar and other earlier black poets in order to develop a new intransigence. Claude McKay, politically the most militant if prosodically among the more conservative of the new black writers, was first with *Harlem Shadows* (1922); then followed Jean Toomer's *Cane* (1924), a loosely knit collection of poems, stories, and sketches expressing the life of the southern black. The most prominent and talented member of the group was Langston Hughes, the only one whose work continued to be published after the stock market crash of 1929 dropped the bottom out of the largely white market for black writing. During the Depression, writers like Richard Wright barely subsisted by working on travel guide books for the Works Progress Administration, and only occasionally published a poem in a socialist newspaper. For some twenty-five years there was just an occasional spurt of attention, as when in 1950 Gwendolyn Brooks was awarded the Pulitzer Prize, to show that black poetry was still alive.

The year 1922 saw many important tendencies in modern verse put into motion. It was the year of *The Waste Land* and of Joyce's *Ulysses* (published in Paris), and of several bursts of concerted activity such as the Harlem Renaissance in New York. It was also the year when a group of teachers and students at Vanderbilt University brought out a literary magazine called *The Fugitive*, in which they published their own and others' poems and urged an alternative to the cosmopolitan modernism centered in London. Of the Fugitives, the central figure was John Crowe Ransom, and the younger members of the group included Allen Tate and Robert Penn Warren. They cultivated an astringent wit as an antidote to Southern nostalgia; politically, through the Agrarian movement, they hoped to keep for the South some of its traditional values. They came to view their provinciality, their remoteness from metropolitan culture, and their sense of rootedness in time and place as sources of strength for their writing. The magazine ceased publication in 1925; Tate had already moved to New York, Warren (after graduate study at Berkeley, Yale and Oxford) went to Louisiana State University, and Ransom joined the faculty of Kenyon College and founded the *Kenyon Review*. As poets, teachers, and critics, these and other poets speaking from the university such as Yvor Winters, continued to write in a style that younger poets liked for its aloofness and its complexity of motives and materials.

The influence of this style began to take shape during the later Twenties and the Thirties, when a number of important critical works were published whose general tendency was applauded by John Crowe Ransom in a book, *The New Criticism* (1941), whose title became a byword for the entire movement. In *A Survey of Modernist Poetry* (1927), by Laura Riding and Robert Graves, Miss Riding had been perhaps the first to try the experiment of reading a poem apart from any historical or linguistic context; her intense appreciation of the semantic complexities of a Shakespeare sonnet encouraged the young William Empson to discover how far one might go in this line, and to read every poem in sight as if it had just been written anonymously. The result was his famous study, *Seven Types of Ambiguity* (1930), which sought to characterize the semantic strategies of multiple meanings which distinguish imaginative writing from straightforward exposition. Another force behind the New Criticism was Empson's teacher, I. A. Richards, who urged that poems be read with active and exclusive attention to what they said and not be distorted by the reader's subjective preferences. Eliot, important for his criticism as well as for his verse, agreed that what was needed in reading poetry was "a very highly developed sense of fact." These prescriptions for readers, and by extension for writers, were codified by Robert Penn

Warren and Cleanth Brooks in their textbook, *Understanding Poetry* (1938), which had a masterful influence on the teaching of verse at American colleges. Taken to extremes, the New Criticism implied that the essence of poetry was not to convey ideas or feelings as such but to create intricate structures of language which would manifest the density of psychophysical experience. Some of Empson's own poems are perhaps the most thoroughgoing exemplifications of this principle; few other poets went so far, but they understood his goal. During and immediately after the Second World War, most poets living in the United States came to write in a way that poets of the Twenties and critics of the Thirties had got ready for them.

In England during the late Twenties and early Thirties, the most important young poets were W. H. Auden, Stephen Spender, Louis MacNeice, and C. Day Lewis, a group which prided itself on "understatement" and "social concern." They were eager to express radical political attitudes, and preferred to do so through older verse techniques. Except for their preference for rhyme and meter, they were strenuously ahead of their time. They proclaimed their support for a socialist revolution. To some extent, the Second World War obliged them to try to preserve rather than to change. Auden, who went to the United States, wrote sharply and sympathetically about the new problems of community in a divided world. In his later years he became orthodox in his religious beliefs and more tender and friendly in his verse. Instead of predicting that something dreadful was about to happen, he preferred to celebrate with great wit what was happening already. For most readers in the Sixties Auden was the principal poet then writing in English, although his ways of using rhyme and meter made him look more like a vigorous survivor from a gentler age.

5. Contemporary Poetry

Perhaps the most accessible way to consider today's poets together is to recognize that they conduct in their work, or in their thinking about their work, a restless dialogue. Behind them is a powerful literature which early in the century registered great innovations and consolidations in verse. As they look back upon this period, they are likely to see as fixed what was then experimental. They would like to invade areas of awareness, both commonplace and exotic, which were largely neglected by their predecessors. The Second World War may not have markedly divided the poetry written before it from that written after, but many poets who were young during the War have written with greater skepticism of accepted personal and social values than those older poets—Stevens, Cummings, Williams, Frost, Eliot, Pound, Marianne Moore—who survived it.

During the War itself a number of British poets emerged whose response to the "age of anxiety," as Auden called it, was vehement and extreme. These were the poets of the New Apocalypse, a rubric which first appeared as the title of an anthology published in 1940. Its editor announced "a new Romantic tendency, whose most obvious elements are love, death, an adherence to myth and an awareness of war." The most notable member of this visionary company was Dylan Thomas.

Perhaps in opposition to the understatement of the Auden school, Thomas, with the most spectacular display of language since Hart Crane, reintroduced intense emotion into English verse. He tried to restore to nature a radiance lost to English poetry since the seventeenth century. In reaction to this Apocalyptic mode there arose during the Fifties a loose association of university poets who called themselves, baldly, "The Movement." Kingsley Amis and Robert Conquest, as editors of the anthology *New Lines*, were their main propagandists, and the chief of them has proved to be Philip Larkin. While objecting to what they saw as the Romantic excesses of the New Apocalypse, the poets of The Movement also rejected the symbolist tradition of Yeats, Pound, and Eliot, and favored wit over prophecy and extravagance, urbanity over commitment. They defined themselves more narrowly in relationship to Graves, Empson, and Edwin Muir, and they aimed to consolidate the achievements of the Auden school, to write a poetry which in its subjects and in its diction would express rather than overthrow the restrictions of ordinary urban life.

A similar situation obtained in the United States, where a generation of younger poets had emerged during the Forties, many of whom were to die—some by suicide—before the Sixties were out. Randall Jarrell, Lincoln Kirstein, Richard Eberhart, and Karl Shapiro wrote poems out of their wartime experiences; they were essentially meditative rather than dramatic. Others, such as Theodore Roethke, Robert Lowell, and John Berryman, began to write in a different atmosphere. For some years after the War, the aesthetic of the New Criticism—itself a condensation of the practice of certain poets—helped to shape most new American verse, even that by writers like Lowell and Berryman who fifteen years later would write in quite different ways. The qualities it enshrines, such as metaphysical wit (exemplified by John Donne and Gerard Manley Hopkins), an irony too complex to permit strong commitments, and a technique which often calls attention to its own dexterity, are characteristic elements of what has been called by its detractors an academic style. Whatever it may lack in gusto, it is not dull, and it served handsomely as a difficult school for some of the best recent poets. If some poets of the New Criticism have gravitated to careers as critics and college teachers, it must be recognized that both criticism and college teaching have become more demanding and exciting pursuits when so many esthetic battles are being waged.

The wry, cultivated quality of much poetry of the Fifties is visible in the work of some university poets. The verse of men like Richard Wilbur, Howard Nemerov, and Louis Simpson, and of women like Elizabeth Bishop and Josephine Miles, gives pleasure by the fertility and deftness of their images and phrases; their work is unsentimental and yet alive to senses and sympathies, well made and careful not to repeat itself or become predictable. These are real values and lead to verse that is often more durable, if less sensational, than what has come from more daemonic talents.

In contrast to the influence of the New Critics, that of William Carlos Williams and Ezra Pound has been more subversive and therefore less easily accommodated by the academy. Williams continued in the life of a physician in Rutherford, New Jersey, and was the object of pilgrimages by young poets including A. R. Ammons and Allen Ginsberg. Pound, under indictment for treason because of his wartime radio broadcasts from Rome, was returned to the United States in 1945, bringing with him the manuscript of the *Pisan Cantos.* Found mentally incompetent to stand trial, he was immured in a Washington sanatorium, and until his release twelve years later (as incurably insane but harmless) he was a magnet for younger American poets who sought in his work an immersion in experience which they found to be lacking in the poetry of Eliot and Ransom and their followers. Finding strength in their association with the old impresario of *vers libre* and the even older M. D. in Rutherford, they preferred open to closed poetic forms, agreeing with Robert Creeley that "Form is never more than an extension of content."

Creeley was one of the poets who gathered around Charles Olson at Black Mountain College, an experimental and unaccredited school in North Carolina which was to become one of the centers of the new American verse. Olson developed the theoretical manifesto of the Black Mountain poets and others of similar aims in his essay on "projective verse," which attempts a dynamism like that of Pound's Vorticism, and offers a conception of "open-field" form. Here, and in his *Maximus Poems* of the Sixties, he constituted himself the heir of Pound and Williams. Like Williams he emphasized the breath, rather than the iamb, as the basis of rhythm. Like Pound, Olson in his verse mixed colloquialism and farflung learning. He opposed the isolation of literature from the rest of experience; the poet must take a stance towards the world.

The faculty of Black Mountain College included Creeley, who also edited the *Black Mountain Review;* during its short run of seven issues it was a major outlet for the antiacademic verse which was to explode into prominence in the late Fifties. Robert Duncan came from San Francisco to join the college staff; Paul Blackburn and Denise Levertov were published in the *Review.* A. R. Ammons, from North Carolina if not from Black Mountain, has much in common with these poets; even LeRoi Jones has acknowledged the fundamental influence of Charles Olson on his kind of poetry.

The Beat poets too align themselves with the "open" prosody of Pound and especially of Williams, who wrote an introduction for Allen Ginsberg's *Howl.* They were featured in the last issue of the *Black Mountain Review,* of which Ginsberg was a contributing editor. The Beats, however, tended to dismiss the Black Mountain poets as too much at ease with authority figures; their own consistent opposition to authority made them the most conspicuous and notorious poetic movement of the Fifties. They set themselves against the stuffy majority culture, the anticommunist inquisitions, and the formalistic poetry of the times, and decided to drop out and create among themselves a counterculture based upon inspired improvisation, whether through jazz, drugs, or transcendence by way of oriental mysticism. Ginsberg, Gregory Corso, and Lawrence Ferlinghetti, exiles from New York, found a congenial milieu in San Francisco, where a poetic renaissance had already been formented within the counterculture. Robert Duncan returned to the San Francisco scene after Black Mountain

College collapsed in 1956; Gary Snyder returned to his birthplace after years in the lumber camps of Oregon and more years studying Zen Buddhism in a Japanese monastery. Following the example of Walt Whitman, Beat writers like Ginsberg and San Francisco poets like Brother Antoninus shape their public utterances out of the private experiences which their first readers found shameful and appalling; they present, often as visionary experiences, confidences of a kind which were once uttered only to priest or doctor. This kind of poetry has come to be known as "confessional," and through the Sixties many younger poets vied with each other in unabashed self-revelation. Others of the Beats, however, have written with less personal intensity, and the poetry of Gregory Corso has less in common with Ginsberg's than with the offhand, witty verse of Frank O'Hara.

O'Hara was a member of what has been called the "New York school" of poets. Others were John Ashbery and Kenneth Koch. The three met at Harvard, where they (and Gregory Corso) were associated with the Poets' Theater, an experimental drama group of the early Fifties. Inspired by the paintings of such contemporary artists as Jackson Pollock and Willem de Kooning, they went to New York and immersed themselves in modern art—Ashbery and O'Hara wrote for *Art News*, and O'Hara worked for the Museum of Modern Art. Although the painters they admired are abstractionists, their verse is not abstract; they practice a calculated effrontery and discontinuity of perception, as if all the rest were pomposity. In their highspirited way they celebrate New York and record its landscape, as when O'Hara, characterisically looking from the window of an art gallery, writes that "the warm traffic going by is my natural scenery." The rootedness of these poets in their locale is as intense as that of the Georgians or the poets of the American south. Like the Beats, the New York poets want to refresh a poetry which they feel has too long been at the mercy of critics and professors of literature.

Surrealism, a mode which exploits as material the distortion imposed upon reality by the unconscious, has until recently been more common to the visual arts, and to European writing, than to American or English poetry. During the Sixties, however, some of these achievements have suggested ways for American poets to exploit new perceptions and arrangements of phenomena. Under the sponsorship of Robert Bly's magazine, *The Fifties* (later *Sixties* and *Seventies*), new translations of the South Americans Pablo Neruda and Cesar Vallejo, as well as other surrealist poets, have been made available, and a "new surrealism" can be found in some of Bly's own poems and in those of W. S. Merwin and Mark Strand. Others, like Diane Wakoski and Jim Harrison, have also periodically been attracted to the dislocation of sense and image that is a feature of surrealism. The reader is invited to experience such visions without the effort of logical construction; in the work of Mark Strand, for example, the very mysteriousness of what is going on contributes to a mounting effect of uncanny power.

In Robert Lowell's work the New Critical tradition of elaborate structure and the Whitmanesque tradition of radical contact with subject approached startling fusion during the late Fifties. As a young man, Lowell had left Harvard to study at Kenyon College with John Crowe Ransom; he and his older friend Allen Tate became Roman Catholics at the same time; his second book, *Lord Weary's Castle*, showed a technical mastery of rhyme and meter, and gave him an established place among young poets. Then followed a long silence, during which Lowell, teaching at the University of Iowa, was struck by some aspects of Beat poetry (and, he says, by the work of one of his students, W. D. Snodgrass). In 1959 he published his first book of "confessional" poetry, *Life Studies*, working for the first time in what appeared to be a looser form. It seemed at first that Lowell might himself be becoming a Beat, but in fact his verse is closely controlled even when it does not seem so; if he writes poems in fourteen unrhyming lines, it is in order to play against the reader's expectations of sonnet form. Other poets who have written in this intensely autobiographical vein, such as Snodgrass, Theodore Roethke, John Berryman, Sylvia Plath (perhaps the best of all in this mode), Anne Sexton, and Adrienne Rich, have either played against conventional form or written free verse in a peculiarly unrelaxed way. These poets are generally melancholy; they have sought in their lives the key moments of pain much more often than of pleasure, and see such moments as epitomes of the general condition of men and women in their time. They present themselves in extraordinarily intimate terms, with little or no extenuation of weakness or alleviation of distress. Three of them, Sylvia Plath, John Berryman, and Anne Sexton, committed suicide.

Black poets since the War have also sought a special rapport with their readers, but on social rather than personal grounds. They regard agonies as imposed from without rather than from within, and against oppression have written the most politically inflammatory verse of the time. Some have also made use of the prosodic innovations of Pound and Williams, for example, in some of Robert Hayden's work. Gwendolyn Brooks, on the other hand, began to use black street language in poems such as "We Real Cool." LeRoi Jones, taking the name Imamu Amiri Baraka, left the white avant-garde during the Sixties to move towards a distinctively black esthetic, which insisted on the importance to black writers of commitment to the needs of the black community and the discovery of their artistic resources in it. He has been followed by younger poets like Don L. Lee, Nikki Giovanni, and Etheridge Knight, both in the celebration of blackness and (except for Knight) in the use of modernist forms developed by Whitman, Williams, Olson, and Cummings. Many have also rejected not only white audiences but white publishers and have instead placed their books with black enterprises like Dudley Randall's Broadside Press, whose list features not only new poets but established figures like Gwendolyn Brooks and Randall himself.

The revolt against academic poetry in America has been paralleled by similar, though less successful, efforts in England. Though The Movement has inspired much of the best verse by younger poets, such as Jon Stallworthy, it has from the beginning been challenged by other initiatives which seek to bring greater technical diversity and intensity of statement to English poetry. A community of poets calling themselves "The Group" held meetings to provide mutual encouragement and criticism; its most notable members have been George Macbeth, whose poems often exploit a mood of dark surrealist humor, and (briefly) Ted Hughes, whom many consider the finest of the younger English poets. He sees the world as violent and himself as having a savage role to fill, and finds emblems of violence in the outer world of animals. Before long The Movement itself lost some of its coherence: Thom Gunn left England altogether and went to the United States, and so did Charles Tomlinson for a time, as his sympathies had always been with such American poets as Marianne Moore and the Black Mountain contingent.

During the Sixties, American modernism came to have many adherents among the younger English poets who lived north of London. One locus is Newcastle-upon-Tyne, where the poet Jon Silkin founded a magazine called *Stand* which was not to be subject to the prevailing London winds; among his contributors has been Geoffrey Hill, whose work is at once distinctively modern and reminiscent of the "metaphysical" poetry of John Donne and other seventeenth-century poets. Another center of antiacademic rebellion is Liverpool, whose poets are like the New York poets in their humorous protests against authority and their sense of their environment, though they write in a simpler-minded way. Inspired by the Beats, the Beatles, and pop art, such Liverpool poets as Roger McGough and Adrian Henri (who is a painter as well) construct humorously savage poems, many of them intended to be read to jazz or rock music.

Since the death of Yeats in 1939, the most notable Irish poets have been Austin Clarke and Patrick Kavanagh. Clarke's strongest verse presents amorous passion against a background of sin and judgment, often in terms of Celtic legends. His technique of off-rhymes, drawn from poetry in Irish, has impressed Auden and other poets. Kavanagh's tough, satiric later work superseded his more lyrical and rustic quality. He conveyed a sense of a plainspoken, unquellable man, mordant yet vulnerable. Seamus Heaney has written poems of Irish country life terse and direct enough to recall Kavanagh. Not surprisingly, the great achievements of Irish literature in the recent past have proved more a hindrance than a spur to younger writers. Many have chosen to live abroad, for example Thomas Kinsella, a forceful, saturnine poet, who has protested that much of his work is not specifically Irish, and who lives in the United States. In Scotland, no poet has appeared to challenge the earlier achievements of Edwin Muir and Hugh MacDiarmid; George Macbeth, perhaps the most talented younger poet from Scotland, has spent most of his life in England.

6. Some Conclusions

As may be seen from this rapid overview, and even more from the poems which follow, ours is a century of poetic diversity probably unequaled in history; the extremes of style and subject available to today's poets are further apart than they have ever been before. It may be useful to picture modern poets as occupying positions at various points between two contrary extremes and as conducting in their work dialogues with each other and with themselves. On the one hand are the "formalists," for whom literature is a definite institution and whose poems are highly worked and perfected items in an established tradition. On the other hand are what might be called the "informalists," for whom terms like "literature," "tradition," and even "poetry" and "poem' are suspect. They debunk qualitative distinctions between literary and non-literary writing. The word "poem" is put aside by at least some of the informalists in favor of the word "composition," specifically—as Olson says—"open field composition" in preference to "closed," a distinction like that which Robert Lowell makes between "raw" and formally "cooked." Against meter, stanza, line, sentence, and rhyme the informalists offer free verse, nonstanzaic and ostentatiously run-on.

These differences extend to the governing life of the poem as well as to its external characteristics; the formalists offer a continuous discourse, while the informalists are likely to present discontinuity and intermittences. In general, the movement of formalism is towards the art world where experience is mastered, and the movement of the contrary school is towards what Pound calls "the green world," where experience is registered. The search of the one group to sift and purify is met by their opponents' search for "impure poetry."

There are, of course, many poets on either side of the dialogue, and few who do not at times take on some of their adversaries' characteristics. Poetry is seldom written merely to support esthetic positions, and even the most ardent polemicist is likely to absorb even as he defies. The further boundaries of poetry have been extended by Pound and Williams, and the nearer ones defended by Eliot and Ransom, but none of these eminent figures should be taken as a generalissimo whom his juniors obsequiously obey. Their rival conceptions derive, at last, from the symbolist contraposition of a heroic and artistic dream to the wasteful, incomplete, yet ever-engendering life around them. The battle lines were drawn in the late nineteenth century, and the combat has been waged fiercely in this one. Although they do not agree upon the answers, the poets of our century share the same questions.

Bibliography

This bibliography lists works by each poet in the anthology, beginning with all the books of poetry, and continuing with verse translations and a very selective list of other books: fiction (f), drama (d), and criticism (c).

KINGSLEY AMIS

Bright November (1947); *A Frame of Mind* (1953); *A Case of Samples: Poems, 1946–1956* (1956); *The Evans Country* (1962); *A Look Round the Estate: Poems, 1957–1967* (1967).

Other:

Lucky Jim (1954) (f).

A. R. AMMONS

Ommateum (1955); *Expressions of Sea Level* (1964); *Corsons Inlet* (1965); *Tape for the Turn of the Year* (1965); *Northfield Poems* (1966); *Selected Poems* (1968); *Uplands* (1970); *Briefings* (1971); *Collected Poems, 1951–1971* (1972); *Sphere* (1974); *Diversifications* (1975).

BROTHER ANTONINUS (William Everson)

These Are the Ravens (1935); *San Joaquin* (1939); *The Masculine Dead* (1942); *The Waldport Poems* (1943); *War Elegies* (1944); *The Residual Years* (1944, expanded 1948); *Poems MCMXLII* (1945); *A Privacy of Speech* (1949); *Triptych for the Living* (1951); *The Crooked Lines of God* (1959); *The Year's Declension* (1961); *The Hazards of Holiness* (1962); *The Poet Is Dead* (1964); *The Blowing of the Seed* (1966); *Single Source* (1966); *In the Fictive Wish* (1967); *The Rose of Solitude* (1967); *A Canticle to the Waterbirds* (1968); *The Springing of the Blade* (1968); *The City Does Not Die* (1969); *The Last Crusade* (1969); *Man-Fate: The Swan Song of Brother Antoninus* (1974).

JOHN ASHBERY

Turandot and Other Poems (1953); *Some Trees* (1956); *The Poems* (1960); *The Tennis Court Oath* (1962); *Rivers and Mountains* (1967); *Selected Poems* (1967); *Fragment* (1969); *The Double Dream of Spring* (1970); *Three Poems* (1972); *The Vermont Notebook* (1975); *Self-Portrait in a Convex Mirror* (1975).

W. H. AUDEN

Poems (1928); *Poems* (1930, rev. 1933); *The Orators: An English Study* (1932, rev. ed. 1966); *Look, Stranger!* (U.S. edn: *On This Island*) (1936); *Spain* (1937); *Selected Poems* (1938); *Some Poems* (1940); *Another Time* (1940); *New Year Letter* (U.S. edn: *The Double Man*) (1941); *For the Time Being: A Christmas Oratorio* (1944); *Collected Poetry* (1945); *The Age of Anxiety: A Baroque Eclogue* (1947); *Collected Shorter Poems, 1930–1944* (1950); *Nones* (1952); *The Shield of Achilles* (1955); *The Old Man's Road* (1956); *Selected Poetry* (1959); *Homage to Clio* (1960); *About the House* (1965); *Collected Shorter Poems, 1927–1957* (1966); *Collected Longer Poems* (1968); *Selected*

Poems (1968); *City Without Walls* (1969), *Academic Graffiti* (1971); *Epistle to a Godson* (1972); *Thank You, Fog* (1974).
Translation:
with L. Sjöberg, *Selected Poems by Gunnar Ekelöf* (1972).
Other:
With C. Isherwood, *The Dog Beneath the Skin* (1935) (d); with Isherwood, *The Ascent of F6* (1936) (d); *The Dyer's Hand* (1962) (c); *Selected Essays* (1964) (c).

MARGARET AVISON
Winter Sun (1960); *The Dumbfounding* (1966).

IMAMU AMIRI BARAKA (LeRoi Jones)
Preface to a Twenty Volume Suicide Note (1962); *The Dead Lecturer* (1965); *Black Art* (1966); *Black Magic: Poetry 1961–1967* (1969); *Spirit Reach* (1972).
Other:
Dutchman and *Slave* (1964) (d); *The Baptism* and *The Toilet* (1967) (d).

JOHN BERRYMAN
Poems (1942); *The Dispossessed* (1948); *Homage to Mistress Bradstreet* (1956); *His Thoughts Made Pockets & the Plane Buckt* (1958); *77 Dream Songs* (1964); *Berryman's Sonnets* (1967); *Short Poems* (1967); *His Toy, His Dream, His Rest* (1968); *The Dream Songs* (1969); *Love & Fame* (1970); *Delusions, Etc.* (1972).

JOHN BETJEMAN
Mount Zion; or, In Touch with the Infinite (1931); *Continual Dew: A Little Book of Bourgeois Verse* (1937); *Old Lights for New Chancels: Verses Topographical and Amatory* (1940); *New Bats in Old Belfries* (1945); *Slick But Not Streamlined* (ed. by W. H. Auden) (1947); *Selected Poems* (1948); *A Few Late Chrysanthemums* (1954); *Poems in the Porch* (1954); *Collected Poems* (1958, 2nd ed. 1962, 3rd ed. 1970); *Summoned by Bells* (verse autobiog) (1960); *High and Low* (1966); *A Nip in the Air* (1975).

ELIZABETH BISHOP
North and South (1946); *Poems: North and South—A Cold Spring* (1955); *Questions of Travel* (1965); *Selected Poems* (1967); *The Ballad of the Burglar of Babylon* (1968); *The Complete Poems* (1969).

PAUL BLACKBURN
The Dissolving Fabric (1955); *Brooklyn-Manhattan Transit* (1960); *The Nets* (1961); *Sing-Song* (1966); *The Reardon Poems* (1967); *The Cities* (1967); *In, On, or About the Premises* (1968); *Early Eelected y Mas: Collected Poems, 1949–1961* (1972).

ROBERT BLY
Silence in the Snowy Fields (1962, rev. 1967); *The Light Around the Body* (1967); *The Morning Glory* (1969); *The Teeth-Mother Naked at Last* (1970); *The Shadow-Mothers* (1970); *Jumping out of Bed* (1972); *Sleepers Joining Hands* (1973); *Point Reyes Poems* (1974).
Translations:
Late Arrival on Earth: Selected Poems of Gunnar Ekelöf (with C. Paulston) (1967); *Twenty Poems of Pablo Neruda* (with J. Wright) (1968); *Forty Poems of Juan Ramón Jiménez* (1969).

ROBERT BRIDGES
Poems (1873); *Carmen Elegiacum* (1876); *The Growth of Love: 24 Sonnets* (1876); *Poems* (1879); *Poems, Third Series* (1880); *Prometheus the Firegiver* (1883); *Poems* (1884); *Nero Part I* (1885); *Eros and Psyche* (1885); *The Growth of Love: 79 Sonnets* (1889); *Palicio* (1890); *The Return of Ulysses* (1890); *The Christian Captives* (1890); *Achilles in Scyros* (1890); *Shorter Poems* (1890); *Eden* (1891); *November Drear*

(1892); *The Humours of the Court* (1893); *Shorter Poems, Book V* (1893); *Nero Part II* (1894); *Invocation to Music (Purcell Ode)* (1895); *Purcell Ode, and Other Poems* (1896); *Chants for the Psalter* (1897); *A Song of Darkness and Light* (1898); *Poetical Works* (1898–1905); *Now in Wintry Delights* (1903); *Poetical Works* (1913); *Poems Written in the Year MCMXIII* (1914); *The Chivalry of the Sea* (1916); *October and Other Poems* (1920); *Poetical Works* (6 vols, 1920); *Poor Poll* (1923); *The Tapestry* (1925); *New Verse* (1925); *The Testament of Beauty* (1929); *Poetry* (1929); *The Shorter Poems* (1931); *Selected Poems* (1941).

GWENDOLYN BROOKS

A Street in Bronzeville (1945); *Annie Allen* (1949); *Bronzeville Boys and Girls* (1956); *Selected Poems* (1963); *In the Mecca* (1968); *Riot* (1969); *Family Pictures* (1970); *The World of GB* (1971); *Aloneness* (1972).

AUSTIN CLARKE

The Cattledrive in Connaught (1925); *Pilgrimage* (1929); *Collected Poems* (1936); *Night and Morning* (1938); *Ancient Lights* (1955); *Too Great a Vine* (1957); *The Horse-Eaters* (1960); *Later Poems* (1961); *Flight to Africa* (1963); *Mnemosyne Lay in Dust* (1966); *Old-Fashioned Pilgrimage* (1967); *The Echo at Coole* (1968); *A Sermon on Swift* (1969); *Collected Poems* (1974).

LEONARD COHEN

Let Us Compare Mythologies (1956); *The Spice-Box of Earth* (1961); *Flowers for Hitler* (1964); *Parasites of Heaven* (1966); *Selected Poems 1956–1968* (1968); *The Energy of Slaves* (1973).

ROBERT CONQUEST

Poems (1955); *Between Mars and Venus* (1962); *Arias from a Love Opera* (1969).

GREGORY CORSO

The Vestal Lady on Brattle (1955); *Gasoline* (1958); *Bomb* (1958); *The Happy Birthday of Death* (1960); *Long Live Man* (1962); *Selected Poems* (1962); *The Mutation of the Spirit* (1964); *There Is Yet Time to Run Back Through Life and Expiate All That's Been Sadly Done* (1965); *Elegiac Feelings American* (1970); *Earth Egg* (1974).

HART CRANE

White Buildings (1926); *The Bridge* (1930); *Collected Poems* (1933); *Seven Lyrics* (1966); *The Complete Poems and Selected Letters and Prose* (1966); *Ten Unpublished Poems* (1972).

ROBERT CREELEY

Le Fou (1952); *The Immoral Proposition* (1953); *The Kind of Act of* (1953); *All That Is Lovely in Men* (1955); *If You* (1956); *The Whip* (1957); *A Form of Women* (1959); *For Love: Poems 1950–1960* (1962); *Poems 1950–1965* (1966); *Words: Poems* (1967); *The Finger* (1968, rev. 1970); *The Charm: Early and Uncollected Poems* (1968); *5 Numbers* (1969); *Divisions and Other Early Poems* (1969); *Pieces* (1969); *As Now It Would Be Snow* (1970); *St. Martin's* (1971); *A Day Book* (1972); *Listen* (1972); *Thirty Things* (1974).

E. E. CUMMINGS

Tulips and Chimneys (1923); *&* (1925); *is 5* (1926); *CIOPW* (1931); *ViVa* (1931); *no thanks* (1935); *One Over Twenty* (1936); *Collected Poems* (1938); *50 Poems* (1940); *I x I* (1944); *XAIPE: 71 Poems* (1950); *Poems 1923–1954* (1954); *95 Poems* (1958); *100 Selected Poems* (1959); *73 Poems* (1963); *Complete Poems, 1931–1962* (1972).

Other:

The Enormous Room (1922) (p).

CECIL DAY LEWIS

Beechen Vigil and Other Poems (1925); *Country Comets* (1928); *Transitional Poem* (1929); *From Feathers to Iron* (1931); *The Magnetic Mountain* (1933); *Collected Poems, 1929–1933* (1935); *A Time to Dance and Other Poems* (1935); *Noah and the Waters* (1936); *Overtures to Death and Other Poems* (1938); *Poems in Wartime* (1940); *Selected Poems* (1940); *Word over All* (1943); *Poems, 1943–1947* (1948); *Collected Poems, 1929–1936* (1949); *Selected Poems* (1951); *An Italian Visit* (1953); *Collected Poems* (1954); *Pegasus and Other Poems* (1957); *The Gate and Other Poems* (1962); *Requiem for the Living* (1964); *The Room and Other Poems* (1965); *CDL: Selections from His Poetry* (1967); *The Whispering Roots* (1970).

Translations:

Virgil, *The Georgics* (1940); *Paul Valéry, Le Cimetière marin* (1946); Virgil, *The Aeneid* (1952); Virgil, *The Eclogues* (1963).

WALTER DE LA MARE

Poems (1906); *The Listeners and Other Poems* (1912); *The Sunken Garden and Other Poems* (1917, rev. 1931); *Motley and Other Poems* (1918); *Poems 1901–1918* (2 vols, 1920); *The Veil and Other Poems* (1921); *Selected Poems* (1927); *The Captive and Other Poems* (1928); *The Fleeting and Other Poems* (1933); *Poems 1919 to 1934* (1935); *Memory, and Other Poems* (1938); *Collected Poems* (1941); *The Burning Glass and Other Poems* (1945); *Inward Companion* (1950); *Winged Chariot* (1951); *O Lovely England* (1953); *Complete Poems* (1969).

JAMES DICKEY

Into the Stone (1957); *Drowning with Others* (1962); *Helmets* (1964); *Two Poems of the Air* (1964); *Buckdancer's Choice* (1965); *Poems 1957–1967* (1967); *The Eye-Beaters, Blood, Victory, Madness, Buckhead and Mercy* (1970); *Exchanges* (1971).

Other: *Deliverance* (1970)(f).

EMILY DICKINSON

Poems (1890); *Poems* (1891); *Poems* (1896); *The Single Hound* (1914); *Complete Poems* (1924); *Further Poems* (1929); *Poems of ED* (1930); *Unpublished Poems* (1935); *Bolts of Melody* (1945); *Poems of ED* (3 vols, 1955); *Complete Poems* (1960).

H. D. (Hilda Doolittle)

Sea Garden (1916); *Hymen* (1921); *Heliodora and Other Poems* (1924); *Collected Poems* (1925); *Red Roses for Bronze* (1931); *The Walls Do Not Fall* (1944); *Tribute to the Angels* (1945); *The Flowering of the Rod* (1946); *By Avon River* (1949); *Selected Poems* (1957); *Helen in Egypt* (1961); *Hermetic Definition* (1972).

Translations:

Euripides, *Choruses from the Iphegenia in Aulis and the Hippolytus* (1916); Euripides, *Ion* (1937).

ALAN DUGAN

Poems (1961); *Poems 2* (1963); *Poems 3* (1967); *Collected Poems* (1969); *Poems 4* (1974).

ROBERT DUNCAN

Heavenly City, Earthly City (1947); *Poems 1948–1949* (1949); *Medieval Scenes* (1950); *Song of the Borderguard* (1952); *Caesar's Gate* (1955); *Letters: Poems 1953–1956* (1958); *Selected Poems 1942–1950* (1959); *The Opening of the Field* (1960); *Roots and Branches* (1964); *Wine* (1964); *A Book of Remembrances* (1966); *Fragments of a Disordered Devotion* (1966); *Passages, 22–27* (1966); *The Years as Catches: First Poems 1939–41* (1966); *Bending the Bow* (1968); *The First Decade: Selected Poems, vol. 1* (1968); *Derivations: Selected Poems, 1950–1956* (1968); *Tribunals: Passages 31–35* (1970); *Caesar's Gate* (1973); *Dane* (1974).

RICHARD EBERHART

A Bravery of Earth (1930); *Reading the Spirit* (1936); *Song and Idea* (1940); *Poems, New and Selected* (1944); *Burr Oaks* (1947); *Brotherhood of Men* (1949); *An Herb Basket* (1950); *Selected Poems* (1951); *Poems 1930–1960* (1960); *The Quarry* (1964); *Selected Poems 1930–1965* (1965); *Thirty One Sonnets* (1967); *Shifts of Being* (1968); *Fields of Grace* (1972).

T. S. ELIOT

Prufrock and Other Observations (1917); *Poems* (1919); *Ara Vos Prec* (1920); *The Waste Land* (1922); *Poems 1909–1925* (1925); *Ash-Wednesday* (1930); *Collected Poems, 1909–1935* (1936); *Old Possum's Book of Practical Cats* (1939); *The Waste Land and Other Poems* (1940); *East Coker* (1940); *Burnt Norton* (1941); *The Dry Salvages* (1941); *Little Gidding* (1942); *Four Quartets* (1943); *Poems Written in Early Youth* (1950); *The Complete Poems and Plays* (1952); *Collected Poems 1909–1962* (1963); *The Waste Land* [Facsimile of MS] (1971).

Other Books:

The Sacred Wood (1920) (c); *Selected Essays 1917–1932* (1932) (c); *The Use of Poetry and the Use of Criticism* (1933) (c) *Murder in the Cathedral* (1935) (d); *The Cocktail Party* (1950) (d).

WILLIAM EMPSON

Poems (1935); *The Gathering Storm* (1940); *Collected Poems* (1949); *Collected Poems* (1955).

Other:

Seven Types of Ambiguity (1930, rev. 1947) (c).

LAWRENCE FERLINGHETTI

Pictures of the Gone World (1955); *A Coney Island of the Mind* (1958); *Tentative Description of a Dinner Given to Promote the Impeachment of President Eisenhower* (1958); *One Thousand Fearful Words for Fidel Castro* (1961); *Starting from San Francisco* (1961); *Where Is Vietnam?* (1965); *An Eye on the World: Selected Poems* (1967); *After the Cries of the Birds* (1967); *Moscow in the Wilderness, Segovia in the Snow* (1967); *The Secret Meaning of Things* (1969); *Tyrannus Nix?* (1969); *Open Eye, Open Heart* (1973).

ROBERT FROST

A Boy's Will (1913); *North of Boston* (1914); *Mountain Interval* (1961); *New Hampshire* (1923); *Selected Poems* (1923, rev. 1928 and 1934); *West-Running Brook* (1928); *Collected Poems* (1930); *A Further Range* (1936); *Selected Poems* (1936); *Collected Poems* (1939); *A Witness Tree* (1942); *A Masque of Reason* (1945); *Poems* (1946); *A Masque of Mercy* (1947); *A Sermon* (1947); *Steeple Bush* (1947); *Complete Poems* (1949); *Aforesaid* (1954); *In the Clearing* (1962); *The Poetry of RF* (1969).

ROY FULLER

Poems (1939); *The Middle of a War* (1942); *A Lost Season* (1944); *Epitaphs and Occasions* (1949); *Counterparts* (1954); *Brutus's Orchard* (1957); *Collected Poems* (1962); *Buff* (1965); *New Poems* (1968); *Off Course* (1969); *Tiny Tears* (1973).

ALLEN GINSBERG

Howl (1956); *Empty Mirror: Early Poems* (1961); *Kaddish and Other Poems, 1958–1960* (1961); *Reality Sandwiches* (1963); *Wichita Vortex Sutra* (1966); *T.V. Baby Poems* (1967); *Ankor-Wat* (1968); *Planet News: 1961–1967* (1968); *Airplane Dreams* (1968); *The Fall of America* (1973); *The Gates of Wrath* (1973).

NIKKI GIOVANNI

Black Judgment (1968); *Black Feeling, Black Talk* (1968); *Black Feeling, Black Talk, Black Judgment* (1970); *Re:Creation* (1971); *My House* (1972).

ROBERT GRAVES

Over the Brazier (1916); *Goliath and David* (1916); *Fairies and Fusiliers* (1917); *The Treasure Box* (1919); *Country Sentiment* (1920); *The Pier Glass* (1921); *Whipperginny* (1923); *The Feather Bed* (1923); *Mock-beggar Hall* (1924); *Welchman's Hose* (1925); *Poems 1914–1926* (1927); *Poems 1929* (1929); *Ten Poems More* (1930); *Poems 1926–1930* (1931); *Poems 1930–1933* (1933); *Collected Poems* (1938); *No More Ghosts: Selected Poems* (1940); *Poems 1938–1945* (1946); *Collected Poems 1914–1947* (1948); *Poems and Satires* (1951); *Poems 1953* (1953); *Collected Poems 1955* (1955); *Poems Selected by Himself* (1957); *Collected Poems 1959* (1959); *More Poems 1961* (1961); *Collected Poems* (1961); *Man Does, Woman Is* (1964); *Collected Poems 1965* (1965); *Love Respelt* (1965); *Poems Missing from "Love Respelt"* (1966); *Poems 1965–1968* (1968); *Poems About Love* (1970); *Poems, 1968–1970* (1970); *The Green-Sailed Vessel* (1971); *Poems, 1970–1972* (1972); *Timeless Meeting* (1973).

Translations:

Homer, *The Anger of Achilles* (The *Iliad)* (1960); *Rubaiyat of Omar Khayyan* (with O. Ali-Shah) (1967).

Other Books:

On English Poetry (1922) (c); *A Survey of Medernist Poetry* (with Laura Riding) (1927) (c); *I, Claudius* (1934) (f); *Claudius the God* (1934) (f); *The White Goddess* (1947, rev. 1966) (p).

THOM GUNN

(Poems) (1953); *Fighting Terms* (1954, rev. 1962); *The Sense of Movement* (1957); *My Sad Captains* (1961); *Selected Poems* (1962); *A Geography* (1966); *Positives* (with Ander Gunn) (1966); *Touch* (1967); *Poems, 1950–1966: A Selection* (1969); *Moly* (1971); *To the Air* (1974).

THOMAS HARDY

Wessex Poems (1898); *Poems of the Past and Present* (1901); *Time's Laughingstocks* (1909); *Satires of Circumstance* (1914); *Selected Poems* (1916); *Moments of Vision* (1917); *Late Lyrics and Earlier* (1922); *Human Shows* (1925); *Collected Poems* (1926); *Winter Words* (1928).

Other:

Far from the Madding Crowd (1874) (f); *The Return of the Native* (1878) (f); *The Mayor of Casterbridge* (1886) (f); *Tess of the D'Urbervilles* (1891) (f); *Jude the Obscure* (1896) (f).

JIM HARRISON

Plain Song (1965); *Locations* (1968); *Outlyer and Ghazals* (1971); *Letters to Yesenin* (1974).

ROBERT HAYDEN

Heartshape in the Dust (1940); *A Ballad of Remembrance* (1962); *Selected Poems* (1966); *Words in the Mourning Time* (1970); *The Night-Blooming Cereus* (1972); *Angle of Ascent: New and Selected Poems* (1975).

SEAMUS HEANEY

Eleven Poems (1965); *Death of a Naturalist* (1966); *A Lough Neagh Sequence* (1969); *Door into the Dark* (1969); *A Boy Leading His Father to Confession* (1970); *Wintering Out* (1973).

GEOFFREY HILL

(Poems) (1952); *For the Unfallen* (1959); *Preghiere* (1964); *King Log* (1968); *Mercian Hymns* (1971).

A. D. HOPE

The Wandering Islands (1955); *Poems* (1960); *Selected Poems* (1963); *Collected Poems* (1966); *New Poems, 1965–1969* (1970); *Dunciad Minor* (1970).

GERARD MANLEY HOPKINS

Poems (1918; rev. 1930, 1948, 1967).

A. E. HOUSMAN

A Shropshire Lad (1896); *Last Poems* (1922); *More Poems* (1936); *Collected Poems* (1939, rev. 1953); *Complete Poems* (1959, rev. 1971).

LANGSTON HUGHES

The Weary Blues (1926); *Fine Clothes to the Jew* (1927); *Dear Lovely Death* (1931); *The Negro Mother* (1931); *The Dream Keeper and Other Poems* (1932); *Scottsboro Limited* (1932); *A New Song* (1938); *Shakespeare in Harlem* (1942); *Jim Crow's Last Stand* (1943); *Lament for Dark Peoples* (1944); *Fields of Wonder* (1947); *One Way Ticket* (1949); *Montage of a Dream Deferred* (1951); *Selected Poems* (1959); *Ask Your Mama* (1961); *The Panther and the Lash* (1967).

Translation:

Gabriela Mistral, *Selected Poems* (1957).

TED HUGHES

The Hawk in the Rain (1957); *Lupercal* (1960); *Selected Poems* (1962); *The Burning of the Brothel* (1966); *Wodwo* (1967); *Recklings* (1967); *Scapegoats and Rabies* (1967); *Crow* (1970); *Selected Poems, 1957–1967* (1972).

RANDALL JARRELL

The Rage for the Lost Penny (1940); *Blood for a Stranger* (1942); *Little Friend, Little Friend* (1945); *Losses* (1948); *The Seven-League Crutches* (1951); *Selected Poems* (1955); *The Woman at the Washington Zoo* (1960); *Selected Poems* (1964); *The Lost World* (1965); *Complete Poems* (1969).

Other:

Poetry and the Age (1953) (c).

ROBINSON JEFFERS

Flagons and Apples (1912); *Californians* (1916); *Tamar and Other Poems* (1924); *Roan Stallion* (1925); *The Woman at Point Sur* (1927); *Poems* (1928); *Cawdor and Other Poems* (1928); *Dear Judas and Other Poems* (1929); *Descent to the Dead: Poems Written in Ireland and Great Britain* (1931); *Thurso's Landing* (1932); *Give Your Heart to the Hawks and Other Poems* (1933); *Solstice and Other Poems* (1935); *Such Counsels You Gave to Me and Other Poems* (1937); *Poems Known and Unknown* (1938); *Selected Poetry* (1938); *Be Angry at the Sun* (1941); *The Double Axe and Other Poems* (1948); *Hungerfield and Other Poems* (1954); *The Beginning and the End* (1963); *Selected Poems* (1965).

JAMES JOYCE

Chamber Music (1907); *Pomes Penyeach* (1927); *Collected Poems* (1936).

Other Books:

A Portrait of the Artist as a Young Man (1916) (f); *Exiles* (1918) (d); *Ulysses* (1922) (f); *Finnegans Wake* (1939) (f).

PATRICK KAVANAGH

Ploughman and Other Poems (1936); *The Great Hunger* (1942); *A Soul for Sale* (1947); *Come Dance with Kitty Stobling* (1960); *Collected Poems* (1964); *November Haggard* (1971); *Complete Poems* (1972).

WELDON KEES

The Last Man (1943); *The Fall of the Magicians* (1947); *Poems 1947–1954* (1954); *Collected Poems* (1962).

THOMAS KINSELLA

Poems (1956); *Another September* (1958, rev., 1962); *Moralities* (1960); *Poems and Translations* (1961); *Downstream* (1962); *Wormwood* (1966); *Nightwalker* (1967); *Nightwalker and Other Poems* (1968);

Finistere (1972); *Notes from the Land of the Dead* (1973); *Selected Poems, 1956–1968* (1973); *New Poems* (1973).
Translation:
The Táin (1969).

LINCOLN KIRSTEIN
Low Ceiling (1935); *Rhymes of a P.F.C.* (1964); *Rhymes and More Rhymes of a P.F.C.* (1966).

ETHERIDGE KNIGHT
Poems from Prison (1968); *Belly Song* (1973).

KENNETH KOCH
Poems (1953); *Ko: or, A Season on Earth* (1959); *Permanently* (1961); *Thank You and Others Poems* (1962); *Poems from 1952 and 1953* (1968); *When The Sun Tries to Go On* (1969); *Sleeping with Women* (1969); *The Pleasures of Peace* (1969); *The Art of Love* (1975).

STANLEY KUNITZ
Intellectual Things (1930); *Passport to the War* (1944); *Selected Poems 1928–1958* (1958); *The Testing-Tree* (1971); *The Terrible Threshold: Selected Poem 1940–1970* (1973).
Translations:
Andrei Voznesensky, *Antiworlds* (with others) (1967) (v); *Poems of Anna Akhmatova* (with M. Hayward) (1970).

PHILIP LARKIN
The North Ship (1945, rev. 1966); *Poems* (1954); *The Less Deceived* (1955); *The Whitsun Weddings* (1964); *High Windows* (1974).

D. H. LAWRENCE
Love Poems and Others (1913); *Amores* (1916); *Look! We Have Come Through!* (1917); *New Poems* (1918); *Bay* (1919); *Tortoises* (1921); *Birds, Beasts, and Flowers* (1923); *Collected Poems* (2 vols, 1928–32); *Pansies* (1929); *Nettles* (1930); *Last Poems* (1932); *The Ship of Death* (1933); *Poems* (2 vols, 1939); *Fire and Other Poems* (1940); *Complete Poems* (3 vols, 1957); *Collected Poems* (2 vols, 1964).
Other:
Sons and Lovers (1913) (f); *The Rainbow* (1915) (f); *Women in Love* (1920) (f); *Lady Chatterley's Lover* (1928) (f).

DON L. LEE
Think Black (1967); *Black Pride* (1968); *Don't Cry, Scream* (1969); *We Walk the Way of the New World* (1970); *Directionscore: Selected and New Poems* (1971).

DENISE LEVERTOV
The Double Image (1946); *Here and Now* (1956); *5 Poems* (1958); *Overland to the Islands* (1958); *With Eyes at the Back of Our Heads* (1960); *The Jacob's Ladder* (1961); *O Taste and See* (1964); *The Sorrow Dance* (1967); *Embroideries* (1969); *Summer Poems / 1969* (1970); *Relearning the Alphabet* (1970); *To Stay Alive* (1971); *Footprints* (1972).
Translations:
In Praise of Krishna: Songs from the Bengali (with Edward C. Dimock) (1967); *Selected Poems of [Eugene] Guillevic* (1969).

PHILIP LEVINE
On the Edge (1963); *Not This Pig* (1968); *5 Detroits* (1970): *Thistles* (1970); *Pili's Wall* (1971); *Red Dust* (1971); *They Feed They Lion* (1972); *1933* (1974).

ROBERT LOWELL
Land of Unlikeness (1944); *Lord Weary's Castle* (1946, rev. 1947); *Poems, 1938–1949* (1950); *The Mills of the Kavanaughs* (1951); *Life Studies* (1959); *Imitations* (1961); *For the Union Dead* (1964); *Selected Poems* (1965); *Near the Ocean* (1967); *The Voyage and Other Versions*

of Poems by Baudelaire (1968); *Notebooks, 1967–68* (1969, rev. 1970); *History* (1973); *For Lizzie and Harriet* (1973); *The Dolphin* (1973).
Translations:
Jean Racine, *Phaedra* (1961); Aeschylus, *Prometheus Bound* (1969).

GEORGE MACBETH
A Form of Words (1954); *The Broken Places* (1963); *A Doomsday Book* (1965); *The Colour of Blood* (1967); *The Night of Stones* (1968); *A War Quartet* (1969); *The Burning Cone* (1970); *Collected Poems* (1971); *A Prayer, Against Revenge* (1971); *The Orlando Poems* (1971); *Lusus: A Verse Lecture* (1972); *Shrapnel* (1972); *A Poet's Year* (1973).

HUGH MAC DIARMID (C. M. Grieve)
Annals of the Five Senses (1923); *Sangschaw* (1925); *Penny Wheep* (1926); *A Drunk Man Looks at the Thistle* (1926); *The Lucky Bag* (1927); *To Circumjack Cencrastus* (1930); *First Hymn to Lenin and Other Poems* (1931); *Scots Unbound and Other Poems* (1932); *Stony Limits and Other Poems* (1934); *Selected Poems* (1934); *Second Hymn to Lenin and Other Poems* (1935); *Cornish Heroic Song for Valda Trevlyn* (1943); *Speaking for Scotland: Selected Poems* (1946); *A Kist of Whistles: New Poems* (1943); *In Memoriam James Joyce* (1955); *Stony Limits and Scots Unbound and Other Poems* (1956); *Three Hymns to Lenin* (1957); *The Battle Continues* (1957); *The Kind of Poetry I Want* (1961); *Collected Poems* (1962, rev. 1967); *Poems to Paintings by William Johnstone* (1963); *The Terrible Crystal: A Vision of Scotland* (1964); *The Ministry of Water* (1964), *The Fire of the Spirit* (1965); *A Lap of Honour* (1967); *A Clyack-Sheaf* (1969); *More Collected Poems* (1970); *Song of the Seraphim* (1973).

ARCHIBALD MAC LEISH
Songs for a Summer's Day (1915); *Tower of Ivory* (1917); *The Happy Marriage* (1924); *Streets in the Moon* (1926); *The Hamlet of A. MacLeish* (1928); *New Found Land* (1930); *Conquistador* (1932); *Before March* (1932); *Poems, 1924–1933* (1933); *Frescoes for Mr. Rockefeller's City* (1933); *Public Speech* (1936); *Land of the Free* (1938); *America Was Promises* (1939); *Actfive* (1948); *Collected Poems* (1952, rev. 1963); *Songs for Eve* (1954); *The Wild Old Wicked Man and Other Poems* (1967); *The Human Season: Selected Poems 1926–1972* (1972).

LOUIS MAC NEICE
Blind Fireworks (1929); *Poems* (1935); *Letters from Iceland* (with W. H. Auden) (1937); *Poems* (1937); *The Earth Compels* (1938); *I Crossed the Minch* (1938); *Autumn Journal* (1939); *The Last Ditch* (1940); *Collected Poems 1925–1940* (1941); *Selected Poems* (1940); *Plant and Phantom* (1941); *Springboard: Poems 1941–1944* (1944); *Holes in the Sky: Poems 1941–1944* (1948); *Collected Poems 1925–1948* (1949); *Ten Burnt Offerings* (1953); *Autumn Sequel: A Rhetorical Poem in XXVI Cantos* (1954); *Visitations* (1957); *Eighty-Five Poems* (1959); *Solstices* (1961); *The Burning Perch* (1963); *Collected Poems* (1966).

EDGAR LEE MASTERS
A Book of Verses (1898); *The Blood of the Prophets* (1905); *Spoon River Anthology* (1915); *Songs and Satires* (1916); *Toward the Gulf* (1918); *Starved Rock* (1919); *Domesday Book* (1920); *The New Spoon River* (1924); *Selected Poems* (1925); *The Fate of the Jury: An Epilogue to "Domesday Book"* (1929); *Lichee Nuts* (1930); *The Serpent in the Wilderness* (1933); *Invisible Landscapes* (1935); *The Golden Fleece of California* (1936); *Poems of People* (1936); *The New World* (1937); *More People* (1939); *Illinois Poems* (1941); *The Sangamon* (1942).

ROGER MC GOUGH

Summer with Monika (1967); *Watchwords* (1969); *After the Merry-making* (1971); *Out of Sequence* (1973).

CLAUDE MC KAY

Songs of Jamaica (1912); *Constab Ballads* (1912); *Spring in New Hampshire and Other Poems* (1920); *Harlem Shadows* (1922); *Selected Poems* (1953).

JAMES MERRILL

The Black Swan (1946); *First Poems* (1951); *Short Stories* (1954); *The Country of a Thousand Years of Peace* (1959, rev. 1970); *Selected Poems* (1961); *Water Street* (1962); *Nights and Days* (1966); *The Thousand and Second Night* (1966); *The Fire Screen* (1969); *Braving the Elements* (1972); *The Yellow Pages* (1974).

W. S. MERWIN

A Mask for Janus (1952); *The Dancing Bears* (1954); *Green with Beasts* (1956); *The Drunk in the Furnace* (1960); *The Moving Target* (1963); *The Lice* (1967); *Three Poems* (1968); *Animae* (1969); *The Carrier of Ladders* (1970); *Writings to an Unfinished Accompaniment* (1973).

Translations:

The Poem of the Cid (1959); *The Satires of Persius* (1961); *Spanish Ballads* (1960); *Selected Translations, 1948–1968* (1968); *Transparence of the World: Poems of Jean Follain* (1969); *Voices: Selected Writings of Antonio Porchia* (1969); *Pablo Neruda, Twenty Love Poems and a Song of Despair* (1969).

JOSEPHINE MILES

Lines at Intersections (1939); *Poems on Several Occasions* (1941); *Local Measures* (1946); *Prefabrications* (1957); *Poems, 1930–1960* (1960); *Kinds of Affection* (1967); *Fields of Learning* (1972); *To all Appearances* (1974).

EDNA ST. VINCENT MILLAY

Renascence and Other Poems (1917); *A Few Figs from Thistles* (1920); *Second April* (1921); *The Harp-Weaver and Other Poems* (1923); *The Buck in the Snow* (1928); *Fatal Interview* (1931); *Wine from These Grapes* (1934); *Conversation at Midnight* (1937); *Huntsman, What Quarry?* (1939); *Make Bright the Arrows* (1940); *Collected Sonnets* (1941); *Collected Lyrics* (1943); *Mine the Harvest* (1954); *Collected Poems* (1956).

Translation:

Baudelaire, *Flowers of Evil* (with George Dillon) (1936).

MARIANNE MOORE

Poems (1921); *Observations* (1924); *Selected Poems* (1935); *The Pangolin* (1936); *What Are Years?* (1941); *Nevertheless* (1944); *Collected Poems* (1951); *Like a Bulwark* (1956); *O To Be a Dragon* (1959); *The Arctic Ox* (1964); *Tell Me, Tell Me* (1966); *Complete Poems* (1967).

Translations:

Jean de La Fontaine, *Fables* (1954).

EDWIN MUIR

First Poems (1925); *Chorus of the Newly Dead* (1926); *Six Poems* (1932); *Variations on a Time Theme* (1934); *Journeys and Places* (1937); *The Narrow Place* (1943); *The Voyage and Other Poems* (1946); *The Labyrinth* (1949); *Collected Poems, 1921–1951* (1952); *Prometheus* (1954); *One Foot in Eden* (1956); *Collected Poems* (1960, 2nd ed. 1965); *Selected Poems* (1965).

HOWARD NEMEROV

The Image & the Law (1947); *Guide to the Ruins* (1950); *The Salt Garden* (1955); *Mirrors & Windows* (1958); *New and Selected Poems*

(1960); *The Next Room of the Dream: Poems and Two Plays* (1962); *The Blue Swallows* (1967); *The Winter Lightning: Selected Poems* (1968); *Gnomes & Occasions* (1974).

FRANK O'HARA

A City Winter, and Other Poems (1952); *Meditations in an Emergency* (1957); *Odes* (1960); *Lunch Poems* (1964); *Love Poems (Tentative Title)* (1965); *In Memory of My Feelings* (1967); *Collected Poems* (1971); *Selected Poems* (1974).

CHARLES OLSON

To Corrado Cagli (1947); *y & x* (1950); *Letter for Melville* (1951); *This* (1952); *In Cold Hell, in Thicket* (1953); *Maximus Poems 1–10* (1953); *Maximus Poems 11–22* (1956); *O'Ryan 2 4 6 8 10* (1958); *The Maximus Poems* (1960); *The Distances* (1960); *Maximus from Dogtown I* (1961); *Proprioception* (1965); *O'Ryan 1 2 3 4 5 6 7 8 9 10* (1965); *Selected Writings* (1967); *Maximus Poems IV, V, VI* (1968); *Archaelogist of Morning* (1971); *Maximus Poems,* Vol. 3 (1975).

WILFRED OWEN

Poems (1920); *Collected Poems* (1963).

SYLVIA PLATH

The Colossus (1960); *Ariel* (1965); *Crossing the Water* (1971); *Winter Trees* (1972).

Other:

The Bell Jar (1963) (f).

WILLIAM PLOMER

Notes for Poems (1927); *The Family Tree* (1929); *The Fivefold Screen* (1931); *Visiting the Caves* (1936); *Selected Poems* (1940); *The Dorking Thigh* (1945); *A Shot in the Park* (1955); *Collected Poems* (1960, rev. 1974); *Taste and Remember* (1966); *Celebrations* (1972).

EZRA POUND

A Lume Spento (1908); *A Quinzaine for This Yule* (1908); *Personae* (1909); *Exultations* (1909); *Provença: Poems Selected from Personae, Exultations and Canzoniere* (1910); *Canzoni* (1911); *Ripostes* (1912); *Lustra* (1916); *Quia Pauper Amavi* (1919); *Umbra: The Early Poems* (1920); *Hugh Selwyn Mauberley* (1920); *Poems, 1918–1921* (1921); *A Draft of XVI Cantos* (1925); *Personae: Collected Poems* (1926, rev. 1949); *Selected Poems* (1928); *A Draft of The Cantos 17–27* (1928); *A Draft of XXX Cantos* (1930); *Homage to Sextus Propertius* (1934); *Eleven New Cantos: XXXI-XLI* (1934); *The Fifth Decad of Cantos* (1937); *Cantos LII-LXXI* (1940); *The Cantos* (1948, 1965, 1971); *The Pisan Cantos* (1948); *Selected Poems* (1949, rev. ed. 1957); *Seventy Cantos* (1950); *Section: Rock-Drill: 86–95 de los cantares* (1955); *Thrones: 96–109 de los cantares* (1960); *A Lume Spento and Other Early Poems* (1965); *Selected Cantos* (1967); *Drafts and Fragments of Cantos CX to CXVII* (1969).

Translations:

Sonnets and Ballate of Guido Cavalcanti (1912); *Cathay: Translations* (1915); *Certain Noble Plays of Japan* (with E. Fenollosa) (1916); Confucius, *The Unwobbling Pivot and The Great Digest* (1947); *The Confucian Analects* (1951); *Translations* (1953); *The Classic Anthology Defined by Confucius* (1954); Sophocles, *Women of Trachis* (1956).

E. J. PRATT

Rachel: A Sea Story of Newfoundland in Verse (1917); *Newfoundland Verse* (1923); *The Witches' Brew* (1925); *Titans* (1926); *The Iron Door: An Ode* (1927); *The Roosevelt and the Antinoe* (1930); *Many Moods* (1932); *The Titanic* (1935); *The Fable of the Goats* (1937); *Brébeuf and His Brethren* (1940); *Dunkirk* (1941); *Still Life and Other*

Verse (1943); *Collected Poems* (1944, 2nd ed. 1958); *They Are Returning* (1945); *Behind the Log* (1947); *Ten Selected Poems* (1947); *Towards the Last Spike* (1952); *Here the Tides Flow* (1962).

A. W. PURDY

The Enchanted Echo (1944); *Pressed on Sand* (1955); *Emu, Remember!* (1957); *The Crafte So Longe to Lerne* (1959); *Poems for All the Annettes* (1962); *The Blur in Between* (1963); *The Cariboo Horses* (1965); *North of Summer* (1967); *Poems for All the Annettes* [selected poems] (1968); *Wild Grape Wine* (1968); *The Hiroshima Poems* (1973).

DUDLEY RANDALL

Poem Counterpoem (with Margaret Danner) (1966); *Cities Burning* (1968); *Love You* (1971); *More to Remember* (1971); *Green Apples* (1972); *After the Killing* (1974).

JOHN CROWE RANSOM

Poems About God (1919); *Chills and Fever* (1924); *Grace After Meat* (1924); *Two Gentlemen in Bonds* (1927); *Selected Poems* (1945, rev. 1963 and 1969); *Poems and Essays* (1955).

Other:

The World's Body (1938) (c); *The New Criticism* (1941) (c).

ADRIENNE RICH

A Change of World (1951); *The Diamond Cutters* (1955); *Snapshots of a Daughter-in-Law* (1963, rev. 1967); *Necessities of Life* (1966); *Selected Poems* (1967); *Leaflets* (1969); *The Will to Change* (1971); *Diving into the Wreck* (1973); *Poems Selected and New 1950–1974* (1975); *AR's Poetry: A Norton Critical Edition* (1975).

EDWIN ARLINGTON ROBINSON

The Torrent and the Night Before (1896); *The Children of the Night* (1897); *Captain Craig* (1902); *The Town down the River* (1910); *The Man Against the Sky* (1916); *Merlin* (1917); *Lancelot* (1920); *The Three Taverns* (1920); *Avon's Harvest* (1921); *Collected Poems* (1921); *Roman Bartholow* (1923); *The Man Who Died Twice* (1924); *Dionysus in Doubt* (1925); *Tristram* (1927); *Collected Poems* (5 vols, 1927); *Sonnets: 1889–1927* (1928); *Cavender's House* (1929); *Collected Poems* (1929); *The Glory of the Nightingales* (1930); *Selected Poems* (1931); *Matthias at the Door* (1931); *Nicodemus* (1932); *Talifer* (1933); *Amaranth* (1934); *King Jasper* (1935); *Collected Poems* (1937).

THEODORE ROETHKE

Open House (1941); *The Lost Son* (1948); *Praise to the End!* (1951); *The Waking: Poems 1933–1953* (1953); *Words for the Wind: The Collected Verse* (1958); *I Am! Says the Lamb* (1961); *Party at the Zoo* (1963); *The Far Field* (1964); *Sequence, Sometimes Metaphysical* (1964); *Collected Poems* (1966).

CARL SANDBURG

In Reckless Ecstasy (1904); *Chicago Poems* (1916); *Cornhuskers* (1918); *Smoke and Steel* (1920); *Slabs of the Sunburnt West* (1922); *Selected Poems* (1926); *Good Morning, America* (1928); *The People, Yes* (1936); *Complete Poems* (1950, rev. 1970); *Wind Song* (1960).

Other:

Abraham Lincoln, the Prairie Years (2 vols, 1926) (p); *Abraham Lincoln, the War Years* (4 vols, 1939) (p).

SIEGFRIED SASSOON

Poems (1906); *Sonnets and Verses* (1909); *Sonnets* (1909); *Twelve Sonnets* (1911); *Poems* (1911); *Melodies* (1912); *An Ode for Music* (1912); *The Daffodil Murderer: Being the Chantry Prize Poem. By Saul Kain.* (1913); *Discoveries* (1915); *Morning-Glory* (1916); *The Old Huntsman and Other Poems* (1917); *Counter-Attack* (1918); *War Poems* (1919);

Picture-Show (1920); *Recreations* (1923); *Lingual Exercises for Advanced Vocabularians* (1925); *Selected Poems* (1925); *Satirical Poems* (1926); *The Heart's Journey* (1927, rev. 1928); *Poems, by "Pinchbeck Lyre"* (1931); *The Road to Ruin* (1933); *Vigils* (1934); *Rhymed Ruminations* (1939, rev. 1941); *Poems Newly Selected, 1916–1935* (1940); *Collected Poems* (1947); *Common Chords* (1950); *Emblems of Experience* (1951); *The Tasking* (1954); *Sequences* (1956); *The Path to Peace: Selected Poems* (1960); *Collected Poems 1908–1956* (1961).
Other:
Memoirs of a Fox-Hunting Man (1928) (f).

DELMORE SCHWARTZ
In Dreams Begin Responsibilities (1938); *Genesis I* (1943); *Vaudeville for a Princess* (1950); *Selected Poems: Summer Knowledge* (1959).

ANNE SEXTON
To Bedlam and Part Way Back (1960); *All My Pretty Ones* (1962); *Selected Poems* (1964); *Live or Die* (1966); *Love Poems* (1969); *Transformations* (1971); *The Book of Folly* (1973); *The Death Notebooks* (1974); *The Awful Rowing Toward God* (1975).

KARL SHAPIRO
Poems (1935); *Person, Place and Thing* (1942); *The Place of Love* (1943); *V-Letter* (1944); *Essay on Rime* (1945); *Trial of a Poet* (1947); *Poems, 1940–1953* (1953); *Poems of a Jew* (1958); *The Bourgeois Poet* (1964); *Selected Poems* (1968); *White Haired Lover* (1968).

JUDITH JOHNSON SHERWIN
Uranium Poems (1969); *Impossible Buildings* (1973).

JON SILKIN
The Peacable Kingdom (1954); *The Two Freedoms* (1958); *The Re-ordering of the Stones* (1961); *Nature with Man* (1965); *Poems New and Selected* (1966); *Killhope Wheel* (1970); *Amana Grass* (1971); *The Principle of Water* (1974).

LOUIS SIMPSON
The Arrivistes (1949); *Good News of Death* (1955); *A Dream of Governors* (1959); *At the End of the Open Road* (1963); *Selected Poems* (1965); *Adventures of the Letter I* (1971); *North of Jamaica* (1972).

EDITH SITWELL
The Mother (1915); *Twentieth-Century Harlequinade* (with O. Sitwell) (1916); *Clowns' Houses* (1918); *Façade* (1922); *Bucolic Comedies* (1923); *The Sleeping Beauty* (1924); *Troy Park* (1925); *Poor Young People* (with S. and O. Sitwell) (1925); *Rustic Elegies* (1927); *Five Poems* (1928); *Gold Coast Customs* (1929); *Collected Poems* (1930); *Epithalamium* (1931); *Five Variations on a Theme* (1933); *Selected Poems* (1936); *Poems New and Old* (1940); *Street Songs* (1942); *Green Song* (1944); *The Song of the Cold* (1945, rev. 1948); *The Shadow of Cain* (1947); *The Canticle of the Role* (1949); *Poor Men's Music* (1950); *Façade and Other Poems 1920–1935* (1950); *Selected Poems* (1952); *Gardeners and Astronomers* (1953); *Collected Poems* (1954, rev. 1957); *The Outcasts* (1962); *Music and Ceremonies* (1963).

STEVIE SMITH
A Good Time Was Had by All (1937); *Tender Only to One* (1938); *Mother, What Is Man?* (1942); *Harold's Leap* (1950); *Not Waving But Drowning* (1957); *Selected Poems* (1962); *The Frog Prince and Other Poems* (1966); *The Best Beast* (1969); *The Scorpion and Other Poems* (1972).

W. D. SNODGRASS
Heart's Needle (1959); *After Experience* (1968).
Translation:
Christian Morgenstern, *Gallows Songs* (with L. Segal) (1967).

GARY SNYDER

Riprap (1959); *Myths & Texts* (1960); *Six Sections of Mountains and Rivers Without End* (1965); *A Range of Poems* (1966); *The Back Country* (1968); *Regarding Wave* (1970); *The Fudo Trilogy* (1973); *Turtle Island* (1974).

STEPHEN SPENDER

Nine Experiments: Being Poems Written at the Age of Eighteen (1928); *20 Poems* (1930); *Poems* (1933, rev. 1934); *Vienna* (1934); *The Still Centre* (1939); *Selected Poems* (1940); *Ruins and Visions* (1942); *Poems of Dedication* (1946); *Returning to Vienna* (1947); *Edge of Being* (1949); *Collected Poems, 1928–1953* (1955); *Selected Poems* (1964); *The Generous Days* (1971).

Translations:

F. Garcia Lorca, *Poems* (with J. L. Gill) (1939); *Rainer Maria Rilke, Duino Elegies* (with J. B. Leishman) (1939); Paul Eluard, *Le Dur désir de Durer* (with F. Cornford) (1950); Rainer Maria Rilke, *The Life of the Virgin Mary* (1951).

Other:

The Destructive Element (1935) (c).

JON STALLWORTHY

The Earthly Paradise (1958); *The Astronomy of Love* (1961); *Out of Bounds* (1963); *The Almond Tree* (1967); *A Day in the City* (1967); *Root and Branch* (1969); *Positives* (1969); *The Apple Barrel: Selected Poems 1955–1963* (1974); *Hand in Hand* (1974).

JAMES STEPHENS

Insurrections (1909); *The Lonely God and Other Poems* (1909); *The Hill of Vision* (1912); *Five New Poems* (1913); *Songs from the Clay* (1915); *Green Branches* (1916); *Reincarnations* (1918); *Little Things* (1924); *A Poetry Recital* (1925); *Collected Poems* (1926); *Theme and Variations* (1930); *Strict Joy* (1931); *Kings and the Moon* (1938); *Collected Poems* (1954).

Other:

The Crock of Gold (1912) (f).

WALLACE STEVENS

Harmonium (1923, rev. 1931); *Ideas of Order* (1936); *Owl's Clover* (1936); *The Man with the Blue Guitar* (1937); *Parts of a World* (1942); *Transport to Summer* (1947); *The Auroras of Autumn* (1950); *Selected Poems* (1953); *Collected Poems* (1954); *Opus Posthumous* (1957); *The Palm at the End of the Mind* (1971).

MARK STRAND

Sleeping with One Eye Open (1964); *Reasons for Moving* (1968); *Darker* (1970); *The Sergeantville Notebook* (1973); *The Story of Our Lives* (1973).

ALLEN TATE

Mr. Pope and Other Poems (1928); *Poems, 1928–1931* (1932); *The Mediterranean and Other Poems* (1936); *Selected Poems* (1937); *The Winter Sea* (1944); *Poems, 1920–1945* (1947); *Poems, 1922–1947* (1948); *Two Conceits for the Eye to Sing, If Possible* (1950); *Poems* (1960); *Poems* (1961); *The Swimmers and Other Selected Poems* (1970).

Other:

Collected Essays (1959).

DYLAN THOMAS

18 Poems (1934); *Twenty-Five Poems* (1936); *The Map of Love* (1939); *Deaths and Entrances* (1946); *Collected Poems* (1952); *Poems* (1971).

Other:

Under Milk Wood (1954) (d).

EDWARD THOMAS

Six Poems (1916); *Poems* (1917); *Last Poems* (1918); *Collected Poems* (1920); *Poems and Last Poems* (1974).

CHARLES TOMLINSON

Relations and Contraries (1951); *The Necklace* (1955, rev. 1966); *Seeing Is Believing* (1958); *A Peopled Landscape* (1963); *Poems: A Selection* (1964); *American Scenes* (1966); *The Matachines* (1968); *The Poem as Initiation* (1968); *The Way of a World* (1969); *America West Southwest* (1969); *Words and Images* (1972); *Written on Water* (1972); *The Way In* (1974).

Translations:

Versions from Tyutchev (with H. Gifford) (1960); *Castilian Ilexes: Versions from Machado* (with H. Gifford) (1963).

JEAN TOOMER

Cane (1923).

DIANE WAKOSKI

Coins & Coffins (1961); *Discrepancies and Apparitions* (1966); *The George Washington Poems* (1967); *Greed: Parts I & II* (1968); *The Diamond Merchant* (1968); *Inside the Blood Factory* (1968); *Some Poems for the Buddha's Birthday* (1969); *The Magellanic Clouds* (1970); *Greed: Parts III & IV* (1969); *The Moon Has a Complicated Geography* (1969); *Black Dream Ditty for Billy "The Kid" M Seen in Dr. Generosity's Bar Recruiting for Hell's Angels and Black Mafia* (1970); *Greed: Parts V–VII* (1971); *The Motorcycle Betrayal Poems* (1971); *Smudging* (1972); *The Wise Men Drawn to Kneel in Wonder at the Fact So of Itself* (with D. Bromige and R. Kelly) (1972); *Sometimes a Poet Will Hijack the Moon* (1973); *The Pumpkin Pie* (1973); *Greed: Parts 8, 9, & II* (1973); *Dancing on the Grave of a Son of a Bitch* (1974); *Virtuoso Literature for Two and Four Hands* (1975).

DEREK WALCOTT

Twenty-Five Poems (1948); *Poems* (1953); *In a Green Night: Poems 1948–1960* (1962); *Selected Poems* (1964); *The Castaway* (1965); *The Gulf* (1969); *The Gulf and The Castaway* (1969); *Another Life* (1972).

ROBERT PENN WARREN

Thirty-Six Poems (1936); *Eleven Poems on the Same Theme* (1942); *Selected Poems, 1923–1943* (1944); *Brother to Dragons* (1953); *Promises: Poems, 1954–1956* (1957); *You, Emperors and Others: Poems 1957–1960* (1960); *Selected Poems: New and Old, 1923–66* (1966); *Incarnations* (1968); *Audubon: A Vision* (1969); *Or Else* (1974).

Other:

Understanding Poetry (with Cleanth Brooks) (1938) (c); *All the King's Men* (1946) (f).

WALT WHITMAN

Leaves of Grass (1855, rev. 1856, 1860, 1867, 1871, 1872, 1876, 1881, 1889, 1891); *Drum-Taps* (1865); *Passage to India* (1871).

RICHARD WILBUR

The Beautiful Changes (1947); *Ceremony* (1950); *Things of This World* (1956); *Poems, 1943–56* (1957); *Advice to a Prophet* (1961); *Poems of RW* (1963); *Walking to Sleep: New Poems and Translations* (1969); *Digging for China* (1970); *Opposites* (1973).

Translations:

Molière, *The Misanthrope* (1955); *Molière, Tartuffe* (1963).

WILLIAM CARLOS WILLIAMS

Poems (1909); *The Tempers* (1913); *Al Que Quiere!* (1917); *Sour Grapes* (1921); *Spring and All* (1923); *Collected Poems, 1921–1931* (1934); *An Early Martyr* (1935); *Adam and Eve and the City* (1936);

The Complete Collected Poems, 1906–1938 (1938); *Paterson, Book I* (1946); *Paterson, Book II* (1948); *The Clouds* (1948); *Selected Poems* (1949, rev. 1963); *Paterson, Book III* (1949); *The Collected Later Poems* (1950, rev. 1963); *The Collected Earlier Poems* (1951); *Paterson, Book IV* (1951); *The Desert Music* (1954); *Journey to Love* (1955); *Paterson, Book V* (1958); *Pictures from Brueghel* (1962); *Paterson* (1963); *Imaginations* (1970).

YVOR WINTERS

The Immobile Wind (1921); *The Bare Hills* (1927); *The Proof* (1930); *Before Disaster* (1934); *Poems* (1940); *The Giant Weapon* (1943); *Collected Poems* (1952, rev. 1960); *The Brink of Darkness* (1965); *Early Poems* (1966).

Other:

Primitivism and Decadence: A Study of American Experimental Poetry (1937) (c).

DAVID WRIGHT

Poems (1949); *Moral Stories* (1954); *Monologue of a Deaf Man* (1958); *Adam at Evening* (1965); *Nerve Ends* (1969).

Translation:

Beowulf (1957).

JAMES WRIGHT

The Green Wall (1957); *Saint Judas* (1959); *The Branch Will Not Break* (1963); *Shall We Gather at the River* (1968); *Collected Poems* (1971); *Two Citizens* (1973).

Translations:

Twenty Poems of Georg Trakl (1963); *Twenty Poems of Cesar Vallejo* (1964); *Twenty Poems of Pablo Neruda* (with R. Bly) (1968); Hermann Hesse, *Poems* (1970).

RICHARD WRIGHT

(No collections of his poetry have been published).

Other:

Native Son (1940) (f).

W. B. YEATS

Mosada: A Dramatic Poem (1886); *The Wanderings of Oisin and Other Poems* (1889); *The Countess Cathleen and Various Legends and Lyrics* (1892); *Poems* (1895, often rev.); *The Secret Rose* (1897); *The Wind Amoni the Reeds* (1899); *In the Seven Woods* (1903); *Poems 1899–1905* (1906); *Poetical Works* (2 vols, 1906–7); *Collected Works in Verse and Prose* (1908); *The Green Helmet and Other Poems* (1910); *Responsibilities: Poems and a Play* (1914); *Eight Poems* (1916); *The Wild Swans at Coole* (1917); *Michael Robartes and the Dancer* (1921); *Selected Poems* (1921); *Seven Poems and a Fragment* (1922); *Later Poems* (1922); *The Cat and the Moon and Certain Poems* (1924); *October Blast* (1927); *The Tower* (1928); *The Winding Stair* (1929); *Selected Poems* (1929); *Three Things* (1929); *Words for Music Perhaps and Other Poems* (1932); *Collected Poems* (1933); *A Full Moon in March* (1935); *New Poems* (1938); *Last Poems and Two Plays* (1939); *Last Poems and Plays* (2 vols, 1949); *Collected Poems* (1950, rev 1956); *Variorum Edition of the Poems* (1957).

Other:

A Vision (1925, rev. 1937) (p).

Biographical:

Autobiographies (1926, rev. 1938).

Index

Index to "Reading Poems"